ORANGE, GREEN AND KHAKI

The Story of the Irish Regiments
in the Great War, 1914-18

ORANGE, GREEN AND KHAKI

THE STORY OF THE IRISH REGIMENTS IN THE GREAT WAR, 1914-18

TOM JOHNSTONE

GILL AND MACMILLAN

Gill and Macmillan Ltd
Goldenbridge
Dublin 8
with associated companies throughout the world

0 7171 2002 3 (hardback)
0 7171 1994 7 (paperback)

Designed by Fergus O'Keeffe
Maps by Thomas Johnstone and Fergus O'Keeffe
Index compiled by Helen Litton
Printed by
ColourBooks Ltd, Dublin

3   5   4

To Oliver, Mike and Jim,
Irishmen
who died in Northern Ireland, the Falklands and the Gulf,
this book is respectfully dedicated.

'Let Ireland weep: but not for sorrow, weep,
That by her sons a land is sanctified.'

Francis Ledwidge
Royal Inniskilling Fusiliers
Killed in action at Pilckem Ridge, 31 July 1917

Contents

List of Illustrations

List of Maps

Acknowledgments

No work of this nature can be successfully accomplished without the assistance of many. May I extend my grateful thanks to the following without whose help and support this book could not have been written.

Mrs M. Brien, for the words of the song 'Dublin Fusiliers'.

Maj. A.P.B. Condon, Ministry of Defence, London.

Monsignor P.J. Corish, St Patrick's College, Maynooth.

Fr Etienne N. Degrez SJ, Calcutta Province of the Society of Jesus, for information about Fr Frederick Peal SJ and his work.

Lt.-Col. John Dorroch, RHQ, the Royal Hampshire Regiment.

Mr J.P. Downs, for sight of a photograph of an Irish green flag carried by 5th Connaught Rangers into Serbia, behind which his father marched.

Fr Oliver J. Doyle, St Peter's College, Wexford.

Maj. Margaret A. Easey, Royal Army Chaplains' Department, Bagshot, Surrey.

Fr S. Farragher CSSp, Blackrock College, Co. Dublin, for permission to quote from his article in *Blackrock College Annual*, 1966.

Mr C. Finnegan.

Mrs Moyra Flanagan, PRONI.

Fr Bernard Funnell.

Mr Nicholas Gander, Leeds University.

Col. M.N. Gill, for permission to quote from a letter by his father, written in hospital while recovering from the Suvla battle.

Sister Eileen Grant, Royal Army Chaplains' Department, Bagshot, Surrey.

Air Commodore the Earl of Granard, for his kind permission to quote from the letters of the 8th Earl of Granard.

Captain H.C. Heather, Irish National Memorial Management Committee.

Lt.-Col. I.G. Henderson.

Brig. W.S. Hickie, for his kindly patience in answering my many enquiries about his uncle, Gen. Sir William Hickie.

Mr Billy Ervine, the Somme Association, Belfast.

Maj. A.H. Johnstone, for explaining some of the mysteries of Blackwater 'Tech.

Dr Peter Liddle, Keeper, the Liddle Collection, Leeds University, for his advice and boundless help in making available relevant documents from his invaluable collection.

Dr Anthony Malcomson, Deputy Keeper, Public Record Office of Northern Ireland, for kindly drawing my attention to and making available documents I would otherwise have missed.

Mr A.K. MacMillan, Queen's University, Belfast.

Mrs Winn McLean, Librarian, Army Apprentices' College, Harrogate.

Fr John McEvoy, St Patrick's College, Carlow.

Monsignor Joseph Mallon, Principal Roman Catholic Chaplain (Army).

Mr Martin Middlebrook, for making available letters and documents in connection with 16th Division during the March 1918 battle.

Mr Kevin Myers, *The Irish Times.*

Maj. M. Murphy, Belfast, for his unfailing help on many queries.

Lt.-Col. Benny Newell.

Fr Michael O'Connor, St John's College, Waterford.

Mrs Bridget Patrick, for her help with obscure references.

Maj. John Pinkerton, North Irish Horse, for the extended loan of 'The Book of the 7th Royal Inniskilling Fusiliers', for which I offer sincere thanks and apologies for its late return.

Fr Kevin Rafferty, All Hallows' College, Dublin.

Fr Sephen Redmond SJ, Jesuit Provincial Archives, Dublin.

Roberta Reeners, for her considerable helpful critical advice which saved me from many errors.

Fr Thomas Rock, for information about his uncle, Maj. C.B. O'Connor.

Mrs Alison Schwalm, for the kind loan of her father's 'Haphazard'.

Mr David C. Sheehy, Diocesan Archivist, Archbishop's House, Dublin.

Maj. G.E.M. Stephens.

Mr Myles Stoney, Mount Nugent, Co. Cavan, for his kind permission to quote from the letters of his grandfather, Gen. Sir Oliver Nugent.

Andrew Swires and the staff of the Reading Room, British Library, Boston Spa, for their courteous assistance during my four years researching this work.

Fergal Tobin of Gill and Macmillan, for his timely words of encouragement in moments of sagging morale.

Maj. M. Wright.

The staff of the Command Library, Bulford.

The staff of the Prince Consort Library, Aldershot.

The staff of the Reading Room, State Library, Victoria, Australia. One of the busiest, friendliest and best-stocked libraries it has been my good fortune to use during walkabout.

To all those, too numerous to mention, who contributed to the making of this book. And, finally, to my wife, whose forbearance at all times has been above and beyond the call of duty. To all these I offer my deepest thanks.

Glossary

ABBREVIATIONS

2i/c	Second in command
ADMS	Assistant Director, Medical Services
ADS	Advance Dressing Station
AOD	Army Ordnance Department
AQMG	Assistant Quartermaster-General
ASC	Army Service Corps
AVC	Army Veterinary Corps
BGRA	Brigadier-General, Royal Artillery
BM	Brigade Major
Bn	Battalion
CCS	Casualty Clearing Station
CRE	Commander, Royal Engineers
DAA&QMG	Deputy Assistant Adjutant and Quartermaster-General
DAAG	Deputy Assistant Adjutant-General
DADOS	Deputy Assistant Director of Ordnance Services
DAQMG	Deputy Assistant Quartermaster-General
DCLI	Duke of Cornwall's Light Infantry
GOC	General Officer Commanding
GSO1	General Staff Officer, 1st Grade
GSO2	General Staff Officer, 2nd Grade
KOSB	King's Own Scottish Borderers
KOYLI	King's Own Yorkshire Light Infantry
MGGS	Major-General, General Staff
RA	Royal Artillery
RAChD	Royal Army Chaplains' Department
RAMC	Royal Army Medical Corps
RAP	Regimental Aid Post
RE	Royal Engineers
RFA	Royal Field Artillery
RHA	Royal Horse Artillery
SLI	Somerset Light Infantry

THE IRISH REGIMENTAL TITLES, ABBREVIATIONS, SHORT TITLES AND NICKNAMES

Irish Guards	IG	Irish Guards	The Micks
Royal Irish Regiment	RIrR	Royal Irish	The Old Namurers

They stormed Namur in 1695 and were granted the first battle honour awarded to a British regiment.

Royal Inniskilling Fusiliers	RInnF	Inniskillings	The Skins
Royal Irish Rifles	RIR	Irish Rifles	The Rifles
Royal Irish Fusiliers	RIF	Irish Fusiliers	The Faughs

From their use of the slogan cry *'Fág an bealach'* (vulgarly, Faugh a Ballagh or 'Clear the Way') in the Peninsular War

Connaught Rangers	CR	The Rangers	The Devil's Own
Leinster Regiment	LeinsR	The Leinsters	The 40-10s
Royal Munster Fusiliers	RMF	The Munsters	The Dirty Shirts

The dirt referred to was sweat, blood and powder grime following the successful storming of a fortress in India.

Royal Dublin Fusiliers	RDF	The Dublins	The Old Toughs, and the Blue Caps

Both names are derived from their long service in India. Once the Blue Cap was as distinctive and honoured as maroon or green berets are in the modern British Army.

MILITARY RANKS AND ABBREVIATIONS

Field-Marshal	FM
General	Gen.
Lieutenant-General	Lt.-Gen.
Major-General	Maj.-Gen.
Brigadier-General	Brig.-Gen.
Brigadier (modern title)	Brig.
Colonel	Col.
Lieutenant-Colonel	Lt.-Col.
Major	Maj.
Captain	Capt.
Lieutenant	Lt.
Second-Lieutenant	2/Lt.
Regimental Sergeant-Major	RSM
Regimental Quartermaster-Sergeant	RQMS
Company Sergeant-Major	CSM
Company Quartermaster-Sergeant	CQMS
Sergeant	Sgt.
Corporal	Cpl.
Lance-Corporal	L/Cpl.
Rifleman	Rfn.
Fusilier	Fus.
Private	Pte.

HONOURS AND AWARDS

Victoria Cross	VC
Distinguished Service Order	DSO
Military Cross	MC
Distinguished Conduct Medal	DCM
Military Medal	MM
Meritorious Service Medal	MSM
Mentioned in Despatches	MID

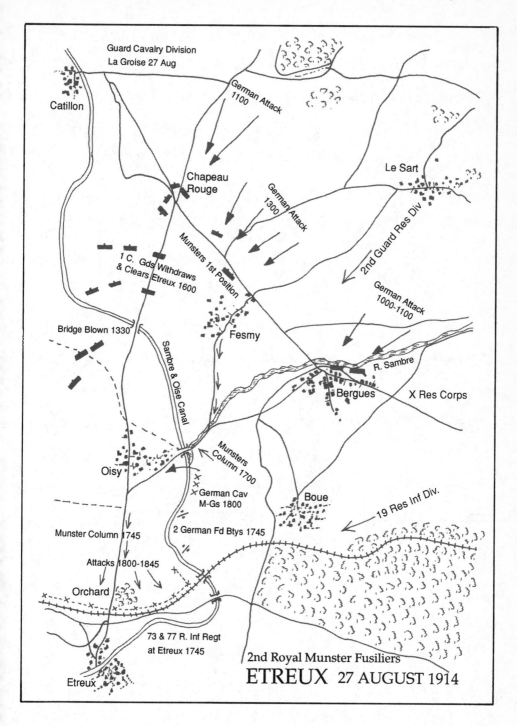

Guard Cavalry Division
La Groise 27 Aug

Catillon

German Attack
1100

Le Sart

Chapeau
Rouge

German Attack
1300

2nd Guard Res Div

Munsters 1st Position

1 C. Gds Withdraws
& Clears Etreux 1600

German Attack
1000-1100

Bridge Blown 1330

Fesmy

R. Sambre

Sambre & Oise Canal

Bergues

X Res Corps

Oisy

Munsters
Column 1700

German Cav
M-Gs 1800

Boue

19 Res Inf Div.

Munster Column 1745

2 German Fd Btys 1745

Attacks 1800-1845

Orchard

73 & 77 R. Inf Regt
at Etreux 1745

2nd Royal Munster Fusiliers

ETREUX 27 AUGUST 1914

Etreux

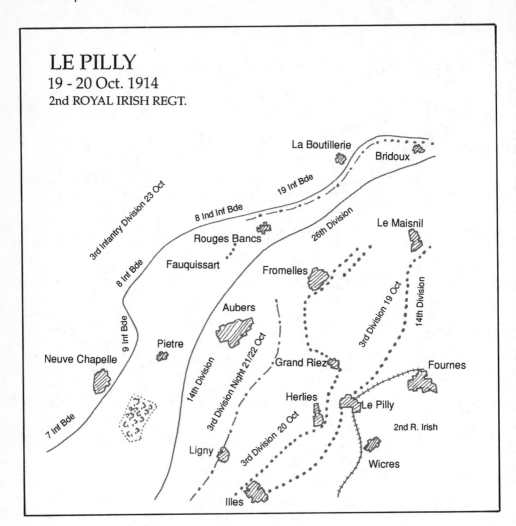

LE PILLY
19 - 20 Oct. 1914
2nd ROYAL IRISH REGT.

La Boutillerie

Bridoux

19 Inf Bde

8 Ind Inf Bde

3rd Infantry Division 23 Oct

Le Maisnil

26th Division

Rouges Bancs

Fauquissart

Fromelles

8 Inf Bde

3rd Division 19 Oct

14th Division

Aubers

9 Inf Bde

Pietre

3rd Division Night 21/22 Oct

Neuve Chapelle

Grand Riez

Fournes

14th Division

Herlies

Le Pilly

7 Inf Bde

2nd R. Irish

Ligny

3rd Division 20 Oct

Wicres

Illes

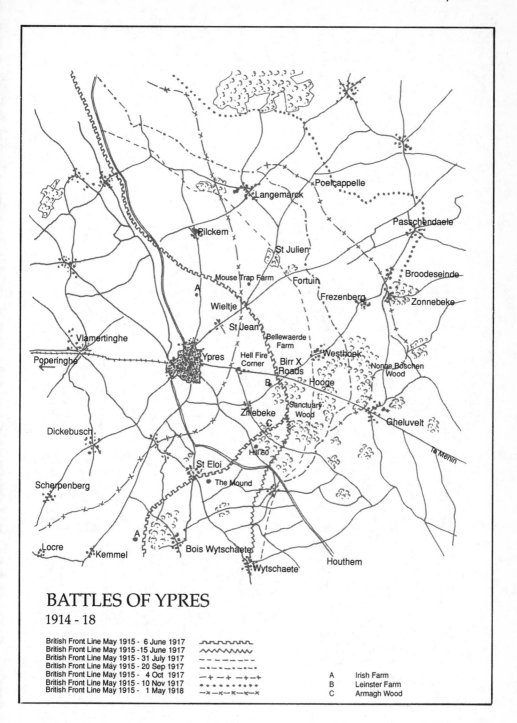

BATTLES OF YPRES
1914 - 18

British Front Line May 1915 - 6 June 1917	
British Front Line May 1915 -15 June 1917	
British Front Line May 1915 - 31 July 1917	
British Front Line May 1915 - 20 Sep 1917	
British Front Line May 1915 - 4 Oct 1917	
British Front Line May 1915 - 10 Nov 1917	
British Front Line May 1915 - 1 May 1918	

A   Irish Farm
B   Leinster Farm
C   Armagh Wood

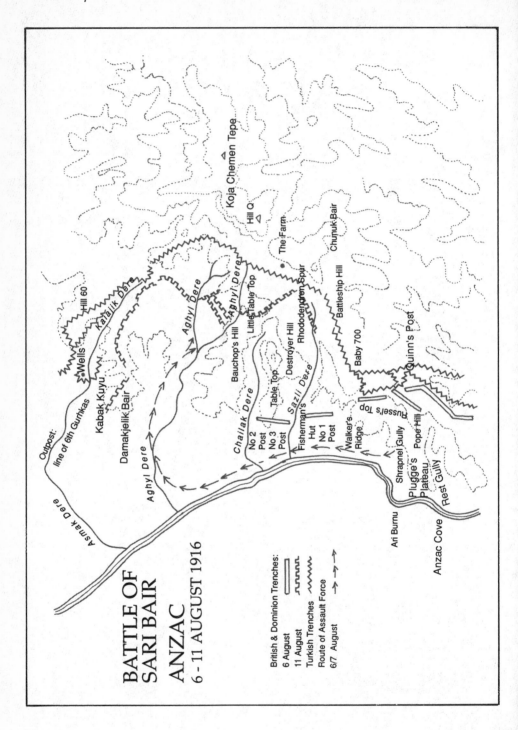

BATTLE OF
SARI BAIR
ANZAC
6 - 11 AUGUST 1916

British & Dominion Trenches:
6 August
11 August
Turkish Trenches
Route of Assault Force
6/7 August

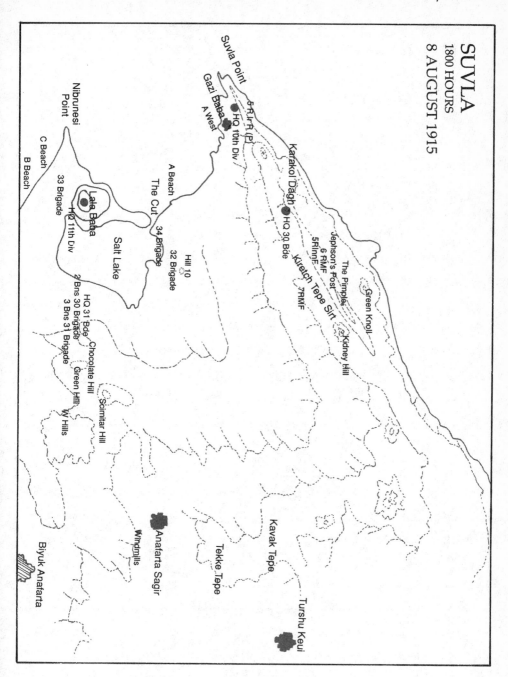

SUVLA
1800 HOURS
8 AUGUST 1915

Suvla Point
Gazi Baba
A West
5 R Ir R (P)
HQ 10th Div
Karakol Dagh
HQ 30 Bde
The Pimple
Jephson's Post
5 RInnF
6 RMF
5 RInnF
Kiretch Tepe Sirt
7 RMF
Green Knoll
Kidney Hill

Nibrunesi
Point
C Beach
B Beach
33 Brigade
Lala Baba
HQ 11th Div
A Beach
The Cut
34 Brigade
Salt Lake
Hill 10
32 Brigade
HQ 31 Bde
2 Bns 30 Brigade
3 Bns 31 Brigade
Chocolate Hill
Green Hill
W Hills
Scimitar Hill

Anafarta Sagir
Wndmills
Kavak Tepe
Tekke Tepe
Biyuk Anafarta
Turshu Keui

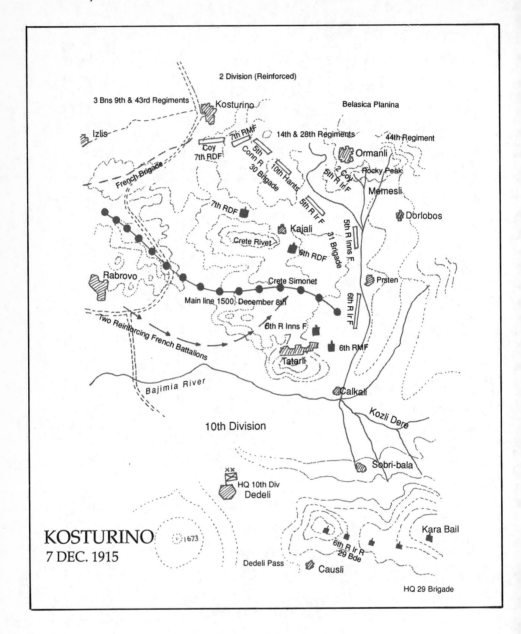

2 Division (Reinforced)

3 Bns 9th & 43rd Regiments

Kosturino

Belasica Planina

Izlis

7th RMF

14th & 28th Regiments

44th Regiment

Coy
7th RDF

French Brigade

5th
Conn R

10th Hants

30 Brigade

Ormanli

Rocky Peak

2 Coy
5th R In F

Memesli

7th RDF

5th R Ir F

Dorlobos

Kajali

Crete Rivet

6th RDF

31 Brigade

5th R Inns F.

Prsten

Rabrovo

Crete Simonet

Main line 1500, December 8th

6th R Ir F

Two Reinforcing French Battalions

6th R Inns F.

6th RMF

Tatarli

Bajimia River

Calkali

10th Division

Kozli Dere

Sobri-bala

HQ 10th Div
Dedeli

KOSTURINO
7 DEC. 1915

1673

Kara Bail

6th R Ir R
29 Bde

Dedeli Pass

Causli

HQ 29 Brigade

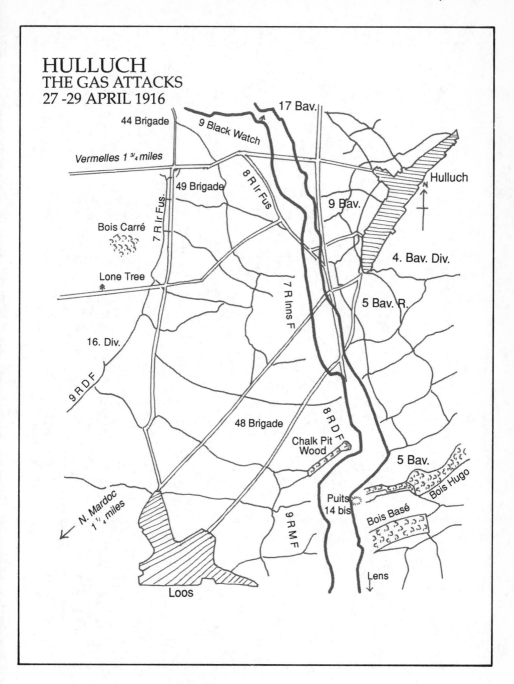

HULLUCH
THE GAS ATTACKS
27 -29 APRIL 1916

44 Brigade

9 Black Watch

17 Bav.

Vermelles 1 ¾ miles

49 Brigade

8 R Ir Fus.

Hulluch

7 R Ir Fus.

9 Bav.

Bois Carré

Lone Tree

4. Bav. Div.

7 R Inns F

5 Bav. R.

16. Div.

9 R D F

48 Brigade

8 R D F

Chalk Pit
Wood

5 Bav.

Bois Hugo

N. Mardoc
1 ¼ miles

9 R M F

Puits
14 bis

Bois Basé

Lens

Loos

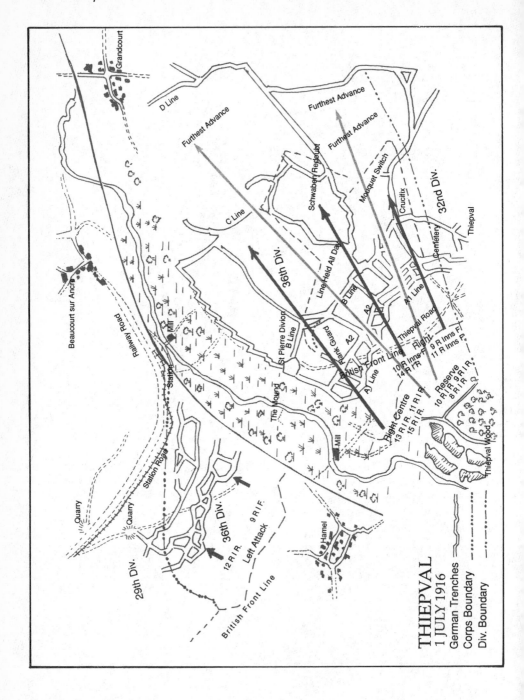

THIEPVAL
1 JULY 1916

German Trenches
Corps Boundary
Div. Boundary

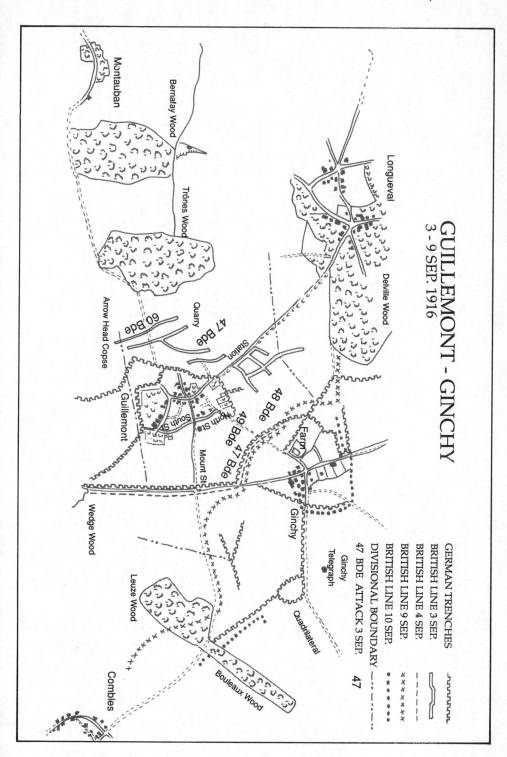

GUILLEMONT - GINCHY
3 - 9 SEP. 1916

Montauban

Bernafay Wood

Trônes Wood

Longueval

Delville Wood

Arrow Head Copse

Quarry

60 Bde

47 Bde

Station

48 Bde

49 Bde 47 Bde

Guillemont

North St.

South St.

Mount St.

Farm

Wedge Wood

Ginchy

Ginchy
Telegraph

Quadrilateral

Leuze Wood

Bouleaux Wood

Combles

GERMAN TRENCHES
BRITISH LINE 3 SEP.
BRITISH LINE 4 SEP.
BRITISH LINE 9 SEP.
BRITISH LINE 10 SEP.
DIVISIONAL BOUNDARY
47 BDE ATTACK 3 SEP.   47

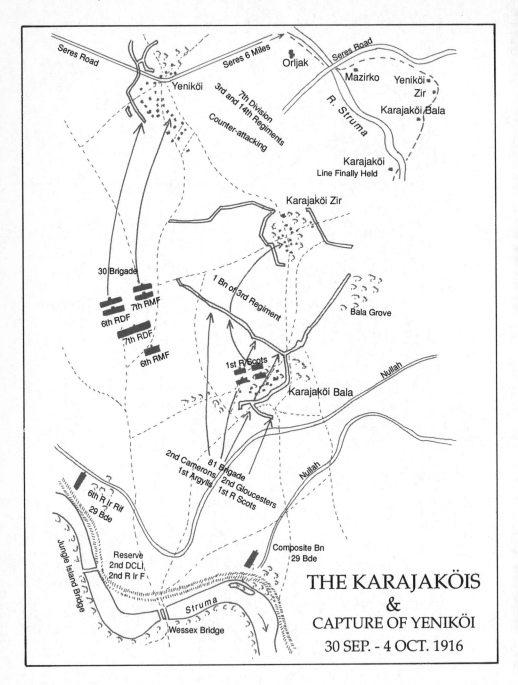

THE KARAJAKÖIS
&
CAPTURE OF YENIKÖI
30 SEP. - 4 OCT. 1916

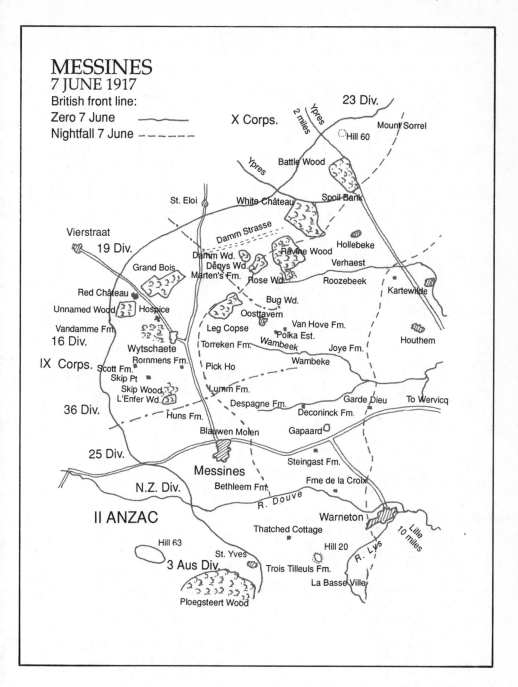

MESSINES
7 JUNE 1917
British front line:
Zero 7 June ————
Nightfall 7 June — — — —

X Corps.

23 Div.

Mount Sorrel

Hill 60

Ypres
2 miles

Ypres

Battle Wood

St. Eloi

White Château

Spoil Bank

Damm Strasse

Vierstraat

19 Div.

Damm Wd.

Dénys Wd.

Marten's Fm.

Ravine Wood

Rose Wd.

Hollebeke

Verhaest

Roozebeek

Kartewilde

Grand Bois

Red Château

Unnamed Wood

Hospice

Bug Wd.

Oosttavern

Leg Copse

Van Hove Fm.

Polka Est.

Houthem

Vandamme Fm.

16 Div.

Torreken Fm.

Wambeek

Joye Fm.

Wytschaete

Rornmens Fm.

Wambeke

IX Corps.

Scott Fm.

Pick Ho

Skip Pt

Skip Wood

L'Enfer Wd.

Lumm Fm.

Despagne Fm.

Garde Dieu

To Wervicq

36 Div.

Huns Fm.

Deconinck Fm.

Blauwen Molen

Gapaard

25 Div.

Steingast Fm.

Messines

N.Z. Div.

Bethleem Fm.

Fme de la Croix

R. Douve

Warneton

Lille
10 miles

II ANZAC

Thatched Cottage

Hill 63

Hill 20

St. Yves

R. Lys

3 Aus Div.

Trois Tilleuls Fm.

La Basse Ville

Ploegsteert Wood

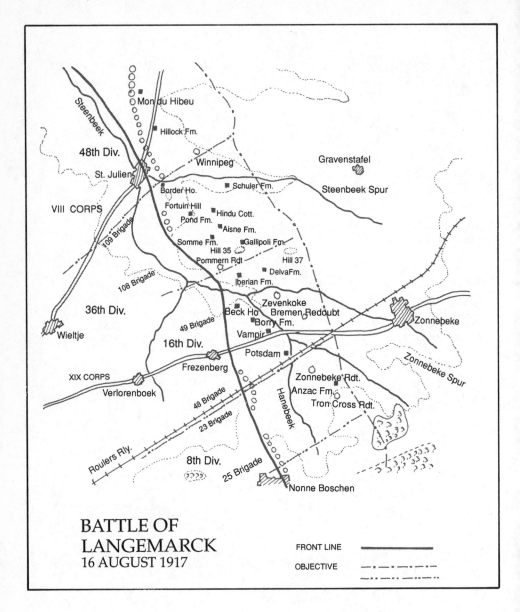

Mon du Hibeu
Hillock Fm.
48th Div.
Winnipeg
St. Julien
Gravenstafel
Steenbeek Spur
VIII CORPS
Border Ho.
Schuler Fm.
Fortuin Hill
Hindu Cott.
Pond Fm.
109 Brigade
Aisne Fm.
Somme Fm.
Gallipoli Fm.
Hill 35
Pommern Rdt.
Hill 37
108 Brigade
DelvaFm.
Iberian Fm.
36th Div.
Zevenkoke
Beck Ho.
Bremen Redoubt
Borry Fm.
49 Brigade
Zonnebeke
Wieltje
Vampir
16th Div.
Potsdam
Frezenberg
Zonnebeke Spur
XIX CORPS
Zonnebeke Rdt.
Verlorenboek
Anzac Fm.
Tron Cross Rdt.
48 Brigade
Hanebeek
23 Brigade
Roulers Rly.
8th Div.
25 Brigade
Nonne Boschen

BATTLE OF
LANGEMARCK
16 AUGUST 1917

FRONT LINE

OBJECTIVE

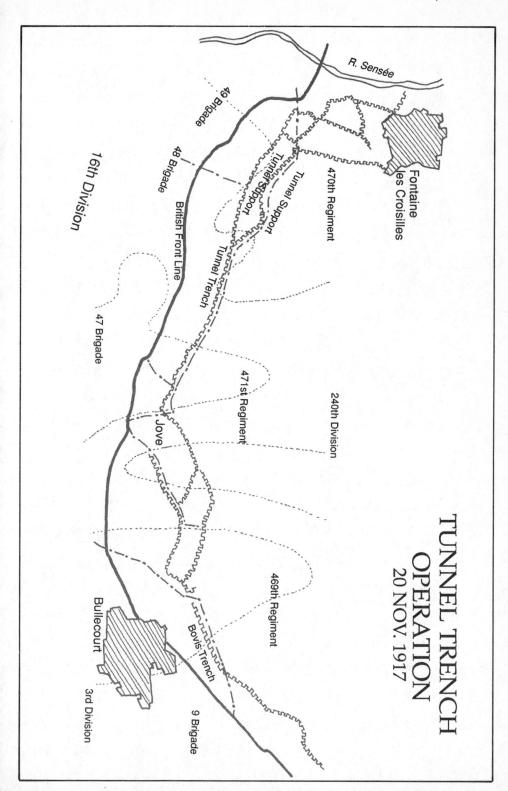

TUNNEL TRENCH
OPERATION
20 NOV. 1917

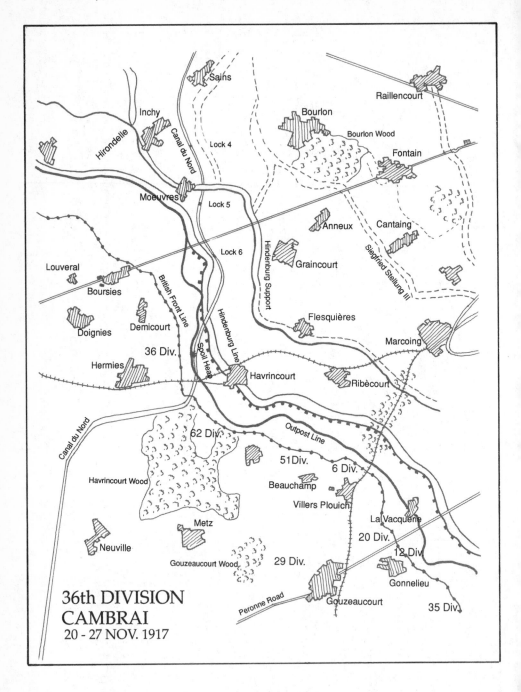

Sains

Raillencourt

Inchy

Hirondelle

Canal du Nord

Lock 4

Bourlon

Bourlon Wood

Fontain

Moeuvres

Lock 5

Anneux

Cantaing

Hindenburg Support

Siegfried Stellung III

Lock 6

Louveral

Graincourt

Boursies

British Front Line

Demicourt

Flesquières

Doignies

Marcoing

Hindenburg Line

36 Div.

Spoil Heap

Havrincourt

Ribècourt

Hermies

Canal du Nord

62 Div.

Outpost Line

51 Div.

6 Div.

Havrincourt Wood

Beauchamp

Villers Plouich

La Vacquerie

20 Div.

12 Div.

Metz

Neuville

Gouzeaucourt Wood

29 Div.

Gonnelieu

**36th DIVISION
CAMBRAI**
20 - 27 NOV. 1917

Peronne Road

Gouzeaucourt

35 Div.

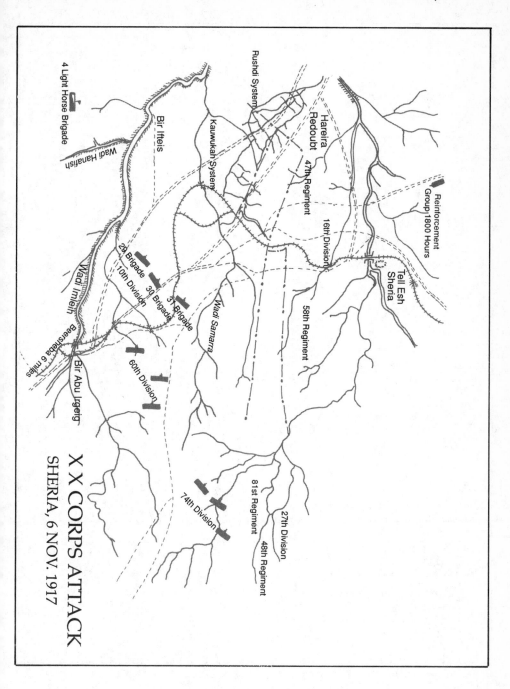

X X CORPS ATTACK
SHERIA, 6 NOV. 1917

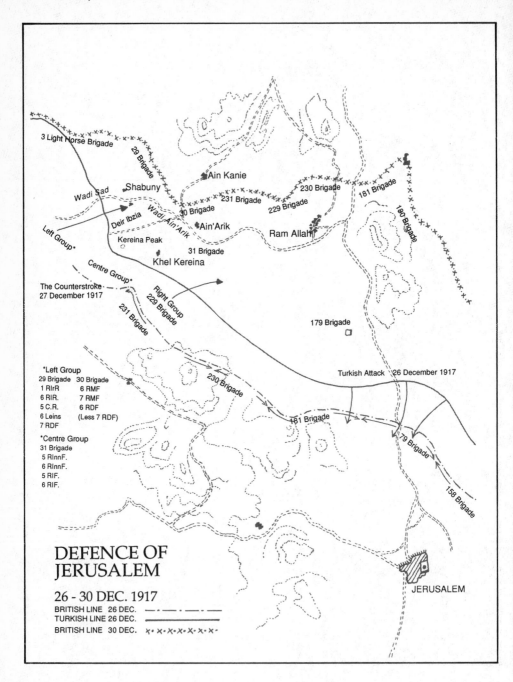

3 Light Horse Brigade

29 Brigade

Wadi Sad

Shabuny

Deir Ibzia

Wadi Ain 'Arik

30 Brigade

Ain Kanie

231 Brigade

229 Brigade

230 Brigade

181 Brigade

180 Brigade

Left Group*

Kereina Peak

Ain'Arik

Ram Allah

31 Brigade

Khel Kereina

Centre Group*

The Counterstroke
27 December 1917

Right Group
229 Brigade

231 Brigade

179 Brigade

230 Brigade

Turkish Attack   26 December 1917

*Left Group
29 Brigade   30 Brigade
1 RIrR   6 RMF
6 RIR.   7 RMF
5 C.R.   6 RDF
6 Leins   (Less 7 RDF)
7 RDF

*Centre Group
31 Brigade
5 RInnF.
6 RInnF.
5 RIF.
6 RIF.

181 Brigade

179 Brigade

158 Brigade

DEFENCE OF JERUSALEM

26 - 30 DEC. 1917

JERUSALEM

BRITISH LINE 26 DEC. — · — · — · —
TURKISH LINE 26 DEC. ▬▬▬▬▬▬▬
BRITISH LINE 30 DEC. ×·×·×·×·×·×·

7th ARMY

Nablus 8 Miles

Flank of
75th Division
12 March

Wadi Lubban

Mezra

10th Division Final Line

Sinjil

Nablus Rd

3rd Cav. Div.

Sh Redwan

Deir es Sudan

74th Division Final Line

Flank of
75th Division

Ajul

Um Suffa Ridge

Wadi el Jib

III CORPS

En Nabi Salih

Um Suffra

1800 8 March

Atara

Deir en Nidham

Jibia

Sh Kalrawani

Nablus Road

Tel 'Asur
4430

1st Div.

Kh Rashiniyeh Plateau

24 Div.

1000   10 March

10th Division
Right Attack
30 & 31 Bde
Less 1 Bn each

74th Division

10th Division
Left Attack
29 Bde

53rd Division

Janiya

Nablus Rd

Bethel

Ain Kanie

L. Balua

Ain 'Arik

Ram Allah

Beitunye

Jerusalem

TELL 'ASUR
8 - 12 MARCH 1918

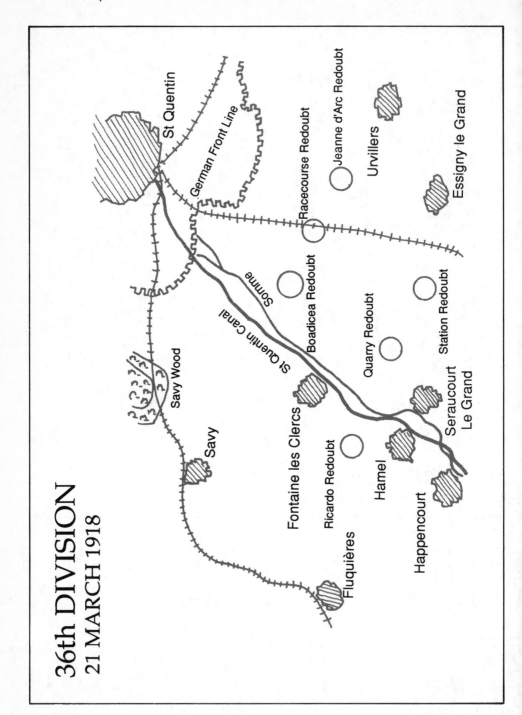

36th DIVISION
21 MARCH 1918

St Quentin

German Front Line

Racecourse Redoubt

Jeanne d'Arc Redoubt

Urvillers

Essigny le Grand

Somme

St Quentin Canal

Boadicea Redoubt

Quarry Redoubt

Station Redoubt

Seraucourt
Le Grand

Savy Wood

Savy

Fontaine les Clercs

Ricardo Redoubt

Hamel

Happencourt

Fluquières

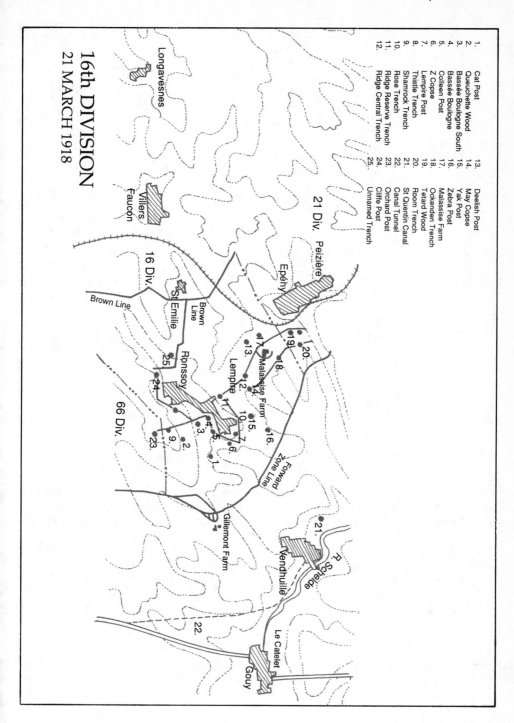

16th DIVISION
21 MARCH 1918

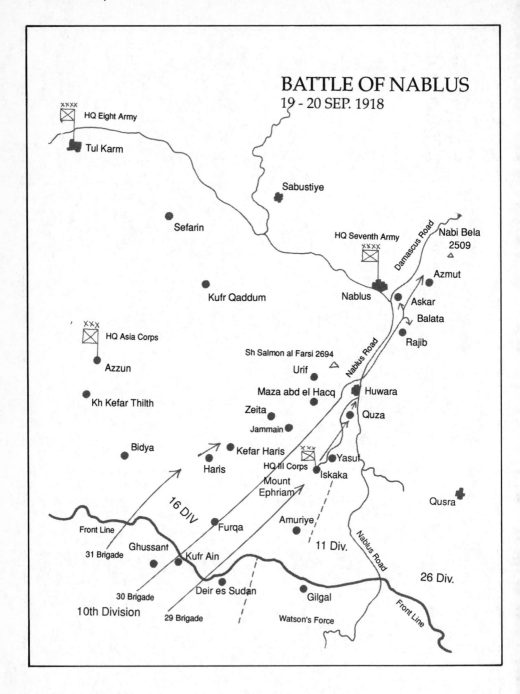

BATTLE OF NABLUS
19 - 20 SEP. 1918

HQ Eight Army

Tul Karm

Sabustiye

Sefarin

HQ Seventh Army

Nabi Bela
2509

Kufr Qaddum

Nablus

Azmut

Askar

Balata

Rajib

HQ Asia Corps

Azzun

Sh Salmon al Farsi 2694

Urif

Kh Kefar Thilth

Maza abd el Hacq

Huwara

Zeita

Quza

Jammain

Bidya

Kefar Haris

Yasuf

Haris

HQ III Corps

Iskaka

Mount
Ephriam

Qusra

16 DIV

Furqa

Amuriye

11 Div.

Front Line

Ghussant

26 Div.

31 Brigade

Kufr Ain

30 Brigade

Deir es Sudan

Gilgal

Front Line

10th Division

29 Brigade

Watson's Force

Army Mobilisation and Expansion, August 1914

Without the Irish regiments, the story of the British army would be impoverished.[1]

Lord Kitchener was at Dover on 3 August 1914. He was returning to his pro-consulship in Egypt when he was summoned by 10 Downing Street. He returned to London to learn of the outbreak of war. The Prime Minister then kept him waiting for forty-eight hours. Mr Asquith would have preferred to have retained Lord Haldane as Secretary for War. Unfortunately, Haldane, like Prince Louis of Battenberg at the Admiralty, was caught up in the wave of anti-German hysteria which was sweeping the country. Haldane at the War Office, with Lord Kitchener as Chief of the Imperial Staff, would have made a formidable team. Together, they might have avoided some of the later politico-military errors of British policy. This was not now politically possible. With deep misgivings on the part of the Prime Minister, Kitchener was offered the seal of Secretary of State for War.

At the War Office, Kitchener entered a military vacuum. Most of the senior desks had been cleared, and their occupants were now filling posts in the British Expeditionary Force (BEF). They had left eagerly, to take an active part in the war, without first ensuring that an efficient staff remained at the War Office to support the field army. Later, some would criticise the very inefficiency which they themselves, by default, had created. At the first meeting of what was to be called the War Council, Kitchener astounded cabinet ministers and fellow generals alike by declaring the nation should prepare for a war of at least three years. He demanded an expansion of the army to seventy divisions. This was accepted, and almost at once recruitment of these new armies began.[2]

Kitchener played no part in the concept of a British Expeditionary Force, in the selection of its operational area or its role. Joint planning with the French to meet the threat posed by Germany's grand scheme for French defeat, the Schlieffen Plan, had largely been conceived and executed by an Irishman, Maj.-Gen. H.H. Wilson. During Wilson's tenure as Commandant, Staff College, and Director of Military Operations, the General Staff was totally tied to French principles of war, especially those expounded by Gen. Foch. Intelligence information and informed opinion concerning German preparations and methods which ran counter to, or failed to conform with, this orthodoxy, were 'ignored and almost resented'.[3]

Kitchener had several options for the expansion of the army. He could retain part of the BEF to train and stiffen the New Army, but this was made impossible by demands to send all the planned BEF to France. The use of the Territorial Force (TF) as a nucleus for expansion was also considered, but not adopted because it was

> only partially under War Office direction and administration, and largely in the hands of local associations in which the civilian element predominated, and in which local influences prevailed and would be sure to assert themselves.[4]

It was this last fact which decided Kitchener. The Territorial Force was operated by County Territorial Associations with little War Office control. Illustrating its methods and limitations is the story of Glasgow Engineer Volunteers. Detached to serve with a Yeomanry Division being raised in Suffolk, they each had only one suit of uniform. It soon showed wear and tear in essential parts. The Suffolk TF Association refused to replace them, on the grounds it was Glasgow's responsibility. Glasgow also refused because they were 'out of area'. The Provost Marshal began arresting the Scots for indecent exposure. Only War Office intervention saved the men further embarrassment.[5]

Kitchener's vision was of an army on a continental scale which was trained and equipped to the highest standards. If necessary, he would use the entire resources of Great Britain and the Empire—its wealth, manpower and material, without limit—to achieve this. He rightly saw that the cumbersome apparatus of county associations, too strongly entrenched for change, was not equal to the task. The New Armies were to be extensions of the Regular Army under War Office control from the outset. There would be no place for private armies, although he would use their manpower where he could.

> Every formation must be standardised so as to fit exactly into its place in the military machine. That condition once observed, Kitchener valued the spirit of clannishness or comradeship which prompted men with social, local or professional ties to serve together. It was the simple and plain desire to secure an unbroken military level which prevented him, to his great regret, from closing with the fine offer made by Mr Redmond to raise a special force in Ireland.[6]

The Regular Army divisions were expanded from an original one cavalry and six infantry divisions to three cavalry and eleven infantry divisions, 1st to 8th Division and 27th, 28th and 29th Divisions. The last five divisions were formed from returned regular battalions from overseas garrisons. To replace them, the 43rd, 44th and 45th Territorial Force Divisions, at Lord Kitchener's request, volunteered to serve overseas as garrison troops, mainly in India.

KITCHENER'S NEW ARMIES

Parliament consented to an increase of half a million men for the Regular Army on 6 August. Five days later, a general proclamation called for 100,000 men to volunteer for three years, or the duration of the war. This force, K1 as it was known, became First New Army. Later, on 13 September, a further 100,000 were called for. This was K2, which formed Second New Army.

First New Army	*Second New Army*
9th (Scottish) Division	15th (Scottish) Division
10th (Irish) Division	16th (Irish) Division
11th (Northern) Division	17th (Northern) Division
12th (Eastern) Division	18th (Eastern) Division
13th (Western) Division	19th (Western) Division
14th* (Light) Division	20th (Light) Division

(*This was originally the 8th Division, but was changed when the 8th Regular Division was formed from overseas garrisons.)

By early spring 1915, five of these six divisions were concentrated in the Aldershot District for final training before embarking for either the Western Front or Gallipoli. When all the difficulties are considered, this must be seen as a remarkable achievement. After the 20th Division, the territorial designation for New Army divisions was discontinued. Exceptions were made only in the case of the 36th (Ulster) and the 38th (Welsh) Divisions.

Third New Army	*Fourth New Army*
21st Division, 24th Division	30th Division, 33rd Division
22nd Division, 25th Division	31st Division, 34th Division
23rd Division, 26th Division	32nd Division, 35th Division

Fourth New Army was broken up to provide replacements for the first two New Armies. The 37th–41st Divisions were renumbered 30th–35th; with the 36th Division they became the Fifth New Army. However, not everyone shared the long vision of the Secretary of State. Maj.-Gen. H.H. Wilson, Deputy Chief of Staff to the BEF, wrote to his wife on 15 September 1914:

> K's shadow armies, for shadow campaigns, at unknown and distant dates, prevent a lot of good officers, NCOs and men from coming out. It is a scandalous thing. Under no circumstances can these mobs now being raised, without officers and NCOs, without guns, rifles, or transport services, without moral (*sic*) or tradition, knowledge or experience, under no circumstances could these mobs take the field for two years. Then what is the use of them? What we want, and what we must have, is for our little force out here to be kept to full strength with the very best of everything. Nothing else is any good.[7]

THE IRISH REGIMENTS

At the outbreak of the First World War, Irish regular regiments of cavalry and infantry of the British Army were old and distinguished. They had emerged from the recent South African War of 1899–1902 with enhanced reputations for bravery and dash. In recognition of this valour, Queen Victoria ordered the distribution of shamrock to all Irish regiments on St Patrick's Day and a new, Irish, Regiment of Foot Guards was formed. The regiments were:

Cavalry

4th Royal Irish Dragoon Guards   5th Royal Irish Lancers
6th Inniskilling Dragoons   8th King's Royal Irish Hussars

Infantry

4th Regiment of Foot Guards, 1st Battalion, The Irish Guards
18th Foot, 1st and 2nd Battalions, Royal Irish Regiment
27th/108th Foot, 1st and 2nd Battalions, Royal Inniskilling Fusiliers
83rd/86th Foot, 1st and 2nd Battalions, Royal Irish Rifles
87th/89th Foot, 1st and 2nd Battalions, Royal Irish Fusiliers
88th/94th Foot, 1st and 2nd Battalions, The Connaught Rangers
100th/109th Foot, 1st and 2nd Battalions, The Leinster Regiment
101st/104th Foot, 1st and 2nd Battalions, Royal Munster Fusiliers
102nd/103rd Foot, 1st and 2nd Battalions, Royal Dublin Fusiliers

Supplementing the regulars was a reserve of two regiments of yeomanry cavalry and twenty battalions of militia infantry.

Throughout the history of the British Army, the Irish regiments had served with honour in almost every campaign in which it fought, from the River Plate to the Imjin, the Somme to the Tugela. Officered mainly by the Anglo-Irish ascendancy, its rank and file were predominantly Catholic Old Irish with a sprinkling of Cromwellian dourness. The first Catholic to achieve the rank of general in the British Army since the reign of James II was Irish, Lt.-Gen. Sir William Francis Butler (his wife, Elizabeth Butler, was a famous military artist). Many field marshals and generals of this class are household names. Less well known is the host of ordinary regimental officers who led their units with loyalty and distinction, enjoying 'being Irish and being different'.[8]

After the South African war, Field Marshal Lord Roberts, first colonel of the Irish Guards and the last Commander-in-Chief of the British Army, was largely responsible for seeing through reforms where serious weaknesses had been exposed. These were mainly in command and staff structure, arms training and leadership. As a result of these reforms, the transition to war was smooth and the British Expeditionary Force which took the field in August 1914, although small by Continental standards, was unquestionably highly trained and well equipped. The development of trench warfare after the initial encounter battles revealed arms deficiencies—notably, grenades, trench-mortars and light machine-guns. To meet the demands of active service, the in-service stocks of shells proved totally inadequate. The British arms industry, adequate for a small professional army and colonial wars, proved incapable of meeting the army's demands for the first two years of war. British industry was not yet fully geared-up to meet the demands of a nation-in-arms at general war with the foremost military power in the world.

All Irish regiments were represented in the BEF, either by their first or second battalions, and not least by the Commander-in-Chief, FM Sir John French, Regimental Colonel, the Royal Irish Regiment.

Irish Units in the British Expeditionary Force August/September 1914

Formation and Commander		*Unit*
Cavalry Division Maj.-Gen. E.H.H. Allenby		4th Royal Irish Dragoon Guards
		5th Royal Irish Lancers
		8th King's Royal Irish Hussars
		The North Irish Horse/South Irish Horse, composite regiment
First Corps Lt.-Gen. Sir D. Haig		
1st Division	1 (Guards) Brigade	2nd Royal Munster Fusiliers
2nd Division	4 (Guards) Brigade	1st Irish Guards
	5 Infantry Brigade	2nd Connaught Rangers
Second Corps Lt.-Gen. Sir H. Smith-Dorrien		
3rd Division	7 Infantry Brigade	2nd Royal Irish Rifles
	8 Infantry Brigade	2nd Royal Irish Regiment
Third Corps Maj.-Gen. W.P. Pulteney		
4th Division	10 Infantry Brigade	1st Royal Irish Fusiliers
		2nd Royal Dublin Fusiliers
	12 Infantry Brigade	2nd Royal Inniskilling Fusiliers
6th Division	17 Infantry Brigade	2nd Leinster Regiment

At the end of July 1914, many of the battalions of the Regular Army were on training exercises, while others were in barracks. But all responded with quiet elation when orders were received to mobilise. For many it was the culmination of a lifetime's preparation. In some cases, like 2nd Leinsters at Fermoy, the arrival of a despatch rider turned their first thoughts to the current situation in Ireland, the Ulster Crisis. The thinking professional officers of the regiments were without illusions as to the consequences of their relative size in any war against Germany. Yet they were confident in their ability, the training and experience of a long-service regular army, matched against a conscript army, however large.[9]

With the slow growth of tensions between Germany and Great Britain in the drift to war, there was a sympathetic leaning towards France because of its defeat in the Franco-Prussian War of 1870. However an uneasy feeling existed that the French were not a match for the German might, although there was a 'generous sympathy which the British officer always feels for an old and honourable opponent'.[10]

Those who had attended Staff College would have had few doubts about the trials ahead. None of the virulent jingoism or racist hatred so evident in the popular press was evinced in the officer corps or ranks of the professional army. They moved in accordance with the mobilisation plan. Spirits were high, but there was no excitement comparable with that seen in the streets of most European or British capital cities. Instead, there was a deep conviction that 'Germany must be settled with once and for all'. A genuine feeling also existed that it would not be accomplished until a 'great deal of blood be shed'.[11]

The initial expeditionary force numbered approximately 70,000 all arms. With the inclusion of the Artillery, Engineers, Medical and Logistic Services, the Irish contingent numbered no less than 15,000 officers and men. More followed as the regulars forming the overseas garrisons were relieved by Territorial Force units and came home to form five new regular divisions.

Irish Units returned from overseas, December 1914

Formation	Unit	Overseas Theatre
8th Division, 25 Brigade	1st Royal Irish Rifles	Aden
27th Division, 82 Brigade	1st Royal Irish Regiment	India
	2nd Royal Irish Fusiliers	India
	1st Leinster Regiment	India
29th Division, 86 Brigade	1st Royal Munster Fusiliers	India
	1st Royal Dublin Fusiliers	India
87 Brigade	1st Royal Inniskilling Fusiliers	India

In October 1914, an army corps of the Indian Army arrived in France. Within its European element was 1st Connaught Rangers in Lahore Division.

On the outbreak of war, the Special Reserve battalions of the Irish regiments were called up. All their officers and men were sent to France in drafts as replacements for the enormous casualties suffered by the regular battalions, demands for which could not be met by regular army reservists alone. Within three months of the outbreak of war, approximately 40,000 Irishmen were, or had been, in action on the Western Front, not including those Irish serving in other British regiments.

To meet the manpower demands of the regular battalions on active service, the twenty Reserve and Special Reserve militia battalions of Irish regiments, unlike the Territorial Force in Great Britain, were retained in Ireland to provide training and reinforcement holding units. This was accepted, although it was a bitter blow to many volunteer officers and soldiers at not being able to go into action under their own unit's identity. Throughout the war these historic formations—the Royal Meath, South Cork, Monaghan and Sligo militia battalions and all the others—proved invaluable, especially training and despatching drafts to the front. Some also formed Garrison Battalions of 'B' Category men which served in Italy, India, Gallipoli, Salonika and Egypt. Many of these men were unfit for front-line duty by virtue of previous line service. All garrison battalions performed an invaluable service by releasing 'battle-infantry' battalions for the front.

Kitchener, highly security conscious, ordered the army to move quietly to France. The BEF left without the wild scenes enacted in Paris, Berlin and Vienna. But there were good send-offs. One draft of the Royal Irish left its regimental depot at Clonmel escorted by the local unit of the National Volunteers under Commandant Drohan.[12] A senior officer of the Royal Irish, Col. Kellet, travelling on the same train on his way to a staff appointment, inspected the volunteers and, to the cheers of the spectators, made a patriotic speech.[13]

A lookout was posted near the barracks of 2nd Leinsters at Cork. Although the battalion left during early morning, Cork rose to give them a rousing send-off.[14] Typically, 2nd Leinsters, the '40-10s', sailed away to the strains of 'Farewell, Isobel' instead of the traditional, 'The Girl I Left Behind Me'. Sometimes Irish regiments sang a parody chorus to the old Irish song, 'I'll do pack-drill in Arbour Hill* for the girl I left behind me.'

The Leinsters' nick-name, the '40-10s', was a regimental family one. In India, turned out one night to meet an emergency, they formed two ranks and numbered from the right. The numbers rattled down the front rank, from one to forty-nine. The fiftieth, who 'had drink taken', shouted 'forty-ten'. Many regiments might have preferred to forget such an occurrence, but not an Irish one. The unfortunate soldier was lampooned from Bombay to Barbados; there, a warship woke up one morning to find '40-10' painted on its side.[15]

The East Surreys of the Curragh Brigade, 5th Division, had been stationed in Wellington Barracks (now Griffith Barracks) in Dublin since 1912 and had been involved in 'unpleasant strike duty' during the Dublin labour lock-out of 1913. A Cockney battalion, the men of the East Surreys very probably understood well the hardship of the strikers' families. They had no trouble with striking workers, and on one occasion when guarding a coal convoy, had been 'unable to stop women scattering the coal'. They were given a rousing send-off. Years later Lt. H.F. Stoneham, who had listened to snipe drumming in the bogs of the Glen of Imaal, had studied lepidoptera on the Donard ranges and had watched a golden eagle, *'aquila chrysaestos*, in

*Arbour Hill Barracks, Dublin.

majestic flight over Keadean mountains towards the Sugar Loaf' recalled leaving Ireland: 'A country that during my several years there I had learned to love, as we steamed down the Liffey, all the ships dipped their flags, accompanied by stupendous cheering from the banks. It was a great and memorable sight.'[16] The East Surreys were commanded by Lt.-Col. John Longley, later GOC 10th Irish Division, during its most successful campaign.

CHAPTER TWO

Ireland Responds

The Irish Home Rule Bill crisis had brought the United Kingdom to the brink of civil war. It was overshadowed by a greater one caused by an assassin's bullets at Sarajevo. On 4 August 1914, Great Britain declared war on Germany in response to the violation of Belgian neutrality. British politicians, realising where their major interest lay, immediately assumed roles in the greater tragedy. The leaders of both Irish factions responded differently to meet the new situation.

> Redmond had no doubts as to where the real interests of Ireland lay. He believed that Ireland should support England to the maximum degree, thereby demonstrating a loyalty and friendship that was certain to be rewarded after the guns were still. He likewise saw the war as an opportunity for welding north and south together. He wanted to raise an all-Irish force with its own officers and colours, to be used both in defence of the state and on the continent. But these plans were frustrated by the War Office.[1]

In the first and second 'Hundred Thousand', volunteers known as K1 and K2, two 'Irish' divisions were formed in accordance with New Army policy, completely under War Office control. There were to be no 'private armies' in Ireland. Ulster Unionist leaders, however, were slower to respond to the call to arms.

> Sir Edward Carson's position was not easy. He was most eager to help by every means in his power. But he had a heavy responsibility towards the people of Ulster. If the fighting men of the province were to go to the war, and in their absence a Home Rule Act, such as they had banded themselves together to resist, were to be forced upon those they had left behind, they would have cause to reproach him.[2]

The Ulster Volunteer Force was not to escape Kitchener's trawl for men to man his New Armies. Although its leaders procrastinated, they were to be brought into the New Army. Already organised in regimental and brigade formations, its initial training was well advanced, if illegally. It could be prepared and committed to active service more easily than any other formation of the New Army. In this Kitchener failed. Carson was playing for high stakes and was prepared to hold out, to the consternation of his supporters at the War Office.

During the Ulster Crisis, Henry Wilson had pressed upon Craig and Carson the need to reiterate at every opportunity that the 'Ulster army' would be at Britain's disposal in the event of war. The time had come, and the Ulster leaders hesitated. However, agreement was eventually reached, with minor concessions to regional pride, and the 36th Ulster Division was formed. But while Kitchener used the Ulster Unionists, he could have no doubt about the threat they could later pose to the government of which he was a minister and to which he was unquestionably loyal. For this reason it is significant that artillery organic to the Ulster Division was not raised: 'At first it had been suggested that the artillery should also be raised in Ulster, but this project was not proceeded with.'[3] This could not have been a popular decision with the Ulstermen and it received 'much attention and gave rise to much discussion'.[4] But inevitably the War Office ruling had to be accepted.

For reasons given by Sir George Arthur in his biography, the Secretary of State for War was unsympathetic to Redmond's requests for a separate Irish army. But Kitchener allowed two minor concessions. The shamrock, which he suggested, was authorised as a divisional emblem for the 16th Division. This was not a difficult decision, as Queen Victoria had *ordered* its distribution annually to her Irish troops on St Patrick's Day. The second concession was the use of 'Irish' in the divisional title. Again, it meant little, for after initially resisting Redmond's request, it became official War Office policy to allow regional prefixes to divisional titles as an inducement to recruiting. Kitchener's rejection of Redmond's proposals now seems difficult to understand. An outstanding Irish fighting general, Gen. Sir Alex Godley, was in favour of Redmond's proposal, and his uncle, John Robert Godley, was Under Secretary of State for War.

> I have always thought that if those in authority had had the vision and foresight in the early stages of the War, to raise three divisions in Ireland—one in Belfast, one in Dublin and one in Cork—and to turn them into an Irish Army Corps under command of John Redmond, the history of my distressful country might have been very different... And what a nucleus for that corps would have been all the splendid Irish regular regiments with their glorious records and traditions. But the English politicians, and I am afraid many English soldiers, were totally unable to understand Irishmen. They would not trust them ...[5]

RECRUITING

In Ireland, the Regular Army reservists reported to their regimental depots, and within twenty-four hours were kitted and despatched in drafts to the

Home Service battalion. With the King's Proclamation, the two cavalry regiments and twenty infantry battalions of the Irish Special Reserve were embodied. The North Irish Horse and South Irish Horse were on summer camp at the outbreak of war. They formed a composite regiment of Irish Horse which, upon going to France, joined the BEF just after Mons; they took part in the retreat, the only Territorial Force unit to do so. The Special Reserve infantry units began training to provide drafts for their battalions in France. So great were the casualties on the Western Front that these had to be sent practically half-trained. These battalions also relieved the Regulars in guarding key installations throughout Ireland. Men flocked to the recruiting offices, but without the wild scenes of enthusiasm seen in Britain because much of the available manpower was already in uniform. Old soldiers volunteered and were accepted. Young men of spirit from all classes joined. Most outstanding were 350 rugby football players from the Dublin area who paraded at Lansdowne Road rugby ground and then marched through the city on their way to the Curragh and 7th Dublins.[6] Another element of 7th Dublins was a company of tough Dublin dockers, called 'Larkinites' after the union leader, James Larkin.[7]

Most recruits were sent to Irish regimental depots. After reception, documentation, medical examination and kitting, they received some training before being passed on to the the next phase. A regiment's reserve battalions were responsible for completing basic training and for advanced training of all recruits. The trained soldier was then drafted to a battalion on active service. However, in the early stages of the war, replacements were so urgently needed at the front that often half-trained soldiers were drafted. Later in the war, drafts intended for Irish regiments were diverted by Reinforcement Holding Units in France to other units or formations whose needs might be desperate. This caused heartache to the depots, regiments and men alike. In his excellent diary of the trenches, *Stand To*, Capt. F.C. Hitchcock, 2nd Leinsters, tells of fifty men destined for his battalion being sent to the Black Watch. Hitchcock also relates how 160 men of the 5th Royal Irish Lancers who had volunteered specifically for 2nd Leinsters were sent to 13th Middlesex, with the Leinsters receiving a draft of Dorset Regiment soldiers. During the battle of Neuve Chapelle, 1st Irish Guards were less concerned about enemy shelling than the fact that a draft of Irishmen under Maj. the Earl of Rosse were discovered to be 'attached to the Scots Guards'.[8]

By May 1915, all regular battalions had repeatedly been heavily engaged, and their losses were horrific. The recruits coming forward were urgently required, not only for the New Army divisions then forming, but also as replacements for battle casualties in the regular battalions. Two examples are shown below: the replacements provided by the Depot, Royal Irish Rifles, for all its battalions, and the replacements provided by Depot, Royal Irish Fusiliers, for its 1st Battalion, after they had embarked at full strength for active service.

| | Royal Irish Rifles[9] | | | | Royal Irish Fusiliers[10] |
| | (All Battalions) | | | | (1st Battalion only)[*] |
Year	3rd Bn	4th Bn	5th Bn	Total	3rd and 4th Bns totals
1914	1098	153	380	1631	768
1915	2469	577	582	3628	1396
1916	1878	439	569	2885	1246
1917	1243	561	206	2010	1235
1918	1381	458	197	2036	1985
Totals	8879	2188	1934	12,191	6630

[*] This includes returned wounded.

There were eight infantry regimental depots in Ireland.

Some men, or all in the case of 36th Ulster Division, were recruited directly into particular battalions for service with one of the three Irish divisions. Recruits who enlisted directly in this way received all their training with those battalions, except for some specialist courses.

RECRUITING THE NEW ARMY DIVISIONS

Available manpower for Irish New Army divisions being limited when spread over three divisions, it was nowhere completely satisfactory. Being first, 10th Division had a decided advantage. It attracted directly to its ranks the first flood of volunteers to the New Army; they came from all sections of Ireland's political and religious communities. All were resolved to ignore previous differences 'for the duration'.[11] Most old soldiers also re-enlisted in the 10th. Additional to this was the surplus from the English Division's First One Hundred Thousand. This was so because the regional system under which the New Armies were organised took no account of mass centres—the Clyde/Forth conurbation in Scotland, the industrial north of England, the Midlands and the London area. Rural England found it as difficult to raise its quota as rural Ireland.[12]

By a tradition existing in the British army since Napoleonic times, English Roman Catholics were usually sent to Irish regiments, in this case the 10th Division New Army battalions. Not unnaturally, most of these were reported as being descended from Irish immigrants of the nineteenth century. This is partially confirmed by the names and places of birth shown in the casualty lists.[13] Notwithstanding this addition, when 10th Division went to Aldershot Command in May 1915 to prepare for overseas, it was understrength because of the weeding out of unfit men. Bringing its units up to war establishment demanded drafts of 300 from all battalions of 16th Division. Hardest hit by this was its 49 Brigade which was already understrength.

Subterfuge towards preparing for the Ulster Division's formation denied recruits which ought more properly have gone to the 10th Division. Capt. A. St Q. Ricardo DSO, recalled from the Reserve of Officers, assumed command of the Inniskilling Depot at Omagh. Before the formation of the Ulster

Division was authorised, he held on the strength recruits for battalions with 10th or 16th Divisions. From these he held back two companies, about 400 men, for a battalion of 36th Division, not then formed, which later became 9th Inniskillings.[14] Ricardo had no authority for this, nor could he affect officer movements. Therefore the officers went as they wished or were sent on War Office instructions; most went to Gallipoli with the 10th Division. But Ricardo was in a position to influence the movements of other ranks from the depot to specific units. This he did, to the detriment of battalions preparing for early active service.

36th Division, drawn from the Ulster Army of 90,000 men, was not without its manning problems. Recruits were perforce accepted from the industrial cities of north-east England and Scotland, sometimes from elements not particularly in keeping with the image of the division. One draft of 300 drunken Orangemen from Glasgow gave its conducting officer and NCO more trouble than they had ever had in all their previous army careers.[15] On War Office instructions, men were allowed to transfer from 10th Division to 36th Division; this affected the two Inniskilling battalions in 31 Brigade: 'The battalion was at full strength and was progressing fast when the War Office wrote to our brigade giving men in it the option of joining the new Ulster Division; about half the men of A Company left us.'[16] The gaps in the Inniskilling battalion were filled by a draft from the Duke of Cornwall's Light Infantry (DCLI), mainly Londoners.

In England and Scotland, the development of industry onto a war footing was sometimes delayed by a shortage of skilled tradesmen, since many had enlisted. This was better managed later; in the Second World War, those in essential jobs had their enlistments deferred. In the First World War, Belfast shipyard and engineering works-management quickly saw this danger, and patriotic fervour was placed second to business needs. Sir George Richardson, commander of the UVF, assisted in this on behalf of employers by persuading highly-skilled UVF men to stay at their workplaces.[17]

Recruiting for the Irish New Army divisions, in itself difficult, was exacerbated by the GOC 16th Division, Sir Lawrence Parsons. His well-meaning and understandable desire to obtain only the finest for his division was not helped by his strictures against 'slum birds' and 'corner-boy elements' which discouraged many and ignored hard recruiting facts. His tactless, not to say offensive, rebuffs of helpful offers and suggestions did nothing to assist recruitment for his division. His rejection of the Tyneside Irish was particularly shameful.[18] Direct recruiting for the 16th Division was slow because the regular battalions needed constant replacements, especially following First and Second Ypres, the landings at Gallipoli and other battles of 1915. Improved recruiting sometimes depended upon the effort, and money, which battalion commanders were prepared to expend. The commanding officer of 7th Inniskillings, Lt.-Col. Michael Hughes, was faced with the possibility of his battalion being disbanded after transferring 300 men to 10th Division. By his own efforts and money, he recruited 670, ninety of whom came from the north of England.[19] The success of his personal efforts can in itself be taken as a poor reflection on the organisation of the official recruiting effort in Ireland.

Officer selection and training also presented problems which were common to all three divisions. The officer corps of 10th Division was found from a variety of sources. Officers of Irish extraction serving with the Indian Army or seconded to colonial forces, who were on leave or courses in the United Kingdom on the outbreak of war, were ordered to report for duty to 10th Division. Many officers came from the reserve of officers or were transferred from the Royal Irish Constabulary. Junior officer vacancies were filled from the ranks of the elite D Company, 7th Dublins or the established Officer Training Corps of Irish universities and colleges. Some retired officers returned specifically to the 36th Division; others were posted in exactly the same was as any other New Army division to the 36th. Some officers of 36th Division were commissioned with the Ulster Volunteer Force and some of 16th Division's officers had been with the National Volunteers.[20] Others came from the reserve of officers; many junior officers were received from the Cadet Company of 7th Leinsters. This, a highly successful innovation of that regiment, was used by Gen. Parsons as the means of selecting and training junior officers for the entire division. Later, when War Office policy changed, this company became an official officer cadet training unit.

There was another way, under authority issued from the War Office in mid September 1914, in which commanding officers could recommend individuals for commissioning which, if endorsed by brigade commanders, would be approved for probationary, then temporary, commissions. From the outset, Parsons appears to have been importuned for commissions. Understandably, he particularly resented recommendations from politicians. The system of commissioning by purchase and promotion by patronage had only recently been discontinued. To many older officers who had memories of this system, it was an extremely sensitive issue. To them, the merest hint of 'political interference' in army affairs was anathema. However Parsons' brusque refusals to excellent potential gave needless offence and created understandable ill-feeling. One person refused in this way was the son of Mr John Redmond MP, who afterwards, without help from his father or Parsons, became a Guards officer who won an immediate DSO.[21] Direct granting of commissioned ceased from February 1916. Thereafter, candidates for commissions had to attend and successfully pass an Officer Cadet Training Unit course.

For a time, divisional badges became another source of friction between soldiers and politicians. Without the knowledge of the Ulster Division, Unionist politicians had somehow obtained approval from the War Office for a distinctive Red Hand cap badge for that division. On discovering this, nationalist politicians were incensed and raised the matter with Parsons for a comparable badge for 16th Division. Sir Lawrence flatly refused to countenance any equivalent for the 16th, pointing out that some Irish regiments wore a harp and a shamrock scroll, and disdainfully dismissed any others as 'silly badges.'[22] The matter was dropped when the Ulster Division, on receiving the badges, raised such an outcry against them that they were quickly withdrawn.[23] The Ulstermen had demonstrated most emphatically to politicians that the badges of the Irish Fusiliers, Inniskillings or Irish Rifles meant more to them than a party badge. The matter of divisional signs was then raised and eventually the Red Hand was approved for 36th Division, while the 16th wore the shamrock. By mid-1916, distinctive signs were worn by almost every division and painted on vehicles throughout the British Expeditionary Force. In World War II, formation signs in most armies became a minor branch of heraldry. Far from these political wranglings, the battalions of 10th Division, with or without official approval, were attaching various distinguishing insignia to their helmets, usually incorporating the shamrock. [24]

EQUIPMENT AND TRAINING

Like all Kitchener army divisions, the development of all three Irish ones was constrained by lack of equipment and matériel. An army order published shortly after the outbreak of war outlined the training requirements and objectives in the altered circumstances of war and mass recruiting. It prescribed All Arms courses of six months' training in elaborate detail, with timetables. The syllabus provided for a basic recruit's course, a trained soldier's course and collective company, battalion, brigade and divisional training. The content was considerable and covered every aspect of military training, from elementary drill, discipline and personal hygiene to brigade and division collective training.[25] Of the Irish divisions, the War Office syllabus was fully carried out only by 10th Division before embarking for active service.

Initially, training progressed slowly and was restricted to basic foot drill and route marches. Lectures on various subjects filled the gaps in the training day and provided an alternative in poor weather. In the organisation of the New Armies, one of the major problems facing the War Office was manufacturers in both the United States and Great Britain who, for their own commercial reasons, promised delivery dates which were hopelessly unrealistic. In the competitive atmosphere of the time, and given a general shortage of raw materials and manufacturing plant, all inevitably failed to meet promised dates.[26] (The Bethlehem Steel works in Pennsylvania received an order for 400 18-pounder guns in 1914, 'for delivery in 1916: one year later this order had not been completed'.[27]) Not only did this cause bitter disappointment and frustration to the New Army; but to the out-gunned BEF it also meant defeat and heavy loss of life. Not until 1916 was the manufacturing economy of Great Britain properly geared for the demands being made upon it.

But the War Office system was also faulty. The desperately needed 9.2 inch heavy howitzers were ordered on 4 September 1914. The contract was not signed until 7 October; and the ammunition for the guns, instead of being ordered, was put out to tender.[28] All the available equipment was required in France, and later in the Middle East, to replace losses and equip reinforcements. Only obsolete and unserviceable arms and equipment could be made available for initial basic training. The frustration engendered by this scarcity and its effect on both training and morale can easily be understood. In Ireland, it might be seen as a desire on the part of the War Office to place the 16th or 36th Divisions low in the pecking order. This, however, is not borne out by the facts.

Less easy to understand in Ireland was the scarcity of horses which affected all arms and services of the embryonic divisions. In this scarcity, the artillery of 16th Division was particularly affected: 'It was some time before the batteries were able to obtain even fifteen horses each for training purposes.[29] A likely explanation for this is that the sudden demand forced up prices. Thus farmers, in a seller's market, held onto suitable animals in the expectation of further price increases. Then, even when horses were obtained, harness was limited.[30]

Yet incredibly, notwithstanding all its difficulties, one Irish division went into action during August 1915 and the other two went to France in the autumn and winter of 1915–16. Ironically, brigades of 16th Division, heavily recruited from the Irish nationalist community, first came under two Irish commanders who had opposed Irish nationalism, Lt.-Gen. Henry Wilson, Commander IV Corps, and Lt.-Gen. Hubert Gough, Commander I Corps.

CHAPTER THREE

The BEF at Mons and Le Cateau, 23–26 August 1914

One of the first disagreements between Kitchener and Sir John French was the concentration area of the BEF in France. Amiens was the planned detraining zone, but shortly after British entry into the war, France's Commander-in-Chief, Gen. Joffre, pressed for a more forward one at Maubeuge. Kitchener was against this: 'Nothing, he urged, could be worse for the *morale* of our troops than that the result of their first meeting for over fifty years with a European enemy should be a compulsory retirement, which he regarded as the too likely sequel to detraining so far forward.'[1]

However, strong military intuition is no match for reasoned planning staff arguments. Had Kitchener been Chief of the Imperial General Staff, as senior Field Marshal he could have over-ruled staff objections. But as Secretary of State, his was a political appointment and he could not do so. Where there was disagreement between the political and professional heads of the army, it has to be resolved by the Prime Minister. It was a nice constitutional point, and Mr Asquith sided with the 'experts'.[2]

Having detrained in the Maubeuge area, the BEF crossed the Sambre and marched forward on Mons. The French, both civilians and soldiers, were delighted to see them and cheered their passing, shouting *'Vivent les Anglais.'* The Irish (and no doubt the Scots) left them in no doubt as to their nationality: 'For my company I gaily corrected them: *"Nous ne sommes pas Anglais, nous sommes Irlandais"*. They liked that and laughed with pleasure, and then shouted: *"Vivent les Irlandais"*, and we cheered and shouted back at them *"Vive la France."* [3] All the BEF sang as they marched at ease along the pavé roads of northern France that blazing summer. Of the many songs they sang, none became more associated with the British arrival as allies, after centuries as enemies, than 'Tipperary'. In 1964 Gen. Charles de Gaulle inspected a British contingent at a commemoration ceremony. He did so almost indifferently until they marched past to 'Tipperary'. As the khaki column swung by to its music, a chord of memory must have been struck, and the flicker of a smile was seen to pass across the general's face.

All battalions of the BEF were nearly 50 per cent recalled reservists. Some had left the army up to seven years before and most were physically unfit. In the rushed mobilisation and movement, there had been no time for fitness or musketry training. Many suffered from foot blisters and shoulder sores from carrying equipment. Some were holding a loaded rifle for the first time in years.

MONS—23 AUGUST 1914

On 23 August, the German Goliath met the British David in an encounter battle at Mons. On the right of II Corps, 3rd Division defended a salient formed by the Conde Canal as it skirted north of Mons and Nimy. 8 Brigade was on the right, 9 Brigade on the left and 7 Brigade in reserve. Brig. Doran deployed his 8 Brigade in a north-south line east of Bois la Haute and facing eastwards. From the right were 2nd Royal Scots and 1st Gordons behind the Nimy–Hermignies road and 4th Middlesex guarding the Obourg Bridge. The 2nd Royal Irish were in brigade reserve. A gap existed between 4th Middlesex and the right battalion of 9 Brigade. Advancing towards them from the north and north-east were 17th and 18th Divisions of the German IX Corps. The Royal Irish had their breakfast interrupted and were ordered to move to support the Middlesex. Having arrived and settled down, their dinner was also interrupted as they were called to move back to their original position.[4] A gap between 9 and 8 Brigades had left the Middlesex flank exposed. To cover it, the Irish moved under fire which became intense as their move was observed.[5] Despite this, the battalion was in position at Petit Nimy at 1330. The German artillery had complete ascendancy, and with good observation from north of the canal, they used their guns effectively. The area was one of small vegetable patches bordered with hedgerows, broken by wire fences and sunken roads. But there was no real cover. The Irish deployed in company positions using whatever shelter they could, digging rifle pits where there were none. That morning, the CO of the Royal Irish, Lt.-Col. St J.A. Cox, had gone to brigade headquarters and throughout the day was separated from his battalion. Maj. St Leger was in command.[6]

The Germans, partly screened by Bois d'Havré, crossed the canal at Obourg and for three hours the Irish and Middlesex defended stubbornly. At first the Germans came in dense formations and offered ideal targets. When this proved too costly, they shook out into extended order. The German IX Corps was throwing its full weight against their exposed position. Firing from their first position, the two Royal Irish machine-guns caught German cavalry emerging from the Bois d'Havré 600 yards away. The Irish fire caused carnage among massed horses and men. In turn, the Royal Irish came under accurate German shell-fire and both guns were knocked out. Under this fire, the machine-gun sergeant salvaged parts from one gun, and, repairing the other, continued firing. Both gun-crews suffered heavy loss, but held tight to their repaired gun. By 1515, the Germans were within a few hundred yards of the Royal Irish and had worked around both flanks.

Early in the fight, OC A Company, the Hon. Fergus Forbes, brother of Earl Granard and direct descendant of the founder of the regiment, was mortally wounded, with the other two officers and many men wounded by shell-fire. Without pause, the sergeant-major and sergeants automatically took command and the fight continued. The Adjutant, Lt. R.E.G. Phillips, was lightly wounded while organising a fall-back line, but he carried on. The wounded were evacuated to a civilian hospital, where the medical officer established the Regimental Aid Post. The hospital came under shell-fire. So, to save the wounded from further injury, the medical officer had the wounded carried down to cellars; he stayed with them when the enemy over-ran the position. During the action, D Company became separated from the rest of the battalion and under its commander, Maj. Daniell, fell back on the Gordons.

An 18-pounder gun-section, attempting to support the Royal Irish and Middlesex, only succeeded in drawing heavy fire on itself, and was lucky to escape. The two infantry battalions, supporting each other well, withdrew fighting to Bois la Haut. Here the Middlesex passed through the Irish and retired to Nouvelles, the second position. When the Royal Irish attempted to follow, they found the Germans had blocked the road. The gun-section was also halted, apparently because the enemy was trying to cut off 8 Brigade. The gunners and infantry entrenched around the guns near the crossroads and waited.

Enfilade covering fire from troops on their right flank saved the Royal Irish and Artillery detachment from complete destruction. The Gordons, Royal Scots and Royal Irish Rifles were entrenched on the Mons–Givry road in good concealed positions. Although they could do nothing to help the Middlesex and Royal Irish from the German northern attacks, they prevented envelopment from the east. RQMS T.W. Fitzpatrick, with the forward Quartermasters detachment of forty cooks, drivers, storemen and batmen, saw the withdrawal of D Company. Accurately assessing the situation, Fitzpatrick gathered his men and led them to the left flank of 1st Gordons and placed himself under its company commander. From here his detachment gave fire-support covering the withdrawal of the Royal Irish and 4th Middlesex. He held this position until 2300 when ordered to withdraw and rejoin the battalion. For his initiative and gallantry, Warrant Officer Fitzpatrick was deservedly decorated with the Distinguished Conduct Medal (DCM) and awarded a battlefield commission.[7]

The brigade commander, Brig. Doran (late Royal Irish), ordered his brigade to withdraw to Nouvelles at 2100. An hour later, he met the Royal Irish just north of Hyron and told them it was imperative to gain contact with the Gordons. After leading two companies himself in a fruitless attempt to do so, Doran ordered St Leger to withdraw the battalion south-eastward to the Mons–Givry road. There the battalion linked up with D Company, the Quartermasters detachment and the Gordons. That night at 2300, the last of 8 Brigade withdrew from its exposed position and retired to Nouvelles.

Earlier that same day at 1600, two companies of the 2nd Royal Irish Rifles were ordered to support 8 Brigade and came up on the right of the Royal Scots. The German artillery discovered their position and shelled it, whereupon the boisterous Belfast and Dublin riflemen watched and commented on the shell-bursts with professional, high-spirited and good-humoured interest: '"Washout", "Another miss". One wag, simulating great terror, cried: "Send for the police, there's going to be a row on here."'[8]

It was evening on 23 August. Anxious to force the British line before nightfall, the Germans attacked the English, Scottish and Irish battalions of II Corps in perfect formation about 1900. Impatient of further delay and determined to crush opposition by weight of numbers before dark, dense columns of Germans advanced, almost disdainful of the opposition. Using favourable ground, they were able to get within 300 yards of the British line. From there, in accordance with their tactical doctrine, they would be able to overwhelm by force of numbers. The German shelling stopped. It was now the turn of the infantry. Watching the German mass advance, the British regulars waited in silence, rifles held casually, each loaded with eleven rounds, one in the breech and ten in the magazine. On the command 'Watch your front' the weapons were brought to the aim. 'At two hundred yards,' safety catches were pushed forward. 'Rapid'—the word was a long, drawn-out yell, and first pressure was taken on the trigger. 'Fire', with a deafening crash the British line erupted. Thereafter, orders were transmitted by whistle.

The 'mad-minute' of at least fifteen aimed rounds a minute struck the enemy with destructive force. Many of the British regular soldiers had become first-class shots; some were even marksmen because it increased their pay. They were able to work a rifle-bolt with a dexterous roll of the right hand, opening the bolt with the index finger and closing it with the ball of the thumb, then squeezing the trigger with the index finger, all in one flowing motion. Rifle slings wrapped around the left elbow held the rifle perfectly tight to the shoulder, allowing the rifleman to hold the point of aim while the bolt was worked. The flat trajectory of the Lee-Enfield at close range against dense masses could find more than one victim. Beside each soldier were several clips of ammunition. Each round fired was counted. At the end of the fill, a fresh clip was placed in the breech-charger guide of the opened bolt. With thumb on top of the five rounds and four fingers under the wooden stock, the rounds were pressed firmly into the magazine; this was done twice. When the ammunition of the second clip was rammed home, the bolt, pushed forward firmly, sent the empty clip flying and a round into the breech. Almost at the same instant, the first shot was fired. With practice, the whole sequence of movements became mechanical: 'Our rapid fire was appalling even to us, and the worst marksman could not miss.'[9]

Under the weight of fire, the German columns staggered. But by their sheer momentum and disciplined bravery, they somehow managed to maintain a forward movement. Struck repeatedly by this savage blizzard, the enemy infantry columns lost cohesion and disintegrated, shattered before a foe they had hitherto dismissed as insignificant. The survivors fell back into the darkness. Cease-fire was ordered to allow the Germans to collect their wounded; they were seen to do so by the light of lanterns.[10]

Unknown to the entrenched troops, the French Fifth Army, on the right of the BEF, had retreated after being attacked in front by the German Second Army and on the right flank by the 3rd. Its commander, Gen. Lanrezac, neglected to inform Sir John French of this. Late that night, Sir John became aware of what had happened and ordered a retirement. The two forward brigades of 3rd Division withdrew through 7 Brigade, and just after midnight they in turn fell back through 1st Irish and 2nd Grenadiers of 4 Guards Brigade. At Mons, the losses of the Middlesex and Royal Irish had been severe—400 and 300 respectively.[11] The Gordons, Royal Scots and Irish Rifles had hardly been touched. The German IX Corps, because of its outdated tactics, had been savagely mauled.

2nd Connaught Rangers were entrenched at a crossroads on a ridge a mile and a half south of Mons. In perfect summer weather, they could see shells bursting and thought it wonderful. It was their first experience of German shelling and shortly all became familiar with heavy German howitzer shells—Black Marias or Coal Boxes which sent up tall pillars of black smoke, while the white shrapnel puffs of 77 mm field-guns became whizz-bangs. All afternoon and late into the evening, the Connaughtmen had an excellent view of the battle. They cheered when dense German columns were repulsed by the single line of British infantry.[12]

Next morning shortly after daybreak, the Rangers were told to stop digging. A retirement was about to be ordered and they would act as rear-guard. They watched as the troops moved back. Not all units were as organised as they might have been. However, the 2nd Royal Irish and the 4th Middlesex, which had been most seriously engaged, were in marked contrast and marched off 'as if on parade'.[13]

At 1100 on 24 August, the enemy shelled the ridge held by 5 Brigade. Then, at about 1200, the Rangers were one of the last units off the field. After all had passed through their position, they fell back, company by company. When all were assembled in echelon, the battalion marched off. Shrapnel followed the column for nearly an hour, although it was 'still too high,'[14] wrote the battalion chronicler with an almost audible sniff of professional disdain. However, greater respect developed for enemy artillery when German heavies caught the battalion transport and destroyed water carriers and mess-wagons, 'which caused considerable trouble', he then moaned.[15] The Rangers passed through 1st Irish Guards, 2nd Grenadiers and other battalions of 4 Guards Brigade who were now the rear-guard. The battalion machine-gun section had been sent to support the Royal Irish and did not return until after the retreat; it would be the Rangers' misfortune to fight an action without them.

Across the BEF's line of retreat lay the obstacle of Mormal Forest through which there were no good north-south roads. Both corps of the BEF had to separate to pass it, intending to unite to its south and make a stand on high ground around Le Cateau. I Corps moved to the east and Smith-Dorrien's II Corps to the west. The greater part of the large and unwieldy cavalry division, four and then five brigades, was acting closely with II Corps, which seemed most vulnerable. Without an adequate cavalry screen, elements of I Corps were surprised by German troops several times during the retreat. The attack on the rearguard, 4 Guards Brigade at Landrecies during the night of 26–27 August, was the most serious. On the 26th, the Connaught Rangers were also surprised at the village of Grand-Fayt when it was again rearguard to its brigade.

One Ranger company was detailed to escort the brigade transport. They withdrew with it until all were clear of Grand-Fayt and then halted for a time. Having rested, eaten and received no orders, the company commander ordered a retirement which was meant to cover the brigade transport and brigade headquarters, his action possibly being prompted by hearing firing from behind. A second company was ordered by the commanding officer to retire to Grand-Fayt, where brigade headquarters was thought to be; they were to hold it and arrange billets. This company endured some shelling during the afternoon. After attempting without success to gain contact with battalion headquarters, it also retired in the early evening.

At midday, Col. Abercrombie covered Grand-Fayt with two companies on a ridge north of the village. From there he sent a message to brigade headquarters, informing them of his position and of his intention to remain there until 1500 unless ordered to the contrary.[16] When the brigade transport and escort had withdrawn through their lines towards Grand-Fayt, Abercrombie, inexplicably, did not retire at 1500 as he had stated. Fifteen minutes later, a French cavalry patrol passed word of a strong enemy force with machine-guns 'quite close'. Abercrombie took two platoons about 600 yards to his left flank, towards the reported enemy, before he was stopped by machine-gun and artillery fire. He ordered his remaining force to fall back to a defensive position while he held that exposed position and waited for developments. It was a fatal error. Having pinned down the British rear-guard, the Germans turned their flank, gained their rear and cut them off.[17]

Receiving no information or instructions, at 1800 Abercrombie belatedly ordered a retirement. Approaching Grand-Fayt, his force was caught by heavy fire from enemy troops positioned in houses and enclosures. The Rangers fought their way through the village, leaving behind one officer and fourteen rangers dead, two officers and over fifty rangers wounded, and an equal number taken as prisoners. A handful under the second-in-command, Maj. W.S. Sarsfield, fought their way south. The remnant, Lt.-Col. Abercrombie with one other officer and about fifty men, reached a position some 600 yards west of the village and remained there until 1930. They retired westward as dark descended.

Some time later on the Maroilles–Prisches road, Abercrombie's remnant met Col. H.N. Thompson RAMC, ADMS 2nd Division. Thompson had been treating wounded in Maroilles and was retiring to Prisches when he met the Rangers. Seeing they were 'lost, and very hungry and weary, in fact absolutely done',[18] he decided to take them to Maroilles where the British had left a considerable amount of rations.[19] In the early dawn of 27 August, Lt.-Col. Abercrombie and his men were surprised at Maroilles and captured. Col. Thompson was also captured nearby.

In the fight at Grand-Fayt against dismounted troops of First Guard Cavalry Brigade and a battalion of Guard Sharpshooters, 2nd Connaught Rangers lost heavily. Their losses, including those captured at Maroilles, were one officer and fourteen other ranks killed or died of wounds and five officers and 180 other ranks taken prisoner. Many of the prisoners were wounded. Among the captured officers was the commanding officer, Lt.-Col. Abercrombie, who died in Germany the following year. Of the other four officers, two were invalided from Germany, and one escaped to England on his ninth attempt and was badly wounded on his return to the Front.

The scattered Ranger companies went their separate ways during the night of 26–27 August and were reunited on 27–28 near Guise. Second-in-command Maj. W.S. Sarsfield escaped with another officer from the debacle at Grand-Fayt. He rejoined his troops on the evening of the 27th and assumed command. That evening, the battalion was once more ready for action. Next day at 0700, 5 Brigade, 'more or less reorganised',[20] continued the retreat.

THE BATTLE OF LE CATEAU, 26 AUGUST 1914

Gen. Smith-Dorrien's II Corps, with its right flank resting on the Mormal Forest and its left flank completely open, was pressed hard by the Germans. Executing their great wheel in accordance with the Schlieffen Plan, the huge enemy columns were dangerously close to II Corps' front and exposed left flank. Squeezed into a narrow corridor between the forest and outflanking Germans, Allenby's cavalry was given no room to manoeuvre.

Despite the difficulties, II Corps withdrew successfully to Le Cateau on the night of 25–26 August. However, Sir John French ordered a further retirement next morning.

Smith-Dorrien's situation was critical. With the enemy almost in contact, Gen. Allenby had come to advise him that the cavalry would be unable to screen him in a withdrawal. GOC 3rd Division also advised Smith-Dorrien that the troops were exhausted. One brigade, the 7th, had just arrived at 0200, and would be in no condition to move again at first light. In fact the last battalion to arrive was the rearguard, 2nd Irish Rifles, which rejoined its brigade at 0400. Faced with these facts, Smith-Dorrien made his courageous decision to stand and fight.

3rd Division stood in the centre on a general line Troisvilles–Audencourt–Caudry which was held by 9, 8 and 7 Brigades in that order. In 7 Brigade, 2nd Irish Rifles formed a support line at Caudry; 2nd Royal Irish was near Audencourt.

On 3rd Division's right flank was 5th Division and on the left the newly arrived 4th Division. In this last were 2nd Inniskillings, 1st Irish Fusiliers and 2nd Dublins. On the morning of the 26th, 8 Brigade stood to arms from 0300 to 0500. The Gordons and Royal Scots entrenched around the northern fringe of Audencourt, with the Royal Irish and Middlesex in reserve. Later that morning, the Middlesex entrenched on the east of the village. Maj. St Leger was then ordered to take two companies of Royal Irish and extend the line to the left of the Gordons towards Caudry. Maj. Daniell with B Company was sent to Caudry to help 7 Brigade hold the town. A Company remained in reserve south-west of Audencourt and dug trenches astride the road. Lt.-Col. Cox was wounded at 1000 but remained in the trenches on a stretcher. St Leger ought to have been informed and should have taken over command, but Col. Cox continued to command from his stretcher, possibly because he had not commanded the battalion in action at Mons and wished to do so now.

In extending the Gordons' line, St Leger posted C Company and a platoon of D Company in a railway cutting. The rest of D Company under Maj. Panter-Downes was thrown back as flank-guard facing Caudry. The men scraped shallow pits with their 'grubbers' in the surrounding beet fields. The knee-high foliage provided cover from view but none from fire.

Daniell's company moved to Caudry where it was ordered to assist 3rd Worcesters in holding the town. He placed two platoons facing north-east, with two platoons in support. A Royal Irish machine-gun section exacted praise from a section commander of 2nd Irish Rifles with its tactics of fire and movement. Word of their fine performance at Mons had spread through the army and 'we were glad to have any of them near us'.[21] A high-explosive bombardment was kept on Caudry until about 1400. It was then that Maj. Daniell discovered the north-west part of the town had been almost completely evacuated and decided to retire. Daniell collected his company and withdrew from Caudry. He circled back to Audencourt where he rejoined the battalion just as the order for general retirement was given.

An extraordinary artillery action began with gunners using 19th century tactics fighting with 20th century artillery pieces. Unlike the British field artillery which only fired shrapnel, the German field-guns fired high-explosives as well. This, however, was offset by the speed with which the British ranged and shot. Although giving a good account of itself, the British artillery was heavily out-gunned and lost guns when its gun-teams were put out of action. In one of these situations, 32nd Brigade commander, Lt.-Col. M.J. MacCarthy, called for volunteers to rescue the guns of 27th Battery, personally leading gun-teams to save them.[22] In a similar action with 37th Battery, Capt. Reynolds and two sergeants were awarded the Victoria Cross.[23]

The enemy shelled the front of 3rd Division and caused heavy damage at Caudry, but otherwise made no infantry frontal attacks. On the flanks, however, the battle was raging furiously. Having greatly superior numbers, Germany's von Kluck sought to turn both flanks of the British, and to envelop and destroy II Corps. By the rules of war, he ought to have done so. The full weight of the enemy attack, therefore, fell on 4th and 5th Divisions until the afternoon.

At 1500, GOC 3rd Division, Maj.-Gen. Walter Hamilton, replaced Brig. McCracken in command of 7 Brigade with Lt.-Col. Bird of 2nd Irish Rifles. McCracken had been concussed by a shell-burst and for a time there were conflicting orders, but Bird established control and Caudry, under heavy shelling, was evacuated. About this time, B Company, 2nd Royal Irish, returned to its battalion. A short time later, 5th Division on the right was forced back by overwhelming pressure and the withdrawal commenced. All 3rd Division withdrew, with the exception of two companies of 2nd Royal Irish, the bulk of 1st Gordons and a company of Royal Scots. All these units did not receive the order from 8 Brigade to retire. The main body of the Royal Irish arrived at Beaurevoir before midnight. Rations were not available and the men 'were starving'.[24] Some food was purchased, and the town Maire presented them with a dozen large hot loaves of bread which were distributed and wolfed down. The condition of the men left behind can therefore be imagined.

At 1330 on 26 August, St Leger's two companies became heavily engaged. Rapid fire repulsed the enemy and, although swept by machine-gun fire, the Royal Irish held their position. At the same time a heavy bombardment descended upon Audencourt. Half an hour later, 7 Brigade was seen retiring from Caudry. The 3rd Worcesters counter-attacked in an attempt to regain Caudry and reached the edge of the village before being forced back. At 1530, when some men and horses were seen moving out of Audencourt, it could be presumed by St Leger that 8 Brigade had begun to retire.

Watching these events, St Leger could be forgiven for feeling uneasy about his own situation, but in the absence of orders he steadfastly held his position. From 1530 to 1700, the enemy bombarded the Caudry–Audencourt road with high explosive. St Leger's men came under fire from the right rear, directly behind the trenches which were supposedly occupied by the Gordons. A scout sent to reconnoitre reported no movement in the Gordon trenches. At the same time, a fierce battle was heard raging on the left. At 1830, St Leger decided to retire towards the left company and ordered his men to move that way. In the gathering darkness, St Leger crawled away and presently found Maj. Panter-Downes, wounded and dying. Around him were sixteen dead and many wounded. Panter-Downes said his company had held up the enemy movement out of Caudry until they occupied the wood on his right rear. Then, without officers or NCOs and he himself wounded, he ordered his men to get out as best they could. At 2130, St Leger made his way to a private hospital near Caudry and arranged for the wounded to be brought in the following morning. Lt. Phillips, the adjutant, was wounded but recovered sufficiently to crawl away in the darkness and eventually joined up with a company of the Cameronian Scottish Rifles.[25] This was not the only instance of a detachment or unit being isolated and cut off at Le Cateau because of an inexplicable breakdown of communications between a brigade headquarters and its battalions. Telephone communications had only been established up to brigade headquarters. However: 'The Le Cateau district, consisting as it does of fine rolling downs, was ideal for visual purposes and extremely good work was done by the signallers during the critical and closing stages of the battle.'[26] But not, it would appear, within 8 Brigade.

Because isolated companies, like those of the Royal Irish, remained in position and fought until darkness relieved them, the Germans were convinced that the British were still holding on. It allowed the greater part of II Corps to slip away, mauled, having lost guns and men. But the Corps was intact and pressure by the Germans halted. Without question, had the enemy pressed hard they might have won a resounding victory. But the Germans had learned something of the British regulars at Mons which induced more respect for them at Le Cateau.

THE RETREAT OF II CORPS

The remnants of the Royal Irish left Beaurevoir at 0200 on 27 August. Because their medical officer and his staff had stayed with the wounded at Mons, and the brigade field ambulance had become separated, the wounded of Le Cateau were left untreated, except for personal dressings. The battalion transport was caught in jams of transport and refugees on the main roads; they could give no assistance in carrying exhausted or wounded men. The march continued all night. Next morning in a deserted bivouac, several tins of biscuit were discovered with some cooking pots. The biscuit was consumed instantly and the tins saved.[27]

The march began again. Along the narrow, winding, dusty third-class roads they trudged, leaving the main roads clear for transport. The day seemed endless. Arriving at Vermand, they found no rations waiting. Wasting no time, root vegetables were dug up in nearby fields and boiled in the biscuit tins; this satisfied them until rations arrived that evening. After a short rest, the retirement of the Royal Irish continued just before midnight. Ham was reached at 0900 next day and after a halt of a little over two hours, the march resumed. It was 28 August, and the men marched all day as though in a trance[28] until they reached Genvry at 1830. The British had reached the Oise on the line of La Fère–Chauny–Noyon. There they had their first good night's rest for a week.

Not far away were 2nd Irish Rifles who had been less involved at Mons or Le Cateau. A typical Rifle regiment, they were proud of their marching ability, but they too were feeling the effects of the long retirement. On the morning of 28 August as they approached their first real resting place since the campaign opened, they were inspected on the line of march by Gen. Sir Horace Smith-Dorrien. As they looked him in the eyes during the march-past, one NCO, Cpl. John Lucy, liked his expression; 'satisfaction' was there.[29]

In the confusion of engagement and retirement, many platoons and companies became separated from their parent units, and with unerring instinct, made for the coast. One company of Dublins, with the stragglers from a dozen battalions, marched to Boulogne, fighting off all opposition on the way; a platoon of 1st Irish Fusiliers got to Rouen. These stragglers and isolated sub-units spread over a wide area, often brushing with enemy patrols and scouts, and confusing German Intelligence. They credited the British infantryman with something like the same skill and resources which the Japanese were believed to have had in the jungle immediately after their entry into World War II. More importantly, after the two British corps had disengaged, it appeared to the German High Command that the BEF was making for the Channel ports. Later, this had considerable strategic importance when the BEF suddenly confronted the Germans on the Marne.

The stand at Le Cateau had won Smith-Dorrien's II Corps time for its withdrawal to Ham. The retirement of Haig's I Corps to Guise had not been pressed by enemy action. The reason for this has to be sought in the action of 2nd Munsters, rearguard to 1st Division of that corps.

CHAPTER FOUR

The Retreat from Mons and the Advance to the Aisne, August–September 1914

Haig's I Corps complied with the orders of Sir John French, and his retirement towards Guise was covered by 1 Guards Brigade (Brig.-Gen. I. Maxse). To relieve pressure on the corps, the brigade stood overnight near Etreux and dug in. 2nd Munsters, the rearguard, was north of Oisy. Behind them, Maxse's three remaining battalions, 1st Coldstreams (guarding the canal bridge north of Oisy) and 1st Scots Guards, were echeloned back to Etreux where 1st Black Watch was entrenched on the railway. Brig. Maxse deployed 2nd Munsters three miles north of Etreux, with two troops of 15th Hussars and an 18-pounder section of 118 Battery RFA. Its commanding officer, Maj. P. Charrier, had shortly before relieved Lt.-Col. J.K. O'Meagher in command of the Munsters.

Paul Charrier, a large, powerful personality in all respects, was regarded as one of the best officers in the army.[1] Charrier decided to defend a line extending about two and a half miles east of the Sambre l'Oise Canal facing north-east. On the right at Bergues was half A Company with a troop of Hussars; on the left at Chapeau Rouge were B and D Companies protecting the crossroads. Along the road between both places, the other half of A Company was spread thinly. Charrier established his headquarters at Fesmy where he held C Company in reserve, less one platoon detached to Oisy as bridgeguard.

Stand-to at dawn on the morning of 27 August began at 0400, after which the cooks prepared breakfast. It was sultry, with a sound of distant thunder. At 0900 the French to the east were seen to be retiring. Shortly afterwards, a German cavalry patrol appeared and stationed themselves at 600 yards. They watched, waited and probably sent back a contact report. At about the same time, a message was received from Brig. Maxse instructing Charrier to hold the position until ordered to retire or forced back. A bit later, German infantry appeared at Chapeau Rouge. Enemy skirmishers, followed by infantry, launched probing attacks in company strength. When the skirmishers opened fire, the Irish held theirs, waiting for the main company attack. When it came it was easily beaten off by rapid fire. Unknown to Charrier, however, leading elements of 2nd Guards Reserve Division were attacking his position, and columns of 19th Reserve Infantry Division, both forming X Reserve Army Corps, were advancing towards Etreux.

About 1100, the Germans mounted attacks in great strength on both flanks and Charrier drew in his flank companies on Fesmy. As they retired, the Fusiliers' rapid fire kept the enemy at a respectful distance. Contact was lost with the detachment at Bergues and a relieving platoon was beaten back. But the half-company there, seeing the danger, had already retired. Skilfully fighting a rear-guard with a combination of attack and defence, they fell back to Oisy and came under command of Capt. Emerson, OC bridgeguard.

At midday, dinner at Fesmy coincided with an enemy attack. D Company was on two sides of the road, so the cooks had to scamper across, laden with dixies of food and drink. Their arrival and antics under fire caused the irrepressible Fusiliers great merriment and banter: 'Don't be emptying all the tay down your trousers'; 'Come out of that, Micky; what are you stopping in the middle of the road for?'[2]

Shortly afterwards, in the middle of a cloudburst and under cover of artillery fire, the Germans attacked down the road from Sart. Again rapid fire drove them back. Then, a German ploy of rounding up cattle and driving herds in front also failed to break the Irishmen. When the enemy concentrated in the open, fire from the two artillery pieces broke them up. In all the guns fired about four hundred rounds. Mustering in strength, the Germans attacked with great courage and determination in the face of the Munsters' fire; they came within 150 yards of the Fusiliers' line. Undaunted, the Irishmen again repulsed the assault. Capt. Rawlinson led C Company in a dashing counter-attack which 'carried all before it'.[3] German cavalry, attacking with their infantry, charged home. Several riders outflanked the Munsters' positions, gained entry and shot two wagon teams before being killed or captured themselves.

During the lulls between attacks, the Irish stretcher-bearers brought the German wounded under cover. In that curious mixture of pathos and hilarity so often associated with soldiers, their groans were added to by animal squeals. One of the Munster cooks, engaged in a foraging operation, 'was chasing a stout young porker round a yard close by'.[4]

Despite their fine stand, the position of the Munstermen was becoming desperate in the face of German determination to break through. With their flanks in the air and the Sambre Canal at their backs, 2nd Munsters' position was untenable. Charrier, waiting for support or orders to retire, would have known the danger as his men resisted the onslaught with cheerful tenacity. Seeing his flanks about to be enveloped, Charrier ordered the battalion to retire on Oisy at 1430. As the company columns set off, one section was found to be missing and an officer was sent back to find them. He ran back under heavy fire and when he told his men to fall back, one pleaded for 'one more crack at them, sir'.[5] The retreat of the main battalion force was slow. Flankguards on each side of the road were held up by bocage-like hedgerows. B Company, thrown out wide on the left, was slow in reaching the rendezvous at the crossroads near Oisy. It was 1730 before they rejoined. The delay was serious.

At 1500, an orderly cycled up and delivered a message for the Munsters to Capt. Emerson. From brigade headquarters and despatched from Brig. Maxse at 1300, it instructed all commanders to 'retire at once'.[6] The message was delivered to CO Coldstreams at the same time. As the orderly had been delayed by enemy fire across the canal, his message was two hours old. It is impossible to know what Lt.-Col. Ponsonby of the Coldstreams thought, but his duty was clear. Having attempted and failed to contact the Munsters, he ordered his battalion to retire. The Munsters now stood alone.

As the French withdrew that morning, the Germans closed in on the right flank. When 4 Guards Brigade retired with none to guard that flank, Etreux was occupied by the enemy at 1745. The Irish fell back across Oisy bridge and left two platoons of C Company for its defence; 'commanded by Lt. Deane-Drake and Sgt. Foley, they supported each other brilliantly'.[7] Occupying two houses on the west side of the bridge, they waited until the enemy were almost on the bridge and then opened fire. Hearing the noise of battle, Charrier sent back asking if they needed help, but this was refused. Against an enemy who came on bravely, the bridge was held until it was heaped with German dead and wounded. Slowly the two platoons withdrew, section by section. The last made a run for it, covered from the rear.[8]

Charrier led his men along the west bank of the Sambre l'Oise Canal and approached Etreux from the north. As he withdrew from Oisy, the Germans gave pursuit. To delay them, the machine-gun section mounted their guns in the centre of the road and Charrier ordered the Fusiliers into the sides. When the guns opened up, the Germans were halted and not a Munsterman was hit in the stream of fire which swept down the road.

Close to Etreux, the Munsters came under enfilade fire from guns, machine-guns and rifles from the east bank. In front was a railway cutting and a group of houses on the western outskirts. One house lying back from the road had been turned into a loopholed blockhouse; another was on fire.

The withdrawal of 2nd Munsters to Guise was blocked; they would have to force a passage. The gunners came up with their two guns and a deluge of fire struck them from battery positions on the opposite canal bank. The lead horses and their driver were struck, plunging the teams into chaos. Charrier ran forward to organise an attack, passing the gunners where they strove desperately against maddened horses, enemy shell fire, the dead and the wounded to get the guns into action. He yelled, 'Come on, Bayly, put a round into that house! We'll soon boost them out of that!'[9] The second gun, manned by infantry and gunners, returned fire but their ammunition was almost exhausted. With only a few rounds left, the gun was dragged into position to fire on the fortified house, but the concentrated German fire killed the crew: 'The last unwounded gunner met his fate struggling to carry an 18-pounder shell to the gun, standing on the road, surrounded by a small heap of huddled-up bodies.'[10]

German fire became intense and the Munsters fell in large numbers. Maj.

Charrier ordered the leading companies to clear Etreux. Quickly they deployed into line and charged. But, in addition to manning the outlying houses of the village, the enemy occupied trenches dug the previous day by the Black Watch on the railway cutting. Concealed by a hedgerow, the German position was a strong one. They now held it as tenaciously as they had once charged against the Munsters so bravely.

Paul Charrier, conspicuous by his great height and wearing a ludicrous khaki helmet with a green and white Munster hackle,[11] seemed to have a charmed life. He organised his attack without hesitation and led the lead platoon into a charge on the blockhouse. Under concentrated fire, they fell around him. Charrier too fell back, unscathed, to gather fresh strength. The support company under Capt. H.S. Jervis[12] was without orders. But seeing the situation, he led his company eastwards through the fields, thus extending the Irish attack towards the railway cutting. Then, as soon as his whistle sounded, 'up got the Irish and dashed forward with a cheer, bayonets fixed. The enemy's fire redoubled in vigour and took heavy toll of the company'.[13] 'Only one officer and one man reached it. There the fusilier fell dead at the side of his officer.'[14]

Meanwhile, Charrier led two more charges against the fortified house. The adjutant, Capt. Douglas Wise, supported him with Lts. O'Malley and Moseley. All fell except Wise. He reached the house and was firing his pistol through a loophole when knocked out. The remnants of all the attacks gathered in the orchard. Charrier, wounded twice but undaunted, formed another attack. This time he fell riddled with shrapnel from a shell-burst. The RSM, WO1 P. Cullinan, fell wounded. The third most senior warrant officer in the army and RSM of the battalion since 1905,[15] he was a tower of strength throughout the action. Drummie Fountaine and the Corps of Drums, who in war became stretcher-bearers, laboured to bring the wounded to a regimental aid post. There, Sgt. Rodgers of the Munsters and Pte. Hall of the RAMC worked tirelessly in the human wreckage.[16]

CSM McEvoy rallied his company with the cry, 'Come on, boys, the Irish never lost a Friday's battle yet.'[17] It was now evening and the Germans attacked, determined to end the battle before nightfall. From all sides they assaulted the last Munsters' position, the roadside ditches of an orchard. The senior, Capt. C.R. Hall, took command and, supported by CSM Browne, led a bayonet charge. The enemy were driven back, but continued the attack with rifle fire. Hall fell wounded and command of the battalion remnant devolved upon Lt. E.W. Gower. Concentrating in the orchard, the Munsters continued to resist. The machine-gun officer, Lt. Chute, was killed. Sgt. Johnson then took over and, with his section, worked both guns until ammunition ran out. He then destroyed the guns.

It was dusk. The Munsters had been resisting with ammunition taken from the dead.[18] There could be only one ending, and the unhappy duty fell to Lt. Gower to surrender the remnant. Early that summer, Gower's platoon had won the Duke of Connaught's Cup and Shield in the Army Athletics meeting at Aldershot.[19] This day at Etreux, something more prized was won—the respect of a brave enemy. A German officer said of them,'Men have never fought so bravely'.[20]

At 2115, the end came in the orchard when four officers and 240 fusiliers, many of them wounded,[21] stood up and surrendered. The 2nd Munsters had been engaged for twelve hours against six battalions of 73rd and 77th Reserve Regiment from 19th Reserve Division, and 15th Reserve Regiment of 2nd Guards Division. Overwhelming odds! The dry words of the official war historian cannot conceal the admiration felt by soldiers who knew the moral and physical courage required in such an action. Having praised the Munsters for their gallant stand, the historian concludes with: 'Beyond question they had arrested enemy pursuit in their quarter for fully six hours, so their sacrifice was not in vain.'[22] Because of the heroic stand of the 2nd Munsters, 1st Division at the rear of Haig's I Corps was able to retire on Guise with trifling loss.

Col. H.N. Thompson DSO, RAMC (later Lt.-Gen. Sir Nevil Thompson), once of Clonmany, Co. Donegal and Trinity College, Dublin, had been captured and taken to a place near Etreux where he was held with the survivors of the Munsters for two nights and a day. Then, taken to Etreux, he was asked to help the doctors of 47 German Field Lazarette treating the Munsters who were severely wounded. Upon his release the following year, he wrote in the *RAMC Journal*:

> Almost every house in the town was full of wounded Germans and Irish and No. 47 German Field Lazarette was working away with two operating tables set up in a large room in the Mayorie [*sic*]. Private Hill, RAMC, attached to the RMF did splendid service now and also during the all day battle; also Sergeant Rodgers, RMF and the surviving stretcher-bearers. The surviving officers and men were loud in their praise of the gallant conduct and work of Pte. Hall, amidst scenes of terrible suffering and misery.[23]

The senior German doctor, Herr Hoppe, was a specialist obstetrician from Emden. He treated Germans and Irish alike, and took them into the theatre in priority of seriousness. With reasoned objectivity, Col. Thompson declared his professional admiration for German medical skilfulness, but compared the German field hospital unfavourably with an RAMC equivalent in basic field hygiene.

> The pure surgery was good, but the administration , sanitation, and feeding arrangements were very poor—in fact, there was no system at all. All the officers of the hospital—six medical and two administrative—had served in cavalry, artillery or infantry, but not in

the Medical Corps until called up for the war. I would like to mention here that I have never seen plaster of Paris so skilfully used. After ten days all fractured legs and thighs were done up in it, and windows cut to enable the dressings to be done. Very few of the wounded died after the first two days and some of the most severe seemed to be recovering when I left.[24]

Thompson's article must have been a severe blow to war propagandists of that time. Possibly for this reason it received little publicity. During his time with the German field hospital, Thompson lived with their officers.

Many German brigades passed through and spent the night; and I never saw any man misbehave in any way, nor did I hear of any—in fact I was astonished at the perfect discipline. There was plenty of wine about, but I never saw a German drunk or war excited.[25]

Col. Thompson was imprisoned in Germany for about six months before being released. He later returned to France, and by the end of the war became Major-General, Director of Medical Services, First Army. It says much for the balanced humanity of the *RAMC Journal's* editorial policy that Thompson's fair-minded article was published at the height of the war. That Thompson could feel able to write it, after captivity in Germany, is perhaps a good reflection on that country also.

The Germans allowed the Munster prisoners of war to collect their dead and bury them in the place around which most of them fell, the orchard. Maj. Paul Charrier was found as he had fallen, facing the enemy. The Germans buried the dead, both Irish and German, in two great trenches within the orchard at the northern end of Etreux. A cross carved with *Freund und Feind in Tod vereint* (Friend and Foe united in Death) was erected over them.[26] In a field nearby, about ten separate graves were dug for the bodies of German officers. The German dead of the morning battle would have been buried at Fesmy. Hearing most were Catholic, the Germans sent to their headquarters for a Catholic chaplain to conduct the burial service. Although congratulating the Irish for their brave stand, the Germans were furious at being held up for so long by such a small force, which had drastically upset their timetable.[27]

The cost of holding Etreux has high. In twelve hours of serious fighting, the Munsters lost nine officers and 118 other ranks killed or died of wounds; most of the rest were wounded to some degree. Almost all the gunners were killed or wounded. Only five escaped. One, Pte. D. Donovan, hid for several months in France, then made his way through Belgium to neutral Holland and back to Britain. He returned to his battalion and won the Military Medal in 1917.[28] The cost to the Germans had also been high. The Munsters saw at least 1500 German wounded collected in Etreux next day.[29] And this would not take account of the numbers gathered in the surrounding villages. The numbers must have been considerable for a German field hospital to request the services of a British doctor.

The Section of 118 Battery RFA had its two officers wounded, Maj. A.R. Bayly and 2/Lt. A. Stewart Cox; twelve gunners were killed and ten wounded. Following the return of the prisoners of war in 1919, an investigation into the conduct of 2nd Munsters at Etreux was carried out by the War Office. As a result of this, the following awards for gallantry were gazetted on 30 January 1920:

Maj. C.R. Hall	DSO	Capt. H.S. Jervis	MC
Capt. F.S. Waldergrave	MC	Capt. C.J.V. Deane-Drake	MID
WO1 (RSM) P. Cullinan	DCM and MSM	WO2 (CSM) J. Browne	DCM & MID
WO2 (CSM) P.W. McEvoy	MM	Sgt. J. Foley	MM
Sgt. G.C.G. Johnson	MM	Fus. A. Metcalfe	DCM
Fus. G. Young	DCM	Sgt.-Dmr. E.J. Fountaine	MID
Sgt. C. Lister	MID	L/Cpl. E.J. Forward	MID
Fus. H.W. Jordan	MID		

Maj. A.R. Bayly, RA, was awarded the DSO. As Maj. Paul Alfred Charrier had died, he received no decoration. The only decoration which could have been awarded posthumously was the Victoria Cross. At this time, the VC was only awarded when the act of gallantry was witnessed by a senior officer. Charrier's reward therefore was fighting and dying to the code of the Munsters: 'Quick off the mark, obstacles brushed aside, losses ignored, straight to the objective.'[30]

In 1921, the orchard at Etreux was purchased by Capt. H. Walter Styles MP, brother of Capt. Styles who was buried there. Two Celtic crosses, similar to one at Killarney commemorating the Munster dead of the South African War, were later erected. The dedication service was conducted by Father Francis Gleeson who had been chaplain to the battalion 1914–18. In affirming the right of the Munsters to erect a memorial at Etreux, the Secretary of the Battle Exploits Memorial Committee wrote:

> The action is likely to become the classical example of the performance of its functions by a rearguard. The Battalion not only held up the attack of a strong hostile force in its original position, thereby securing the unmolested withdrawal of its Division, but in retiring drew on itself the attacks of very superior numbers of the enemy. It was finally cut off at Etreux by five or six times its numbers, but held out for several hours, the remnant only surrendering when their ammunition was practically exhausted and only a small number of men remained unhurt. The survivors were warmly congratulated by the Germans on the fine fight they had made. No other claim to a memorial near Etreux is likely to be advanced—certainly nothing which would not take second place to the Munsters.

(Signed) C.T. Atkinson, Historical Section, Committee of Imperial Defence.[31]

The retreat of the BEF continued, but without pressure from the Germans. II Corps' stand at Le Cateau and the sacrifice of the 2nd Munsters at Etreux had won respite. The retirement continued from 28 August 1914, day by day, with little to eat or drink in the blazing sun. With only a few hours' snatched sleep, most were exhausted, yet somehow the spirit of the battalions held. Bonds of friendship were tested to the limit and not found wanting. Some, unable to march, had to be helped or placed in wagons. Some battalions like 2nd Irish Rifles prided themselves on holding every man in the ranks.

Eventually, on 5 September, the final retirement of the BEF was made to the vicinity of Melun. The next day the BEF advanced towards an enemy by now convinced that the BEF had ceased to exist as a fighting force. The battalions marched only a short distance that day, then halted for the night. But it was enough for the soldiers to realise that the retreat was at an end, then 'an amazing cheerfulness came over the men'.[32] This may have been helped by a desire to 'get their own back', especially the Rangers, who had cause to remember Grand-Fayt.

THE ADVANCE TO THE MARNE

The initial over-confidence of the German High Command suddenly changed to doubt. Their field commanders modified the Schlieffen Plan and manoeuvred in front of Paris instead of enveloping it. This completely exposed their right. Joffre, who had kept his nerve, saw the opportunity and ordered a general attack by the French armies round Paris.

Von Kluck's army, over-eager to destroy Lanrezac's Fifth Army and the BEF, had crossed the Marne, leaving only a reserve corps to protect its Paris flank. Maunoury's Sixth Army, reinforced by the Paris garrison, attacked and defeated the surprised German flankguard. Its commander delayed sending the bad news until the situation was critical. Faced with imminent danger, von Kluck withdrew two corps facing the BEF to meet the new situation. Franchet d'Esperey, who had replaced Lanrezac in command of the Fifth Army, attacked von Bülow, who reacted by pivoting Second Army on its centre to face south-west. The moves of von Kluck and von Bülow to meet the French counter-attacks opened a 30-mile gap between their armies. To screen it, each commander sent a cavalry division supported by Jägers with machine-guns.

Using the short breathing space granted by Maunoury's attack, the British force concentrated just north of Melun. There, Sir John French refitted and reorganised the BEF into three corps, with the formation of III Corps. This consisted of 4th Division (Maj. Gen. D'O Snow) and 19 Brigade, with 6th Division expected shortly. A second cavalry division was formed under Brig.-Gen. Hubert Gough by detaching 5 and 6 Cavalry Brigades from Allenby. It was there that FM French, reacting to an emotional appeal by Marshal Joffre, issued orders to his army for a general advance. At 0500 on 6 September the advance began, with I Corps on the right, II Corps in the centre and III Corps on the left. The cavalry of Allenby and Gough, containing the Royal Irish Dragoon Guards, the Royal Irish Lancers and the Irish Horse, probed ahead. The British Expeditionary Force advanced cautiously but steadfastly. The German cavalry screen proved no match for British regulars schooled in tactics by the Boers of South Africa.

In 3rd Division, the Royal Irish was advance guard to its division. Behind them were the Royal Irish Rifles, with 5th Division on their left and 2nd Division containing 2nd Connaught Rangers and 1st Irish Guards on the right. On the right of the line 1st Division had no Irish contingent since the destruction of 2nd Munsters. On the extreme left of the British line, 4th Division had most Irish units—2nd Inniskillings, 1st Irish Fusiliers and 2nd Dublins. 2nd Leinsters of 6th Division were hastening to France, fearful only of missing the war.

THE MARNE, 6–10 SEPTEMBER 1914

On 8 September 1914, 2nd Royal Irish came up with enemy rearguards near Orly. Having fixed the enemy to his position, the Gordons attacked on the right and the Royal Scots on the left. German shelling of the approach road held up the British artillery and prevented them from supporting the infantry, who attacked without it. 2nd Division on the right were asked to co-operate on that flank. At long range, the Royal Irish supported the attack by rifle fire. The Royal Scots, having worked round the enemy's right flank, entered Orly and captured the position assisted by a unit of 2nd Division. Two platoons of Royal Irish helped clear the village and a number of prisoners of a Jäger regiment were taken. Next day, the Royal Irish assumed guard duties on the prisoners and entertained the German officers to breakfast before they were marched away to captivity.[33]

In the taking of Orly by 3rd Division, 2nd Connaught Rangers played a small but significant part on the right flank. When 2nd Division crossed the Petit Morin, the Rangers and the 43rd/52nd Light Infantry were sent to assist 3rd Division. The Rangers passed through the Worcesters on the Morin, and near Orly the lead platoon came under fire. About half an enemy battalion was seen withdrawing through Orly, and in an exchange of fire, the platoon commander and two men were wounded. The senior NCO, Sgt. W. O'Brien, assumed command and ordered the platoon to advance. He placed it north of the village, cutting off the German retreat. When the Royal Scots assaulted Orly, the retreating Germans were caught by O'Brien's men at point-blank range.[34] The German wounded were brought in and it was discovered they were from the Garde-Schützenbataillon which had overcome Col. Abercrombie's party at Grand-Fayt. Sgt. O'Brien was commissioned and later won the Military Cross and Bar.[35]

The retirement of 4 Guards Brigade ended at Fontenay. There, some much needed equipment was issued and the guardsmen heard again the voice of their RSM. Next day their advance towards the Marne began. Marching through Rozoy, 1st Irish Guards passed a church before which stood an old priest watching the marching column. The Irish Guardsmen, passing a Catholic church, automatically saluted it by removing their hats or crossing themselves. The old priest 'openly surprised, gave them his blessing'.[36]

At the passage of the Petit Morin, heavy machine-gun fire from a wood held up the advance of 4 Guards Brigade. The Irish Guards sent two companies to support 3rd Coldstream Guards and the brigade crossed and occupied a village. Then, in a deluge of rain, the Irish Guards, under cover of artillery fire, charged German positions in the wood and destroyed a Jäger machine-gun company. A wounded German major, two other officers and ninety men were captured. The wounded officer was given over to the care of mess servants; the men were locked up and two unwounded officers entertained to dinner. The Marne was crossed uneventfully on 9 September by a bridge which although wired for demolition, was not destroyed. The Aisne was crossed by pontoon bridge at Pont Arcy, and the Guards hurried forward to Cour de Soupir.[37]

THE AISNE, 13–28 SEPTEMBER

By 12 September the Germans had retired to a line of entrenched positions behind the Aisne. At the same time, their divisions, released by the fall of Maubeuge Fortress, reached and filled the gap and came strongly against the BEF.

At Aisne, the Connaught Rangers, who were the leading battalion of their division, came to Pont Arcy where the bridge had been destroyed. Examination showed some of the girders were above the swollen river and these were used to cross. Pte. Hayes was the first Ranger over, and soon a complete company formed a bridgehead guard. Under their cover, the Royal Engineers built a pontoon bridge and by evening the whole of 5 Brigade had crossed. Once over the river, 5 Brigade prepared defensive positions to hold off an expected German counter-attack. To cover the crossing of 4 Guards Brigade, the Rangers were ordered forward to the ridge above the river, and late that evening had gained Cour de Soupir just beneath the ridge. No enemy were encountered and the place was practically deserted. Heavy firing could be heard from the direction of Soissons.

Scouts were posted and the battalion bivouacked on the lower slopes of a hill to the north of Soupir. Maj. Sarsfield ordered Capt. C.J. O'Sullivan to take his company before daylight and occupy and hold the Manoir de Soupir on the hilltop. This was a strongly-built farm just on the edge of a spur which stretches northward from Aisne valley towards the Chemin des Dames. The remainder of the battalion arrived about 0500 on 14 September.

COUR DE SOUPIR, 14 SEPTEMBER 1914

About 0900, under cover of artillery and machine-gun fire, the Germans attacked in the morning mist. Advancing boldly, they attempted to crush the centre and envelop from the right by pushing through an adjacent wood. Although held in front and despite heavy losses, they made considerable progress on the right and were stopped only 100 yards from the farm buildings. Heavy fighting continued. By late morning, the situation had become serious when German reinforcements arrived and pressed forward on each flank. At a critical moment, two companies of Coldstream Guards reinfoceed the Rangers; with their help the Germans were repulsed. The fight ended in an extraordinary way—when they had evidently had enough, the enemy suddenly stopped firing and put up their hands. About 250 were taken prisoner.[38]

But the attack was far from over. In divisional strength the attack was renewed, but the arrival of the complete Guards Brigade and a strong counter-attack changed the situation

The Irish Guards attacked a wooded ridge on the left. In fighting throughout the day and evening, they took and cleared the wood. But a treacherous white flag *ruse de guerre* enticed some into the open where they were shot by the enemy. In all, the Guards suffered significant casualties, including the medical officer, Capt. Watson, RAMC, who was wounded while attending the casualties. [39] Both sides dug in and this remained the front along the Aisne until the British left. Had the Rangers not secured and held the position, the Guards Brigade would undoubtedly have suffered heavy casualties in taking that ridge. But their own losses were severe. In the fighting on the Aisne, 222 officers and men were killed or wounded. Both the brigadier and GOC 2nd Division congratulated the Rangers on their fine exploit. In the minds of the old 94th, the memory of Grand-Fayt faded. Sarsfield, the acting commanding officer, survived this action but was killed shortly afterwards.

By the evening of 14 September 1914, the British had advanced forty miles to the Aisne and were holding a line Troyon–Chivy–Cour de Soupir–Vailly–Chivres–Bucy, a front of about twenty miles. Having forced the passage of the Aisne, the BEF found itself clinging precariously to the edge of a plateau with strong German positions in front and an unfordable river at its back, all under heavy shell-fire. Newly-arrived German 8-inch howitzers, called 'Jack Johnsons', made it essential to dig in for protection. Because of the losses of equipment during the retreat from Mons, there was a shortage of tools apart from 'grubbers'. Entrenchments were therefore far from satisfactory.

Further British advance was impossible. The trench line was just held against repeated counter-attacks as the Germans attempted to drive the BEF into the river. Rain fell heavily and continuously and it turned cold. The Germans were strongly reinforced by troops released by the capture of forts on the frontier. With these, they intensified their attacks and heavy guns were brought up to smash the British line. Successive waves of Germans attacked under heavy shell fire, but all attacks were driven back with heavy losses. British losses were also heavy. The BEF had dug in on what was to be the Allied Front until the last year of the war.

During the advance to and crossing of the Aisne, 2nd Rifles had seen little fighting and had suffered only a few casualties in crossing by a footbridge. But in succeeding days they were heavily engaged in repelling the German assaults and suffered considerable losses in the fierce bombardments. The dead included the CO, Lt.-Col. Bird DSO, the adjutant, Lt. Dillon, and three other officers. In all, three officers and sixty-three NCOs and riflemen died on the Aisne.[40]

THE ARRIVAL OF 6TH DIVISION
2nd Leinster Regiment on board the *Lake Michigan* arrived at the mouth of the Loire in a fever of impatience.[41] Eventually they disembarked and marched through St Nazaire with the drums playing 'Tipperary' to trains garlanded with flowers by the locals. Two days later, after a journey that seemed interminable, they detrained behind the Marne and marched forward. So little had the country changed in appearance that they unknowingly crossed the battlefield of the Marne. Everywhere they saw first-hand evidence of a hasty German retreat—abandoned vehicles, unfinished meals, half-empty wine glasses. But they were struck by the absence of wanton damage to houses recently occupied and left 'in good condition and clean.'[42]

The Leinsters reached the Aisne on 16 September. During the preceding day, spirits had been raised by news of the Aisne battle. They would not miss the war after all. In hot, sultry weather punctuated with downpours, they marched singing 'Tipperary'. The only hardship was a shortage of cigarettes and matches ('lucifers').[43] The first wounded were seen on lorries as they approached the Aisne; most had head or neck wounds. Having hurried forward, there were then several days of frustration as they waited for orders. Eventually the Leinsters marched northwards on the 19th and bivouacked a mile south of the river in pouring rain. Next morning, when the rain ceased, the officers and troops climbed to vantage points to watch the shelling on the heights opposite. That night, 6th Division crossed the Aisne by the Pont Arcy pontoon bridge to relieve 2nd Division. In pitch darkness, the Leinsters took over from the 43rd/52nd Light Infantry at Cour de Soupir and dawn was breaking when the operation was completed. For the first time in its history, 2nd Leinsters was on centre stage in a European war.[44]

THE RACE TO THE SEA
In a letter to Kitchener on 24 September, Sir John French first proposed that the BEF should move back to its original position on the French left. Sir John's lines of communication from the Channel ports to the Aisne were over-extended. His proposal coincided with fears being expressed in London

for the safety of Antwerp, which King Albert and the Belgian army were barely holding. A hastily-formed corps under Sir Henry Rawlinson landed at Ostend and Zeebrugge to relieve Antwerp. Consisting of the 3rd Cavalry Division and 7th Infantry Division, it had little artillery, engineers or signals. At the same time, the Germans committed several newly-created reserve corps to their right in a fresh attempt to outflank the Allies, thereby threatening the Channel ports. This heightened threat to his continental base increased Sir John's fears.

In an attempt to stiffen the Belgian resistance in Antwerp, elements of an Allied naval division had landed in early September. It was half-trained, but full-spirited nevertheless. The effect was morally greater than its material, and Antwerp fell on 9 October. Its fall released large numbers of German troops to reinforce their right wing. Against them stood Rawlinson's skeleton corps, practically the only Allied force positioned to defend the Channel ports. Their timely presence covered the retirement of the Belgian army under King Albert.

By the end of September 1914, fighting on the Aisne had developed into trench warfare. Seeking a way out of this stalemate by a decisive battle of envelopment from the north, both Allies and Germans began the 'race to the sea'. Joffre agreed to the redeployment of the BEF from the Aisne to Flanders and the move began during early October. Smith-Dorrien's II Corps and two cavalry divisions moved from the Aisne at the same time, with the infantry going by rail and the cavalry by road. At the end of the move, while covering the concentration and deployment of II Corps at La Bassée, the two divisions of cavalry were formed into I Cavalry Corps under Lt.-Gen. Edmund Allenby.

CHAPTER FIVE

La Bassée,
10–31 October 1914

LA BASSÉE, 1914

By 12 October, the move of the BEF from the Aisne to Flanders was well under way. First to move was the Cavalry Corps, followed by Smith-Dorrien's II Corps. At a meeting between Sir John French and Gen. Foch, it was agreed to co-operate in the north for a combined advance eastwards 'with the BEF passing to the north of Lille'.[1] Their intention was to envelop the German right flank, and Sir John French committed II Corps and Cavalry Corps to battle without waiting for the rest of the army. II Corps advanced towards La Bassée and made contact with the retiring enemy cavalry screen who fought a skilful rearguard action. Two German cavalry corps last seen on the Marne opposed the Allied advance, but these were reinforced and II corps soon was met by dense infantry masses of two newly arrived reserve corps. The Allied commanders had seriously under-estimated enemy strength. Almost within hours, the Allied plan went wrong. The French lost Vermelles, leaving Gen. Smith-Dorrien no choice but to redirect the line of advance of his corps east, towards La Bassée and Aubers Ridge. 3rd Division moved on the right, or north, of 5th Division.

The ground was marshy, patterned by hedgerows and intersected with dykes, ditches and sluggish streams. It was ideal for defence which the retiring Germans made good use of, disputing every building, hedgerow and stream and always with artillery advantage. Near the village of St Vaast, the Germans made a stand. After an artillery exchange, the Royal Irish stormed the enemy trenches and drove them back through St Vaast at the point of a bayonet. Again the enemy made a stand at the main road from Estaires to Neuve Chapelle. Lt. Laing, with a machine-gun section, reinforced the right flank and swept the Germans with enfilade fire while the advance continued. Against stiffening enemy resistance, 3rd Division attacked and captured the village of Aubers.

A draft of six officers and 353 men arrived from Ireland on 15 October, bringing the Royal Irish nearly up to establishment, with the battalion again reorganised into four companies. This was the seventh draft to reach the battalion since Le Cateau.[2] At the same time, 2/Lt. T.W. Fitzpatrick DCM, who had been RQMS at Mons, returned to the battalion (he was later wounded but survived the war). Maj. St Leger was wounded and Maj.

Daniell assumed command. About the same time, the divisional commander, Maj.-Gen. Hubert Hamilton was killed during a visit to the battalion.

On the night of 17–18 October, 3rd Division held Illies and Herlies with 7 and 9 Brigades, keeping 8 Brigade in reserve at Aubers. The 56th Chasseurs *à pied* Alpins, co-operating with 3rd Division, were before Fromelles. Next day a company of Royal Irish was detached to support an attack which captured Fromelles. Later that day, the same company reached Le Riez under heavy fire from Le Pilly. An enemy counter-attack was beaten off with rapid fire and the remainder of the battalion reached Le Riez at dusk. By dawn they had consolidated their hold on the village. 4th Royal Fusiliers filled a gap between Le Riez and Herlies on the right. An attack on Fournes by the Chasseurs failed and they withdrew to Fromelles, exposing the left flank.

LE PILLY, 19–20 OCTOBER 1914

On the morning of 19 October, 2nd Royal Irish was ordered to attack Le Pilly at 1430 in conjunction with another French attack on Fournes. Two machine-guns, a troop of 15th Hussars and one section of field artillery were placed at Maj. Daniell's disposal. At 1400, the gun section shelled the village of Le Pilly for an hour, but most of the shells appeared to go to the left and the village itself was only shelled for about ten minutes. At 1500, the battalion attacked the village with all four companies, two in the first line, one in support and one in reserve. Under cover of the battalion machine-guns, the Irish advanced. In a most gallant attack, delivered with great dash, they succeeded in capturing the place despite heavy fire from dominating positions. The supporting gun section did not lift its fire and for a time held up A Company.[3] The time had not come when troops would charge into their own shell-fire to avoid a hail of enemy machine-gun fire when the barrage lifted.

Just as the last elements of the battalion were launching their attack, a draft of two officers and sixty-three men reached it. Anxious not to miss the action, they joined the last two platoons of D Company. Both officers and about forty men were sent to A Company. At dusk, the battalion was holding the line of the road running through Le Pilly, with both flanks thrown back. The enemy had withdrawn 400 yards from the village. The French had not succeeded against Fournes, but premature reports that they had done so were received and accepted by HQ 3rd Division. It had dire consequences for the Irish. After dark it rained and the wounded, two officers and 161 men, were evacuated; two other wounded officers remained on duty. The dead lay on the battlefield throughout a night which remained quiet except for harassing artillery fire. Knowing the French attack had failed, Maj. Daniell asked 4th Middlesex to fill a gap on the left. Their commanding officer felt unable to comply, but promised to hold his position at Le Riez. After daybreak, German shelling forced the Middlesex back 400 yards, leaving the Royal Irish isolated.[4]

At 0645, outflanked on their extreme left, a platoon of the newly-arrived draft under 2/Lt. W.E. Bredin (commissioned from Sandhurst on 1 September), extended the line of A Company. The adjutant, Lt. M.C.C. Harrison, placed them in position and in doing so discovered the Germans were only 150 yards from the left of Le Pilly. A Company were cut off, so he placed Bredin's men to their rear. On the way out, a bullet smashed the bone of Harrison's left arm; on the return he was severely wounded in the hip. Hit in two places, probably suffering from shock and bleeding badly, Harrison crawled on his back to battalion headquarters where his wounds were bandaged. With so many wounded to treat, the MO had no time for anything else, and he was carried to the cellar of a nearby cottage.[5]

By 0730, the attack on the left was repulsed and fire slackened for the first time since dawn. But not for long. It reopened with greater intensity on the right. Braving the fire, Daniell went to stiffen D Company and returned about noon to battalion headquarters. The Irish, of course, realised their isolation but refused to retire without orders. They fought on, hourly expecting a British counter-attack to restore the situation.[6] Dead piled up and the wounded were carried to the cellars of the village houses. Ammunition began to run out and had to be collected from the dead and wounded. The machine-guns were located by enemy artillery and put out of action. At 1500, Daniell sent a messenger to brigade headquarters reporting the situation. Then, seeing A Company were about to be attacked from their rear, he raced down himself to warn them. Daniell died in the process. Almost leaderless, the survivors continued to hold their untenable position until few could hold a rifle and little ammunition was left to fire. Feeling the fire slacken, the Germans rushed the position and it was all over.

The fate of 2nd Royal Irish at Le Pilly was sealed when it believed that French cavalry had occupied Fournes, roughly a mile north-east of their position. When Fournes was not taken, Smith-Dorrien moved his left back for fear of being enveloped.[7] The Germans learned that an Irish infantry battalion was located near Le Pilly, well in front of the British line. Seeing its isolation, the local German commander despatched a battalion of 56th Infantry Regiment to reinforce three battalions of 16th Regiment with orders to surround Le Pilly and cut them off.[8] This was done, and the German batteries at Fournes ranged on the Irish entrenchments, pouring shrapnel on them at about 2000 yards. The Germans attacked in converging directions. Despite the resistance of the Irish, they eventually got snipers and machine-guns into all surrounding houses and commenced shooting all who showed themselves. At 1600, they finally pressed their attack home under cover of machine-gun fire and overran the village.[9] The Royal Irish casualties at Le Pilly were seven officers and 170 NCOs and men killed or dead from their wounds. 302 were taken prisoner, the large majority of whom were wounded, some very severely; 'barely 100 could walk'.[10] These losses were in addition to the 163 wounded and evacuated the previous day: 'After a fight lasting until 3 P.M., some three hundred survivors of the Royal Irish, nearly all wounded, were forced to surrender.'[11]

Only the Germans could give adequate testimony to the steadfast bravery of the Irish at Le Pilly. One such was Lt. Matens, 56th Infantry Regiment, who was present at Le Pilly and by an extraordinary coincidence was captured by 2nd Royal Irish early in 1915. He recognised their badges and gave an account of the action which was taken down and forwarded to the War Office. One of the officers taken prisoner at Le Pilly, Lt. M.C.C. Harrison, escaped from Germany in 1917. On his debriefing, he submitted an after-battle report to the War Office which agreed with that of Matens.[12]

On 25 October, Maj. St Leger arrived from Ireland with a draft of 100 men to take command. The next four months were spent refitting and retraining as Guard Battalion at Army HQ, where their Regimental Colonel was the Commander-in-Chief, Sir John French.

The German counter-offensive against II Corps began on 20 October, directed mainly against the French on the left of II Corps and the Royal Irish. This gave the rest of II Corps a day's respite to prepare for the German attack. On the evening of 21 October, 3rd Division withdrew two miles to prepared positions. The line II Corps held, from east of Givenchy running east of Neuve Chapelle to Fouquissart, was to remain the front, almost unchanged, for the next four years.

Fierce fighting continued for three days after the action at Le Pilly and the Germans broke the front of 2nd South Lancashire. On the flanks of the break-through, 1st Wiltshires and 2nd Irish Rifles 'held on unflinchingly'. The gap was sealed off by 7 Brigade Signals and a company of 3rd Worcesters who 'shot the invaders down at 50 to 100 yards range'.[13] A counter-attack by units of 7 Brigade, including 2nd Irish Rifles, retook the lost trenches. In the stand of the Irish Rifles:

> That bit of trench became sulphurous with plaintive blasphemy, until a Dublin soldier incongruously checked it by vehemently demanding: 'For the sake of the sufferin' Saviour, can't yez shut yer bloody blasphemy, even in the face of sudden death?'

A sardonic Belfast voice commented: 'Listen to yon.'[14]

With so many officers dead the delegation of responsibility for holding the line descended upon the surviving warrant officers and non-commissioned officers. That the line held is testimony to their success. One such was Sgt. J. Kelly, a Dubliner.[15] At Neuve Chapelle in October 1914 after the heavy German bombardment, he commanded the remnants of two Irish Rifle platoons facing imminent attack. With curses, blasphemy and sheer force of will, he drove his half company remnant to clear the trench of dead and battle-wreckage. Kelly organised his reduced numbers to man the trench evenly and in leadership by example inspired his men to repulse repeated German attacks. 'He was a great man in a way, and a good war leader.'[16] Eventually even such men were struck down. Kelly fell mortally wounded by a shell splinter. There were many such as Sgt. Kelly who died, their gallant leadership unrecorded.

TREATMENT OF WOUNDED PRISONERS

German losses in the attack against the British were enormous. Because of this, little could be done for the captured wounded of the Royal Irish. Placed in the waiting room of the local station, they ate the emergency rations collected by the doctor from their dead. The Germans, overwhelmed by their own wounded, could give scant attention to the needs of their prisoners. The medical officer of the Royal Irish worked 'incessantly day and night for three days, attending to the wounded of both sides. With such an enormous number of casualties, there was really nothing the Germans could have done during this period to improve conditions. Naturally their own wounded had to receive primary consideration.'[17]

On 23 October the Irish wounded were evacuated to the rear and fell into the hands of a brutish head doctor. He accused them of using 'dumdum' ammunition, claiming to have found a quantity of it on one of the Irish. To Harrison's request to produce this man for his explanation, the head doctor replied it was off a dead man. He then proceeded to demonstrate how the British rifle could supposedly be used to manufacture dumdum ammunition using a German newspaper diagram.

> He placed the butt on the floor and forced the nose of the bullet into the hole at the end of the cut-out, and then using all his force managed to break a bit off the nose. It was a difficult operation, and only succeeded with the ammunition manufactured in certain years. He continued doing this for three days and gave orders they [the prisoners] were to receive no medical attention.[18]

The prisoners' greatcoats were removed although the nights were now bitterly cold; some of the wounded had had their uniforms cut to expose their wounds for dressing. Except for a cup of soup once a day, they received no food or drink. One German doctor, Herr Scherning, attended the worst cases contrary to orders.

> Finding my arm was broken in two places, he got hold of a young specialist to set it. That I subsequently recovered the use of my left hand is entirely due to the skill of this man. In order to avoid detection by the head doctor, he had little time at his disposal. Holding my hand

securely he placed a foot against my shoulder, pulled as hard as he could, turned the arm outwards and then carefully attached a splint. Primitive as the method was, there was practically no pain till he released his grip.[19]

The evacuation of prisoners to Hamburg began on 26 October, a long, harrowing journey for the wounded, made infinitely worse by the vindictive action of the head doctor. He had the British and Irish wounded crowded onto a cattle truck, while the German wounded occupied the rest of the train. He personally distributed the dumdum ammunition which he himself had made to the German wounded. On the many stops, the Germans were fed and showed the ammunition to crowds of spectators and Red Cross workers. As a result, the prisoners were given no food or drink on the journey and were subjected to considerable suffering: 'I have never known a train have so many or such long halts. I felt as if I would die of thirst.'[20]

The condition of Harrison and another officer deteriorated so badly that they were taken off at Dortmund and put into the Krankenhaus Barmherzigen Brüder. There, their treatment underwent dramatic improvement, except during the short stay of two unpleasant Prussian officers. Harrison describes the head brother as 'one of the finest specimens of the human race that I have ever come across.'[21] German wounded mingled with them but were naturally full of the German successes, a fact which grated on Harrison. Not all his visitors were welcome. Their most obnoxious visitor became an Englishwoman living in Germany. She instructed her wounded countrymen in 'all the atrocities perpetrated by England and told us how ashamed she was of the country of her birth'.[22]

Eventually, on 14 December 1914, an escort arrived to take Harrison to Fort Brükenkopf at Torgau on the eastern bank of the Elbe. For Lt. Harrison it was not the end but a beginning of adventures.

The dumdum bullet, one with its nose cut off, opened in flight and disintegrated on impact with the human body, causing dreadful wounds. Its use is forbidden by the Geneva Accord. In almost every war, accusations of its manufacture and use are directed by one side against the other. The German government made such a claim in 1914.

Professor Dr M. Kirschener, senior surgeon of the III Bavarian Army Corps, published an article in *Münchener Medizinische Wochenschrift* on 29 December 1914, in which he questioned supposed medical evidence of their use. He argued:

When the German government can officially state that special machines have been found in Belgium for the manufacture of these projectiles, when… dumdum bullets are taken from enemy dead or prisoners, then no doubt can exist as to the use of this illegal type of bullet. On the other hand, medical statements, and since the outbreak of the present war such statements have been published, sometimes fail to provide such conclusive proof.[23]

Professor Kirschener's article tells how he had various normal infantry rifle bullets—German, French and British—dissected and describes their construction. The probable action in flight and impact on tissue and/or spongy bone is analysed and the types of wound inflicted by each bullet, in regular and malformed shape, in ordinary and abnormal conditions, at long and short ranges, is given in detail. In his conclusion he stated:

> Extensive destruction of the tissues, particularly large and lacerated wounds of entry and exit, do not of themselves afford proof of a dumdum bullet; they occur rather with the use of the regular infantry bullet. They can, in fact, when only soft tissues have been wounded, have been due to the bullet striking sideways (with or without ricocheting), or to the ingress of a foreign body, or to a bullet wound inflicted at point-blank range, or to the ingress of the gases of the explosion. If bones are involved, the resultant action may be due to the usual explosive action of the regular bullet at close range.[24]

It was, noted Lt.-Col. E.M. Pilcher DSO, RAMC, 'a fair presentation of the comparative effects of the modern pointed composite rifle bullet and of the so-called dumdum bullet.'[25]

ARMENTIERES, 1914

In early October, rumours circulating in the ranks of 2nd Leinsters said they were off to Belgium, although officers scoffed at this with good humoured incredulity. However, the rank and file, 'not for the first time, had it right'. Shortly afterwards, the Leinsters began marching north-westwards in 'the race to the sea'.[26]

Allenby's Cavalry Corps covered the concentration of III Corps at Hazebrouck and some high ground had to be cleared to accomplish this. The Mont des Cats was taken by dismounted 4th Hussars and 5th Irish Lancers and among the German casualties was Prince Max of Hesse. He was treated by Dr O'Brien-Butler of 5th Lancers; before he died, Prince Max presented the medical officer with his gold watch.[27]

Conforming to the orders of Sir John French, issued in the mistaken belief he had found the enemy flank with superior numbers, III Corps advanced eastwards. 6th Division on the right moved towards Vieux Berquin–Merris; and 4th on the left marching on Flért. At Meteren on 13 October, III Corps became involved in the prelude to the first battle of Ypres and a general attack by 4th and 6th Divisions began. In 4th Division, 2nd Dublin Fusiliers, ordered to attack the right flank of its brigade objective, were wrongly directed by a cavalry patrol and to their disgust arrived at Meteren after it had been taken. However, 1st Irish Fusiliers had the satisfaction of a frontal assault with 2nd Seaforths. The Germans' rearguards retired before their charge and the trenches were captured without loss. Meteren was occupied that night.

The British advanced steadily and methodically; at times the action resembled a pre-war 'field day'—the bolted breakfast of scalding tea, a hurried march, cavalry reports and study of maps on a windy hill and rain while the troops watched and waited. Then quick orders, and a rush to carry them out, only to have them countermanded minutes later. Every move and halt of the forward units was reciprocated down the long columns, like a shunting train. Intelligence reported the enemy retiring in disorder, but on the ground there was no evidence of this. Indeed the veterans compared the meticulously cleared bivouac areas favourably with their own such areas in South Africa many years before.[28]

A bridge on the Lys was taken intact and the British crossed on the morning of the 15th. That night, a piquet of the Leinsters encountered a French cavalry patrol which, failing to answer a challenge, was fired on. A lot of firing in the darkness followed, with no casualties.[29] Armentières was reached on the evening of 17 October. In the four days since Meteren, little had happened, but now a sense of impending action prevailed with the great fortress of Lille so close and in German hands.[30]

Gen. Pulteney, III Corps commander, ordered 6th Division to probe the enemy line on the Pérenchies ridge from La Valleé to Pérenchies and push them back if possible. To do this, 18 Brigade was sent against the line La Vallée–Pérenchies. 16 Brigade was in reserve. 18 Brigade reached its objectives without opposition, but 2nd Leinsters and 3rd Rifle Brigade of 17 Brigade met 'continuous opposition' in their move up a ridge, which was actually the glacis of an outwork of the fortress of Lille. By mid-morning, 2nd Leinsters had captured Prémesques and were in sight of Lille. There they were stopped by heavy fire from Germans in entrenched positions. On their flank, the Rifles were forced back.[31] The Leinsters were now actually within the outer defences of Lille. Lille, the strongest fortress in the defences of northern France created by Marshal Vauban, was not unknown to Irish regiments. Some two hundred years before, the 18th Royal Irish had been one of five British regiments which took part in the siege which captured the place under Prince Eugene of Savoy. One of its officers had written at the time: "Tis a hard case that our poor Regiment must always be pick'd upon [for] all extraordinary commands.'[32]

On the right, one Leinster company reached the vicinity of Batterie Senarmont and a small party crossed the ridge between Prémesques and Pérenchies. For a few moments they were actually within the body of the fortress of Lille, '… the Leinsters had got nearer to Lille than British troops were to be for many a long day'.[33]

That night, the Leinsters dug in and 18 Brigade came up on their right. It was the firm belief of the Leinster Regiment that everything of special significance to the regiment occurred on the Lord's Day. On Sunday 18 October they were to have their first serious engagement of the war. On that day three officers were mortally wounded and ninety-nine other ranks were killed and wounded. German artillery shelled the Leinsters throughout the day. Although many enemy shells proved to be duds, the Leinsters felt let down by their own artillery not replying. But the German batteries were probably out of range and the RFA in 1914 were very conscious of ammunition conservation. Next day, a quiet one, was spent in evacuating the wounded and organising the defence. The battalion were now convinced they were up against stiffer resistance than any they had met since leaving the Aisne.

At precisely 0800 on the 20th, the Germans opened an artillery bombardment on Prémesques and the trenches in front of it. One company evacuated their shallow trenches without informing their flanking companies. Simultaneously, three battalions of 179th Saxon Infantry burst from the woods near Prémesques and Batterie Senarmont. Advancing regardless of loss, they overran a detached post, stormed Prémesques and streamed down the Bas Trou road. The Leinster defenders suffered heavily and the company commander, Capt. R.A. Orpen-Palmer, was shot in the eye and captured; he remained completely blind for several hours. The company near Batterie Senarmont came under fire from the right flank and rear. It fell back to the support line in front of Bas Trou. The second line was by this time wiped out and the company almost ran into those Germans now holding it. Capt. Whitton, the company commander, was wounded and captured. Farther to the left, the enemy had come down in force against B Company. Here the fighting was especially severe. Capt. Maffett, the company commander, was killed, Lt. Cormac-Walshe mortally wounded, and 2/Lt. Budgen, carrying a message to a company of the East Yorkshire Regiment, was severely wounded. Capt. Maffett, writing a hurried note, was killed. (Curiously, the note and other effects were picked up by a German and returned to Maffett's family after the war.)[34]

The Leinster centre was broken. Part of the left was overrun and forced back, but the right fought on. A Company quickly discovered their left was in the air and the enemy had penetrated around the flank. Acting decisively, the commander, Maj. Mather, refused his left flank. He occupied the edge of the wood facing Prémesques and sent off two messengers to warn 18 Brigade. At about 0900, when the situation became clear, Mather determined to retake Prémesques. His left platoon with a few North Staffs from brigade reserve recaptured some ground and took a few prisoners. A Saxon battalion coming out of Prémesques stopped this; but so effective were the Leinster machine-guns that the Germans were also checked.

Meanwhile, 18 Brigade sent a company of East Yorks against Prémesques and a gallant attempt to recapture the place by the Yorkshiremen failed. A

Company of the Leinsters were now in serious difficulties. The platoon holding a farm at Mont de Prémesques suffered heavy casualties, and the Saxons pushed strongly against them. By noon, the enemy had got a machine-gun into position, sweeping the trench of A Company, who clung tenaciously to their position. However, by this time the Saxon advance had stalled. For the Irish, the situation was 'desperate but not serious'. D Company had been overrun in the first rush and C Company pushed back, but B and A Companies, although suffering heavy casualties, had stood fast. The right had been reinforced by a second company of East Yorks. Battalion headquarters, with the remnant of D and C companies, had established and held the line in the centre; the enemy were in a cul de sac. When the Saxon commander realised this, he became alarmed and in the early afternoon ordered a retirement from the pocket. It was then that Capts. Whitton and Orpen-Palmer escaped.

> Too badly wounded to be sent to the rear, they were kept in a cottage during the fight and abandoned by the Saxons while the latter were streaming back in retreat. They stayed with German wounded until darkness when they stole away. Capt. Whitton, unable to walk, was carried by and guided Capt. Orpen-Palmer who could not see, until they reached the British line held by the 1st Royal Fusiliers.[35]

Both officers survived the war. Lt.-Col. Whitton became the regimental historian and Lt.-Col. Orpen-Palmer commanded 2nd Leinsters on the last parade in Saint George's Hall, Windsor Castle. Orpen-Palmer, son of Rev. Abraham Orpen-Palmer, a noted biblical scholar of Killowen, Co. Kerry, had a brother who later commanded a battalion of the Royal Irish Fusiliers. To their friends throughout the army, they were 'Opee 1' and 'Opee 2'.[36]

That evening, A and B Companies were ordered to fall back. It is to their credit that they made every attempt to evacuate all the wounded, Saxon and Irish, before they did so. At 0230, the remnant of the battalion assembled and retired south-east of Armentières.

The Germans attacked again during the evening of 22 October but were driven off by rifle and artillery fire. Resuming his attacks during the night, the enemy was exposed in the glare of burning villages, farms and hayricks and was driven back with heavy loss. At dawn on the 23rd, the attack was resumed in greater strength but was again repulsed. That night, after five days of unremitting fighting almost without rest, the Leinsters were relieved. In three days' fighting which included the capture and loss of the Prémesques salient, 2nd Leinsters suffered a total loss of 434, of whom five officers and 150 other ranks were killed. Three officers were severely wounded and three captured. Another battalion of 6th Division fared worse. 2nd Sherwood Foresters in 18 Brigade were surprised in the act of withdrawing and the greater part of the battalion surrendered, with 576 taken prisoner.[37] The Prémesques ridge was not regained for four years.

Foch and French had seriously underestimated the German strength above and below the Lys. Sir John French's orders to advance coincided with Crown Prince Rupprecht's to his Sixth Army to advance below the Lys. This advance coincided with that of German Fourth Army above the Lys. Out-gunned and heavily outnumbered, the Allies south of the Lys fell back, but III Corps managed to hold on to Armentières and some ground around it. North of the Lys, the situation was more critical.

CHAPTER SIX

First Ypres

The IV Corps consisted of 7th Division which was made up of regular battalions returned from India and 3rd Cavalry Division. Both divisions were supported by poorly equipped Territorial Force artillery and engineers. Commanded by Lt.-Gen. H. Rawlinson, it felt its way forward and made contact with the Germans in front of Ghent. Unsure of British strength, the Germans hesitated and allowed the vast bulk of the Belgian army to escape. Rawlinson skilfully disengaged and withdrew on Ypres. Sir John French, still unaware of the danger, ordered IV Corps to join the march eastwards. Rawlinson, like Smith-Dorrien at Le Cateau, chose to disobey the CinC; he stood and fought at Ypres after a token advance on Menin.

Fourteen German divisions were advancing through Flanders. To meet the shock, the tiny Belgian army stood behind the Yser and IV Corps before Ypres, with a thin blue line of French marines between. The marines were shortly reinforced by two French Territorial divisions. Coming up, Allenby's Cavalry Corps extended the line between IV and III Corps. At first the British cavalry attacked the German line, but making little progress against firm opposition, they dug in on the line of the Lys between Armentières and Menin. There was now a continuous front line, however tenuous in places, from the Swiss frontier to the Channel.

FIRST YPRES

On 21 October, 'a cold raw ould day,' I Corps arrived at Ypres to relieve the hard pressed IV Corps. In pursuance of Sir John French's new-found belief in the offensive, I Corps pushed forward. The battered 7th Division was almost at breaking point but had nevertheless crucially resisted the overwhelming German attack. It was relieved by 2nd Division which then advanced in a general attack on St Julien-Langemarck-Zonnebeke. Its 5 Brigade contained 2nd Connaught Rangers; in 4 Guards Brigade were the Irish Guards.

The Irish Guards supported 22 Brigade of 7th Division and 5 Brigade during a heavy attack on 23 October. With 2nd Grenadiers, they cleared Polygon Wood. Shell-fire caused heavy loss to one platoon, but the attack continued and the battalion fought alone to 300 yards north of Reutel. Patrols sent out in darkness to gain touch found only Germans. A double line of picquets to the rear maintained a precarious link with the Worcesters

600 yards behind and prevented the Irish being completely cut off. Next morning, 3rd Coldstreams came forward on the right. Again the Irish attacked the enemy to its front and gained ground but found themselves in a salient enfiladed by machine-guns. Having captured a couple of farmhouses, they were counter-attacked and after heavy loss one farm had to be evacuated. In treating the wounded, Lt. Hugh Shields, RAMC, was killed. 'He had been remonstrated with only a few minutes before for exposing himself too much, and paid as much heed to the rebuke as did the others who succeeded him in his office.'[1]

Shields was replaced by Capt. A.H.L. McCarthy, RAMC, the third medical officer since the campaign started. Having had no food for forty-eight hours, 'the night was memorable inasmuch as the battalion... was allowed to eat its emergency rations'.[2] The 2nd Division, encountering very stubborn resistance, was brought to a standstill. Eventually, Haig was compelled to order his corps to consolidate and hold its ground. As German reinforcements arrived, Haig's divisions became heavily engaged, repulsing incessant German attacks although they could barely do so.

On the right of 5 Brigade, 2nd Connaught Rangers flanked the Guards. For three days, heavy assaults were beaten off. In the attack on the 23rd, the enemy almost got into the Rangers' trenches before being repulsed.[3] That night they were withdrawn into reserve and reached a rest area at Halte a mile and a half from Ypres. So desperate was the need for reserves that after an hour's rest and breakfast, they were placed on two hours' standby to move.

The Rangers were still tired when they moved off at 0900 along the Menin Road. Meeting a long stream of wounded from 7th Division, they advanced steadily towards the roar of gunfire. The enemy had broken through the thin line of 7th Division. Three battalions of 5 Brigade were to clear Polygon Wood. The fourth battalion, the Rangers, were sent to support 7th Division. Overcoming fatigue, they marched to fill a gap in the line at the crossroads on the Menin Road, later called Birr Crossroads. They were overtaken by the corps commander, Gen. Haig, riding at a slow trot with one officer and an orderly carrying his corps pennant. To the watching troops he looked unconcerned and untroubled by the battle chaos and was 'immaculately' dressed. Haig's appearance was a tonic to his men.[4]

In the following days of desperate fighting at the end of October and early November, weary men of the BEF, often cold, hungry and mud-coated, repelled successive waves of German infantry attacks. There was no reserve behind and it was therefore useless to ask for reinforcements. With only their own determination to sustain them, they fought on. Corps and divisional commanders were reduced to the level of scavengers, garnering tiny groups with which to plug holes in the line. And when there were no more reserves, they would ride forward as Haig was doing to stiffen the resolve by sheer example. As in so many battles, it became a soldiers' affair, as at Inkerman where the 1st Connaught Rangers had captured a stand of Russian drums and a battery of cannon. Such was the effect of the controlled rapid fire that only once did courageous Germans succeed in forcing an entry into the Rangers' trenches. Even then they were driven out at bayonet point.[5]

At the same time, the Irish Guards were also heavily engaged. Like the Rangers, they, with the 43rd/52nd Light Infantry, had been sent to fill a gap between the Klein Zillebeke–Zandvoorde road and the trenches of 2nd Gordons. The gap was filled just before the enemy drenched the area with heavy shell-fire. But the Gordons, Light Infantry and left flank company of the Irish were driven back. To save their guns, their supporting artillery 'limbered up and went off as though it were a "Military Tournament"'.[6] However a counter-attack restored the line before nightfall.

The German bombardment was renewed on 1 November. This time heavy artillery joined in against the British rear areas. The front-line trenches suffered heavily. The Irish Guards' machine-guns were put out of action and the forward companies fell back to a support line on the fringe of Zillebeke Wood. One platoon failed to get the message and stayed in its trenches. By its collective gallantry, it was instrumental in breaking up a heavy attack. Every officer and guardsman who could hold a weapon took his place in the line knowing there was little behind. The brigadier was wounded; his headquarters staff had moved and could not be contacted for help. The commanding officer, Lord Ardee, was wounded and Maj. Stepney assumed command. Casualties mounted in both officers and men killed and wounded. Relief eventually arrived in the shape of a French Territorial regiment, with some 2nd Grenadiers and cavalry. They strengthened the line allowing the Irish, not to leave it, but to contract their front. Heavy fighting continued. The commanding officer, Maj. Stepney, was killed. So short of officers were the Irish that Capt. Orr-Ewing of the Scots Guards assumed command until the remnant were relieved. In all, sixteen officers and 597 men were killed or wounded. Reduced to four platoons, about 200, the Irish Guards were relieved on the night of 9 November.[7] It was due to this determined resistance that the enemy opposite 2nd Division were so 'fought out' that they were easily subdued by artillery fire. At times, however, the Germans continued with local attacks. In one of these, the enemy gained a position in a house just a few yards in front of 2nd Connaught Rangers in the south-west corner of Polygon Wood. They tormented the Rangers with fire from a Minenwerfer, in action for the first time against the BEF. But a British gun was brought up on the night of the 7th and the next day the gunners of 70th Battery blew the enemy out of their position with the new high explosive shell which kept the Germans quiet for the rest of the day.[8] That night a welcome draft of forty-seven men arrived just in time to help beat off two more attacks—the first at dawn, the second in the evening. Afterwards, heavy shelling continued remorselessly until, on 9 November, they were relieved by the Worcesters while the remnant of 2nd Rangers moved to Polygon Wood for a day's rest. One company remnant rested at the south-west corner of the wood and was still there at a critical moment on 11 November when the Prussian Guards attacked.

THE BATTLE OF MESSINES, 12 OCTOBER–2 NOVEMBER 1914

The 1st Battalion of the Rangers, the old 88th Foot, had arrived in France with the Indian Corps. The Connaught Rangers were therefore the first Irish regiment to have both regular battalions on the Western Front. They, with the 57th Rifles of the Indian Army, were detached on 23–24 October to reinforce Allenby's hard pressed cavalrymen and to man trenches south and east of Messines. Parties of Connaughtmen erected barricades in Messines' village streets, which soon proved useful in a last ditch defence. Battalion headquarters moved into Messines convent. That afternoon its church was shelled by the enemy in the mistaken belief that its tower was being used for observation purposes. The church caught fire and with so few men at hand, little could be done to save the building, although a few did all they could to save the artifacts. Everything which could be moved was, although they were defeated by a large crucifix. Despite all efforts it could not be moved and eventually the men had to be ordered out to save themselves.[9]

The battalion was only a few days at Messines, but it was long enough for them, fresh and full of fight, to introduce themselves. Orders were received at noon for the battalion to take part in an attack at 1630 on the German trenches near Gapaard. 2nd Cavalry Division, with the Rangers and 57th Rifles, attacked over open ground almost devoid of cover and which, because of recent heavy rain, was now a quagmire.

Three and a half companies strong, the Rangers assembled a quarter of a mile south-east of Wytschaete. Two companies attacked with two platoons in support. When the first objective was gained, the attack was discontinued. But one company, C, did not receive the order and was left behind when the battalion fell back and moved to Wytschaete. Isolated and without orders to the contrary, C Company continued its attack. As they approached the German support trenches, they came under a 'smart' fire. After a burst of rapid fire, they charged with traditional élan and, with a 'Connaught yell',[10] closed with the bayonet. Three trenches were captured in succession, considerable losses were inflicted and an officer and two men captured for interrogation. Eventually at midnight an order came to discontinue the attack and retire. Passing back through the outposts of 5th Cavalry Brigade, Maj. Murray, the commander, handed over the prisoners to Hubert Gough in person. Gough gave his thanks and compliments to Murray who then led his men back to the battalion at Wytschaete.[11] At the end of October, the Rangers left the Cavalry Corps and returned to Lahore Division.

GHELUVELT: THE CRISIS, 29–31 OCTOBER 1914

The Messines-Wytschaete ridge dominated the surrounding area. Realising its importance, the German commander facing the BEF, Gen. von Fabeck, decided upon its capture and directed the main weight of attack against Brig. Gough's 2nd Cavalry Division.

On the extreme right, the 57th Rifles were in the process of being relieved by 2nd Inniskilling Fusiliers when the German attack struck early on 31 October. 2nd Inniskillings had been involved in fighting since III Corps' arrival. At Le Gheer, the Inniskillings had sustained heavy loss, especially in officers. They were forced out of the line and, in a counter-attack to retake the position, they again lost heavily and had been relieved to regroup. This was their first subsequent action.

At 0245, a company of Inniskillings was already in the trenches on the Douvre when two German regiments struck and overran the Indian troops of the 57th Rifles. Part of the 57th, with troopers of various cavalry regiments, held the German attack at the barricade in the centre of Messines village. At the same time the Inniskillings made a flank attack, and as dawn broke the enemy retired.

A reinforcement group from II Corps, consisting of the Yorkshire Light Infantry and Scottish Borderers with the recently arrived London Scottish, counter-attacked. The Yorkshiremen and Borderers were positioned at Messines and the London Scottish on the left flank, with 2nd Inniskillings on the right flank. The Inniskillings swept the Germans out of the trenches captured from the 57th Rifles and their enfilade fire held off 119th Grenadiers with heavy loss.[12] However, sustained heavy German pressure made Messines ridge untenable. Allenby, with the agreement of Sir John French, withdrew the Cavalry Corps to prepared positions facing the ridge. To conform with this movement, HQ 4th Division ordered 2nd Inniskillings to retire to the line of the Douvre. As so often happened, the order failed to reach two companies. Unlike previous similar situations, however, this was fortuitous. The enemy Guards Cavalry Division had received a special message: 'By Order of HM the Kaiser, Douvre Farm is to be stormed today'.[13] In their shallow scoops, the two Inniskilling companies, with well directed bursts of rapid fire, enfiladed Douvre Farm and successfully denied it to the German Guards Cavalry throughout the day. The Germans brought up a mortar battery and two howitzer batteries and pounded the deserted farm without touching the Inniskillings who remained concealed. They achieved '... a decided triumph'.[14]

In fierce fighting, 3rd Worcesters, attached to 4th Division, gave way and the Germans pierced the line of 4th Division. To regain the lost trenches, a company of 1st Irish Fusiliers brought from the Armentières sector, with 2nd Inniskillings, made a desperate counter-attack to retake the position. The Irish Fusilier company lost all its officers and half its men, but the line was restored.

NONNE BOSCHEN, 11 NOVEMBER 1914

Air reconnaissance on the 10th disclosed German reinforcements moving into the line at Ypres and additional artillery moving up to add to the enemy's established preponderance. Among the reinforcements were the fresh Guards Division and 3rd Prussian Division. This latter, mainly composed of Pomeranians and West Prussians, was regarded in the old Prussian army as being the best fighting formation they had. At field training they were probably better than all the other German troops including the Guard Corps.[15] That evening, most enemy troops were withdrawn from the forward areas preparatory to the expected bombardment. Long before the wintry dawn, a bombardment began which in weight and volume of fire had never been seen before. From 0800 to 0900 it intensified. The British artillery, short of ammunition, did not engage in counter-battery fire but made ready. Strongpoints and redoubts were manned by whatever personnel could be scraped together from headquarters staffs. Infantrymen who had been fighting almost continuously for three weeks, without relief and with very little rest, spaced at about two men to five yards, crouched in their poor cover. Among the many items they were short of was rifle oil. Rifles, once clean, bright and slightly oiled, were mudcoated, dry of oil and wet with rain. They tended to jam at crucial moments; a batch of poor ammunition heightened the problem.

'A welcome reinforcement also sent up by General Haig was the 2nd Royal Munster Fusiliers.'[16]

2nd Royal Munster Fusiliers, over 800 strong, returned to front-line duty the day before what was to become the turning point in the First Battle of Ypres, which has been likened to the attack of the Imperial Guard at Waterloo.

After Etreux, 2nd Munsters were re-formed with drafts from its Special Reserve battalions and Regimental Depot at Tralee, Co. Kerry. However, it was divided by companies and posted for duty at the headquarters of all the corps of the BEF, until Lt.-Col. A.M. Bent assumed command in October. Following his 'representations'[17] to Sir Douglas Haig, the battalion assembled as a single fighting unit and was posted again to 1st Division. Such was the desperate need for troops to man the over-stretched line that no time could be given for collective training. The Munsters marched into the line on 9 November and relieved a battalion of Grenadiers on the 10th, between the 3 Brigade and 1st Irish Guards. No entrenchments existed. The front was too great to construct a continuous trench system, so each man dug a shelter at a spacing of two men to five yards.

So reduced was I Corps that brigades were called 'groups' corresponding to their commanders. In Lord Cavan's Group, the Irish Guards, one of four Irish battalions destined to take part in this historic engagement, could only muster two companies of 148 men each, and this only after reinforcements of an officer and 100 guardsmen had arrived. The other units of the group, 2nd Grenadiers, 1st Royal Sussex, and 43rd/52nd Light Infantry, were only a little better off.

Heaviest shelled was McCracken's Group in 3rd Division. It mustered four battalion remnants which included 2nd Royal Irish Rifles. McCracken's numbered 1500 rifles, which was about average.

Part of 3rd Prussian Division and the right of 30th Division struck McCracken's Group. The 2nd Royal Irish Rifles at Heronthage Château was hard hit. The Rifles, barely 230 men, had suffered very badly in the concentrated bombardment. By this time, most battalions were composed of half-trained militiamen with a stiffening of regulars: 'Some of these men could not even fire a rifle properly, and at times our hearts quailed for our safety and theirs.'[18]

But now the time had come. Somehow their native hardihood and the example of the few old regulars prevailed. All ranks of 2nd Rifles poured their fire into the massed ranks of the Pomeranians and West Prussians who faced them. RSM John Kearns of 2nd Rifles, a large man over six foot four and a crack-shot, 'bowled over' seventeen Prussians himself.[19]

Against Shaw's Group in Heronthage Wood, the Prussians suffered heavy casualties while achieving less than elsewhere. German shell-fire had splintered the fringe of the wood, forming a natural *chevaux-de-frise*. Behind, Shaw's men lay concealed. With rapid fire they almost destroyed 1st Grenadier Regiment which could not penetrate the barrier constructed by their own artillery.

South of the Menin road, Count Gleichen's Group, containing units which had recently been preparing to engage the UVF in Belfast,[20] likewise more than held its own. The Prussians became so dazed and shocked by the fire they encountered that they marched steadily to their deaths 'with arms at the secure'.[21]

North of the Menin road, 1 Guards Brigade was attacked by the Imperial Guard Division and 54th Reserve Division. Composed of the pick of the German army, the Imperial Guard was led by sons of the noblest and proudest houses in the German Empire. Their advance began with the *paradeschritt*, a high-kicking goose-step. Their coming was heard long before it could be seen—loud words of command, shrill whistles and the singing of 'Die Wacht am Rhein'.

> On came the enemy in masses. As they appeared a withering fire was opened on them; the attack was stopped, only to be renewed as another wave appeared. The men fought in groups of two or three. They knew there were no reserves, so they gritted their teeth and prepared to 'die hard'. Again and again the wave of enemy advanced, but each time faltered, stopped, and then ebbed. For three-quarters of an hour the enemy pressed the attack, but were defeated by the dogged pluck of the rain-sodden, scattered groups of Fusiliers trying in vain to keep the mud from clogging their rifles, and then taking those of their wounded comrades when all else failed.[22]

At Ypres, 2nd Munsters were not the long-service and highly trained regulars of Etreux, but part-time soldiers of militia battalions hastily sent to France to reconstitute the annihilated regular battalion as a matter of urgency. However, what these Munstermen lacked in training was more than adequately compensated for in courage and determination, against which the Kaiser's guardsmen failed. Later, little boys in Cork sang:

> Oh the Kaiser Bill tried very hard
> When he lined our front with the Prussian Guard.
> But the brave old Munsters still fought hard,
> And held them back at Ypres.

On the flank of the Munsters the attack of the Prussian Guard was more successful.

> Early in the morning we heard a very intense bombardment taking place, but we were still in mobile reserve and did not occupy any trenches. Suddenly someone came running in to say that the Germans had broken through.[23]

No news travels faster than that of military disaster; it loses nothing in the telling. North of the Menin road a section of the line had cracked and for a time it seemed the Guard Division had broken through. It was inevitable that at some part of the British line the artillery fire would concentrate with grater accuracy than elsewhere. This happened on the front held by 4th Royal Fusiliers, who were driven out of their trenches by the weight of shell-fire. Here, the 1st and 3rd Guard Regiments crossed the British line.

Swiftly the British commanders responded to the crisis. 2nd Connaught Rangers and 5th Field Company, Royal Engineers, in local reserve, were ordered by Col. Westmacott, the group commander, to form a defensive flank opposite Nonne Boschen. Gen. Monro, GOC 2nd Division, sent forward three companies of Highland Light Infantry and 1st Coldstream Guards, his last reserve; help was requested from Corps Headquarters.

The Rangers could see the enemy advancing between the two woods. To them there was no mistaking the Prussian Guard. Coming up on their left, the Highlanders opened fire on the enemy at the same time as the Irish. It may have been for that reason that the attack edged off and went through the Nonne Boschen Wood. Some of the Rangers and a few of 5th Field Company, RE, moved farther forward towards the wood and continued to fire into the enemy flank. Eventually the Prussians emerged from the wood and made for Westhoek about eleven hundred yards behind. Had they reached this, they would have been right through the British position in that sector. Only cooks, batmen and clerks of a brigade headquarters stood in their path. It was then that the British had one of the few strokes of luck during the early stages of the war. The ground sloped downwards for about five hundred yards from the wood and then rolled gently upwards towards the village. Monro was able to muster an entire brigade of field artillery and a group (one regiment) of French 75s to meet the threat; these were deployed just north of the village. Over open-sights the guns fired at the Prussians in scenes reminiscent of the Napoleonic Wars. Undaunted, these devoted guardsmen advanced to their death with extraordinary discipline, pressing home their attack in more or less close formation which made a perfect target. Their generals had learned nothing from Mons after all.

Some thirty guns firing shrapnel at point-blank range as fast as gunners could load was an awe-inspiring sight for the watching infantry. It was more than flesh and blood could stand and eventually the Prussians were forced to withdraw to Nonne Boschen Wood.

A counter-attack by 43rd/52nd Light Infantry, Northhamptonshires, part of HLI and Connaught Rangers and 5th Company, RE, took part, but the enemy, many wounded and exhausted, had already given their best and did not offer much resistance. The Irish Guards, who supported the Light Infantry, captured thirty prisoners in the wood. On that day the Rangers suffered sixty-six all ranks killed or wounded. 2nd Irish Rifles, caught badly in the early bombardment, ended the battle with less than a company strength, 130 all ranks. These were sent in groups of little more than sections or platoons, as the situation dictated, to reinforce the other units of McCracken's Group. At the end of the battle of First Ypres, 2nd Irish Rifles could muster only forty who could hold a rifle.[24]

No Irish regiment suffered heavier losses in 1914 than 2nd Royal Irish Rifles. Like its 1st Battalion, the 2nd was recruited heavily from Belfast and Dublin. At the end of the battle of La Bassée, the original battalion had practically ceased to exist. Although it had been reinforced several times during the opening battles, by the end of First Ypres less than a platoon stood to arms. Like any unit coming out of the line in the Ypres salient, they did not halt before passing through the city. Then, as the pitiful remnant of Irish Rifles marched through the support areas, artillery men deserted their guns, lined the roads and cheered and clapped them as they passed. John Lucy who was there and who had lost a brother with the battalion on the Aisne wrote: 'The tribute from fighting soldiers is the hardest to bear.'[25]

2nd Irish Rifles suffered 344 officers, NCOs and men killed or died of wounds;[26] the rest were mainly wounded. Throughout the war on the Western Front, only one Irish battalion exceeded such terrible casualties in a similar period. By early January, 2nd Rifles had rebuilt its strength to 850 with drafts from the reserve battalions (the 3rd in Dublin, and 4th and 5th Battalions in Belfast). It was a new battalion.

On the night of 11–12 November 1914, 2nd Munsters deepened their rifle-pits to four feet, got whatever rest they could and stood-to long before dawn.

The bombardment resumed at 0630 and although under heavy attack themselves, help was sent to 'adjacent troops' which filled a gap in their line for twenty-four hours. It was on this day that, because two senior warrant officers in succession became casualties, 'the redoubtable John Ring'[27] became RSM. Ring retained this appointment throughout the war, seemingly bearing a charmed life and winning the MC, DCM and bar; he repeatedly refused commissioning. His photograph, taken in Limerick, shows his square jaw, waxed moustache and steely eyes. He was the epitome of an infantry RSM and became well known throughout the BEF, from the army commander down. His last parade with the battalion colours in 1922, still RSM, was their final parade at Windsor.

Although the woods at Nonne Boschen had been searched after the battle, 2nd Rangers were detailed on 13 November 1914 to search them yet again for enemy wounded. About twenty Germans were collected and their wounds treated. The action at Nonne Boschen was to prove the last battle of 2nd Connaught Rangers in the Great War. First Ypres cost the battalion eleven officers and 159 rangers dead.[28] Since arriving in France they lost twenty-three officers and 230 rank and file dead. The remainder of the original battalion had been wounded or were prisoners. Hundreds of reinforcements had also become casualties. The Rangers moved into reserve at Bellewaarde and received a reinforcement of seventy-eight men. From there they were posted from 5 Brigade.

The Indian Corps had arrived in northern France at the crisis of the Ypres battle and took its place in the line on the Neuve Chapelle sector where the British and German trenches were only fifty yards apart. For two days, the front remained quiet until a fierce attack on 2/2nd Gurkhas brought an urgent appeal for support. The Ranger support company was ordered to help and sent two platoons. The Gurkha trench was restored after fierce fighting in which the adjutant, Capt. Frederick George, was wounded. L/Cpl. T. Kelly cleared the parapet and brought him in under heavy fire, but Capt. George was hit again and killed. Kelly was subsequently recommended for a Victoria Cross but was awarded the DCM. In his post-war memoirs, the corps commander, Gen. Sir James Willcocks, wrote of Kelly: 'I should have liked to have seen him get the Victoria Cross, but as it was he was awarded the DCM. It was never better earned. He died of wounds in January 1916.'[29]

Vigorous trench warfare began towards the end of November 1914. In company strength, fierce attack and counter-attack took place in which the Germans had a decided advantage with their 'stick grenade'. This gave them efficient service throughout the war, against which the British had no effective reply until late 1915. In the meantime they made do with jam-pot varieties which regimental histories variously described as '… useless.' For weeks in snow and rain, the Indian soldiers of Lahore and Meerut Divisions strove to hold a line in conditions of mud, sleet, slush, snow, and frost which their English, Irish and Scottish comrades in each brigade found almost unendurable. Outgunned and outnumbered, the Indian soldiers, Hindu and Moslem, stood their ground against some of the finest troops in Europe. In such company, the European battalions were expected to set an example of courage and resolution; there is no record of them failing to do so. But the cost was high. By the end of November 1914, in a little over a month of trench warfare, the 1st Connaught Rangers were down to 351 all ranks.

By this time, after weeks of almost continuous fighting, both battalions of the Rangers were weak in officers, NCOs and men. (Of the original fifty combatant officers of the Rangers who had arrived in France with two battalions, six remained of the 1st and one of the 2nd Battalion.) Two service battalions of Connaught Rangers were in training in Ireland, and the Regimental Depot at Galway, faced with the enormous casualty rate in France, found it difficult to keep two regular battalions up to efficient fighting strength. In view of this it was decided by GHQ to amalgamate the 1st and 2nd Battalions. On 5 December the two battalions merged, an event which coincided with the arrival of another draft from Galway. The strengths were:

	1st Bn	2nd Bn	Draft	Totals
Officers	8	6	4	18
All other ranks	343	440	130	913 [30]

As 1st Connaught Rangers, the battalion remained with Lahore Division for the remainder of the war, serving in France, Mesopotamia and Palestine.

Just as the defeat of the Imperial Guard at Waterloo signalled the end of that battle, the attack of the Prussian Guard at Nonne Boschen was almost the last try of the German high command at Ypres in 1914.

At the cost of their own destruction, the soldiers of BEF held the line at La Bassée, Armentières and Ypres. Training and discipline played some part; so also did regimental pride and tradition; and that indefinable and over-used word, 'morale', derived from the sum. But assuredly all these intangibles would not have succeeded without the soldiers' dauntless courage. Commenting on the battle of the Marne, Liddell Hart wrote: 'For the profoundest truth of war is that the issue of battles is usually decided in the minds of the opposing commanders, not in the bodies of the men.'[31] Like many other 'soldiers' battles', the first battle of Ypres proved this precept erroneous. The outcome of *wars* may be decided in the minds of commanders, but *battles* are won, and lost, by men, although their commanders will undoubtedly achieve fame for success, or be blamed for failure.

The French and German General staffs had learned nothing from the battles of 1870 regarding the effects of modern rifle and machine-gun fire, as witnessed particularly by the destruction of the Prussian Guard Corps at Gravelotte-St Privat. Yet this had entered the psyche of the French common soldier. As late as the mid 1960s, the writer heard French soldiers describing very heavy rain as 'just like at Gravelotte'; they at least had remembered. Before the rapid fire of British and Irish regulars, the flower of German manhood was killed in what their historians have described as the *Kindermörder*, the 'slaughter of the innocents'. At the same time in north-eastern France, the cream of the French army was being annihilated in pursuance of their Battle Plan 17.

The proportional cost to the British army was very high. Except for the divisions formed from the returned overseas garrisons, the old army was destroyed in the battles of 1914; the rest died at Gallipoli and Second Ypres in 1915. Irish regiments had correspondingly high losses. Total killed in action and died of wounds to the end of 1914 was 122 officers and 2012 other ranks.[32] On a 3.5–1 ratio (the accepted estimation of wounded to killed), this indicated that battle casualties could be estimated at at least 10,000 all ranks killed and wounded.

CHAPTER SEVEN

1915: Winter in the Trenches

The last German attack of 1914 began on the afternoon of 20 December. It was carefully directed against the weakest part of the British line, the Meerut Division of the Indian Corps at Givenchy-Festubert. The Indian troops were all forced out of their trenches, except for those held by 1st Manchesters which hung tenaciously onto Givenchy village. Haig's I Corps, resting and refitting after the Ypres battle, was in reserve and stationed in the centre of the British line. Responding to urgent appeals, 1st Division was sent to relieve the Indians and retake the lost trenches. The march of 1 Guards Brigade and 3 Infantry Brigade from Bailleul to Festubert began at 1830—at one hour's notice and in the worst possible weather. Later, 2 Infantry Brigade were bussed to the sector.

In pelting rain and hail, the brigades force-marched for twenty miles in three hours. Resting in a muddy field, they ate a hurried breakfast and, across a desolation of muddy fields and water-logged shell holes, they attacked under shell and machine-gun fire. Passing through the Indians, 1st Coldstream Guards and 2nd Munsters recovered the lost trenches in the teeth of savage machine-gun fire.[1] Having sustained cruel losses, little groups of Munster survivors, isolated, without reserves and often without officers or NCOs, somehow hung on for over forty-eight hours until relieved.

Eight officers were killed; three others, including the commanding officer, were wounded and two hundred NCOs and men were killed and wounded. Col. Bent had a shell-splinter wound from which his entrails protruded. He fell on a dead German in a shell-hole which saved him from drowning. Stretcher parties, helped by the chaplain, Father Gleeson, heroically scoured the fire-swept battle field for the wounded. Miraculously, Bent survived his wound, eighteen hours' exposure, frostbite and pneumonia; he ultimately survived the war.[2] In an order of the day, Sir Douglas Haig expressed his appreciation to 1st Division, singling out 2nd Munsters, 2nd Welch Regiment, 1st Gloucesters and 1st Coldstream Guards for special mention.[3] Christmas was spent improving front-line trenches and digging new communication trenches. It could hardly have been a merry one.

More British reinforcements landed in France during November and December. 1st and 2nd Indian Cavalry Divisions arrived and a second cavalry corps was formed before Christmas under Maj.-Gen. M.F.

Rimington. The two cavalry corps were therefore commanded by former officers of 6th Inniskilling Dragoons. 27th Division arrived in France on 23 December; its 82 Brigade contained 1st Royal Irish, 2nd Royal Irish Fusiliers and 1st Leinster Regiment, all newly back from India. In addition to these regular army formations, twenty-two Territorial Force infantry battalions and six Yeomanry regiments, including the main element of the South Irish Horse, landed in France.

The King and Lord Kitchener inspected 27th Division before the departure for France on 19 December. A few days later, they feasted on 'ducks, chickens and fresh vegetables provided by the kindly inhabitants'[4] before going into the line in the Ypres Salient. 82 Brigade took over the sector which included St Eloi and 'the Mound'. Because of its hasty formation, and the urgent need for replacements on the Western Front, 27th Division went into action weak in field artillery and without its establishment of howitzers and heavy guns.

Reinforcement drafts for Irish battalions at the Front poured over to France. Typical perhaps was the experience of a draft for the 2nd Royal Irish Rifles:

> … headed by our pipes and our band, we entrained at Holywood. At Belfast we boarded trams, and I had some difficulty in keeping the women who surrounded us from passing the men bottles of stout and whiskey… On board the boat I found awaiting me 50 men and young [2/Lt.] Calverly of the 3rd Battalion, who are quartered at Dublin, Col. M'Cammon, Jack Curran; and several other officers of the 3rd Battalion were at the quay to wave their Au Revoirs to us. Detrained at Southampton. The men behaved awfully well on the journey and gave me no trouble.[5]

REORGANISATION OF THE BEF

With the inflow of reinforcements, it became necessary for administrative and operational reasons to reorganise the BEF into two armies. This became effective on Christmas Day 1914.

Reorganised BEF, 25 December 1914

First Army	Second Army
Gen. Sir Douglas Haig	Gen. Sir H.L. Smith-Dorrien
I Corps (Lt.- Gen. Sir C.C. Monro)	II Corps (Lt.-Gen. Sir C Ferguson)
IV Corps (Lt.-Gen. Sir H.S. Rawlinson)	III Corps (Lt.-Gen. W.P. Pulteney)
Indian Corps(Lt.-Gen. Sir J. Willcocks)	27th Division(Maj.-Gen.T.D'O. Snow)
Cavalry Corps (Lt.-Gen. Sir E.H.H. Allenby)	Indian Cavalry Corps(Maj-Gen. M.F. Rimington)

When 28th Division arrived, it, together with 27th Division, formed V Corps (Lt.-Gen. Sir H. Plumer) under Second Army.

That same day, an unofficial truce was declared and fraternisation took place between Germans and Allies. All took advantage of the respite to bury their dead and clean surrounding areas. Songs were sung by both sides in turn and applauded by all. At the end of the day, both sides sang 'Auld Lang Syne'. The war then resumed. The Germans requested two Irish battalions to prolong the cease-fire without success.[6]

THE TRENCHES, WINTER 1914–15

The expansion of the BEF placed heavy demands on Royal Engineers for improved road-rail infrastructure, port facilities and communications which fully stretched their manpower and material resources. Consequently, little effort could be released to improve front-line and communication trenches and defences. The trenches occupied by the troops in Flanders generally consisted only of shallow scoops in the ground with built-up parapets of unbagged soil. These afforded little protection from fire; in heavy rain the parapet slid into the trench. Troops stood up to their knees in liquid mud; unless they moved from time to time, they gradually sank. Brushwood, straw and planks were all tried to make a secure flooring for the trenches but these, too, sank. There was no timber, shovels or sandbags; simply no material of any sort existed to improve the trenches. Most stood or crouched motionless in water for two days. Men slept, if they could sleep, leaning against the back of a trench in a standing position. A tour of duty was forty-eight hours. However, the march into the line, at a mile an hour and out of it again, could take up to eight hours. Many of the troops exposed to these conditions were just home from the baking climate of India or Aden.

Trench latrines were non-existent, and bodily functions for the fastidious were a nightmare. Bully beef tins were used and the contents flung out into no man's land. Those suffering gastric complaints lived in perpetual torment. One Leinster officer wrote: 'It was purgatory to me... I had diarrhoea very badly... fourteen times during daylight... I was in a dreadful state when I got to hospital, but it was not my fault.' That final sob can be imagined. The cold, wet, slime, filth of trench life in Ypres Salient during the early months of 1915 could never after be erased from the minds of those who survived.[8]

Every rifle had to be carried for the entire tour of duty; to put it down was to rest it in water or mud, rendering it inoperative. Supplies of food were carried into the line; jars of rum, tins of army biscuits; cases of jam, a sack of charcoal, bags of tea and sugar, cheese and bacon; reserve ammunition. On the journey into the line, soldiers were over-burdened with kit, ammunition, entrenching tools, full water-bottle, rifle, wearing a rain-sodden and clay-caked overcoat. Nevertheless all carried an additional share of platoon rations and stores. Some inevitably slipped and fell in deep mud or water, ruining food and (woe betide him) breaking rum jars. There was no provision for rest. Fires for heating were out of the question, and only one bag of charcoal per twenty-four hours was supplied to each company for cooking purposes.

There were also other stomach-churning inhabitants of a trench. The French, who had previously occupied the trenches, had buried their dead under the floors. In the muddy conditions of the winter, decomposing bodies floated to the surface and had to be disposed of.[9]

The British artillery was short of ammunition and gave insignificant support to the infantry in those early days. German artillery fire, on the other hand, was constant and accurate. It ranged with methodical nerve-racking slowness; fortunately for the receiving troops, there were many duds. German infantry were better equipped for trench warfare than either French or British troops. Their trench-mortars and grenades were excellent and plentiful. They were quicker to manufacture barbed wire on a vast scale; this, with well sited machine-guns, was soon to make their trench systems almost impregnable. Added to this was their overwhelming manpower strength, much of which could be devoted to improving their defences, generally on higher and drier ground. The British had no efficient trench-mortar until 1916 and the only grenade available to the troops in 1915 was the jampot type. The manufacture of this was remarkably simple, and just as inefficient. A jampot was filled with shredded gun-cotton and nails, a detonator and short length of fuse. After lighting, the user was well advised to 'throw for all you are worth'.[10]

The relief march out of the line was slow and painful, at about one mile an hour. For some, their feet and legs swollen by long immersion in water, every step was agony. Strong men wept like children on this journey.[11] Ruined houses or barns were the only shelter out of the line. But these were welcome nevertheless, giving some the opportunity for sleep and dry conditions: 'The other day after marching 5–6 miles after three days in the trenches, we were put in rest billets; ours was a barn. Next night we were all wetted through owing to defective or inadequate roof of barn.'[12]

There was no rest in the front line and little out of it. When not on line duty there were fatigues, communication trench digging, road improving, and the task which all infantry came to detest above others, digging six-foot trenches to protect Signal Service cable networks from shell-fire. Very little time existed for drying clothing or cleaning up. All uniforms remained mud-caked for weeks; they never dried completely unless the weather turned fine—in which case they dried on the body. Eventually divisional bathhouses were organised where every man could get clean at least once a week and receive a clean set of underclothing. While the soldiers bathed, their uniforms were pressed to 'destroy insect life'.[13]

Yet morale somehow remained high throughout the BEF, especially in the Irish battalions: 'The Irish soldier is at his best when things look blackest.'[14]

Those who have a full right to speak affirm that, in absolutely impossible situations, the Irish could be trusted to 'play up' beyond even a Cockney battalion.[15]

This was due to an irrepressible spontaneous humour, exemplified especially by the Dublin and Belfast 'crack', that dry, understated biting wit, which, almost unconsciously, sees humour even in the most dreadful circumstances.

In dangerous situations, the Irish had a contempt for danger bordering on the reckless. It angered and exasperated officers and NCOs who were responsible for their safety and for keeping casualties low to reduce 'wastage'. 'It drove any English officer or NCO half mad, and it made every professional wild.'[16] There was also a traditional, easy affinity between officers and men in an Irish regiment which before then was quite rare, although more common throughout the army in World War Two and since.

> The Celt's natural poise and manner, his gift of courtesy and sympathy, and above all the curious and incommunicable humour of his outlook in those days made it possible for him and his officers to consort together upon terms perhaps debarred to other races.[17]

> There existed a camaraderie extending through all ranks, a cheery good-fellowship, with perhaps little thought for the morrow, and a disregard for consequences verging almost on recklessness... Familiarity extended to the rank and file never caused the latter to forget their instinctive good manners.[18]

They found pleasure in unexpected ways, as one soldier wrote home:

> Have been lucky to get on the organ at the Roman Catholic church in this village. A little beauty, just what I would like at home... Have asked the nuns who kindly let me have three hours!!![19]

Their generals, from Marlborough, Saxe and Wellington, had always appreciated their worth in war, if perhaps not always in peace.

> The men were stout fighters, good marchers, and splendid workers, their trenches were always kept as well as circumstances permitted, and, as I saw myself, when blown in by artillery fire, the men set to work at once, without orders, on rebuilding them. They were always wonderfully cheerful, and always ready with some quaint answer to a question, or a witty remark on some remarkable incident. Though apt to be somewhat reckless in attack—in raids they showed individually the strict obedience and restraint by which alone a raid can be brought to a successful conclusion.[20]

Through the bitter opening months of 1915, the round of trench tours ground on remorselessly, broken only by relief for a brief rest and clean-up before returning to the trenches. Sapping forward to obtain positions closer to the enemy line for observation was a hazardous but necessary task; preventing the enemy from doing the same was constant. The drain of casualties relentlessly drained the strength of line companies. A normal day's routine in the trenches began with stand-to for an hour before daylight, during which time parapets were manned in anticipation of a possible surprise attack. When day broke, the order was passed along to stand-down. One man in four remained on lookout, the remainder, officers and men, had hot tea or coffee. Little was done during the day. Rations, letters and home parcels came up from the rear echelons in the evening. At night, sentries watched in the corners of the bays, and patrols and working parties went out into no man's land. In sectors of that muddy, water-soaked wasteland, no discernible trench-line or defences existed; only a few rain-drenched, mud-coated figures stood between the Germans and the keep-areas, or strongpoints.

> 'Sergeant Byrne, take me down to your trench, I don't know it.'
> 'Right, Sir, this way, Sir. Look out, Sir,' as plop I go, up to my knees in a regular lake. 'Better get out of the trench, Sir, and come along the back. Just here, the man was killed this morning, Sir.' I literally clamber, hands and knees, out of the quagmire of clay and water, over a claey heap into which my hands plunge to the wrists, in and out, round about, for fifty yards which seem like 500 yards, through some ruined cottages, past a smelly evil-looking pond, and a slither down into the bottom of the ditch in front of which is a straggly hedge.
> 'Here's my left, Sir, one man here.' I peer into the gloom and discover an object huddled up half kneeling in the mud, half crouching against the rain-sodden bank, with no head cover and little cover from view. Rifle on the bank, his bleared eyes straining out into the dark, from where I saw two tiny spurts of flame come, as a couple of bullets sung overhead.[21]

Casualties by enemy action and illness relentlessly sapped the strength of the line battalions, but their spirit was unshaken, as a diary entry shows.

> Got relieved awfully dark night had to pass a farm to get to dug-outs dead horse and cattle here and dead Frenchman which we buried in the adjoining field. And then to 'rest' in dug-outs behind the line. Bags of rain. Just going to sleep. Boys singing 'Grey Home in the West' ...[22]

Several times the Germans attacked fiercely, usually accompanied by heavy artillery bombardments or exploding mines. To celebrate the Kaiser's birthday on 25 January on I Corps front, where conditions were little better than on the salient, 1st Division in the La Bassée-Givenchy sector was assaulted and many trenches lost. The right of 2nd Munsters on the La Bassée Canal fell back to conform with the movement on the right. Giving the enemy no time to consolidate their hold, after dark the Munsters support company counter-attacked and regained their trenches.[23] South of the canal, the deployment of reserves was far behind the front line. This delayed the counter-attack by 1st Division until the following day, and when it was delivered it failed.[24] In the fighting to regain the lost positions, L/Cpl. Michael O'Leary, 1st Irish Guards, almost single-handedly captured two barricades in the trench system, killing eight enemy and taking two prisoners; he later received the Victoria Cross.

St Eloi

In the St Eloi sector of the Ypres Salient there was little respite. 28th Division had come into the line and, with 27th Division, formed V Corps. The enemy, realising both divisions were new to the Front, gave them little rest. On Sunday 14 February 1915 there was a sharp enemy attack on 'the Mound' directly in front of St Eloi village. This, a 30-foot high spoil heap about half an acre in extent, commanded the surrounding flat country and was usually held by a platoon with two machine-guns. It was the 'Mound of Death' to all who held the Salient.[25] The battalion on the left of the Leinsters were driven in. The Mound and St Eloi village were systematically shelled. One trench, only twelve yards from the Germans and a notorious death-trap, was overrun.

Just as the Royal Irish were about to relieve the Irish Fusiliers, word came that the battalions on the left of the Fusiliers had lost several trenches. Brigade Headquarters at once ordered the Royal Irish to counter-attack and recover it. On the Mound, the machine-guns were mud-coated and out of action. The Royal Irish were consequently forced to assault without covering fire. Across the morass-like ground, lit by German star shells and under bombardment, three under-strength companies, about 200 officers and men, attacked. The first attack was repulsed and Col. Forbes, having regrouped, waited until 0200. Then, in a concerted attack with 1st Leinsters, all the lost trenches were regained.

A month later on 14 March, another German attack, fiercer and better co-ordinated, took place. Mines were exploded under 'the Mound' and adjacent trenches. In the mine eruption, the machine-gun detachments were buried. Simultaneously, heavy artillery fire swamped the British line. This was quickly followed by infantry attacks supported by trench-mortars. Assault troops armed only with hand grenades, deadly in trench warfare, led the German attack.

Despite a stout defence, by evening the trenches on each flank of the Mound had fallen. The village of St Eloi was taken shortly afterwards.

Behind the lines, Brig. J.R. Longley's 82 Brigade had 1st Royal Irish and 1st Leinsters in reserve and these were brought up. The Leinsters were ordered to recapture the lost trenches and the Royal Irish were given the task of recovering St Eloi and the Mound. However, it transpired that the situation was not as bad as reported. Although many trenches were lost, 2nd Irish Fusiliers had held their own and recovered others. Only one trench remained untaken and a Leinster company carried this out 'with a neat piece of tactics'.[26]

The Royal Irish recovered St Eloi, but their attack on the Mound was brought to a standstill. Typically the Germans mounted not two but three machine guns on the positions. Repeated efforts were made to get forward but an advance could not be made beyond the house nearest the Mound. In this, a few men established themselves and held the position throughout the day. A most gallant attempt was made by 2/Lt. R.D. Ford, Sgt. Brown and four men to rush a barrier the Germans had constructed at the end of the street. All were killed except Sgt. Brown who was wounded in the head. Lt.-Col. George Forbes (a descendant of the founder of the regiment) was wounded slightly in the head and severely in the thigh. He died on the 17th. Maj. Milner took command and was ordered to hold St Eloi 'at all costs'.

When fighting died down, German and Irish dead and wounded were lying in the street of St Eloi. With astonishing audacity, CSM T. Kelsey and L/Cpl. W. Carroll walked up the street of the village towards the German road barricade and began to bring in some wounded. They were stopped by the Germans, called up to the barrier and told to 'come in.' Kelsey replied that they had already helped two German wounded to safety and now wanted to get in their own men. The German officer signalled to them to go away, which they did only after taking their wounded with them.[27] It was a bold, brave effort which succeeded, reflecting credit on Kelsey, Carroll and the unknown German officer.

Neuve Chapelle, 10–13 March 1915

Planning began early in 1915 for an offensive to conform with French strategy—the elimination of the great German-occupied salient in France which the Western Front had assumed. The French were to attack northward from Champagne, the British eastward from Artois. Notable as a milestone in the development of the BEF, the battle of Neuve Chapelle was the first offensive operation planned and executed by the British. Carried out by IV Corps and the Indian Corps of Haig's First Army, it won some initial success by surprise. But the enemy were allowed time to recover and the attack ultimately failed to achieve its objectives—Neuve Chapelle village and Aubers Ridge. 1st Royal Irish Rifles in 25 Brigade of 8th Division was the only Irish unit involved in the fighting. 1st Connaught Rangers, in reserve with Lahore Division, were not committed to battle.

The initial assault was to be delivered by 8th Division, the last all-regular formation to arrive on the Western Front supported by the greatest concentration of artillery the British had thus far assembled. After a short intense artillery bombardment which took the Germans by surprise and shattered their defensive wire, 25 Brigade (Brig.-Gen. A.W.G. Lowry-Cole of Fermanagh) of 8th Division, in its first engagement, assaulted the German defences on a frontage of four hundred yards with two battalions and a further two in support. 2nd Royal Berkshires and 2nd Lincolns crossed no man's land without loss. The Germans, not for the first time in the war, had under-estimated the British and had allowed their line to become seriously weakened. The second phase now began.

Behind concentrated shell-fire directed on the village itself, 2nd Rifle Brigade and 1st Royal Irish Rifles advanced in artillery formation across open ground against little opposition. The Rifle Brigade took Neuve Chapelle and passed through. Waiting for the barrage to lift, they then pressed on to their final objective. On the right, touch was gained with an Indian brigade. Almost at the same time the Irish Rifles reached the Armentières road. Pivoting on their right the Irishmen, now under intense fire, with great steadiness wheeled right and passed north of Neuve Chapelle. However, because the advance of 23 Brigade had been held up, their left flank was open. There, German machine-gun and rifle fire took them in enfilade, inflicting heavy losses. Nevertheless within an hour the Irish Rifles had taken their objective and were in touch with the Rifle Brigade on the right. They then swung back a company to guard their left, or open, flank. Having won its objectives, 25 Brigade consolidated its gains. In doing this 1st Irish Rifles unearthed bodies of their 2nd Battalion, recognised by their uniform buttons and badges.[28]

At this point, the divisional attack began to go wrong. Several batteries of 23 Brigade's supporting artillery were late arriving in position and its bombardment left the enemy wire untouched. The attack failed before uncut wire and machine-gun fire from the trenches held by a few dozen dauntless Jägers who held on determinedly, just as the British had at Ypres.

The reserve, 24 Brigade, was sent forward to renew the assault in this sector. Advancing through communication trenches choked with wounded, it was slow in reaching the jump-off position. When its attack came, it also failed. At an early stage in its offensive operational development, some elements of the General Staff were learning to reinforce failure instead of exploiting success. Meanwhile, the Germans reacted with accustomed skill and energy. The break into their line was sealed off by local reserves and reinforcements were hurried forward.

Haig renewed the attack on the 11th; this also failed. The German counterstroke delivered on the 12th recovered lost trenches and the village of Neuve Chapelle. A final assault on Aubers Ridge by the Indian Corps was to be made. Lahore was brought up, and relieving Meerut, they massed for an assault at 1800 that evening. At the last moment the attack was postponed; next morning it was cancelled. 1915 had begun inauspiciously for the Allies.

CHAPTER EIGHT

1915: the Spring Battles

Plumer's V Corps, 27th and 28th regular Divisions and the Canadian Division took over, from the French, the northern and north-eastern sectors of a now notorious Ypres Salient. 2nd Irish Fusiliers and 1st Leinsters of 27th Division relieved the French in trenches astride the Menin road. Hill 60 dominated the area. The Germans had captured it from the French in December, and the British retook it in April, but it was retaken by the enemy in fierce counter-attacks. Now held with many machine-guns, the Germans sprayed fire at every movement.

Before the trenches could be improved, the British and Irish had the unpleasant task of digging out rotting corpses from the trench floor where the French had buried them, packing them into sacks for removal and reburial elsewhere. Chloride of lime was liberally used to disperse the stench of decomposition and fumigate the trench system.

In divisional reserve, 1st Royal Irish bivouacked in woods near Hooge Château lake. Shells bursting in the lake left shoals of dead fish, which the Irishmen gathered enthusiastically as a welcome change from bully-beef. Behind Ypres, 2nd Dublins and 1st Irish Fusiliers of 10 Brigade were resting. Farther south, 1st Connaught Rangers with Lahore Division were training behind the lines. The front was unusually quiet.

SECOND BATTLE OF YPRES, 22 APRIL–25 MAY 1915
On 22 April 1915, the Germans opened an intense artillery bombardment and at the same time began the first effective modern chemical warfare attack. Opposite the French line on the north-western sector of the Ypres salient, a green cloud of chlorine gas drifted down upon trenches manned by the 87th French Territorial and 46th Algerian Divisions. Within minutes, the positions were occupied by men choking in the last extremities of agonised life; the survivors were streaming away in terror, carrying rear details and artillerymen with them. A gap five miles wide opened in the French line from the Ypres Canal to St Julien. The Germans, who had suffered terrible losses to their bravest manpower in the first battle of Ypres, seemed determined to win the second by artillery and terror weapons. In the opening assault, only self-imposed objective limitations and a scarcity of local reserves to exploit a startling success prevented the Germans from capturing Ypres.

On the French right, the Canadian Division was also affected by the gas although less severely. Nevertheless they gallantly stood their ground and delayed the Germans' methodical advance while hastily assembled reserve units formed a patchwork of defence. Spurred by their success, the German commanders rushed reserves to the scene and resumed the attack with gas on 24 April. Only ferocious fighting by the Canadians and British kept the line intact. But the salient became almost a death trap and suggestions on the part of Second Army commander, Gen. Smith-Dorrien, to retire on the Ypres Canal and the ramparts of Ypres resulted only in his dismissal. The scene was inexorably set for the horrendous British casualties at Second and Third Ypres.

St Julien, April 1915

On 24 April the German attack was accompanied by a heavy bombardment of salient rear areas. This was also accompanied by a drenching of those areas with tear-gas, particularly on the artillery positions. So grave was the situation that the antiquated artillery of 27th and 28th Divisions was reinforced by a battery of 60-pounders and one 9.2-inch howitzer from the meagre army reserve. For once, the restriction on artillery and ammunition to three rounds per gun per day was relaxed. It was this support which largely stabilised the Ypres front.

When the Canadians were compelled to withdraw from St Julien, 1st Royal Irish from 27th Divisional reserve were ordered to 'make good Fortuin and stop the Germans coming on.'[1] Moving from Hooge Wood, they came under heavy shell-fire near Wieltje. Ignoring this, they deployed into two lines of half platoons and advanced rapidly. The leading company just managed to beat the advancing Germans to the high ground north of Fortuin crossroads 600 yards from St Julien. They beat off the enemy and held the position until the arrival of 4th Green Howards and 4th East Yorkshire Regiment.[2] Both Territorial Force battalions, fresh and at full strength, attacked at once and drove the Germans back on St Julien. Despite their gallantry, the village was not taken. That night the Yorkshiremen and Royal Irish were relieved and withdrew into reserve to await reinforcements.

On Sunday 25 April, as the 1st Dublins were landing at Gallipoli, their sister battalion, 2nd Dublins, were force-marching with 1st Royal Irish Fusiliers as part of a large force comprising ten Territorial battalions. 1st Royal Irish and 10 Infantry Brigade (Brig.-Gen. C.P.A. Hull) had orders to retake St Julien. But so hurriedly had the concentration been ordered that most of the battalions were not in position on time, despite a postponement of two hours. This was hardly surprising, considering the short notice and the distance covered to reach the concentration area. An officer of 1st Irish Fusiliers later recalled:

> It was indeed a performance of outstanding merit. The distance covered by road before the actual attack was thirty miles, during which

not an officer nor a man succeeded in snatching more than a few minutes' sleep.[3]

Only Hull's five battalions attacked the objective at Zero Hour, 0530. But the postponement had fatal consequences. In the confusion of orders and counter orders, some artillery batteries failed to receive notification of the delay and carried out their bombardment from 0245 to 0315, according to the original timetable. Other batteries fired over the place in the mistaken belief that some Canadians were still in St Julien. Consequently Hull's brigade attacked a heavily defended place across open ground largely without artillery support.

Under cover of a morning mist, 1st Irish Fusiliers, 2nd Dublins, 2nd Seaforth Highlanders and 1st Warwickshires advanced in the first line supported by 7th Argylls. It was almost a mirror image of the attack of the Prussian Guard at Nonne Bosschen without the goose-stepping. From column of route they deployed into line and advanced by alternative 'rushes'. Observers noted they advanced in 'faultless order'[4] until they were 100 yards from the outskirts of St Julien. Then, deluged with withering machine-gun fire, the leading lines were swept away. A few managed to crawl back under cover, but the vast majority never moved again. The losses were dreadful—73 officers and 2826 other ranks, all highly-trained regular soldiers and at that stage of the war irreplaceable.[5] 2nd Dublins alone had 510 all ranks killed or wounded. Despite their cruel losses, the Irish Fusiliers and Dublins reached the outskirts of St Julien and some elements of the Dublins actually succeeded in getting into the village.

> Captain Tobin Maunsell, with Corporal (now Sergeant) Lalor and a few men, got into the village up a ditch, but the rest of the company under me was mopped up trying to get there in extended order.[6]

One company remnant of Dublins, having lost its officers and NCOs, fell back. Others followed, and as they did so, they were confronted by a single slight figure. Dressed in an ancient 'British warm' and armed only with a blackthorn stick, he was instantly recognisable to his Dubliners, Lt.-Col. Loveband, the commanding officer. As he walked towards his men he made the lie-down signal with hand and stick. They obeyed and dug in. Then they were shelled and more gas was released: 'The effect was instantaneous, and for hundreds of yards along the front the men dropped and used their entrenching tools.'[7]

However the Dubliners were undismayed by the repulse and heavy losses. A cry arose, 'three cheers for Jim Larkin'[8] and was responded to with cheers and laughter. It was the six months' Dublin lock-out of 1913–14, led by James Larkin, the leader of the Irish Transport and General Workers'

Union, which had forced many of them into the army and thus to their
present condition.

> The only satisfaction I got out of that day's fighting was to see the
> disgusted face of a German officer captured by Sergeant Cooke, a
> Dublin Fusilier. Posted as look-out on a farm he was above the main
> force of gas and saw an enemy section of fourteen creeping along a
> ditch. He shot each man from the rear at a range of fifty yards until
> only the officer was left. He [Cooke] then got down and captured him.[9]

Sgt. W. Cooke was awarded the DCM two months later.

The Irish Fusiliers also lost heavily. Among their 122 dead and dying was
Pte. R. Morrow from Co. Tyrone. Barely two weeks previously, on 12 April
at Messines, the Irish Fusiliers had come under severe shelling by huge
German siege guns which totally destroyed the front-line trenches. Morrow,
without waiting for orders, dug out several buried men and carried them to
comparative safety. He repeatedly returned, under intense fire and with total
disregard for his own safety, to save others buried in the debris. For this
most conspicuous bravery he was posthumously awarded the Victoria
Cross.

The gallant Canadian Division was relieved in the line on 4 May by the
remainder of 4th Division. With them came 2nd Royal Irish Regiment which,
re-formed and retrained after Le Pilly, was back in the line on the left of 2nd
Dublins. With 1st Royal Irish back at Fortuin, four Irish battalions were now
holding the St Julien front.

THE LAHORE DIVISION ATTACK, 26 APRIL

Without warning, on 26 April, Lahore Division was ordered to move quickly
for an undisclosed destination which proved to be Ypres. It was an
emergency move at a forced-march pace to the threatened sector. The roar of
artillery ahead of them told all it was likely to be a bloody affair. Father Peal
SJ, chaplain to 1st Connaught Rangers, marched with the doctor and medical
orderlies in the battalion tail. As they marched through burning, battered
Ypres, Father Peal did *his* duty.

> At 3 am on Monday the 26 April we were astir. For this once I was
> allowed to follow the regiment going into action. As the companies
> passed me I raised my hand; the men understood the signal. Heads
> were bared and I gave a general absolution. Many passing then never
> returned. Dead horses and dogs met us at every turn; shells screamed
> and hissed and crashed over and around us. Presently, as the Doctor
> and I walked along behind the Regiment, we noticed the Staff-Captain

with his bleeding arm in a sling, helped along by an orderly. He told us that a shell had struck the head of the regiment. We hurried up and there were two of my boys on the pavement.[10]

During the previous three days, the Germans had established themselves along Pilckem Ridge from the Ypres Canal to St Julien, four miles north-east of Ypres. Lahore was ordered to retake the ridge. Without time to reconnoitre for an attack delivered in daylight up a glacis-like slope under enemy observation, it was a desperate venture. When the advance began, only two batteries of divisional artillery were in position and these were without forward observation officers. Exact enemy positions were unknown, save that they were over the crest of Pilkem Ridge. Lahore Division attacked with Jullundar Brigade on the right and Ferozepore on the left; 1st Manchesters were on the extreme right of Jullundar and the Rangers were on the extreme left of the Ferozepore line. Between were the Indian battalions, 40th Pathans, 47th Sikhs, 129th Baluchis and 57th Rifles. In a second line were 59th Rifles, 4th Suffolk (TF), 4th London (TF) and 9th Bhopal. On the left of the Rangers was a French Moroccan brigade.

The artillery barrage opened at 1230 just as the assault troops crossed the start line. Forty minutes were allowed for the attacking troops to reach the German line. Then, after five minutes of intense bombardment, the troops would storm the German line.

Lahore Division advanced steadily through close country to Hill Top ridge, then across a shallow valley where they crossed the British front-line trenches and up a gentle slope to Mauser Ridge. Before them, protected by barbed wire and dominating the approach, were the enemy trenches. As Lahore Division crossed Hill Top ridge, a withering artillery fire met them; heavy German howitzer shells knocked out whole platoons, 'literally falling in heaps'.[11]

German machine-guns were well-sited in enfilade positions to sweep up to a 1000-yard frontage and a blast of fire met the assaulting troops as they neared the crest. Part of the Jullundar Brigade, edging away from the fire-blast, blundered into the second line of Rangers. Causing bunching and offering perfect targets for the enemy machine-guns, they drew fire and suffered badly. Before the advancing troops had reached an assault position, the artillery fire stopped without cutting the enemy wire. The German infantry manned their parapets unmolested and fire poured into the attackers. Against withering fire, the Irish and Mancunians somehow struggled on and nearly reached the German wire on the crest of the ridge, just in front of the enemy trenches. The wire, uncut and impenetrable, checked the advance. Worse followed. A light north-westerly wind was blowing; the men scarcely felt it as they struggled forward against the machine-gun hail. But on that gentle breeze came a yellow-greenish cloud and it rolled down onto the right battalion of the Moroccan and the Ferozepore Brigade. It was chlorine gas.

The gas attack broke up the assault everywhere. Without respirators, the troops wetted handkerchiefs or cloth and pressed them over nostrils and mouths.

> The ground became covered with bodies of men writhing in torture. The enemy redoubled its fire. The whole French line went to pieces, exposing the Rangers' flank. Large numbers of surviving Indians streamed back to La Brique shouting, 'Khabardar, Jehannam pahunche!' (Look out, we've arrived in Hell!)[12]

Despite torture and death, the surviving Rangers held a position 80 yards from the German wire and dug in. A group of forty from 1st Manchesters under a lieutenant joined D Company and were directed to go into a ditch and dig in. This they did and stood with the Rangers through the night of 26–27 April until relieved by 1st Highland Light Infantry at 0300.

The Indian troops lost sixty-eight officers and 1106 soldiers from four battalions; the Manchesters twelve officers and 277 men; the Connaught Rangers eighteen officers and 351 men. On the following afternoon, the attack was resumed, ostensibly in concert with the French. But when their attack failed to materialise, Lahore, advancing in isolation, again suffered heavily for no gain.

German gas attacks occurred again on 2 May and settled into a pattern of artillery bombardment and gas release, followed by infantry attack. Hoping, apparently, to occupy ground vacated by the retreating British, they were often disappointed. Covering their faces with moistened flannel, their only protection, the stubborn infantrymen, British, Canadian, Indian and Irish, beat off repeated attacks. The Germans then adopted a policy of switching attacks to different parts of the front, grinding down the opposition with concentrated artillery fire of all calibres.

After the assault on the Canadians, the German attack switched to 28th Division on Frezenberg Ridge between 6–8 May. It again succeeded in breaking the British line, but exploitation was prevented by an heroic stand of regular and Territorial troops. 10 Brigade was again hurried to the scene. Shortly after their arrival a night attack by 2nd Dublins, 1st Irish Fusiliers and 1st Warwicks swept obliquely from Mouse Trap Farm sector, driving back the German garrison of Hill 33. As they fled, they carried with them the German XXVI and XXVII Corps. An entire German army retired from positions they had captured and went immediately onto the defensive; it was an incredible result for a brigade attack.[13]

The Germans switched direction again, and 27th Division felt the weight of enemy artillery and gas from 9–12 May. All attacks were beaten off successfully, except on 11 May when the 2nd Cameron Highlanders and 1st

Argylls were subjected to gas; after a hard fight the Camerons were driven out of their trenches on the Menin Road. 1st Leinsters in divisional reserve were sent to their relief and attempted to restore the position. A fight with alternate attack and counter-attack went on well into the night of 11–12 May. Although the Leinsters gave and took heavy punishment, including the loss of their commanding officer Lt.-Col. C. Conyers, the Germans held to their gains.

MOUSE TRAP FARM, 24 MAY 1915

Early on the morning of 24 May, many sectors of the British line were deluged by German shell-fire and saturated with gas. On the left of the British front, the line of 4th Division was held by 10 and 11 Brigades, 1st Fusiliers, 7th Argylls, 2nd Dublins, 2nd Royal Irish.

The much-disputed, aptly named Mouse Trap Farm was only thirty yards from the German lines. Called 'Shell Trap Farm' by the Dubliners,[14] it was held by two platoons. The Dublins had just finished stand-to at 0400 and rum was being issued, a tablespoonful a man, when a loud explosion and bombardment began and a wall of gas rolled down each side of the farm. 'The colonel shouted "Get your respirators boys, here comes the gas!"'[15] So close together were the German and Dublin trenches at this point that there was little time to put on respirators. For once the German assault infantry followed close behind their gas and were able to gain entry into the trenches. Col. Loveband was shot dead, his second in command, Maj. Mangan, was gassed and dying. All company officers fought on, either dying or gassed at their posts. The farm was taken and retaken in a day of heavy fighting which reduced it to a heap of 'mud and rubbish'.[16]

The Dublins held the line until after midday when 'organised defence came to an end, leaving little more than headquarters details and transport men'. That night in response to brigade orders, the remnant, one officer and twenty soldiers, marched out and reported to brigade headquarters. Of the remainder of the battalion, the commanding officer and eleven other officers were killed; four officers, including the medical officer, were wounded or gassed; one, the machine-gun officer who had stayed by his guns to the end, was taken prisoner. 583 other ranks, practically all the battalion, were killed, wounded or gassed.

Within a month, 2nd Dublins had lost thirty-three officers, nineteen dead, thirteen wounded and one prisoner (2/Lt.W.J. Shanks, the machine-gun officer). 1078 other ranks were casualties, of whom 439 were dead. Taken together with the terrible losses suffered by 1st Dublins at Gallipoli (569 dead), this constituted the complete destruction of both regular battalions of the Royal Dublin Fusiliers. Throughout the war, no other Irish regiment, and only one British regiment, suffered such fearsome casualties in so short a time.[17]

When the wounded were sent away after dark there were no Dublins in front of Battalion Headquarters. From about 2.30 pm there was no fighting in our trenches; everyone held on to them to the last; there was no surrender, no quarter given or accepted.[18]

1st Irish Fusiliers, on the right farthest away from the gas discharge and with maximum warning, were least overcome. They stood firm although heavily engaged. During the attack the resourceful bravery of Pte. G. Wilson was outstanding. When all the men of a machine-gun team were blown out of an emplacement, Wilson carried the gun to a new position and brought it into action. Its fire helped repulse the enemy assault. Wilson was awarded the Distinguished Conduct Medal, but died of wounds on 18 June.[19]

On the left of the Dublins were 2nd Royal Irish. Apart from the Dublins, they were nearest the point of gas discharge and suffered heavily. After the fall of Mouse Trap Farm, one company, hard hit by the bombardment and seriously affected by gas and enfilade fire, fell back. But a counter-attack by the other three companies restored the position. However, the Germans soon renewed the attack and again took the trench. In all the Royal Irish lost their commanding officer, sixteen other officers killed and wounded; 378 other ranks were killed, wounded or gassed. That night the Divisional Commander decided not to counter-attack to retake Mouse Trap Farm, so the line was adjusted accordingly. For some time French officers regarded the British waste of men in futile attacks much as they viewed the charge of the Light Brigade: 'C'est magnifique, mais ce n'est pas la guerre.'[20]

AUBERS RIDGE, 6–9 MAY 1915

Shortly after the end of the second battle of Ypres, Sir John French ordered Gen. Haig's First Army, comprising I and IV Corps and the Indian Corps, to break through the enemy line to his front and gain the La Bassée–Lille road (a distance of three miles). The first phase of Haig's plan was a simultaneous assault by 1st Division and the Meerut Division to be followed by a rapid advance to gain a footing on Aubers Ridge, 4000 yards behind the enemy's front-line trench system.

Following the lessons of Neuve Chapelle and not to be taken unawares a second time, the Germans had intensified their preparations. An additional line of defences was constructed and their front-line trenches strengthened with accustomed energy and engineering skill. Because the water table was only two to three feet below the surface, high parapets and parados were constructed of sandbags, each course supported in strength by large mesh wire. The parapets, doubled or trebled to fifteen to twenty feet across and heightened to six or seven feet, were considered to be proof to all but shells of the heaviest calibre. An excavation in front of the parapet, dug during its construction, was filled with barbed wire which was invisible to British observers. At intervals of a few yards, two-man dug-outs were built into parapet and parados. At twenty yard intervals, steel shuttered machine-gun emplacements were fixed into the parapet at ground level, so strong that a direct hit by heavy artillery was required to knock them out. At salient positions, additional strongpoints were sited to fire in enfilade.

Support trenches of similar design were constructed 200–300 yards to the rear of the front line. In every regimental sector, up and down, communication trenches were made to allow free passage both ways. In some cases these were roofed or 'blinded' to conceal movement. All the preparations were constructed in line with the old German adage 'sweat saves blood'. So it was to prove.

THE ATTACK ON 6 MAY

The Indian Corps objective was Aubers Ridge. Meerut was to attack with Lahore Division in support. Lahore, recently back from its trial at Ypres, had the task of holding the line and giving covering fire to fix the Germans to their positions. Just before the battle, a draft of three officers and 300 men arrived for the Connaught Rangers; although the Rangers were very weak in numbers, it was decided the new arrivals should be left out of battle. After a short postponement, Meerut attacked at 1520; by 1800 they were back at their start line, having been beaten back with severe losses. The Rangers remained in the support trenches throughout the battle, the enemy replied to Lahore Division's small arms fire with heavy trench-mortar and artillery fire. It was a very one-sided contest. After relief the Indian Corps was moved to the Rue du Bois for the next phase.

THE RIGHT ATTACK AT RUE DU BOIS, 9 MAY

After Ypres and Givenchy, 2nd Munsters had reconstructed and retrained at Taleuvriere. Part of this training was the religious ethos fostered by the battalion chaplain, Father Gleeson, and encouraged by the officers and NCOs. Nearby, in a fifteenth century Benedictine abbey, the battalion hung the company standards presented by Lady Ishbel Gordon, wife of the recent Lord Lieutenant of Ireland. (She was author of *Ireland's Crusade Against Tuberculosis* and was made a freeman of the City of Limerick.)

> We hung our four beautiful green flags (dark green with golden harp in the centre, and Munster under). The tricolour (with sacred heart in the centre) and the green hung side by side, and it reminded us of the 'Wild Geese' and of Fontenoy.

'The flags we conquered in that fray, look lone on Ypres choir they say.'[21] The men were very proud of the honour shown to the Irish flags by the local curé and all the French people. When the curé allowed the Munsters to guard the Exposition of the Eucharist, Father Gleeson was overjoyed.

I wished it could have been seen by our friends in Ireland.[22]

On the evening of 8 May, under command of Lt.-Col. V.G.H. Rickard, 2nd Munsters once again marched towards the front. At a French wayside shrine, Rickard halted the battalion and formed a hollow square before it. On three sides were the rifle companies, and facing them on horseback were Col. Rickard, his adjutant, Capt. Filgate and the chaplain, Father Gleeson. Gun flashes added to the semi-light of a spring evening; gunfire and shell explosions reminded all of the ordeal to come. All bared their heads and the light breeze ruffled hair and caused to flutter the green company standards. Father Gleeson's stole made a splash of soft colour. The chaplain raised his right hand and intoned general absolution and all sang the Te Deum. Then, to the barked commands of RSM Ring, the march resumed towards the sound of the guns.[23]

After a restless night, the Munstermen massed in the front-line trenches at 0530. It was the intention to go over the top during the final intensive period of the bombardment, establish themselves eighty yards from the enemy positions, and be ready for the charge directly the bombardment lifted. So poor was the bombardment that German lookouts were in position and gave the alarm. Fully expecting the bombardment to neutralise the enemy machine-guns, no covering fire was arranged. This allowed the Germans time to man their machine-guns and gave them full freedom to sweep a deadly fire into the attackers.

The bombardment was ineffectual. Only thirty minutes were allowed for wire-cutting; the Royal Artillery used shrapnel for this crucial fire-mission. The wire was largely uncut and where it was, machine-guns covered the gaps. There were too few heavy guns in the bombardment and 18-pounders lacked sufficient punch to effect a breach in the massive parapet wall. This, six feet in height, presented a formidable obstacle.

The guns lifted at 0540. The leading British assault waves rose and rushed the enemy defences. The charge was met by devastating machine-gun and rifle fire and there was nothing to suppress it. Courageously the charge was pressed home by all battalions of 1st Division. The leading waves reached the enemy wire before being stopped. The few gaps which existed were raked with fire, yet through these death traps, a handful out of thousands succeeded in getting through. These dauntless stormers were now confronted with the enemy's six-foot-high breastwork. Twenty of 1st Northamptons and the right flank company of the Munsters, about 100 strong, somehow managed to force their way through and reach the German parapet. The Northamptons entered the German positions through a gap and, according to a later German account, were all killed by bomb or bayonet.

The charge of the Munsters began with a cap being tossed into the air and a shout of 'Yoicks, Tally ho'. [24] Col. Rickard was killed almost at the outset as his men dashed at the enemy. Overcoming all difficulties, fifty Munsters crossed the enemy parapet. One intrepid soul stood upright on the wall, faced the British lines and waved a green company flag. Having captured the first German trench, the gallant band pressed on to the second line in accordance with their orders. The survivors halted at a broad water-filled dyke, but this had been foreseen and 'bridges' (long duck-boards) were taken forward. However those who carried them were dead or wounded before the wire. The 'bridge' which ought to have come forward to bridge the dyke could not be got through, and the gallant stormers took cover.

> By this time, it had become apparent to all that the attack had failed. Word was sent to the British artillery that no troops had reached the German trench, and that the attack was to begin again. Shortly afterwards down came the British barrage on to the German lines and back areas. The unfortunate Munsters could not go forward and would not go back. They took cover as best they could, but life in the open was impossible. The heroic company was wiped out. Two men got back to tell the tale.[25]

The mass of wounded hanging on the enemy wire had stopped a second wire-cutting bombardment. But finally the order to fire was given. Artillery forward observation officers, of whom the future FM Lord Alanbrooke was one, were horrified by the futile slaughter of gallant and helpless infantryman sheltering by the wire.[26]

In the short period of the attack, casualties suffered by the two brigades were heavy, eighty-five officers and 2135 men. The Munsters lost nineteen officers and 374 men, eight of whom were taken prisoner. 'Comment seems superfluous.'[27] That afternoon, another attack by 1st Division delivered by 1st Guards Brigade was equally unsuccessful.

In the Indian Corps, the Dehra Dun Brigade of Meerut Division attacked twice and was repulsed each time. Whole lines of men fell before machine-guns and the assault infantry could only establish themselves half-way across no man's land. German artillery pounded the unfortunate Indians into mud and blood. Having suffered the loss of thirty-seven officers and 856 men, the Meerut divisional commander stopped all further attacks by his division. That night another assault by the Indian Corps was ordered. Lahore Division was brought up and relieved Meerut at 1800. The orders of its new divisional commander, Maj.-Gen. H.D'U. Keary, was that the attack was to be pressed and the position carried 'at all costs',[28] a cliché destined to become infamous. No artillery bombardment took place and eventually at 0100 on 10 May, the attack was cancelled.

AUBERS RIDGE—THE LEFT ATTACK AT FROMELLES

On the left at Fromelles, the attack on V Corps front was made by 24 and 25 Brigades of 8th Division. 1st Royal Irish Rifles in 25 Brigade were in position by 0230. Considering the concentration was made at night, it had been reasonably orderly. At 0500, the bombardment began and as elsewhere on the army front, it was a failure. In this sector, failure was mainly due to defective barrels of the ancient 8th Divisional artillery and faulty shells. Some fell short of the enemy defences while others failed to explode. The wire was largely uncut, the parapet unbreached and the enemy fire unsuppressed. During the final intensive period, the leading companies moved out into no man's land, here about 200 yards wide. In 24 Brigade, the East Lancashires found two gaps. Despite terrific enemy fire and being caught in the open by their own bombardment, the leading company got through the gap and about thirty men entered the German trench. They were never heard of again. In the other battalion, 2nd Northamptons, one company reached the wire where no gaps existed. All were shot down.

Despite all the odds against it, 25 Brigade under Brig. Lowry-Cole attacked successfully. 2nd Rifle Brigade and 1st Royal Irish Rifles charged across no man's land and, getting through gaps in the wire, stormed the unbroken breastwork. In scenes reminiscent of the breach of Badajoz, this time in daylight and before machine-gun fire, men helped each other to scale the obstacle while others fell all around them. Those successful pressed on to their first objective. Seeing their success, the support companies of the Rifle Brigade and Irish Rifles charged forward together and also reached the enemy line. Brig. Lowry-Cole advanced on hearing the attack was successful, but on reaching the German line, found that all forward movement had stopped. The enemy in the untaken part of the line were now sweeping no man's land with heavy fire. In the inevitable confusion and maddening din of battle came a shouted order, 'Retire! Retire!' Some of the Rifles and Rifle Brigade came back and carried back two companies of 2nd Lincolns. To restore order, Brig. Lowry-Cole stood on the German parapet in plain view of the Germans; he was mortally wounded. Yet, resolutely, the Rifle Brigade and Irish Rifles maintained their lodgment in the German lines, although elsewhere the attack was a costly failure. The Rifle Brigade had lost twenty-one officers and 632 men, the Royal Irish Rifles twenty-three officers and 454 men. The two regular battalions of the Northamptonshire Regiment engaged in the battle lost twenty-nine officers and 951 men killed and wounded.[29]

BATTLE OF FESTUBERT, 15 MAY 1915

The battle of Festubert dispensed with land objectives and initiated instead the policy of attrition. This involved wearing down the stubborn foe by resolute use of superior numbers, never allowing him rest, and unrelenting grinding of the enemy until his will to fight was broken and his defences destroyed, irrespective of cost.[30]

It was initiated, not by dour Scottish Sir Douglas Haig, but by imaginative Irish Sir John French. Principles of war treasured by great captains, such as surprise, economy of effort and flexibility, were discarded in the process. It was the policy which was the beginning of the road to the Somme, Arras, Passchendaele and the victory of exhaustion. Unfortunately at this stage of the war, the BEF did not yet possess the means of pursuing the policy totally.

The initial bombardment began on 13 May and continued until the morning of 15 May. A night attack by 6 Brigade achieved total surprise and advanced to the German support line with little loss. The 5 Brigade, where 2nd Inniskillings attacked on the right with 1st Worcesters on the left, could achieve no such surprise. By Corps' order, Lahore Division just north of their attack fired 'to deceive the enemy'. This alerted the Germans, who put up fire balls and detected the light bridges over the dyke in front of the Worcester positions. At 2300 when the British batteries lifted, the enemy manned their parapets and brought a searchlight into play in addition to light balls and flares. This illuminated the battlefield for machine-gunners and riflemen, and simultaneously rocket-signals brought artillery fire. The deluge of fire stopped the Worcesters and prevented the advance of the support lines. 2nd Inniskillings, attacking on the right of the Worcesters, had mixed fortune. The right half of the Inniskilling attack reached and captured two German lines of trenches. The brigadier endeavoured to exploit this by sending the 2nd Battalion 43rd/52nd Light Infantry forward in support; in all, ten platoons were gradually sent up. But the left of the Inniskillings, influenced by the failure of the Worcesters, could not make headway. All attempts failed to penetrate the German line and eventually the survivors were forced back. The Inniskillings lost nineteen officers and 630 men.

In the continuation of these futile attacks at Festubert between 16–17 May, 2nd and 7th Divisions achieved nothing and sustained heavy casualties. Under Brig. Lord Cavan, 4 Guards Brigade of 2nd Division was to attack at 0430 on 16 May following an intensification of the bombardment. The 1st Grenadiers and Irish Guards led the assault, but the Germans were already alerted. A new German position extending at right angles along the entire front escaped artillery fire. From there, enfilade machine-guns at short range opened up on the advancing Guards and stopped them dead. The leading companies lost half their strength in minutes. Across 100 yards, the Grenadier Guards lost five officers and eighty-three men, the Irish Guards fifteen officers and 415 men. To pursue such costly attacks would be imbecility; Lord Cavan wisely ordered the attack to discontinue. At 0730, headquarters 2nd Division ordered him to dig in and consolidate.[30]

The battle of Festubert was no more than a series of costly and abortive attacks which rarely broke into the enemy front line. They served only to exhaust the British on the Western Front at a time when Gallipoli was soaking up considerable manpower. The Irish regular battalions were for the most part shattered and it was left to the young service battalions of 10th

Division, now entering the field, to carry on the fight. The battles coincided with an order from Lord Kitchener to Sir John French to send 20,000 rounds of 18-pounder shells from his reserve stocks to Gallipoli where they were urgently needed. These were replaced immediately from England. The double shift of ammunition made no difference to Sir John's battles in France, but provided him with political ammunition which he made use of several weeks later. The 'shell scandal' raised such a storm that the Liberal government was brought down. In the formation of a new coalition administration, Sir Edward Carson, the Ulster Unionist leader, and Mr John Redmond, leader of the Irish Nationalist Party, were offered ministerial positions. Redmond declined; Carson accepted.

CHAPTER NINE

Raising and Training 10th Division

A proclamation was issued on 11 August 1914 asking for an immediate addition of 100,000 men to the Regular Army. Army order 324 of 21 August authorised the addition of six divisions (9th–14th and Army Troops to the Regular Army). This formed the First New Army, and late in August 1914 the 10th (Irish) Division began to assemble in Ireland. The infantry of the Division was comprised of service battalions of all Irish line regiments. Its men drawn from all classes, creeds and political opinions.[1]

The General Officer Commanding (GOC), Lt.-Gen. Sir Bryan T. Mahon, a Galway man, first commissioned into the Connaught Rangers, transferred to the 8th KRIH and became adjutant. He was seconded to the Anglo-Egyptian Army. Under Kitchener, he took part in the reconquest of the Sudan and was present at the battles of Firket, Atbara and Omdurman. In addition to his duties as intelligence officer, he commanded a cavalry squadron with distinction at Omdurman and was awarded the DSO. Under Wingate, Mahon commanded the mounted force which harried and destroyed the Khalifa. Seconded for a year's special service in South Africa, he commanded a mounted brigade and relieved Mafeking.

Mahon returned to the Sudan as Military Governor of Kordofan. Then he was sent to India were he ended his army career as GOC the Lucknow Division before retirement early in 1914. He was fifty-two years of age, bronze and lithe, relaxed, a heavy smoker; he was rarely seen without a cigarette which he smoked in a holder. He mixed easily with troops at sports where he usually appeared riding a magnificent chestnut and was soon easily recognised throughout the 10th. 'Everything about him appealed to them—his great reputation, the horse he rode, his Irish name and his Irish nature, all went to their hearts. Above all, he was that unique being, an Irishman with no politics.'[2]

Brig. Cooper, 29 Brigade, was commissioned into the Grenadiers in 1880. Having served in Egypt in 1882 and in South Africa, he transferred to the Irish Guards in 1900 and later commanded the 1st Battalion. He had been private secretary to the Lord Lieutenant of Ireland 1904–5.

Brig. Nicol, 30 Brigade, a Scot, was commissioned into the 94th of Foot which later became 2nd Connaught Rangers. He transferred into the Rifle Brigade with whom he saw active service on the North West Frontier and in South Africa.

Brig. Hill, 31 Brigade, had a long and distinguished career in Royal Irish Fusiliers. With them he served in the eastern Sudan and was present at the battles of El Teb and Tamai. He had been commanding at Belfast 1910–14 when the army and UVF confronted each other. Possibly his greatest personal moment came after the war, when in 1922, he met his old battalion of the Royal Irish Fusiliers returning from India with the news they had been saved from extinction.

Regular cadres for the new battalions were available at all regimental depots. In almost every case, the senior major commanding the depot was promoted to lieutenant-colonel and assumed command of the senior service battalion, the exception being the Royal Irish. The regular battalion on home station was ordered to detach three officers and at least ten senior NCOs. Many officers were Indian Army or had been seconded to colonial forces and were on leave or on UK courses; on the instructions of the War Office, they were retained for duty at home. Those officers on Staff College courses became brigade majors. Battalion quartermasters, regimental sergeant-majors and regimental quartermaster-sergeants were usually pensioners. The company sergeant-majors and company quartermaster-sergeants were drawn from promoted sergeants from the regular battalions. It was around these cadres that 10th Division was created. Being the first Irish division, it had the pick of officers and NCOs and its rapid development reflects this. In Ireland, 'fortunately there was no lack of martial material.'[3]

Implementing a War Office Order of mid September, commanding officers selected candidates for temporary commissions, subject to approval by brigade commanders. After this, vacancies were quickly filled. Some had experience from officer training corps; nevertheless all studied and learned as they taught their men. Later, nearly all newly commissioned temporary officers attended courses at the Officer Training Corps, Trinity College, Dublin, and 'compared well, after nine months, with regular subalterns'.[4]

Heady words, but the fact stands that they accomplished the astonishing feat of raising, training and taking a good division to war in less than a year.

From all over Ireland old soldiers returned to the colours. The best were those who had volunteered for and served in South Africa. These men proved invaluable in helping and setting an example for the recruits. Inevitably there were some incorrigibles who were discharged or drafted elsewhere. Unlike Britain, where every class was represented in the ranks, with the notable exception of D Company, 7th Dublins, the ranks of the 10th were filled with men from working-class backgrounds.

Large numbers of British Catholics were transferred to the Irish Division from all over the country, although they were mainly from the industrial areas of the north and miners from the south-west. Many were second or third generation British, sons and grandsons of Irish immigrants, perhaps of those who were British grass-root supporters of Parnell in the crucial 1885 general election. They were staunch trade unionists and not accustomed to accepting orders readily from bosses. But once they settled down they proved excellent soldiers and in many cases were quickly promoted.[5] Their Irish, and British, names and places of birth are on the rolls of the dead of all Irish regiments who served in the Great War. The divisional historian whimsically records: 'One English habit, however, never deserted them: they were unable to break themselves of grumbling about their food.'[6]

A Scottish contingent deserving mention was led by Pte. James Scollan, a Glasgow shipyard worker. Scollan, who was Fermanagh born, decided to join his county regiment. Such was his 'wholly deserved popularity with his workmates' that about a hundred enlisted with him and served together throughout the war in 5th Inniskillings.

> Scollan won no honours in the field, but he was the salt of the earth; a miniature Harry Lauder, with a very good voice and irrepressible cheerfulness and humour, who could always be relied on to keep up his fellow's spirits when things looked—or were—bad.[7]

Another notable element within 10th Division was D Company, 7th Royal Dublin Fusiliers. An address by Mr F.H. Browning, President of the Irish Rugby Football Union to over three hundred young professional men of Dublin rugby clubs, brought in many middle and upper class volunteers. They included barristers, solicitors, engineers and businessmen from many spheres. Some were shortly commissioned, while others selected by their peers became NCOs. In addition to forming D Company, they became the battalion specialists—signallers, machine-gunners and medical orderlies. A high 'tone' was set, and remained. One barrister who had seen service in the South African war refused a commission for eighteen months because it would separate him from his friends. They became the 'Toffs in the "Old Toughs"'.[8]

Although there were many Irish serving with the support arms and services in the Regular Army, it is true to say that a proportion of those serving with the Artillery and Engineers were either English or Scottish, although many had obvious Irish names.[9]

Initially the division concentrated in barracks within the Dublin area but some soon moved away: 29 Brigade went to Fermoy; 30 Brigade, the Curragh; 31 Brigade remained in Dublin. However, with the formation shortly afterwards of 16th Division, the barracks in Munster were vacated and 29 Brigade scattered temporarily. 6th Royal Irish Rifles were formed at Wellington Barracks, Dublin, during the last week of August and moved to Fermoy, Co. Cork. 6th Leinsters went to Birr and the 5th Royal Irish to

Longford. The latter afterwards became the Divisional Pioneer Battalion and were replaced in the line by the 10th Hampshire Regiment.

The Hampshires were army troops, that is troops at the disposal of the Army Commander. Having mustered in Hampshire, they were moved to Dublin, destined to become the Pioneer battalion of the 10th. They first paraded 1070 strong at Beggar's Bush Barracks, the headquarters of Brig. Hill. On parade he told them, 'You have the mark of class about you'.[10] It was a good start. They were shortly afterwards transferred to Mullingar where they were joined a month later by 11th Hampshires formed for the 16th Division. Both battalions created so good an impression on the town that on their departure the following year, the town commissioners gave them a vote of thanks. A local ladies' committee organised by Mrs Patrick was remembered by the Hampshires long after, for kindness and hospitality during their stay at Mullingar.[11]

The division's support and service units were initially scattered for organisation and training, but were later concentrated for divisional collective training. The artillery was stationed on the Curragh and at Kildare, except for 54 Brigade, Royal Field Artillery (RFA regiments were at this time known as 'brigades') which formed at Dundalk.

The engineer field companies, one for each brigade, the divisional cyclist company and the divisional train of the Army Service Corps were at the Curragh, the signal company at Carlow and the RAMC field ambulances at Limerick. The cadre of the divisional signal company came from the Engineer Depot at Chatham. Among them was Sapper J.C. Dart, one of three post office telegraphists from Bristol who became instructors in the company. He found:

> Carlow extremely pleasant after Chatham. The barrack-room was large and spacious, plenty of good food and sleeping accommodation better than we could have hoped for …Telegraph operators were from north and south Ireland, motor cyclist dispatch riders from south-west Ireland, particularly Co. Cork.[12]

Sapper Dart was surprised how quickly his trainee telegraphists picked up Morse and were soon competent at ten words a minute. At flag signalling, they 'were extremely competent and well worth watching for their speed and gracefulness'.[13]

Depots in Ireland were not overwhelmed as were the British ones, and most recruits were fully equipped at once. The recruits from Britain had joined their battalions in civilian clothes, but all with the exception of Medical Corps units were fully equipped by mid-October, with the exception of greatcoats; this was partly relieved by purchasing tweed overcoats until proper greatcoats arrived in January.

Basic platoon training began at once and they 'worked pretty hard, with physical training 7.00–8.00, parades 8.30–12.30 and 2.00–5.00 pm. There were lectures in the evenings'.[14] They worked conscientiously on the *Manual of Infantry Training and Field Service Regulations*. 'We rarely went over to the town.'[15] This soon developed into company training. By the end of 1914, the basic musketry course was fired by all battalions. Training lectures and battalion route marches broke the monotony. Battalion training started early in 1915 when the weather of the awful winter of 1914–15 allowed. With this, the six battalions in Dublin were beginning to feel the constraints of their training area, the Phoenix Park. Afterwards the smell of roasting malt which lingers heavily on the air by the Liffey in west Dublin, was long remembered by soldiers who marched to and from that great park.[16] To ease training constraints, landowners volunteered their demesnes. These were used but distance and lack of transport restricted their use.

In the new year, despite rain and slush, battalion training commenced; long route marches of 70–80 miles were done in four days. Trained soldier courses were organised. Those for 31 Brigade were held close to the ranges at Dollymount, where the men were in 'quite decent huts' and the officers were billeted 'in the club houses or in small cubicles'.[17] Battalions of this same brigade quartered in west Dublin barracks, Richmond and Royal Barracks, took part in a series of schemes which built up to brigade exercises. 'Quite a good attack west of Tallaght, satisfactory palaver with [Brig.] Hill afterwards' and 'fought encounter battle against skeleton enemy at Cromwells Fort' or 'defended convoy from Ballyfermot to Irishtown'. 5th Inniskillings 'fought quite good rear guard action' against 6th Inniskillings.[18] By spring, night training and major exercises had begun and were practised twice weekly. In one, 31 Brigade defended the Grand Canal at Clondalkin; they were possibly influenced by the action of 2nd Royal Irish behind the Conde Canal at Mons.

As the training of the soldiers went on, officer training was carried out supplementary to it. Some of the wounded officers from the Western Front lectured during their convalescence, and many lessons were learned and applied in trench siting and digging. Curiosity was excited about new battle novelties such as steel helmets and hand grenades, none of which had yet been seen within the division.

But it wasn't all work. 7th Dublins won the soccer competition, 5th Inniskillings the boxing and 6th Inniskillings the long distance running. The officers frequented the Gaiety, Royal and Empire theatres. A performance of *Tannhäuser* by the O'Hara company was well received. Some even managed breakfast at the Kildare Street Club after a night on the town.[19] For the men, in addition to sport, there was the famous Dublin pub society which tempted many to overstay evening pass. One orderly officer at Richmond Barracks recorded in his diary: 'Only 16 absentees at tattoo'.[20]

In mid February, just before brigade exercises started, something of a novelty occurred for service battalions when they lined the streets of Dublin for the departure of Lord and Lady Aberdeen. Almost exactly two months later in mid April, 31 Brigade lined the streets for the arrival of Lord Wimborne, the penultimate Lord Lieutenant of Ireland.[21]

Shortly after Lord Wimborne's arrival parade, 29 Brigade moved to the Curragh, one battalion in barracks and three in huts. Two brigades were now concentrated at the Curragh, but the third, 31 Brigade, remained in Dublin and no doubt were happy to do so. Some divisional troops also remained in the capital; the divisional cyclists and Service Corps Reserve Park were stationed at the Royal Barracks. Brigade day and night exercises went on throughout February, and fitting into what must have been a tight schedule, the battalions fired a second musketry course. The final phase of divisional training started early in March when Gen. Mahon held a series of brigade exercises which included brigade and divisional support units—three brigades of field artillery and the heavy battery; three engineer field companies, the signal company and divisional cyclists. Later, because of the social activity which usually accompanied them, these were considered the high points in the division's training for war and were remembered as the most pleasant in the division's history.

At last, after months of training, units became as one, with that feeling of corporate pride which is the hallmark of good battalions. All had formed fife and drum bands at their own expense; some battalions also had Irish pipes. That spring they marched many miles to their music along the wet lanes of Kildare and Co. Dublin. They saw hedges bursting into leaf or flower under skies where clouds always drifted overhead, water in abundance in still springs or bubbling streams, the air always filled with varieties of fresh scents of the land keen on their nostrils. These memories gave them comfort in dreadful moments during harsh times ahead.

On 16 April 1915, barely seven months after its formation, Gen. Mahon held a divisional parade at the Curragh at which he formally inspected the complete division for the first time. After his arrival and a general salute, with his personal staff behind him he inspected on his favourite hunter. Mahon had become well known to his troops. His easy, informal manner relaxed them and gave all an added pride. The units then passed in review to the music of their regimental marches. In battalion mass, followed by the artillery in line of close interval, they paraded before their divisional commander. It marked the final welding of diverse units into one fighting formation of all arms and services, ready, almost, for war. All were proud to be the first Irish division to take to the field. One officer of 6th Royal Irish Rifles wrote: 'It was a tiresome day but being one of such a stalwart body of men filled one with elation. We felt we would be quite invincible.'[22]

Following this, battalion specialist training was intensified for machine-gunners, transport men, medical orderlies and signallers. Stringent medicals weeded out the unfit and often, to their chagrin, they were left behind.

The time came for the 10th to move to Britain for final training before active service, and as yet no one knew their ultimate destination. In accordance with Kitchener's policy, the division was to go quietly and in secrecy, since German submarines were reported in the Irish Sea. Many battalions took the short sea crossing via Larne and Stranraer. However, 7th Dublins were to march through the city during daylight to represent the division. After parading in the Royal Barracks (now Collins Barracks) close to Parkgate, the Commanding Officer, Lt.-Col. Downing, the largest man in the division, told the assembled spectators, 'We will do our best; judge us by our deeds'.[23]

Led by the band of 12th Lancers and the pipers of the Officer Training Corps, Trinity College, the 'Pals' marched off. Along the Liffey quays, crowds on the pavements and spectators in windows cheered and waved. Outside the Four Courts a large group of barristers, solicitors, officials and judges shouted goodbye to their friends. To the watchers the Pals

> looked exceedingly fit, and presented a fine military bearing. As they marched by in perfect order and in swinging, rhythmic step, every one felt that they were worthy of the city and of a country noted for its soldiers.[24]

It was nearly impossible to march to attention. Little boys strutted alongside the marching column, chanting their street songs:

> Left, right; left, right; here's the way we go,
> Marching with fixed bayonets, the terror of every foe,
> A credit to the nation, a thousand buccaneers,
> A terror to creation are the Dublin Fusiliers.[25]

Not for them the direct route along the Liffey quays. Diverting across Essex Bridge, they marched through the commercial centre of Dame Street, then College Green, passing the Bank of Ireland and Trinity College where many of the battalion had been students and one a professor. Flags bedecked those palladian buildings giving colour to their smoke-begrimed eighteenth-century stone, in the shadows of which stood statues of Burke, Grattan, Goldsmith and Tom Moore. Spectators became dense as the marching column crossed O'Connell Bridge and right-wheeled onto the quays, skirting the statue of O'Connell the Liberator. Emotion rose when well-dressed ladies from the fashionable Georgian and Regency squares of south Dublin mingled with their poorer sisters in shawls from the Liberties and lesser squares of north Dublin. Together they joined their husbands and sweethearts in the ranks to keep step with them the last few hundred yards.[26] Almost on cue, the band broke into the traditional Irish trooping air, 'The Girl I Left Behind Me', as they passed the stately Custom House along the North Wall, where many of A Company had worked, towards the waiting steamer.

Possibly the only person along the route of the battalion unaware of its passing was stone-deaf George Vanston, in his office on the first floor of the Custom House overlooking the quay. Six years later, as Sir George, he failed to hear the crackle of flames as the Custom House, set alight by the IRA, burned about his ears. On that occasion he had to be 'knocked-up and escorted out'.[27]

An overnight ship and train journey brought them from Dublin to Basingstoke in Hampshire after a long journey through a warm night and lovely morning of late April or early May as unit after unit of 10th Division departed from Ireland. A quarter of its fighting men would never return. The English countryside struck them as pretty but too orderly and cultivated compared with their own country's natural beauty.[28] The division moved into vast tented camps which then surrounded Basingstoke. For the first time they lived under canvas which other troops had used until recently. At first the people of Basingstoke were 'stand-offish' but they thawed under the cheerful friendliness of the Irishmen who were more polite than the previous units.[29] Possibly 10th Hampshires, now on *their* home ground, had something to do with this in telling of the hospitality *they* had received in Ireland. The division was to spend two months there in glorious weather.

Unlike the 16th and 36th who followed them, Aldershot Command found no weakness in their training except in the comparatively new art of bombing. Twenty-four men were selected from each company and despatched to the grenade training area of Lord Curzon's Hackwood Park, 'requisitioned for the duration' to learn the techniques of bombing. The British grenade was poor compared with the German stick type. Most were 'jampots' with a fuse, or the 'Orange' iron variety which were little better. They would however have been familiar to a grenadier of the Royal Irish from Marlborough's time.

The battalion machine-gunners went to Bordon training areas for practise; selected good shots went there for sniper training. Each brigade marched to Aldershot in turn and spent several days on the Ash Ranges. Extended exercises took place, usually of three or four days' duration, bringing to life the training of barracks and camp. Mahon exercised his complete division in the field. The entire division would leave camp, march on day one and bivouac at night. On day two were exercises, with the enemy represented by the cyclists and pioneers. Occasionally, night attacks were made on the camp areas. For the first time, brigade and divisional logistics staff officers and Army Service Corps units were exercised in their operational role, organising and supplying the division in the field. The infantry learned to take care of themselves individually, away from barracks.[30] Indeed the

Munsters were alleged to have poachers in their ranks who kept them supplied with pheasant.[31] Such a concentration of Irish fighting men, never before seen in England, was so improbable that it raised a chuckle: 'I thought of what Oliver Cromwell would say if he could come back to earth to hear the tune ['The Wearing of the Green'] played by Irish pipers in the Basingstoke district.'[32]

In these long marches that boiling summer, strict march and water discipline was taught to men unaccustomed to unslaked thirst. The friendly Hampshire people were mystified and sometimes hurt when offers of lemonade to the obviously thirsty troops were refused.[33] But their thirst here was nothing compared with what was to come.

Four weeks after the division arrived in England, on 28 May, they were inspected by HM King George V, accompanied by Queen Mary. After the arrival and a royal salute the King's inspection was followed by a march-past in column of platoons. This was followed by the mounted massed South Irish Horse, artillery, engineers, field ambulances and the supply column. One brigade was away on the Ash Ranges, but the King, wanting to see them, had the party driven towards Aldershot and was able to take the salute of 31 Brigade on the line of march as they returned.

Four days later, Lord Kitchener arrived for his inspection. Kitchener's inspection of the division on 1 June was like a reunion of old comrades, with Hunter, Mahon, Hill and many others besides to remind him of the Sudan campaigns which had begun his march to fame. The parade formed up in Hackwood Park, drawn up in a gigantic hollow square, reminiscent no doubt of the squares in the desert. At noon, FM Lord Kitchener arrived, trotting with his entourage onto the parade ground; it seemed to watchers he looked pleased. No doubt he was, as he was viewing closely one of the first divisions of the New Armies he had called into being such a short time ago. Despite all difficulties, and the sneers of some, it was now ready for war. It must have been a relief as well as a pleasure. The risks he had taken in pressing for New Armies had been fully justified.

> The Royal Irish Regiment, senior of the Irish line, marched to stirring 'Garryowen'. The Hampshires followed, marching to the tune which carried the old 37th from Minden to Pretoria; then came the Connaught Rangers to their rousing 'Saint Patrick's Day'. The Leinsters marched to 'Come Back to Erin', then the Fusiliers, all of them to the fusilier march, 'The British Grenadier', which the Inniskillings, Irish Fusiliers, Munsters and Dublins, all marched past to.[34]

The band was probably an Aldershot duty band with limited sheet music available. They had assumed the Inniskilling, Irish, Munster and Dublin Fusiliers' marches were the same as other fusilier regiments; they didn't have 'The Sprig of Shillelagh', 'Killaloe' and 'The Wearing of the Green', the alternative march music of Irish fusilier regiments. To break the repetition of 'The British Grenadiers' the Dublins suggested to the Rangers that they might use 'St Patrick's Day'. Such is regimental pride that the reaction was an instant and furious refusal.[35] The parade of the complete division, horse, foot, guns, engineers and service troops, was an overwhelming success and 'a magnificent spectacle'.[36]

Divisional order no. 34, 1 June 1915, stated:

> Lt. General Sir B. Mahon received His Majesty's command to publish a divisional order to say how pleased His Majesty was to have an opportunity of seeing the 10th Irish Division, and how impressed he was with the appearance and physical fitness of the troops.
>
> His Majesty the King recognises that it is due to the keenness and co-operation of all ranks that the 10th Division has reached such a high standard of efficiency.
>
> The General Officer Commanding 10th Irish Division has much pleasure in informing the troops that Secretary of State for War, expressed himself as highly satisfied with all he saw of the 10th Division at the inspection today.[37]

To Gen. Mahon, the efficiency of his division transcended national pride. 10th Hampshires were fully up to establishment and from the beginning their bearing had been remarked upon by the brigade commander. The 5th Royal Irish was a battalion commanded by a peer of the realm, a recent junior minister and a member of the royal household (and a friend of Gen. Mahon), a descendant of the founder of the regiment. Nevertheless, at Mahon's order, 5th Royal Irish became the divisional pioneers and 10th Hampshires went to 29 Brigade as a line battalion. The brigade's range-training continued uninterrupted, despite a royal visit and inspection, and showed a determination to place divisional operational training and efficiency above all else, something not all divisional commanders would have insisted on. But George V, a no-nonsense, forthright monarch, would have approved.

The division was fully-trained and equipped. Gaps in its ranks after weeding out the unfit had been filled by large drafts from its sister division, the 16th. It waited impatiently for orders. At last on 27 June, the warning order arrived, confirmed on 1 July. It was to be the Dardanelles.

Re-equipping began for the Middle East. Sun helmets and khaki drill clothing were issued, fitted and altered. Pagris (cotton bands around the helmet) to the Wolsley helmets with regimental insignia occupied much attention. Proper 1908 pattern web equipment was issued to replace the earlier American-made leather equipment. All documentation and medical inspections were brought up to date. Officers' chargers were returned to the remount depot. The Heavy Battery and the squadron of South Irish Horse were transferred to other divisions. 10th Division Ammunition Column went to 36th Ulster Division. Divisional and regimental transport were ordered to remain at Basingstoke. All this caused consternation, but none more so than to those officers who had recently purchased tight-fitting riding boots, ill-suited for marching.[38] The usual outsize tropical clothing was issued to the men and had to be tailored in a rush. Consternation spread also in the machine-gun sections when they realised they would now have to physically carry those heavy weapons themselves. Certain officers worked late into the night on regimental and public fund accounts until they balanced and were audited. The 10th (Irish) Division was finally ready for embarkation.

During the first week of July 1915, final orders came for the division to move to ports of embarkation. Most of the division sailed from Liverpool aboard Cunarders, each taking almost a complete brigade, except for 5th Inniskillings which embarked on HMT *Novian*, 'a wretched iron-decked cattle-boat'[39] and 5th Connaught Rangers on HMT *Bornu*, a small and elderly West African liner. The Rangers boarded her at Devonport on 9 July and she sailed shortly after midday. As the *Bornu* steamed away, the naval training ships saluted and spectators along the shore cheered the departing battalion. The Ranger Drums struck up 'Brian Boru', which Irish regiments traditionally played in great or desperate moments. It was a regimental custom for a Rangers' band, or the Drums, to pause half-way through the score of this march for several beats while the men gave a 'Connaught yell'.[40] This was done now, and a high-pitched soaring yell from a thousand throats echoed across the water in reply to the cheers. When the Irish Fusiliers and Connaught Rangers, the 87th, 88th and 89th of the Line, were raised during the Napoleonic Wars, attempts had been made to get them to cheer in the British fashion; they failed. Of the high-pitched cry the Rangers now gave Napier, in his *History of the Peninsular War*, wrote, 'Nothing so startled the French soldiery as the wild yell with which the Irish regiments sprang to the charge'. In America during the Civil War, it became the 'Rebel Yell', and among Australians at Anzac it was 'C-o-o-e-e'.

THE GREEK ISLANDS

The division called at Alexandria where some battalion equipment and stores were landed. The artillery and ammunition columns disembarked and became separated from 10th Division. Without artillery support, the division sailed for the Greek islands. Part of 29th Division was resting, and the remnant of its attenuated battalions related something of their experiences for the benefit of the newcomers.

There was considerable confusion at disembarkation, due mainly to shortage of transport lighters. Ashore there were no roads save dusty tracks. Battalions were allotted bivouac areas, which quickly became dust-covered. Such heat, never before experienced by troops from a temperate zone, soon had its exhausting effect. Fly hordes were indescribable and multiplied; there was a shortage of disinfectants. All the food was instantly covered with insects. Sleep in daylight became impossible. Added to this was a shortage of water, a particular hardship in the July heat of the eastern Mediterranean to unacclimatised men. All water came from Egypt in water lighters. It was lukewarm and heavily chlorinated. Needless to add it was in limited supply—one gallon per man per day was the allowance. But because there were few containers, wastage was high.

Fly-infested food, lack of water, infected fruit purchased from local sources, all combined to bring enteritis; at this stage it was not severe but very widespread. Men were reluctant to report sick for fear of being thought malingerers.

There were, however, compensations. Bathing was magnificent, but on the advice of the medical authorities, swimming was allowed only in the early morning and late evening. For those who could appreciate it, there was the superb scenery of beautiful islands.

To ease the water shortage, it was decided to keep half 30 Brigade and the complete 31 Brigade on board troopships and send them to Mytilene. These were fortunate, enjoying better food, water and the absence of dust. Boredom became the chief enemy, with speculation and rumour the chief occupation. Finally signs came of impending action. Orders were received on 4 August for each battalion to despatch three officers, including second-in-commands and 180 other ranks to the Divisional Base Depot. All knew what this meant and those selected were highly disgusted at being left out of battle.

That evening, further orders warned all to prepare to embark at 0900 hours the following morning. Company commanders were told their destinations. 29 Brigade was going to Anzac to support the attack there. 30 and 31 Brigades were for Suvla to support 11th Division in its assault landing. Before dawn on 5 August, the divisional chaplains held services; Holy Communion for Protestants and Mass and general absolution for Catholics. It had been decided that chaplains would remain at the field ambulances. This brought general regret to both chaplains and men.[41]

Troops were heavily loaded in field service marching order with greatcoat and two blankets; 200 rounds of ammunition, entrenching tool or dixie, but only one water bottle with three days' rations. Dress was slacks, puttees, khaki drill shirts and helmet with regimental sign or fusilier hackle on one side.[42]

A sound, efficient base is essential to a successful military campaign. One experienced officer was so struck by the disorganisation he saw on Mudros that he felt grave doubts about the campaign before the Suvla landings. Writing from Mudros, Lord Granard, commanding 5th Royal Irish, wrote home on 28 July: 'The way this campaign is being run is an absolute disgrace. I wish somebody was sent out to pull things together. Otherwise it might run on for any length of time.'[43] It was an early criticism fully justified by time and history.

By 0530 on 6 August, 10th Division embarked on ferries and sailed shortly afterwards. They were so tightly packed none could move around. They lay beside their kit and tried to sleep. Hot water was freely available, so most troops made tea and ate bully beef and biscuits. They neared the peninsula at dusk and for the first time had proof of impending action. Flashes of guns became visible and a broad searchlight beam stabbed the sky from the summit of Achi Baba.

On board the ferries carrying 29 Brigade to Anzac, men dozed throughout the night and were woken when the engines stopped and anchors dropped. A Leinster was hit in the chest and a Ranger in the hand by chance shots, the first casualties.[44] Disembarkation under fire had not been rehearsed and in the dark, all sub-units were mixed up. Yet there was no confusion among the heavily-laden soldiers. Disembarkation into lighters for landing was slow despite whispered urging to hurry; but it went smoothly. By the time the last ship began to unload, dawn was breaking and the sailors became anxious, not only because it was desirable to deny the enemy knowledge of reinforcements but also to avoid landing in daylight under fire. In the event, almost all got ashore safely.[45]

10th Division had arrived. But it was not to fight as a complete formation at Gallipoli.

CHAPTER TEN

Gallipoli: the Landing at Helles

In a catalogue of historical might-have-beens, the failure of the Allied campaign to force the Dardanelles passage in 1915 is outstanding. Success could have ended the Great War in 1916 by negotiated settlement without the intervention of the United States; it could also have avoided the Communist interregnum in Russia. The consequences of its failure are a matter of dismal record in world history. Each would be reason enough for fascination, but its close geographical association with the classical Greek triumph, tragedy and heroic failure enhances historical context on another dimension.

Conceived early in January 1915 by the First Lord of the Admiralty, Winston Churchill, and supported by all the Sea Lords and CinC Mediterranean Fleet, Churchillian eloquence persuaded the cabinet to accept the proposed naval operation to force the Dardanelles, bombard Constantinople and evict Turkey from the war, opening a short sea-route to Russia. Kitchener had no answer to Churchill's assertions on the power and effectiveness of battleship guns against land forts and batteries, but he resisted all attempts to involve the army at this stage. His New Armies were undergoing training and were under-equipped. The spring offensive was about to open on the Western Front and only one regular division, the 29th, remained uncommitted. Determinedly Kitchener retained this within his hand until the situation on the Western Front stabilised.

Spurred on by Churchill, the naval operation began prematurely. On 19 February 1915, Anglo-French naval forces attacked and silenced the outer forts of the Dardanelles. Marines landed unopposed on the Gallipoli peninsula and withdrew after a few hours. Complete strategic and tactical surprise was achieved. But this was wasted as the attack, which was not followed up, only served to alert the Turks and send political shock-waves reverberating across Europe, particularly throughout the Balkans and Russia. Scheduled to commence in mid-March, the planned attack was estimated to require fourteen days of continuous bombardment to reduce the forts and enter the Sea of Marmara. With the repulse of the German second offensive at Ypres, Kitchener, recognising army support was essential to the success of the operation, appointed Gen. Sir Ian Hamilton Commander of the Mediterranean Expeditionary Force. This consisted of 29th Division, the RN Division and an Australian and New Zealand Army

Corps (ANZAC) in Egypt. With one attached French division, these were considered sufficient for the limited subsidiary nature of army involvement.

After granting the Turks a month's reprieve, the naval offensive restarted, and ended on 18 March when, having all but silenced the forts commanding the Narrows at a cost of three old battleships sunk by floating mines, the naval commander withdrew and asked Gen. Hamilton to assume primary responsibility for clearing the straits. Hamilton accepted. His hastily assembled staff began planning an early amphibious assault on a defended beach in an area of great natural strength, with inadequate intelligence of the enemy's forces and dispositions. Hamilton divided his staff into two elements, Operations and Logistics, each working independently and with little consultation or liaison between elements. It was his second error; his first was to accept complete operational responsibility without consulting London.

Following the March bombardment, the Turks were not idle. FM Liman von Sanders was appointed CinC Dardanelles; defences were heavily reinforced and skilfully strengthened with energetic German help.

The Gallipoli Peninsula was not so much a natural fortress as a series of fortresses in a gigantic defensive work fashioned by nature during millions of years of heat, cold, flood and fire. Its gullies, ravines and gorges which criss-crossed the foothills were the moats, ditches and fosses. Thick masses of impenetrable thorn scrub formed the *chevaux-de-frise.* Its stony precipitous foothills were the outworks, ravelins, horn works to the main ramparts and double ramparts of the 800-foot-high Sari Bair. Chunuk Bair, Hill Q and Hill 60 were its advance works. It was a fortress which would have delighted the heart of that master of siege warfare, Marshal Vauban: 'A better example of a coast for defence than I have ever seen explained in the military academy by teachers of tactics.'[1] Correlatively, no worse place could have been chosen for an assault landing.

On 25 April Hamilton feinted at Bulair with units of the RN Division. At the same time the French division landed at Kum Kali on the Asiatic shore in a diversionary attack which took 600 prisoners before re-embarking shortly afterwards. The main landings at Ari Burnu and Cape Helles were conceptually different from each other. Gen. Birdwood, commanding ANZAC at Ari Burnu, insisted his best chance of success was to land silently in darkness without preliminary bombardment. Depending upon surprise to gain the beaches, he would then go all out for the commanding heights of the Sari Bair range. It almost succeeded; only the presence of the redoubtable Mustafa Kemal who rushed his division forward in defiance of von Sanders' standing orders halted, then repulsed, the scattered and exhausted Australians and New Zealanders. There followed several critical weeks of furious fighting before a precarious beachhead was secured at what came to be called Anzac.

Farther south at Cape Helles, 29th Division with elements of the RN

Division landed at a number of widely scattered beaches in daylight after naval bombardment. In places they landed unopposed; at others they suffered terrible losses without gain until nightfall. Hamilton intended to confuse the Turkish command by multiple simultaneous landings. He achieved this at the cost of losing control of the landings. On board a warship without ship-shore communications, the CinC was cut off from the troops, unable to control or influence the battle. The divisional commander positioned to observe one landing was unaware of the success and failure elsewhere until it was too late; opportunities were lost, never to recur.

The story of the landing at Sedd-el-Bahr has been told often and very well, not least by John Masefield. It is a harrowing story, painful to write or read about. The rapid-fire of British and Irish regulars in the opening battles of World War One, and the resulting slaughter of German conscripts, can be told and read dispassionately. When such fire strikes our own grandfathers and great-grandfathers, by men bravely defending their homeland, that too has to be seen objectively, and learned from.

In keeping with the classical arena in which the campaign was fought, a Trojan horse was to be used. The collier *River Clyde* had been prepared as an assault ship. Sally ports were cut into her sides, gangways were in position and lighters were tied to her sides. Armoured cars from the Naval Division were sandbagged on deck and in the bows. Their machine-guns would give close fire-support. Into the holds were packed four companies of 1st Munsters, two companies 1st Hampshires, one company 1st Dublins, a West Riding field company, a signal section, elements of a field ambulance and a Naval Division platoon to work the armoured-car guns. With the ship beached, lighters would form a bridge to the shore across which the troops would dash, arriving dry-shod to fight the Turks. In addition to the assault ship, four picket boats would tow twelve cutters packed with troops of 1st Dublins to the beach. In all there were about 3000 troops. Such was the plan.

The evening before the landing, Brig. S.W. Hare commanding 86 Brigade made an appeal to the regimental pride of his men:

> Fusiliers, our Brigade is to have the honour to be the first to land and to cover the disembarkation of the remainder of the Division. Our task will be no easy one. Let us carry it through in a way worthy of the traditions of the distinguished regiments of which the Fusilier Brigade is composed, in such a way that the men of Albuhera, Minden, Delhi and Lucknow may hail us their equal in valour and military achievements, and that future historians may say of us as Napier said of the Fusilier Brigade at Albuhera—'Nothing could stop this astonishing infantry.'[2]

Soldiers have an unerring instinct rarely expressed outside their immediate group. But a first principle known to all is that when their general appeals to regimental traditions, a hard fight lies ahead.

> That night there were not many who slept. Cocoa was issued to the men just before dawn.[3]

At 0500 the naval bombardment started. The battleships *Albion* and *Queen Elizabeth* directed their fire upon the Turkish positions around Sedd-el-Bahr. The much-vaunted guns of the latter which had silenced Kitchener's arguments against Churchill in the cabinet debate were again put to the test. When they ceased firing, no movement was seen around the Turkish positions.

Seen from the sea, the beach at Sedd-el-Bahr is a small amphitheatre-like bay about three hundred yards across, with a shelving beach. On the right is the village and an old castle; on the left are cliffs, about fifty feet high and steep; behind them in dead ground a fort. Liman von Sanders had used his time well, and the Turks, who were natural soldiers, had been skilful military engineers for centuries. This, one of the most obvious landing places, had been well fortified. Lines of well-dug and concealed trenches ran just under the crest, with three well-staked transverse wire entanglements in front, 'the wire so thick that the ordinary wire-cutters could make no impression'.[4]

The collier grounded at 0625 and in a blizzard of fire the naval party struggled gallantly to tow and anchor the lighters into position to form the landing bridge. Some of the Munsters helped and L/Cpl. Quinault and Ptes. Slattery and Flannery distinguished themselves. Eventually Lt.-Col. H.E. Tizard, commanding the Munsters, was told the gangways were ready, and the leading company of the Munsters made ready, X Company on the port and Z on the starboard. Z Company ran into a wall of fire and many dropped at once; others struggled on and some, in defiance of all odds, gained the shore. At that moment the lighter nearest the beach broke away. Without hesitation Capt. Geddes, the company commander, jumped over the side and, finding the water too deep to stand, swam for the shore. The more heavily-laden troops behind followed his example; they also jumped and sank like stones. The men in the following platoons issued from the sally-ports and ran the gauntlet until the lighters were a shambles of heaped dead and wounded. A naval party again went out to fix the barges to the beach. Many died in doing so.

The few Munsters ashore took cover behind a shingle bank eight feet high, ten yards from the water-line. Twenty-five yards in front was the barbed wire. The beach was swept by cross-fire from the forts on the left and the right and from the trenches in front. Capt. Geddes led his four remaining men to the right under a wall of the old castle. Within minutes two were killed and one wounded. Geddes was wounded high in the shoulder. Only one man of X Company reached the objective unscathed. About fifteen minutes later Geddes was joined by his second-in-command, Capt. T.S.

Tomlinson, and by Sgt. Ryan with three men of Z Company.

OC X Company, Capt. Henderson, had been badly wounded getting ashore and was succeeded by Capt. R. Lane. In landing, Lane judged the barge platform a death trap, so he led his platoon over the side. The water came up to their shoulders and all reached shore safely. Ashore, the beach was heaped with dead and wounded. They crouched behind the shingle bank; anyone who raised a head was shot. Another platoon followed Lane's lead and reached the bank. Lane attempted to lead his men up a small nullah towards the barbed wire, but fell wounded. One of his men dragged him to safety: 'I had only been on the beach five minutes and never saw a Turk'.[5] All further movement was stopped.

Those within the *River Clyde* were not safe either. In directing the landing on board the vessel, the second-in-command, Maj. R.H. Monk-Mason, and the adjutant, Capt. H.S. Wilson, were wounded. In No. 1 Hold, Lt. G. Pollard was killed. Lt.-Col. Carington-Smith of the Hampshires was killed on the ship's bridge.

The 1st Dublins had transhipped three companies into cutters, arranged in 'tows' of four boats towed by naval pinnaces. Each tow carried about two platoons, packed tightly. When tow-lines were cast off on the cutters, the sailors rowed for the shore, each side of the *River Clyde* as she grounded. They too were caught in the storm of fire and within minutes almost all had been killed or wounded, including the commanding officer, second-in-command and most company officers. The rowers being dead, the boats drifted helplessly under the unrelenting Turkish fire. So great was the• slaughter that the sea along the shore was dyed pink; around the boats it was deep red. Many Dublins jumped from the boats, sank and drowned; others in shallow water were shot before they could penetrate the barbed wire stretched in the water. From this horrific carnage, fourteen heroes survived, reached the shore and joined the few Munsters under the beach-ridge. One, Lt. C.W. Maffett, later wrote:

> When the picquet boat cast us off we all rowed for the shore as hard as we could. The Turks let us get very close, and then they opened a terrible fire on us with machine guns and pom-poms, the shells of which contained an incendiary mixture. They began to hit the boat I was in very frequently, and killed many of my men as we were rowing ashore. We were also unlucky enough to lose several of the blue-jackets who were rowing us in, and the men had to take over their oars, and as they did not know much about rowing the result was that we often got broadside on to the shore and presented a better target for the enemy.[6]

Saved from drowning by his platoon sergeant, Sgt. Willis, Maffett got under cover and looked behind to see the remnants of his platoon trying to reach the shore

> ...but they were shot down one after another, and their bodies drifted out to sea or lay immersed a few feet from the shore.[7]

The Catholic chaplain of 86 Brigade, Father William Finn, insisted upon landing with the battalion despite appeals to remain in safety on the *River Clyde*. 'The priest's place is beside the dying soldier,' he replied, and embarked on one of the first boats; he was shot dead on landing.[8]

> The men never forgot him and were never tired speaking of him. I think they felt his death almost more than anything that happened in that terrible landing.[9]

Within minutes two and a half companies of 1st Dublins were annihilated without striking a blow in return.

One tow had taken two platoons of Dublins to Camber Beach, just north-east of Sedd-el-Bahr castle, from where they could threaten the Turkish left flank. An experienced war correspondent, Henry Nevinson, who covered the Gallipoli campaign, wrote:

> The Irishmen with great skill crawled from cover to cover till they reached the village windmills and the entrance to the houses. There they were overwhelmed by the crowd of snipers. Many were killed, some cut off, and twenty-five returned.[10]

With the repulse of the landing Turkish fire died down at about 0800. In the stillness which followed, 'the dead lay upon the lighters, and below the water, and awash upon the edge of the beach. The ripple of the tormented sea broke red against the sand.'[11]

When lighters were again anchored to the shore and Turkish fire had died down, the commanding officers of the Munsters ordered Maj. Jarrett to take Y Company ashore. The command was obeyed instantly. Again the Turkish fire-storm broke out and although the company reached the beach, it was only with very severe casualties. Once ashore, Jarrett, seeing the desperate situation and having no other way of communicating with the ship, sent Lt. Nightingale back through the shambles, asking Lt.-Col. Tizard to send no more ashore. This was done. An hour later, Brig. Napier (88 Brigade) accompanied by his brigade major, attempted to land; they too were shot dead. The Munster CO assumed command and Maj. Hutchinson took command of the battalion. It was decided nothing further could be done until darkness.

Commander Josiah Wedgwood MP, a friend of Mr John Redmond, was in command of the armoured cars[12] and proved himself a valued friend of Ireland that day. The machine-guns of his armoured cars playing on the Turkish trenches saved the Irish ashore from complete annihilation. They and the guns of the fleet now took up the battle where flesh and blood had failed. But some Turkish machine-guns in dead ground on the left continued to sweep the beach, preventing movement to succour the wounded. They endured agonies from wounds and thirst until nightfall.

Night fell about 1900 and in the darkness shortly afterwards, the last Munster company landed carrying with them four machine-guns. They were followed by the companies of Hampshires, Dublins and West Riding Engineers. Shortly after midnight, all the troops from the *River Clyde* were ashore and all the wounded collected and taken back to the ship. During the night, many fierce struggles took place as the Turks at last came out of their trenches.

At dawn on the 26th, small detachments which had gathered on the right under the castle wall prepared to attack the old fortress. Commanded by Lt.-Col. Doughty-Wylie of the staff, the senior officer ashore, they rushed the castle and gained entry. First in was Pte. T. Cullen of the Dublins. Ferocious hand-to-hand fighting took place in semi-darkness, but by 0800 the castle was won. Pte. Cullen was later awarded the DCM. The remnant of Dublins and Munsters, together with 1st Hampshires, fought their way through the castle and into the village. Close-quarter fighting of savage ferocity seldom equalled on the Western Front followed. Since the landing had started, all the officers of the Dublins save three were killed or wounded and twenty-one warrant officers and NCOs were dead. Leading the remnant was Maj. Molesworth. Under him, those who distinguished themselves were Sgts. Ferguson and Doyle, Cpl. Cummins, and Ptes. Oliver and O'Toole. By midday the village was won. Ferguson and Cummins were later awarded the DCM.

W Company of the Munsters remained pinned down under the shingle bank on the beach. The wire was still intact, since all attempts by the infantry to destroy it failed. Why it was not blown apart by naval gunfire is difficult to understand. This can only be explained by the loss of so many officers, poor navy/army co-operation and no direction of naval gunfire support. Maj. Jarrett was killed by a single shot shortly after dawn. Because all Munster officers were dead or wounded, command passed to a staff officer, Capt. Stoney, King's Own Scottish Borderers. At midday, word came that, having fought their way through the village, Doughty-Wylie was going to lead his little force against the hills behind. A naval bombardment was arranged and carried out by HMS *Albion*.

The attack started at 1330 when the bombardment ceased, the combined force consisting of the Munsters, less W Company, two companies Hampshire and one company Dublins. The Turks resisted stubbornly and caused heavy losses to the attackers, but were driven off the position by a furious charge led by Doughty-Wylie. 'All he carried was a small cane. He walked about in the open under a continuous fire talking to the men, cheering them up, and rallying them together.'[13] He too was killed, and was later awarded a posthumous Victoria Cross.

Seeing the right attack go forward, Capt. Stoney led the men out from the bank to its support. But all were halted by the wire which remained untouched by the bombardment and took cover. Cpl. William Cosgrove of the Munsters ran forward. In full view of the enemy, he desperately strove to cut the wire. Failing in this he started to uproot the wooden stakes, with complete disregard for his own safety. He succeeded in making a gap and through this the attack went. Sgt.-Maj. Bennett was killed and Cosgrove took over, leading the Munstermen in their desperate charge. For his gallantry that day Cpl. Cosgrove was awarded the Victoria Cross. Hill 141 was taken by 1400 and the beachhead advanced half a mile in front of the Old Castle. That night the Turks counter-attacked twice but were driven off and the beachhead was at last secured.

> The prolonged, renewed and seemingly inexhaustible efforts of the survivors of these three battalions, their persistency, their will-power, their physical endurance, achieved a feat of arms certainly in these respects not often, if ever, surpassed in the history of either island race.[14]

The remainder of the RN Division and the French Division were withdrawn from Kum Kale, and reinforced Cape Helles. The Munster, Dublin and Hampshire remnant were relieved at dawn and withdrawn to the beach. As battalions they had practically ceased to exist.

Elsewhere the landings had met better success. On the right at S Beach, in Morto Bay, a force had landed and scaled the cliffs at Eski Hissarlik Point and secured their position with few casualties. On the left at W Beach, Lancashire Landing, 1st Lancashire Fusiliers met stiff opposition. Just when it appeared that another slaughter would ensue, by a stroke of luck one company was carried by the current to a concealed landing place from where the well-led company took the defenders in rear. Further north at X Beach, 1st Royal Fusiliers had led 87 Brigade ashore without opposition; they were followed by 1st Inniskillings and the Border Regiment. It was the most successful of the landings. 87 Brigade advanced 500 yards, took the cliff line against stiff opposition, beat off a counter-attack and then bivouacked for the night. To the north-east at Y Beach, a marine battalion and 1st KOSB landed, again without opposition, and sat down. That night they were attacked by Turkish reinforcements and re-embarked the following day having accomplished nothing.

Maj.-Gen. Hunter-Weston, 'Hunter-Bunter' to his officers,[15] remained on board HMS *Euryalus* which carried the Lancashire Fusiliers. He concentrated on W Beach to the neglect of the landings elsewhere. Gen. Hamilton was aware that a dangerous situation was developing; nevertheless he failed to intervene to correct it. Incredibly, while 86 Brigade was being slaughtered at the tip of the peninsula, nothing was done to relieve their agony, although adequate forces existed on the flanks to envelop and destroy the Turkish defenders from the rear. On the following day, 87 Brigade advanced about a mile and made contact with the exhausted 86 Brigade.

By the evening of 26 April, the situation had improved and a firm foothold gained at the tip of the peninsula from X Beach to De Tott's battery. On the 27th, a general advance against slackening opposition secured a beachhead some two miles in depth, giving V and W beaches security against small arms and machine-gun fire. That night, Hamilton issued orders for 29th Division to advance next day on Krithia; the French were to conform to the British movement. The advance began—the French on the right, 88 Brigade in the centre, 87 Brigade on the left and 86 Brigade in reserve. At midday, 86 Brigade was ordered forward to support 88 Brigade which was in difficulties. The real battle had just begun.

Lt. H.D. O'Hara of the Dublins, 'little more than a boy',[16] had much responsibility suddenly thrust upon him:

> Lieutenant O'Hara, who rose to every occasion with the greatest coolness and competence, from commanding a platoon at the terrible landing from the *River Clyde* to the command of a company the next day, and after 28 April to commanding the Battalion.[17]

The Allied advance was not only halted by the Turkish counter-attack but also thrown on the defensive.

On the night of 1 May, the enemy attacked in great strength and was repulsed. Repeatedly the Turks were driven back at bayonet point, only to return to the charge. At dawn the Irish, reinforced by 1st Essex, finally forced the Turks to retire, leaving piles of dead before the trenches.

> It was an awful time, and at the end I was the only officer left in the battalion… The Turks made no attempt to follow up their advantage, and we were able to dig in. We remained there for two nights, and on the third the Turks advanced 20,000 strong, and tried to break through the line. The fight went on from 10.30 at night till 5 o'clock next morning—a desperate fight the whole time. My regiment alone got through 150,000 rounds, and they were only 360 strong…[18]

The Munsters were pressed just as sorely. Platoons were now led by sergeants, and one, Sgt. R. Rice, 'put up a great fight; it was mainly through this platoon that the enemy failed to take the Battalion in rear'. Capt. E.C. Dorman 'was killed exhorting his men to die like Irishmen'.[19] (To an English battalion in extremity, the ultimate appeal is the Regiment—'Die hard 57th, die hard!'[20] In Scottish and Irish ones, final inspiration comes from pride of race.) Lt. T. O'Sullivan died next day of his wounds. It was in this battle that the Turks made use of grenades in large numbers; 'each man carried about six, hooked onto his belt.'[21]

In the left brigade, the Inniskillings, still strong and fresh, repulsed the Turks with concentrated rapid fire.

> There was long grass in front of our lines and a single strand of barbed wire. At about ten o'clock we heard the swish-swish of the Turks' feet as they advanced towards us and the voices of their officers as they gave orders. Somebody sent up a Very light, and there they were , advancing in a solid mass towards us. Somebody shouted 'Give them hell'. A terrific fire burst out from our lines. The effect was deadly. We could hear the shrieks of their wounded and the shouts of their officers as they urged them on; but they never reached our line.[22]

So great had been their casualties that the remnants of Dublins and Munsters were formed into a composite battalion, affectionately named the Dubsters. With its strength of eight officers and 400 men, they returned to the line. A week's intensive fighting followed as the Turkish command rushed reinforcements to the scene and sought to drive the invaders into the sea. The brigade major of 86 Brigade declared: 'The fiercest fighting was against the Irish regiments who were defending the weakest part of the line and bore the greatest weight of the attack.'[23] 'The twenty-one men who garrisoned one particular bit of trench died to a man... One man, I recollect, a signaller, had as many as nineteen wounds. Of course, it was hand-to-hand fighting—no quarter was asked or given.'[24] Capt. Geddes of the Munsters, who had been awarded an immediate DSO, recovered from his wound sufficiently to assume command of the Dubsters.

On 12 May, 29th Division was withdrawn for five days' rest and reorganisation, at the end of which both Dublin and Munster resumed their battalion identities. A few days later, mutual Turkish and British exhaustion brought a lull in the fighting and a four-day truce to recover wounded survivors and bury the dead on each side. The clearing operation, however, failed to remove the all-pervading stench of death from the battlefield, mixed incongruously with the scent of thyme growing there with other flowers in wild profusion.

By mid May, after heavy fighting, the lines at both Helles and Anzac stalemated into attritional trench warfare dominated by barbed wire, bomb and machine-gun. Yards were gained only at high human cost. Finally, Kitchener asked Hamilton what he wanted for success. Getting his reply, Kitchener promised fifty per cent more men than requested.[25] It was with these that Hamilton planned the stroke which he believed would break the stalemate. In the meantime, the fighting went on.

BATTLE OF KRITHIA, 28 JUNE–2 JULY

Krithia, the core of Turkish resistance and valuable for its water, was a bare mile away; taking it would prove tangible evidence of success. An attack to capture it made on 28 May had advanced on the right, but having initially gained ground, the centre was flung back on its start line. Another attack on 4 June failed, principally because of the strength of the Turkish position on Gully Spur. To improve co-ordination of effort, a reorganisation on 5 June concentrated the Royal Naval Division, 29th and 42nd Divisions into VIII Corps, under Maj.-Gen. Hunter-Weston. Maj.-Gen. H. de B. de Lisle became GOC 29th Division. A further attack in the centre and right proved successful on 21 June. The next phase was to be on the right at Gully Spur, a narrow strip between Gully Ravine and the sea, and the wide deep cleft of the ravine itself. The objective was five lines of Turkish trenches, with redoubts capable of all-round defence. The attack was to be covered by the largest concentration of British and French artillery yet assembled at the Dardanelles. As this would not be ready until 27 June, the attack was timed for 28 June. Further reinforcements arrived, 52nd Lowland Division and an Indian Brigade, but they barely made up for battle casualties.

28 June dawned 'fiercely hot, with scarcely a breath of wind'.[26] Under cover of the heaviest bombardment yet experienced on the peninsula, the attack started at 1100. The 156 Lowland Brigade attacked on the right of Gully Ravine, supported by 88 Brigade. The 86 Brigade attacked up Gully Ravine; 1st Lancashire Fusiliers supported by 1st Dublins, 1st Royal Fusiliers supported by 1st Munsters. The left attack was carried out by 87 Brigade; 2nd South Wales Borderers and 1st Borderers, with 1st Inniskillings and 1st King's Own Scottish Borderers in support. On the extreme left, Gurkhas of the Indian Brigade were to advance along the sea-cliffs.

On the right, east of Gully Ravine, 156 Brigade ran into trouble. Part of the Turkish lines were untouched by the bombardment and machine-guns lashed the advance. Despite great gallantry by the Scots, the left attack failed, with heavy losses including their brigadier and his brigade major. 88 Brigade, with the remnant of the Scots, attacked in the afternoon but fared no better.

The attack in the centre and left began well. Under cover of a bombardment by French mortars, 1st Border Regiment stormed a Turkish redoubt just before Zero Hour, upon which the guns ranged on the Turkish rear areas and the troops on both sides of Gully Ravine lunged forward. 87 Brigade captured all objectives according to plan. With fanatical determination, the Turks reacted strongly to regain their lost trenches on Gully Spur. Unrelenting bombing attacks covered by heavy machine-gun and rifle fire began, and 86 and 87 Brigades were driven back. At dusk, Gurkhas and Munsters were ordered to retake the lost sections of trenches and succeeded after hard fighting. In the darkness, the Turks renewed the attack with showers of bombs and 'after heavy fighting, the ends nearest the Nullah remained in Turkish hands.'[27]

As the Gurkhas and Munsters were attacking, the Dublins were ordered to attack up Gully Ravine and the Nullah to the junction with the Gurkha trenches. Against heavy opposition, the Dublins were driven back. They dug a trench line along the western bank to connect with the Gurkhas against fierce opposition. The Turks launched frequent counter-attacks. Although the Dublins were unable to connect with the Gurkha trench, they dug and held a line near it in a night of intense fighting. 'This line they held despite the loss of nearly all their officers.'[28] 2/Lt. A.G. Cripps was one of six officers of 9th Somerset Light Infantry attached to the Dublins. He brought with him his own hunting rifle and was instantly dubbed 'the mad mullah' by the Dubliners when he volunteered for sniping duty.[29] After a few days of this, he was given command of the machine-gun section for the Gully Spur attack.

In response to orders, the Dublins counter-attacked into the Nullah and were met by a blast of fire. The company commander, Capt. L.E. George, 9th SLI attached to the Dublins, fell almost at once. The leading platoon was totally destroyed while the rest of the company fell back: 'The leading platoon charged around the corner of the Nullah and were never seen again, except one who crawled back in darkness, dragging his guts in the sand and dying almost immediately.'[30] In darkness, it was now the Turks' turn to attack with their very efficient bombs. Calling 'Allah, Allah', they lay down in the scrub throwing bombs into the Dublins trench.

Runners were sent to collect bombs whilst we were gradually forced back. At last some bombs turned up and we started the most effective counter-bomb attack I have ever witnessed... The Tommies started cheering and the Turks at once climbed out of the trench. This was a golden opportunity for my machine-guns; out of a 500 strong enemy battalion few other than prisoners of war returned. One wounded Turkish conscript spoke excellent French. He had no real desire to fight and was sent back under guard for interrogation. Captain George, who had been thought killed in the attack, was seen to move and Lance Corporal O'Reilly with two men were sent out to bring him in; the two men were hit. Corporal O'Reilly calmly stood there firing at Turks we could not see, then he dropped his rifle picked up Captain George placed him on his shoulder and brought him back. It was then that I saw that the corporal had a very ugly wound in the shoulder. Captain George died immediately on being put down. His [O'Reilly's] name was sent back for very gallant conduct but nothing came of it, in fact the RDF were apparently not in favour with the general of the Division. Since the landing only one medal had been allotted them. How the RDF kept the vital position that night I do not know. Officers kept being hit and the men were getting thinner and thinner. Words will never describe the horror of that night. In front of us the bodies of Turks and RDF were literally piled into heaps. At dawn the line was found to be held by scattered groups of Dublins, a large body of Turks were holding an exposed flat area, when they realised their position some ran, some attacked, and some tried to surrender. As they retired across perfectly flat ground they were mown down.[31]

Of the Dublins, eleven officers and 97 men were dead and 199 all ranks were wounded. Lt. A.G. Cripps was wounded two days later, the forty-ninth officer killed or wounded since landing. His name was 'sent in', but nothing came of it. L/Cpl. James O'Reilly, a Dubliner, died of his wounds two days later; he received no award for his valour.[32]

Fighting continued intermittently in the captured trenches which changed hands several times on the 30th. On the following night, the attacks intensified against trenches held by 6th Gurkhas. Next day, attacks were made against trenches held by 10th Gurkhas and the Inniskillings set to work on a new trench to support them, called 'Inniskilling Inch'. That night, 1–2 July, the Gurkha trenches and 'Inniskilling Inch' were heavily attacked.

> Again, owing to lack of bombs, the troops were forced to give ground. But 1½ companies of the Inniskillings, under Captain G.R. O'Sullivan, restored the situation, and recaptured the whole of J12 as far as the Nullah. Owing to an unfortunate misunderstanding, the garrison of J12 (10th Gurkhas) fell back to the old barricade in that trench at daybreak without further pressure from the enemy, and shortly afterwards the empty portion of the trench was reoccupied by the Turks. For their gallantry on this occasion, Captain O'Sullivan and Corporal James Somers were awarded the VC, and Somers was specially promoted to sergeant in the field.[33]

Cpl. Somers refused to fall back when his section was bombed out but fought on with his rifle. Bombs were brought up and he then climbed over into the Turkish trenches and bombed them clear. Later, while a stop barricade was being built, he fearlessly held off the Turks until the work was done. Somers continued to serve with the Inniskillings until he was downgraded medically and transferred to the Army Service Corps in 1917. He was gassed and invalided home where he died in Cloghjordan, Co. Tipperary.

Soldiers accept that the award of medals for bravery is a lottery in which many deserving cases are overlooked. Yet, considering the ferocious fighting, the appalling sacrifices and outstanding bravery of the regimental officers and men, there is a distinct paucity of honours and awards at Gallipoli. Taking just one example, 1st Dublins were awarded one DSO (Maj. H.D. O'Hara), one Military Cross (Capt. H.C. Crozier), ten Distinguished Conduct Medals and two Military Medals (the Military Cross and Military Medal were instituted in December 1914 to 'save' the DSO and DCM), for the loss of over 2000 casualties of whom 569 men were killed or died of wounds in eight months. This gives some substance of fact to the assertion by Lt. Cripps, SLI attached RDF, that 1st RDF were 'not in favour'. It is fair to add that with so many officer casualties, few citations for awards could be written. But if Cripps is correct (the case of L/Cpl. O'Reilly has to be remembered), it is a further dreadful indictment of gross mismanagement at Gallipoli. Lt. Cripps received a Military Cross for later service on the Western Front with his own regiment and ended the war a major.

CHAPTER ELEVEN

Gallipoli: Anzac, 6–12 August 1915

By 6 August, all was ready for Hamilton's decisive offensive, a co-ordinated surprise landing at Suvla and attack on Sari Bair. His plan was brilliant in some respects. But it relied too heavily on inexperienced troops attacking easily defended dominating heights to a tight timetable, making small allowances for difficulties and inadequacies—harsh terrain, heat fatigue, inadequate transport and water supply, and at Suvla, poor artillery support. The CinC planned two subsidiary land attacks, one at Helles and one on the right at Anzac to fix the Turkish reserves. Then, with this accomplished, the main thrust would be delivered on the left at Anzac, timed to coincide with a landing at Suvla.

Gen. Birdwood, the ANZAC commander, had carefully briefed his divisional commanders. His intention was to mount a diversionary attack in the afternoon in the southern sector at Lone Pine and that night to march the main attack force up the ravines towards Sari Bair, the crest of which he hoped would be taken at dawn. The attack of the Australians at Lone Pine succeeded in what must have been the most savage and bloodiest hand-to-hand fighting of the campaign, if not the war. By 1800 the Turkish front-line trenches had been taken.

The attack on Sari Bair was less straightforward. Because of the nature of the ground, it entailed a long approach march through broken, difficult country dominated everywhere by Turkish-held heights.

Scores of Deres, or gullies, four to six feet high, let into the Sari Bair Range. In spring, flash flooding during torrential rains made these raging torrents. In August they were dry. The country between the gullies was covered by almost impassable thorn scrub and criss-crossed by ravines. The gully sides were steep and lined by olive trees and scrub. Long stretches were under fire from Turkish guns on Sari Bair. Generally, the gullies could only be used in safety at night. The principal gullies were Asmak Dere, Aghyl Dere, Chailak Dere and Sazli Dere. Towering between these last two gullies was a spur from Sari Bair's main ridge at Chunuk Bair down to the sea, Rhododendron Spur. The ground was so difficult that the Turkish commanders had discounted the ability of the British to attack at night.

Gen. Godley, GOC 1st Australian and New Zealand Division and the attack force commander, had 20,000 men under his command, with attached troops. These he divided into four columns: covering force right and left, and assault group right and left. The right covering force was four New Zealand regiments under the command of Brig. A. Russell. The right assault group consisted of the New Zealand Brigade, an Indian mountain battery, and a field company of New Zealand engineers under Maj.-Gen. F.E. Johnston. It was to advance up Sazli Dere and Chailak Dere, go through the covering force and attack Chunuk Bair and Hill Q. The left covering force, two battalions of 13th Division under Brig. J.H. Travers, was followed by the left assault group: 29 Indian Brigade, 4 Australian Brigade, an Indian mountain battery and a field company of New Zealand engineers, under command of Maj.-Gen. H.V. Cox. They were to march northwards along the flat ground between the foothills and the sea, then strike inland up the Aghyl Dere, go through the left covering force and attack Koja Chemen Tepe or Hill 971, the highest and culminating-point of the Sari Bair Ridge. Six battalions of 13th Division were in reserve at the mouth of the two main deres.

The right and left covering forces attacked superbly and gained all objectives, but they took too long. The assault groups advanced, but the guides trying to make up lost time took short cuts, lost their way and many battalions found themselves back at the starting point. Others had made their way along Rhododendron Spur and settled down to await the lost battalions. When dawn broke, the assault on the main crest had not begun.

A flank guard precautionary attack by the Australian Light Horse at the foot of Battleship Hill was delivered, knowing it was a desperate venture. The knowledge that the Sari Bair objectives had not been taken failed to deter the commander of what was probably the most aggressive of all that brave Australian force. The 1200 Light Horse troopers charged, and in less than ten minutes half were dead.[1]

At midday on the 7th, the New Zealanders on Rhododendron Spur, reinforced by two companies of Gurkhas, attacked the crest of Chunuk Bair. It was too late. The Turkish defence, commanded in person by Col. Kannengisser, although only of platoon strength were alert and waiting and drove off the exhausted attackers.[2] There was no further fighting on the 7th. This gave Kannengisser time to bring up the main elements of his division to strengthen the defences on this crucial position until the Turkish reserves were committed under the redoubtable Mustafa Kemal.

29 BRIGADE AT ANZAC

On the morning of 6 August, 29 Brigade landed at Anzac and concentrated in Shrapnel Gully, a wide deep, dried river bed with high, steep slopes covered in parts with thorn scrub. Here some cover had been prepared. Battle-noise was incessant. White strips were issued and men began sewing them onto clothing; to the knowledgeable it indicated a night march or operation of some kind. The unwary stood and watched the shell burst overhead as the Turkish guns sought out the reserve holding positions until they realised the danger and sought cover. Thereafter the brigade was left to get whatever rest it could. Orders were given for all to rest, easier given than obeyed. During the wait, one battalion, 6th Irish Rifles, suffered about thirty casualties from shrapnel.[3] At a Brigade 'Orders Group' at 1630, the battalion commanders were told for the first time that the brigade was operating independently under command of the Australian and New Zealand Army Corps. All units were warned to be ready to move by 0100.

In the early hours of 7 August, in pitch darkness, the march began. 6th Leinsters led, followed by 6th Rifles, 5th Rangers and 10th Hampshires. Progress was slow and halts frequent. At last the column cleared the gully and turned north towards Russell's Top. In the blackness of a moonless night, the heavily-laden troops stumbled over the rough ground. Once on the move tension eased, and the 'crack' began, with remarks about 'the blind leading the blind';[4] 'I even heard a laugh or two. It was a terrific relief.'[5]

Offshore, the naval monitors shelled the Turkish position. Far ahead of the Irish, the forward assault columns were working up Chailak and Aghyl Deres to attack Sari Bair. Then, without explanation, came an order for the brigade, with the exception of 6th Leinsters, to return to Shrapnel Gully.

BATTLE OF SARI BAIR, 7–12 AUGUST

Throughout 7 August the three battalions of 29 Brigade waited at instant readiness to move. Brigade staff knew as little as battalion riflemen. No information was received, and every passer-by was eagerly questioned. Only the sound of battle told them of the fighting at Lone Pine and Sari Bair. Wounded streamed past. Little was said by either sweating stretcher-bearers or wounded, save a laconic 'pretty tough up there.'[6] At last orders came, and Brig. Cooper sent 5th Connaught Rangers to Victoria Gully near Anzac Cove. One company was detached to Brown's Dip on burial detail. There they remained for forty-eight hours.

As the Rangers were moving to Victoria Gully, the remaining two battalions of 29 Brigade were summoned from Shrapnel Gully at 1000 on 8 August. Brig. Cooper led his battalions to No. 2 Post where Gen. 'Alex' Godley had established his headquarters. Commissioned into the Dublins, he had commanded Mounted Infantry in the South African War.[7] Here under Godley's hand, they waited until late afternoon, then moved to occupy captured ground.

The two battalions advanced against a flood of wounded coming down the choked Deres. Despite orders to the contrary, men gave water to the wounded in response to their piteous pleas and were themselves to suffer for this later. One platoon of the Rifles was caught in an exposed area and almost totally destroyed by a hail of rifle fire.[8] In the gathering darkness, a halt was made and all rested on the shoulders of the gully. Most slept immediately until roused at 2115 for an assault on Chunuk Bair, under the command of Brig. A.H. Baldwin.

On the evening of 8 August a new attack was commenced. Throughout the night five columns were formed up. Their orders were brief, too brief: '"Make good Hill Q at dawn. Farm B is already in our hands." That was all and now I have been through a few properly organised attacks, I realise how totally inadequate they were.'[9]

The Rifles and Hampshires, tired and confused by the sameness of the landscape, blundered forward in the darkness.

> The most nerve-racking night I have been through. We blundered forward, now halting, now moving at a snail's pace, now struggling forward as fast as we might over uneven ground. As the night wore on the halts became more and more distressing. The men slept in their tracks. There was a continuous stream of wounded back, and ammunition mules back and forth.[10]

The attack came incredibly close to success, even with the confused and exhausted state of the assault columns. That night two companies of Gurkhas succeeded in gaining a position just below the crest of Hill Q and two companies of New Zealanders were just below the crest of Chunuk Bair. Then for a fleeting moment came glorious success. At dawn on the morning of the 9th, Gurkha troops of 29 Indian Brigade, with a few companies of 13th Division, gained the summit of Chunuk Bair. But by a tragic error, they were blasted off by their own heavy artillery, either naval guns or army howitzers. Whose guns they were has never been satisfactorily explained.

On 9 August, the attack restarted. The objectives were reduced to Hill Q and Chunuk Bair. Brig. Baldwin led the main attack force of four newly-arrived British battalions: 6th Irish Rifles, 10th Hampshire, 6th East Lancashire, 5th Wiltshire. To their right was a column of New Zealanders under Johnston. On Baldwin's left was Brig. Cox's force of 4 Australian Brigade, 29 Indian Brigade and another brigade of 13th Division.

In a complicated manoeuvre which took no account of ground, time and state of troops, Baldwin's column moved up Chailak Dere to attack south-west of Hill Q. The New Zealand guides lost their way, and having marched all night, Baldwin's force at dawn on the 9th were only in the Aghyl Dere at the foot of Chunuk.

Unsupported by Baldwin's force, the attacks by the right and left columns failed. Despite previous lessons, Brig. Baldwin formed up his force for a daylight assault. The ground rose in a gentle concave slope covered by young wheat. The last fifty yards to the Turkish trench were steep, almost perpendicular. Without hesitation, the men went forward under heavy shelling and enfilading machine-gun fire which almost wiped out 6th East Lancashire. Many of the Irish Rifles were down and Baldwin's men were held on the lower slopes of Chunuk. The two battalions of 29 Brigade reached a point 300 yards above the Farm in the shelter of a small, jutting feature. Two companies of Hampshires under Maj. Pilleau contacted the New Zealanders on the right. Under shrapnel fire, they forced their way to the New Zealanders' positions and held this throughout the 9th. The remainder of the Hampshires were deployed down the seaward slopes of Chunuk Bair in a line which was continued by the two battalions of 38 Brigade.

Two companies of 6th Irish Rifles assaulted a line of Turkish trenches. The rapid order rang out:

> Assault enemy trench. Numbers one and three platoons leading; two and three in support... There was scarcely a square yard of the hillside which could not be observed and brought under fire. They had an ideal target and continuously raked it with rifle and machine-gun fire and shrapnel.[11]

The two companies which attempted the assault were annihilated; dead and wounded strewed the hillside. One wounded officer attempted to crawl under cover and was shot a second time by a sniper. He lay still and feigned death. Later he was picked up by a young Gurkha and carried for over an hour to a Regimental Aid Post. The Gurkha put him down without a word, and before he could be thanked properly, trotted off. [12]

Maj.-Gen. Cox's Australians had taken Hill Q, but, driven off it, made contact with the left of Baldwin's force.

Throughout 9 August, the British, Dominion and Irish soldiers lay in the blistering sun, scraping out whatever cover from fire they could in the scorching hillside of Chunuk Bair. There was no cover from the sun save the thorn bushes, and by midday the temperature had risen to over 110 degrees. Bully beef and dry biscuit inflamed thirst and the scarcity of water brought agony and dehydration. Overlooked by the Turks on the crest, their positions were under constant shell and machine-gun fire and the casualties steadily mounted throughout the day. Nightfall brought relief from the sun and some relief from the Turkish fire, but none from raging thirst.

Throughout the night of 9–10 August troops of Baldwin's force entrenched where they stood, usually under shell-fire which the Turks maintained throughout the night. The New Zealanders on Rhododendron Spur to their right were relieved by the Loyal North Lancashire, Wiltshire and Leinsters battalions. Above them loomed the mass of Chunuk which they hoped to take at dawn. But events were to decree otherwise.

From dawn on 7 August to the morning of 9 August, 6th Leinsters moved from place to place achieving nothing but losing men from shell-fire. Ordered to relieve the New Zealanders on Rhododendron Spur, Lt.-Col. Craske led his battalion to the foot of the ridge and waited until dark.

Rhododendron Spur (so called because those who had named it mistook the wild oleanders for rhododendrons) was connected to the main Chunuk Bair ridge by a col. In front of this the shallow trenches of the advance line had been dug. Not deep or well-sited, they served only to indicate a line to hold. In most places the lines of opposing trenches were a bare thirty yards apart.

On the right of the Leinsters were 8th Royal Welsh Fusiliers; the left on

Chunuk was held by 6th Loyal North Lancashires. Throughout the night of 9–10 August, enemy artillery maintained a continual fire, launching a counter-attack at dawn. Mustafa Kemal has described how he himself had personally brought up a Turkish division and had led this attack, advanced alone into no man's land and gave the signal to charge with his whip.[13]

At 0430, just as dawn was breaking on Chunuk, the Turks charged against the three British battalions. The Loyal North Lancashires were overwhelmed in the enemy rush; the Wiltshires were caught in the open and annihilated. On their right, not quite in the main flood of the Turkish charge, the Leinsters stood firm. The two line companies held the first Turkish wave at the point of the bayonet in furious hand-to-hand fighting. The hard-pressed Leinsters were then joined without delay by the support companies led personally by Col. Craske. Alerted by a shout of 'fix your bayonets, boys, they're coming'[14] they grabbed their weapons. In whatever dress they slept, the supporters flung themselves with a cheer into the mêlée. They arrived at a critical phase and after a desperate hand-to-hand fight, the Turks were driven back. Craske was wounded in the arm and several other officers were killed or wounded. One, a noted Irish tennis player, Capt. J.C. Parke, who had represented the UK in the Davis Cup before the war, was also wounded in the arm.[15] Many men were dead, but as the Leinsters tended their wounded they could see the area to their left was covered with dead enemy.

The Turks, having overwhelmed the Loyals and Wiltshires, pressed on towards Rhododendron Spur to envelop the flank of the Leinsters. They were caught in the open in full view of the guns of the fleet and a deluge of fire cut them to pieces. Survivors of the shell-fire struggling gallantly onwards were caught in the fire of New Zealand machine-guns and totally destroyed. Rhododendron Spur remained firmly in the hands of the Leinsters.

Throughout the 10th, the Leinstermen dug fresh positions to meet the threat from Chunuk. Under cover of darkness, the Turks crept forward to open fire at close range. After two hours, a platoon was sent to drive the enemy off. They found the enemy in strength and a grim hand-to-hand struggle took place, with no quarter given or asked. The platoon fought its way out, leaving half its strength behind dead or badly wounded; the lightly wounded came back. The Turkish attack developed in strength; A and D Companies came forward in support. In pitch blackness, the Turks repeatedly attacked and were driven back each time. At dawn they made a final effort. On they came with great determination, calling upon the name of God, 'Allah, Allah, Voor, Voor' (Strike, Strike). Realising they stood completely alone, the Irish resolved to meet the enemy with a bayonet charge. With a wild yell, the Leinstermen, their exhaustion and thirst forgotten, flung themselves on the advancing Turks, who, faltering, were swept away. Unfortunately, as often happens in an Irish counter-attack such as at Fontenoy and Busaco, the pursuit went too far. Capt. D'arcy Irvine and Lt. Willington leading their men in that wild charge were cut off and never returned.[16]

The Turks, broken by the charge, left those intrepid fighters alone for the remainder of 11 August. That evening the Leinsters were relieved after being in constant action for thirty-six hours and having delivered two bayonet charges against an unbroken and very determined enemy. Although their losses had been heavy, they went into reserve with that elation which comes to men after their first successful action. But the overall feeling was that they, a young service battalion fighting in isolation, had not let down their race or regiment.[17]

THE FIGHT AT THE FARM

Meanwhile, under the near cliffs of Chunuk, Baldwin's dwindling force came under heavy fire. Helplessly they watched the destruction of the Loyals and Wiltshires, but with grim satisfaction they saw the guns of the fleet destroy the Turkish infantry in their turn. The annihilation of the Loyals and Wiltshires had left the two Hampshires companies under Maj. Pilleau dangerously exposed, but they held their ground. On the right of the Farm, the remainder of the Hampshires were heavily shelled. Col. Bewsher was wounded in the head; his second-in-command took over. But as Bewsher was on his way to the beach for treatment, he was told by a wounded CSM that there were no officers left in the line. He returned at once to his battalion where he found only two junior officers left. Nearly all the senior NCOs were also killed or wounded. One machine-gun had been knocked out; nevertheless, the almost leaderless remnant hung on resolutely.

To the left of the Hampshires, mingled with the Rifles under Col. Bradford was a pitiful handful of the East Lancashires and Gurkhas and a very weak company of 9th Warwicks. Baldwin's force was reduced to less than 1000 all ranks to hold the Turkish counter-attack. With furious courage, the Turks attempted to drive them off the slopes. But the dwindling British force fought with stubborn courage to hold their position. In this grim fighting, Brig. Baldwin was killed and Brig. Cooper severely wounded. (He survived because Gen. Alex Godley, walking along the beach, recognised him, a fellow Irishman, lying on a stretcher with the rest of the wounded. Scribbling a note to the head doctor, Godley had Cooper carried at once to a lighter.)[18] Col. Bradford of the Rifles was also seriously wounded. As their commanders fell, the next level of command took over but they too fell; Maj. Morphy and Maj. Eastwood of the Rifles and the battalion adjutant were killed; the brigade major was hit in the face, a bullet piercing both cheeks and breaking his jaw; Maj. Wilford of the Rifles was severely wounded in the head. Col. Bewsher, reaching the line once more, was again wounded but in the storm of fire he assumed command and continued to fight. Now all the junior officers were down. Contact with the Turks was often at hand-to-hand. In one place, a 29 Brigade Staff Captain, Capt. Gerald Nugent, was killed leading a counter-attack to restore a local position. His death deeply affected all around. He was regarded as 'a man in a thousand, kind, charming, bright, cheerful and unselfish. His gallant death it was said fitted his life.'[19]

In the entire Baldwin force, only about eight officers and 450 men remained, less than a fifth of those who had set out.

Finally, Col. Bewsher, deeming the position untenable, ordered a general retirement which was carried out in an orderly manner. Yet the men were still not done. At the foot of the hill, a brigade staff captain, bringing up a water-carrying detail, called on the men to return with him to the position. The surviving men of the Rifles, Hampshires, Wiltshires and Warwicks followed him. Their efforts were in vain; the implacable Turkish fire drove them off. Both Hampshires and Rifles suffered grievously. The former had one officer and about 200 rank and file; the latter had one junior captain, two lieutenants and about 200 men left standing. The quartermasters of both battalions, as so often in critical situations, became towers of strength. Lt. Dowling of the Rifles and Lt. Saunders of the Hampshires stepped into the breach. Acting as adjutants, they brought up rations, water and ammunition. The doctor of the Rifles, Lt. Adams, RAMC, worked continuously throughout the battle at a Regimental Aid Post under a deluge of wounded.[20]

Birdwood and Godley watched their plans fall apart. Although a vast area of ground had been taken, the dominating ridges remained in Turkish hands. As long as they did, the offensive could not be termed successful. Only a single battalion remained uncommitted, but it could hardly be expected to accomplish what two divisions had failed to achieve. Nevertheless the last battalion of 29 Brigade, 5th Connaught Rangers, was sent hurrying to the scene.

At 0700 on 10 August, the Rangers received orders to move. The outlying companies were quickly recalled. Less than an hour after the warning order to move came, the battalion moved off. On the way to No. 2 Post, they passed through saps full of wounded, mostly Leinsters, Hampshires and Irish Rifles. As usual in such circumstances, the worst possible news was given. The brigade staff had been wiped out, Hampshires and Rifles were practically wiped out. The air was full of disaster rumours. The Rangers hurried on.

Lt.-Col. Jourdain personally received orders from Gen. Godley to place his battalion under Maj.-Gen. Cox. Progress to the new position was slow, in competition with mule transport and wounded. But eventually they reached the new headquarters, only to be told to pass on to the headquarters of Brig. Cayley under the Farm. Cayley welcomed Jourdain, gave him a cup of tea, explained the situation and gave orders. They were to climb the slopes of Chunuk and occupy the Farm. The Rangers rested, ate and drank and were replenished with water. Then, loaded with extra ammunition, the battalion advanced.

THE FARM: 5TH CONNAUGHT RANGERS

A and B Companies led the way up Aghyl Dere. Climbing the slopes of Chunuk Bair as far as the Farm, they occupied the position, supported by C and D Companies. Snipers and machine-guns poured fire into them as they advanced through the scrub. At one place, an open strip of sand 300 yards wide, covered with bloated bodies and equipment, was crossed under fire. OC A Company with his signallers and a rifle section ran across into the gully. Of the twelve, half fell in crossing. Capt. Massey was wounded but carried on. The remainder, in platoons, worked their way through the scrub to a flank and the advance continued slowly. About a platoon and a half of each company reached the steep slopes of Chunuk Bair. Sun-baked and dehydrated, the shortage of water began to tell. Company commanders, not knowing what lay ahead, conserved the strength of their men as much as possible for the final assault should the enemy be found on the objective. At the Farm, the Rangers moved in fast but in the event it was unnecessary. The place was deserted. However, distant machine-gun fire quickly sent them to cover. Defensive positions were established and picked shots returned fire. A patrol captured a Turkish sniper and brought him in. The first Turk any Ranger had seen, he was observed with curiosity and given a cigarette.[21]

The officers took stock of the situation. Their chief concern after defence was water, now very scarce since so many men had given theirs to passing wounded. The Rangers entrenched the position and waited for orders. These, when they came from Brig. Cayley, were to retire at dusk. But before that there was other work to be done. The position was covered with wounded, but when the Turks saw what was happening, they mercifully held their fire. At dusk the last covering party withdrew.

Despite his wound, Capt. Massey remained with his company until all wounded had been removed. For his performance that day he was later awarded the Military Cross. Withdrawing to Aghyl Dere, all were delighted to find the other two companies of Rangers had strengthened the gully walls and sand-bagged traverses to cover its open places. The Rangers had also gone into the exposed part of the gully to remove the wounded. The battalion MO, Lt. J.J. O'Sullivan, RAMC, and his orderlies worked in the bloody remnants of two brigades. At one time O'Sullivan had 320 stretcher wounded, mainly from 13th Division or 29 Brigade, huddled in a small area. The battalion stretcher bearers carried the human wreckage four miles to the beach hospital, then returned once again to the fire-swept zone for more wounded. The exhausting operation was repeated until all the wounded were evacuated from the battlefield.[22] 5th Connaught Rangers took no part in the battle of Sari Bair, but their action in collecting, treating and evacuating the wounded, sharing precious water with them, won the appreciation of hundreds crippled in that battle.

THE LANDING AT SUVLA

As night fell on 6 August, 11th (Northern) Division sailed from Imbros; about the same time 10th Division sailed from Mudros and Mytilene. To meet the threat of a landing, two Turkish divisions had initially been covering the Anafarta plain, but by this time most had been drawn into the battle at Helles and Anzac. Three battalions, two gendarmerie and one infantry battalion, supported by a cavalry squadron and four artillery batteries, were left to defend Suvla. One battalion was on Kiretch Tepe Sirt with a gun-battery. The other two were thinly scattered across the plain. Only at Chocolate Hill were they entrenched in force.

For the initial assault, Gen. Sir Ian Hamilton intended landing Lt.-Gen. Hon. Sir F. Stopford's IX Corps at Suvla. But of the three New Army divisions in Stopford's corps, almost half, 13th Division and 29 Brigade of 10th Division, was ordered to Anzac in support of Gen. Birdwood's corps. Sir Ian expected the assault force to occupy the inner semi-circle of Suvla Bay and the outer semi-circle of commanding heights, or at least the vital points of Kiretch Tepe Sirt, Scimitar and W Hills, in the first twenty-four hours. To achieve this, Stopford had five brigades, only one of which had any war experience. The assault force was almost without artillery support, except for the fleet, the guns of which had no land-based observers. They were pitted against an enemy of proven courage and tenacity, under commanders known to react with vigour to the unexpected. Secrecy became so obsessional that only Gen. Stopford and his GOC divisions were briefed on the commander's plan. Orders with accompanying maps were issued to brigades and battalions the afternoon before the landing when the troops had already carried out their normal day's training; or, in the case of 10th Division, in ferries just before the assault. Brigade and battalion commanders were not briefed on the concept of operations, their role in it, or the vital need for speed to exploit surprise. Brigadier and soldier had an equally scant knowledge of the operation.

Hamilton originally planned to land the whole of 11th Division at the continuous beach just south of Nibrunesi point. It was an ideal landing place, large enough for the entire division to beach simultaneously. The brigades, after capturing Lala Baba promontory, would then advance along the marshy but passable ground south of the salt lake, or over the centre of the lake itself, to capture the high ground to the east. The second wave, two brigades of 10th Division, were to land on the northern side of the bay near Suvla Point and occupy Kiretch Tepe Sirt, a commanding whale-back ridge. However, because the defences of Chocolate Hill appeared less on the northern side, Gen. Stopford wished to land a brigade inside the bay, apparently intending an advance across the plain north of the salt lake. This was accepted and 34 Brigade was to be put ashore within the bay at A Beach. At the same time, 32 Brigade and 33 Brigade were to land south of Nibrunesi Point. This, a long continuous beach, was divided into C for artillery and B for infantry. A rapid advance by the route Stopford now intended to take depended upon a successful landing by 34 Brigade to clear Hill 10, Ghazi Baba and Karakol Dagh to secure the beachhead. However, for security reasons, the navy were not permitted to reconnoitre the bay to confirm the old charts they were operating from. Once again, excessive secrecy denied naval and army officers at operational level a proper briefing, especially the paramount necessity for speed in securing the high ground of Kiretch Tepe Sirt and Anafarta Ridge.

32 and 33 Brigades landed on time at 2130 on 6 August at the correct place

with no casualties. Almost immediately after landing, two battalions from 32 Brigade took Lala Baba with the bayonet in darkness, 'with loud cheering.'[23] One battalion had losses of fifteen officers and 250 other ranks. Apart from this battalion, casualties in both brigades were insignificant and the southern side of the bay was won. Six battalions of 32 and 33 Brigades concentrated around Lala Baba. No further advance was made for several hours.

Inside the bay, 34 Brigade's touch-down was less smooth. Instead of finding A Beach, landing craft headed for a point deep within the bay 200 yards from the Cut. There they ran into shoals and beached a long way off-shore. Troops landed with difficulty but suffered few casualties. Time was lost in counter-marching along the beach to reach their respective objectives. 11th Manchesters, well-led and confident, captured their first objectives, Suvla Point and Gazi Baba. They then began climbing Karakol Dagh. Turkish skirmishers fought a steady rearguard, inflicting significant casualties while retiring on their main positions on the crest. Only this battalion showed initiative and daring. The remaining battalions, losing their way, scattered, hugged the beach and suffered many officer and NCO casualties as Turkish 'stay-behind' snipers shot the obvious leaders.

Hill 10, a scrub-covered sand-mound, one of the early objectives, remained untaken at dawn. In daylight, fire from its redoubt further disrupted the landing at A Beach. The plan was well out of phase, and all hope of an advance on Chocolate Hill under cover of darkness was gone. The situation on the beaches by the Cut was becoming chaotic chiefly because of a mass of thirsty men of all units. Hill 10 was finally located and taken about 0600 in a converging attack by half 9th Lancashire Fusiliers. The Turkish garrison, about 100 strong, made good their escape. As the sun rose, Turkish batteries on the hills on the eastern side of the lake opened fire, most of which was directed at incoming elements of 10th Division. Brig. Haggard of 32 Brigade was wounded. Shortly before this, he had cheerfully called to his men to ignore the shelling and carry on: 'I saw and heard him, he waved a hand at us and shouted, "There's nothing to worry about, men, they are only balls of sawdust." Very shortly one of the balls of sawdust took the old General's leg off and off the peninsula.'[24]

The brigadiers were ashore by 0300. By late morning, they had allowed their men to drift into inertia; the divisional commander, Maj.-Gen. Hammersley, failed to halt the drift. The commanders ashore were already losing sight of the CinC's aim, and the Corps Commander, lying off-shore in a yacht, failed to intervene and restore it.

Gen. Stopford had left his staff at Imbros, although communications essential for a tactical headquarters were immediately available at Suvla. None of the Corps' staff arrived to use its facilities to control the battle and unravel the chaos of the beachhead until it was too late for their action to influence the outcome of the Suvla operation.[25]

CHAPTER TWELVE

Gallipoli: 10th Division at Suvla, 1915

10TH DIVISION AT SUVLA

Just before dawn on 7 August, leading elements of 10th Division arrived off Suvla, including 31 Brigade and two battalions of 30 Brigade. Stopford had intended landing 10th Division at A Beach, taking its objective at Kiretch Tepe Sirt and advancing as far as possible along the ridge towards Ejelmer Bay. This would turn the Turkish flank on the hills of Tekke Tepe and Anafarta Ridge. Had this aim been achieved, success would have been assured. However, because of landing difficulties, Brig. Hill's battalions were diverted from A to C Beach, far from the division's objective. Disembarkation began at 0530 and Hill was taken by picket boat to Jonquil where he was ordered to place himself under the command of Gen. Hammersley. Stopford could give Hill no information as to the situation ashore; he himself had none. As the sun rose, the Turkish batteries opened fire and struck the leading elements of 10th Division. In one boat, an officer and seventeen men of 7th Dublins were killed or wounded.[1]

Two battalions, 6th Inniskillings and 5th Irish Fusiliers, were soon ashore and concentrated around Lala Baba with the rest following. Brig. Hill landed at 0630 and reported to Gen. Hammersley; delay followed. Order and counter-order flowed between Jonquil and HQ 11th Division and its brigades as to what Hill should do. A new beach at Suvla point was discovered, and Gen. Mahon had arrived with his remaining three battalions. Stopford refused to change his orders. Hill was eventually told by Hammersley to pass his battalions along the sand spit, go through 32 and 34 Brigades and, with their co-operation, to attack Chocolate and Green Hills. This conflicted with previous written orders to 32 and 34 Brigades and caused further delay. For Hill's battalions, it meant an approach march around almost three-quarters of the salt lake.

Landing 5th Inniskillings at C Beach was stopped because of increased Turkish shelling. They landed later that day at Suvla point, on a beach later called A West. On disembarkation, 5th Inniskillings came under command of Brig. Nicol on Kiretch Tepe Sirt. As a result of this change, Brig. Hill was left with five battalions.

By midday, Hill's five battalions were ashore and concentrated near Lala Baba. Crossing the spit began shortly afterwards. In traversing the long, narrow sandy neck of the spit and deep muddy ditch of the Cut, they had to bunch up and plod the gauntlet of accurate artillery fire from well-laid guns on Chocolate Hill. In the barrage, the three foremost battalions, 6th Inniskillings, 5th Irish Fusiliers, 7th Dublins, suffered casualties. One shell in particular fell in the middle of a company of Irish Fusiliers, creating a shambles. The troops behind opened ranks around the dead and dying and marched steadily on. Lt.-Col. Neil Malcolm, GSO1, 11th Division, was sent by Hammersley to 'explain' his orders to Sitwell. He watched Hill's battalions march by Sitwell's headquarters. Struck by their excellent bearing Malcolm turned to Sitwell with the Parthian shot, 'You cannot stay here and refuse to support the advance.' But Sitwell did refuse.[2]

Near the beach, Hill's troops removed their large-packs and stacked them before advancing in a double line of companies—6th Inniskillings on the right, 7th Dublins in the centre and 5th Irish Fusiliers on the left. The German commander noted how they marched 'bolt upright as though on parade without using cover'.[3] One therefore assumes they were advancing boldly, with as much speed as circumstances permitted in the torrid heat, to make up for the delay. Each man had landed with one full water-bottle. After a sleepless night on crowded ferries, the tension of landing and the prolonged wait by the shore, how much water remained as the march began is open to speculation.

When they reached the north-east edge of the lake, no support from 32 Brigade had arrived, and a wheel towards Chocolate Hill would have exposed their left flank. They halted and waited. Hill appealed to Sitwell and got a promise of support; but mistrusting this, Hill sent forward one of his reserve battalions, 6th Irish Fusiliers. He informed Hammersley of this by signal, which was received at 1530. It arrived in the middle of the distribution of fresh orders, cancelling Hill's attack and ordering a converging attack on Chocolate Hill for 1730, Hill's battalions from the north and two battalions of 33 Brigade from the south-west. 32 and 34 Brigades were to support. Sitwell, who had consistently opposed all advance, was placed in overall command.

Hill's troops lay out on the Suvla plain and entrenched against fire from Anafarta Ridge and Chocolate Hill. When they could do so safely they advanced, the Dublins a little in front. The Inniskillings, who were holding to the edge of the salt lake, advanced in alternate rushes. The Irish Fusiliers, harassed by a tough enemy, formed a flank guard. Wheeling right, or southwards, they faced Chocolate Hill. Hill's left was now exposed towards Anafarta Ridge, his right rested on the lake. Turkish rifle and shell fire from Chocolate Hill and the Ridge inflicted light casualties on the advancing line. This, however, was ignored as the excitement of the advance grew; tired and thirsty they may have been, but their spirit was intact. Col. Downing, a large man with an enormous girth, ignored danger as he cheerfully led on the Dublin Pals.

Brig. Sitwell not only failed to support Hill but two mountain guns sent across the Cut to support Mahon on Kiretch Tepe Sirt were commandeered by him for his own brigade. When Sitwell finally did detach units to co-operate with 10th Division, he issued tactical orders himself and withdrew them without notification to 10th Division commanders.[4] Brig. Haggard was seriously wounded at midday. Command of 32 Brigade then devolved on Lt.-Col. J.O'B. Minogue, 9th West Yorks, but he was forward with his battalion and until he returned to assume command, Sitwell also issued orders to 32 Brigade. Eventually two battalions from 33 Brigade, 6th Lincolns and 6th Borderers, started out to co-operate with Hill. They were so late in the day that these two units marched straight across the Salt Lake from their positions on Lala Baba. It was only good fortune that their arrival and Hill's attack coincided well.

Hill's brigade attacked in orthodox formation, two battalions in the first line with two behind, each battalion on a two-company front with two behind in support. It made a good target but also gave good weight to shock action. On the right against the lake were 6th Inniskilling Fusiliers; behind them, in support, were 6th Royal Irish Fusiliers. On the left, 5th Royal Irish Fusiliers had formed a flank guard and a gap opened; to fill this, 7th Dublin Fusiliers moved up A and D Companies. The Inniskillings came up against a swampy obstacle, where the water of the lake had not yet evaporated, and found its path strewn with landmines where the going was good. They suffered severely and their advance slowed.

Gen. Hill seemed to appear everywhere, always cool and cheerful.[5] The sun was beginning to fall when the Irish formed for the assault at 1700, only 300–400 yards from Chocolate Hill. The infantry halted as artillery, naval and field, bombarded the hill. When this ceased as dusk was falling, the charge began. 7th Dublins went directly at Chocolate Hill, A and D Companies leading in competition with each other. D Company, the 'Toffs in the Old Toughs', raced towards the objective with the exhilaration and impetuosity of a wild forward rush at Lansdowne Road, the scene of their first parade.[6] Together, the two companies swept triumphantly over the crest at sunset. On the left, 5th Royal Irish Fusiliers continued the assault half a mile farther on and took Green Hill, a smaller eminence to the east of Chocolate Hill, which the Faughs carried in their time honoured style, probably shouting their regimental war cry, 'Faugh-a-Ballagh', more properly in Irish, 'Fág an bealach'—'clear the road'.

The Lincolns and Borderers hurried across the salt lake in columns. Disregarding losses of over two hundred, they attacked from the south simultaneously and joined hands with the Irish on the hill. Both these battalions were withdrawn before dawn on the 8th. The battalions of 32 Brigade, drawn forward behind Hill's advance, were recalled to the beach by Sitwell that evening. The taking of Chocolate Hill and Green Hills was a clear demonstration of what New Army troops were capable of, given the right leadership and definite orders.

That night, Hill's tired and thirsty battalions bivouacked on and around the newly won hills. But there was no rest for them. Wounded had to be collected and tended to, dead found and buried, water, rations and ammunition brought up and the position entrenched against an expected Turkish counter-attack. In this work around the captured hill, the devotion of the doctors and medical orderlies was remarkable. Most of the wounds were from shrapnel fire; amongst the officers, casualties were the commanding officer and second-in-command of the 6th Inniskillings, and about six others, including the quartermaster.

> It is no disparagement of Colonel Cliffe, wounded while leading his men against the Turkish defences, to say that the loss which the battalion was to feel most acutely during the next two years was that of its white-haired Quartermaster, Lieutenant Dooley. He was its first casualty—wounded while still on the beach. No amateur Quartermaster, however hard working, can replace a first-class member of the fraternity of Quartermasters. He has not the experience—or the guile— required to find the extra rations and comforts that the old hand seems able to produce for his unit in mysterious and no doubt perfectly legitimate ways.[7]

A message was despatched to Gen. Hammersley telling him of the capture of the hills and requesting orders. No reply was received.

CHAOS ON THE BEACH

It was the task of 6th Dublins in reserve to bring up rations, water and ammunition. In doing so, they found the greatest difficulty. Only fifty mules were landed on the first day and these were totally inadequate to supply the needs of two divisions. No provision had been made to provide bulk containers for water, and all the regimental water carts were in Egypt. This lack of water was the greatest source of danger. At the beachhead, horrific scenes began to take place. The navy had expected the army to find wells ashore and that these would provide the bulk of its water requirement; little provision had been made for bulk watering on the beachhead.

Quartermasters did what they could. Using his camp kettles as containers, Lt. Byrne of 6th Dublins supplied all that was possible. But the amount of spillage from open camp kettles carried over a distance of three miles can easily be imagined. Hamilton's operation order had instructed battalions to return collective cooking utensils to Ordnance depots before embarkation,[8] presumably to reduce the stores to be carried in battalion lifts. Lt. Byrne, with the practical foresight of a quartermaster, disobeyed this instruction; Hill's force was grateful that he did. Details which carried the water not unnaturally suffered thirst in the operation and helped themselves from what they carried. It was normal for a water carrier to arrive with about half of what he had started with. Later, biscuit tins and petrol cans were pressed into this service for want of anything better. For his energy and efficiency Lt.

Byrne was later awarded the Military Cross. Not for the first time in the history of the British army, disobedience to orders was rewarded.

KIRETCH TEPE SIRT, 7–8 AUGUST 1915

Gen. Mahon, arriving from Murdos at 0730 with his headquarters, assumed command of a much depleted division. Only two battalions of 30 Brigade (Brig.-Gen. L.L. Nicol) and the divisional pioneers, 5th Royal Irish, remained under command. 29 Brigade was at Anzac. Brig. Hill had five battalions committed to an attack on a distant position, and a last battalion of Hill's brigade was about to disembark to follow him. Mahon had no support troops; the divisional artillery was in Egypt and the engineer field companies had not arrived. The Pioneers were immediately detailed for beach duties. With his two remaining battalions, Mahon was faced with what ought to have been the divisional objective, Kiretch Tepe Sirt. However, the immediate problem was to get ashore. As Hill had earlier discovered, A Beach had been declared unfit for disembarkation. Further confusion was added by an order from Corps HQ that disembarkation would not take place until 'special orders' were received.[9] This delayed the disembarkation for several hours.

Eventually the navy gave the order to disembark on the northern side of Suvla point. 6th Munsters were first off and, like 34 Brigade of 11th Division, the troops dropped over the side of the lighters and waded ashore. The Turks had sown the beach with landmines, and as the Munsters landed these exploded on contact. Fortunately the mines, although frightening at first, caused few casualties. 7th Munsters followed their comrades ashore nearly two hours later. The orders given to both battalions were to secure Kiretch Tepe Sirt and to protect the left flank of the troops on Anafarta Plain.

Under a blazing sun, unacclimatised troops stood with full equipment: 'being five weeks without exercise had made us rather soft'.[10] They began the steep climb up the rugged 600-foot ridge. The shattered and exhausted remnant of 11th Manchesters, still determinedly hanging on after their early success, were leap-frogged; 5th Inniskillings came forward that evening to relieve them. A shower of rain in late afternoon gave some welcome relief.

Turkish troops of the Gallipoli Gendarmerie Battalion, about 500 strong, with two guns, defended the high ground around the Pimple. With their fire, they dominated the long whale-back ridge of Kiretch Tepe Sirt. This was their home ground; they knew it well and fought stubbornly defending it. Resisting fiercely, the Turks inflicted heavy casualties, especially among officers. Despite this, the Munsters were within 100 yards of the crest when darkness forced a halt. That night, they strengthened their positions and prepared for an assault at dawn. Then, led by Maj. Jephson, the second-in-command, they stormed the Turkish line with bayonets. On the crest, the enemy rearguard bravely defended to the last the position which became known as Jephson's Post. The support of the destroyer *Grampus* was invaluable, especially at night with its searchlights and machine-guns. Fire support was not its only contribution. On the 8th, learning the critical condition of the Munsters because of lack of water, the destroyer rushed ashore two water tanks fitted with taps and water to fill them. Such was the urgency of the sailors' magnificent response that their whaler sped across the water and on landing was propelled half its length onto the beach.[11]

The cost of capturing half Kiretch Tepe Sirt ridge was not light. Together, both Munster battalions lost forty-eight all ranks dead and over 150 wounded. More significantly, the battalions were exhausted not only by fighting, but also by the sheer effort of movement in terrible ground conditions and torrid heat, and lack of water. Having captured Jephson's Post, the Munsters could do no more. This was the moment for fresh troops to continue the attack. But there were none to hand. For the lack of reserves, the assault along Kiretch Tepe Sirt stalled. The presence of Hill's battalions or 29 Brigade (soon to be destroyed at Anzac to little gain) would have been decisive. Just behind the enemy lines, plentiful water gushed from a spring. At the end of this ridge was the main Turkish ammunition dump for the Gallipoli Peninsula; its capture would have been disastrous to the enemy. Both prizes went begging.

In their newly-won positions the Munsters dug in on 8 August. The dead lay where they fell—Turks, Manchesters and Munsters, down inaccessible gullies or in the midst of fire-swept scrub. The whole area stank of death. On 9 August, the Munsters attempted to advance but were beaten back. Enemy reinforcements had arrived and came under the command of Maj. Kadir, the Turkish commander on the ridge. All hope of an easy Allied victory faded. Aggressive patrol activity began by both sides. In this, Capt. R.W. Oldnall was seriously wounded and 2/Lt. L. Gaffney was mortally wounded. Gaffney was carried in by Lt. Waller, RE, who displayed most conspicuous courage in going out three times under fire to rescue him and two other wounded men.[12]

Water remained desperately short. Apart from two wells at Lala Baba, all springs and wells were either inland or on the untaken heights. A quart water-bottle was all that was available to each man and by early afternoon on 7 August all were enduring agonies of thirst. A water tanker and two lighters had arrived with the fleet, and although the lighters were grounded out in the bay, water was pumped ashore through hoses. But there was nowhere to put it. The containers and troughs, along with well-digging and water distribution equipment, were in an engineer storeship (*Prah*) out in the bay. Under the landing timetable, this was not to come ashore for several days.[13] No one on the spot short-circuited this order. Thirst-maddened men crowded the beach. Unable to get to the hose-heads to fill water-bottles, they pierced water hoses with bayonets.[14] This helped to assuage thirst but wasted vast quantities of the precious liquid. Because no watering facilities were ashore, of 800 valuable mules available to transport supplies, only fifty were landed on the first day. Unit water-carts had been off-loaded at

Alexandria. Without these, quartermasters used any receptacle, even ammunition boxes with a high spillage factor for want of anything better to get water to the forward positions.[15] Lacking transport mules, ammunition and rations together with these dixies and cans were carried up to three miles to the inland positions by fatigue parties which drained fighting manpower by 25 per cent.[16] Without water for the gun teams little of the available artillery was landed on the 7th.

The suffering of the wounded was piteous. In the heat, wounds rapidly became infected and within hours crawled with maggots. Men lay where they fell until taken to collection points. They were carried on stretchers by tired and thirsty men with sweaty, slippery hands several miles over rough ground, often under fire, to field ambulances at the beachhead. Here they usually received their first professional treatment, sometimes twenty-four hours after being hit, but their suffering continued. Because of the great numbers, sheltered accommodation was scarce and most lay in the sun. Many died waiting. The fortunate were eventually floated by lighter to hospital ships for evacuation to Imbros. The story of one officer, Lt. O.G.E. McWilliam, 5th Inniskillings, *Suvla and After*, published under the pseudonym 'Juvenus', is a harrowing tale. An untold number, possibly a high proportion of 'missing believed killed', died of wounds or thirst, alone in the scrub, down deep gullies or ravines. The stench of putrefying dead was thereafter never absent from Suvla; flies were of plague proportions.

Compounding the thirst problem was the two days' rations issued to the troops before landing, consisting of bully beef and dry biscuit. No food was manufactured better to increase thirst. In the intense heat, the 'bully' turned into a gooey mess upon which fly-hordes settled and stuck fast. Most of this was thrown away in disgust; Lala Baba was littered with opened, unconsumed tinned bully.[17] Hunger added its torment to troops already dehydrating fast. Diarrhoea and gastric complaints which had become manifest among the troops on the Greek islands spread like wild-fire. Dysentery followed quickly.

Of the field ambulances, only the 30th arrived on the 7th. For ten days they had to tend all 10th Division battle-casualties at Suvla. In addition to this was the rising number of dysentery and enteric fever cases. Mysteriously, illness appeared to fade when an attack was in the offing; none wanted to report sick until they were forced to. In mid-August, the 31st and 32nd Field Ambulances arrived and the pressure eased, but by that time the numbers of casualties and illness cases were rising. 30th Field Ambulance was later cited for its performance in the dreadful conditions prevailing during the early days at Suvla.[18]

The beaches were a disorganised chaos where information was difficult to obtain. The erection of piers, without which the disembarkation of heavy equipment could not begin, was delayed because landing-craft could not take the pier parts into A Beach. When the navy found a suitable place close to Suvla point, the Corps Chief Engineer was not told; he was evacuated through illness two days later.[19] The commanding officer of an artillery brigade, keen to disembark and asking his brigadier the reason for the delay, was told with mordant wit, 'We are waiting for Turkish reinforcements'.[20]

The night of 7 August all over Suvla tired and thirsty battalions bivouacked where they were at nightfall. But there was no rest for them. Wounded had to be collected, tended to and evacuated. Dead had to be found and buried. Water, rations and ammunition had to be brought up, and the position entrenched against an expected Turkish counter-attack. Darkness fell and as the air chilled, cold and hunger added their torment to the dehydrated troops; a heavy rainstorm was a mixed blessing. Where springs and wells were found, hundreds of men festooned with water-bottles jostled to replenish them. Cold, hungry and thirsty, for nearly all it was their second sleepless night.

> Personally it was an extraordinary night. The Signal Office was fixed on a boulder strewn hillside and consisted of a table and a hurricane lamp with a vibrator [Morse transmitter]. Some time during the night the divisional commander, General Sir Bryan Mahon, and one of his staff found the Signal Office.[21]

All day on 8 August, IX Corps did little except maintain their positions. Receiving no orders from Gen. Hammersley, Brig. Hill ordered his battalions to entrench on the positions captured the previous evening. Throughout 8 August, Hill's force laboured to fortify their positions on Chocolate Hill and on Green Hill. It was a quiet day for the troops, but they suffered much from sunburn and severe thirst. The wells they had found the previous evening came under heavy Turkish fire and their use was restricted. By now, because of inadequate containers and mule or horse transport, it was necessary to deploy a quarter of the troops available[22] to supply water from the beach, over three miles distant, a round trip of nearly six miles which was in itself exhausting. On this day Lt. Ernest Lawrence Julian, 7th Dublins, until recently Reid Professor of Law at Trinity College, Dublin, died of wounds received the previous evening. Many of D Company 7th Dublins were to die at Suvla. Among the most intelligent, vigorous and capable of their generation, they would be sorely missed in the shaping of post-war Ireland.

The troops dug trenches and sweltered while officers chaffed impatiently and waited for orders. Near the beach they swam. Stopford congratulated his troops on having landed. One battalion of 32 Brigade, now under Col. Minogue, protected Nicol's right flank under Kiretch Tepe Sirt; the others came up into line with Hill's force, facing Anafarta Ridge. Then, two units of 32 Brigade with commendable initiative began to scale the high ground. 6th East Yorks occupied Scimitar Hill and 9th West Yorks began climbing Anafarta Ridge. The West Yorks had almost reached the top when Turkish reinforcements began to resist furiously. On the right of the lake, 33 Brigade extended the line southwards, but showed no further initiative although within striking distance of W Hills. Brig. Sitwell's 34 Brigade remained at the beach. From Anzac they were observed swimming and this started an ill-founded legend among Australians about British lethargy.

Meanwhile, Gen. Liman von Sanders and Mustafa Kemal, the Turkish commander, urged their troops to the scene with an energy which was totally lacking in Hamilton or Stopford. Finally Sir Ian Hamilton arrived at Suvla on the evening of 8th but it was already too late. His arrival did more harm than good. In response to his orders for an immediate attack on the heights, 32 Brigade was ordered to concentrate. 6th East Yorks, named particularly by Hammersley, withdrew from Scimitar Hill, which was instantly reoccupied by the enemy. Failure to hold this vital position was to prove costly. Kiretch Tepe Sirt, Scimitar and W Hills, which could have been gained on day one with determined leadership and more troops, were to remain untaken.

On 9 August an attack called by Gen. Hamilton on the Anafartha heights was made by 11th Division. They were supported by two battalions of 30/31 Brigade, with two further battalions acting as carrying parties. The attack was delivered disjointedly by battalions of brigades hopelessly mixed across Suvla Plain. With no unified command, little cohesion and poor co-operation, it had small chance of success. Despite the gallantry of the troops, each phase of the attack was defeated by the Turks, who were now present in hourly-increasing strength. Fresh infantry of two Territorial divisions landed. Like a butcher feeding a meat-grinder, 53rd Welsh and 54th Eastern Divisions were committed piecemeal to the battle on 10, 11 and 12 August with no better results. Indeed on the 12th several hundred men of 5th Norfolks followed their CO and sixteen officers into the bush and were never seen again; their fate was never discovered. On 10 August, Lord Granard wrote home:

> As was to be expected all the arrangements for the landing were faulty, but the resistance offered by the Turks was not very great. If it had been otherwise, the casualties would have been terrible. Our losses in the fighting after the landing have been very heavy and I attribute this to the stupidity of Ian Hamilton in starting operations before he had sufficient troops and, what was more criminal, starting the fighting without any artillery whatever. If this campaign had been properly run we ought to have gained the position we are attacking and cut off a great portion of the Turkish army. The troops have suffered very much from the want of water and they have been much more uncomfortable than conditions demanded.[23]

For his part in these attacks, Brig. Hill was ordered on 9 August to detach two battalions to 11th Division. 6th Irish Fusiliers and 6th Dublins were despatched, their objective Hill 70. Despite losses, the two Irish battalions obtained a lodgment on their objective and succeeded in holding on against a determined counter-attack. But on their left, 32 Brigade were driven off. Taken in the flank the Irish were forced off the position, and the adjutant of 6th Irish Fusiliers, Capt. Johnston, and Lt. MacDermot of the same regiment were killed. In the engagement, a Regimental Aid Post had been established under a tree in captured territory. It was noticed that wounded men were hit a second time after they arrived, and a quick search revealed a sniper above the RAP in the tree.[24] He was given short shrift. The remainder of Hill's force suffered lightly from shrapnel and rifle fire, as they were employed in carrying forward supplies of ammunition and water. Lt. J.F. Hunt of the Inniskillings was awarded an MC for cool courage. Sometimes the ammunition parties, having delivered the supplies, would join in the fight. A party led by Capt. R.P. Tobin of 7th Dublins stayed to fight with an English regiment throughout the day. It was an example of the high morale and eagerness of the men who, despite the appalling heat and thirst, were still eager to advance and take on the Turk. They were restrained only by poor generalship in deciding the aim, giving clear objectives with decisive orders to brigade and battalion commanders.

For the remainder of that first week, Hill's men took no further part in the fighting, simply holding the line they had captured on the 7th. However their suffering was not over; to shell-fire were added the discomforts of living. Flies were appalling, exposed food was instantly covered, latrines infested. Rest was impossible during the heat of the day since flies covered every part of exposed flesh. Everyone was dirty, unshaven, soiled with sweat, blood and filth. In such conditions it is not surprising that by now most men were suffering from diarrhoea, enteritis, or various degrees of sunburn and heat cramp occasioned by exposure and inadequate fluid intake. Yet, despite all this, they had a new-found confidence in themselves as soldiers and their morale soared when ordered back to the beach to concentrate for a new attack. Relief began on the 10th and was completed on the 13th. At the beach they cleaned up, swam, rested and drank their fill of water which was not carried laboriously three miles. On the evening of the 14th, orders were received to take Kiretch Tepe Sirt.

The two brigades under Gen. Mahon were ordered to take a ridge which, in the week since the landing, had been heavily reinforced by the Turkish command. Had Gen. Hammersley's division accomplished its mission without taking Hill's battalions under command, Mahon's two brigades would have been free to carry out the original plan of taking Kiretch Tepe Sirt on Day One. Now, one week later, the situation had significantly changed.

15 August, Lady Day in Ireland, began with divine services. Canon Maclean celebrated Holy Communion for Protestants in a marquee of a field ambulance, and Father Murphy of 7th Dublins said Mass and gave general

absolution in the open air, his vestments making a splash of colour.

At 1210 the attack began. 30 Brigade on the left were to advance along the ridge proper. 31 Brigade on the right had the task of moving through the southern foothills. The crest of the ridge was bare and rocky, one and a half miles long. It was mostly 600 feet high but in parts rose to 750 feet, the centre marked with a cairn known as the Pimple. The Turks, now very strong, had entrenched half way between Jephson's Post and the Pimple.

Both northern and southern faces of the ridge fell away sharply for 300 feet, then made a gradual descent. The entire face was laced by gullies and covered by thorn shrub, in places fire-scorched. The operation was painfully slow. Maj. Jephson was mortally wounded on the peak bearing his name. Seeing the advance on the ridge held up, Brig. Hill ordered two companies of 6th Munsters and two of 6th Dublins to advance along the northern slope of the hill. They did so and gained 250 yards to a point halfway to the Pimple. With 250 yards to cover, and the Turkish positions in sight, the company commanders decided to charge. Within sight of the enemy, and despite crags and cliffs, thirst and fatigue, the young Service battalions of the 'Old Toughs' and the 'Dirty Shirts' bounded forward despite heavy fire. Led by Maj. Tynte of 6th Munsters, they went at the enemy with irresistible élan and fought their way into the Turkish positions. The enemy not killed at the first bayonet thrust fled or surrendered.

On the summit, the exuberant Irish yell cheered all who heard it. It was echoed by cheers at their great feat from the watchers on ships in the gulf and soldiers on the lake. Its effect on the Turks was even more remarkable, since they fled from a position they believed impregnable. The whole of the northern stretch of Kiretch Tepe Sirt and beyond the Pimple was cleared: 'There was a yell. I looked up and saw figures racing along the crest with sun glinting on their bayonets.'[25]

On their right, or southern or landward side of the ridge, the attack was less successful, where 5th and 6th Inniskillings, supported by a single mountain battery, were held up. The artillery found it impossible to locate the position of the enemy machine-guns on Kidney Hill against which 5th and 6th Inniskillings, with 6th Irish Fusiliers in support, assaulted in vain.

> At 1.15 pm, supported by one mountain battery, three battalions moved forward along the landward side of the ridge. Within an hour we had suffered some 350 casualties; and although the two battalions above us gained some ground temporarily along the top of the ridge, the enemy, with five battalions in line and two in reserve, were far too strong for us. Of the six officers in my company, three were killed and the rest wounded.[26]

In broken scrub-covered ground, the stubborn, courageous Turk showed his best qualities. Manning positions which gave perfect observation of the advance, the Turkish machine-gunners stopped every attack with a withering hail of bullets. Nearly all the officers were down. The commanding officer of 5th Inniskillings, with five of his officers, were killed; both majors, two captains and ten lieutenants were wounded; rank and file dead and wounded lay all over the scrub-covered hill. The surviving Ulstermen, knowing they could not advance, would not retire without orders. They huddled in small groups in the scrub and waited. After dark, Lt. G.B. Lyndon went out and led many of these groups. Officers were brought in from other battalions; Capt. J. Grant and Lt. J. Comerford of the Munsters came to help; one died and the other was wounded. The battalion was temporarily shattered.[27]

A medical corps detachment landed, arriving that afternoon by destroyer. Without briefing or information, they were marched off in the gathering dusk to the scene of the fighting. With bullets flying around them, they made their way through a nullah, up the scrub-covered hill to the newly-won position. One of these, Pte. Harold Thomas MA (Oxon), RAMC, once a curate of the Church of England and now a medical orderly, later described the scene.

> It was very dark now... Two sergeants and an officer were busy over an indistinct blur under the gully bank, a 'hand' was needed and I ran up to find it consisted of three Turks, one dead and two badly wounded... After this a connected account of that first night becomes impossible... Between the bursts of fire the silence was broken by agonising cries which will always haunt me. Seemingly from all about that hill there were voices crying 'Ambulance', 'Stretcher-bearers'. It was horrible, we would start for a voice and it would cease and another far away would begin. That hillside was a shambles. Evidently there had been fierce hand-to-hand fighting there a few hours ago... we came suddenly on a half-dug trench which an RAMC officer had made into a combined mortuary and first aid station. As we set furiously to work sorting the dead from the living, there reeled among us out of the darkness an officer raving 'My men have taken that bloody hill and now they're dying of thirst.' He passed on and we continued our ghastly work.[28]

Pte. Thomas and six others, apparently without stretchers, linked hands to carry a badly wounded man to the beach.

> The poor fellow moaned piteously at every stumble. The hot night was thick with the whirr of bullets, the sharp metallic cry of crickets, the ghastly calls of undiscovered wounded and the sickly smell of Gallipoli thyme... Now and then we would catch a glimpse of Suvla Bay with the hospital ship aglow with the lamps of fairyland, but try as we would we did not seem to get nearer them.[29]

At the end of the day, the northern edge of the ridge had been taken but no progress had been made along the southern side. On their side of the ridge, the Dublins and Munsters were now exposed to the full weight of the Turks on the other side. The two reserve battalions were already hurrying to the scene. As they came, the CO of 7th Dublins, the out-sized Col. Downing, was shot in the foot by an enemy sniper and was relieved by Maj. Harrison. The position, along a line just below the crest of Kiretch Tepe Sirt, was held from the left by 6th Irish Fusiliers, 6th Munsters, then three companies of 7th Dublins. Their B Company had been detached. 6th Dublins, who suffered heavily in their charge, were relieved. In the darkness the Turkish counter-attack began.

The first Turkish attack came at 2200. A savage fight began in the moonlight and continued until musketry and close-quarter bayonet work eventually drove back the enemy. Listening patrols were sent over onto the other side of the ridge. The exhausted troops got what rest they could. Long before dawn, the listening-posts were driven in and the line stood to with bayonets fixed. First to come was a hail of grenades, followed by a wave of attackers which was again thrown back. From their side of the ridge, the Turks began to hurl over scores of their excellent grenades of German design. These highly effective missiles became the best weapon in that situation. The Turks began to rain grenades onto the Irishmen. With mounting casualties, Maj. Harrison ordered Capt. Poole Hickman to take part of D Company over the crest and clear the bombers. Their charge, from which only four returned, gained only a short respite.[30] Similar attacks by 7th Dublins and 6th Munsters, elsewhere along the line, had no better results.

Throughout the 16th, 30 Brigade remained on that bare bloodstained ridge. Under scorching sun, they were ravaged by hunger, thirst and enteritis which they endured stoically. Hand grenades rained upon them in increasing numbers. To go forward was death, to remain was death, to go back was unthinkable. The noise of battle was incessant. With the stench of death all around them, somehow they clung on. Their dominant feeling was helpless rage. Some tried to catch the Turkish bombs and return them; Pte. Albert Wilkin of 7th Dublins accomplished this five times, but the sixth exploded in his hand. Wilkin, serving with the elite D Company, must have considered the risks and could have 'flicked on' to save himself, but his catching and returning demonstrated a desire to fight back. Elsewhere he would have won a Victoria Cross for his heroism; here, such gallantry was so commonplace he was 'mentioned in despatches'. In their fury of exasperation, the men even threw rocks back at the enemy and rolled boulders over the crest, exposing themselves to Turkish fire to do so. The few remaining officers did what they could to calm and lead. In doing so they inevitably exposed themselves to greater risk and suffered accordingly. Capt. 'Paddy' Tobin of the Dublins, Lt. FitzGibbons of the Munsters, the son of the Nationalist MP for South Mayo, and Lt. Wetherill, a descendant of King William's ADC at the Boyne, all died this way and not far from each other.[31]

On the right, 6th Irish Fusiliers exposed in front and flank were almost annihilated. Their sister battalion, the 5th, came forward to their relief but shared their fate. Three officers of this battalion were awarded the Military Cross for their heroic example, Capts. Panton and Kidd and 2/Lt. Heuston. By dusk, nearly all the officers of the three battalions on the ridge were either dead or wounded. Still the men, now almost leaderless, held on. They would not retire until ordered to do so. Here there were no visible symbols of regimental tradition and honour, only their own stout hearts with their feeling of regimental, national, not to say personal, pride. At last the sun set on that awful day, easing their suffering slightly, but the fighting went on after sunset.

In the darkness, 6th Dublins and 5th Royal Irish Pioneers came into the line and the remnants of the 7th Dublins, 6th Munsters and 5th Irish Fusiliers fell back. All night the fight carried on relentlessly and mercilessly, but the line held. 6th Dublin lost six of their best officers, including the adjutant, Capt. Richards, and 2/Lt. W. Nesbitt, so highly regarded that he was called the soul of the battalion. Ammunition supplies dwindled, yet the Turks had a plentiful supply to blaze away, sometimes unaimed 'funk firing'.

At last, although that splendid spirit which had taken them this far might have kept the remnant in position until all died, their commanders considered they had done more than could be expected without support or reinforcements. Flesh and blood could not do or stand more. Brigs. Hill and Nicol ordered the pitiful remnants of their battalions to retire to their original start line. On the 15th, Lord Granard wrote:

> This campaign is going as badly as it can. You have doubtless seen our losses in the papers. 10th Division has lost over 114 officers and c. 3,000 men killed and wounded. Ian Hamilton is entirely responsible... and the sooner he is recalled the better. He has run the whole show like a madman. He will take no advice, and unless he is soon recalled it is difficult to know what will happen... owing to General Hamilton's action we have not the number necessary for an advance. I believe that the 11th Division have lost about 205 officers and 5,000 men. This could have been avoided by proper generalship.[32]

Lord Granard's letter was written at the beginning of the campaign, before the battle of Kiretch Tepe Sirt, and before the heavy losses sustained there became known.

At the critical stage of the battle for Kiretch Tepe Sirt, Hamilton, apparently unaware that this was taking place, decided to shake-up the senior command structure of IX Corps. Stopford, Hammersley and Sitwell were relieved and sent home. GOC 29th Division, Maj.-Gen. de Lisle, was brought in from Helles as temporary corps commander, pending the arrival of Gen. Byng from France. Mahon, on being told of de Lisle's appointment, resigned and went to Imbros. It was at this stage that Brig. Nicol's appeal for reinforcements came. Gen. de Lisle, not yet familiar with the situation, delayed his decision, which, when it came was too late. Nicol and Hill had withdrawn their shattered remnants, now virtually without officers, to their start lines. The Turkish command regarded this as the critical period of the entire campaign. One German commander wrote: 'These were again days of the heaviest fighting on which the balance of success seemed to tremble to and fro. The Marshal was again personally on the spot. Reinforcements from Asia dropped their packs at the foot of the heights, and scrambled up the heights to help their comrades.'[33] Maj. Prigge, ADC to Marshal von Sanders, wrote at the time: 'The chief danger lies at present on our right wing, by Edje Liman (Ejelmar). The English [*sic*] have suffered enormous losses and the battles were far more bitter than any we have had so far.'[34]

Bitter indeed: with incredible ill-judgment, Hamilton's operational order had stated that the 'enemy's stock of ammunition is low'.[35] On the bloody crest of Kiretch Tepe Sirt, lashed by a hail of Turkish bombs, the Irishmen could reply only with rocks, boulders and bayonet charges 'in default of anything more deadly'.[36]

Gen. Liman von Sanders regarded the situation as 'very dangerous'. Since the offensives at Cape Helles and Anzac had petered out, the Turkish command were free to move reinforcements to its defence, and they did so with their accustomed rapidity and vigour. Winston Churchill might well comment: 'This action does not bulk very largely in British accounts, and its critical character seems scarcely to have been appreciated.'[37]

Liman von Sanders was alive to the danger and his appreciation was: 'If during their attacks on 15 and 16 August the British had captured and held Kiretch Tepe, the whole position of the 5th Army would have been outflanked. The British might have then achieved a decisive and final victory.'[38]

Hamilton, somehow, was unaware of the battle. It was therefore hardly surprising that he failed to inform London of its nearness to victory. But the War Office eventually could stand no more. Maj.-Gen. C.E. Callwell, the Director of Military Operations, spoke frankly while briefing Gen. Monro's Major-General General Staff, Maj.-Gen. Lynden-Bell, before departing on a Dardanelles inspection tour at Kitchener's behest: 'We don't think Ian Hamilton and his crowd are telling the truth about the situation in the Dardanelles—and we are confirmed in our view by a letter from an Australian War Correspondent called Murdoch.'[39]

Keith Murdoch, an Australian on his way to London to represent a group of newspapers, had been commissioned by the Australian government to report on postal facilities at Anzac.[40] Horrified by what he saw there, he consulted the war correspondent of the *Daily Telegraph*, Mr E. Ashmead-Bartlett, who concurred with his views:

The authorities and the public at home, he said, were in complete ignorance of what was going on, and under the existing censorship at Imbros there was no way of enlightening them—unless, of course, one broke the rules and sent out an uncensored letter. After some discussion they agreed this must be done. Murdoch was due to leave for England in a day or two; it was arranged that he would take a letter written by Ashmead-Bartlett and get it into the hands of the authorities in London.[41]

CHAPTER THIRTEEN

Gallipoli: the Last Days

At the close of the Sari Bair battle, 29 Brigade less 5th Rangers withdrew for reorganisation. The Hampshires and Leinsters had suffered very severe casualties but the Rifles were shattered. Of the 1000 officers and men who had left England, a sergeant and thirty-five men remained and were attached to 10th Hampshires. So poor was their physical condition that the acting CO of the Hampshires, Maj. Morley, ordered them into reserve to recuperate. They spent the last of their time at Anzac unloading ships.[1]

Lt.-Col. Jourdain of the Rangers acted as brigade commander until relieved by a senior lieutenant-colonel, G.K. Agnew MVO DSO, Royal Scots Fusiliers.

29 Brigade headquarters and its remaining units withdrew into the Olive Grove. This was officially a rest area, but like every other place at Gallipoli, it was under sniper fire and occasional shell-bursts. First-line reinforcements who had been left out of battles at Mudros rejoined and were heartily welcomed. Most of the majors arriving with the drafts found themselves commanding their battalion.[2]

The final phase of the combined August battles took place on the 22nd for Scimitar Hill and was co-ordinated with Anzac's attack on Hill 60. For this offensive the 29th Division was brought from Helles and 2nd Dismounted Yeomanry Division from Egypt. 11th Division was the right attack, 29th Division the left, with 2nd Yeomanry in reserve at Lala Baba. After fierce going, elements of the left brigade of 29th Division won the top of Scimitar Hill, where they were met with concentrated Turkish artillery and machine-gun fire. Once again misfortune dogged the luckless 11th Division. Losing direction in thick smoke, 32 Brigade blundered to the left across the path of the right brigade of 29th Division, creating confusion and delaying their attack. The unit on the crest, 1st Inniskillings, unsupported, was forced off. In this action, Capt. G.R. O'Sullivan who had won the Victoria Cross at Helles in June, was killed. The last reserve, five brigades of the very understrength Yeomanry, went forward. Their left brigade (2nd South Midland), led personally by its brigadier, stormed the hill at sunset with extraordinary bravery and gained the crest. For a while it seemed they might have won, but the Yeomanry, like 29th Division, were annihilated in a torrent of fire. The brigadier, Lord Longford, and his brigade major died among 5300 casualties out of 14,300 assault troops.[3] Elsewhere the Yeomanry fared little better than 11th Division. The last throw had failed. From this time until the evacuation of Suvla on 19–20 December, the front line was the same as the advance positions of 10th Division on the evening of 7 August.

The death in action of Capt. Gerald O'Sullivan VC had a profound effect on the three battalions of his regiment at Suvla.

> From men of the 1st Inniskillings, Jimmie heard of the death of Captain Gerald ('Micky') O'Sullivan. This young man had become a legendary figure in a regiment not given to panache or hero-worship. He was last seen leading a small party of men in a desperate charge on Scimitar Hill and disappearing, never to be seen again, into the third line of Turkish trenches. He did not live to receive the Victoria Cross which he had earned by great gallantry on two separate occasions at Cape Helles earlier that year.[4]

Gen. Birdwood's Anzac force, in a co-ordinated offensive with IX Corps, aimed at capturing Hill 60 (also known as Kaiajik Aghala). Holding it would give domination of the Anafarta Gap, the ground west of Hill 60 and the wells of Kabak Kuyu. These latter were extremely important to the Turks who were also desperately short of water. Maj.-Gen. H.V. Cox, Indian Army, was to command the force responsible for its capture. Cox's force consisted of elements of three brigades. An Australian and New Zealand (ANZ) brigade under Brig. Russell was the right attack; its objective was Hill 60. Cox's own 29 Indian Brigade was the left attack, tasked with capturing the low ground close to the sea and establishing contact with units of IX Corps at Suvla. Two battalions of 29 Brigade were separated. The Hampshires on the extreme right were to feint an attack while the Rangers, positioned between the Indian and ANZ brigades, were to capture Kabak Kuyu wells.

The co-ordinated assault by the Suvla and Anzac forces had a planning weakness. Because of limited artillery, IX Corps wished the Anzac force to provide enfilade covering fire for the advance of 11th Division. This could only be done by denuding the Anzac troops of support, or alternatively, delaying their attack. No decision had been reached as the troops moved to their start lines. An hour after sunset on 20 August, the Rangers began their move as silently as possible across open ground to Aghyl Dere. Arms and equipment were carefully wrapped with cloth or paper to prevent rattling.

> There was a strange evening glow after the sun went down that night and for a while the towering summit of Sari Bair showed up in the dim light. Many wondered if the Turks had already seen the column and what would the effect be when they reached the open country.[5]

Additional bombs, sand bags and entrenching tools were issued. With this increased load, the troops deployed to their concentration areas and got as much rest as possible. Next day Gen. Godley spoke to the Rangers. He told them one regiment (9th Warwicks on 12 August) had failed to take the wells, but 'he looked to the Rangers to do so in a way that was known to all, by the cold steel and an Irish yell'. He wished them God speed and left. Godley knew his men and 'his words appealed to the gallant Irish to whom they were addressed. They would have cheered but for commands to remain silent.'[6]

The Connaught Rangers had taken many casualties holding the line since landing, but this was their first attack at Anzac. Such was their spirit that, although some were suffering from what might have been dysentery or enteric fever, on the morning of the attack not one man reported sick. The Rev. J.W. Crozier celebrated Holy Communion and Father Tom O'Connor gave general absolution at Mass. The whack of bullets overhead or striking the ground was a constant reminder to the kneeling Rangers of the ordeal to come.[7]

Shortly before the assault it was finally agreed that the Anzac attack would be delayed for thirty minutes to allow its artillery to support 11th Division. Thus Zero Hour at Suvla was fixed at 1500 and for Anzac, 1530. News of the change of time reached the Rangers at 1330. The decision was unsatisfactory on two counts. First, it gave the Turks at Anzac assault thirty minutes' warning of a possible attack; and secondly, it forced 11th Division to attack with its right flank exposed to enfilade fire from Hill 60. Like many military compromises, it achieved the worst possible end.

From the heights of Anzac, the Suvla attack could be plainly seen, with enemy shrapnel bursting over the lines of advancing infantry. Part of 11th Division struck by enfilade fire from Hill 60, was seen veering to the left, leaving a wide gap between them and 5th Gurkhas.

At Zero, the Anzac batteries and Monitors in the bay of Saros bombarded Hill 60, then ceased firing at 1540. To achieve surprise, the guns had not registered, which affected the accuracy of the shooting. It was largely ineffective and served only to alert the Turks further.

The feint of the 10th Hampshires succeeded, but not without heavy losses; again the officers took a disproportionate share. Their commanding officer, Maj. Morley, and Capt. Hellyer, the only officers of that battalion to survive the battle of Sari Bair unhurt, were both killed. One hundred and fifty NCOs and men were killed and wounded out of a total strength of 335.

The Australian and New Zealander attack started at 1530 when the bombardment ceased. The 400 men of Canterbury Mounted Rifles and the Otago Mounted Rifles advanced in lines of successive troops across 500 yards of open ground. Alongside them, 500 Australians from 4 Australian Brigade tried to cross the 200 yards of open ground in an unbroken rush. The New Zealanders, in small parties, reached the lowest Turkish trenches on Hill 60 shortly after 1545, and at 1600 had reached their first objective. However neither the Australians on their right nor the Indian Brigade on the left had caught up with them. The Australians had met a withering fire from positions untouched by the bombardment. The Indian brigade, weak in strength after its previous ordeal, made little headway in the gap between the Suvla and Anzac force.

KABAK KUYU WELLS AND HILL 60, 21–28 AUGUST 1915

The 5th Connaught Rangers, about to take part in their first attack, filed by platoons down a narrow gully to the jumping off area facing the objective, Kubak Kuyu wells. Once in position, the Rangers formed up for the assault which was to be delivered in successive platoon waves. Each platoon formed an extended line, one platoon behind another, then settled down to wait for the bombardment. The air became filled with the noise, dust and smoke of explosions.

> Here and there a man murmured a prayer or put up a hand to grasp his rosary… At last the bombardment ceased, the word came and the leading platoon dashed forward with a yell like hounds breaking covert.[8]

No man stopped save the dead and crippled. With levelled bayonets they raced forward as they 'vied with each other which should reach the objective first'.[9] 2/Lt. T.W.G. Johnson, an association football amateur international, had the distinction of being first into the enemy, where he killed six Turks with his bayonet before his men joined him. (He was later awarded the Military Cross.)[10] True to their reputation for stubborn bravery, the Turkish infantry stood fast and fought well, but were finally overwhelmed. The entire trench system guarding the wells, together with a communication trench to Hill 60, fell in the whirlwind charge.

The CO of the Rangers, who throughout led his men 'finely', followed the assault companies with his HQ staff; behind him were B and A Companies. Of battalion headquarters only Jourdain and Pte. Tuite came through unscathed. The CO's orderly, Pte. Michael Judge of Ballina, was shot in the face at a range of three yards.[11] It was a measure of how well the Turks stood to receive the charge.

The success of the Rangers' attack affected other parts of the line. 5th Gurkhas on the left followed the Rangers when the wells and part of Hill 60 were taken. On the right of the Rangers, the New Zealand attack was making poor progress against stubborn defenders on Hill 60. The crest was ringed with trenches. The foremost on the edge of the slope had a perfect field of fire and was supported by those behind. Well sited in dense prickly scrub, these positions were concealed from attackers. Realising its importance to the British, 'the Turkish command had heavily fortified it for defence to an extent not appreciated by the British commanders'.[12] Hardly surprising, therefore, the attack made such little progress. Acting in response to the tactical situation, Jourdain decided to help the attack on Hill 60 from his position.

Allowing his men only a breather at the wells, Jourdain ordered one company to attack the western side of the hill. Men from other companies, filled with battle-madness, could not be restrained and went forward also. Led by their surviving officers, the Irish line surged up the bare slope in full view of IX Corps at Suvla and the troops at Anzac. Their Turkish enemy met them with a blast of rifle and machine-gun fire. Under this blizzard the Rangers suffered severely. Bodies on the slope, in sight of their comrades below, were in ordered ranks facing the enemy, and could be thought to be taking cover except for their stillness.

While the main body of the Rangers closed in on the wells, the survivors on Hill 60 entrenched on the captured position and attempted to keep down the enemy fire. Not a man of the assault troops retired from his position. Indeed some penetrated into the Turkish positions. Most were killed and six were taken prisoner, the only prisoners captured from the Connaught Rangers at Gallipoli. The little groups on the hill made attempts to contact the New Zealanders on the other side of the hill, and a sap in that direction was begun.

At 1645, Brig. Russell ordered the Australians and Hampshires to push forward on their right. He asked the Rangers to assist the New Zealanders on the other flank, an action which CO Rangers had already put in motion. The Australians and Hampshire men made one more gallant attempt, but met such fierce fire their efforts failed and were not resumed until after sunset. Just after 1700 hours, 5th Gurkhas, unable to advance earlier, came up and took over the extreme left flank including a sunken road to Anafarta. Gen. Godley sent his congratulations at once:

> Personally, as an Irishman who has served in two Irish Regiments, it gives me the greatest pride and pleasure that the Regiment should have performed such gallant deeds under my command.[13]

Enemy artillery bombarded the wells and took a heavy toll until the Rangers were able to dig in. Nevertheless before nightfall, the positions around the wells were secure. Every effort was made to supply the men that night. Ammunition, food and water came up as soon as darkness fell. By daylight the whole area was in a good state of defence, well supplied with ammunition, food and water. But on the hill that night a desperate struggle took place. The remnant of A Company joined the New Zealanders and fought the enemy in the darkness. The Turks kept up a hail of bombs, interspaced with bayonet charges in fierce counter-attacks to regain their positions. Lt. Blake was killed; the platoon sergeant, Nealon, led a mixed force of Irish and New Zealanders to an abandoned trench and held it until relieved. Sgt. John O'Connell, an Irish-American who returned for the war, went out under heavy fire to bring in a wounded New Zealander. For this and his extraordinary courage throughout the action, he was awarded the DCM.[14]

Next night, the Rangers were relieved by the 18th Australian Infantry battalion and concentrated in South Wales Borderers Gully. Later they were visited there by Gens. Birdwood, Godley and Cox. Gen. Birdwood congratulated the Rangers on their gallantry. But the praise had been won at heavy cost; eighty-seven all ranks were killed and 159 wounded, including the RSM. Six Rangers had been taken prisoner.

Months later, a party of convalescing Australians was being shown around the House of Commons. Approaching them, Mr John Redmond MP asked them if they had come across any of the 10th Irish Division. He was told by them of the charge of the Connaught Rangers at Kabak Kuyu, which was described to him as the finest they had ever witnessed.[15]

But Hill 60 still remained to be taken. Gen. Birdwood decided it should be assaulted again on 27 August with Brig. Russell in command. The attacking force was to consist of

> 350 Australians—right attack against enemy trenches at the base of the hill; 300 New Zealanders and 100 Australians—centre attack on hill itself; 250 Connaught Rangers—left attack against the trench system from the crest of the hill northwards towards Anafarta village.

Because of the shattered condition of all units at Anzac, it had become necessary to stipulate numbers rather than battalions or brigades. The strength of the 5th Connaught Rangers after three weeks in action had been reduced to seven officers and 300 men, of whom half were suffering from diarrhoea and enteritis.

An hour before Zero, the Rangers were on the start line and a bombardment lasting an hour began at 1600. The instant it stopped, the stormers were over the top led by Lt. S.H. Lewis, and gained the enemy trenches with little loss. The support lines were less fortunate. In the interval, the Turks rushed to their positions and shot down whole sections of the support company as they cleared the parapet.

Although isolated, Lt. Lewis and his party did not wait for support. They fought their way along the 500-yard-long Turkish trench system. Half full of dead enemy, the Turkish survivors disputed every yard with great determination. As the stormers advanced, more Rangers succeeded in pushing forward, until all 250 had cleared the start trench. With this added weight, the stormers fought their way through the Turkish trenches towards the objective. Impeded in the narrow trench by dead Turks and debris, some Rangers impetuously climbed out and advanced on each side in the open, ignoring enemy riflemen hidden in the bush. Most Turks held their positions with dour resolution. They would not surrender and died where they stood in close-quarter, brutal fighting. The objective was taken at 1730 and by nightfall the objective was secured.[16]

The Australians on the right had been held up by concentrated machine-gun fire and made no progress in spite of great gallantry which cost them heavily. But opposite the New Zealand troops, the bombardment had been more effective in reducing the Turkish positions. The moment the bombardment stopped, the New Zealanders rose and went straight for the top of the hill and carried all the known trenches south of the crest. Over the crest was a shallow trench choked with Turkish dead and wounded, and fierce fire from a support trench halted the attackers. Nevertheless, a few New Zealanders worked their way along the hill and joined up with the Rangers. At nightfall, the whole south face of Hill 60 was in Allied hands. Now the Turkish counter-attack began, and wave after wave was hurled forward. The remainder of the Rangers were sent forward to reinforce their comrades, all forty-seven, weakened by illness.[17] Again and again the Turks attacked, mad with religious fanaticism shouting 'Allah, Allah, voor, voor'. When the Turkish attacks stopped, the bombing continued; trenches were a tangled chaos filled with dead. Every Ranger officer was either dead or wounded. Lt. Lewis, who had led the attack, was wounded in two places, an elbow and a knee. Despite his agony, he ordered himself lifted up to direct the last defence. After five hours' fighting, at 2230 hours, a body of Turks forced a way into the Rangers' trench held by Lewis's devoted little band. All died defending it. The enemy was held and the battle developed into fire-fights and bombing. The Rangers, fewer now and with ammunition running out, were in desperate straits. No more local supports were available. At midnight the exhausted remnant of Rangers at the northern extremity of the captured line blocked the trench and fell back to the southern end. At 0330, the 9th Australian Light Horse arrived just too late. Nevertheless they attacked this northern part of the trench but found the Turks too strong. The Turkish losses were estimated to have been 5000, almost all at close quarters. When the New Zealanders eventually took this part of the trench in a combined attack, nearly 60,000 rounds of ammunition, three machine-guns and three trench-mortars were taken. The entire attack force had barely reached 1000 men. At the end of the action, the Connaught Rangers had less than 100 men unwounded; almost all of these had some form of gastric complaint. Lt.-Col. Jourdain was awarded a CMG.

> On the left, 250 men of 5th Connaught Rangers excited admiration of all beholders by the swiftness and cohesion of their charge. In five minutes they had carried their objective, the northern Turkish communication trench. At once there began a lively bomb fight against strong parties which came hurrying up from the enemy supports and reserves. At midnight fresh troops were to have strengthened the grip on the hill, but by that time the Irishmen had been out-bombed.[18]

Sadly, little was known outside Gallipoli of the very gallant exploits of the 5th Connaught Rangers. Gen. Hamilton's despatches had told nothing of their capture of Kabak Kuyu wells and had credited 29 Indian Brigade with more than they had in fact accomplished. In his diary Hamilton wrote:

> The Indian Brigade have seized the well at Kabak Kuyu and that fine soldier, Russell, fixed himself into Kaiajik Aghala and is holding on there tooth and nail. There was fighting going on there at the moment but Russell is confident... The success of old Cox's is worth anything. The well alone, I suppose, might be valued at twenty or thirty thousand a year seeing it gives us beautiful spring water in free gift from Mother Earth instead of the very dubious fluid conveyed at God only knows what cost from the Nile to Anzac Cove... Turns out that Cox and Russell did even better than Birdwood had thought in the fight on the 21st and the morning of the 22nd. They have killed more Turks and the line held runs well out to the north-east and quite a way to the north of Kaiajik Aghala.[19]

When Hamilton's despatches were published in January 1916, Col. Jourdain, with understandable indignation but commendable reticence, wrote to Gen. Godley asking him to rectify the error. Godley replied and enclosed a copy of his letter to the Military Secretary MEF.

Headquarters
2nd Australian and New Zealand Army Corps.
Ismailia 20th April 1916.

My Dear Jourdain,
I am very glad you wrote to me about the taking of Kaiajik Aghala. I had noticed it myself, but as later on your battalion was so favourably mentioned, I had not thought it necessary to draw attention to the obvious mistake, but you are perfectly right, and I enclose copy of a letter which I have written on the subject, which may lead to the necessary alteration being made.
I thank you very much for your very kind congratulations. In return I am very glad to be able to congratulate you. I should be proud if I have a Battalion of your Regiment serving under me again.
Yours very sincerely,
(Sd) Alex Godley

Lieut-Colonel H.F.N. Jourdain, C.M.G.
The Connaught Rangers.

Memorandum for
The Military Secretary
Mediterranean Expeditionary Force

I enclose herewith a letter from Lieut-Colonel Jourdain, who commanded the 5th Battalion Connaught Rangers at the attack on the Kaiajik Aghala in August last. His contention is correct, and I should be glad if the necessary correction may be made. If, in the last two lines of page 44 of the Despatch as published in pamphlet form, the words 'Connaught Rangers' were substituted for 'Indian Brigade', the matter would be put right.

(Sd) Alex Godley,

Lieut-General.
Late Commanding
New Zealand and
Australian Divisions.[20]

THE END AT GALLIPOLI

The attacks on Scimitar Hill and Hill 60 were virtually the end of the offensive operations at Gallipoli. From August onwards, the Allies were content to hold their positions. Following the failure of the attack for Kiretch Tepe Sirt, the remnants of 10th Division's troops, both at Suvla and Anzac, settled down to the monotonous tedium of line duty and fatigues, of which the most hated was the unloading of stores from the stifling holds of lighters. Enemy shell-fire was constant and no place at Gallipoli was safe. Drawing rations was considered one of the most dangerous jobs, involving a long trek over exposed ground. Swimming in the blue waters of the Aegean was highly popular; it was the one opportunity to cool off and be clean, free of sweat and dust.

Brig. Hill was invalided with dysentery and his place was taken by Col. King-King of the divisional staff. Poor diet began to tell on the general health of the troops. Apart from prevalent diarrhoea, multiple boils were common. A high proportion were on medical 'light duties', which in essence made little difference to their daily lives. Adding rice to the diet improved it. Originally brought for Indian troops, there was now a surplus because of their high casualties. Cooked with water instead of milk, the rice was less palatable to troops accustomed to rice pudding, but as an alternative to heat-liquidised bully-beef it proved invaluable. At the beginning of September, the divisional artillery arrived at last. They had been sent to Cairo; unfortunately they had no further connection with the 10th. One brigade went to Helles, one to Suvla, but not under the 10th. By this time the Turks were content to hold their positions.

Since arriving on 7 August, 5th Royal Irish, mostly miners and artisans, had been employed in the defence of the headquarters area and on construction work on the beachhead. From time to time they had been called into the line to fill gaps during the crisis of the first two weeks. When these calls came they had responded eagerly, but they too had suffered battle casualties. Of the officers Maj. Fulda, Capt. Morel and six subalterns were wounded and Lts. Costello and MacAndrew and many rank and file were killed in action.

In September, reinforcements arrived from Ireland. The recovered wounded from the French battles comprising some regimental drafts were particularly welcome as they included excellent battle-hardened regular soldiers. Most of these were perforce sent to the regular battalions of the Irish regiments with the 29th Division, but some found their way to the 10th.[21] Often a draft would be larger than the battalion it relieved. When this occurred, the old hands felt they were being swamped by the new arrivals. Most of the battalions had lost their machine-gunners and signallers; few of these came with the replacements. On-the-job training had to be carried out by the senior specialists of the battalions, an unwelcome, time consuming, inefficient chore on active service. It was the same with the officers, since it was rare to find a battalion where both the machine-gun officer and the signals officer had survived. Usually, if they had, then the adjutant probably had not.[22]

THE EVALUATION

With typical understatement, the official historian says: 'It can be no matter for surprise if he [Gen. Mahon] felt… that neither he nor his division had been given a fair chance.'[23] After the initial limited gains by 11th Division on 6–7 August 1915, all advances on Day One were made by 10th Division. Deployment of 29 Brigade at Kiretch Tepe Sirt on 8 August, when reserves were desperately needed to maintain momentum, could have been decisive. Its fighting qualities were well proven; the counter-charge of 6th Leinsters on Rhododendron Spur and the charge of 5th Connaught Rangers at Kabak Kuyu wells showed the excellence of its offensive spirit. The dour stand of 10th Hampshires and 6th Irish Rifles at the 'Farm', in which Brig.-Gen. R.J. Cooper and all the officers of 29 Brigade Headquarters became casualties, gives testimony to its resolute steadiness in defence. Whatever the reasons for sending this brigade to Anzac, even if it appeared they were for sound military ones, it was a grave error of enormous consequence. The main Turkish ammunition depot for Gallipoli was at Ak Bashi. Had Kiretch Tepe Sirt been taken and Ak Bashi exposed, its capture would have meant defeat for the Turks.[24] This was the worst fear of Marshal von Sanders, which is why he was present there encouraging his soldiers on 15 August. Almost at the same time, Gen. Hamilton was at Imbros, throwing IX Corps' command structure into confusion, unaware that a crucial battle was taking place. This epitomises the fundamental grasp of situation and style of each commander.

There is reason for conjecture on the necessity for deploying 29 Brigade to Anzac. In Gen. Birdwood's correspondence, a letter he wrote to Col. Fitzgerald (Lord Kitchener's Military Secretary and an old friend) dated 10

August, gave a detailed account of the battle, knowing it would be relayed to Kitchener. In it, Birdwood tells of the critical water shortage and reveals:

> On the 5th I was almost on the point of wiring to say not only could I not receive reinforcements, but must contemplate sending off some of my troops.[25]

The 29 Brigade was not in action at Anzac until 9–10 August, by which time Birdwood had hoped Sari Bair would have been captured. Had it been at Suvla, Kiretch Tepe Sirt would probably have been taken on the 7th or 8th and von Sanders' worst fears realised. He would have been compelled to reinforce his Suvla front at the expense of Anzac. Mustafa Kemal would probably not have been present to deliver his devastating attack on 11 August. The possibilities are easy to see.

Even with post-event wisdom, it remains difficult to understand why 10th Division was divided; reasons other than operational ones must be sought. Personality clashes between commanders are as old as war. During the South African conflict, the dispute between the followers of Buller and Roberts, the senior British commanders, was bitter and public. It caused deep division within the army and Hamilton was involved. Ian Hamilton's courage and intellectual ability were beyond question, but he appears to have been highly partisan, not to say unscrupulous, in his loyalties. It is alleged that his vindictive whispering campaign in South Africa brought down Redvers Buller, to Lord Roberts' advantage.[26] For these reasons, his treatment of Gen. Mahon has to be examined.

Hamilton's indecision as a commander has long been accepted and criticised. What is not so readily apparent is professional jealousy. In South Africa, Mahon's relief of Mafeking had made him an Empire hero. Hamilton's failure to cut off Christian de Wet's Boer commando at Olifant's Nek infuriated Kitchener; his career was saved only by the intervention of Lord Roberts.[27] The operation at Suvla was to be decisive and Hamilton was determined it should be his victory, with no dashing intervention by Mahon to steal the limelight. If this was a possibility, Mahon's wings could be clipped by detaching one of his brigades to Anzac, even if it reduced the effectiveness of 10th Division at Suvla.

Mahon had tea with Gen. Hamilton at Imbros shortly after joining Hamilton's force. Mahon told him 'either he should be given a Corps or his Lieut-General's rank should be reverted to that of Major-General.' Hamilton agreed with him.[28] With or without foundation, among the senior officers of 10th Division it was rumoured that Mahon was to have command of a Corps.[29] Although there appears to have been no open friction between Mahon and Hamilton, undoubtedly Mahon was unwelcome at the Dardanelles and Hamilton tried to prevent his coming. Moreover in his letters from Imbros, Sir Ian informed Kitchener that Mahon, with five battalions, had failed to take Kiretch Tepe Sirt held 'by *only* 500 Turks.'[30]

Having failed to prevent his arrival, on one hand Hamilton kept Mahon sweet with promises; on the other he sought to undermine his position by dividing his command and reporting unfavourably on him to London.

One part of Lord Granard's letter of 15 August is of particular significance: 'Owing to General Hamilton's action, we have not the number of troops necessary for an advance.'[31] This possibly refers to the deployment of 29 Brigade to Anzac.

Some military commentators have assumed that Mahon, on learning both that Stopford had been sacked and that de Lisle had been given command of IX Corps, resigned and was sent by Gen. Hamilton to Imbros to 'cool his heels'.[32] Lord Granard, in letters to his wife, casts doubt on this account. According to him, Mahon was sacked at the same time as Stopford and Hammersley. Restored to command on Kitchener's order, Mahon refused to serve under de Lisle, then resigned, but later changed his mind. What is certain is that Maj.-Gen. W.E. Peyton assumed command of 10th Division from 19–23 August.[33]

Lord Granard wrote in an undated letter, probably 15 August: 'I am sorry to tell you that General Mahon leaves the Division tomorrow for England. I cannot tell you what I think of the way he has been treated.'[34]

On 16 August he wrote again: 'De Lisle has just been put over Mahon's head and he has just resigned. I shall probably do the same as the treatment accorded to him and his 10th Division makes it impossible for me to stay on. Mahon was asked to serve on by de Lisle but he refused.'[35]

On 25 August, Lord Granard again wrote on the subject:

> You will be glad to hear that General Mahon, who had been ordered home by General Hamilton, has been put back in command of his division by Lord Kitchener. Everybody is delighted.[36]

Whatever happened, it is apparent that considerable indignation existed in 10th Division at the treatment of Mahon and his division, which is hardly surprising. Fragmented, the 10th was destroyed piecemeal to little purpose; concentrated at Suvla, it might have changed the course of history. Unlike 16th and 36th Divisions later, on the Somme and at Messines, 10th Division received little recognition for its valour and sacrifice. Yet, at that time, the survivors of the Irish battalions had feelings of deep pride in their achievements. One officer of 7th Dublins proclaimed: 'I am proud to be Irish; Ireland may mourn, but the Irish may hold up their heads and be proud of their Tommys.'[37]

Killed in Action and Died of Wounds at Gallipoli (not including officers) Mainly in the period 7–16 August 1915.

10th Division	2017 —mainly during 7–16 August 1915		
1st Inniskillings	428	1st Munster 397	1st Dublins 569
Total	3411		

CHAPTER FOURTEEN

The Battle of Loos,
25 September–15 October 1915

The 2nd Battle of Ypres flickered and died out, but British Second Army continued to endure a daily grinding in the Salient. Although the Irish battalions moved from sector to sector as the situation dictated, there was no relief from the constant battle of attrition. At the end of May 1915, with the arrival of the first complete formations of the New Army and Territorial Army, a system of 'roulement' began. By this, divisions were moved into the Salient where they would serve for a time before moving to quieter sectors. Until almost the end of the war, the Salient bore a fearsome reputation for slaughter. Because of their early service there, many places were named for an Irish connection. 'Irish Farms' proliferated; 'Birr Crossroads' is close to 'Leinster Farm'. After the war, some names became associated with British Commonwealth War Cemeteries, ensuring they would endure in perpetuity.

The move of 27th Division at the end of May to trenches north of Houplines in the Armentières sector was welcomed by 1st Royal Irish, 2nd Irish Fusiliers and 1st Leinsters. The trenches were excellent, dry and clean. It was a star sector of the British front. Politicians and other civilian visitors who wanted to see conditions at the Front were directed here by a public-relations-conscious GHQ. The Saxon troops opposite, although doughty fighters when necessary, were also happy to live and let live given the opportunity. However the divisional commander, Gen. Milne, declared it was his intention to make the enemy exclaim: 'Gott straff the 27th Division'.[1] The Irish, after Ypres and the loss of so many comrades, were 'looking for some of their own back',[2] unlike the 'live and let live' practised by the French army on their sectors.

> The thrifty French held the trench line on the 'Live and let live' principle as far as possible; the motto of the prodigal British was usually 'Kill and be killed'.[3]

The battles of May left many battalions of the BEF weak in officers and men. So critical had the state of reinforcements become that regular cavalry officers and men were drafted into the ranks of infantry battalions. The Irish depots, with fifteen battalions on their way or at Gallipoli, were stretched to keep their thirteen battalions in the BEF up to strength. At unit level, the laborious task of reconstructing the shattered units began. It was a time when the surviving regular warrant officers and NCOs laboured to pass on the almost extinguished torch of tradition and excellence. Some regular line battalions, such as 2nd Munsters, were lucky to have old regular army stalwarts who would somehow survive and become famous such as RSM John Ring. His battalion had been destroyed several times and its 'esprit de corps almost crushed out of existence,'[4] so Ring had to labour long and hard to revive its spirit.

Many regular warrant officers and NCOs were commissioned and although for a time this weakened the middle rank structure of discipline, the officers commissioned in this way did remarkably well. One, Sgt.-Maj. Joseph Frederick Plunkett DCM, Royal Irish Regiment, was commissioned into the Royal Dublin Fusiliers. He became a lieutenant-colonel, commanding a battalion of Royal Inniskilling Fusiliers, and won a DSO, MC and French Croix de Guerre avec Étoile en Vermeil; to his brigade commander he was 'good old Plunkett'.[5]

It would have served the BEF well to have waited until the New Armies were fully trained, and industrial capacity fully mobilised and harnessed to the needs of the new concept of war, as suggested by Smith-Dorrien. However the commander-in-chief was dominated and influenced by Foch on the one hand and Henry Wilson on the other. Foch never wavered, from the beginning of the war to its end, in his belief in the offensive *à outrance*. Wilson was an obedient disciple and his influence upon Sir John French outweighed that of his Chief of Staff, Sir William Robertson and his army commanders.[6]

The Army Ordnance Department, severely constrained by the Treasury in peace-time, took some time to shake off its old habits of contracting. Despite failure by manufacturers to meet contractual obligations, production levels rose to heights hitherto undreamt of by the British army. However, a second front at Gallipoli raised demands to unsupportable levels and all through the summer of 1915, ammunition stocks in France were never up to establishment.[7] Arms production was generally unsatisfactory, because the War Office found difficulty in shaking off peace-time procurement practices; production delays ensued.[8] Not until the formation of a ministry charged with overseeing war production, headed by David Lloyd George, was demand fully met. And only then because: 'the Chancellor of the Exchequer became lord-paramount of a great spending Department of State; its chief was on velvet... "Copper" ... turned footpad, he knew the ropes, he could flout the Treasury—and he did.'[9]

After the opening battles, the year 1915 was the most dangerous period for the Allies. Fortunately, the Central Powers failed to take advantage of their strength and Allied weakness; instead they turned away from the Western Front towards Russia and the Balkans. The preoccupation of the British government with the Near and Middle East, to the apparent neglect of his own front, caused grave concern to Sir John French, even though New Army divisions were arriving in France in increasing numbers. By the end of the summer, there were twenty-eight British, Canadian and Indian divisions on the Western Front, and the Guards Division was in the course of formation. Sir Henry Wilson was offered command of a corps but refused, preferring to remain chief liaison officer with the French.[10]

The Guards Division was formed in August 1915, and to it went the first Irish New Army battalion to reach the Western Front, 2nd Irish Guards. It had been formed in July of that year and was commanded by Lt.-Col. the Earl of Kerry MVO DSO. Lt.-Col. the Hon. L.J.P. Butler assumed command just before the battalion left for the Front. Although the Guardsmen were essentially Irish, most officers were not; some came from overseas as Special Reserve officers. Others were the sons of notables, and included 2/Lt. John Kipling, son of the poet Rudyard Kipling, and Lt. William Redmond, son of the Irish Nationalist Party leader. The battalion left for France in mid August after inspection by its Regimental Colonel, FM Lord Kitchener, but such ordeals paled into insignificance when they found themselves drilling under the critical gaze of their 1st Battalion. Father Simon Knapp OP joined the battalion at the end of August and was soon loved by all ranks.[11]

BATTLE OF LOOS, 25 SEPTEMBER

In June 1915, planning had begun for a major Allied offensive which was to eliminate the great German-occupied salient which ran from Verdun to the channel coast and bulged deep into the industrial heartland of France. In addition to the loss of production in this area it was, understandably, of deep emotional concern to the French. Joffre won Kitchener's support for the offensive and Kitchener ordered Sir John French to take part.[12] Gen. Joffre intended attacking the region on its southern face, northwards from Champagne and eastwards from Artois. He demanded British co-operation and selected the time and place of their attack, neither of which suited either Sir John French or Sir Douglas Haig, whose First Army would be responsible. The offensive eastwards from Artois, using Haig's First British Army and Foch's Army Group North, was to be the main Allied effort. Tenth French Army was to begin its attack by capturing Vimy ridge. So ambitious was the project that Joffre aimed at nothing less than the destruction of three German armies.

From the limited options for First Army's area of operation, Sir John French chose the Lens area, from the junction with Tenth Army to the La Bassée canal, in the Loos-Hulloch sector. Gen. Haig, following a personal reconnaissance, declared it was not favourable for an attack. The enemy defences in open country were so strong that it would require substantially more artillery to reduce them by siege methods. He pointed out that the Germans still had artillery superiority; the ground was so open and under so much enemy observation that concentrating troops for an attack would be difficult. Haig was not against attacking and showed this by submitting alternative proposals. However his main fears were shortage of heavy artillery and shortage of ammunition for all guns.[13]

First Army's I and IV Corps were to attack on a six division frontage between Loos and La Bassée. It was to be supported by the greatest artillery mass which could be mustered by borrowing from Second Army. A division on each flank, 47th London on the right and 2nd Regular on the left, was to attack on a limited objective and act as both flank guard and pivot. The main assault was to be launched by four divisions; from the right 15th Scottish, 1st and 7th Regular and 9th Scottish Divisions. Attacking under cover of chlorine gas and smoke cloud, their mission was to break through the German first and second defensive systems between Loos and Haisnes. Behind in GHQ reserve was XI Corps, containing the Guards Division and two New Army divisions, the 21st and 24th. Subsidiary attacks were to be carried out elsewhere on the First Army front and by Second Army as far north as the Ypres salient. Joffre intended capturing the industrial town of Lens and its surrounding mining area by envelopment, the British coming from the north and Tenth Army from the south. Once the German defences were broken, Joffre planned rapid exploitation. On the British front, three cavalry divisions would pour through. The French had prepared a cavalry mass together with lorry-borne infantry to follow their break-in. A bombardment of four days' duration was to precede the attack, rising to great intensity in the final hour. But the heavy guns were each limited to ninety rounds a day and the field artillery to 150 rounds.[14] Unfortunately the bombardment had little effect on the German trenches and only succeeded in cutting some lanes through massed wire; German infantry in deep dug-outs suffered slight losses.

THE BATTLE OF LOOS, 25 SEPTEMBER–10 OCTOBER 1915

On the morning of 25 September the Allied gas taps were opened at 0550, but only on the left did gas roll down on the German line. Forty minutes later, at 0630, the British attack began.

On the right, 1st/18th London Irish Rifles led 47th London Division. In high spirits, the London Irish dribbled a football towards the German lines and within minutes gained them after a stout bayonet fight. According to plan, the second waves of 140 and 141 Brigades went through.[15]

15th Scottish carried all before it and captured the defences of Loos. It then went through the village, by-passed Hill 70 on the Lens road and went beyond it. In the confusion, however, they drifted southwards, leaving the Chalk Pits uncovered.

Two brigades of 1st Division were to attack Hulluch astride the Vermelles-Hulluch road. In support was 3 Brigade (2nd Munsters). On the right, Lone Tree sector (from a single shot-torn cherry tree) 2 Brigade was held up. The gas which failed to blow over the rising ground rolled back on the British trenches and affected both the assault troops and the gas section; no advance was made. By the time the second wave went through, the German trench garrison had been reinforced. Moreover, the wire and trenches had been untouched by the bombardment. These trenches, holding out to midday, secured Hulluch's defence.

On the left, 1 Brigade had succeeded in getting almost to Hulluch; a few actually got into the village but were evicted. By evening, 1st and 7th Divisions had reached the Lens-La Bassée road. 9th Scottish captured the Hohenzollern Redoubt and broke into the German second line in front of Haisnes. 2nd Division failed completely and were obliged to return to their trenches.

When 2 Brigade's attack failed, the Munsters, supported by 2nd Welch Regiment, were ordered to advance in that sector already captured by 1 Brigade (north of Bois Carré). Having crossed the German lines, they were to roll up the flank of the Germans holding up 2 Brigade.[16]

The divisional commander evidently intended supporting the successful attack of 1 Brigade while at the same time outflanking and breaking down the solid defence opposing 2 Brigade. The Munsters, barely 250 strong under Maj. A. Gorham, attempted to advance along trenches choked with gassed and wounded men going to the rear. Finding it impossible, Gorham gave the order to get out of the trench and advance in the open although it was under fire. The two leading companies received the order and followed him. The succeeding two companies, under Maj. Considine, evidently did not get the order and the two wings became separated.

Maj. Considine led his two companies into the Lone Tree sector and attacked the unbroken German line opposite 2 Brigade. Into this inferno of a failed brigade attack, Considine led his two under-strength Munster companies, attacking an entrenched position garrisoned by a German battalion which up to that time had defied a brigade. Across open country, the Munster Fusiliers moved by alternate waves. When crossing the British front line, the occupants cheered them on. In no man's land, men fell at every yard. They passed Lone Tree and came up to the unbroken German wire. Struggling to get through, man after man fell and hung on the wire or lay beneath. It was a futile slaughter, and the remaining officer, 2/Lt. B.D. Conran, ordered the handful of survivors back.[17] Almost annihilated, their casualties were 118 killed and wounded. It was an heroic attempt but a complete waste of gallant men.

The attack of 1 Brigade had been successful and Maj. Gorham led his wing of 2nd Munsters, barely 125 strong, to occupy the empty British front line trenches with little loss. Advancing into the captured German trenches and making use of a communication trench, the Munsters gained a position about 300 yards from Hulluch. Since Mons, successive battles of destruction had destroyed their best officers, so this surely must have been the nadir of the leadership of 2nd Munster for which their renowned valour could not compensate. It was left to the 2nd Welch Regiment, advancing behind Gorham's Munsters, to surround and capture the Germans who had held up the morning's advance and cost 1st Division over 2,500 casualties.[18]

The results of the first day's fighting had largely been successful, although optimistic French expectations had not been realised. The German first lines had been completely broken and the New Army divisions had proved their fighting worth. However, only by maintaining a vigorous offensive could the German second line be broken. It was time for Gen. Haig to commit his reserves, but they were not readily to hand. Sir John French's decision to retain control of XI Corps is inexplicable. Since it could only have been used on the First Army front, it ought to have been under Gen. Haig's command from the outset. 21st and 24th Divisions were released on the 25th, but FM French still retained control of the Guards.

The roads behind the Front were in chaos, principally caused by massed cavalry waiting to exploit the breakthrough. The artillery of the reserve divisions, who could not reach their positions, were caught in the open by German counter-battery fire and suffered heavy loss. The 21st and 24th Divisions attacked unsupported and with only half their strength. It became a scene as horrific as the worst shambles at Gallipoli. Caught by fire from untaken positions on both flanks and defilade fire from positions to their front, the two unfortunate New Army divisions suffered over four thousand casualties each; with most officers dead, their units practically disintegrated.[19]

Late that afternoon, the Guards Division arrived but could do nothing to retrieve the failure. The best they could do was relieve the shattered 21st and 24th Divisions. 2nd Guards Brigade, with 2nd Irish Guards, took over the front along the edge of the Loos–La Bassée road, on its right the Scots Guards and on the left 1 Guards Brigade. To secure the newly won positions, Lord Cavan was ordered to capture the Chalk Pits, Puits No. 14 bis and Hill 70. 2nd Irish Guards were to lead the assault at 1600 and capture Chalk Pit. When the Pit was secured, 1st Scots Guards were to attack 14 bis covered by rifle and machine-gun fire provided by the Irish.

Under cover of smoke, the Irish Guards reached the western edge of Chalk Pit Wood and the Chalk Pit with few casualties. This accomplished, the Scots doubled forward under shell-fire and reached the Loos-Hulluch road without loss. Crossing the road, they descended the slope and were joined by two companies of Irish. Together the Scots and Irish stormed forward against the withering machine-gun fire from Bois Hugo and the Puits. Few reached the Puits. Those who did managed to establish themselves after savage hand-to-hand fighting, but so intense was the fire between the Chalk Pit and the bis that they could not be reinforced. The Irish in the Chalk Pit were relieved by the Coldstreams, allowing them to concentrate on holding Chalk Pit Wood. Lord Cavan knew that with 14 bis untaken, the assault on Hill 70 was hopeless; he had made it a condition of the assault on Hill 70. Despite this injunction, the attack went ahead and failed. Late that night, the detachment of Scots in the Puits withdrew and the Scots Guards formed a line running southward from Chalk Pit Wood to Loos.[20] During the battle, 2nd Irish Guards suffered heavily in its baptism of fire and had 324 casualties, of whom 146 all ranks were killed or died of wounds.[21]

It had been the intention of the German High Command to use their Guard Corps in a counter-attack to recover Loos on 27 September. Instead, they were forced to use their corps d'élite to hold Vimy ridge. Not until 8 October could the Germans mount the intended counterstroke against the British. Then, after a four-hour bombardment of great intensity, the Germans struck the British front against 1st Division held by 2nd Munsters on the right, 1st Gloucesters in the centre and 1st/9th King's Regiment on the left. The main weight of the attack delivered in massed formation was centred on the Gloucesters and King's, and was finally stopped about forty yards from the British trenches. Against the Munsters, the Germans issued from Puits 14 bis in extended order, but were stopped almost at once by fire from the Munsters. Firing continued until the German survivors reached the safety of their own trenches.[22]

Four days later, the Guards Division began a bombing operation opposite the Hohenzollern Redoubt. What made this different was the first massed use of the British Mills grenade; 8000 had been delivered to the Guards. But even this innovation was not enough during the intense fighting from 13–16 October, which did nothing to improve the position of the British and only resulted in 'useless slaughter of infantrymen'.[23] Although Haig persevered with his efforts until 4 November, it was practically the end of the battle of Loos, but not of the recriminations. In his report, FM French disguised the time he released the Guards Division to Haig, who indignantly refuted this. By his use of the shell scandal after Festubert which brought down the government, Sir John French lost political support; after Loos he lost the confidence of the government and part of the BEF.

The Guards' divisional artillery and engineers, which until six weeks before had been 16th Division's, won special praise.

> The divisional Artillery, after its baptism of fire, made rapid strides in efficiency, and the close liaison, which was set up from the beginning between the infantry leaders in the line and the gunners responsible for the protection of their troops, helped to bring a mutual understanding between the two arms without which any kind of effective co-operation between them is impossible. The divisional RE, too, did yeoman service both in and out of the line. The construction and maintenance of the defences and communications trenches in a modern battle are tasks which test the courage and endurance of the most seasoned troops...[24]

THE DEPARTURE OF THE REGULARS

Before and during the early stages of the battle, rumours had proliferated throughout the rest of the BEF of an early advance, 'and maps far in advance of their present positions were studied carefully'.[25] After this advance failed to materialise, other rumours of impending moves abounded, until finally 27th Division went into reserve and began to prepare to move to Macedonia. It embarked on a fleet of transports at Marseilles on 26 November, reaching Salonika between 5 and 11 December. With 27th Division went 1st Royal Irish, 2nd Royal Irish Fusiliers and 1st Leinsters.

The Indian Corps also moved. The India Office was anxious not to let Indian troops endure another winter on the Western Front; at the same time, events in Mesopotamia had demanded reinforcements. Kitchener, having at first objected, then made a virtue out of necessity and the War Office began moving the Indian Corps thither in early December. The Connaught Rangers embarked at Marseilles, its strength, 24 officers and 813 men. But of the 1000 officers and men who had disembarked at Marseilles just a year earlier, only 242 re-embarked; the rest of the battalion were replacements.[26]

During November 1915, John Redmond MP made a tour of the Western Front visiting the Irish battalions where he was very well received, not least by the army establishment. Corps as well as Divisional commanders accompanied him on his tour. 'John Redmond inspected our battalion late in the year, and everyone—Orangemen as well as Nationalist—gave him a cheer. We buried the hatchet of bigotry during the war.'[27] Redmond's son also won distinction. The citation for his immediate DSO read:

Captain William Archer Redmond. For conspicuous gallantry and devotion to duty who in command of a company holding a line of posts, when, following a heavy barrage, the enemy attacked in strength and a bomb fell on his post, knocking out half the occupants, he immediately led the survivors out and drove the enemy back, which enabled him to establish a new defensive line and to hold it until day broke.[28]

CHAPTER FIFTEEN

Salonika, October–November 1915

By September 1915, Turkish resources became severely strained as a result of Allied pressure on the Turkish army at Gallipoli and Mesopotamia. Its rash and disastrous offensives into the Caucasus Mountains against Russia and against the British in Egypt further compounded its problem. Alarmed, von Sanders advised the German High Command that the Turkish army could not be maintained in the field unless a direct supply route was urgently opened through the Balkans. This could only be achieved by Serbia's defeat. Berlin accepted this advice and planned accordingly for a concomitant political and military operation to achieve both aims.

Bulgaria, bitter from her Second Balkan War defeat (when the victors of the First Balkan War fell out and quarrelled over the spoils of Turkey), felt affronted by the annexation of Macedonia to Serbia and Greece. Biding her time, she trimmed her political sails and demanded the best possible price for her support. The Allies, unable to offer Macedonia, promised Turkish territory after victory. This was rejected by Sofia. Influenced by the failure of Suvla, successive Russian defeats and the nearness of German and Austrian strength, the Bulgarian government signed a military convention with the Central Powers. Conditional upon Bulgaria's entry into the war against Serbia, considerable undertakings were given—a loan of 200 million francs; the annexation of Serbian Macedonia; and restoration of land lost to Greece and Romania in 1913 (in the event of those countries entering the war on the Allied side). Satisfied with this combination of immediate hard cash and future promises, Bulgaria mobilised on 22 September 1915.

Already fighting Austria, Serbia now had to face German troops massing on her northern frontier and Bulgarian mobilisation on her south-eastern border. She appealed to France and Great Britain for help and asked Greece to honour their mutual defensive treaty obligations. Greece agreed, providing the Allies landed 150,000 men as a bulwark against German intervention. France, hoping to draw both Greece and Romania into the Allied camp, agreed to do this. However, in a rare show of unanimity, the British Foreign Office, Admiralty and War Office were against further British involvement in the Balkans. Russia, champion of the Slavic people, pressed the Foreign Office in London to support Serbia and the British gave way. On 25 September, Kitchener signalled Hamilton to prepare one British and two French divisions for Salonika. On 3 October the Greek government asked that Allied troops be sent at once. 10th Division, under the command of Lt.-

Gen. Sir Bryan Mahon, plus one French division and a brigade, were despatched from the Dardanelles. Considering Gen. Hamilton's complaints about his lack of troops, such was the alacrity with which 10th Irish Division was despatched from his command a suspicion arises that Hamilton was glad to see it go, possibly as a way to get shot of its commander.

Unlike the successful German politico-military offensive, Gen. Mahon, for political expediency, was thrust into a situation which took no account of the military requirement. For its success, an overseas operation depends on either long-term contingency planning or time to prepare adequately before the operation is mounted. The haunting memory of the Crimean tragedy may have dimmed, but Gallipoli shines brightly to remind all soldiers of the foolhardiness of rushing ill-prepared into action. Even those troops despatched hurriedly to the South Atlantic in 1982 and the Gulf in 1990–91, notwithstanding possessing the advantages of modern logistics, still required time to reload and position stores tactically, as well as to redeploy and acclimatise troops before engagement.

Of the Macedonia terrain, FM Robertson, Chief of the Imperial General Staff, who had visited the area on a Staff College tour in 1906, declared: 'Of all the countries in Europe, none were more defensively stronger, and therefore none less favourable to an offensive than the Balkan Peninsula'. He was also suspicious of the French motives for involvement: 'I am not at all moved by France sending troops there; that is political intrigue'.[1] The General Staff stated its firm opposition to Balkan operations. The French, they argued, underestimated the difficulties, terrain, number of troops required, and most important, the time necessary to effect the plan.[2] On their part, the Admiralty insisted that insufficient shipping existed to adequately supply more than one overseas operation. Macedonia, or more particularly Salonika, was to prove a quartermaster's and medical officer's nightmare. Gen. Archibald Murray, once of the Inniskilling Fusiliers and one of the army's best administrators, succinctly outlined the logistical problems: port limitations, lack of landing facilities, insufficient railway carrying capacity, poor transport arrangement for troops and equipment.[3] He could also have added atrocious roads into the interior and almost non-existing telegraph and telephone communications throughout the country. It suffered extremes of heat and cold, and was then one of the most unhealthy areas of Europe, particularly the swampy Struma valley which was highly malarial.

On 29 September, 10th Division (less that part of its artillery which had disembarked at Suvla) was ordered to prepare to move from Gallipoli. On the 30th, divisional headquarters, three infantry brigades, field companies, pioneers, cyclist company and field ambulances embarked and reached Mudros on 1 October. By the 2nd, the division was reorganising in camps near Mudros. It was far from being the superb division which had paraded for Kitchener in Hackwood Park. At least 90 per cent of its infantry were dead, wounded or ill, and the major part of its support arms and services were in France, England and Egypt. Its own excellent Divisional Train and

Divisional Ammunition Column had been left at Basingstoke and had to be replaced from that of 13th Division. Part of its regimental transport and equipment had disembarked in Egypt. Artillery consisted of that which could be scraped together—13th Division Artillery Headquarters, 67 and 69 Brigades RFA from Alexandria and its own 54 Brigade from Mudros. However, not a single howitzer battery or mortar, essential for mountain warfare, was included.[4]

Because of the independent nature of its role in a new theatre of operations, various Service detachments were required which were additional to a division's normal establishment. These included an ammunition park, supply column, reserve horse park, field bakeries, field butcheries, ordnance detachment, casualty clearing station, base hospital, base medical store, sanitary section, veterinary hospital—in fact the tail of an army, so often ignored or derided, but without which an army cannot function. All had to come from Mudros, Imbros or Egypt; most went direct to Salonika. The time of their arrival had little bearing on priority of use, since by the unplanned nature of the movement, no priorities of loading could be allocated. Ships arrived at Salonika and unloaded unwanted stores which piled up on the dockside before transport to move them arrived. Essential stores were late in arriving. 500 transport animals arrived from Mudros with few nosebags and no picketing pegs or ropes, indescribable chaos ensued. Drily, the official history comments: 'This gave the army mule one of those opportunities to display his variability of temperament of which he never failed to take advantage.'[5]

As the staff laboured to bring 10th Division up to operational establishment, there was intense activity among the units of the division. Due to heavy casualties and illness, all were weak; recent drafts had brought their average ration strength to 500 all ranks, or about half war establishment. Khaki serge clothing, two blankets per man and tents were issued, but not to all battalions. Because of shortages, some battalions, notably 6th Munsters and 6th Dublins, were not equipped to full clothing scale, especially greatcoats. Beards grown on the peninsula were shaved off,[6] and daily parades and inspections brought a sudden change of appearance to many.

On 4 October, 29 Brigade began to embark for Macedonia. 6th Leinsters led, boarding HMT *Albion*, a small transport which took one closely packed battalion. Departing on the evening of Monday 4 October, they arrived at Salonika the following morning; 6th Irish Rifles were close behind. The remainder of 29 Brigade disembarked at Salonika on the 5th or shortly afterwards; the last, a delayed wing of the Connaught Rangers under Capt. Bryan Cooper, arrived on 10 October. Having landed, 29 Brigade created a British camp five miles from Salonika east of the Serres Road; this was Camp Lembet, near a Greek refugee camp. There the division concentrated and immediately began training. The divisional pioneers, 5th Royal Irish, still commanded by Lord Granard, arrived on 5 October and were attached to 29

Brigade. They set to work at road-making and camp construction. The weather in the eastern Mediterranean was still hot but pleasant to work in and for a time the troops enjoyed the country. However within days the weather changed for the worse and heavy rain turned the tented camps into an uncomfortable morass.

Not all ships' movements went smoothly. Divisional headquarters, the signal company, 30 Brigade headquarters together with 6th and 7th Dublins and a wing of 5th Connaught Rangers crammed into *Aeneas*. The packed vessel became involved in a series of mishaps, delaying their departure for five days. Gen. Mahon disembarked and, going into a destroyer, left for Salonika only to have the ship recalled by wireless. After a further twelve-hour delay, Mahon embarked on another destroyer for the overnight journey. His later interview with the port admiral can be imagined. 31 Brigade arrived on 16 October. One officer of 5th Inniskillings recorded arriving on a misty and dreary morning, 'but the gloom could not entirely conceal the charm of the old city, with its still numerous minarets, rising up the hillside'.[7]

In the move, a most serious loss to operational effectiveness occurred when the troopship *Marquette* was torpedoed on 23 October. Apart from various battalion details, the ship contained 29th Divisional Ammunition Column which had been left in Egypt when that division had embarked for Gallipoli and which was now to join the 10th as replacement for the DAC left in England. Of twenty-two officers and 588 men on board, 130 of these as well as all the animals and equipment were lost. Ten nursing sisters for the New Zealand base hospital were also drowned. The personnel picked up by rescue craft were scattered over a wide area of the Mediterranean and took some time to reassemble. Later, the equipment and animals were made good from Egypt, but the men could not be, and the Brigade Ammunition Columns had to be stripped to find replacements.The Divisional Train, Army Service Corps, upon which a division relies for supply in the field, had also been left in England. It was replaced by that of the 52nd (Lowland) Division. This did not arrive until 22 November. In the meantime, the division managed as best it could. No. 4 Canadian Base Hospital arrived at the end of November, mainly staffed by doctors and nurses from Toronto General Hospital. Fifty years later, they were well remembered by at least one former patient, Sir Thomas Harley, in his memoirs.[8]

While the despatch of the first contingents was going on, political upheaval in Greece brought a confrontation between the pro-Allied Prime Minister, Venizelos, and the pro-German King Constantine, which resulted in the downfall of the Greek government. On their arrival at Salonika the troops of 10th Division were met with mass hostility. Although the movement of the division was allowed to continue, it was decided in London to send no further reinforcements. Instead of 150,000 Allied troops to meet the Bulgarian invasion, there would now be just less than 30,000. At the same time, on 6 October, the Austro-German armies attacked across the

Danube. Faced by gallant Serbian resistance on their own ground in terrain which admirably suited defence, the invaders were checked.

As Mahon and his staff moved the division to its new operational area, preparing to meet whatever demands might he made upon it, politico-military events were occurring in London which were to have profound effects on the course of the campaign. As a result of successive costly failures on the Western Front and at Gallipoli, elements inside and outside the government were clamouring for changes in strategy and command, but they could only agree on the necessity for a change of commanders. Haig replaced French on the Western Front, and Sir Charles Monro, a firm Westerner, relieved Ian Hamilton. After this, Lord Kitchener himself set out to visit the Near East, including Salonika and Athens.

The change of command coincided with Bulgaria's entry into the war on 14 October 1915. With strong forces, they attacked and drove a wedge between the Serbian army and the Allies in Macedonia. Shortly afterwards, Britain and France declared war on Bulgaria, but were unable to agree on their military policy. The French under Gen. Sarrail pushed up the Vardar Valley in an attempt to link with the Serbs. Gen. Mahon, on the other hand, was ordered to remain at Salonika while diplomatic attempts were made to induce Greece to join the Allies. Finally on 22 October Kitchener signalled Gen. Mahon authorising him to co-operate with French attempts to relieve the Serbian army.[9]

One of Gen. Mahon's major initial difficulties was communications. Mahon had only his 10th Divisional Signal Company to maintain command and control of his scattered Brigade HQs and communicate with GHQ MEF and the War Office in London. Only field cable and visual signalling by heliograph were available for communications between headquarters in Salonika and the divisional camp. Because of the non-co-operation of the Greeks, little use could be made of the civil telegraph or telephone in Salonika. The staff's immediate needs were met by constructing line routes with field cables through the streets. Worse, Mahon's staff were unable to communicate directly with either GHQ MEF or War Office, except over the counter at a civil post office, by Eastern Telegraph Company. This continued until, following a visit by the Director of Army Signals Egypt, a new submarine cable between Headquarters Salonika and GHQ Mudros was laid and connected in December 1915. There were severe shortages of communications personnel, stores and equipment which took months to overcome. It is a matter of historical interest how, notwithstanding all these difficulties, the force was able to operate.[10]

Large infantry drafts arrived from the UK and battalion strengths were brought up to near establishment. But a shortage of officers existed because of Gallipoli casualties. Commissioning soldiers from D Company 7th Dublins, that forcing house of excellent junior officers, was to prove successful and no less than over 180 of the Gallipoli survivors and recovered wounded were commissioned to fill vacancies in all the Irish regiments.

Training was an urgent priority and had to be quickly tackled, especially the battalion specialists—signallers, machine-gunners, medical orderlies. Rain continued to fall at Salonika until 22 October, creating a sea of mud and water which did nothing for the morale of the troops. On the 20th, brigade route marches commenced, but the first of these was interrupted by torrents of rain which drenched the men, forcing the battalions to return independently after a roadside dinner. It was a poor start, and it got worse. The weather turned cold, adding to the misery of men already debilitated by their Gallipoli experience. Following a period of route marches, brigade inspections and field days, transport was made up although most wagons and harness needed repairs before use. The problem of assimilating the new drafts into the battalions and creating afresh the corporate regimental spirit had to be dealt with urgently. Each commanding officer dealt with it in his own way. One battalion, the Connaught Rangers, again raised a fife and drum band and this led the battalion on route marches. By hard work the battalions were ready within two weeks to take the field.

On his arrival, Gen. Sarrail ordered forward three battalions, supported by artillery, into Serbia. These took up a position around Strumica Station on 15 October to protect the railway and maintain a link with the Serbs. Shortly afterward, another French regiment was sent to Gevgeli, the first station in Serbia. But without transport, this regiment was tied to a railway of limited capacity, only six small trains daily in either direction up to the Greek frontier, and the Greeks were most unco-operative. The Bulgarians became active and a force of about six battalions, testing Allied strength, attacked Strumica Station and were repulsed. Following up, the French drove the Bulgarians out of Rabrovo, seven miles east of the railway. Sarrail had now secured Serbian communications from the sea to thirty miles up the Vardar Valley. Anxious to do everything possible to aid the Serbians, Sarrail sent a brigade to Krivolak twenty miles south-east of Veles. 'By the 27th, the whole of the French 57th Division had formed a front of fifteen miles between Gradec and Krivolak.'[11] Sarrail, given the numbers available to him, could do no more. Indeed his communications with the advance elements were very tenuous. By the 24th, the Bulgarian Second Army had taken Veles and cut off the main Serbian army from the French. Sarrail now looked to his ally, Gen. Mahon, for support.

Gen. Mahon, although pressed hard by Gen. Sarrail for assistance, was forbidden by the British government to move from Salonika until the 22nd, and even after that was instructed not to cross the frontier. In the meantime, the British build-up continued. By 24 October the bulk of the 10th (400 officers and 13,000 men) had landed at Salonika. With it came 13th Division's Artillery Headquarters and two 18-pounder brigades. Using what he had, by 23 October Mahon had created a mobile force of infantry and support arms under Brig. Nicol, ready to advance into Serbia. To achieve this, transport had to be stripped from 29 Brigade and issued to 30 Brigade. On 29 October, Nicol's force left by train for the frontier. Considering all of Gen. Mahon's difficulties, it was a remarkable achievement. By way of a departure party, the officers of 7th Dublins held a dinner night on 23 October at Salonika's Romeo Hotel. The party ended at 2330 with everyone returning to their units in open GS wagons in pouring rain, which no doubt prepared them for the morrow.[12]

On 3 November a company of 5th Royal Irish was sent to the railhead at Gevgeli and began repairing the road between there and 30 Brigade headquarters at Bogdanci. Such was the awful state of the roads and the need for speed that on the 7th, another company of Pioneers had to be sent to assist.

Nicol wasted no time in relieving the French. Two days after arrival, two battalions relieved the French ones in reserve at Hasanli and Causli, followed next day by another going to Tatarli. Because of poor roads and the scarcity of pack animals, the brigade group was tied to the railway for a time. Bridges were almost non-existent except for railway ones; these had no footways between the traverses to which the rails were fixed. Because of this, transport moved forward with difficulty from the railhead at Gevgeli. Later, when the Greeks became more co-operative, the use of Doiran as railhead eased the problem.

During early November, units of XII Corps began to arrive from France. With the arrival of its staff, Gen. Mahon created an army headquarters at Salonika and was able to release the staff of 10th Division, allowing it to become operational. When 22nd Division came ashore on the 5th, Mahon felt able to send the rest of 10th Division to Serbia. He ordered it forward under the temporary command of Brig. Nicol. 31 Brigade left for the front at the same time as the Divisional Headquarters. But to maintain his essential headquarters communications, Mahon had to retain 10th Signal Company at Salonika until Corps Signals arrived.

Without its own Signal Company, Divisional Headquarters had no means of communicating with Salonika Headquarters except by despatch rider travelling to Doiran and back on the daily train service between Salonika and Constantinople, an enemy capital. Despatches from Division to brigades and battalions were carried by Yeomanry couriers, in almost the same way as gallopers in the Peninsula and Crimea.

However, the arrival of 12th Corps Signal Company relieved the overstretched 10th Divisional Signals allowing it to revert to its original role. It immediately undertook the construction of a cable route along the line of advance of the division, a distance of forty-five miles. The cable link was completed by the third week in November. Suspended from telegraph poles along the line of the railway, it was initially constructed very carefully to reduce maintenance and repair, which would have been difficult. It proved successful, but nevertheless to provide for emergencies, two intermediate detachments were left along its route manned by two operators and two mounted linemen, to inspect the line daily and repair faults. With them were Yeomanry posts to act as relays should the cable be cut. As a matter of technical interest the line was used for both telephony and telegraphy. When Staff officers were not using it for telephoning, the Signal Office connected it to a telegraph signalling device for sending messages by Morse code.[13]

By 12 November, three French divisions had arrived and Sarrail had formed a front resting upon the forks of the rivers Crna and Vardar below Veles (the Crna loop). It was defended by 57th and 122nd Divisions, while 156th Division held a line east of the Vardar facing the Bulgarians in the Strumica Valley. Nicol had two brigades on the right of the French from Lake Doiran to Robrovo and 29 Brigade was on the move to join them. The 6th Leinsters and one company of 6th Irish Rifles marched to the military station and entrained for the Front with the brigadier and his headquarters staff. The last unit of the division to leave Salonika for the front in Serbia was 5th Connaught Rangers. Its departure was in keeping with the rollicking tradition of that splendid regiment. The Rangers marched to the military station on 14 November 1915. On the way they passed the French camp and as they did the drums played 'Killaloe'.

> Ye may talk of Boneyparty. Ye may talk of Decarty.
> Or any party that 'commont tu parley voo'
> We larned to sing it aisy,
> That song the Marshallaisy.

As the battalion marched past the French lines, the drums struck up 'Killaloe' and the 'Marseillaise', which delighted the French troops, who not only cheered and joined in the chorus, but embraced the big drummer in their delight. The two green flags with a huge harp, which were carried by two companies, were received with great ceremony...[14]

Cheers from the Rangers and the French lining the road greeted the demonstration of affection. Service battalions had no Colours until after the war; however two companies carried at their head a green flag with an embroidered harp. To the great joy of the Rangers, the French units gave full military compliments due to regimental Colours to these company standards; all guards turned out and presented arms as they marched past.[15]

In the middle of his operational difficulties, Mahon was suddenly faced with uncertainty about the chain of command, indeed even his own position as Army Commander. Lt.-Gen. Sir H.F.M. Wilson and the staff of the XII Corps landed at Salonika on 12 November. Wilson was junior to Mahon, who, asserting his seniority, assumed command. Two days later, however, orders were received that Gen. Sir Charles Monro was to take over command of the army with the staff of the XII Corps. Monro never did so. This was part of many ploys during Kitchener's tour of the Near East. Kitchener, however, suspecting the government might take advantage of his absence from London to supersede him, had prevented this by taking with him his seals of office.[16]

Kitchener arrived and saw things for himself. He spoke to Mahon and Sarrail and left for Mudros. After Kitchener's inspection of Gallipoli, Monro replaced Hamilton. It was an ironic twist to Hamilton's manoeuvring to get shot of Mahon. But the replacement of Ian Hamilton arrived too late to affect the outcome at Gallipoli.

In the meantime, the War Office assumed that Monro had taken command at Salonika until 19 November when Kitchener telegraphed what he intended from Mudros. Then he placed Salonika under command of GHQ MEF. The War Office objected to this added link in the lengthy chain of command and continued to deal with Mahon directly until Kitchener returned to England, when it was forced to comply with the Secretary of State's wishes: 'Had Salonika not been placed first under Mudros and then Cairo, much administrative muddle would not have arisen.'[17]

The problem of Greek non-co-operation was not resolved for some time, but the situation improved somewhat in November. Monro's chief of staff, Maj.-Gen. Sir A. Lynden-Bell (of Brookhill, Co. Wexford), while on a visit to Salonika together with Gen. Sarrail, gave the Greek military representative, Col. Pallis, an ultimatum:

I informed Colonel Pallis as quickly as I could that unless the Greeks cleared off, the British Fleet then in harbour would bombard the town. Sarrail took a different line. He shook his fist in Pallis' face and said, 'Franchement je ne suis pas aimable.' I should translate it as 'you can go to hell'.[18]

At last the order for which all had been waiting arrived. And with it, 10th Division was committed to a second campaign in its short history.

10th Division Order No 1.
18th Nov 1915.

I. The 10th Division will relieve the French troops in first line on night 20–21 November as follows:—
31st Inf Bde from Kozlu Dere through Prstan and Memisli to Rocky Peak just S of Ormanli.
30 Inf Bde from same Rocky Peak exclusive to Kosturino. Cyclist Company will hold the knoll on the Serbo-Bulgarian frontier just E of main Rabrovo-Strumnitza Station. 29th Inf Bde will be General Reserve

at Rabrovo less two Battalions respectively at (a) Pozarli, (b) Causli.

II.The following moves will take place:—
(a) The two battalions 29th Inf Brigade, now on Dojran-Dedeli Road, will move to Rabrovo, one Battalion relieving the 7th RMF holding the heights NE, N and NW thereof. The two remaining battalions of 29th Brigade will relieve the two battalions of the 31st Infantry Brigade, now holding (a) Pozarli, (b) Causli-Gokceli Bala.
(b) The company, 29th Infantry Brigade, now at Dojran will remain there until further orders. These moves to be carried out on the 19th instant. 31st Infantry Brigade will be concentrated about Calkali by 12.00, 20th instant.
(c) The troops Yeomanry will remain at Hasanli covering the right flank.
(d) A. Section 68th F.A.B. Ammunition Column, will move to Dedeli on 20th after 31st Infantry Brigade has cleared the Dojran-Dedeli Road.

III. Brig-General A.B. Helyar having arrived, he will assume command of the Artillery units of the Division.

IV. The three Field Companies and 5th Royal Irish Regiment Pioneers will not move and will continue the work upon which they are now engaged.

V. Reports to Dedeli, after noon, 20th instant.
Issued at 18.00.

(Sd) G.E. Lemon, Lt-Col.
General Staff, 10th Division.

CHAPTER SIXTEEN

Serbia, 15 November– 8 December 1915

The last elements of 10th Division reached Salonika on 24 October. Despite all difficulties on arrival, Nicol's Brigade Group crossed the frontier on the 29th. A week later, a second brigade joined it and by 15 November, all the division was in Serbia. With divisional headquarters situated at Dedeli, 10th Division relieved the French on a line from Kosturino to the shores of Lake Doiran during the night of 21–22 November. The French line extended deep into Serbia and the security of three French divisions depended upon 10th Division holding its line. Meanwhile, the Bulgarians were massing in the Strumica Valley.

The line of 10th Division was in savage hill-top country broken by deep gullies, barren rock and scree, its only vegetation scant grass, scrub and scarce stunted oak. There was a sudden change in weather conditions when a cold rain then a raging blizzard struck the Balkans as far south as Gallipoli. The exposed infantrymen, their health already undermined by privations on the peninsula, deteriorated. Hundreds suffered frostbite and exposure, hundreds more collapsed with the ailments associated with debilitation, cold and under-nourishment. Yet despite their suffering, most of the infantryman held on and remained cheerful.[1] In the week up to 3 December when the weather changed for the better, twenty-three officers and 1633 men were evacuated to Salonika. Of these, 998 were admitted to No. 4 Canadian General Hospital with frostbite; 'some cases were very severe'.[2] As a result of this, special instructions were issued by the Army Medical Services for the prevention of frostbite and trench foot.[3]

> Fortunately we had been issued with serge at the base, but one unfortunate brigade were still in drill, and, with temperatures below zero, suffered severely from frostbite. Fortunately, too, my company HQ was in a village; and patrols were able to unfreeze themselves at a fire, whilst their greatcoats remained standing like boards on the floor.[4]

The village houses which the troops occupied when not in the front line were, to one officer of 6th Dublins, recently home from the colonies:

> Rather like a native house in Ceylon with fireplace; we have a fine log

> fire and plenty to eat. I wonder if you could send me some little thing
> for each man in my platoon (I have 50 men) for Xmas... They are a fine
> crowd and stick the cold very well.[5]

'Awfully cold' is a recurring phrase.

> Boots get wet then frozen. If one sits still your feet get frozen. I feel
> sorry for the men, some of them have only one blanket... I never want
> to see snow again.[6]

Yet the spirit of the troops was irrepressible. On 29 November, 7th
Munsters relieved 6th Dublins by tracks deep in snow, almost impassable in
places. They came to the final stage which

> was made when the battalion in file, every man hanging on to the tunic
> of his neighbour, slid down the track amid great merriment.[7]

For the weary and cold battalion coming out, it was less high-spirited. After
relief, the march of 6th Dublins to Kajali was described as being

> path icey nearly all the way; we had to wait 1/2 an hour in some places
> while the men one by one got across, my word, worst march I have
> ever done in my life, wind went straight through one... Everyone kept
> falling down.[8]

The trench line had been sited and constructed by the French. In some cases
it was badly positioned and in most cases was inadequate and shallow.
Contemporary photographs show front-line trenches waist deep with waste
soil thrown forward unbagged as a parapet, without dug-outs or fire bays. In
the heavy rain, such trenches soon became little more than muddy ditches.
Where wire existed in front of the trenches, and this was rare, it consisted of
at most a couple of strands. Rain was followed by hard frost; this and
scarcity of tools made late improvement impossible. Picks and shovels
(limited to six sets to a company) only chipped the ground, and when force
was used the handles broke. The battalions in reserve were put to work
improving tracks and gun-hauling. Front-line positions in 30 Brigade area
were named by the Dubliners after areas of Dublin Bay; their front-line
trenches became 'Dollymount', with forward peaks called 'Bray Head' and
'Hill of Howth'.

Artillery support was restricted to 18-pounder field pieces. Their flat
trajectory, only 16 degrees elevation, limited their value in mountain
country. To improve this, two batteries, C/67th at Kajali and B/68th west of
Prsten, were dragged with the help of large infantry working parties to hill-

top positions. Although increasing effectiveness, it exposed them to considerable danger in the event of a withdrawal. The new Commander Royal Artillery concurred with the positions taken and Brig. Nicol had no choice but to take the risk for the sake of gun-fire support.[9] Despite the best efforts of the gunners, without mortars or howitzers, artillery support was poor and counter-battery fire ineffective. Moreover, inaccurate maps hampered artillery direction by forward observation officers. Lines of communications were along a few goat tracks along which telephone lines were laid from division to brigade and down to battalion headquarters. But the cables, because they were of necessity ground laid, were exposed to damage by enemy artillery fire. Inevitably, this could be expected to occur at a critical phase of the battle and would adversely affect artillery support.

Brig. Nicol, alive to the danger of the Bulgarian concentration, warned Mahon of it on 29 November and asked for an additional brigade. Mahon and Sarrail agreed on the necessity of a general Allied withdrawal. The French started on 3 December, but Sarrail insisted that all equipment should be back-loaded to Salonika.[10] Mahon sent a battalion of Pioneers to Nicol and warned a brigade of 22nd Division for a move into Serbia. The Pioneers, 9th Border Regiment, Nicol placed under Vandeleur on the extreme right by Lake Doiran where it was put to work improving tracks. On this day, Nicol relieved two battalions which suffered worst in the appalling weather. The 6th Dublins and 6th Munsters were relieved by 5th Rangers and 10th Hampshires.[11]

Lt.-Col. Cox of 6th Dublins, acting commander of 30 Brigade, ordered the reliefs to take place on the night of 29th–30th. While it was going on, Bulgarian artillery fire caught stretcher-bearers carrying the worst frostbite cases rearwards.

The French retirement down the Vardar began on 3 December. Preparations for it had begun over a week before and most stores, transport and some artillery were sent back. On the line of retreat, two strong intermediate positions were prepared. Their retreat began just in time. Good intelligence indicated to Sarrail that the Bulgarians had been strongly reinforced and were about to launch 120 battalions, in five huge divisions, against the Allied front held by a total of fifty British and French battalions. The major Bulgarian effort was directed against Kosturino and would, if it succeeded, trap the French.

The Serbian army, cut off from the French and hard-pressed by the Austrians and Germans, retreated westwards across the Albanian mountains in the depth of winter on its dreadful journey to Macedonia. When they arrived, the survivors were taken to the island of Corfu for reorganisation, re-equipping and training.

During the skilful retirement of the French down the Vardar Valley, one of 10th Division's engineer field companies played a significant part. With the exception of the bridge at Veles, none existed over the turbulent Vardar. To help the movement problem, two bridges were built at Krivolak, one by the French and the other by a bridging detachment of 10th Division. Under Maj. B. Borradaile, RE, they overcame considerable difficulties. They cut their own timber, hewed stone, launched and anchored pontoons and erected trestles on a fast-flowing river. The bridge was completed in a week. On completion, the company withdrew, leaving Lt. J.E. Gill, RE, with a small party to work it. Then, when the French retired over it, Gill dismantled the bridge, recovered the pontoons and trestles, moved them by rail, and in the course of the retreat, with the aid of a French working party constructed another bridge across the Vardar farther south. When they passed over that, Gill's men again dismantled the bridge and withdrew. Back at Salonika after the retreat, Gill was summoned by Gen. Sarrail to receive his personal thanks.[12]

10TH DIVISION IN SERBIA

On 30 November and 1 December, the enemy shelled 30 and 31 Brigade positions in a way which seemed to the experienced officers and men to be ranging fire. Bulgarian activity increased; shelling and sniping went on by day and night, and battle casualties mounted. Freezing cold following rain froze greatcoats solid; 'they could stand upright unsupported and split if beaten.'[13] The cold snap continued until 2 December when the frost broke. With a thaw, low ground became a sea of mud. In their hilltop ditches, the troops bore their misery with cheerful fortitude. On the 4th, the Bulgarian artillery changed targets and began to search the rear areas, the tracks leading to the front and headquarters. When the shelling stopped, Bulgarian infantry attacked shortly after 1330 against the right centre of 30 Brigade; they were thrown back by well directed rifle and machine-gun fire. Shelling resumed and became intense. Some battalions vacated the exposed front-line trenches and fell back behind to escape the fire. Acting as markers, the trenches continued to be shelled. That night the wounded were evacuated to Tatarli.

On 5 December, Divisional Headquarters issued orders for the withdrawal of heavy equipment for backloading to Salonika. At the same time, warning orders were issued for a withdrawal on the night of 11–12 December. At a divisional conference held at Headquarters 30 Brigade, the withdrawal plan was outlined by Brig. Nicol. During the questions-after session, the CO 5th Connaught Rangers, Lt.-Col. Jourdain, voiced the opinion that the Bulgarian attack would pre-empt the withdrawal. He was possibly articulating the thoughts of many, for it had become apparent that an attack was imminent.[14] Bulgarian prisoners had told of a planned attack on 3 December which was postponed because of fog, but the respite would not last for long. Brig. Nicol and his subordinate commanders must have been aware that if their front were to break, their French allies would be trapped. Nicol, however, could only repeat his orders.

10th Division's position on the morning of 6 December was:

Right: 29 Brigade (Brig. R.S. Vandeleur) from Kozli Dere River along the Kara Bail ridge to the shores of Lake Doiran; 6th Leinsters on the right, and 6th Rifles on the left; 5th Royal Irish were in reserve at Hasanli.

Centre: 31 Brigade (Brig. King-King). The front of two miles ran almost due south, by the villages of Memesli and Prsten, to the Kozli Dere River. 5th Inniskillings on the right, 6th Inniskillings in the centre, 5th Irish Fusiliers, with one company holding a forward detached position which dominated the line, Rocky Peak; 6th Irish Fusiliers was in reserve.

Left: an exposed flank, barely in touch with the French at the head of the Kajali ravine, a mile south of Kosturino. This was held by the Cyclist Company supported by a company of 7th Dublins as flank-guard. 30 Brigade (Lt.-Col. P.G.A. Cox) held a line from the Kajali ravine south-eastward along the Kosturino Ridge up to and including the Serbian Frontier House. *Right:* 10th Hampshire; *centre:* 5th Rangers; *left:* 7th Munsters; in reserve, 7th Dublins less one company.

Two battalions which had suffered severely from exposure on 28–29 November, 6th Dublins and 6th Munsters, were in divisional reserve at Tatarli. 9th Borders detached from 22nd Division were road-working south of Lake Doiran. In support were twelve four-gun 18-pounder batteries of 54, 67 and 68 Brigades RFA, each with a battery in a central hilltop forward position.

Considering the atrocious conditions, the morale of the troops was quite high. At half strength on arrival at Salonika, the ranks had been filled up by infantry drafts 'from all the regiments of the army'.[15] And despite strenuous efforts, some had still not been assimilated into their new units. Nearly all the original officers and NCOs were casualties, either dead or wounded, or had been invalided. Some of the Gallipoli wounded and sick officers had returned, but most of the other regimental officers were attached or had been newly commissioned from D Company, 7th Royal Dublin Fusiliers. All company commanders had led platoons at Gallipoli and none had more that fourteen months' military service. They faced an offensive in overwhelming strength by a tough, hard-hitting enemy, experienced by several Balkan wars.

THE BATTLE OF KOSTURINO

Early on 6 December, stand-to in the trenches was followed by a hasty meal. At 0715, small-arms, machine-gun and artillery fire opened against the Irish line. At the same time, heavy rifle fire was heard from French sector, but the French, well supplied with howitzers, replied with these. Mustering in great strength behind the 'Hill of Howth' 1000 yards in front, the Bulgarians brought well-handled light guns into action, pouring destructive fire into the Irish positions, specifically against the machine-guns. By 1430, Bulgarian fire from Hill 850 and Kosturino was raking the front. One battalion holding a hard-hit sector drew back to avoid casualties, leaving only scouts until the enemy advanced; then going forward, they manned the trenches again. At 1525, the enemy attacked, coming on with great determination, particularly on the front of the Connaught Rangers which appeared to be the main thrust. Here they reached to within forty yards of the Rangers' positions before being driven back. Caught by the enfilade fire of 5th Irish Fusiliers on Rocky Peak and the rapid fire of the Rangers, the enemy suffered heavily as they retired to regroup.

At dusk the entire front was subjected to heavy shell-fire; many men were hit but could not be evacuated. The Bulgarians massed in dead ground, then advanced under cover of the shell-fire. As they closed, their artillery lifted off the front and searched the ground behind the Irish line, hoping to catch the reserves but unaware there was no reserve. Once again in the open, the attackers were driven back by the mad-minute rapid fire. Those wounded in the bombardment fought as long as they could, knowing there could be no evacuation.[16] Darkness came and the attack subsided. Against this part of the front, the Bulgarians had committed the 21st, 27th and 28th Regiments, each of three battalions.[17] These were so roughly handled by 30 Brigade that they had to be withdrawn for reorganisation before a fresh attack could be mounted.

Part of 6th Dublins were sent to reinforce 31 Brigade and a company was sent to reinforce 5th Irish Fusiliers. One platoon went to Rocky Peak, a treeless, shelterless, boulder-strewn height just south of the village of Ormanli held by a company with a machine-gun. During hand-to-hand fighting, its commander, Lt. R.C. McBryde Broun, RDF, was killed. The Irish were forced back but counter-attacked and drove the Bulgarians off Rocky Peak. Some of Broun's men survived and Ptes. C. Martin and F. Barrow later gave the family details of his death and burial.[18] The Christmas presents which Richard Broun had so thoughtfully requested from home for his men were never delivered.

Patrols were sent out and some firing was exchanged; many enemy dead were seen in the area of 'Hill of Howth'. Heavy artillery kept up harassing fire throughout the night, but otherwise the Bulgarians were quiet. The inevitable and reviving tea was made behind the ridge. Wounded were evacuated and the dead buried behind the trench line. Under their young officers, the soldiers prepared cheerfully to renew the battle. As an officer of the Leinster Regiment wrote: 'The Irish soldier is at his best when things are blackest.'[19] Ammunition was getting low and orders were issued to conserve it by holding fire until the enemy were near, then to close with the bayonet.[20] The acting brigade commander congratulated the battalions, at the same time arranging a fresh supply of ammunition.

7 December was very misty. Under its cover, the Bulgarians climbed the heights of Rocky Peak and were into the Irish Fusiliers before they had a chance to fire. Shouts and cries of close-quarter fighting heard plainly by troops in the main positions gave evidence of a gallant defence by the 'Faughs'. Eventually, however, an ominous silence descended. The loss of

the advanced position was to prove costly to the defence of the main line. At once the enemy mounted machine-guns to enfilade the front of 30 Brigade.

At 0650, enemy artillery fire struck the 'Dollymount' trenches. Patrols were sent forward at once and the remainder of the troops had an early breakfast and were given a fresh supply of ammunition. The Bulgarian attack began with small arms fire; heavy artillery and machine-guns joined in, mainly searching for the machine-guns. Minutes later, masses of enemy infantry charged forward under cover of light artillery and machine-gun fire. Six Bulgarian regiments or eighteen battalions were now directed against the three battalions of 30 Brigade, the main weight falling on the Rangers and Hampshires. British artillery replied but was largely ineffective.

All morning the battle raged on the right and centre. Every assault was repulsed with rapid fire. Every man who could hold a rifle was in the line. The battalions, each holding a front of nearly a mile, were under heavy pressure by mid-morning, but thus far all had stood firm, giving the commander time for a second line to be constructed at Crete Simonet. About 1100, fresh enemy infantry infiltrated through gullies into dead ground close to the front. Without the plunging fire of mortars or howitzers, it was impossible to stop it or break it up. Again the enemy attacked the stubborn British and Irish infantry, who first held them off, then drove them back. Again the Bulgarians took up the battle with their superior artillery and a Connaught Rangers' machine-gun was put out of action.

Having gained positions near the British line, the Bulgarians attacked along the entire line of 30 and 31 Brigades. The British artillery was silent and 30 Brigade headquarters moved back from Kajali. Telephone lines were torn beyond repair. 'The telephone wire was cut many times until it was impossible to repair it more. The signallers however gallantly held their posts, and rendered excellent service.'[21]

A second machine-gun received a direct hit; ammunition was getting low. Enemy machine-guns on 'Rocky Peak' proved particularly galling, sweeping fire down the poor trench line holding down the defence while the Bulgarian infantry massed once again before 30 Brigade. Under pressure from the machine-guns, one Hampshire company, in full view of the Rangers, fell back disorganised to Crete Simonet. Unseen by the Rangers, the left Hampshire company stood firm, refused its right flank and held its position until about 1530. But the Connaught Rangers mistakenly thought the whole battalion had retired. The retreating Hampshire company fell back in confusion through the guns of C/67th Battery near Kajali. That detachment, thinking that the whole front had caved in, abandoned their guns but removed the breech-blocks and dial-sights.

At 1400, the enemy attacked from a strong position 100 yards from the front of the Rangers and remaining Hampshires. Bulgarian masses streamed down the 'Hill of Howth' under cover of machine-gun and artillery fire. At the same time, two Rangers, Ptes. Martin and McDonnell, ran to the Bulgarian advanced positions and bombed them back. The end came for the Connaught Rangers at 1430 when Bulgarian masses poured forward, disregarding their losses. As they closed, the Rangers rose from the trenches, emptied their magazines into the enemy and closed with the bayonet in a desperate encounter. Against overwhelming numbers, there could be only one result: 'The enemy in overpowering numbers and admirable fierce courage surged into the two centre companies.'[22]

The remnants of B, C and D Companies retired. Part of A Company, under Capt. D. Kelly, was outflanked, but gallantly held on to its position for a further hour until it and the Hampshire company withdrew to Crete Simonet and fought with 30 Brigade before rejoining its battalion on the 8th.

7th Munsters, on the left of 30 Brigade, were attacked in lesser numbers than elsewhere on the brigade front and successfully beat off all attacks throughout the day. When the Rangers retired, Lt.-Col. G. Drage swung his right company back to deny that flank and held on until 1540 when he received orders to retire. The Munsters retired company by company, falling back with admirable steadiness. As they reached a hill completely bare save for three stunted trees, the mist lifted and exposed them to enemy artillery. In the defence and withdrawal under fire, they lost one officer and nine men killed; two officers and thirty-eight men were wounded. Twelve men got cut off and were taken prisoner. In the darkness the medical officer of the 7th Munsters, Capt. Bremner, courageously went back 'to make doubly sure that no wounded had been left behind'.[23]

The Munsters withdrew down Kajali Ravine, covered by Lt. Bright's platoon. When they were relieved on 8 December, 7th Munsters withdrew through Tatarli, 'only pausing long enough to extract a few tins of bully beef from a blazing pile of stores; Tatarli and Valandova were both blazing'.[24] In the meantime the remnant of 5th Connaught Rangers, 324 all ranks, many severely wounded, less one company still fighting, had rallied and reorganised in the Kajali-Rabrovo ravine.[25] From there, acting on orders from divisional headquarters, they retired to the head of the Dedali defile.

The Bulgarians made no attempt to follow up that night, giving Cox time to consolidate his position on Crete Simonet with 6th Munsters and 7th Dublins. They were soon joined by the main element of 10th Hampshires. On the front of 31 Brigade, with the exception of the loss of Rocky Peak and a sector held by 6th Irish Fusiliers about Prsten, the line held. Late on the 7th, Nicol allowed Brig. King-King to withdraw 31 Brigade which then took up a position on high ground north of Tatarli, to the right of Crete Simonet. A gun-battery in a high exposed position near Prsten was also abandoned, again in the mistaken belief that the entire front had collapsed. But here an attempt was made on the 8th to bring off the guns, although this was aborted when a further withdrawal was ordered. A total of eight guns was lost. It was the price of having no howitzers.

When the effects of the blizzard had worn off, the expected advance by the Bulgars began, and in such strength that retreat to the safety of the Greek frontier became inevitable. On 8 December, after heavy fighting in fog had developed away to our left, we withdrew at nightfall from our ridge, across a valley, and up on to another ridge almost on the frontier. As we stumbled up the steep path, it was eerie to see the flares and hear the bugles of the enemy, who had occupied our former position. We spent that night out in the open, in severe frost, in what we stood up in, but so tired we slept soundly, even though frozen stiff. And at dawn, the sun rose in a glorious sunburst on a sheet of cloud over Lake Doiran far below us.[26]

Gen. Mahon had come forward to watch the battle and had spent the night of 6–7 December with the 10th Division. Seeing the seriousness of the situation, he telegraphed GHQ Salonika for another brigade as quickly as possible. The leading battalion of 65 Brigade, 22nd Division, reached Doiran that night, 7 December.

Brig. Nicol ordered the new line to be held at all costs and was hopeful that the Bulgarian advance could be checked. Knowing a further withdrawal would imperil the French, he informed Gen. Bailloud of the situation. Bailloud at once ordered a mountain battery and two battalions to Tatarli, to strengthen the Allied line. The leading French battalion came into the line between Crete Simonet and the Kajali ravine at 0100 on 8 December.

On Crete Simonet, the Dublins and Hampshires built sangers of rocks and boulders. Next morning, 8 December, Lt.-Col. Cox discovering that Crete Rivet, a hill in front of his position, was unoccupied, sent up two companies of 6th Dublins to hold it and a French company to extend their left to the Kajali ravine, making contact with the line of the French 156th Division.

A Bulgarian attack was broken by the French howitzer battery, but by 1100 the enemy had massed in front and flanks of Crete Rivet and opened heavy rifle and machine-gun fire. For the defenders it was a strange experience; only the peaks of Crete Rivet and Crete Simonet could be seen above the swirling mist. Occasional breaks showed the hills around black with troops. From the mist came incessant firing. A determined attack was beaten off by rapid fire just before noon, but an hour later the French company was withdrawn. Cox ordered his Dublins to fall back should they be heavily attacked, and at 1400 a mass of Bulgarian infantry under cover of machine-gun fire rushed the hill. Retiring, the two companies of Dublins fought their way back to Crete Simonet losing ten dead and fifty-four wounded on the way. 'However, Crete Rivet being only an outpost, the work of the Bulgarians was still in front of them.'[27]

Then came a bolt from the blue. At 1530 Brig. Nicol received a report that the Bulgarians massed on the front of 31 Brigade were working their way down Memesli-Prsten-Calkali ravine, attempting to out-flank the division. Half an hour later he was told by his Signals officer that 31 Brigade was about to retire. Brig. Nicol telephoned Brig. King-King and discovered that orders had actually been issued for retirement, as King-King believed his brigade was in danger of being surrounded. The enemy had not only worked round the right of 31 Brigade, but also penetrated between 6th Irish Fusiliers on the right and 5th Inniskillings in the centre.

Brig. Nicol ordered 7th Munsters to King-King's support and informed Gen. Bailloud that he would be forced to uncover the French right. At 1700, learning 31 Brigade had begun to retire on Causli, Nicol ordered Cox to withdraw 30 Brigade on Dedeli. Withdrawal began at 1745 and in the closing darkness the Bulgarians charged Crete Simonet; five rounds rapid fire drove them back disordered. Before they could recover, the 7th Dublins' rearguard scrambled and slid down the back of the hill. The cheering enemy rushed the forward slope. Having gained the position, the Bulgarians stopped, 'as if his duty for that day were done, and neither the 30th nor the 31st Brigade was pressed in its retirement'.[28]

A more likely explanation is that the Bulgarian commander had no wish to expose his men in darkness to the doughty fighters they had come to respect in three days' heavy fighting.

CHAPTER SEVENTEEN

The Retreat to Salonika, 10–18 December 1915

For over a month, 10th Division stoically endured terrible privations, operating in a freezing mountain wilderness for which they were not equipped or trained. Scantily covered and poorly fed, they held a line of untenable defences in appalling conditions—freezing snow, rain and deep mud on mountain tops over twice as high as any in the British Isles. Their exposure casualties were equal to battle ones. Then, having repeatedly flung back assaults by a valiant enemy which attacked in overwhelming numbers, the 10th Division withdrew. By doing so, they became engaged in the most demanding of all military operations, a withdrawal in the face of a victorious enemy. In the history of the British army to that time, there had been three memorable retreats: Sir John Moore in Spain, Sir John French in France, and a disastrous retreat from Kabul to Jelalabad in 1842. The first two saved their armies, albeit with heavy losses, by forced marches. In the poorly conducted retreat from Kabul, the only person to complete the journey was Surgeon Brydon.

It can only have been a major disappointment for Brig. Nicol that, having held the main weight of the Bulgarian attack, he should now have to retire. Yet the line would have to be adjusted if his division was to be saved. Nicol's actions suggest that, in addition to concern for his own position at all stages of 10th Division's retirement, he honourably consulted the French divisional commander on his left, Gen. Bailloud of 156th Division, before he did so. And almost at the very end of the withdrawal into Greece, one of his brigadiers was prepared to disobey orders so as to remain alongside his French ally. It was a type of co-operation which Sir John French had not received from Gen. Lanrezac at Mons.

On the night of 8–9 December 1915 the line of 10th Division ran from the shore of Lake Doiran along the Kara Bail Ridge north-east of Causli to the Dedeli Pass. It was held by 29 Brigade—6th Irish Rifles, 6th Leinsters and 5th Royal Irish (P) with 9th Borders attached in reserve. Dedeli Pass was held by Lt.-Col. Fair, the divisional chief engineer officer, with a force consisting of 5th Rangers, 7th Munsters, Divisional Cyclist and his own 66th Field Company RE. Col. Fair's force was both rearguard and demolition guard; as such it made good sense to place them under the division's Chief Royal Engineers. Fair's engineers were now preparing the bridges and culverts of the Dedeli Pass for demolition. The remainder of 30 Brigade bivouacked in the pass. In the rear of the division, 31 Brigade halted for the night at Pazarli and withdrew into reserve after falling back through 29 Brigade. Two battalions of 65 Brigade, 9th King's Own and 14th King's Regiment came under the orders of Brig. Vandeleur on reaching Causli.

Bailloud's division withdrew behind the Bajimia Dere in the early hours of 9 December and began the long ascent to the Dedeli Pass. The Kosturino-Doiran road rises sharply from Bajimia to the Dedeli Pass and was under enemy observation from the former Irish positions. It was therefore vital that the pass be cleared by first light. 'The French transport moved with painful slowness and many halts on the steeper parts of the hill, so that when day broke a large proportion of the column had not yet reached the pass.'[1]

However, the morning mist which previously favoured the Bulgarians now helped the Allies and all crossed safely by midday. When the French passed through, the rearguard of 10th Division remained steadfastly in position, awaiting orders to move.

The Bulgarians, after regrouping, did not pursue and the night passed uneventfully. Normally the troops might have slept undisturbed, but in their ragged and exhausted state, in bitter weather, their officers feared that they might die of exposure and thus allowed only fitful sleep.[2] Next morning, Brig. Nicol drew the line of the new British positions, dividing it into three sectors: Lake Doiran to Pazarli-Dorutli track, 29 Brigade; from this track to the neighbourhood of Causli, 65 Brigade (Brig.-Gen. L.N. Herbert); Causli to the Dedeli Pass, 30 Brigade and 10th Hampshire. The pass itself was still held by Lt.-Col. Fair, although 7th Munsters withdrew and rejoined its brigade. 31 Brigade was in reserve on the Doiran road. The enemy, clearly spent by the effort to break the line of 10th Division, paused on the 9th and 10th, giving the French time to withdraw down the Vardar.

On 10 December, Gen. Mahon brought up Maj.-Gen. the Hon. F. Gordon, commanding 22nd Division and placed him in command of all British troops in Serbia (65 Brigade was part of 22nd Division).

Mahon's imposition of a link in the chain of command between himself and Nicol has been mildly criticised by the official historian. It may have been Mahon's intention to take some strain off Nicol by imposing a buffer between him and the French, allowing him to fight his division's battle without having to worry about an ally.

Although events on the British front had influenced the French, the Bulgarians had subjected them to such pressure that the French divisional commanders pressed Sarrail to allow them to retire. This he did, but only an adjustment of the line, allowing him time to evacuate all stores and equipment. Sarrail achieved this with the same determination with which he had saved Verdun in 1914. While this was taking place, the CinC ordered a second line prepared behind the Serbian frontier. Secret intelligence had reached Gen. Sarrail that the Bulgarians would not infringe Greek territory.[3] On 10 December, under cover of mist, the Bulgarians pierced the French line in several places. Gen. Bailloud was allowed a slight withdrawal and moved back three miles south of Dedeli. Gen. Gordon was informed and ordered to extend the French line from Kara Uler to Lake Doiran and to withdraw all other troops behind this line.

At Gordon's command, 65 Brigade formed the line as directed. Arranging his own withdrawal in ordered stages, Nicol instructed his reserve, 31 Brigade, to take up a position at Pataros in Greece and cover Doiran Station from the east. 29 Brigade was to follow and bivouac south of the station. 30 Brigade was to withdraw from the Dedeli Pass at 0400.

When these moves had been completed, Col. Cox's 30 Brigade crossed the start line on time. 7th Dublins led. Behind them came 5th Rangers, then 6th Dublins, followed by 6th and 7th Munsters in that order; at the rear of the column were 10th Hampshires. Behind as rearguard was the Cyclist Company covering the last demolition parties of Royal Engineers. At 0615 on the misty morning of 11 December 1915, 30 Brigade marched away from the head of the pass as explosions behind announced to all the blowing of the bridges and culverts. The rearguard and engineers fell back and Doiran was reached at 0710. The men of 10th Division were in mud-coated tatters, their boots falling apart. Few had slept properly in five nights. Despite this, there was no demoralisation; units maintained their discipline, and morale was high.

The battalions marched to the frontier, passing on the way the newly-arrived 65 Brigade, all fitted with leather jerkins and sheepskin coats. They were grouped around large fires, unmindful or uncaring that the Bulgarians were within artillery range. The feelings of the men of the 10th Division can be readily imagined. Indeed the worst fears of the troops were realised when, later that day, a company of 9th King's Own was surprised by the Bulgarians, cut off and captured.

5th Rangers and 10th Hampshires returned to 29 Brigade and Brig. Vandeleur ordered both battalions to an airfield close to Doiran Station. 30 Brigade rested for a time near the station, then continued their march to Kilindir. That night they entrained for Salonika, which they reached next afternoon.

Acting boldly on 11 December, the Bulgarians forced the French back in some haste east and west of the Vardar. Bogdanci was taken just after midday and the enemy captured a column of French ammunition wagons. Two French brigades then began a precipitate retreat and the whole mass descended upon Doiran.

In the way usual to confused withdrawals, few knew clearly what was going on. That night, Brig. Nicol was told by a French regimental commander that 10th Division ought to withdraw at once as 'everybody was retiring'[4] and he had orders to clear the roads. Convinced, Nicol prepared a warning order for all troops to move back shortly on Kilindir. But before the order was released, Nicol communicated the information to Gordon at Doiran Station. Gordon was incredulous, especially as he had just learned that 65 Brigade had been relieved by the French as arranged. 'But a solid stream of marching French heading for the frontier convinced him.'[5] It was in this confusion that a company of 9th King's Own was cut off and captured.

65 Brigade were flung into a headlong retreat. Getting mixed up with French transport columns, they became jammed on a narrow mountain road. Bordered by a cliff wall on one side and a cliff drop on the other, the road ran along the edge of Lake Doiran. 'Had the enemy brought to bear but a single gun or even a machine-gun from a boat on the lake, he could have turned it into shambles.'[6]

There were two urgent problems—extricating 29, 31 and 65 Brigades from the chaos of Doiran Station, and forming a defensive line to the south, in Greece. Nicol sent for Brig. Vandeleur; two of Vandeleur's battalions, attached to 30 Brigade, had borne the brunt of the Kosturino battle, but the other two, 6th Leinsters and 6th Rifles, remained untouched. Vandeleur was ordered to move 29 Brigade into Greece and to form a defensive line from the lake on the right to a point about a mile and a half south-west of it, linking up with the French.

The railway station where 29 Brigade was resting became jammed with a dense confusion of Allied troops, loaded wagons and stores. Notwithstanding the noise and the cold, officers and men lay asleep on the ground. Just after midnight, Vandeleur summoned his battalion commanders to brigade headquarters where he informed them of the situation and issued orders for the march.

The roads were choked by French transport and troops, with hordes of refugees and animals adding to the congestion. Brig. Vandeleur knew it would be senseless to attempt movement along such a route. He decided to take his brigade across country, marching on a compass bearing. The night was dark and foggy. The compass bearing was fixed on the Greek frontier-stone on the Doiran road and the march began at 0100. The Leinsters led, followed by the Rifles, then the Rangers; last came the Hampshires. Before 0300, the head of the column reached a selected line and was deployed in position. As they marched up to the finishing line, the rear battalions were given their positions. The line was completed just inside Greek territory at 0600. After daybreak, it was found necessary to adjust the line by moving the Leinsters from just within Serbian territory to a position in Greece; the Leinsters would be on the right, Rifles right centre, Hampshires left centre, Rangers left. Supporting was A Battery, 68 Brigade RFA and a troop of Yeomanry. It was a brilliant little piece of night movement and positioning. The French 235th Reserve Regiment of Clermont-Tonnerre's brigade came up on the left of the Connaught Rangers.

By the early hours of 12 December, the whole British force which had entered Serbia was now back in Greece. The last elements of the French 57th and 122nd Divisions were across by late in the same day. With 29 Brigade guarding their right, the French held a line just inside Greek territory.

The question now was, would the Bulgarians respect the Greek frontier?

The Allied line waited expectantly. Behind the line, the withdrawal of 10th Division went on. The divisional artillery crawled along the congested roads, got clear of the traffic and bivouacked north of Kilkush for a night before marching to Salonika. Incomprehensibly, 65 Brigade, well clothed and barely in action, entrained at Kilindir while 31 Brigade, in a far worse state: 'marched to Salonika, where it arrived at a camp outside Salonika on the 17th completely exhausted, and some of the men could not even eat the hot food which had been prepared for them. Their one desire was to sleep.'[7] The suspicion must be that this was done as punishment for 31 Brigade's failure to hold the line at Kosturino on the night of 7 December when they fell back without orders or permission from Nicol.

One battalion of 31 Brigade, however, was hardly affected by the march. 6th Inniskillings is reported to have... 'Rolled into camp at Salonika at 1600 on 18 December as if it had only been on an ordinary route march'[8]...with the Drums, no doubt, playing one of the battalion's favourite marches, 'Rory O'Moore'.

Gen. Leblois was in command of the British and French rearguard. On 14 December Leblois was much upset by a signal from Gordon telling him of the decision to withdraw 29 Brigade. Leblois told Vandeleur, who, although knowing the poor condition of his troops, honourably assured Leblois that since the brigade was under his orders, Leblois could rely on 29 Brigade not moving until Leblois gave consent. That night, orders arrived for a general withdrawal the following morning.[9]

Under cover of darkness, 29 Brigade retired to Kilindir at 0400 on the 15th, reaching there four hours later; the Hampshires and Rangers remained and entrained later. The Leinsters and Rifles continued the march a further fifteen miles to Sarigol Station where they arrived on the morning of the 17th and entrained. Waiting for an engine, they sheltered from the pouring rain in boxcars, resting and watching the French troops stream past. The Irishmen were deeply impressed by the cheerfulness of the French in the conditions.[10] But they could take comfort knowing that but for their stand at Kosturino, the French could not have escaped. When the train moved at last, all lay down on the floor of the boxcars and slept soundly for the first time in weeks.

10th Division took over the tented camp of the 22nd Division, sited in a sea of mud. Sheepskin coats and leather jerkins were issued and all were gratified that nothing was being spared to make them comfortable. Soon the hardship and the strain of the previous month was forgotten as all prepared for Christmas.

The troops of the division which checked a Bulgarian offensive in overwhelming force at Kosturino, and which then retreated in appalling weather through the mountain passes of Serbia, were not the long-service professional soldiers of Mons and Le Cateau. The regulars were fresh, well trained, superbly equipped and led by experienced officers they had served under for years. The British regulars, at Mons and Le Cateau, fought the Germans to a standstill on a summer's day, then slipped away with great professional skill. The men of Kosturino were at best half-trained temporary soldiers, experienced in fighting but wasted in health by their Gallipoli experience; at worst they were newly-arrived raw recruits from regimental depots. All were led by young men whose only war experience five months previously had been in the depths of a rugby scrum. They were commanded by just a handful of experienced officers, some of whom were chronically ill. Notwithstanding their professional limitations, the retreat through Serbia's mountains, in the words of a Spanish historian, had been 'capably directed and marvellously executed'.[10]

Within ten days of their return to Salonika, exhausted and in soaked, mud-caked tatters, the men of 10th Division were refitted, re-equipped and again operational. They had their place in the defence line of an 'Entrenched Camp'.

BATTLE CASUALTIES
The official history gives all British losses in Serbia as

	Killed	Wounded	Missing*
Officers	1	20	12
Other Ranks	98	366	712

*Including 2 officers and 125 men, prisoners from a company of 65 Brigade.

'Of the 1209 casualties given above, just over half were suffered by the 5/Connaught Rangers and 10/Hampshires.'[12]

Actual 10th Division casualties were: killed and died of wounds—302; wounded and evacuated—366; missing (mainly wounded prisoners) 384.

On 19 December, Brig.-Gen. J.R. Longley, commanding 82 Brigade, 27th Regular Division, assumed command of 10th Division with the rank of major-general. Gen. Mahon had recommended to Gen. Monro, Commander MEF, that Brig. Nicol, who had performed so well in Serbia, should be given command of the 10th. Gen. Monro, however, refused on the grounds that Nicol had been on the retired list in 1914. Gen. Longley was also an Irishman, son of an Indian Civil Service official, commissioned into the East Surrey Regiment; he was married to Iva Molony of Kiltanon, Co. Clare. Longley had commanded 82 Brigade with distinction at First Ypres and proved an exceptional commander of 10th Irish Division.

Special Order
Lieut General Sir B.T. Mahon, on relinquishing the command of the 10th Irish Division which he had the honour of raising and commanding until he received command of the Salonika Army, desires to express his thanks for the loyal and faithful support he has received

from all ranks, during the hard work and severe strain caused by heavy casualties on active service, whilst serving on the Peninsula and in Serbia. He wishes the Division good luck in the future, and feels convinced that all members of it, knowing how highly their work in the past has been appreciated by His Majesty, will redouble their efforts to maintain the noble traditions of their regiments and corps, and by good discipline and cheerfully meeting and overcoming all difficulties, help to bring the war to a successful and early end.

(Sd) D. Sapte, Colonel

AA and QMG, 10th Irish Division. 23 Dec. 1915

On 23 December, Divisional Orders published a special message.

Message from HM the King

The Army Commander has received a gracious telegraphic message from His Majesty the King, in which His Majesty expressed his appreciation of the manner in which the 10th (Irish) Division carried out the operations entrusted to them in Serbia. His Majesty also graciously inquires after the welfare of the sick and wounded. To the royal message of appreciation, the Army Commander has replied as follows:

The King—Buckingham Palace, London

All ranks 10th Division respectfully thank His Majesty for his gracious message, which will stimulate them to renewed exertions. Sick and wounded doing well.

General Mahon.

Mahon continued to command what came to be known as the Macedonia Army until the spring of 1916 when, upon the outbreak of rebellion among the Senussi people, Mahon was sent to command in the Western Desert. He collapsed of a stroke on arrival at Port Said and was invalided home. The official history is at great pains to stress that his conduct at Salonika was highly praiseworthy and was not the reason for his being replaced.[13]

CHAPTER EIGHTEEN

Raising and Training 16th Division

The War Office issued Army Order No. 382 on 11 September 1914 authorising six divisions numbered from 15th to 20th. It was 2nd New Army, and during September 1914 the formation of 16th (Irish) Division began. Lieutenant-General Sir Lawrence W. Parsons was appointed to command on 23 September 1914.[1]

Gen. Parsons opened his headquarters in Dublin. But because 10th Division had priority in organising and first claim on accommodation and training areas, 16th Division was sent south to Munster. Divisional Headquarters moved on 8 October 1914 and established itself at Mallow, Co. Cork. The headquarters of its three infantry brigades were: at Fermoy, 47 Brigade; Buttevant, 48 Brigade, all in Co. Cork; and in Tipperary town, 49 Brigade. The artillery was at Cahir, Fermoy and Kilkenny; the engineers at Moore Park, Kilworth; the Cyclist Company at the Old Barracks, Fermoy; the pioneer battalion, 11th Hampshire, went to Mullingar with its sister-battalion, the 10th.

Lt.-Gen. Sir Lawrence W. Parsons KCB CB was born on 25 March 1860, the only son of Lawrence Parsons of Parsonstown, King's County. He was educated at Cheltenham College and RMA Woolwich, from where he was commissioned into the Royal Artillery. Seconded to the Anglo-Egyptian Army, he served under Kitchener in the reconquest of the Sudan. In Natal, he served under Buller during the South African war where he commanded the artillery at Colenso and other battles. He was Inspector-General of Artillery in India 1903–06 and commanded the regular 6th Division 1906–09 and was promoted lieutenant-general on his retirement in 1909. Following his tenure of command with 16th Division, he became Colonel Commandant Royal Artillery in 1917.

47 BRIGADE, BRIG.-GEN. P.J. MILES
6TH ROYAL IRISH REGIMENT, LT.-COL. FITZR. E.P. CURZON
The battalion was raised at Fermoy in October 1914. It shared New Barracks with 6th Connaught Rangers. By spring 1915, each battalion numbered about 1600 men.[2] In its ranks was a company of Guernsey Militia which had asked for drafting to the Royal Irish, so impressed had they been with 2nd Royal Irish during its stay on the island just prior to the war. The Guernsey men formed D Company under Maj. L.C. Lloyd. Half of them spoke only French;

all were completely enthusiastic and were to prove invaluable when the battalion went to France. B Company was composed of nationalists from Co. Derry.[3] When William Redmond, MP for Waterford, was commissioned into the battalion, he influenced many of his constituents to enlist, particularly from the parish of Trinity Without.[4] Capt. Redmond and Capt. Stephen Gwynn of 6th Connaught Rangers were 'an enormous influence for good'.[5] Among the older officers in the mess, both were the only nationalists. It was a restricted and conservative society, without the wide intellect and diverse interests and debate of the House of Commons, where Redmond felt at home.

> At the mess he [Redmond] was quiet, reticent and rather shy. The regular officers could not believe that this quiet and reserved man was the turbulent leader of revolt. Stephen Gwynn tried to draw him out to reminisce on the House of Commons, a place he loved and where he was at his best, but he refused to be drawn. All there grew to love him, quite literally.[6]

6TH CONNAUGHT RANGERS, LT.-COL. J.S.M. LENOX-CONYNGHAM

The formation of 6th Connaught Rangers began at Kilworth Camp in September 1914 when 5th Rangers of 10th Division moved from Fermoy to Dublin. 6th Rangers then moved to Fermoy and its main development really began when Lt.-Col. J.S.M. Lenox-Conyngham, a veteran of thirty years' service with the Rangers, assumed command. He came on 10 October, like many others from the army reserve of officers. However, unlike most early commanding officers of 16th Division, he had the honour of leading the battalion he had founded into action. Five other officers from the reserve of officers and a handful of regular NCOs transferred from the regular battalions formed its cadre. The Connaught Rangers, which to many epitomises an Irish regiment, attracted Irishmen from all over the world. Its casualty list contains names of soldiers from as far away as Argentina, Australia and the United States, in addition to England and Scotland.[7]

7TH LEINSTER REGIMENT, LT.-COL. H. WOOD

On the departure of 6th Leinsters from Old Barracks, Fermoy, sixty-seven NCOs and men were left behind and sent to the New Barracks, Fermoy, to form the nucleus of 7th Battalion. They were under command of Lt. (QM) P.J. Ahern of the Leinsters, 'an exceptionally good Quartermaster who had done much to assist the formation of the 6th. Unlike the 6th Battalion, the 7th was completely Irish.'[8]

Recruiting was slow initially, and the intakes of recruits chiefly consisted of drafts from the Regimental Depot at Birr and direct from Belfast. In November 1914, Lt.-Col. H. Wood assumed command and the pace of work increased considerably. Responding to the need to train young officers,

Wood initiated an officers' cadet company which became an instant success (later it became 7th Cadet Battalion, Moore Park). From this company, several hundred young officers graduated and were gazetted to various regiments of 16th Division. Stephen Gwynn, the well-known Nationalist MP, joined as a private soldier; his example showed the way to many other prominent Irish people.

Like other battalions of the New Army, the Leinsters had its share of vicissitudes of fortune, but its most trying early experience was undoubtedly the move from Fermoy to Kilworth, when, due to overcrowding, the junior battalion had to move. Early in February, in the teeth of a near-blizzard, the battalion marched seven miles from Fermoy with full equipment and arms, four miles of which, from Downing Bridge to Kilworth Camp, was a steady uphill climb. They arrived to discover little had been done for their reception.[9] It must be wondered why an advance party was not sent to organise a proper reception, especially if the quartermaster was as good as the regimental historian insists. This might possibly explain the retirement of Col. Woods shortly afterwards, who was relieved by Lt.-Col. G.A. McLean Buckley. A New Zealander and adventurer, Buckley had explored Patagonia in 1897 and had taken part in Shackleton's Antarctic expedition of 1908. Undoubtedly he was the right leader for the 'Forty-tens'.

7TH ROYAL IRISH RIFLES, LT.-COL. D.L. HARTLEY
Formed at Belfast during early September 1914, the cadre moved to Mallow, Co. Cork, where they spent their first year at Ballyvonare Camp. They did much of their training on the excellent training areas in the Ballyhoura Mountains. In March 1915, six officers and 225 men of the Jersey Militia joined, bringing the battalion up to war establishment.[10] In the summer of 1915, the battalion moved to summer camp at Ballyhooly on the southern Blackwater before the brigade as a whole was concentrated at Kilworth for collective training.

48 BRIGADE, BRIG.-GEN. K.J. BUCHANAN
In September 1914, 48 Brigade was formed in Co. Cork. The Brigade headquarters was at Mallow and the infantry battalions, as follows, at Buttevant.

> 8th Royal Munster Fusiliers, Lt.-Col. J.K. O'Meagher
> 9th Royal Munster Fusiliers, Lt.-Col. H.F. Williams
> 8th Royal Dublin Fusiliers, Lt.-Col. Sir F.W. Shaw
> 9th Royal Dublin Fusiliers, Lt.-Col. W.E.G. Connolly

With four battalions in Buttevant barracks, the accommodation was crowded and uncomfortable until hutted training camps were constructed at

Ballyvonare, Fermoy and Mitchelstown. Despite overcrowding, hard basic training went on: 'The work was strenuous enough—eight hours on the parade grounds in field training every day whatever the weather might be—and for the most part it was frightful.' Later, training took place in the Galty Mountains where the work was 'hard but healthy enough'.[11]

In May 1915, Lt.-Col. M. Williamson, Indian Army, assumed command of 8th Munsters and had the honour of taking the battalion on active service.

9TH ROYAL MUNSTER FUSILIERS

The battalion was raised at the same time as the 8th Munsters, by Lt.-Col. H.F. Williams, at Buttevant Barracks, and followed the movements of the 8th Battalion. Col. Williams also had the honour of taking the battalion to France.

His second-in-command, Maj. Sir Francis Vane Bt, had a disagreement about recruiting with both his brigade commander and the divisional commander.[12] As a consequence, he was relieved before the battalion left for active service. Sir Francis Vane, an Englishman, was later instrumental in exposing an atrocity committed by an army officer of Irish birth during the Easter Rebellion in Dublin.

The officers came from a variety of backgrounds. There were experienced officers from the Reserve of Officers and young officers from London Territorial regiments whose function it was to provide officers for any regiment in war. Additionally there were elderly officers from Irish militia battalions and probationary officers given temporary commissions. Many of its best officers would later come from the Cadet Company of 7th Leinsters. In 8th Dublins the adjutant, Capt. E.A.C. Bellingham (later as Brig.-Gen. Sir Edward Bellingham, Bt, he became a member of the first Senate), was promoted rapidly, first to major, then to lieutenant-colonel. It was he who took the battalion to France.

A noted officer, junior in rank but senior in age, wisdom, and experience and of great influence, was Lt. T.M. Kettle KC, former Nationalist MP for East Tyrone, economics professor at UCD, and poet. Present in Belgium at the outbreak of war on an arms procurement expedition for the National Volunteers, Kettle became a correspondent for the *Daily News* and witnessed German atrocities in Louvain. Convinced of the justice of the Allied cause, he also became convinced that:

> Used with the wisdom which is sown in tears and blood, this tragedy of Europe may be and must be the prologue to the two reconciliations of which all statesmen have dreamed, the reconciliation of Protestant Ulster with Ireland, and the reconciliation of Ireland with Great Britain.[13]

Kettle saw the Irish, north and south, taking part in a crusade and linked this romantically with the 'Wild Geese'. These were Irishmen forbidden because of their religion to bear arms in their own country who left and found employment for their dash and courage in most armies of Europe in the seventeenth and eighteenth century.

49 BRIGADE, BRIG.-GEN. R.D. LONGE

49 Brigade was formed on 1 October and Brig. R. Douglas Longe appointed to its command. His headquarters was established in Tipperary Barracks, and next day, personnel sufficient for four battalion cadres moved in alongside the Brigade staff. The local 'Union' was used as overflow accommodation until a new hutted camp, at Scalaheen a mile west of the town, was constructed. By the end of October, the barracks was almost full. Nearly 1800 officers and men had joined. The barracks, designed for one infantry battalion, was crowded and cramped. However, nearby married quarters were handed over as additional space for officers; this relieved some pressure.[14]

> 7th Royal Inniskilling Fusiliers—Col. R.C.C. Cox
> 8th Royal Inniskilling Fusiliers—Lt.-Col. H.J. Downing DSO
> 7th Royal Irish Fusiliers—Col. R.S.H. Moody CB
> 8th Royal Irish Fusiliers—Col. J.G. Brown

The cadre of each battalion initially consisted of six officers and assembled in Dublin early in September. They arrived in Tipperary on 2 October as part of a group for the brigade. With this nucleus of officers was a group of ex-regular warrant officers and NCOs who formed the basic training staff.

The thousands of recruits who enlisted and joined 16th Division in those early days, unlike the 10th and 36th but in common with most other New Army divisions, found great scarcity of proper khaki uniforms. Not for several months could the clothing industry meet the sudden demand for army uniforms. In the meantime, their dress, an admixture of civilian clothing and uniform, made an unusual spectacle on barrack squares. Those of average size were in temporary uniforms known as 'Kitchener Blue'; a few were dressed in a combination of 'Blue' and civilian clothing; some outsize men wore only 'mufti', civilian clothing. Perhaps the strangest figure was Sgt. Taylor, a re-enlistment of 7th Inniskillings, who drilled a squad while dressed in bowler hat, civilian jacket and khaki trousers, with boots and puttees.[15] Cynical regulars, not perceiving the enthusiasm to learn shown by recruits to the New Army, disdainfully called the motley battalions 'Fred Karno's Army'.

Daily routine was simple and repetitive. Reveille was at 0600, followed by a morning run on the square. Breakfast at 0730 was followed by drill (0900–1230); dinner (1300–1400); drill (1400–1630); tea (1630). About three times weekly there was a four or five mile route march or minor exercise beginning at 1400. A lecture about three times a week was held at 1800 in the gymnasium, usually on regimental history. Sometimes a night exercise enlivened the week.[16] For a division preparing quickly for war, it was not an intensive programme.

Notwithstanding a general shortage of essential equipment, there were other areas where training could have been done, pending the arrival of material. In the artillery, instruction began on horsemanship, gun-team handling, stables, gun-drill and map-reading. Until February 1915, the howitzer brigade only managed to obtain an old 12-pounder gun to use for drill. Usually wooden 'Quaker' guns were used for gun-drill in place of anything better. When guns eventually arrived, they were without dial sights.[17]

The cadres of the engineer field companies were formed at the RE Depot, Chatham. After basic training in England, they moved to Moore Park, Fermoy, where their ranks were filled up.[18] They were glad to be away from the 'flea infested blankets and breakfasts of bread and dripping' at Chatham.[19] They trained 'very intensively constructing field works'.[20] Building bridges over a trout stream running through the park, they 'started off with light foot bridges, then trestle bridges, working up to high pier bridges to carry heavy traffic.'[21] Later they moved west and practised throwing a pontoon bridge across the Shannon at Ardnacrusha.[22]

Basic foot-drill, with its demands for instant obedience and precision, occupied infantry for weeks and laid the basis of discipline and military order from the beginning. Fitness training was held in gymnasiums and on the sports field. Route marches were an important part of training. Except for rapid strategic deployment by train, and later, by bus and lorry, the army generally moved by foot. Regiments took pride in holding their ranks together without stragglers, even to the extent of carrying exhausted men on long marches.

Drill purpose rifles, usually rifles with worn-out rifling, or older types or marks, were issued at the end of November. These, with bayonets, added to the drill which could be taught and gave that soldierly feeling in ranks which only the carrying of arms can impart. It also added to the 'patter' of drill-instructors, whose favourite, 'when I sez fix you don't fix; but when I sez bayonets, you whips 'em out, and yeh put 'em on' was always good for an initial grin.

American-made leather equipment arrived in March 1915. Although unlike the standard 1908 webbing pattern, units could carry their kit into the field on extended marches and exercises.

The 16th Division was composed of high-spirited young men, and its training was not without its lighter moments. A demonstration of battalion in attack was arranged for the Inspector-General of Infantry Training, Maj.-Gen. Vesy Dawson by 7th Inniskillings. One company thought not to be up to standard was left out and given strict instructions to stay well away. However at the critical moment, the 'left out of battle' suddenly captured the limelight: 'Through the hedge appeared B Company, who determined not to miss the "show", charged with fixed bayonets oblique to the main attack.

Dumbfounded the CO and 2/IC said nothing, but the general was delighted: "A well-planned flank attack, delivered just in the nick of time".'[23]

In the spring of 1915, the pace of training speeded up. Long route marches took place with rigid march discipline in field service marching order. Short magazine Lee-Enfield (SMLE) rifles arrived and the companies went daily to the ranges to fire musketry courses with ball ammunition. Brigade shooting competitions were organised and engendered fierce rivalry. Shooting activity inevitably brought complaints about butt duty—the long hours in deep butts, listening to the crack of passing bullets and the distant thump of the report, marking shots and pasting over holes in targets was an essential aspect of range duty, but all who did it found it tedious. It could, however, have its lighter moments: 'Tell the man on number one target, if he wants to hit anything to fix bayonets and charge'. It was hard luck if the rifleman turned out to be the RSM.

Officer training took place mainly in the evenings, often just before the same lecture was delivered by platoon commanders to their men. In addition to the common subjects, they covered tactics and topography; operation order and report writing; billeting exercises and map reading. This training was usually carried out or supervised by the second-in-command or adjutant and kept the young gentlemen busy on winter evenings.[24]

Beginning in April 1915, officers and NCOs were selected for battalion specialist appointments and despatched on courses in England and Ireland. On their return, they assumed responsibility in preparing their element of the battalion for war—the transport, machine-gun and signals sections. Proper equipment for these sections was not yet to hand. In the interim, the officer in charge would have to select specialists from within the battalion and begin training with whatever equipment was available.

As they became better organised and the weather improved, battalions arranged concerts, games and sports. For the latter, training started in May and some commanding officers presented sports prizes; at meetings, their wives presented prizes, promoting the family atmosphere which is never absent from good regiments. Morale usually rose in the competitive spirit of inter-company competition.[25]

Battalion Corps of Drums were raised with issue equipment; some also had Irish pipers who were paid for either by donations from civilian well-wishers or by the officers. Piping had lapsed in Irish regiments in the mid-19th century, but was revived in 1903 by Lt.-Col. Lord Castletown for the Queen's County Militia battalion of the Leinster Regiment. In a few years, piping had spread to all battalions of the Leinsters, as well as to the Dublins and Munsters. One officer, Capt. G. de M.H. Orpen-Palmer of the Leinsters, wrote a book on the subject in 1913.[26]

At least one commanding officer, Lt.-Col. M. Hughes of 7th Inniskillings, who had taken over from Col. Cox in April, presented a brass band to his battalion, adding to the drums, fifes and pipes they already had. All these played at a battalion 'at home' on 2 August, which coincided with an athletics meeting. Hughes, a former Life Guards officer, had clearly raised the 'tone' of 7th Inniskillings considerably. Later in France, they became known as 'the Fighting Seventh'.[27]

In the British army, the sergeants' and officers' messes are central to its regimental tradition. The sergeants' mess, commonly referred to as the backbone of the battalion, is usually more conservative than its officer counterpart; both institutions properly run are essential to the life of a battalion, and mess-spirit can usually be indicative of a unit's morale. The officers of 6th Connaught Rangers and 6th Royal Irish messed together and about 80–100 sat down to dinner each evening. At Tipperary, the officers of Irish Fusiliers and Inniskillings also shared an officers' mess, at least until the Innikillings moved. It would be unnatural if initially the older officers did not at first look askance at these 'temporary officers' (there was no hint of a 'temporary gentleman' sneer as existed in some English regiments). The majority were totally inexperienced in either soldiering or war. But the enthusiasm and energy of the newcomers, aided by a desire and ability to learn, amazed the regulars and soon broke down any barriers which may have existed 'and the atmosphere was thoroughly friendly throughout'.[28]

In the mess of the 8th Dublins Lt. Tom Kettle KC possibly had the largest wine bill, but the conversation in the company of this noted wit and experienced raconteur would probably have been amusing and stimulating. The New Army officers of 16th Division as a whole were smartly turned out and took great pride in this and in their regiment. They were readily accepted by regular officers of their regiments.[29]

It became War Office policy to relieve the shortage of officers by commissioning experienced NCOs and warrant officers from the regular battalions on active service. The newly commissioned officers were welcomed in their battalions in Ireland. Typical was that given to ex-Sgt. Lucy when he joined the officers' mess of a reserve battalion of the Royal Irish Rifles. He was greeted warmly by officers he had served under for many years. At dinner he sat at the 'top' table with the commanding officer who 'was very gracious and astonishingly chatty'. Lucy noted that the atmosphere throughout was a family one and the conversation had a 'homely touch'. For all this friendliness, however, there was a rigid code of practice, but Lucy found it simple to understand and easy to follow, 'based on a genuine respect for one's elders, for the customs and traditions of the regiment. The subjects of religion, politics, and women were taboo.'[30] He might have noticed that after dinner, the water was removed from the table, lest anyone pass his glass over it during the loyal toast, signifying that the toast was 'to the king across the water'.

In June–July 1915, the War Office paid 16th Division an unwelcome back-handed compliment. The elite Guards Division was then forming in France. Its GOC, Irish-Guardsman, Maj.-Gen. the Earl of Cavan, demanded the best support troops possible from the War Office: 'The infantry of the division is so good that nothing but the best and closest artillery support will be good enough.' As a result, 16th Division had its three Artillery Brigades (18-pounders), the Divisional Ammunition Column, two Engineer Field Companies, and the Divisional Signal Company transferred to the Guards Division. Significantly, the artillery commander, Brig. Gouldburn, was replaced almost as soon as he arrived in France, when it was discovered that: 'Although the material was excellent, the personnel as a whole had had but little training'.[31]

At the same time, the third Field Company was sent to France to join the 7th (Regular) Division which had suffered so severely in the spring battles. The three field ambulances, badly needed on the Western Front, had already been transferred. These reached France in early August, and two went to the Guards Division. It was a decided blow to the division. Just when it appeared they were ready for active service, their support units over which they had laboured for almost a year, recruiting, organising and training, were taken away. However it has to be said that training progress and the standards reached by the division as a whole may have influenced this unpopular decision.

Behind all the activity of training, recruiting for 16th Division was unsatisfactory. To help it, Gen. Parsons invited prominent nationalists, John Redmond MP and Joe Devlin MP, to speak to his division.[32] Both came and addressed the troops as requested; resulting from this publicity, many recruits were attracted. Redmond and Devlin did this despite disagreements with Gen. Parsons on his attitude to recruiting from the Irish in British industrial centres. Gen. Parsons had delivered strictures about them to Redmond, referring to some of the Irish as 'slum birds' and 'corner boys'.[33] Only when personally confronted by one commanding officer, Hughes of 7th Inniskillings, did Parsons allow recruiting in Britain; even then it was at Hughes' personal expense.[34] By the time 16th Division got around to recruiting on Tyneside in December 1915, after Parsons' supersession, it was too late. The Tyneside Irish had formed a brigade of their own as part of 34th Division. Sadly, the Tyneside Irish Brigade was totally and uselessly destroyed on the first day of the Somme battle, attacking from positions which they called, with Celtic nostalgia, the 'Tara-Usna Line'.

49 Brigade, the Ulster brigade, was very understrength, although 6th Royal Irish, a Munster regiment, was over establishment and had a company of Co. Derry nationalists.[34] In the spring of 1915, Brig. Longe arranged for 7th Irish Fusiliers and 7th Inniskillings to sweep their regimental areas. There, despite hospitality given and received, few recruits came forward. This is hardly surprising, as both 10th and 16th Divisions had recruited heavily in Ulster and the available manpower of the province had already enlisted. What does surprise is that a Service Battalion raised in southern Ireland outside 10th and 16th Divisions, served in another formation. 10th Dublins went to the army brigade of 63rd Royal Naval Division and took part in the closing stages of the Somme battle in 1916. Clearly Parsons did not fight his corner very well with HQ Ireland or the War Office in securing

10th Dublins to fill the ranks of his understrength units.

Training within 16th Division was patchy. The standards and training objectives were set by commanding officers with no overall direction from Divisional headquarters, except in the matter of dress and lectures on regimental history. Consequently, training tended to be outdated and unrealistic, with no proper preparation for conditions on the Western Front. The most successful aspect of the division's training was at unit level. Battalion training fostered a traditional regimental spirit, moulding a unique corporate feeling into rank and file; without it they could not overcome the trials of battle, borne together along with the personal distress at political events in their homeland.

Commanding a division is 'one of the four best commands in the service... a division because it is the smallest formation that is a complete orchestra of war...'[36] A musical orchestra requires frequent, regular practise to perfect harmony; to achieve harmony in war, a division needs practise in peace. As a former general officer commanding 6th Division which had been stationed and trained pre-war in Munster, Gen. Parsons would have been familiar with the requirement and the excellent training areas available to his division. Yet it was never concentrated for collective training until November 1915, almost immediately before Parsons' departure from command and then only at the instigation of Aldershot Command for a Royal parade. Parsons did not visit some of his infantry battalions until September 1915, almost a year after their formation. Yet, paradoxically, his demand for high standards of recruits and officer selection and training (if narrowly so) indicates a particular, almost proprietary, pride of command.

To Redmond, Parsons proclaimed his Irishness and claimed to know the Irish.[37] But by his remoteness from his troops, Parsons showed that he obviously did not know soldiers generally very well, or the Irish soldier in particular, to appreciate that *he*, like the Scot a 'Celt', responds better than any other 'tribe' of the army to close personal leadership.

It is evident that at least one brigade, 49, received no trench warfare training before going to Aldershot; this has to be accepted as a major failure of Parsons and his staff. As a former Inspector-General of Artillery, India, he must have appreciated field fortifications in defence. In addition to his experience in South Africa, the mass of feed-back from returning officers, either wounded or on leave, which permeated the army must surely have indicated to him and his staff the need to teach basic trench siting, digging, revetting and training, even without War Office directives. The only equipment required is a spade. Little equipment is needed for teaching trench routine and reliefs. But these essential aspects of preparation were completely overlooked in 49 Brigade, and this was not corrected by divisional headquarters. The officers had lectures on static warfare in France, but the lessons were not hammered home or put to practical use.[38] The basic tactics and practicalities of trench warfare were not taught, nor were they intimated to regimental officers, the majority of whom were inexperienced, as necessary or desirable. Not until they went to Aldershot Command and discovered there the emphasis placed upon trench warfare did they realise its importance. Well might they wonder, once on the battlefield, why it had not been taught previously.

Following the German gas attacks in the spring of 1915, the use of gas by the British army was advocated and later implemented. Rudimentary gas masks were issued and various precautionary measures to be taken were circulated. Yet, no introduction to gas warfare or anti-gas training or drills were given or instituted. Within a month of becoming operational in France, 16th Division was subjected to the heaviest gas attack for a year.

Parsons brusquely refused to accept political or private nominations for commissions in 16th Division. His lack of tact and snobbery are indefensible, although his insistence on high standards for officer commissioning was right. Following from this, the only way to achieve a high common standard is to see all candidates in competition with their peers. For this reason, 7th Leinster Cadet Company (through which all candidates for commissioning had to pass, even Stephen Gwynn MP) was quickly adopted and its success is unquestioned. The subsequent renowned élan of 16th Division in action can be attributed in no small measure to the dashing leadership of its junior officers. It was a creditable reflection on the high standards set for their selection and training. This, undoubtedly, was Gen. Parsons' greatest contribution to 16th Division.

16th Division arrived at Aldershot Command for intensive training during September. Initially, much of its time was spent on ranges. Because concurrent activity was not organised for those troops not actually on the firing point, much precious time was lost. Hundreds of troops spent hours in boring inactivity, simply awaiting their turn to fire.

In mid November, the division was concentrated to prepare for a ceremonial review by Queen Mary shortly before embarking. Gen. Hunter, the Army Commander, must have been horrified to discover the division had not been taught rudimentary ceremonial drill. Within weeks of going to France, with much training still to be carried out, two weeks had to be allocated to ceremonial drill and rehearsal for the Queen's parade. It is not hard to imagine the report Gen. Hunter, who had served with Parsons in the Sudan under Kitchener, sent to the War Office on the training standards of 16th Division. Possibly as a direct consequence of this, quite apart from his age and seniority, Parsons was relieved of his command before the division went to France. Brig. Longe's 49 Brigade was retained at Aldershot for a further two months' intensive training before being allowed to embark. Longe was replaced on 7 February, just before his brigade departed for France. The two other brigade commanders had been replaced in January shortly after arriving in France.

Before the age of mass communication, a general feature of army life was the spread of rumours, those connected with impending moves being particularly rife. In Kitchener's New Army divisions, such was the eagerness to get to the Front that these rumours were particularly prevalent. Not until early September did the long awaited and frequently predicted move of 16th Division materialise, and then only to the Aldershot area of England. In accordance with Lord Kitchener's policy, the move of the division proceeded quietly without fuss or parade. Battalion followed battalion on trains to Dublin, usually arriving very early in the morning. They then boarded the steamer to Holyhead and the train to Woking, Blackdown or Bordon. Upon arrival, the division underwent a sudden transformation. Equipment long awaited miraculously arrived—machine-guns, transport, engineer and signals equipment, stores of all kinds and in such vast quantities as to make quartermasters appear more harassed than usual. New 1908-pattern equipment was issued and fitted. Weeks were spent on the ranges under musketry experts; route marching over extended distances in full field service marching order occupied much time and showed a marked improvement. And digging, digging!

THE QUEEN'S PARADE, 2 DECEMBER 1915

On 19 November 1915, 16th Division concentrated and paraded as a division for the first time. On Cobham Ridges, the battalions paraded in a rehearsal for a review by the King. Under its GOC and his staff, the division formed up for inspection. In bad weather, with snow on the ground, the parade mustered too early and had a long wait. At the appointed hour, Lt.-Gen. Sir Archibald Hunter, the army commander, inspected and took the salute. The parade was not a success. 'Orders incoherent and inaudible. Brigades tried to drown each other. Company commanders "paddled their own canoes". On uneven ground the march past was ragged'.[39]

For the next fortnight, all concentrated on ceremonial drill. The diverse regimental origin of senior officers, with their own customs which did not agree with the drill book, complicated training and caused some hilarity.[40] After a week, however, the standard of drill was raised considerably; but to achieve this, all other training had to cease. It could not have failed to reflect on the division in the minds of the Command staff, especially when taken together with evident training gaps in other areas.

The King would normally have personally reviewed the division. Unfortunately, on a recent visit to the Western Front, his horse had fallen and twice rolled over him as he lay on the ground. His injuries were more serious than was realised, and Queen Mary carried out his public engagements.[40] What became known as the Queen's Parade was held on 2 December, and 16th Division was inspected by Queen Mary in good weather. In the extraordinary way of such events, 'on the day' it was a remarkable success. They marched past by battalion in line of companies to their regimental music and presented a smart appearance; all were congratulated. It was a significant fillip to their pride as a division. Lord Kitchener, who had inspected 10th Division once and 36th Division thrice, did not inspect or visit 16th Division at all. To be fair, in early December 1915, Lord Kitchener was in France, visiting GHQ and discussing with Gen. Sir William Robertson the terms of his appointment as Chief of the Imperial General Staff.[42] 'Wullie' Robertson, ever his own man, was determined to be Chief at the War Office. Kitchener, meeting a man as bluff and plain spoken as himself, gave way gracefully and Robertson got the appointment on his own terms.

Just before the Queen's parade, orders for embarkation for France arrived; the division, less 49 Brigade, would leave within two weeks. Long before the orders arrived, officers of 49 Brigade, knowing their standard of training, discounted rumours of an impending departure for France. Now they were told officially; they would remain in Aldershot Command for intensive training and additional drafts.

Before their departure, the Catholic Primate of England and Wales, Cardinal Bourne, gave an impressive address to the Catholics of the division 'who were in the vast majority'.[43]

Gen. Parsons had received news that he was not to accompany the division to France. He spoke to his troops in farewell and in sorrow at not accompanying them. He congratulated all on their smart appearance and good behaviour in England. The men cheered him as he left. It is in the nature of command that he was thoroughly disappointed; his men were also sad at losing him.

> It was a great disappointment to everyone; he was very much liked and had raised the division. I was talking to his daughter yesterday and she told me he and Lady Parsons were very much cut up about it. He is old but everyone thought he would at least take the division to France... The new general is William Hickie, so we can't complain.[44]

Parsons might have been able to devote more of his time to his troops and their training had there been no political dimension to his command. His training, soldierly career and temperament had ill-equipped him to deal with politicians. Indeed, considering party politics had recently deeply divided whole sections of the army during the Ulster crisis, it is hardly surprising that Parsons was deeply suspicious of politicians. He may have thought that political manoeuvring had something to do with his supersession. The truth is more prosaic. Gallipoli had clearly shown the War Office the danger of allowing worn-out, recalled generals to command troops on active service. The best commanders of New Army divisions would be successful regular brigade commanders who had somehow survived the battles of 1914–15, and who were familiar with the tactics of the Western Front. Maj.-Gen. William Hickie, the new general officer commanding, 16th (Irish) Division, was one. He completed the division's training, made it battleworthy and quickly impressed his officers. 'Our new divisional General seems to be very efficient and has had much experience at the Front.'[45]

Just before Christmas 1915, their spirits high, the battalions of 16th Division, less 49 Brigade, marched out of their camps on their way to war. They marched to the music of pipes and drums. 'Garryowen', 'Come Back to Erin', 'St Patrick's Day' and all the other regimental marches were played, except 'Brian Boru', which was reserved for great and terrible moments and would come later.

Some officers and men proved over-age and unfit for active service and much heart-aching was suffered when the final lists for overseas service were published. It was especially hard for those over-age officers and NCOs who had given so much to their units during the early days when their experience was so badly needed. However many of those left behind served very usefully in recruiting appointments. Lord Fingall of the Leinsters went to Drogheda. Capt. William Redmond MP, Royal Irish, went to the divisional staff. Lt. Tom Kettle, 9th Dublins, was sent to Newcastle-upon-Tyne on a recruiting drive. Tom Kettle was over-age for frontline service. Indeed because of his poor health, it is difficult to know how he came to be accepted for the army and can only be explained by his own enthusiasm and the heady atmosphere of the time. Other officers, NCOs and men were returned to regimental depots and probably found their way into garrison battalions of their regiments.

49 Brigade, which had been held back to complete their neglected training, marched in pouring rain to Bordon ten miles south-west of Aldershot. There, training intensified and not surprisingly focused on preparation for the trenches. The battalions laboured at siting, digging and improving trench works; wiring at night under fire; and practising trench manning and relief routine. Suddenly it appeared to them strange that such aspects of warfare had not been taught before: 'True, we had many lectures about the life and routine of stationary warfare in France, but we needed some practical work in this branch to appreciate it thoroughly.'[46]

This was all put right during their stay at Bordon. At least twice a week, companies were detailed to dig and improve the model trenches in the training area at Hogmoor. By the end of December, quite a fair system of trenches and redoubts had been completed and it became part of the weekly programme to conduct all-night exercises in its lines. They practised inter-company relief and trench improvement. Telephone communications were established, tested and used by the commanding officer, from his headquarters about 400 yards behind the front line, to exercise the companies. They were visited occasionally by the brigadier, and the brigade major was always in attendance with advice and criticism.[47]

Brig. Longe departed and a new brigade commander arrived. Brig.-Gen. Philip Leveson-Gower came from a family which had provided two Secretaries of War in the nineteenth century. He had served on the North-

West Frontier and in South Africa, won a brevet lieutenant-colonel and colonel in France and was to remain with 49 Brigade until it ceased to be Irish.

At last, in mid February 1916, the final section of 16th Division's orchestra was ready for the overture. As they sailed for France, a piper of 7th Inniskillings, playing solo, sent 'A Sprig of Shillelagh' trilling across Southampton Water.[48]

CHAPTER NINETEEN

The Loos Salient

THE NEW COMMANDERS
In February 1916, with all its brigades in France, the headquarters organisation and skeleton order of battle of 16th Division was:

GOC	Maj.-Gen. W.B. Hickie (5 December 1915)
GSO1	Lt.-Col. L.C. Jackson
AA&QMG	Lt.-Col. G.A.C. Webb
BGRA	Brig.-Gen. E.J. Duffus
CRE	Lt.-Col. W.L. Palmer

47 Infantry Brigade, Brig.-Gen. G.E. Pereira (20 January 1916)
48 Infantry Brigade, Brig.-Gen. F.W. Ramsay (23 January 1916)
49 Infantry Brigade, Brig.-Gen. P. Leveson-Gower (7 February 1916)

Maj.-Gen. William Hickie CB, who assumed command of 16th Division, was of Slievoyre, Borrisokane, Co. Tipperary and came of an old Irish military family. Born 21 May 1865, he was educated at Oscott College and Sandhurst. Throughout his stay at Oscott he competed with his brother for first place every year. Commissioned into the Royal Fusiliers in 1885, he later passed Staff College where 'his only study was done on the early morning train from London'.[1] Stationed for a time with his regiment in Egypt, he had an affair with an Austrian archduchess, and was the 'penniless subaltern' mentioned in the memoirs of Marie de Vetsera.[2] Hickie served during the South African War on the staff of Le Gallais' Mounted Infantry Brigade which nearly destroyed the combined commando of Steyn and De Wet.[3] Promoted brevet lieutenant-colonel, he commanded a Mobile Column in the elusive war against the Boer commandos. After the war, he was DAQMG 8th Division 1903–06, following which he commanded 1st Royal Fusiliers. Promoted to the rank of colonel, he became AQMG at HQ Ireland during 1912–14. Promoted brigadier-general in 1914, he commanded a brigade in France 1914–15 and was wounded. Hickie had a brilliant mind, but preferred regimental life with its opportunities for action and sport rather than the greater opportunities for career advancement offered by comparatively dull service on the staff.

16th Division was despatched to the Loos Sector of First Army (Gen. Sir Charles Monro), where its brigades were placed under divisions of either I or IV Corps of Monro's army for its initiation to front-line duty. All units of the division had their introduction to the trenches in conditions of frozen snow and ice which in itself brought their first casualties, from exposure. Each brigade was allocated to a division, battalions to a brigade and companies were allocated to battalions. In this way, the division was quickly given its final polish and suffered its first losses, one officer and five men killed, seventeen wounded and two missing. There followed several tours of duty in the line under this well established procedure which gave New Army formations their baptism of fire and 'blooding' before being committed fully. In addition to their front-line duty, over the Christmas period they provided engineer working parties improving trenches and defences and burying communications cable. All the generals under which the brigades were serving inspected them with great interest, but no visit was more historic than that by Gen. Joffre. After a century and a quarter, an Irish brigade was again fighting for France.

In January shortly after arrival in France, Brig. G.E. Pereira assumed command of 47 Brigade. Pereira had led possibly the most adventurous life of any in the division. An eccentric character, a lame Guards officer who spoke Chinese, he had commanded a Chinese regiment and taken part in the fighting to relieve the Peking Legations during the Boxer Rebellion. After this he travelled extensively in China before going to South Africa. A temporary attaché in Seoul, Korea, he witnessed a naval action and the Manchurian campaign during the Russo-Japanese War. Then, appointed attaché at Peking, he remained there until 1910. Returning to the army in 1914, he had worked on the staff and commanded a battalion before going to 47 Brigade. His career with 16th Division was still before him. After the war, he was to journey from Peking to Lhasa mostly on foot, the first European to reach the city since two French Lazarist missionaries in 1846. The Irish of the Four-Provinces Brigade were to discover they had a brigadier worthy of them.

The battalions of 47 Brigade disembarked at Boulogne and Le Havre between December 18–19 and detrained near Bethune just before Christmas, coming under 15th Scottish Division of IV Corps. Gen. Hickie inspected them and could not have been more impressed. Just before Christmas 1916, on the occasion of a church parade, in congratulating one battalion he told its commanding officer, 'You should have seen what I had to look at twelve months ago'.[4] They were inspected on 5 January 1916 by the corps commander, Lt.-Gen. Sir Henry Wilson. He was no friend of Irish Nationalists; however as his diaries contain no record of his inspection, he could have found nothing hurtful to say of 47 Brigade.

Wilson, the pre-war Director of Military Operations and arch-intriguer of the Ulster crisis, neglected his prime duties. Under him, the British General Staff had not studied semi-siege warfare. Following the lessons of the Russo-Japanese War, it was practised by the Germans at their annual manoeuvres and duly reported upon by British observers. The Operations Staff, under Wilson's direction, ignored this and other intelligence and failed to discern the necessity for heavy artillery in these operations and the need to initiate an operational staff requirement for its procurement. For over a year the BEF suffered from a lack of heavy artillery as a direct result. Wilson was 'content to follow French doctrine'.[5]

Now commanding troops in action for the first and last time, Wilson was under a cloud with GHQ for upsetting IV Corps by telling his divisional commanders 'the French were better fighters than the British and the Germans were better leaders'.[6] When Sir Charles Monro returned from the Near East and assumed command of First Army, Haig instructed him to examine the morale in IV Corps.[7]

The Irish Division had its baptism of fire in the salient captured during the battle of Loos in the previous October. Next to the Ypres salient, it was probably the most harrowing part of the Front. Within the sound of guns and small arms, the battalions billeted either in farmhouses, barns or under canvas on muddy fields. The first taste of war occurred to 6th Connaught Rangers on 26 December 1915, when a German mine was exploded and buried a machine-gun sergeant for thirty minutes. Lt. O'Brien, with the battalion bombers, supported the Scottish riflemen in holding the lip of the crater. Their first casualty was Pte. P. McTernan, wounded in action.

IN THE LINE

At the end of January 1916, front-line training began in earnest under artillery fire. The battalion machine-gun section took over the left subsector held by the 10th Scottish Rifles with battalion headquarters at Philosophe. In their first experience of a German attack, the Rangers behaved with commendable steadiness; their machine-guns in particular under Lt. E.E. Beatty were praised by the Scots for the way in which they handled their guns. B Company had two killed and thirteen wounded. The total casualties for the battalion's first four days in the trenches were seven killed and twenty-nine wounded.

At the same time, the Royal Irish entered the trenches at notorious Puits 14 bis north-east of Loos, where in early February the enemy exploded two mines and laid down a heavy bombardment. However the battalion Lewis guns prevented the Germans from entering the craters of the mines and the bombers occupied the near lip of the craters and held the line. The Irishmen improved their fire trenches and with small arms fire, grenades and supporting artillery fire, fought to prevent the Germans from constructing saps towards their positions. The use of these saps was to become clear much later. The Germans for their part replied with intermittent bombardments. In one of these, 2/Lt. Bowen was wounded on 3 February. Four days later, the battalion had its first officer death casualty when Capt. G.S.R. Stritch, who had already won a name within the battalion for his daring, was killed. The Leinsters and Irish Rifles followed the Royal Irish and Rangers. Their blooding experience was very much the same.

48 Brigade, which had come under command of Brig. F.W. Ramsay, was attached to 12th Division of I Corps (Lt.-Gen. Sir H. de la P. Gough). As with 47 Brigade, a series of inspections inevitably followed. After Gen. Hickie came Sir Hubert Gough, then Gen. Monro. This last inspection took place in a blizzard after which 48 Brigade moved into the line for their period of instruction. On the night of 29 February (it was leap year) the battalions moved into the line on the Hulluch sector with Home Counties battalions of Essex, East Surrey and Middlesex.

In early March, a thaw turned the frozen ground into a sea of mud. Rain followed, trenches became knee deep in water or mud, and all were soaked. But work on the trenches continued through days and nights of wet and bitter cold. Their fortitude and endurance, like all the others who manned the front line on both sides, was admirable; it demonstrated the remarkable resilience of the human spirit. After a few days from the line clean and refreshed by a full night's sleep, they were again ready to return.

One of the problems facing battalions out of the line was to get farmers' wives to provide billets for soldiers. In 8th Munsters, because he spoke good French, 2/Lt. J.H. Hall was appointed billeting officer; his tact was to stand him in good stead in the diplomatic service after the war (he became Sir J.H. Hall GCMG DSO OBE MC).

> My procedure is always the same. I first compliment them on the beauty of their children, the gallantry of their soldiers and the cleanliness of their stores (they are always grumpy and disobliging and singularly unembarrassed by the ordinary conventional decencies of life). Then after a few more sugary compliments and patting all the children on the head, I suggest... They grumble but I always prevail.[8]

In mid February, 49 Brigade arrived in France and after a short time in the rear areas, joined the division. Almost on arrival they were inspected by the GOC, Gen. Hickie. He inspected each battalion separately in snow a foot deep. However as each company was inspected he gave instructions for it to fall out. It was a type of consideration which impressed the men. Afterwards, Hickie spoke to the officers of each battalion, explaining the nature of trench warfare and his policy, 'maintaining the aim'. After line duty with several battalions at Givenchy and Festubert, their period of 'on the job training' finally over, 49 Brigade became fully operational and relieved one of 15th (Scottish).

FULLY OPERATIONAL

At last, after months of frustration, 16th Division became fully operational on 1 March in I Corps of First Army. I Corps divisions, 1st (Regular), 12th

Light, and 15th (Scottish), were regarded as among the finest in the army. 16th (Irish), in good company, moved into Corps reserve and its training continued uninterrupted. Within two weeks, the division concentrated and took over the notorious Hulluch and Puits 14 bis sectors of the Loos salient. Opposite them in the line were 4th Bavarian Division, who proved to be worthy opponents.

Sir Hubert Gough asked for the Irish Division to be sent to his Corps and genuinely welcomed and praised them for their 'loyalty, devoted sense of duty, and gallant spirit'. But an insensitive qualification, 'Home Rulers though they were', nullified this praise, although the slur was probably unintentional.[9]

In addition to serving as an introduction to the Front, it also introduced the Irish to life behind the lines in the division's billeting areas, as well as to the sparse delights of innumerable small cafés. The beer was 'weak, wine like vinegar and spirits forbidden. In addition, commanding officers dealt severely with any cases of drunkenness which came before them. In the circumstances these were few.'[10] There was a small compensation, however; being in a mining area, the sector had the finest bath-houses on the Western Front.

The Irish fraternised freely and amicably with the French. They tried the language and, as with all strangers to French, caused much amusement. But 'it was not long before the men got quite enough working knowledge of the language to carry on a conversation with "Madame" to get whatever they required.'[11] Every effort was made to make St Patrick's Day a holiday; after Mass, brigade sports competitions were held and football matches took place. That evening battalion concerts helped momentarily to forget the trenches. That day, a message was received from the Army Commander, Gen. Sir Charles Monro:

> Please convey to all ranks my best wishes on St Patrick's Day, and my feeling of confidence that they will prove themselves to be the stern, hard fighters that Irishmen have always shown themselves to be.[12]

Trenches in the sector were in a poor condition. The stench and the rat swarms were common to all trench lines but 'Tenth Avenue', the main support line, was an example of some nightmare from the Brothers Grimm. Suffering unrelenting bombardment, the trenches required constant repair. The wiring on the Front was totally inadequate, but bright moonlight and alert German sentries prevented improvement. At this stage of the war, the German heavy artillery dominated its British counterpart. It saturated the British front with such a preponderance of fire that the troops were hard pressed to maintain their trenches. This inevitably caused a constant drain of casualties.

The division held its sector on a two-brigade frontage, with the third brigade in reserve; the Front was a continuous line of considerable depth. Each brigade held a two-battalion frontage with one battalion in a support line behind and one farther back in reserve. Front-line battalions operated with two companies actually in the line, with a company in support trenches 100–200 yards behind and another in reserve 400–500 yards farther back. Each battalion manned the Front for equal specific periods during the brigade's front-line tour of duty of eight days. This was followed by four days in reserve behind the lines. Such was the distance between the Front and rear areas that the journey between front and billeting areas might take up to twelve hours. During the period of 'reserve' duty, battalions provided work parties for division and brigade, on the constant fatigue of maintaining and repair of roads, trenches and communication lines. Those not on fatigue duty continued training; grenade-throwing, sniping, wiring and general trench routine.[13] The time a soldier might actually rest was therefore limited. The routine, however, could be severely interrupted by the inconsiderate enemy:

> On 4 April the CO and his company commanders went to Philosophe to inspect trenches in the Hulluch Sector to be taken over from 8th Dublins on 6 April. On that day the Germans heavily bombarded that front, delaying the takeover to the disgust of the Dublins.[14]

A change of corps commanders took place when Lt.-Gen. C.T. McMurrough-Kavanagh took over from Gen. Gough who left to form a new Corps which grew into an army.

Brigade and battalion headquarters were located in cellars at Loos. Each headquarters was connected to its subordinate and superior headquarters by telephone. Battalions had no fixed number of companies in the line or in support or reserve. This would depend upon a number of factors, frontage of the line held, strength of the battalion and enemy activity being the most important.

Every period of duty, even 'quiet' spells, had its casualties.

> On 6 April, 47 Brigade relieved 48 Brigade in the trenches before Hulluch. The Royal Irish had three companies in the support line and one in reserve. On the 9th, the battalion relieved the 6th Connaught Rangers. Three companies took over the front line, with one in reserve. When relieved on the 16th, they took over billets in Philosophe. 1 officer, 8 men killed, 1 and 19 wounded.[15]

The bald statement of facts hides the grim terror of the awful moment and bloody reality of death and destruction. There was the hurried handover and long trudge in drenched, muddy clothing, stumbling with fatigue, back to billets through crowded zig-zagging communications trenches which seemed endless. This was followed by a march on slippery, shell-torn pavements to billets in barns and byres, if they were lucky. The colliery baths of the Loos area were put to good use and each man was provided with a clean set of underwear in exchange for his own. These were then washed and passed on to another unit in their turn at the bath. While the men were bathing, their uniforms were cleaned, pressed and had insect life removed by locally employed women.[16]

THE GAS ATTACK AT HULLUCH, 27–29 APRIL 1916

Events in Dublin during the last part of April 1916 might have cast something of a shadow over the division, but they had their own concerns which gave little time for thoughts other than their own survival. The most serious enemy gas attack since Second Ypres a year before was now to take place on a wide front, striking the whole of 48 and 49 Brigades and a part of 15th Scottish on their left.

At Easter, a German deserter gave the first indications of a pending gas attack. This was confirmed by Intelligence from aerial reconnaissance showing gas cylinders within the enemy lines and swarms of rats leaving German trenches for no man's land as they sought to escape leaking gas. Divisional headquarters issued warnings and instructions which were relayed down to companies and platoons. Gen. Hickie ordered the strengthening of defences, especially wire. Blankets soaked in Vermorel, an anti-gas agent, were to cover entrances of all dug-outs. Vermorel sprayers were checked and ready for use and personal respirators made ready. Compared to those which were to come later, the sack gas-helmet then available was of inferior quality and would only reduce, not prevent, the possibility of asphyxiation, but this was not generally known at the time.[17] As they waited, many must have considered their fate, for all knew its horrible choking effects from the experience of others. Heavy shelling on 26 April swept the Front searching out artillery forward observation posts and lines of communication as the enemy guns registered. It confirmed all other indications of an impending attack.

16th Divisional front was from the right, 48 Brigade, 9th Munsters, 8th Dublins up; 9th Dublins and 8th Munsters in support. 49 Brigade, 7th Inniskillings, 8th Irish Fusiliers up; 8th Inniskillings, 7th Irish Fusiliers in support. 47 Brigade; 6th Royal Irish, 7th Irish Rifles, 6th Connaught Rangers and 7th Leinsters in reserve on stand-to awaiting orders to move forward. On the left of 8th Irish Fusiliers was 9th Black Watch. The divisional artillery stood by their guns; engineers toiled at last-minute efforts on defences; signallers crouched in dug-outs over switchboards or at cable distribution points. At their headquarters in Loos, Gen. Hickie, his brigadiers and their staffs waited for reports. During the first major gas-attack at Ypres, whole battalions had abandoned their positions and fled choking from the green clouds. Being human, Hickie and his staff must have wondered whether the same thing would happen now to their young troops.

A slight easterly breeze was blowing as the dawn showed its first streaks in the eastern sky. Then, at 0435, to draw the Irish from their dug-outs, the enemy opened intense rifle and machine-gun fire. Ten minutes later, when they expected the trench line to be fully manned, a deluge of shell-fire descended. Almost simultaneously gas was released from forward German saps. The gentle breeze, strong enough to carry but not to disperse, caused a gas cloud in which smoke had been mixed to drift lazily across no man's land. Such was its concentration that visibility was reduced to three yards. Hanging over the Front and support trenches for a while, it then drifted slowly south-westward. After half an hour, as the gas lingered over the Irish trenches, the bombardment lifted and moved rearward; the barrage now included heavy quantities of gas-shells, 'lachrymatory' or tear-gas chiefly directed towards the artillery positions. The divisional artillery replied at once and was joined by the Corps 'heavies'.

The Irish infantry opened fire, but under cover of gas and smoke, the Germans advanced through saps close up to the Irish trenches before assaulting. Lodgments were gained in several trenches and grim close-quarter fighting began. Touch was briefly lost between the Inniskillings and Dublins but restored within fifteen minutes. In fierce and confused hand-to-hand fighting, some prisoners were taken and hurried out towards the German lines. Those who struggled against this or attempted to escape were killed, or caught in the descending counter-barrage of their own artillery and killed with their German captors. Numerous gas casualties were inflicted. However, most casualties were caused by the heavy concentrated initial bombardment which had knocked trenches to pieces on a front of half a mile. This cut telephone communications and blocked communication trenches. It meant runners in their gas-masks had the greatest difficulty in getting through to headquarters. Many support company commanders, acting on their own initiative, sent forward reinforcements which helped to restore the situation. Eventually all the enemy were ejected from the Irish trenches. As they withdrew, the enemy blew a small mine between two large craters from previous mines, nicknamed Tralee and Munster, and under cover of this they gained their own lines. Enemy dead counted in front of 48 Brigade were approximately 200, and 49 Brigade 250. Two hours later came a repetition of the gas attack and bombardment, followed by a renewed assault which was beaten off before it could reach the Irish trenches. The wind changed and blew the gas back into the faces of the Germans and into their crowded trenches. Caught in their own gas, they tried to escape by jumping out of the trenches. The corps commander switched the entire corps artillery onto the Irish sector and a deluge of fire descended on the exposed Germans. Battalion machine-guns joined in and added their own retribution.

The front-line trenches of 16th Division were smashed. Parapets were blown down, trenches filled in, material and equipment lay scattered all over the battlefield. Pervading all else was the stench of chlorine. Fire-bays and dug-outs were filled with dead and badly wounded to whom comrades and medical orderlies gave succour. Walking wounded and gas cases, blinded, choking and retching green bile, supported each other or, leaning on fit friends, formed long lines down the choked and chaotic communication trenches, making their painfully slow way back to the Regimental Aid Post before being evacuated to the Casualty Clearing Stations. Father Willie Doyle, chaplain to the Dublins, had a narrow escape.

> I had never tried the helmet on and did not know if it were in working order. In theory, with the helmet on I was absolutely safe, but it was an anxious moment waiting for the scorching test, and to make things more horrible, I was absolutely alone. But I had the companionship of One who sustained men in the hour of trial, and kneeling down I took the Pyx from my pocket and received the Blessed Eucharist as Viaticum. I had not a moment to spare and had my helmet just fixed when I was buried in a thick green fog of poison gas.[18]

Father Doyle's helmet worked perfectly, but not all helmets worked quite as well.

> As I made my way slowly up the trench, feeling altogether 'a poor thing', I stumbled across a young officer who had been badly gassed. He had got his helmet on, but was coughing and choking in a terrible way. 'For God's sake,' he cried, 'Help me to tear off this helmet—I can't breathe. I'm dying'.[19]

Father Doyle half carried him through the choked communications trenches to an aid post. By 1100 the battle was over. The guns fell silent and the cleaning up and the evacuation of the wounded and gassed began.

On 28 April at 1500 hours, advance parties of the Rangers entered the trenches to take over from 9th Dublins. During the night of 28th–29th, the Rangers moved into the support line and relieved 9th Dublins in brigade support. On the right were 8th Irish Fusiliers, on the left 8th Munsters. At 0500 on the morning of 29 April, the enemy released gas on the left sub-sector and many 8th Dublins and 8th Irish Fusiliers were gassed. Some of the Rangers machine-gun section were caught in the gas; the section commander, Lt. E.E. Beatty, and three men died and five were seriously gassed. Realising the importance of keeping the machine-gun in action. Pte. D. Lynch, although gassed himself, gallantly refused to leave his gun for some hours. He continued to work effectively against the attacking enemy after the companies on his flank had almost all been put out of action. Later he stopped a fresh enemy attack and knocked a gas cylinder back into the enemy trench. Lynch was later awarded the Distinguished Conduct Medal.[20]

8th Munsters were in the process of taking over a sector from 8th Dublins and lost three officers and seventeen men. Lt. H.M. Mitchell showed very conspicuous gallantry and was awarded a Military Cross, the first awarded to the battalion. Among the dead was Lt. John Nevill, attached to 8th Munsters, a former President of the Cambridge Union and history scholar of Emmanuel College.[21]

Casualties, 27 and 29 April

	Shelling	Gas	Total
Killed	232	338	570
Wounded	488	922	1410
Total			1980

The Black Watch suffered 107 officers and men killed and wounded.[22]

The enemy, massing behind their lines to support the attack, were caught by their own gas when a sudden change of wind carried the gas back on them, forcing them out of their trenches. There the Germans were caught in the open by the Irish divisional artillery and dispersed. 30 April was quiet, but on May Day an attack was expected. 8th Munsters were resolved to meet them halfway.

> We expected them over on the 1st again as it is a great day in Bocheland, but the wind changed and the swine daren't come without gas. My little company, only eighty strong now, was standing by to go over the top to meet them and were awfully disappointed when they didn't come.[23]

The following days were spent cleaning up the mess of the battle. Gas alarms were sounded on three succeeding days, but gas attacks did not materialise. Clearly the Germans had had enough of their own gas. The Hulluch Sector remained quiet for some time thereafter.

On the effects of gas, a fusilier of the Inniskillings wrote with feeling: 'It is, I can assure you, worse then being wounded or even killed, as the agony is terrible.'[24]

In the battle analysis, it was found important to discover what had caused such high gas casualties. In the short term, so as not to undermine confidence in equipment, it was at first 'unjustly attributed to bad anti-gas procedures in 16th Division.' But all gas-dead were found to have their helmets on correctly. Eventually the truth had to be admitted and the production of the more effective box respirator was rushed ahead.[25]

Shortly afterwards, the Germans on the front of 8th Munsters erected placards in connection with the Easter Rebellion. The Munsters, Catholic and nationalist to a man, reacted with that extraordinary characteristic which bemuses and bewilders Englishmen. First the Munsters replied by firing shots into the placards. Then they sang 'God Save the King', confounding their enemy's 'knavish tricks'.[26] That night a fighting patrol under Lt. F.J. Biggane 'cut their way through the enemy wire, straffed the Huns and captured both placards'.[27] The two placards were later presented by Lt.-Col. Williamson to King George V at an investiture, 'To which the King replied: "The oft-repeated gallantry of the Munsters, Colonel Williamson, will never be forgotten by me, or those who follow me."'[28]

John Lucy, then a sergeant with 2nd Royal Irish Rifles, expressed what was perhaps the general feeling of Irish soldiers concerning the Easter rebellion: 'My fellow soldiers had no great sympathy with the rebels, but they got fed up when they heard of the executions of the leaders.'[29]

DIVISIONAL REORGANISATION

At the end of May 1916, by coincidence four battalions of the Royal Munster Fusiliers were within miles of each other 'in the field in the presence of the enemy'.[30] The 1st, 8th and 9th battalions were with 16th Division and 2nd Battalion with 1st Division on their right flank. Shortly afterwards, 9th Munsters were disbanded to replace casualties in the other three battalions. Three officers and 146 soldiers joined 1st Munsters; seven officers and 140 soldiers went to 2nd Munsters in 1st Division, and twelve officers and 200 joined 8th Munsters. 1st Royal Munster Fusiliers had been transferred from 29th Division to 47 Brigade. At the same time, 7th Royal Irish Rifles went from 47 Brigade to 48 Brigade on 28 May 1916. To meet the changing situation on the Western Front, all infantry divisions lost their cavalry squadron and cyclist company. Therefore, C Squadron, South Irish Horse, was posted to the Corps Cavalry Regiment. The Cyclist Company was disbanded and its personnel distributed to the infantry battalions. Following the introduction of the Stokes trench-mortar, brigade trench-mortar batteries were organised and trained, to be put to good effect later on the Somme.

TRENCH WARFARE, JUNE–AUGUST 1916

Working in great secrecy, divisional headquarters planned retribution for the April gas attack and in June made its riposte as part of the Somme Battle deception plan. With a favourable wind, it was the turn of the Germans to receive the green choking cloud, together with a storm of shell-fire. Behind this, 7th Leinsters executed successfully a brilliantly planned raid.[31]

Battalions became proficient in the continuous turmoil of active trench warfare—raiding, countering enemy raids, improving trenches, cutting saps to forward craters used as listening outposts, the laborious and heart-pounding staking and wiring in the heart of no man's land under fire at night. Even out of the line there was no rest; working parties for the Royal Engineers was a hated fatigue. Roads and communication trenches had to be constantly maintained and repaired after shell damage. Sentries became adept at spotting and giving warning of the approach of the heavy, slow-moving 'coal box' type of heavy mortar projectile which landed with devastating effect.

New weapons arrived. On courses behind the lines and with on-the-job training in the line itself, men quickly became expert in the use of Mills bombs, Stokes medium trench-mortars, Lewis guns and Bangalore torpedoes (lengths of zinc tube six feet long filled with explosives and connected together with bayonet type sockets) which were used for destroying barbed wire entanglements. All began working in teams, becoming confident in their own abilities and that of their comrades. Mutual bonds of trust were forged, not least between officers and men. An example of this occurred during a raid of 6th Rangers. When, returning through enemy wire, L/Cpl. Leary was badly wounded, his sergeant, Paulin, attempted to bring him in but was himself wounded. Going for help, Sgt. Paulin then guided the battalion second-in-command, Maj. R.J.A. Tamplin and his company commander, Capt. J.J. Kavanagh to where Leary lay. Under intense fire from the alerted enemy, the two officers brought him in, although Leary died later of his wounds.[32] It was this willingness of self-sacrifice which drew all together in a common bond of membership of that most exclusive fraternity in the world—the front-line club.

When no official recognition of gallantry was made, 16th Division awarded a 'Parchment Certificate'. This, headed 'The Irish Brigade' in Celtic script, read:

I HAVE READ WITH MUCH PLEASURE THE REPORTS OF YOUR REGIMENTAL COMMANDER AND BRIGADE COMMANDER REGARDING YOUR GALLANT CONDUCT AND DEVOTION TO DUTY IN THE FIELD ON ... AND HAVE ORDERED YOUR NAME AND DEED TO BE ENTERED IN THE RECORD OF THE IRISH DIVISION.
MAJOR-GENERAL, COMMANDING 16TH IRISH DIVISION

The Irishmen called them 'Hickie's Medal'.[33]

The 16th Division remained at Loos until 24 August, taking its share of the successive tours of duty in the line. Raiding the German positions and being raided themselves, they were under constant shell, machine-gun and rifle fire; their casualties mounted steadily. But all had changed during their eight months at Loos. Their enthusiastic, irrepressible high spirits had hardened with experience. As they perfected their battle-craft, their self-confidence grew and they were supremely ready for anything the war might bring. The advance party of the last sub-unit arrived. This was the heavy Trench Mortar Battery which joined by 5 September 1916, just in time. 16th Division departed for the Somme and its first major battle. They left, fit, battle-worthy and confident after five months at the very tip of the Loos Salient, but the cost of this was not light. 1496 dead[34] were left behind at Loos. Their total battle casualties were not less than 6000, more than most Kitchener Army divisions sacrificed in their first battle.

Later a memorial statue of Our Lady of Victories was erected in the church at Noeux-les-Mines in memory of the fallen of 16th Division.[35] Sadly there is now no trace of this in the churches of the area.

CHAPTER TWENTY

Raising and Training 36th Division, September 1914–May 1915

36TH (ULSTER) DIVISION HEADQUARTERS AND ORDER OF BATTLE

After the declaration of war with Germany there was a delay of some weeks, probably on political grounds, before the order was issued to form an Ulster Division.[1]

The 36th Division was authorised on 28 October 1914. Maj.-Gen. C.H. Powell assumed command the same day and began to form his headquarters staff at 29 Wellington Place, Belfast.[2]

Maj.-Gen. Charles Herbert Powell CB, Indian Army, came of an army family and was educated privately. Aged fifty-seven, Powell had served on the North-West Frontier with the Malakand Field Force, the Buner Field Force and in China during the Boxer Rebellion as a staff officer. His rise had been steady and unspectacular. The War Office appointed Powell to command 36th Division; the Ulster Unionists had hoped Gen. Sir George Richardson, Commander of the UVF, would command the Ulster division. Probably Powell was above politics and for this reason one of his first tasks was to 'knock the beer and politics out of them'.[2]

The brigades were raised in mid-September 1914. Initially called 1, 2 and 3 Brigades, they were subsequently renumbered 107, 108, 109 on 2 November 1914 when the division was officially authorised. However, the battalions of the division, based on the Ulster Volunteer Force (UVF) order of battle, had been in existence since before the war.

The UVF had no artillery and consequently had no partially trained force upon which to draw. It was thought that the raising and training of artillery in Ulster would take so long that it might delay the departure to the Front of the Division for several months. In those days it will be remembered, the one feverish anxiety of the men of the New Armies was lest the war should be over ere they were able to play their part in it![3]

Artillery specifically for 36th Division was raised in the London boroughs of Croydon, Norbury and Sydenham in May 1915.[4] After training in England

and France, it joined the division during 1916. The 10th Division Ammunition Column, left behind when 10th went to Gallipoli, was transferred to 36th Division and became 36th Divisional Ammunition Column (DAC). Probably because 36th Division Artillery was not raised in Ulster, a manpower surplus existed in 1915 and six reserve infantry battalions were formed. These were the 17th, 18th, 19th and 20th Battalions Royal Irish Rifles; 12th Royal Inniskilling Fusiliers; and 10th Royal Irish Fusiliers.

36th Division was initially recruited from the Ulster Volunteer Force, the 'Ulster Army' created as an armed manifestation of resistance to Irish Home Rule.

> The Ulster Division was not created in a day. The roots from which it sprang went back into the troubled period before the war. Its life was a continuance of the life of an earlier legion, a legion of civilians banded to protect themselves from the consequences of legislation which they believed would affect adversely their rights and privileges as citizens of the United Kingdom—the Ulster Volunteer Force.[5]

Two days after Lord Kitchener's appointment as Secretary of State for War, Friday 7 August 1914, he sent for Col. T.E. Hickman MP, President of the British League for the Defence of Ulster, latterly Inspector-General of the UVF. Kitchener told him, 'I want the Ulster Volunteers.'[6] Hickman bluntly told Kitchener to see Carson and Craig. Kitchener saw Carson, but with no result.

In the words of the division's historian, 'a short delay ensued'.[7] It was widely believed at the time that the war would be over in a few months. All pre-war planning assumptions and war preparations by the countries involved had been made on this premise. Any delay in providing a fighting contingent from the Ulster Volunteer Force in response to Lord Kitchener's call could result in their missing the war. The Ulster Unionist leaders stood in danger of losing the moral high ground of patriotism they so fervently wished to occupy during the previous eighteen months. Indeed, men who would otherwise have joined an Ulster division refused to wait and joined 10th Division.

> The trouble is that, although it has been decided on principle that the UVF should become, if possible, an army corps of the regular army, details have not been arranged... It was rumoured that the delay was being caused by some political bargain being struck in regard to Home Rule, by Sir Edward Carson. About that I know nothing, but many hundreds of men of Tyrone, exasperated by the delay, marched to the depot and enlisted on their own... I think these men were right; Lord

Kitchener had called for men for the King's service and they responded.[8]

As a result of a meeting at Carson's house, attended by the Ulster Unionist MPs and Lord Roberts, Col. Hickman took a letter to Kitchener offering the aid of Carson and the Ulster Unionist Council in raising a force from the UVF. Capt. Craig and Col. Hickman were appointed chief recruiting officers for the Ulster area.

ACCOMMODATION FOR THE DIVISION

The majority of military establishments in Ireland were in the south, and some of these had been vacated by the departure of the BEF. The barracks were, however, occupied by the already established 10th and 16th Divisions. Consequent upon the formation of the 36th Division, a shortage of army accommodation existed in Ulster. Craig went directly to Kitchener for help, and was told that such details were not for him. Craig persisted. Eventually Kitchener summoned the Adjutant General, Director of Personnel Services, Quartermaster General, and Director of Fortifications and said to them: 'Take Craig away and see that he gets what he requires.'[9] Clearly, Capt. Craig had considerable persuasive powers.

But other factors, totally divorced from military ones, delayed construction of the camps which Capt. Craig had asked for. The Ulster Division was fiercely Protestant.

> One factor in this group-spirit and in the whole life of the Division, which is here approached with diffidence, but which could not be omitted from a faithful record, was the element of religion. It is sometimes forgotten that the Covenant of the seventeenth century was taken almost as widely in Ulster as in Scotland. Undoubtedly something of the old covenanting spirit, the old sense of the alliance of 'Bible and Sword', was reborn in these men.[10]

There was a less praiseworthy aspect to this covenanting spirit. When Headquarters Irish Command sent a Catholic 'Q' Staff Officer to liaise with HQ 36th Division on the construction of hutted camps, his religion became known to the Ulstermen and he had to be withdrawn.

> He...is well disposed and helpful and has, as his primary task, the quartering of the new division and the erection of vast camps of corrugated iron. But the fates are against him. It is discovered in the Ulster Club (how, goodness only knows) that the man from Dublin is a papist! A hurried line to an influential general in England and he disappears...[11]

As a result of this, the camps built at Ballykinler for 107 Brigade, at

Clandeboye and Newtownards for 108 Brigade, and at Finner for 109 Brigade, were tented. During the cold and wet winter of 1914–15, they could have only been highly unsatisfactory accommodation. The ground around them turned into quagmires. Pre-war regulars subjected to such atrocious conditions would have gone sick in droves. Such was the fibre of the Ulstermen that they remained generally cheerful in the appalling conditions. There is no evidence that, because of the dismissal of one of its staff, GHQ Ireland deliberately delayed construction of the hutted camps. But it could hardly have helped. The semi-permanent camps were not completed until early summer 1915, just as the division was departing for England.

ILLNESS IN THE DIVISION

During the cold, wet winter of 1914–15, there was considerable illness among the battalions of 36th Division, most probably because of its tented accommodation. Records show that there were more deaths in Ulster Division at 'Home' (that is, in the British Isles) in the period 1914–15 than in either 10th or 16th Divisions.[12] Concern grew about the state of health within the division to such an extent that eventually something had to be done.

> Because of growing unease about the state of health, those units which were still under canvas were moved to the available barrack accommodation.[13]

Most Irish old soldiers, and with them the NCOs, were Catholic and had enlisted in either the 10th or 16th Division. The 36th were therefore chronically short of NCO instructors. Many of the volunteer NCOs from the UVF kept control initially and in the majority of cases they were confirmed in their rank.[14] The more experienced had been those employed with the UVF as mercenaries, but they had either been recalled to the colours or enlisted. To replace them, a UVF officer of the 'Citadel Force', Maj. F.P. Crozier (later Brig.-Gen. F.P. Crozier CB CMG DSO) was despatched to London to interview re-enlistments on Horse Guards Parade to choose the best and entice them to the 36th. He stayed for several weeks in London and despatched drafts to Ulster almost daily. But most of the recruits were old men who had disguised their true age to enlist, and despite their keenness were out of date.[15]

However, in common with all New Army formations, the enthusiasm displayed by the volunteers for the military life deeply impressed all who encountered it. The interest in acquiring military knowledge became a passion which persisted into their off-duty hours, not least because of the bonds which existed between them from civilian life: 'The infantry of the 36th Division was formed on perhaps the most strictly territorial basis of any division of the New Armies.'[16]

Because the infantry structure of the division was based on the Ulster Volunteer Force, it was highly localised. Belfast streets, town districts or little villages provided whole platoons in a way which made them enlarged families. There are good reasons against this form of recruitment, as events were later to prove. When a unit recruited heavily from the same sparsely populated rural area suffers severe battle casualties, the instant effect on a small community is terrible. But in the heady atmosphere of 1914, this possibility was in the future and not then a consideration.

Almost immediately after Capt. Craig had met Lord Kitchener, Craig placed an order for 10,000 suits of uniform with a military outfitter with whom he had had dealing on behalf of the UVF. The cost of this was borne by friends of Ulster in England, who had created a special fund for this purpose.[17] The result was that, unlike many other divisions of the New Armies, the 36th did not have to train initially in mufti or motley uniforms.

Because of the basic training with the Ulster Volunteer Force, most had a rudimentary knowledge of foot-drill. They could number, form fours, stand at ease, attention, and could march in step. Many men of Kitchener's armies could do the same from previous service with the very popular Boy Scouts and Church Army Brigade. What made the 36th different was that many also had a knowledge of arms drill and musketry, having handled arms illegally imported for the UVF during the Ulster crisis.

Like all New Army formations, in the early days the 36th's chief military activity was marching. In the absence of webbing equipment, canvas rucksacks were purchased and carried fully loaded with kit. Despite the display of enthusiasm, the units were not up to war establishments and numerous recruiting marches were made, adding to the march discipline training. Because of the shortage of rifles (at this time they had only drill purpose rifles), little musketry training was carried out save on the Mauser rifles borrowed from UVF sources. They used UVF ranges for musketry practise, to which 'inspecting generals turned a blind eye'.[18] It was not until the division went to Aldershot Command that proper range courses were fired. Trench digging was neglected: 'Eighteen inches wide and straight down' was the dismissive comment of one Engineer officer.[19] Realistic training for war was as neglected in 36th Division as it was in 16th Division.

On 8 May 1915, the division was inspected at Malone on the outskirts of Belfast by Maj.-Gen. Sir Hugh McCalmont. Afterwards it marched through Belfast in a farewell parade to its native province. The *Lusitania* had been sunk by enemy action the previous day, but this failed to dampen the festive air of that Saturday morning. Sir Edward Carson and many Unionist supporters crossed from London to witness the event.[20] Belfast was *en fête* for the occasion and all Protestant Ulster turned out to say farewell to its division. The streets of Belfast along the parade route were bedecked with bunting and special trains were run to bring thousands of spectators from all over Ulster. The entire division marched past, including the divisional field ambulances, which, because the division lacked its own artillery, was equipped with the best horses and horsemen Ulster could provide. Unfortunately the motor ambulances, purchased by voluntary subscription throughout Ulster, were not yet ready. It must have been disappointing that when they were finally ready in December, the War Office allocated them to a Motor Workshop from Croydon, who then took them to France.[21]

For two more months, men of 36th Division waited in eager expectation before they finally moved to Seaford on the Sussex coast. The 9th Inniskillings were perforce left behind at Ballycastle to recover in quarantine with German measles.[22]

Lt.-Gen. Sir Archibald Murray, Deputy Chief of the General Staff, inspected the division during the last week in July. He reported favourably to Kitchener, who decided to visit them. This he did at 1100 hours on 28 July. He again inspected the division in September, after which he declared to Sir Edward Carson, 'Your division of Ulstermen is the finest I have yet seen.'[23] It was as a result of these visits that the Ulster division was given priority in the allocation of machine-guns and ranges to complete its training courses. A fully trained divisional artillery from the London area, 1st London Territorial Artillery, was transferred to the division on Kitchener's orders.[24] However when the state of 36th Division's training became apparent to the staff in France, the London Artillery was transferred elsewhere in December 1915. 36th Division Artillery did not join the division until March 1916.[25]

On 23 September, Maj.-Gen. C.H. Powell, the GOC, was relieved by Maj.-Gen. Sir O.S.W. Nugent. His home was at Mount Nugent, Co. Cavan. Distantly related to the Norman-Irish Earls of Westmeath, Nugent was educated at Harrow and commissioned into the King's Royal Rifle Corps. He had served on the North-West Frontier and South Africa where he had been seriously wounded. He had recently commanded a brigade on the Western Front and his appointment was in keeping with War Office policy, that only vigorous, experienced general officers would command the New Army Divisions. A week after Nugent assumed command, the King reviewed the 36th (Ulster) Division on 30 September. Kitchener accompanied His Majesty, who was smiling and well pleased. The King congratulated Gen. Nugent and turning to Sir George Richardson, CinC UVF, told him what a fine division had been given by his Ulster Volunteers.[26]

As with Gen. Parsons of 16th Division, the manner of Gen. Powell's supersession aroused sympathy. But with Gen. Powell there was an odd twist. Accompanied by senior officers of the 36th, he had toured the Front in France shortly before his supersession. Apparently the staff in France were aware of his imminent removal, even before the War Office had officially informed Gen. Powell. The last to know was the unfortunate general himself, and anger was felt by those officers who were aware of this.[27]

In the first two weeks of October 1915, the 36th crossed the Channel and moved to its concentration area around Flesselles, 10 miles north of Amiens, where divisional headquarters was established. With several moves, it remained in the general area of the triangle Abbéville–Amiens–Doullens for the winter of 1915–16. Each brigade was attached to either 4th Division or 48th Division for training. They held a quiet sector north of the Ancre where they 'suffered less from the enemy than the elements'.[28]

From the more experienced divisions, the 36th received training in the line. When in rear areas, they were trained in bombing and gas warfare by instructors from the host division. One bombing instructor commented 'that the national sport of the Ulsterman, throwing kidney-stones in street riots, was an admirable preparation for bombing'.[29] Anti-gas training was less well received.

> Passing through a gas chamber in these bags was unpleasant, though accepted as a necessity, but 'doubling' and marching in them, as ordered by some more zealous instructors, was purgatory.[30]

After these attachments, GHQ decided that 36th Division was not to go into the line and should be moved instead near Abbéville. At the same time, 107 Brigade and 12 Brigade of 4th Division were exchanged for three months. Throughout the winter of 1915–16, the remainder of the division was employed on work connected with the 'Big Push'.

Under Third Army engineers, the 36th converted village barns into troop accommodation and made horse lines. At the same time, the Pioneer Battalion constructed a broad-gauge railway between Candas and Acheux. In an area newly taken over from the French, the 36th were creating an infrastructure necessary for occupation by a vast army which would later move into the area of the Somme. It was, however, not the occupation they had expected.

> For the time it was concerned more with sanitation than with war. Never was such cleaning of streets, such draining of middens, such wholesale carting away of manure-heaps, as when the Ulster Division marched into an area.[31]

In early spring 1916, the Somme front was the quietest part of the British line when the 36th, now completely 'Ulster' again, assumed responsibility for a sector behind the Ancre near Mailly-Maillet. On its right was 32nd New Army Division and on the left 4th Regular Division. This last had three regular Irish battalions—2nd Inniskillings, 1st Irish Fusiliers and 2nd Dublins. By mid-march, 36th Division was fully operational and responsible for the sector astride the Ancre between Thiepval and Beaumont Hamel which will now always be associated with the historic province of Ulster. At that time of the year, the valley of the Ancre was idyllic; for about six weeks the sector was quiet, and many went fishing. Thiepval Wood was not completely quiet, however, and 10th Inniskillings had its baptism of fire on 10 March. For all that, the deepest discomfort the men suffered was trench foot, caused by water-logged trenches which in places were sometimes knee-deep.

The long awaited divisional artillery took its place in the line. However, the gunners' training was still incomplete and the artillery brigades took turns doing their final training shoot at Cayeux. Not until mid March was the artillery fully operational. As spring became summer, rumours of the 'Big Push' proliferated. It became the general subject of conversation until preparations for it began. One brigade held the line, one was held in reserve, the third trained. Later, a brigade of the 49th West Riding Division, the 147th, relieved one of the brigades. This enabled two brigades to train together on an elaborate system of dummy trenches representing the German system which was to be assaulted. The weather turned bad. Rain fell heavily and turned the tracks into impassable quagmires, making movement of huge stocks of ammunition to new gun positions difficult. At the last moment, a French artillery regiment with their famous '75s' joined the division to support the attack; gun-pits and shelters had to be constructed at short notice. 11th Inniskillings were given this task. They helped their allies so enthusiastically that they brought praise from Gen. Nugent. By the last week of June all was ready. In the expectation of an early battle, spirits were high. All were supremely confident.[31]

The divisional command structure on 14 May 1916
GOC   Maj.-Gen. O.S.W Nugent
GSO1   Lt.-Col. C.O. Place
AA&QMG   Lt.-Col. L.J. Comyn
BGRA   Brig.-Gen. H.J. Brock
CRE   Lt.-Col. P.T. Denis de Vitré
ADMS   Col. F.G. Greig
107 Infantry Brigade, Brig.-Gen. W.M. Withycombe
108 Infantry Brigade, Brig.-Gen. C.R.J. Griffith
109 Infantry Brigade, Brig.-Gen. H.G. Shuter

CHAPTER TWENTY-ONE

The Somme: Thiepval

THE BATTLE OF ALBERT

A great British offensive using the New Army divisions had been envisaged as early as 1915. Planning for the 'Big Push' began in January 1916. It was to be carried out by Fourth Army using five corps, with another three armies playing subsidiary roles. The crisis of the Verdun battle and the need to relieve the French brought the date forward by about six weeks. The selection of the Somme as its battleground was made to suit French convenience (Haig would have preferred to attack farther north in mid August).[1] Because the Somme area lacked great centres of communication, roads or railways, considerable preparatory work had to be carried out by the BEF in building the required infrastructure. Preparations had to begin at an early date once the decision had been reached. 36th Division became heavily involved in these preparations.

The Royal Artillery, which entered the war in France with 318 field guns and howitzers and 16 heavy guns, now had over 3985 all calibres, with an additional 200 heavy and medium mortars.[2] Once strictly limited in their ammunition usage, sometimes as low as three rounds per gun per day, the guns now had an almost unrestricted ammunition supply. Enthusiastic with their new power, the gunners filled the Higher Command with confidence in the ability of their weapons to reduce the enemy defences and break the German soldiers' will to resist. This overlooked, or ignored, the known limitations of the artillery arm at that stage of the war. Many heavy guns were of the 1895 pattern and dated from the Boer War. Some ammunition suppliers had poor quality-control in their manufacturing process, especially in the fuse which was prone to failure. Poor communications between the forward observation officers, gun-battery positions and commanders restricted the arm's flexibility. Finally, the enthusiasm of New Army divisional artillery brigades could not compensate for experience.

The precise timing of the initial attack was a matter of disagreement between the Allies. The British, mindful of the power of enemy machine-guns, wished to assault at dawn in near-darkness. The French, depending on their powerful artillery to dominate the battlefield, wanted a full-light attack to get good observation. Gen. Foch, commanding the army group attacking on the British right, insisted. As at Loos, Foch had his way.

The 36th was the left division of X Corps. It was flanked on the right by

32nd Division of the New Army and the left by 29th Regular Army Division (VIII Corps), recently back from Gallipoli. In X Corps reserve was 49th West Riding, a Territorial Force division.

Before the attack, elaborate training exercises were held by every division to accustom all ranks to the enemy lines they would assault and tactics they would use. In X Corps, brigades of 49th Division relieved those of 32nd and 36th to allow training over an elaborate system of dummy trenches, marked in outline with plough and spade to represent the divisional objectives, to familiarise all ranks with the objectives. This training proved of considerable value later.[3]

However, the army commander, Gen. Rawlinson, neglected one crucial aspect which had been the main tactical lesson of Neuve Chapelle—what to do if a position proved too tough and remained untaken after the first assault. No instructions were issued on the use of reserves.

Haig, a cavalryman, was conscious of his limitations in infantry tactics. During the initial conference with subordinate army commanders, he posed several interesting questions. Should the infantry advance in line, or probe to find weak spots and infiltrate? How near the barrage on the enemy parapet should infantry creep before it lifted and then charged? To the first question, his infantry generals answered 'in line', ignoring what might happen if defensive wire was only partially cut, a frequent experience. To the second question, 100 yards was considered safest. Commanders were influenced by the over-optimism of senior gunners. Gen. Rawlinson assured his corps commanders that 'nothing could exist at the conclusion of the bombardment in the area covered by it.' Sapping into no man's land to make a 'covered way' was left to divisional discretion; most opted against it.[4]

In VIII Corps area, a mine was to be sprung opposite the fortress village of Beaumont Hamel. The corps commander, Lt.-Gen. Hunter-Weston, wanted to spring it ten minutes before Zero Hour to allow the debris to settle before his troops advanced. This was agreed, with effects on the Ulstermen which will later be seen.

At the western end of Poziers Ridge, the Thiepval Plateau stands out like a great natural bastion. It slopes down sharply to the river Ancre on its west and north face. Its south-western face is more convex and thus offered some cover from view to the British positions. The upper Ancre flows westward to Hamel and makes a bend through a narrow valley containing the villages of Miraumont, Grandcourt, Beaucourt and St Pierre Davion on a railway alongside the Ancre. This railway was used to good effect by the Germans for rapid troop movement.

No man's land was open and bare of cover, save for high nettles and other weeds, especially around barbed wire which gave cover from view but also concealed the wire from observation. The German front everywhere overlooked the British front line. An already strong natural position was turned into a formidable fortress by deep-mined shelters under a maze of trenches. In the village of Thiepval, buildings collapsed over deep cellars reinforced with concrete. German military engineering skill, barbed wire and machine-guns made it a masterpiece of concealed strength. Opposite the Ulster Division was a particularly strong system of trenches, the Schwaben Redoubt, dominated and covered by the machine-guns of Thiepval.

The right flank boundary with 32nd Division ran from the north-east corner of Thiepval Wood to the German trench, D8. The divisional left boundary, which was also the junction with VIII Corps, ran from the redoubt called the Mary Redan to two houses half-way between Beaucourt and its railway station, then along the river to the railway bridge. The 3000 yard frontage of 36th Division bestrode the river Ancre; it held an area 1000 yards north of the river and 2000 yards to the south, 1000 yards of which was marshy. Therein lay an inherent weakness. It is military practice not to have boundaries resting on a natural or man-made feature; the natural weakness of a 'joint' is then made more vulnerable. Sometimes, however, this is unavoidable. Before radio, a formation attacking astride a natural feature invariably increased its communication problem. The 36th was to attack astride the Ancre with a gap of nearly 1000 yards between the two attacks.

On the southern bank of the Ancre, the ground rose sharply up from the river, 250 feet to the Thiepval plateau. The crest was crowned by a parallelogram of trenches, extending from the German B line to the C line, the Schwaben Redoubt. To reach it, the convex curve of the rising ground gave no cover. The German trenches were defended by masses of wire, particularly on the Ancre flank where it was sixteen rows deep; to its front it had five rows. Like all the German dug-outs on the Somme, those of the Schwaben Redoubt were at least thirty feet deep and bombproof. The divisional objective was the fifth line of German trenches.

The marshy banks of the Ancre, unsuitable for operations, were to be saturated with gas shells from the French 75s. On the left or north bank of the Ancre, the Ulster trench-line was between two strongpoints, the William and Mary redans. (The significance of the names William and Mary may have been lost on the Germans, but not on the 36th.) The corps boundary, river and Ulster trench-line formed a perfect triangle. Within this was the objective, a triangle of German trenches up to Beaucourt station. Here no man's land was about 400 yards deep; about half way across was a ravine seventy yards wide and twenty feet deep with steep banks.

Gen. Nugent divided his front into four sectors: right, 600 yards wide; Right centre, 600 yards wide; left-centre, the marsh, 800 yards wide; Left, 1000 yards wide. By saturating the marsh with gas, Nugent denied it to the enemy, leaving the right, right-centre and left sectors for his attack. He decided to concentrate the weight of the assault on the right and right-centre. There, seven battalions would attack with three battalions in reserve. On the left, two battalions were to attack with no reserve. He deployed his division accordingly.

Right Sector: 109 Brigade. The first line, 9th Inniskillings on the right and

10th Inniskillings on the left, were to go through all enemy lines to the C Line, halt and consolidate.

The second line, 11th Inniskillings on the right and 14th Irish Rifles on the left were to follow the first line, hold A and B lines and maintain contact with the first wave. It was important that 11th Inniskillings should fortify the position 'Crucifix' on the Thiepval-Grandcourt Road.

Right-Centre Sector: Two battalions, 108 Brigade and one battalion, 107 Brigade. The first line, 11th Irish Rifles on the right and 13th Irish Rifles on the left, were to go through all enemy lines to C line, halt and consolidate. 13th Rifles were tasked with forming a flank guard and clearing the approaches on the left, especially those covering the Grandcourt-Davion road. Two platoons were to clear the left up to Davion

The second line, 15th Irish Rifles, 107 Brigade, was in support.

Left Sector: The remaining two battalions of 108 Brigade. 9th Irish Fusiliers on the right was to take the mill on the river, Beaucourt station, the trenches and two houses immediately behind. 12th Irish Rifles were to attack the German salient on the left of the objective and clear trenches down to the railway. They were to establish strongpoints at B26 and B21. 12th Rifles were further tasked with detaching one platoon to take a sap on the railway: another platoon was to patrol the marsh in the Ancre valley.

Reserve: 107 Brigade (less one battalion), was to advance through Thiepval Wood, pass through 108 Brigade and 109 Brigade and capture the final objective, the D line from D8 to D11.

First line: 9th Irish Rifles on the right and 10th Irish Rifles on the left. On reaching D9 and D10, they were to expand the front to D8. Second line: 8th Irish Rifles was to advance to D line and occupy D10–11.

The assault battalions were to advance in eight successive waves, at fifty yard intervals. 107 Brigade was to advance in the more dense 'artillery formation' (columns of platoons in extended order).

Supporting artillery consisted of 36th Divisional artillery and one artillery brigade of 49th Division, a regiment of French field artillery and a concentration of corps heavy artillery. The artillery bombardment was to last five days; because of rain, it was extended for a further two days. All the wire in front of 36th Division southern sector was cut. To the artillery observers, the results looked magnificent. The results on the northern sector were less certain.

After a final intensive period of sixty-one minutes, the guns fired intensively upon each German line in a succession of timed 'lifts'. These were designed to concentrate on a succession of German trenches and allow the infantry to catch up just as the barrage lifted. At this stage of the war, the barrage was inflexible; it was not a proper creeping barrage and could not be halted and brought back should it 'run away' from the infantry. At one stage, there was an extended barrage to support the passing through of 107 Brigade. At each 'lift', the barrage 'walked up' enemy communications trenches to its next barrage line.

Stokes mortars joined in a final hurricane bombardment for wire cutting just prior to zero hour. They were assisted by the French 75s using high explosive shells, unlike the Royal Artillery which used shrapnel at this time.

Two machine-guns accompanied each battalion in the attack; the remaining eight of each machine-gun company were held in Brigade Reserve. On 27–28 June it rained. The attack was postponed for two days. Assembly was also postponed, and inter-brigade reliefs were arranged to relieve the troops in the front line who had endured the bombardment.

One order by X Corps headquarters was to have profound consequences—no commanding officers were to accompany their battalions. Since second-in-commands were also left out of battle with ten per cent of battalion strength, it meant no senior officers would be present with the troops during the battle.

As a result of the postponement, the assault would now take place on the anniversary of the Battle of the Boyne, the holiest day in the Orange calendar: 'On the 1st July, an old landmark in the History of ULSTER, the day so long looked forward to...'[5]

Z-day dawned clear and sunny, 'a glorious summer morning'. Zero hour was at 0730, four hours after dawn. In the closing minutes of the bombardment, Stokes mortars laid down smoke. South of the Ancre, the troops lined the Thiepval-Hamel sunken road.

At 0715, the leading companies surged through the gaps in their own wire, extended to intervals of two paces to within 150 yards of the German A trench. At 0720, the earth shook with the explosion of a mine before Beaumont-Hamel. More than anything else, it told the Germans the assault was under way; ten minutes later the bombardment on the German line lifted. Whistles blew, and the men advanced steadily at marching pace with rifles sloped. The troops were in 'fighting order', that is with no large pack. However, all were weighed down with additional ammunition, barbed wire, stakes, entrenching tools, parts of machine-guns or belts of ammunition and other extra equipment. This slowed the pace of the advance.

Battalion commanding officers, majors and sergeant-majors who by divisional order would not accompany the assault, bade their men an emotional farewell. Two battalion commanders disobeyed orders and accompanied their men. One, Lt.-Col. Bernard, cousin to the Anglican Archbishop of Dublin, was killed leading his men. The other, Lt.-Col. Crozier, performed sterling service. Another commanding officer wrote: 'They got going without delay; no fuss, no shouting, no running, everything solid and thorough—just like the men themselves.'[6]

Before the attack started, an act of heroism which typified the gallantry of the Ulstermen on that day was enacted near Thiepval Wood. Pte. William M'Fadzean, a bomber of 14th Rifles, dropped a box of grenades into a crowded trench and two safety pins fell out. In an act of supreme sacrifice,

Pte. M'Fadzean threw himself into the bombcluster and was blown to pieces, but in doing so he saved the lives of many. Only one other was wounded. For his conspicuous bravery, M'Fadzean was awarded the Victoria Cross.

NORTH OF THE ANCRE—THE BLOODY ANGLE

> The order was for the leading wave to get within 150 yards from the German line by 7.30 am to be ready to assault the instant our barrage lifted at 7.30 am. To do this the leading waves went over our parapet at 7.10 am, the second wave at 7.15 am, the third at 7.20 am and the last waves at 7.30 am.[7]

At Zero hour, the two battalions in the line between the William and Mary redans assaulted in four waves of companies in platoon echelon. The 9th Irish Fusiliers, recruited almost exclusively from Armagh, Monaghan and Cavan, advanced with great spirit. The first wave of platoons got away with few casualties. The second wave had many casualties, but the third and fourth waves were met with heavy machine-gun fire which cut down whole ranks like corn before a scythe. Undaunted, the survivors charged on. Not for them the steady advance of other battalions. With that fiery spirit traditionally associated with the 'Faughs' since they captured the first Napoleonic eagle taken by Wellington's army, the Irish Fusiliers swept over the enemy front-line trenches. One platoon in the right centre company under Maj. T.J. Atkinson carried all before it,[8] and with dashing impetuosity penetrated through the German third line to the objective, Beaucourt Station. None returned. There were no reserves to exploit their success.

On the left of the Fusiliers, 12th Irish Rifles began the assault with shouts of 'No Surrender'[9] and then, 'We were now running forward to get the job done'.[10] The wire around the German salient was not completely destroyed. Many gaps were cut, which only served to canalise the attack into killing grounds covered by machine-guns. Beaten back at the first rush, the Rifles lost the barrage, but with heroic fortitude worthy of their regiment at Ypres, the remnants twice re-formed and renewed the attack. Led by the remaining officers, they again advanced twice, but under withering machine-gun fire, all chance of success melted away. Yet somehow a few intrepid souls gained the German line. 'There were two brothers Smith [*sic*], I can remember seeing these two brothers in contact with the Germans using their bayonets.'[11] There were indeed two Smyths in 12th Rifles that day; both were killed.[12] Pte. R. Quigg had been one who had charged three times against the unbroken wire. Early next morning, hearing that his platoon commander was wounded but alive near the German wire, Quigg went forward to search for him. Seven times he went out without finding his officer, but each time he returned with a wounded soldier. The last time he dragged a casualty in on a groundsheet from close to the German wire, under machine-gun and shell-fire. Robert Quigg well deserved his Victoria Cross.

On the left of the two Ulster battalions, the 29th Division advanced across the front-line trenches, but were assailed by fire from machine-guns in the salient redoubt.

In an artillery observation position, 'Brock's Benefit', a young forward observation officer saw the lines of prone men, apparently under cover. He asked, 'Why don't they advance?' He received a sad reply from his more experienced companion, 'They will never more rise'.[13]

> For four nights after, parties went out and searched for the wounded and brought in several... Cather (the battalion adjutant) was killed bringing in wounded in daylight... He was wonderful as Adjutant... He brought in one wounded man from about 150 yards from the German wire in daylight and was killed going out to a wounded man who feebly waved to him on his calling out to see if there were any more near.[14]

Capt. Cather was later awarded a posthumous Victoria Cross. 'For conspicuous bravery near Hamel, France, on 1st July, 1916. From 7 p.m. till midnight he searched no man's land and brought in three wounded men...'

At 0800, the divisional commander was informed of the total failure on this sector.

The mine explosion in front of Beaumont Hamel had fatally given the German machine-gunners ten minutes' warning of Zero hour. They won the race for the German parapet.

SOUTH OF THE ANCRE—THE SCHWABEN REDOUBT

> The German third line of trenches was the objective; and it was reached, though with such dear sacrifice of men that there was won nothing but glory.[15]

On the front south of the Ancre, so successful had the wire-cutting barrage been that all the enemy wire was flattened; 'there was little but the posts left'.[16] 9th Inniskillings, the senior battalion, had the place of honour on the right of the line and advanced to a bugle sounding the regimental call, followed by 'advance'. The leading waves reached the sunken road in no man's land without great loss. Hardly were they across, however, when the German barrage caught the rear companies and those of the second line. When the enemy barrage lifted, they were raked by machine-gun fire from Thiepval cemetery.[17]

Emerging from Thiepval Wood, 11th Inniskillings and 14th Irish Rifles in the second line of 109 Brigade suffered heavily. No man's land was littered with dead and wounded. On the left of the line, 13th Rifles, under long-range fire from the Beaucourt Redoubt across the river, suffered heaviest of all. Most officers were killed or wounded before reaching the German lines. Behind them marched their commanding officer, Lt.-Col. F.W. Crozier, who had disobeyed orders and was now ushering forward his stragglers.[18]

Despite heavy casualties, the attack went home and the German B line was reached on schedule. There was not much fighting here; the enemy infantry surrendered immediately and large numbers of prisoners were taken. C line, including the north-east corner of the Schwaben Redoubt, was taken at 0848. The enfilade fire from Thiepval was unrelenting; even in the shelter of trenches the Ulsterman were cut down. Yet despite fearful losses, the assault waves of 108 and 109 Brigades had captured their objectives. A 'mere handful' of 9th Inniskillings under 2/Lt. McKinley held onto C line for about an hour until forced to retire.[19]

It was now time for 107 Brigade to pass through and take D line. The situation on the ridge overlooking St Pierre Davion quickly became critical. The garrison of Davion mounted repeated bombing attacks against the flank of 108 Brigade under cover of enfilade machine-gun fire from the heights north of the Ancre. Col. Crozier of 13th Irish Rifles, the only commanding officer to succeed in coming forward, commanded in person.[20] His battalion losses that day were to be the greatest in the division, but the remnant succeeded in holding that vital left flank until reinforcements arrived. Even so they were not to prevail.

11th Inniskillings and 14th Irish Rifles moved up. Like the leading battalions, they suffered very severely from the machine-guns of Thiepval. The 11th Inniskillings crossed the first line of enemy trenches; on reaching the second line, a platoon under Lt. Gallagher was left to consolidate; the remainder of the battalion advanced to the third line.[21] That was the high point of the day.

On the right, 32nd Division had broken itself against Thiepval. The advance elements of 109 Brigade had an open right flank; they were raked by enfilade fire and by Germans infiltrating behind 9th Inniskillings. Lt. Gallagher led his consolidating party and destroyed the infiltrators with bombs. Throughout that day, Gallagher fought with 'singular resolution and gallantry; at one time he met single-handed and killed six Germans. He survived the Somme to fall in the Battle of Messines.'[22]

Sgt. S. Kelly of 9th Inniskillings dashed across open ground near the Crucifix to gain contact with troops of 32nd Division and returned the same way. Later, when all the officers were dead or wounded, Kelly assumed command of the defence at the Crucifix and held out until he too was wounded. L/Cpl. D. Lyttle, 'isolated with a Lewis gun and a Vickers gun ... fought the Lewis gun until all his ammunition was exhausted, then destroyed both guns and bombed his way back to our main body near the Crucifix.'[23]

Across the battlefield, men like Kelly and Lyttle fought and died, their gallantry unrecorded. However, one officer of 9th Inniskillings, Capt. Eric Bell, was deservedly rewarded. The trench-mortar officer, he single-handedly took out a machine-gun with his pistol, then attacked a trench with grenades. When these ran out, he threw trench-mortar bombs into them. When the enemy were advancing in counter-attack, Bell stood on a parapet completely exposed and fired a rifle to repel the invaders. He died rallying men who had lost their own officers. He was awarded the Victoria Cross.

The attack on Thiepval village by the 32nd Division had failed because the artillery bombardment had not cut the wire or silenced the enemy machine-guns; the place was too strong and the British artillery was not strong enough. Gen. Nugent, seeing the situation, judged it best not to commit his reserve. He requested permission from Corps HQ at 0832 to halt the advance of 107 Brigade. This was refused. Almost forty-five minutes later, Corps headquarters instructed 36th to withhold 107 Brigade until the situation on their flanks became clear. It was too late. 107 Brigade was already committed. Far too few returned.

Because of a bend to the right in the British line, as they advanced through Thiepval Wood the men on the right of 107 Brigade could see the battalions of 32nd Division being swept away by machine-gun as they emerged from their trenches. By now the wood was bare of foliage. 10th Irish Rifles came under fire from their front, flank and rear simultaneously before they reached their jump-off position. Massed as they were, casualties were high, and Col. Bernard was killed. So intense was the fire that the final move to their jumping-off position had to be carried out in short rushes. The enemy machine-guns could be seen and were engaged by Lewis gun teams. These, however, were outfought and destroyed. No Vickers guns were in close support. Four of the brigade Vickers machine-guns had been deployed in the Hamel sector, and four were in Thiepval Wood. All were tasked with firing enfilade into German positions opposite the 36th.[24]

When the order came to go, 107 Brigade advanced unswervingly across 1000 yards of fire-swept zone. Men fell at every yard of the way. The survivors pressed on to the D line, only to find it full of German reserves. Too weak to take it, the Ulstermen retired slowly to C line. Here they were subject to repeated attacks from German bomb-throwing grenadiers emerging from St Pierre Davion. These were beaten off time and again by the 8th and 15th Rifles and that handful of the 13th Rifles who had survived from the original flank guard.

The ground won on the Schwaben had to be consolidated, but the remnants of ten battalions were scattered across its face. They needed to be pulled together and given leadership and direction. But there were only two senior officers present. One was Crozier, and he was tied down on the left flank. The other was Maj. Peacocke of 9th Inniskillings who had braved the fire of no man's land at 1000 and joined his battalion at the Crucifix on the right flank. In the afternoon, Peacocke took command of the remnants of 9th and 11th Inniskillings and held out until nightfall.

> He fought hand to hand with the enemy, repeatedly leading his men to repulse their bombing attacks. His was the life and soul of the defence and it was entirely due to his example of coolness and gallantry that our unsupported troops held on to the position for the length of time they did.[25]

The decision to keep commanding officers at battalion headquarters was an error of judgment.[26] It deprived the troops on the battlefield proper of direction, and brigade commanders of intelligent situation reports. Additional experienced officers on the spot could have saved the situation by galvanising the defence in more areas. By getting information back to divisional headquarters earlier and demanding support, more of the ground gained by the gallant initial assault might have been held. A scout of 14th Rifles based on battalion headquarters, Rfn. James McRoberts (a Queen's University science undergraduate and later the Armagh county surveyor), went forward for information and found the remnant of his battalion on their objective, the B line.

> They had lost nearly all their officers. There seemed to be nobody who had any authority and groups of men were sitting in clusters everywhere, doing nothing at about noon.[27]

McRoberts was wounded in the neck and took no further part in battle. That vital information, it seems, never got back to battalion headquarters.

Water and ammunition were desperately needed at the front, but to cross no man's land in daylight was very difficult. Gallantly, two companies of divisional Pioneers attempted to dig a communication trench for resupply, but enemy fire forced them back.[28] Critically, ammunition and water for the water-cooled Vickers guns began to run out. During the afternoon, attacks began to develop from the right flank. The 11th Inniskillings at the Crucifix and 9th Inniskillings in the Schwaben Redoubt became hard pressed. A bombardment on the right flank was ordered to relieve them. Elements of 49th (West Riding) Division attacked Thiepval under cover of a bombardment, but they were stopped in the face of concentrated machine-gun fire. Two enemy companies counter-attacked towards C11 on the left, but were caught in the open and destroyed by artillery fire and small arms fire from 8th Irish Rifles.

Behind the lines, there was considerable confusion in the communication trenches because of the failure of the traffic control system in the face of an unforeseen flood of wounded. The RAP of 11th Inniskillings was inundated;

there were 1000 cases of all units[29] and the RAMC stretcher bearers could not cope. Battalion bearers, having collected wounded from the Front, were then forced to carry men farther back after treatment. An officer and the RSM of 11th Inniskillings stood on the parapet and directed the oncoming support troops to climb into the open to make way for the wounded.[30]

Conflicting information about the role of 146 Brigade of 49th Division led to confusion. Nugent was told it was at his disposal, and Brig. Withycombe was ordered to send two of its battalions to the Schwaben Redoubt to help 9th Inniskillings. However, two battalions of this brigade were already committed to the Thiepval attack, and the remaining two battalions had already moved up behind them into the trenches of 32nd Division. By the time the situation was corrected, it was too late. The Yorkshiremen advanced into a hail of machine-gun fire and were beaten back.

The reserves which might have been decisive at Schwaben were thrown uselessly against Thiepval. That night, just before midnight, 148 Brigade of 49th Division was placed at Nugent's disposal. They came under command of Withycombe. 4th Yorks and Lancs arrived shortly after this, but 4th and 5th Yorkshire Light Infantry had not arrived by 0100. Withycombe submitted: (a) it would not be possible to organise an attack by daylight; (b) if they did advance before dawn, they might have difficulty in maintaining direction across unknown ground; and (c) if Schwaben Redoubt were taken, it could not be held while Thiepval was still in German occupation.[31] Gen. Nugent accepted these views and submitted them to Gen. Morland, the corps commander, who replied that the man on the spot must take the decision.[32] The operation was cancelled. Two battalions of Yorkshiremen were sent back to Aveluy Wood, while 4th Yorks and Lancs were held in Thiepval Wood.

Next morning at dawn, a summer ground mist obscured visibility. The mist did not disperse until 0700, at which time observers on the Mesnil Ridge saw that British troops in small numbers were in the first two German lines of trenches. Gen. Nugent ordered Withycombe to support and reinforce these troops, and to send forward supplies of bombs, ammunition and water. Withycombe collected a force of 400 men of the four battalions of his own brigade, together with two machine-guns of 107 Machine-gun Company. Not until 1400 did these begin to move forward; then, it lost a third of its number going across open no man's land, although the remainder reached its objective. Later, two small parties of the 16th Rifles (Pioneers) gallantly braved the German barrage with more bombs and ammunition. What might have been accomplished in darkness or in misty dawn without loss proved impossible in daylight under machine-gun fire.

On the left flank, Maj. Woods of 107 Machine-gun Company found Cpl. Sanders, of the 7th West Yorks, with a party of forty men, whom he described as 'played out but still full of fight'.[33] Sanders had been beating off German bombing attacks all night, had rescued several wounded Ulstermen and had taken several prisoners. He was subsequently awarded the Victoria Cross.

On the night of 2–3 July, the Ulster Division was relieved by 49th Division. 148 Brigade relieved 107 Brigade in the two lines of trenches now held between A12 and 19. The relief was not complete till after 1000 on the 3rd. A weary, pitiful remnant marched into Martinsart and dropped down to sleep. They had brought to Thiepval Wood fourteen prisoners. The total number captured in the offensive on their front was 543.[34]

36th Division's casualties in the two days amounted to 5500 officers and men killed, wounded and missing. Some battalions had almost disappeared. The two battalions which flanked the Ancre, 9th Irish Fusiliers and 12th Irish Rifles, suffered most. Their dead amounted to 244 and 256 respectively out of the 1944 who were killed or died of wounds that day.[35] Because of the concentration of its recruiting area, whole areas of Belfast and many little towns, villages and townlands across Ulster were cast into deep mourning.

On 5 July the division moved back to Rubempré and its surrounding villages and five days later to the Bernaville area. After a few days' rest in the back areas of the Somme which gave the survivors time to absorb the shock of losing so many friends in a very short time, the 36th entrained for Flanders. On 12 July, they detrained and marched to their new concentration area. In bright sunlight they marched, with 'marigolds in caps to honour the day; the bands played "King William's March".'[36] The 14th Rifles had a pipe band; it might also have played the Border lament, "The Flowers of the Forest were a' wede awa'".

Inevitably there are many might-have-beens which ought to have been seen at the time and which were probably discounted for various reasons. 'Had X Corps used the 49th Division to reinforce the success of the 36th instead of adding to the failure of the 32nd, the outcome on this sector might have been very different.' The armchair soldier has said this since that awful day, with all the knowledge of hindsight.

There was, however, one general officer who thought this at the time and said so. Maj.-Gen. Perceval, GOC 49th (West Riding) Division, had gone forward shortly after Zero hour to see and assess the situation at the Front for himself. His division was in corps reserve. Observing the repulse of the 32nd and the growing stalemate before Thiepval, and seeing for himself the advance of the 36th, he suggested his whole division should be used to support the success of the latter. Feeling the urgency of the situation, Perceval went to Englebelmer two miles away to urge his proposal on the corps commander, Gen. Morland.[37] Morland was in an observation post situated high in a tree and had just ordered the 49th to move one of its brigades forward to Thiepval Wood where it would be ideally positioned to support either the 36th or 32nd as the situation demanded. He declined Gen. Perceval's suggestion, being more interested in helping the 32nd. Morland's OP must surely have been up a gum-tree.

Historically, the junction of armies and corps is the weakest sector of a front. Although first principles dictate that a boundary should not rest on a natural obstacle, problems of communications, logistics and fire support have to be measured against this. The problem was foreseen on the right of X Corps where the boundary with III Corps was drawn through the centre of Blighty Valley. Given this, it is impossible to understand the attack of 36th Division astride the Ancre. All we now know is that 'the action on the north side of the Ancre was separate from the other and of lesser importance'.[38] The decision to treat that attack in this way led directly to the destruction of two splendid battalions of 36th Division to no purpose.

Neuve Chapelle had shown the danger from the swift German counterstroke which was usually delivered after the British assault had shot its bolt. The attackers had to support and resupply their troops across ground made nearly impassable by their own artillery, and in the face of enemy machine-gun fire. On the other side, German reserves, moving on 'green ground', could move faster. On the Somme, the Ulstermen carried rolls of barbed wire into the assault, but only two machine-guns per battalion were taken forward; the other eight from each of the machine-gun companies were taken into Brigade reserve. It was an error of judgment. In the firefight against the German machine-guns at Thiepval, the British Lewis gun proved ineffective against heavy, sustained enemy fire. Without heavy machine-guns to reply, the Ulstermen were at a grave disadvantage, and lost the fight.

The battle was not without its poignant notes. Lt.-Col. F.P. Crozier, CO 9th Royal Irish Rifles, was in Aveluy Wood on the evening of 30 June just before the advance to Thiepval Wood. There he spoke with Lt.-Col. H.C. Bernard, CO of 10th Royal Irish Rifles, who said to him:

> I hope this war will settle the Irish question. The Ulster and the Irish Divisions, shoulder to shoulder in France, should consolidate the home front afterwards, despite the Easter Rebellion. I know nothing of politics, I hate them—they are the curse of every land, but I know the Irish question is an unreal, politically-inspired game of bluff and office-seeking expediency.[39]

Col. Stewart Blacker, in a letter to the officer commanding the depot of the Royal Irish Fusiliers, confessed himself 'heartbroken'. With the indignation of the fighting man who has seen friends and hundreds of his own men killed in action, he was upset by some press reports: 'There has been a lot of extravagant stuff written and published in the press which is a great pity. The division behaved magnificently and the point does not want labouring.'[40]

CHAPTER TWENTY-TWO

The Somme: Guillemont, 2–4 September 1916

At the end of August 1916, 16th Division moved from Loos. They were assured by friendly villagers and railway staff that their secret destination was the Somme. At a new divisional concentration area around Bray in the Somme valley, they enjoyed several days' rest and relaxation, including bathing parades in the River Somme. Following a briefing of the officers by brigade commanders, the battalions advanced into XIV Corps reserve. Before the opening of the offensive on 1 July, Guillemont, a village on high ground between Longueval and Combles, had been a strongpoint in the second line of the German defences. It was surrounded by bastions at the railway station, the quarry and a farm on the face of the village. On high ground to its rear, it was covered by more strong positions—the flattened village of Ginchy, Ginchy Telegraph and in the relatively unshattered Leuze Wood. Between the last two was a trench bastion, the 'Quadrilateral'. All bristled with reinforced concrete machine-gun emplacements. Approach to Guillemont could only be made across a bare valley, significantly known as 'Death Valley'. The entire area, being devoid of cover, was admirable for defence. Since July it had defied assault; fine British divisions had gallantly broken themselves against its defences. 2nd and 3rd Regular Divisions, the 24th (which included 2nd Leinsters), 30th and 34th New Army Divisions and the 55th Territorial Division had all failed in some measure to pierce its defences. On the evening of 1 September, XIV Corps had consolidated a position before the village.

In the current battle, 5th Regular and 20th New Army Divisions of XIV Corps and 7th Regular Division (with 2nd Royal Irish) of XV Corps were about to assault Leuze Wood, Guillemont and Ginchy. The battalions of 16th Division were to provide additional support and came under command of the commanders on the spot.

The battalions advanced in their brigades. First to move was 47 Brigade, coming under command of 20th Division. In the approach, they marched through the choked towns of the back areas. Because it was close to the boundary with French Sixth Army, French soldiers were much in evidence, and friendly troops and civilians turned out to exchange greetings and good wishes.[1] Approaching the Front, traffic intensified and roads became jammed, choked with wagons, guns, staff cars and ambulances going in both directions. To avoid this, the troops advanced along tracks just off roads to their allotted rest areas in the midst of vast rear-area stores and ammunition dumps, called with the unfailing sardonic wit of soldiers 'Happy Valley'. There, each battalion was granted a patch of bare ground. In the hot, humid weather it mattered not. All rested until evening when they moved into the line under cover of darkness.[2]

Brig. Pereira's 47 Brigade was in support of 20th Division, tasked with the capture of Guillemont. 20th Division was so weak in numbers from previous fighting that only one brigade could be assembled with sufficient strength to assault the southern part of Guillemont. 47 Brigade was brought up to replace 60 Brigade for the attack on the northern part of the village. The attack was to be delivered in three stages to its final objective on the Wedge Wood–Ginchy road. Succeeding waves of infantry battalions would leap-frog after a barrage which became intense before beginning to creep forward at 100 yards in four minutes. This intensification was a signal for the assault troops to get as close to the barrage as they could before the advance began.

The 47 Brigade rested at Carnoy for the night. The valley seemed to become a fairyland of twinkling lights from the campfires of units going into and coming out of the line. Father Joe Wrafter SJ gave general absolution. As the men prayed, the noise of battle could be heard and with it occasional snatches of plaintive songs which some later generations interpreted as anti-war. But to the listeners they were merely those grim soldiers' jests which originate in all wars: 'Oh my! I don't want to die! I want to go home', or (in mock mourning for their sergeant-major), 'I saw him, I saw him, hanging on the old barbed-wire'.[3]

Commanding officers went ahead with their adjutants to a brigade conference. Nearby, battalion quartermasters and the Brigade AA&QMG hammered out supply arrangements. At the Regimental Aid Post (RAP), the medical officers had their own necessary, if grim, preparations to make. Early next morning, the battalions got orders to take over the line before Guillemont. After a bustle of activity to prepare themselves, they moved forward, heavily laden with ammunition, arms and entrenching tools. Intermittent shell-fire came, but growing accustomed to it, the soldiers soon took no notice in their struggle to get forward. During the advance from Montauban, an enemy bombardment struck them and gas was detected. Respirators were donned, adding to the difficulties of marching in semi-darkness. At the same time, significant casualties were inflicted by enemy cocktail-shelling, gas, high-explosives and shrapnel. To advance in such conditions was impossible. 47 Brigade halted and waited for two hours. When the straffing ended, the troops removed their respirators and the advance continued.

Through Bernafay Wood and the northern part of Trônes Wood, the soldiers plodded towards the assembly areas before Guillemont. As they advanced under shell-fire across the desolation of the battlefield, their hardening experience at Loos stood them well. It was enough to frighten, if not deter, all but the most insensitive on a slow, seemingly interminable journey. Just before dawn, the front-line positions were near; six hours had been spent on the approach march. It was a Sunday and traditionally, unusual events occurred to the Leinster Regiment on the Sabbath.

GOC 16th Division sent a message to his brigades the evening before the attack: 'The divisional commander sends his best wishes to the officers and men of the Brigades and knows that their action tomorrow will go down to history. W.B. Hickie, Major-General'.

The battalions massed in a sector of three shallow, parallel trenches bisected by others; from its layout it was known as the Gridiron. The men, warned that the trenches would be under enemy observation in daylight, crouched low. Any sign of their presence would have brought a hail of destruction upon them. By 0400, the assault battalions were ready, but Zero hour was not until 1200. In the waiting period, their experience at Loos was again invaluable. Because of faulty shells, many 'unders' exploded over or among the waiting troops, causing heavy casualties. But instead of being cowed and disheartened, their adrenalin pumped and battle-madness overcame many. One officer likened them to 'lions in their lairs thirsting for blood'.[4]

Because of intense German artillery fire, hot rations had not come up on the previous evening, but thirst and lack of water were the greatest problems. A platoon from each battalion had been detailed as 'carrying party'. Throughout the battle these units would be completely depended upon for their efficiency, courage and determination for resupplying with rations, ammunition and water over the open, fire-swept battlefield. Carried in petrol cans, the water was heavily tainted, but highly welcomed. Because of the known water problem in the battle area, those huge armoured objects covered by canvas, which had just arrived, were readily acceptable as 'tanks'. In front, across the ground strewn with human flesh from previous assaults, lay a heap of discoloured rubble, all that remained of Guillemont. But underneath the rubble, the deep-mined dug-outs were intact, and tunnels connected these with all the village wells.[5]

Safe within their dug-outs and trenches, the undaunted Germans of 73rd Hanoverian Regiment (which carried the British battle honour 'Gibraltar' as a shoulder flash) waited for yet another assault.

> This churned up battlefield was ghastly... The sunken road and the ground behind was full of German dead; the ground in front of English. Arms, legs, and heads stuck out stark above the lips of the craters... Guillemont was only distinguishable by the lighter colour of the craters, due to the white stones of the houses, now pulverised. Before us lay Guillemont station crumpled up like a nursery toy... It was the days at Guillemont that first made me aware of the overwhelming effects of this war of material. The communications

between the troops and staff, between the artillery and the liaison officers were utterly crippled by the terrific fire.[6]

The Artillery Fire Plan for the assault was detailed, its timing precise. Commanders at all levels on the spot would need to watch the time carefully.

Time	Unit	Detail	Remarks	
0	RFA	Open barrage on objective.		
0	7th Leinsters	Leave	Advance, in quick	
0	6th CR	trenches	time. Double time	1st
0	8th RMF	for objective	towards quarries	Bound
0 + 3 min.	RFA	Lift barrage in front of 6th CR		
0 + 4 min	RFA	Lift barrage in front of 7th Leinsters		
0 + 25 min.	RI Regt	1st move		
0 + 50 min.	RFA	Roll barrage E at 100 yards for 4 mins.	To E of Village	2nd
0 + 50 min.	7 Leinsters	Remain to consolidate		Bound
0 + 50 min.	6 CR	Advance		
0 + 50 min.	8th RMF	Advance and pass through 6th CR		
0 + 2 hours	RFA	Roll barrage at 50 yards per minute		3rd
0 + 2 hours	6th RI Regt	Advance. Infantry to follow barrage		Bound
0 + 2.45	RFA	Lift barrage		4th
0 + 2.45	8th RMF	Advance through 6th RI Regt		Bound

At 1159, the aspect of Guillemont was quite still in its awful horror. Precisely at 1200, a tremendous bombardment was opened by the British artillery. This was followed by a creeping barrage of divisional 18-pounders behind which the storm battalions advanced, and the German counter-barrage began. The leading companies went over the top in perfect lines through the enemy shelling, men of Leinster, Munster, Connaught. With the Royal Irish was a company of Ulstermen from Derry and a company of Channel Islanders. Their reckless bravery saved lives by giving the Germans no time to come from their dug-outs and fire their machine-guns. Before the Germans could resist, the stormers were on top of their positions, bombing them out.

The part played by the bombers of 7th Leinsters, under their commander Lt. J.V. Holland, was crucial to the victory. Not content with bombing enemy dug-outs within the specified zone, Holland fearlessly led his bombers through their own barrage and cleared a great part of the village in front of the moving fire-wall. He started with twenty-six bombers and of these, only five were left standing after the battle: all others were either killed or wounded. The citation of his Victoria Cross ended, 'By this very gallant action he undoubtedly broke the spirit of the enemy and thus saved us many casualties when the battalion made a further advance.' Holland had a near-miraculous escape when a shrapnel shell burst yards from him and the steel hail missed him completely.[7] The Leinster Bombing Platoon won a Victoria Cross (Lt. J.V. Holland), two DCMs, six MMs; and one man, Pte. John Ford, was recommended for a battlefield commission.[8]

Holland personally bombed several dug-outs and forced out the garrison: two were badly wounded, and he shot several with his revolver. A German officer shot one of Holland's men, then raised his hands in surrender, just in time to avoid being shot himself.[9] Seven Germans, including the officer, were captured. Holland detailed Cpl. Finney to take the prisoners back to the rear with his compliments. Holland then carried on with the battle. Hours later, he returned: 'I found this poor devil lying outside the place I bombed. He cried out "You English, you English, don't leave me here to die."'[10] Holland got a Royal Irish soldier to give the man water. Between them, they carried the German, seated on a rifle, back for assistance. In the history of war, the chivalry of John Holland VC to a wounded enemy on the battlefield in the heat of action has undoubtedly been equalled; but rarely, if ever, can it have been surpassed.

The Connaught Rangers, with the Leinsters on their left and a battalion of the Staffords on their right, assembled in Rim Trench. They were to attack in three waves, with D Company on the right and C Company on the left. Behind in two waves were B and A Companies, in that order. The trenches were packed, and many 'unders' from British artillery, particularly trench mortar bombs, caused heavy casualties; the Rangers alone suffered 200 casualties.[11] The two leading companies of the first wave were so seriously weakened that the commanding officer ordered the second and third waves to reinforce the first waves in case of a pre-emptive enemy attack. When the barrage lifted, the Rangers cleared the parapet. Lt.-Col. Lenox-Conyngham, with his pistol still in its holster and carrying only a cane, was in the front-line trench with his leading companies. Not for him the safety of a dug-out while his men stormed the enemy line. Pointing his cane in the direction of the quarries, he called to those nearest him 'that Connaught Rangers is what you have got to take', then he fell dead.[12] The Connaughtmen reacted as their forefathers had at Salamanca with Sir E. Pakenham's 3rd Division. There, the death of Maj. Barnaby Murphy had so maddened his men, Pakenham had called to the brigade commander, 'Unleash them, Wallace'.[13] Once again the slips were off. Like hounds upon a quarry, they dashed into the enemy lines. Completely disregarding machine-gun fire, the Rangers were into the enemy before they had fully recovered from the bombardment.

Many surrendered at once; those who did not were killed when cellar-clearing began with bomb and bayonet. The first objective was won by 1209. The second objective was gained at 1220 and the third, North Street, was captured at 1255. Pte. Tom Hughes was wounded. On getting his wound dressed by a regimental medical orderly, he returned at once to the line and joined the fight. Seeing an enemy machine-gun, he dashed out in front of his company, shot the gunners and single-handedly captured the gun. Despite being wounded again, he brought back three prisoners. For this he was later awarded the Victoria Cross.[14]

When the Connaught Rangers reached their objective, 8th Munsters passed through and reached the line of North and South Streets on schedule at 1315. Here they mopped up before continuing the next 'bound'.

At Fontenoy, in May 1745, Irish pipers had played 'The White Cockade' to the Irish Brigade as they advanced to attack the victorious English columns.[15] Fifty miles from that battlefield, at 1255, the 6th Royal Irish attacked to the skirl of their war-pipes playing the stately 'Brian Boru', traditionally played by some Irish Regiments in desperate moments to lift heads and square shoulders or in honour of great occasions. The Royal Irish, senior regiment of Ireland, responded, advancing in excellent order towards the brigade's final objective, the infamous sunken road. Despite heavy losses in both officers and men, so swift was their advance that all objectives were taken according to the timetable. About 150 of the Connaught Rangers, who more properly ought to have remained in the captured area to 'mop-up', could not be restrained and accompanied the Royal Irish in their headlong advance.[16] They were not alone in this: with them went some of the Munsters whose 'ardour could not be restrained'.[17] Then 8th Munsters went through the Royal Irish, making the final bound to that sunken road described by the German officer, Lt. Ernst Jünger. There they consolidated at 1445, precisely to the staff timetable. Their historian noted, 'The Chaplain Rev. J. Wrafter SJ accompanied the battalion during the whole operation.'[18]

Behind the assault infantry came their support, a Field Company of Royal Engineers and a company of Pioneers from 11th Hampshires. Theirs was the inglorious but essential work of consolidating the captured ground—digging new trenches, often simply by connecting a string of shell holes and revetting, or strengthening their sides and wiring the front. Signallers laid cable to battalion headquarters and artillery forward observation posts. All were under the same shell, machine-gun and rifle fire as that suffered by the battle-infantry, but without the excitement of the assault. Often when the battalions were relieved, these support troops remained behind. It called for a special kind of courage. The supporting engineers and Pioneers dug new trenches which the infantry manned, ready for the inevitable counter-attacks.[19] These, when they came, were beaten off.

On the left, the attack of 7th Division captured Ginchy. However, troops of 47 Brigade could see a German counter-attack forcing a withdrawal and reported this to brigade headquarters, who in turn reported to Gen. Smith, GOC 20th Division. The failure of 7th Division to hold Ginchy was to have tragic implications for 47 Brigade.

More than 700 German prisoners, both wounded and unwounded, were taken. Dead Germans 'lay thick on the captured ground'.[20] But the cost had been heavy. In the Royal Irish alone fourteen officers and 311 men were killed and wounded. So short were the Royal Irish in officers that four were borrowed from 7th Leinsters before the next operation at Ginchy. All four were destined to die.

The battalion medical officers established Regimental Aid Posts close to battalion headquarters in whatever cover they could find, usually shell holes. There, the medical officers and their dedicated helpers toiled under shell and machine-gun fire to relieve the suffering. One MO, Lt. Cheeseman, 8th Munsters, was wounded. So great was the number of wounded that insufficient stretchers were available to take them all away as casualties occurred, although each battalion by now had more than the war establishment permitted. There were simply not enough stretchers to cater for all the wounded, even if there had been bearers to carry them. German prisoners were pressed into this. One German officer was detailed for this duty in error and protested vigorously, but 'this was not the time to conform to any punctilio of military etiquette. The fiery Hun was ordered to do what he was told and he did it.'[21]

It is to the credit of these doctors and medical orderlies that all wounded, British and German, were treated alike. One doctor, Capt. G.D. Watkins, RAMC, 7th Leinsters, had only arrived in France on 1 September and worked continuously for twenty-four hours in a shell hole, regardless of the danger. He was remembered with particular affection long after the battalion ceased to exist.[22]

Even after they were treated at the RAP, stretcher cases had to be carried 500 yards across Death Valley to the field ambulances in Trônes Wood; 'After darkness fell, rain began adding to the trials of the troops and promised to make movement difficult on the morrow.'[23]

7th Irish Rifles and 1st Munsters of 48 Brigade relieved the exhausted Rangers and Leinsters. They took over responsibility for 47 Brigade front and consolidated. German shell and mortar fire went on unceasingly. A battalion of the King's Liverpool Regiment did sterling work protecting the left flank which had been left open by the failure of 7th Division against Ginchy. The King's, with the Royal Irish and Munsters, repelled three counter-attacks, two between 1730 and 1830. Finally, the last assault battalions were relieved at 0200 on the 4th by 12th King's Royal Rifle Corps and 12th Rifle Brigade. Trudging through the rain back to Carnoy, they went into bivouac. They had suffered terrible losses. Drafts of replacements came forward for some battalions. The Royal Irish had a draft of ninety-one; others did not, and would have to renew the battle with reduced strength when called upon. Despite their losses, the entire brigade was in the highest spirits and 'it was difficult to say whether the camp was German or Irish; nearly everyone sported a German helmet and a German greatcoat'.[24]

After the battle, the Rangers recovered the body of Lt.-Col. J.S.M. Lenox-Conyngham. 'It was buried in a little churchyard just behind the lines, amidst every possible manifestation of grief and respect, deeply lamented by all the battalion he had raised and led for just two years.'[25] In 1927 a memorial to him was erected by his wife in the Royal Irish Fusiliers Memorial Chapel of St Patrick's Anglican Cathedral, Armagh, where it still is. With it is the original wooden Celtic cross which first covered his grave near the battlefield. It is interesting to note that the account of the Somme battle given in the Irish Fusilier Chapel is that of 16th Division's capture of Guillemont and Ginchy.

Headquarters of 16th Division watched its brigades and battalions committed to battle piecemeal, under 20th and 5th divisions, without regard to either losses or whatever fresh tasks 16th Division might be given: 'Sir Douglas Haig visiting Army Headquarters, although emphasising the importance of capturing high ground and Leuze Wood, stressed that new divisions must be economised'.[26] The economy of manpower ordered by the CinC does not appear to have taken place, especially in relation to 49 Brigade under command of 5th Division.

Throughout Sunday 3 September, 48 and 49 Brigades waited in Happy Valley, listening to the noise of battle and wondering when it would be their turn to go forward. Their arrival in the area of the Somme had been greeted by French troops singing a 'quaint version of "Tipperary" which afforded us much amusement, and brought back the memories of a comfortable fire and bed'.[27] As they waited, battalions held impromptu concerts to pass the time. The hot, humid weather broke on the night of 3 September; for those sleeping in the open, what had been a pleasure now became a misery.

Next day, 48 Brigade were ordered forward under 20th Division and two battalions of 49 Brigade, 7th and 8th Irish Fusiliers under 5th Division. Brig. Leveson-Gower briefed the officers on the situation in front at Guillemont and the area they would enter.

At 1900 on the evening of 4 September, after waiting a day in heavy showery conditions, the last two battalions of 49 Brigade, 7th and 8th Inniskillings, relieved 59 Brigade. It was a 'slow and difficult process'.[28]

In life there is no scene more forgettable, yet so haunting, as that of an uncleared battlefield. Natural sensitivity forbids full stomach-churning descriptions even if, vicariously, it could be drawn. An eye-witness cameo suffices.

By 2 am we reached Arrow Head Copse and the battlefields of the fighting which had taken place a day or two previously. Here we beheld for the first time the awful and ghastly spectacle of an uncleared battlefield—absolute chaos and utter desolation everywhere. Shapeless masses of human beings lay strewn over the ground. The very air reeked with the smell of putrefying flesh and blood.

Occasionally the flares in front would show up the grim horror of it all, then dwindle and die out, leaving us to pick our way through the abandoned material as best we could. Friend and enemy were the same there. Broken rifles, ammunition boxes, equipment, all bore testimony of the terrible wastage of war. Still we plodded through the mud and stench. Fortunately, the rain cleared away about 3 a.m. Even this had but little effect on the 'going', as the shell holes by now were water-logged.

Certainly, it was the most cheerless night we had yet experienced for a relief. To add to our discomfort, the guides were uncertain as to the way; in fact, looking back over it all, it almost seems a mystery how we arrived in Guillemont as soon as we did.[29]

CHAPTER TWENTY-THREE

The Somme: Ginchy, 5–10 September 1916

Ginchy, about a mile north-east of Guillemont and situated at the intersection of six roads, stands on a high plain holding the right flank of Combles, two and a half miles to the south-east. This fortress village covered Guillemont and dominated all approaches; it was bare and without cover, save shell holes. Just south of Ginchy, in a fold of ground, German military cunning had built a strongpoint, the Quadrilateral. Ginchy itself, in its strength of machine-gun emplacements, was next only to Guillemont. A forward bastion in the German Braune Stellung, their second line, it was stronger than the first line positions stormed on 1 July. Repeated gallant assaults on Ginchy had all been bloodily repulsed. It had been taken, but not held, by 7th Regular Division on 3 September. The Quadrilateral, which was to prove even more formidable, was a strong loop-trench bristling with machine-guns and covered by wide belts of barbed wire. Some of these belts were sixty yards wide. In dead ground covered by long grass and tall weeds, they were completely concealed from observation. Deceptively, that wire to its front, which could be seen, appeared to have been cut.

Unlike the 36th at Thiepval, the brigades of 16th Division were thrust piecemeal into a continuing battle under command of other divisional commanders. Often the commanders, under whose orders they came, flung the Irish battalion against strong positions to retrieve failure by their own troops. This was notable in the case of 49 Brigade under the command of 5th Division. It could only have been galling for Gen. Hickie to watch, helplessly, as his brigades were used in this way. Hickie and his staff then had to take over command of a tired, shattered and scattered division and to prepare it for a major operation: the capture of Ginchy.

On the morning of 5 September, command of the front before Ginchy and the Quadrilateral passed to Gen. Hickie. Under command he had two battalions of 48 Brigade and four battalions of 49 Brigade in the line, but these were scattered along the fronts of 5th and 20th Divisions. The remaining two battalions of 48 Brigade, 8th and 9th Dublins, were on their way and would arrive after dusk that evening. Shattered 47 Brigade was regrouping in Carnoy.

Hickie's first task was to have 49 Brigade relieved by 56th Division and to rest it before its next mission. The brigade had suffered heavily, particularly 7th Irish Fusiliers. Hickie also had to resist XIV Corps' orders for a premature attack on 6 September: 'At 8.15 p.m the Corps ordered an attempt to be made to secure the German trench between Leuze Wood and the Quadrilateral, but the incoming battalions were not ready to do so.'[1]

Two 48 Brigade battalions, 7th Irish Rifles and 1st Munster, had both suffered heavily from shell-fire in Trônes Wood before they advanced. After three days in the line, consolidating the Guillemont position and linking with the Inniskillings, they too were very weak in numbers. The Dublins came into the line after dark on the 5th and found touch with elements of 55th Division. There was no shelter from rain except in a few dug-outs where, 'in the darkness, men sometimes happened upon strange and grisly house-mates.'[2]

THE INNISKILLINGS IN LEUZE WOOD

The morning mist of 5 September 1916 covered the two Inniskilling battalions from enemy observation and the relief of the front before Guillemont was accomplished without casualties. 7th Inniskillings consolidated positions around the southern and western edges of Leuze Wood along the Ginchy-Wedge Wood road and the Guillemont-Leuze Wood road. 8th Inniskillings continued the line, connecting the trenches before Guillemont to Leuze Wood. Heavy enemy shelling began in the afternoon, interrupting the work, and several officers and men were wounded, but 8th Inniskillings consolidated the line during the night of 5–6 September. Finding part of their line in full view of the Quadrilateral, they dropped below the contour line into cover. Extending the line southwards, 7th Inniskillings linked up with 5th Division. During the same night, 7th Inniskillings established themselves firmly in Leuze Wood. At dawn, they lost their CO, Lt.-Col. H.N. Young, who was seriously wounded by a sniper. Young's wound was very serious and only the speed with which his devoted men got him out saved his life. He returned to the battalion in 1917.[3] Command was assumed at once by Maj. A.D. Reid, the second-in-command who, although left out of battle, came forward on a visit during the night.

Throughout 6 July, the two Inniskilling battalions were subjected to intermittent shelling which seemed to be registering on their positions. At 2000 hours, a hurricane bombardment was followed by a heavy attack on Leuze Wood. SOS rockets brought a counter-barrage, and with rifle and machine-gun fire they beat off the attack. During 7 September, shell-fire wounded the acting CO, RSM and three headquarters staff. Because of casualties, a captain now commanded the battalion and all companies were led by young lieutenants. That night, both Inniskilling battalions were relieved by incoming units of 56th Division and moved back to Bernafay Wood. 'A good tot of rum' helped all sleep soundly.[4]

The taking of Leuze Wood is credited in the Official History to patrols from the Devonshires. As Maj.-Gen. Ramsay, who had been present, said when he presented colours to 7th/8th Inniskillings on 29 August 1919: 'It was you who captured Leuze Wood, on the Somme in 1916, though the credit of it was given to another division.'[5]

5th Division, south of Guillemont and 1000 yards from the forbidding bastions of Ginchy and the Quadrilateral, had been able to advance the line during the 4th and night of 4–5 September, taking severe casualties as they did so. A line was formed linking Leuze Wood with the French left in Savenake Wood. On the afternoon of 5 September, 7th Irish Fusiliers under command of 5th Division was ordered to attack Combles trench. The Fusiliers advanced, but found solid belts of wire in standing corn and high weeds covered by machine-guns against which they could make no headway. In response to orders, another attempt was made that evening, which also failed to break through the wire. Both attempts cost the 'Faughs' heavy casualties. They were relieved during the night by a battalion of Kensingtons who tried a flank attack which also failed. A French attack along Combles ravine was likewise unsuccessful.

On the same night, 8th Irish Fusiliers, also with 5th Division, came into the line. Advancing across the Ginchy–Combles road, they entered Bouleaux Wood. But both their flanks were open, and throughout the 6th they were heavily bombarded. Seeing an enemy counter-attack develop, to avoid being isolated they fell back on the main trench at Leuze Wood. That evening they were relieved by the London Scottish. Both Irish Fusilier battalions reverted to command of 49 Brigade that night. The division front was now held by 47 Brigade on the right at Guillemont and 48 Brigade on the left facing Ginchy, with 49 Brigade out of the line resting. 49 Brigade had suffered heavy losses under command of 5th Division and received little credit for their share in advancing the British line on the right of Guillemont after that place had fallen.

Orders for a resumption of the attack on 9 September were received from Fourth Army. XIV Corps was to secure the line Combles–Leuze Wood–Quadrilateral and Ginchy. Other corps taking part were: XV Corps, objectives Beer Trench and Ale Alley; III Corps, Wood Land and the eastern corner of High Wood.

Gen. Hickie now had all his division under command. But they were tired and reduced after six days in action. Notwithstanding this, they were to be tried against the formidable Ginchy, so often tested and not found wanting in the resolution of its defenders. And the Quadrilateral was as yet untested.

The right attack of XIV Corps was 56th London Division. Their left, 168 Brigade, was positioned within and to the left of Leuze Wood. It was given the task of making a flank attack on the Quadrilateral, timed to coincide with the Irish frontal assault.

16th Division was the left attack. Gen. Hickie tasked 48 Brigade with the capture of Ginchy. Brig. Ramsay had explained the condition of his men and was promised they would be relieved shortly after the position was taken.[6]

Although the strength of the Quadrilateral was unknown, it was thought to be the weaker of the two positions and for this reason Gen. Hickie assigned its capture to 47 Brigade.[7] 49 Brigade, in support, had two battalions behind each brigade.

48 Brigade were to attack in two waves: in the first, 7th Irish Rifles, 1st Munsters; the second, 8th and 9th Dublins; 8th Inniskillings and 7th Irish Fusiliers were behind in support. 47 Brigade had 6th Royal Irish and 7th Leinsters in the first wave, 8th Munsters and remnant 6th Rangers in the second wave; behind in support were 7th Inniskillings and 8th Fusiliers. To replace Col. Lenox-Conyngham came Maj. R.C. Feilding, Coldstream Guards, who assumed command on 6 September. The principal reason for his selection to command the Rangers appears to have been his religion; he was a Catholic. 'He fitted in very well with the Irishmen, they liked and trusted him.'[8] 'His battalion nick-name became "snowball".'[9]

Because of casualties, two battalions, 7th Inniskillings and 9th Dublins, would go into action commanded by captains, neither of whom had seen action before Loos. One of these captains was destined to die in the action. Most of the companies were commanded by lieutenants, some by second-lieutenants. Some of the men were newly-joined replacements. But what they lacked in experience was made up for in part by high-spirited fighting zest.

During the early morning of 9 September the last units of the division moved to their assault positions. On the right, 47 Brigade went into the trenches hastily dug by the Engineers and Pioneers. The Connaught Rangers were reduced to eleven officers and 231 men, of whom eighty were newly arrived replacements.[10] Some were young officers who had joined on 3 September and had been left out of battle. Each company was no more than platoon strength. The adjutant became a casualty and was replaced by the signal officer, 2/Lt. Seymour Jourdain, a stripling of eighteen years and seven months. On commissioning just two days after his eighteenth birthday, he had 'just beaten the ban on front-line service under nineteen years of age'.[11] There were many like him in the 16th.

The night of 8–9 September was quiet, save for desultory enemy machine-gun fire directed on Guillemont. Conditions were ideal for getting into position. Before dawn, supporting artillery opened up. The enemy counter-bombardment was constrained by bad visibility and the Royal Flying Corps had swept the sky clear of enemy observation balloons. It is not clear why 'Zero Hour' was fixed so late in the afternoon, but there are several possible reasons. It may have been meant to vary the time from the usual dawn attack, or to allow the enemy insufficient hours of daylight to organise his counterstroke.[12] This, in turn, allows early relief of the assault troops in darkness. However it was fraught with danger for the waiting troops.

Assembly trenches were dug on the night of 8–9 September by 7th Irish Rifles west of Guillemont–Ginchy road and by 1st Munsters east of that road. In the time available, these trenches were little more than ditches, in four lines, forty yards apart, each capable of holding a company. As the support battalions came up behind they too dug in. All day on the 9th, they waited in trenches visible to enemy observers, taking nine hours of 'hard pounding' in daylight before Zero. Adding to this were the very numerous 'unders' from the British artillery. So great were the casualties during this phase that Lt.-Col. Francis of the Irish Rifles told Brigade he was reduced to 150 bayonets for the assault.[13] 1st Munsters, which had entered the line with twenty-seven officers and 675 strong, had lost 169 all ranks.[14] Some Munster platoons were led by sergeants. 7th Irish Fusiliers were ordered to support the Rifles, and had to get into position under heavy fire.

Zero Hour, fixed for 1645 was changed in defiance of an old army adage, 'order, counter-order, disorder'. Corps headquarters decided on a last-minute change to the bombardment plan. The message making the change reached 47 Brigade, but not 48 Brigade and, it appears, not 168 Brigade of the right flanking division. It was to have disastrous consequences for the complete success of the commanders' plan. It also brought near-destruction to 47 Brigade. The substance was that the assault battalions were ordered to wait a further two minutes after Zero Hour, for a final intense barrage, before advancing.[15]

The division on the right of 16th Division, 56th (London), was on its second tour of the Somme battle. On 1 July it had carried Gommecourt in great style, one of the few successes of the day. In doing so, however, it had sustained 4314 casualties; by 9 September it had not recovered. 168 Brigade attacked at Zero on a two battalion front; right 1st/4th Royal Fusiliers, left 1st/12th London Rangers. The Fusiliers advanced and achieved their objective on the German trench south-east of the Quadrilateral, but the London Rangers (who lost 467 at Gommecourt) advanced slowly against machine-gun fire and lost the barrage. They then lost direction and failed to find their objective, the Quadrilateral. The German counter-barrage interrupted 56th Division's communications. Nothing was known at divisional headquarters of this failure: 'As attempts to bomb up the Quadrilateral failed, nothing was accomplished on the front of 56th on this day.'[16]

Not having received the order to wait a further two minutes at Zero, 48 Brigade and 168 Brigade advanced on time. In Ginchy the Germans were caught unprepared. Seeing the movement, however, enemy observers elsewhere gave the alarm and the Germans manned machine-guns and signalled for artillery fire. The British artillery barrage had completely missed whole sections of the German front. Many shells failed to explode; many were 'unders' which fell among the waiting troops. Immediately in front of 47 Brigade the bombardment was so 'ineffective' that the Germans continued to man their trenches throughout.[17] This, adding to the failure of 168 Brigade's flank attack, allowed the German machine-gunners to man their parapets in time to meet the assault.

47 Brigade attacked in accordance with orders. Waiting until the intensive phase of the barrage ended before advancing, they rose from the trenches and advanced into a storm of artillery and machine-gun fire from the now-prepared Germans. They were caught on the open slopes of no man's land, exposed to the cross fire of machine-guns on Ginchy Telegraph and the Quadrilateral, added to by machine-guns in shell-holes; the 47th had entered a 'veritable hornets' nest'.[18]

The leading lines of 6th Royal Irish and 8th Munsters were swept away in a hurricane of fire. Behind them, 6th Connaught Rangers, 7th Leinsters and a company of Hampshiremen vainly attempted to come to their support. They too were slaughtered. Col. Curzon of the Royal Irish fell dead leading his men. But some Royal Irish, with great fortitude, somehow reached and captured an advance German trench.

The survivors of the support lines succeeded in reaching the front-line trenches, but found them already crowded with the Munsters and Royal Irish, dead, wounded and barely living. The deadly fire forced the Leinsters, Connaught Rangers and Hampshires to take shelter with them. Despite the terrible fire, a handful of Hampshiremen bravely followed the Royal Irish into the captured trench.

7th Inniskillings were brought up, but in their weakened state, they could not be expected to succeed where a brigade had failed. They sought shelter and waited for further orders. Eventually, in the early hours of 10 September, the survivors of 47 Brigade were relieved by elements of 4 Guards Brigade and retired to Trônes Wood.

THE CAPTURE OF GINCHY, 9 SEPTEMBER 1916

48 Brigade succeeded in penetrating Ginchy because the swiftness and dash of their assault caught the German machine-gunners still under cover during the intense final minutes of the barrage. 1st Munster, the right assault battalion of 48 Brigade, felt the check on its right by enfilade fire from that sector. This briefly affected the advance of 48 Brigade. But 1st Munsters were not new to the business of war. X Company wheeled to their right, dug in and formed a flank-guard. The first two waves of this company were wiped out, leaving twenty-eight men. CSM Harris, the warrant officer commanding, wheeled the left of Z Company and charged, driving the enemy from their positions. He then joined X Company and dug in with a machine-gun. This prevented a German flank-attack on the right rear of 48 Brigade. The remnant of W and Y Companies carried on to the objective. It was a brilliant feat of minor tactics in the face of stout resistance by men of 1st Battalion, 19th Bavarian Infantry Regiment.

Behind the Munsters, 8th Dublins under Lt.-Col. E. Bellingham ignored the check and carried on through the Munsters into the village which they entered at 1725, punctual to the minute. Hot on their heels were 8th Inniskillings. To their left, in the western part of Ginchy, 7th Irish Rifles were strongly assisted by 7th Irish Fusiliers. Going with great dash, they reached the German line and quickly took it, killing or taking prisoner most of its garrison. Some Germans, however, fell back and gallantly began setting up a line of resistance with machine-guns. A light trench mortar section which had advanced with the Rifles set up their Stokes and with a short barrage forced the Germans to surrender.[19] Hans Crescent, the objective of the Rifles, was reached by 1700. On time, 9th Dublins passed through the Rifles at 1725. Leading the advance of 9th Dublins was Lt. Tom Kettle, commanding B Company. More properly, he ought to have been left out of the battle because of his advanced age and ill health, but he insisted on taking his place with his men. He fell leading his company, killed instantly by a shot in the chest. The company behind was led by Lt. James Emmet Dalton, aged eighteen. Dalton paused long enough to see his friend was dead, then led his men on. Six years later, Dalton, by then an Irish Army general, witnessed another friend, Michael Collins, die at Béal na mBláth, Co. Cork. Kettle's personal crusade to secure Irish independence was not over when he fell at Ginchy. His time would more properly have come after the war. It was a tragedy for Ireland that this was not to be.

The 8th and 9th Dublins had passed through and were leading the assault through Ginchy. Their objective was the German support line on the northern outskirts of the village. The Dublins, attacking with a headlong rush which took all before it, carried with them troops of the Inniskillings, Rifles and Irish Fusiliers. Few stayed to mop up. About two hundred Germans surrendered; others fled towards the rear, hotly pursued by the eager victors. Not for the first time in battle, the Irish were in danger of pursuing too far. Because so many officers were dead or wounded, too few were left to restrain and lead. Eventually, however, control was established and the troops were brought back to the objective to consolidate positions around the edge of the ruined village.

Consolidation became the imperative. A swift counterstroke always followed a German withdrawal, and Lt.-Col. Bellingham of 8th Dublins, almost the sole surviving commanding officer, did sterling work organising the defence. The divisional engineers who had accompanied the assault, 156 Field Company with two companies of 11th Hampshires, were detailed to construct a strongpoint at the Corps boundary on the Delville Wood road. On the left flank of 16th Division, units of XV Corps were unable to make progress. It was therefore essential that defensive preparations be taken. By its capture, Ginchy formed an awkward and provocative salient in the enemy line, who responded that evening with their customary vigour. This time the Germans failed, but not before sharp fighting took place to repulse the 19th Bavarian Regiment when they came at 1820 and again at 2100. In defending their newly-won line, a distinguished part was played by the divisional Royal Engineers and 11th Hampshire.

That night, 9–10 September 1916, the exhausted units of the 16th in

Ginchy were relieved by 3 Guards Brigade. The Irish dead were collected by the guardsmen. Among them was the body of Tom Kettle which had been recovered by the Welsh Guards. The Irishmen withdrew through Trônes Wood to Carnoy from where they were bussed back to Happy Valley and the sleep of exhaustion. On their way back, they had a 'first glimpse of strange objects apparently trying to secrete themselves in the wood'. One battalion war diary described them as 'new pattern armoured machines'.[20]

On 11 September the joyful brigades of 16th Division marched behind their pipes to Vaux sur Somme and went into billets.

The price of 16th Division's success had been a heavy one. In the week's fighting, the infantry, engineers and pioneers of the 16th suffered the loss of over fifty per cent officers and forty per cent men out of its strength of 435 and 10,410.

On 9 September, the capture of Ginchy was the only success on the entire front. Unquestionably this success was due to the courageous dash of the Irish into their own barrage. All the brigades had won renown throughout the Western Front. Thereafter, Guillemont and Ginchy were linked inextricably with 16th (Irish) Division.

The casualty figures given by the Official History:

> 5th Division, 26 August–7 September, 133 officers and 4100 men
> 20th Division, 22 August–8 September, 129 officers and 2830 men
> 16th Division, 3 September–9 September, 224 officers and 4090 men

In a successful assault there are no 'missing'—or prisoners. Therefore all the above in relation to 16th Division were killed in action, died of wounds or wounded in action. Fifty years later, a singular tribute was paid to the efficiency of the RAMC at Ginchy by ex-Pte. M. Kane, 7th Royal Irish Rifles. During an interview in 1976, Kane told how he had his left foot completely blown off, and had suffered other injuries to his back, buttocks and head. Within minutes he was picked up, and under fire, a tourniquet applied to his leg before he was carried to an RAP. After field treatment, he was evacuated to Rouen where he was operated upon before being evacuated to Southampton for further operations. Following these he was evacuated to the Ulster Volunteer Force Hospital at Victoria Barracks, Belfast, near his home. He lived into his eighties at the Erskine Hospital in Scotland.[21]

The Battle of the Somme continued its bloody course. The Guards Division, supported by tanks, making their first appearance in war, succeeded in capturing Ginchy Telegraph and the Quadrilateral on 15 September. In this battle, 1st and 2nd Irish Guards were, not for the first time, almost destroyed, and a certain Capt. the Hon. Harold Alexander won an immediate DSO. Of his battalion only 166 all ranks came out of the action.[22] Next day Thiepval fell to an assault of five divisions.

Beaumont Hamel, where 1st Dublins and 1st Inniskillings of the 29th

Division died against unbroken wire on 1 July 1916, was the last German fortress to fall in the Somme battle. This defiant fortress repulsed all attacks until it finally fell in mid November 1916. It was fitting that, when Beaumont Hamel was captured by 51st Highland and 63rd Naval Divisions, an Irish battalion was part of the army brigade in the latter division. In a driving snowstorm which turned to sleet then rain, 10th Royal Dublin Fusiliers, a battalion of shopkeepers, supported by two tanks which stuck in chalky mud, rounded up 400 prisoners. It was at this point that the Battle of the Somme ended, at last, in mutual exhaustion.

> As the bloody angle south of Beaumont Hamel will be for ever associated with the Ulster Division, so Guillemont was a triumph for the troops of Southern Ireland. The men of Munster, Leinster and Connaught broke through the intricate defences of the enemy as a torrent sweeps down rubble. The place was one of the strongest of all the many fortified villages in the German line and its capture was the most important achievement of the British since the taking of Pozières. It was the last uncaptured point in the old German second position between Mouquet Farm and the junction with the French. It was most resolutely defended, since, being close to the point of junction, it compelled a hiatus in the advance of the Allied front. With its fall the work of two years was swept away and in the whole section the enemy were now in new and improvised positions.[23]

The men of Connaught, Leinster and Munster who fought there would proudly acknowledge the part played in the battles of Guillemont-Ginchy by the men in their ranks from the historic nine counties of Ulster.

After the battle, a wooden Celtic cross made by 11th Hampshires was erected at Ginchy in memory of the fallen of 16th Division. After the war, it was replaced by a cross of Irish granite which stands in the churchyard of Guillemont. The original 'Ginchy Gross' is preserved at the War Memorial Gardens, designed by Lutyens, at Islandbridge, Dublin.

Death Casualties
16th Division—1496 at Loos and 1167 on the Somme
36th Division—1944 at the Somme [24]

The official historian says of the Battle of the Somme:

> For this disastrous loss of the finest manhood of the United Kingdom and Ireland there was only a small gain of ground to show.[25]

Because of the casualties suffered at Loos and the Somme, certain Service units of 16th Division were disbanded or amalgamated. Other regular battalions joined the division. 8th Royal Munster Fusiliers was disbanded on 26 November 1916. Its personnel, twenty-one officers and 446 other ranks, were absorbed by 1st Royal Munster Fusiliers. The 7th and 8th Royal Irish Fusiliers amalgamated on 25 October 1916 and became 7th/8th Royal Irish Fusiliers. 2nd Royal Irish Regiment were in 22 Brigade, 7th Division through the Somme battle until 24 October 1916. They then joined 49 Brigade. 1st Royal Munster Fusiliers were transferred from 48 and 49 Brigade. 2nd Royal Dublin Fusiliers joined 48 Brigade from 10 Brigade, 4th Division on 11 November 1916.

Meanwhile, 16th Division had departed from the Somme and into Second Army where it took up a position alongside its sister division, 36th (Ulster), opposite Messines Ridge. The largest town in the area, Locre, was a pleasant Flemish community and it had many canteens and good cafés which were used by both divisions. As they settled down to the attrition of the trenches, during their rest periods they began to get to know each other through sports, exchange visits and dinner parties. A feeling of mutual regard grew out of shared experiences of war and its horrors. The sacrifices and supreme examples of human courage which both divisions had witnessed in the horror of the Somme abated that animosity between Unionist and Nationalist. The politics of the Home Rule crisis could now be discussed in different circumstances. Gen. Sir Alex Godley commanded an ANZAC corps close to the two Irish Divisions. He had many friends in both. On New Year's Eve 1916, he invited to dinner Oliver Nugent and Somerset Saunderson MP from the 36th, along with Stephen Gwynn MP and Willie Redmond MP from the 16th. His Maj.-Gen. General Staff, Charles Gwynn, was brother to Stephen.

> On the last day of the year, we had the first of several most interesting and amusing dinners, when we got the four of them together. The talk and arguments between the two Unionist Orangemen of the black north, and the Southern Home Rulers, egged on by Charles Gwynn and myself, would become rather heated; but I need hardly say that they always finished by falling on each other's necks, and were in reality the best of friends.[26]

Had Tom Kettle been alive it could have been even more amusing. He and Saunderson had been electoral opponents in 1908. Kettle won by sixteen votes (but resigned later). In one of his bolts during the hustings, Kettle told his audience: 'Mr Saunderson has declared so often he is the son of Colonel Saunderson, I am inclined to believe him.'[27] It was said of Kettle that 'Only he could have won the seat in the Nationalist interest.'[28]

Life in those far off days was full of surprises completely removed from the war. On route marches, units of 16th and 36th Divisions inevitably passed each other. One former officer of 8th Irish Rifles recalled: 'During the march we met a battalion of the Irish Brigade marching in the opposite direction with the band playing 'She's the most distressful country', which produced on our part loud cheers.'[29]

An Orange Lodge of 14th Irish Rifles, meeting in a Flemish farmhouse, had a unique experience, over which one member mused many years later: 'It was strange for an Orange Lodge to meet in a room with Roman Catholic pictures and statuary on the walls.'[30]

CHAPTER TWENTY-FOUR

Macedonia, 1916–17

Following the Serbian campaign, several changes in command took place within 10th Division. Brig. E.M. Morris took over 31 Brigade from Brig. King-King. King-King may have been disappointed but not surprised at his own replacement. Excellent and understandable reasons there may have been for the precipitate withdrawal of 31 Brigade from the Kosturino position, but King-King's failure to give prior warning to the divisional commander was inexcusable and irredeemable. His relief would have followed as a matter of course. Less understandable is Monro's refusal to confirm Nicol in command of 10th Division because he was on the retired list in 1914. Precedents existed for promoting general officers from the retired list. Later in 1916, Nicol went on leave and was succeeded by Col. A.D. Macpherson. Nicol never returned to Macedonia and Macpherson was confirmed in command of 30 Brigade. Brig. W.B. Emery assumed command of the divisional artillery in February 1916. At the same time, Lt.-Col. E.M.S. Charles became Chief Royal Engineers. All retained their appointments until the end of the war.

With effect from 15 January 1916, Maj. G.M. Grogan was promoted lieutenant-colonel and assumed command of 5th Battalion, Royal Irish, from Lt.-Col. Lord Granard, who was promoted colonel and became Military Secretary, Headquarters Salonika Army. Shortly after this, 500 men of the Greek Labour Corps were attached for manual labour under the battalion's specialists and all began the repair of old roads and the construction of new ones. In addition to roads, bridges and railways were constructed and laid. This work continued until 10th Division left Macedonia.

In view of the dangerous situation which existed following the conquest of Serbia by the Central Powers and the rise of an anti-Allied government in Athens, the Salonika army began to fortify a perimeter around Salonika. It was to become known as the Entrenched Camp. Some cynics called this the 'bird cage'. 10th Division could only be allowed ten days for refit and reorganisation before returning to the line at the end of December. Then it deployed in defence of the right of the Allied line from the mouth of the Rendina River to the eastern edge of Lake Langaza. 29 Brigade was shipped from the mouth of the Rendina River in the Gulf of Orfano and fortified the line Skala Stavros-Lake Beshik along the front of the Rendina Gorge.

Brig. Vandeleur, commander 29 Brigade, was beginning to emerge as the character of the division. 29 Brigade, however, was not altogether delighted with his eccentricities. His brigade fortified its line and trenches were begun on sites personally selected by him. Later, when these trenches were half-dug, he then changed the sites and had them re-dug.[1] This was possibly connected with an order by Gen. Sarrail (a keen archaeologist) for all to protect and report antiquarian finds, and the find by 6th Leinsters of a sarcophagus which is now in the British Museum.[2]

30 and 31 Brigades marched to their allotted positions on a line between Lake Beshik and Lake Langaza. Rain started to fall on the morning of 1 January as the brigade began constructing defences and its infrastructure of roads which was to form the 'Entrenched Camp'. Fortifying the front was not easy with their depleted numbers and a shortage of essential tools and stores. The weather turned bitterly cold again and the 'Vardar wind' pierced even the goatskin coats they now wore. However they were not to remain there long. The very capable and conscientious Army Surgeon-General, W.G. Macpherson CB CMG, inspected the battalions in January. Possibly resulting from this, 10th Division was relieved by 27th Division at the end of January and remained out of the line for four months.

Brought back to Salonika, 10th Division concentrated on the Ortiach Plateau in the area of Kirechkoi, east of the city. Here they settled down to a long period of training, varied by road-making and the construction of a second line of defences. As the weather warmed up in spring, a new timetable was adopted which was better suited to avoid working during the heat of the day. Reveille at 0330 was followed by a mug of tea. After a march to its area, work started at about 0500 which went on until breakfast at 0800. All rested until 1500, when dinner was served. Work restarted at 1630 and went on until 2200.

Several mobile columns were formed in late spring to test the new pack-mule transport establishment. All personnel were issued with slouch hats which gave the division the appearance of an Australian one. The period of exercising provided a useful break from the monotony of work. Some brigade commanders had their own ways of breaking monotony which were not always welcome. In addition to the strenuous mountain warfare exercises the division was engaged in, Brig. Vandeleur began to tighten up administrative procedures in his brigade. As a result, the commanding officer of the Rangers was ordered to remove his adjutant, Capt. Martin, who was replaced by Capt. C.J. Lyster of the Leinsters.[3] 'Vandy'[4] inspected his battalions several times in April and May before eventually declaring himself satisfied.

Martin was not the only officer lost by the Connaught Rangers. Its treasured Medical Officer, Capt. O'Sullivan, RAMC, was transferred to 30th Field Ambulance. His work among the wounded at Gallipoli and Kosturino would never be forgotten by the men of the battalion.

The departure of the MO left only the CO and the QM of the original 5th Rangers officers. Several days later the CO, Lt.-Col. H.F.N. Jourdain, collapsed. He had raised and commanded the battalion, without interruption, although suffering acutely from gastric complaints in Gallipoli and exposure in Serbia. Several times he had temporarily commanded 29 Brigade. Such was the esteem in which he was held that, on the journey to the hospital, he was accompanied by all the officers of his battalion. By some incredible contrivance, possibly helped by Lord Granard, Jourdain continued to command 5th Rangers on paper until February 1917. His health never recovered, and after he was invalided home, Jourdain was not allowed to serve in the East again. He later temporarily commanded 6th Connaught Rangers in France and 16th Battalion, Royal Welsh Fusiliers. When at the end of the war the 5th Battalion became the regular 2nd Battalion, he commanded it for two years in Silesia from 1921 until its disbandment. Jourdain was the last lieutenant-colonel of the Connaught Rangers, as well as its historian.

The static, almost tranquil, situation in Macedonia was broken at the end of May 1916, when the Bulgarians, with German support, advanced into the Struma valley. Gen. Sarrail decided to take the offensive and Gen. Milne assumed responsibility for almost the entire Allied line east of Lake Doiran.

10th Division remained on the Ortiach Plateau until June, when Gen. Longley was ordered to relieve the 26th Division in the line west of Lake Langaza between Tumba and Aivatli. But when the British responsibility was extended, 10th Division advanced to the Struma early in June.

Having had its longest period of training and refitting since leaving Basingstoke, the 10th advanced along the Seres road in early June. The troops were still carrying winter-scale equipment and they suffered severely from heat exhaustion. Many of 29 Brigade fell out and one man of 10th Hampshires died.[5] 'A bloody march, hot as hell, a fearful time getting men along. 27 of ours fell out, 60 of the Leinsters, 80 of the Connaught Rangers, 119 of the Hampshires'.[6] Next day, the brigade staff arranged marches during early morning and late afternoon, having learnt that 'the falling out was due to the issue of orders to march through the hottest part of the twenty-four hours.'[7] When this was done, fewer men fell out than previously. The battalions averaged ten miles a day and marched ten days to reach the Struma. On the way they were tasked with quarrying road-making material from nearby sites before marching on. The abundance of insect life on the line of march, apart from the mosquito, was remarkable, 'especially dazzling butterflies'.[8]

The art of long-distance route marching had been lost in France, but in the east it was still an essential part of campaigning. When they became acclimatised on long marches, the battalions swung along in a tireless, rhythmic way, wasting little energy, never shuffling. Sometimes they accomplished marches of up to twenty-five miles in the heat of Struma, which in September 1916 rose to 114°. At the end of a day's march in battalion staging areas, 'bivvies' were quickly erected and neatly 'dressed', tea was made; those not on guard or fatigues soon got 'down to it'.[9]

On 11 June 1916, 10th Division relieved the French along the line of the Struma River between Lakes Tahinos and Butkova. Each brigade had three battalions in line and one in reserve. Battalions had a frontage of about four miles. The level of the river had fallen and defensive field-works, breast-works and trenches were constructed around various bridges and at fording places. Roads and tracks were made between divisional and brigade headquarters and down to battalion headquarters. It was essential but hard work in the stifling heat of a marshy valley, bare of shade and infested with mosquitoes. Virtually the only recreation for off-duty troops was bathing at specially-selected spots. But the area was green and more attractive than Gallipoli, and fresh vegetables, fruit and eggs were obtainable.[10]

Six months previously, the Director of Medical Services, Salonika Army, Surgeon-General Macpherson, had warned Sir Bryan Mahon of the possible ill effect upon the army caused by its operations in the highest malarial region of Europe. Mahon instituted anti-malarial precautions which included the draining of a 1,500 acre swamp during February. The Quartermasters' branch was instructed to requisition mosquito nets and gloves and other anti-mosquito material. The DMS also requisitioned quinine in large quantities, both for the army and Greek refugees from Turkey for humanitarian reasons. Following the correct chain of command, all requests went through GHQ MEF, Egypt. At first they ridiculed the requirement, then procrastinated.[11] Gen. Macpherson, in profound exasperation, passed the entire correspondence to the War Office Medical Directorate. The matter was resolved, possibly by Lt.-Gen. Sir Alfred Keogh, the Director General of Army Medical Services, through Surgeon-General T.J. O'Donnell, Deputy Director Medical Services, and spokesman to the Adjutant-General on medical matters. But the matter was not yet ended. When eventually the material arrived in Egypt, much of it was held there for the benefit of its own resources.[12] In the meantime, the men of the 10th Division were struck down by a malarial plague.

Cases of Malaria 1916

	July	August	September	October
	4580	7511	894	6872
Deaths	88	26	112	70

The command comparative figures for malaria, per 1000 of strength[13]

Year	Egypt/Palestine	Macedonia
1916	8.10	331.47
1917	44.66	353.18

Average days' treatment for recovery	19.9	41.3

'The tortures we suffered that summer are beyond description.'[14] On visiting one of his outposts which he had positioned the previous evening, a company commander could hardly recognise his men, so badly disfigured were they from insect bites.

> So swollen and red were they that I could scarcely recognise one of them. They had been attacked by mosquitoes during the night and almost eaten alive. They must have suffered agonies.[15]

The mosquito nets issued at this time were small, 2 feet by 2 feet. Protective cream and face veils were issued for use by sentries in 1917.

At first there were no Bulgarians within eight or nine miles of the River Struma line. Then, during early July 1916, the Greek government handed over to the Bulgarians the fort blocking the Rupel Pass. The enemy thronged into the villages on the eastern side of the Struma. To meet the threat, the British commander quickly moved part of his reserves, 27th Division, extending the British defensive line fifty miles, down to the mouth of the Struma into the Gulf of Orfano. A further problem was created by demobilised Greek troops attempting to cross the Struma into the entrenched camp. Orders were received from Paris to prevent this, even to the extent of opening fire. This did little to reduce a local crisis and eventually the order was rescinded.

Meanwhile, the effects of malaria upon the strength of the exposed battalions was such that 10th Division's front was seriously under-manned. Eventually in late July 1916, British forces were withdrawn from the Struma valley to high ground. But before withdrawing, crossing points on the river were wired and patrolling was established. The area was cleared and cleaned before the withdrawal between 23–28 July. The march to the hills was a painfully slow one for troops weakened by illness. Battalion strengths were down to about 450 all ranks.

In the cooler high ground, training began. Range practise and field firing were followed by collective battalion training and brigade exercises. Courses for specialists were organised including Lewis gun, grenade throwing, and signalling. The scale of transport which Mahon had requested eight months previously had finally been introduced and each battalion obtained new pack-harness and mules, handing back its remaining wheeled vehicles. That unlovable beast, the army mule, had at least one who loved his charges. Pte. Dollahan of 6th Inniskillings, a transport driver, had charge of two company mules. At every stop of some duration, Dollahan insisted on digging a sloping pit in which his charges were perfectly safe from anything but a direct shell-hit.[16] During August, Gen. Longley inspected the units of his formation, paying particular attention to its transport. Slowly, as the heat and malaria effects waned, the units recovered. Throughout all this, the endless road construction and maintenance went on.

The Karajaköis and Yeniköi, 30 September–4 October 1916

Early in June, the Serbian army, which had been reconstituted and re-equipped on the Island of Corfu, landed at Salonika and began offensive preparations to retake Monastir. In the operation designed to fix the Bulgarian reserves and to prevent them from moving to resist the French and Serbians at Monastir, the XVI corps was ordered to attack across the Struma and capture Karajaköis Bala and Karajaköis Zir. Because 10th Division was weakened by malaria, the corps commander, Lt.-Gen. C.J. Briggs, tasked 27th Division with the operation. 10th Division was in support. However, 27th Division was scattered. Its chief artillery and engineer officers could not be contacted in time and the artillery commander and chief engineer of 10th Division were placed in command of Artillery and Engineers for the operation.[17] Moreover, two battalions of 27th Division, 1st Royal Irish and 1st Leinsters, were thirty miles away on road-building tasks.

29 Brigade, consisting of two composite battalions, crossed the Struma by assault boats and provided flank guards while 10th Division engineer field companies built two foot bridges and an artillery bridge across the Struma in a remarkably short time. The artillery bridge was especially important.

> This was a good piece of work by the 66th Field Company. The company had at noon on the 27th finished a trestle footbridge 540 feet long. By noon on the 29th this had been converted to an artillery bridge. A screen of maize straw on each side hid movement on the bridge.[18]

At 0515 on 30 September, 81 Brigade of 27th Division attacked across the Struma and captured the villages of Karajaköis Bala and Karajaköis Zir by the end of that day. During the evening, the 10th Division engineer field companies wired the captured position. From 30 September to 2 October, several counter-attacks were made by the Bulgarians but all were repulsed in front of the wire. During this phase, 2nd Royal Irish Fusiliers was sent to reinforce 81 Brigade.

Following the success of his minor operation, Gen. Briggs decided to widen the bridgehead by capturing Yeniköi, a large straggling village astride the Seres road. 30 Brigade was ordered to attack at 0530 on 3 October. The acting brigade commander of 30 Brigade was given little time: 'Colonel Macpherson only learnt, from General Briggs in person, that he was to undertake the capture of Yeniköi at 10 a.m. on the 2nd.'[19] At the same time, 28th Division were to widen the bridgehead on the left flank of 30 Brigade, but this appears to have been casually arranged: 'Presumably General Briggs telephoned to Major-General Croker, commanding the 28th Division, that he desired Mazirko to be occupied; for the village was actually seized without opposition… before XVI Corps issued orders.'[20]

30 Brigade crossed the Struma early on 3 October and deployed on the line held by 6th Royal Irish Rifles on the left of 27th Division. After a half hour's bombardment, Yeniköi was attacked by 7th Munsters and 6th Dublins, supported by 7th Dublins and with 6th Munsters in reserve. 6th Irish Rifles followed behind. By 0700, Yeniköi had been captured. 7th Munsters found touch on the right with 1st Royal Scots on the road from Karajaköis Zir; 6th Dublins gained contact with an Armoured Motor Battery which had advanced along the Seres road. The armoured cars were followed by 1st Suffolks of 28th Division. The inevitable counter-attack followed.

An immense bombardment was directed against Yeniköi. Under its cover, the Bulgarians again massed for an attack. The Bulgarian column debouched from the north of Kalendria Wood, led by an officer on a white charger. Instantly they were met by a storm of artillery and rifle fire from the Irish line. The enemy column was enveloped in smoke and dust in which the horse and rider vanished.

> They were in line of companies. I could see the officers mounted on their chargers. On they came, line upon line of them. The sight should have struck terror into our hearts but it had the opposite effect. It filled us with exhilaration and in less than no time we were blazing away. So also were the machine-guns. At the same time like a clap of thunder or one thousand claps of thunder, our guns opened up. Never had artillery such a target, a mass of troops, closely packed together and in full view. I don't believe the Bulgars had a chance of firing a shot.[21]

An intense bombardment was directed against Yeniköi by the Bulgarians. But in the bombardment, the two Dublin battalions suffered heavily, not only from the enemy artillery but also from 'unders' from their own. The telephone cables were cut, and with no communications between the artillery observers and the battery positions, this could not be corrected. The Dublins fell back to a sunken road in the centre of the village. Carrying parties returning from Yeniköi were mistaken by watchers on the heights above the valley for a retirement and caused some heart fluttering. The Munsters, on the right, unaffected by the bombardment, held their position.

Because of the supposed withdrawal of the Dublins, 6th Irish Rifles were ordered to advance through the bombardment.

> The first wave had almost reached its objective when it came under scattered rifle fire. Then with a crash like thunder the enemy artillery opened up. So intense was the barrage and so dense the clouds of smoke created that those in the front wave were completely lost to

view of those in the second wave. But there was no hesitation in the ranks of the latter. On it came as steady as if on parade until it too was enveloped in a pall of smoke, in that hell of bursting shells.[22]

Throughout all this, two Dublin companies were in possession of the village. One company remained there throughout the night. Next morning, Yeniköi was again reoccupied in strength.

6th Inniskillings and 5th Irish Fusiliers of 31 Brigade went to the relief of 30 Brigade and crossed the Struma in canvas boats which were powered across by the soldiers pulling a rope fixed to both banks.[23] Three days after the battle, when 1st Royal Irish relieved 5th Irish Fusiliers, many fowls and melon patches were found having somehow been missed by the Fusiliers. They provided a welcome addition to a diet of bully-beef and biscuit.[24]

On a ridge high above the valley in which the attack and counter-attacks took place, the reserve troops had a splendid view. There the regular battalions of the Royal Irish and the Leinsters watched and cheered on their young 'Service' battalions as though spectators to a sporting engagement. 1st Leinsters had been road-mending on 1 October when ordered to rejoin their brigade with all possible speed. They began marching next morning and arrived 'long after midnight after a march of thirty-two miles in which not a man had fallen out.'[25] Next day the Leinsters provided carrying parties across the Struma.[26]

The success of the Yeniköi operation, and the mauling at Zir and Bala by 81 Brigade of 27th Division, forced the Bulgarians to withdraw to the high ground east of the Struma valley. 10th Division now held the Seres road up to the railway line west of Seres, with 27th Division on the right and 28th Division on the left. It was the largest battle fought in Struma and the Bulgarians were routed. 'Had there been five to six divisions instead of three, under strength by illness, we could have swept over the mountains and knocked Bulgaria out of the war.'[27]

An officer of 6th Inniskillings commented on how the British CinC and Gen. Sarrail, as guests of the corps commander, observed the battle. They with their staffs, accompanied by nurses and Greek ladies, watched the 'event' from a ridge where the Corps had set up a tactical headquarters. In coloured tents the guests were entertained by a divisional band. The officer's comment is acerbic:

> It seemed horrible that the British Commander in Chief should bring up from Salonika, over 100 kilometres away, a party to whom to give a lunch and tea, and let them watch three battalions crossing a river and losing men killed and wounded.[28]

This gathering possibly explains how 28th Division attacked before written orders were issued, and why Col. Macpherson of 30 Brigade had little warning of his brigade attack, and was in fact told of it by the corps commander in person and not through the corps and divisional chain of command.

During the period 30 September–6 October 1916, when 10th Division was in action, the admittance to hospital figures for the operation were:

Wounded	836
Sick (Malaria)	554
Total	1390[29]

The total killed was 189 all ranks.[30]

The Bulgarians remained quiet. The British, their strength reduced by malaria by over twenty-five per cent in addition to battle casualties, were forced into a long period of inactivity. For the battalions, the inevitable road improvements, the battle against mosquitoes and the training began again.

Such were the effects of malaria and the slow rate of replacements from depots in Ireland (which also had to find replacements for the casualties of the Somme battles) that brigades became composite battalions. Finally, in an effort to build up the strength of 10th Division without altering its national character, in November 1916 GHQ ordered the three Irish regular battalions in 27th Division to transfer to the 10th. At first this was not popular with the regulars, who had been through much hard fighting with their comrades of 27th Division and who were reluctant to leave them. However, they settled down quickly in the 10th.[31]

Two battalions of the Leinsters were brigaded together for the first time when the 1st Battalion joined 29 Brigade. 1st Royal Irish went to 30 Brigade when 6th Munsters absorbed 7th Munsters. 1st Irish Fusiliers went to 31 Brigade, and 5th Irish Fusiliers absorbed 6th Irish Fusiliers. 10th Hampshires, which had served with 10th Division from its foundation, left 29 Brigade to join 27th Division. Bonds forged in war remain very strong. On Gallipoli Day 1965, 1st Battalion Royal Hampshire Regiment invited survivors of the old Irish regiments to the fiftieth anniversary of their great annual celebration. This was in memory of the service of their 10th Battalion with 10th Division and 11th battalion with 16th Division, and their 1st Battalion which fought and died alongside 1st Dublins and 1st Munsters at Sedd el Bahr.

The Irish battalions of 27th Division, much reduced from the battles on the Western Front, were composed of long-service regular soldiers of between five and fifteen years' service. Having returned from India, they then served in France and moved as a division to Salonika. Nearly all had not been home for up to five years. Home leave to the Salonika Army was now being granted. The numbers allowed were necessarily small, and it was quickly seen that it would be years before the entire force could obtain home leave. It brought considerable grumbling, especially among the regulars of 27th Division who had been on active service, without home leave, since December 1914. They had been offered three days' leave, but when the travelling time was calculated, they considered it not worth the effort. But the allocation to staff officers appeared unduly high to the ever-suspicious regimental warriors: an unfair allocation was suspected.[32]

At the end of 1916, 10th Division command and senior divisional staff was:

GOC	Maj.-Gen. J.R. Longley
GSO1	Lt.-Col. H.L. Knight
AA&QMG	Lt.-Col. C.W. Pearless
BGRA	Brig.-Gen. W.B. Emery
CRE	Lt.-Col. E.M.S. Charles

29 Brigade, Brig.-Gen. R.S. Vandeleur
30 Brigade, Brig.-Gen. A.D. Macpherson
31 Brigade, Brig.-Gen. E.M. Morris

The Reverend Skilbeck-Smith, then a young platoon commander with 1st Leinsters, describes his Irishmen as a 'sturdy type, resolute and hardy'. They were ignorant of Near East geography, with little notion of the relative position of Macedonia, and unable to correlate the relationship between Bulgar and German.

> They easily assimilated the principles of individual efficiency as fighters, knowing that if each man is wise in his own particular sphere, the platoon must necessarily be an effective unit. So it was not necessary for the officer to rush around yelling out orders. Each man had been trained in his job, and the elementary principles of warfare; if he were to lose touch with his officers he could still act on his own initiative with good results.[33]

Like all Englishmen who served with Irish troops, Skilbeck-Smith was struck by one particular aspect of his men.

> There is a humorous strain about him too, perhaps of a peculiar type. He doesn't sing on the march, or give vent to his feelings generally, except perhaps when his anger is aroused. Here in battle he is supreme, and, from my experience doesn't require any leading, particularly in any case of open fighting. He is yet humorous enough to enjoy a joke and to make one, and sometimes he is unconsciously funny. I served only with one unit; but I have been brigaded with an Irish brigade for

two years in service, and I would not wish to have spent that time with any other brigade or unit.[34]

The war in Macedonia had not the same awfulness as the Western Front, Gallipoli or Serbia. Despite the daily toil of hard manual work and an unceasing battle against malarial mosquitoes, and indeed the illness itself, the toll of battle casualties was low. There were particularly good concert parties, boxing matches, sports, team games of many sorts, and swimming in the Struma. For those optimistic officers who had brought shot-guns, reasonable rough shooting could be found in the hills. Others had more intellectual pursuits. One, Lt. Pickup of 6th Leinsters, to the amusement of his battalion, created a magnificent collection of butterflies and beetles during the campaign; his collection boxes and naturalist equipment, however, left little living space in his bivouac.[35] The eccentricity of Pickup could only have existed in the '40-10s'.[36] Intellectual pursuits were not confined to the Leinsters; Capt. Terence Verschoyle of 6th Inniskillings learned Greek.[37]

During 1917, 10th Division operated in the upper Struma valley where they attacked and captured Prosenik. 6th Dublins raided Keupri and every battalion patrolled vigorously. The men of 10th Division built roads, improved railways, exchanged artillery fire with the Bulgarians and waged a ceaseless war against mosquitoes. On 14 May, 6th Irish Rifles, with 5th Rangers in support, captured and held Keupri, driving off counter-attacks.

For health reasons, Gen. Longley decided to withdraw across the Struma. Everything of potential value to the enemy was salvaged and removed; even the front-line wire was taken away without the enemy detecting any signs of withdrawal. New camps and access roads were constructed on high, wooded hills where life was more pleasant. Constant training went on when they were not in the front line. By 14 June all troops had been withdrawn from the Struma valley, except for Yeomanry patrols. Enemy patrols which attempted to exploit the situation were driven out of villages by battle-patrols.

Stringent anti-malaria precautions were now in operation. At daily parades, each man took five grains of liquid quinine; shorts had deep turn-ups which could be lowered and tucked into puttees at night; two-man bivouacs with mosquito netting were issued; face veils and gloves were worn at night by sentries; skin cream was issued to all. Had the Salonika Army Medical Services been listened to eighteen months previously, these measures could have been introduced sooner and prevented much illness and death.

On 18 August the 10th Division received orders to concentrate at Salonika. This heralded a move from Macedonia to yet another theatre of operations, Palestine. On the route march to the port area of Salonika, 6th Inniskillings

sent a party of men badly affected with malaria ahead from the final bivouac
fifteen miles from the town. Under command of Lt. T.T. McCartney-Filgate,
the march began late at night, to escape the worst heat, and the party got
lost. Finding a railway station with a train standing outside, the officer
inquired of the Greek staff about its use, with little satisfaction. Two
corporals of the Royal Engineers Railway Transport were more helpful and
expressed a willingness to drive the train to Salonika if the Greek staff were
'distracted'.[38] The Irish created a disturbance. The Greeks, enticed into the
darkness by the commotion, found themselves set upon, tied up, locked up,
and their train stolen. Next afternoon, it was discovered at the 'English
dock', Salonika, by which time the Inniskillings were on the high seas.
Months later, in Sinai, a file recording the investigation into the occurrence,
growing heavy in the process, made the rounds of 10th Division units
without the culprits being discovered.[39]

Embarkation began on 1 September. The first units of the division reached
Ismailia on the banks of the Suez Canal on 5 September, in time to take part
in a decisive battle in Sinai. The troops on the Macedonian front regarded
theirs as a sideshow, and had the feeling of 'being left out in the cold which
was general throughout the army'.[40] This view was not helped by the Army
Staff, who remained completely isolated from the forward units. Upon their
departure for Palestine and a new campaign, neither a representative of the
CinC nor his staff took the trouble to visit the departing ships and wish the
troops well. There is no regimental record of letters or messages of farewell
or appreciation.

> And here we were. My division, 10th Irish, had been in Salonika from
> the very beginning, nearly two years, and not a single officer of GHQ
> or Salonika staff came down to the quay to see the battalion and wish
> them bon voyage and good luck. At the time we didn't think about it,
> but now looking back on it, it seems a peculiar thing.[41]

10th Division was not to see the fruits of the patient build-up of a sound
Macedonian base in the years 1916–17. From Macedonia was launched the
Balkans campaign of 1918 under Gen. Franchet d'Esperey, 'Desperate
Frankie' to the British, which forced Bulgaria then Austria out of the war. In
October 1918, Gen. Milne marched his Salonika Army to Constantinople; the
10th would have enjoyed that. But the 10th Hampshires were there as their
representatives. As the Hampshiremen marched into Bulgaria across the old
battlefield of Kosturino, they were met by the survivors of those men of 10th
Division who had been wounded, captured and survived that dreadful
Serbian campaign.[42]

Maj.-Gen. Sir William Hickie of the 16th Division. (Courtesy of Brig. W.S. Hickie)

Stretcher bearers of the 16th Division under fire at Ginchy, September 1916. (Imperial War Museum)

Neuve Chapelle, 1915, by Col. E.A.P. Hobday, 16th Division Artillery. (Liddle Collection, Leeds University Library)

Some of the dead of the Dublins and Munsters on V Beach at Sedd-el-Bahr on the evening of 25 April 1915. The SS River Clyde *is in the background. Taken by Sgt. J. Bareille, 4ème Regt. Mixed Colonial, French Army. (Liddle Collection, Leeds University Library)*

Captured German pill-box, seen from the rear. (Imperial War Museum)

The Royal Irish Regiment of the 16th Division resting before assaulting Tunnel Trench. (Imperial War Museum)

The Menin road, October 1918, two days before 2nd Leinsters had advanced in this area with 29th Division. (Imperial War Museum)

The capture of Wytschaete by the 16th and 36th Divisions, June 1917. (Imperial War Museum)

A 16th Division advance dressing station, Guillemont, September 1916. (Imperial War Museum)

Defensive position at Ginchy, September 1916. (Imperial War Museum)

The Ypres Salient, near where Francis Ledwidge died on 31 July 1917. (Liddle Collection, Leeds University Library)

A drawing by Lt. McPeake, 5th Connaught Rangers, of a dressing station near Serain, 8 October 1918. (Liddle Collection, Leeds University Library)

A drawing by Lt. McPeake, 5th Connaught Rangers, of C Company caught in an explosion in a railway cutting at Le Cateau, 10 October 1918. (Liddle Collection, Leeds University Library)

Troops of the 16th Division returning from the capture of Guillemont. (Imperial War Museum)

10th Division records section Egyptian Expeditionary Force, October 1918, showing a group of officers and NCOs from the Royal Irish, Connaught Rangers, Leinsters, Dublins and Munsters. The officer seated on the left is from the Royal Irish Regiment. The other officers are Norfolk Regiment, Royal Artillery and Scots Fusiliers; the warrant officer is Cameronian Scottish Rifles. The photograph belonged to Sgt. Harry Downes, Connaught Rangers (seated, bottom right). (Mr J.P. Downes L.C.)

CHAPTER TWENTY-FIVE

Messines, 1917

During Christmas Day 1916, Gen. Hickie visited every battalion in the division.[1] His booming, hearty voice[2] was a tonic to his men and he 'had the knack of cheering up everyone with whom he came in contact'.[3] The Irishmen had come to appreciate Locre. Its camps had Irish names—Birr, Curragh. It had a cinema where many concerts, film shows and boxing tournaments had been held since the previous September. It was regarded as a comfortable billeting area, 'with many shops and cafés and also a YMCA'.[4]

The convent and its nuns became known to all the division, and after the war the Reverend Mother visited Gen. Hickie's estate near Borrisokane, Co. Tipperary.[5] Finally, after a pleasant stay of seven months recuperating from the battles of Loos and the Somme, the time came to march by brigades behind battalion pipes and drums to the training areas around Tournehem. Battle preparation for the new offensive was to begin.

The 16th and 36th Divisions of IX Corps were preparing for an offensive against Messines Ridge. The aim was to pinch out a well-fortified German salient on high ground south of Ypres, in a carefully defined limited operation. It was to be carried out by Gen. Plumer's Second Army. Haig regarded the capture of the ridge as the necessary prelude to the Ypres offensive, planning and preparation for which were already in progress by Gough's Fifth Army headquarters.

At the beginning of April 1917, 16th Division left the Locre/Kemmel sector for training in a rear area. Training, which never stopped when out of the line, now intensified. Replicas of the Wytschaete Front were constructed with dispositions, objectives and distances all clearly marked to scale. Artillery creeping barrages were simulated by flag-waggers and massed Brigade Drums moving according to the artillery plan. 16th Division's practise attack was attended by all senior commanders from Gen. Plumer, the corps commanders and their staffs downwards. It was a dazzling display of red tabs and gold braid. The exercise was followed by a critique opened by Gen. Plumer. 'Daddy' Plumer relaxed all the junior officers by saying he never 'straffed' anyone under general rank.[6] Although Plumer disagreed with a few minor tactical points, positions of Lewis guns being one, on the whole he agreed with the divisional tactics. He then spoke on his own overall concept of operations in the coming battle and asked all those present to pass on to their men the details of the plan; only the date-time was kept secret.[7]

During the training phase, 16th Division enjoyed their longest period out of the line since arriving in France and passed off-duty time with games and sports most afternoons. Rugby and soccer were the favourites. The artillery dug their guns into new positions during April. An engineer field company under Capt. J. O'Sullivan, RE,[8] and large infantry working parties carried out the work. On completion, elaborate camouflage was draped over the positions. This gave the songsters of the Blackthorns' divisional concert party their opportunity.

> Oh! Paddy dear an' have you heard the news that's goin' round?
> Our guns are hid, just where we're bid, by diggin' underground.
> A camouflage so fine and large, prevents their bein' seen,
> For they're hangin' nets, with trimmin' up, a wearing of the green.

> I met with Gen'ral Hickie, and I took him by the hand,
> And I said, 'How's our artillery?' 'Sure,' said he, 'they're doin' grand,'
> With guns in pits, all makin hits, with shell-dumps in between,
> Get fine disguise, from pryin' eyes, by wearing of the green.

> They love the ould Division in the land the boys come from,
> And they're proud of what the boys have done
> at Loos and on the Somme.
> So if by chance we all advance to Wytschaete and Messines,
> They'll learn our guns that straffed the Huns
> were wearing of the green.[9]

The painstaking detail of Second Army headquarters staff planning was reflected in their operations order. As the date of the attack on Messines Ridge neared, parties of officers, NCOs and men went to inspect a gigantic scale model of Messines Ridge near Scherpenberg Hill. After this, the detail plan was distributed, usually in multi-page complicated annexes of fire-support plans, communications instructions, transport arrangements, and march tables. Vast amounts of detail had to be absorbed by commanders and passed on to their staff or unit subordinates for implementation. Nothing could be overlooked; where interaction with other units or formations occurred, liaison had to ensure close harmony. Right up to the last moment minor adjustments had to be made as the plan was 'massaged'. All had to be informed of these changes, for action or information. Several days before the attack, commanding officers were informed of the date. The time remained most secret.

Particular care was taken for the evacuation of the wounded. One-way road systems were established over good roads behind the front for motor ambulances. Even Zero Hour was carefully studied and only arrived at following consultation between headquarters staff and infantry commanders. The final criterion was the ability to see across 100 yards. The time was finally fixed at 0310.

Raids were carried out behind the barrage as part of the deception plan. 36th Division mounted two successful daylight raids on 3–4 June each in company strength. On the 3rd, 13th Irish Rifles carried an enemy trench at Peckham and took nineteen prisoners. Next day, a similar raid by 9th Irish Fusiliers on Spanbroek salient bagged an officer and thirty soldiers. 16th Division mounted a heavy raid on the night of 3rd/4th by 290 all ranks of 6th Connaught Rangers under the command of Lt. Tuite. Its objectives were two enemy trenches, Nancy Switch and Nancy Support. The attack was launched in two waves; the first wave bypassed Nancy Switch and secured the second objective, Nancy Support. The second wave, coming up behind, took Nancy Switch. Both attacks were completely successful. At Nancy Switch, an officer and a platoon of sixteen young soldiers were taken prisoner with little fighting. Nancy Support, more strongly held, put up a stiff fight in which a machine-gun was destroyed and seven prisoners taken; about sixty enemy were killed. Casualties to the Rangers were comparatively light: one officer and two men killed, one officer and five men missing, presumed killed, one officer and thirty-four men wounded. For his inspiring leadership, Lt. Tuite was later awarded the Military Cross.

The Second Army attack was to be mounted on a broad front from St Yves to Mount Sorrel by three corps. II ANZAC Corps (Sir A. Godley) on the right were to assault north-eastwards and capture the southern shoulder of the ridge, including Messines. In the centre, IX Corps (Sir A. Gordon) was to advance due east astride the Spanbroekmolen saddle between the heights of Kemmel and Wytschaete. It was to capture the central sector of the ridge, including the village of Wytschaete. On the left, X Corps (Sir T. Morland) was to assault south-eastwards and capture the northern part of the ridge between the St Eloi-Oosttaverne road and Mount Sorrel. Behind in GHQ reserve was XIV Corps (Lord Cavan).

The preparatory artillery bombardment began on 20 April, with a limited barrage by corps and divisional artillery. After the Arras battle, army heavy and medium support artillery brigades moved to Second Army front. Before the battle opened, 2266 guns, including 756 heavy and medium weapons, had been assembled. The artillery mass was organised into forty bombardment and counter-bombardment groups. Twelve, four to each corps, were specifically for counter-battery fire. Enormous stockpiles of ammunition were created; in all, 144,000 tons of ammunition was located in dumps behind the lines. No less than 1000 rounds was positioned in each gun-pit.

When it opened, the barrage was maintained by two-thirds of the available guns, with one-third resting. The guns in action fired 180 rounds per gun per day. On each divisional front, four two-inch trench-mortar batteries joined in on a wire-cutting fire-mission, dropping 600 rounds per day each. So effective was this fire that vast belts of enemy wire were destroyed so that 'in no case did it form an obstacle to our infantry'.[10] Batteries of heavy trench-mortars, shooting 250 lb projectiles called flying-pigs by the troops, fired 150 rounds each on enemy strongpoints. Identified by aerial reconnaissance, this action was particularly effective: 'This was most effective and dug-outs and machine-gun emplacements of great strength with 6" of concrete as overhead protection were in practically every case completely demolished.'[11]

Three practise barrages were carried out before the pre-assault barrage. These were 'useful drill, but the enemy was not drawn into counter-battery fire'.[12] However under cover of the barrages, battalions all across the front carried out frequent raids by day and night to take prisoners for information.

The actual barrage opened, 'punctual to the second'.[13] Divisional artillery had some latitude and in 16th Division, Gen. Hickie decided that one shell in ten would be smoke. To ensure maximum flexibility in support fire, a battery of 18-pounders and 4.5" howitzers was at the disposal of each infantry brigade commander. The advance of the artillery behind the infantry was carefully prepared and carried out by batteries under their own brigade commanders. Problems only arose over the replacement of artillery pieces during the battle. Because the Australian division in the corps made such demands on Army Gun Parks, 16th Divisional artillery had five guns out of action at one time.[14] It was a minor criticism, but interesting that notice was taken of the detail. Daily air reconnaissance photography was carried out and examined carefully for results; where necessary, further bombardments were ordered.

In November 1916, after nearly five months' fruitless assault, Beaumont Hamel, the last of the original Somme fortress villages, was magnificently assaulted by 51st Highland Division. A novel feature of that attack was the massed deployment of divisional machine-guns, situated on a little eminence and firing over the heads of the attacking troops. The concentrated machine-gun fire swamped the defences there, as effectively as Napoleon's grand battery had at Austerlitz. At Messines, Second Army used the concept on a grand scale. Four mortars and six machine-guns were to accompany each brigade. The remaining divisional machine-guns, sixty-six guns to a division, were to provide a creeping barrage of machine-gun fire, which was aimed ahead of the artillery creeping barrage directly onto the ridge's main defence strongpoints. Sections of tanks, forty-eight machines in all, were to support the infantry attack on strongpoints. 16th and 36th used them mainly against Wytschaete. It was planned that, when Black Line was taken, engineer field companies were to move up after dark and lay wire around newly-won strongpoints and along Black Line. Overhead, aircraft of the Royal Flying Corps were to act in co-operation with the advancing infantry and to relay information and intelligence back to commanders. Each infantryman carried two water-bottles. In 16th Division, one was filled with tea.[15]

Excellent co-operation and understanding were fostered by the Army Commander, one of the few commanders who was originally an infantryman. Under his Major-General General Staff, Maj.-Gen. C.H. Harington, considerable trust was generated between the staffs at all levels of command and also between the Artillery, Infantry and Royal Flying Corps. A remarkable atmosphere permeated Second Army[16] which undoubtedly enhanced its fighting ability.

16TH DIVISION AT MESSINES, 1917

In the central sector, IX Corps had 36th Division on the right, 16th Division in the centre and 19th Division on the left. Each division was to attack on a two-brigade (four-battalion) frontage. The brigades had two battalions in line, with two behind in support. All divisions retained their third brigade, ready for counter-attacks when the Germans were usually at their most dangerous.

16th Division held the Vierstraat-Petit Bois sector, with 47 Brigade on the right, 49 Brigade on the left, and 48 Brigade in reserve. By early June 1917, all were ready. The essence of the plan was for each brigade to gain five objective lines: Red, Blue, Green, Black and Mauve. The leading companies, advancing in two lines, would take the Red Line; the second line would leap-frog and go through to Blue Line and halt. The support battalion would then go through to Green, then Black, where it would consolidate. A fresh brigade (from 11th Division) would then go through to the final objective on Mauve Line.

Before the attack, the divisional commander issued an order of the day:

> The Big Day is very near. All our preparations are complete, and the Divisional Commander wishes to express his appreciation and his thanks to all the officers and men who have worked so cheerfully and so well. The 16th Division is fortunate in having had assigned to it the capture of the stronghold of Wytschaete. Every officer and man— Gunners, Sappers, Pioneers, RAMC, ASC, and infantry of historic Irish regiments—knows what he has to do.
>
> Let all do their best, as they have always done, continuing to show the same courage and devotion to duty which has characterised the 16th (Irish) Division since it landed in France, and it will be our proud privilege to restore to Little Belgium, the 'White village', which has been in German hands for nearly three years.
>
> (Signed) W.B. Hickie, Major-General
> Commanding 16th (Irish) Division
> 5 June 1917

At 0100 on 7 June the troops moved into assembly positions:

Right attack, 47 Brigade: 6th Royal Irish on the right and 7th Leinsters on the left. 1st Munsters in the second wave. 6th Rangers in the rear as moppers-up and carrying parties.

Left attack, 49 Brigade: 7th/8th Irish Fusiliers on the right and 7th Inniskillings on the left. 2nd Royal Irish in the second wave. 8th Inniskillings in the rear as moppers-up and carrying-party.

48 Brigade was in divisional reserve.

Each battalion had two machine-guns and two Stokes mortars attached to protect flanks and overcome local opposition during the advance and to support resistance to counter-attacks afterwards. It was the duty of the carrying parties to help move forward their weapons and ammunition.[17]

The heat was intense. To refill personal water-bottles, arrangements had been made for water to be carried forward in petrol cans immediately behind the assaulting infantry. Consequently, heat exhaustion was not suffered. A rain shower the previous night had laid the dust and conditions were said to be 'perfect'. 'Nightingales in Rossignol Wood were still finishing their nights song when suddenly hell was let loose in the bowels of the earth.'[18]

Early in 1916, decisions were taken to begin extensive deep mining operations under the German lines as the personnel and material became available. In all, twenty-four mines were commenced: four came outside the eventual sphere of operations; one was discovered by the enemy and destroyed; nineteen were completed and exploded successfully at Zero Hour.

At exactly 0310, nearly 1,000,000 pounds of high explosives made the greatest earthquake ever in northern Europe, accompanied by the mightiest crash ever made by humanity to that date. Immediately, from the whole enemy's trench system arose his coloured lights—the signal that the attack has begun, which surely was unnecessary as the explosion was so loud it was heard in England. Four mines were exploded in front of 16th Division and four in front of 36th. Although all ranks were aware of what was to happen, the actual effect was greater than any of the waiting troops had imagined. Great columns appeared out of the earth and rose slowly, awesome in their destructive power.

The senses of many refused to believe that these explosions were what they had been told to expect. All had lain down to receive the shock; it would have been impossible to stand or even kneel. Higher and higher the columns rose, until gradually the most beautiful colour effect was observed. All the colours of the light spectrum seemed to emerge in flames from the brown columns. Then each volcano, gradually collapsing, fell in a shapeless mass. For minutes, falling earth and stones rained upon friend and foe alike; it was almost impossible for anyone to move. Officers and NCOs got busy rousing the men to their duty. Under great difficulties, the massed troops struggled forward. In the blinding dust and gaseous fumes, many men were violently sick, or lost direction by disorientation. Visual or oral communication was impossible. Units crossed each other, and sub-units intermingled in skirting the gigantic craters. In such circumstances, it was inevitable that the leading waves lost the creeping barrage; but so weak was the enemy response, demoralised by the horrific mines, that this hardly mattered then. Resistance would depend upon how quickly the enemy might respond. Unlike the Somme, in this instance the attackers were more vigorous. Somehow the commanders of the leading platoons and companies reorganised the units and brought order out of chaos. Slowly the fog lifted and the troops could identify features and advance. Casualties were inflicted by enemy machine-guns in concrete pill boxes among the ruins of Wytschaete village, firing on fixed lines.[19] Enemy SOS rockets showed the way.

THE 47 BRIGADE ATTACK

6th Royal Irish advanced with A and B Companies up, C and D behind. Almost at the outset, Maj. W. Redmond MP, commanding A Company, was wounded in the wrist but continued forward until wounded a second time; he fell and, unable to stand, cheered on his men.[20] Immediately to their front, one of the great mines exploded under Macdelstede Farm. The final objective of 6th Royal Irish was the northern outskirts of Wytschaete. The leading companies captured the first objective. C and D passed through to secure the village of Wytschaete and to mop up the Bois de Wytschaete. Germans in concrete machine-gun posts within the wood put up considerable opposition. In storming one of these posts, Capt. O'Brien-Butler fell dead. All objectives were taken on schedule. Left of the Royal Irish, 7th Leinsters attacked the front manned by the 4th Grenadiers and 33rd Fusiliers. A few moments after Zero hour, 7th Leinster battalion headquarters dug-out received a direct hit. Most of the occupants, the commanding officer, Lt.-Col. T. Stannus, the adjutant, a brigade trench-mortar officer, two artillery liaison officers and four orderlies were either killed or wounded. The second-in-command, Capt. J.A.J. Farrell, only severely shaken, assumed command and appointed a second-lieutenant as his adjutant and carried on. Hand-to-hand fighting took place in Nancy Switch and between Petit Bois and Wytschaete village. Some prisoners were taken and sent back. Battalion headquarters then moved forward to Petit Bois. The leading companies reached Red Line on time, reorganised and pressed on to Blue Line until C Company was held up by a machine-gun post. Its support company sent forward two Lewis gun sections and, with their help, the post was taken after a stiff fight. As a result, C Company arrived on Blue Line just behind schedule. A section reconnoitred L'Hospice, but it was already covered by 7th/8th Irish Fusiliers of 49 Brigade. The Leinsters reached their objective, the edge of Wytschaete village, precisely on time, at Zero + 3 hours 40 minutes, without their supporting tanks which had broken down.[21]

Barely had the Royal Irish and Leinsters reached Blue Line when 1st Munsters, the second wave, went through 'in splendid order'. The Leinstermen, impressed, gave them a rousing cheer.[22] 1st Munsters, having gone through the Leinsters and Royal Irish, stormed Wytschaete. Supported by the only tank with 16th still operational, it broke German resistance. The Munsters continued to the Black Line, marching, in the words of a captured German officer, 'as though they were on parade'. On the Black Line, they consolidated until relieved. Such was the impetuosity of the Munsters that on the Wytschaete-Oosttaverne road, one company overtook the barrage. Seeing this, 2/Lt. E. Hussey rushed forward to warn his men and was killed by a shell-burst.[23] Behind the Munsters, 6th Connaught Rangers, the 'moppers up', discovered a strongpoint just outside Wytschaete which had been bypassed. Here, the Rangers took ninety-eight prisoners, including an officer. In deep dug-outs within the ruined village, two machine-guns were taken and placed on the parapets 'for the Munsters to collect'.[24]

In his after-battle report, Brig. Pereira wrote, 'As is usual with the Irish, the difficulty was in restraining them.'[25] Having gained the objective, 2/Lt. Moloney of the Munsters, a fifty-two year old, led a patrol into Oosttaverne Wood and clearing it, 'took many prisoners'.[26] The divisional artillery, moving forward by alternate batteries, kept up a steady fire. That evening at 2000, 6th Royal Irish extended to the left, relieved 7th Leinsters and held the position until next day, when relieved by 7th Irish Rifles. Throughout 8 June, completely undisturbed by the Germans, the Irish Rifles consolidated their trenches. Connaught Rangers improved the position of the supporting mortar and machine-gun batteries before withdrawing that night to Rossignol Wood. That same day, 33 Brigade of 11th Division continued the attack to the final objective, Mauve Line, and 7th Irish Rifles withdrew.

THE 49 BRIGADE ATTACK

The attack of the 7th/8th Irish Fusiliers on the right was delayed slightly by the nearness of the mine at Petit Bois salient. Gaseous fumes from the mine explosion affected nine men. Some fire met the 'Faughs', which they disregarded, and the Red Line was reached 'well up to time, and touch being obtained with battalions on either flank'.[27] An enemy machine-gun on the northern edge of Wytschaete Wood gave some trouble before being rushed by A Company. L'Hospice, a very strong position, was covered, to be taken later and bypassed. 2nd Royal Irish passed through the Fusiliers who then regrouped, consolidated the position and advanced again in artillery formation. On reaching Black Line, the Fusiliers extended into waves and passed through the Royal Irish and occupied Sonnen Farm. A machine-gun at Leg Copse gave trouble, but with neat tactics, the Fusiliers engaged it in front with Lewis guns. Under their cover, a platoon delivered a flank attack and after a 'short but fierce fight',[28] captured a machine-gun and thirty prisoners. Touch was gained on the left with a battalion of Gloucesters. In the afternoon, a company of Dublins relieved the Fusiliers: 'This company during its advance to the Mauve Line captured two guns, two machine-guns and forty-six prisoners, including two officers, a canteen and an artillery group headquarters, complete with telephones, etc.'[29] The war diary of 7th/8th Irish Fusiliers does not record what happened to the stock of the canteen. The losses to 7th/8th Irish Fusiliers were the highest in the division, thirty-five dead and 158 wounded.[30]

7th Inniskillings on the left had the Red and Blue Lines as their objective. Nail Switch trench was carried within twenty minutes; it had been blotted out by the bombardment, and was now a swamp. No pause was made there. To this point the 7th, by keeping close to the barrage, had suffered no casualties. A Company met some opposition on the Red Château line, where some enemy resisted. This was overcome and prisoners were sent to the rear. The Inniskillings found breakfast in many enemy dug-outs; some found beer.[31] C and D Companies passed through, continued the advance and, keeping up with the barrage, stormed the ridge. Despite machine-gun fire, D Company went on to capture 'Unnamed Wood'. Later, by Gen. Hickie's order, it was renamed 'Inniskilling Wood'.

With almost clockwork precision, 2nd Royal Irish passed through the Irish Fusiliers and Inniskillings. Advancing with C and D Companies up, B Company in support and A as 'moppers up' in the rear, the Royal Irish took all objectives on schedule, together with 200 prisoners. L'Hospice, which had been converted into a strongpoint with all round defence, held out until 0648. It had, however, been isolated and bypassed, to be taken later. Royal Irish casualties were light, one officer and seventeen soldiers dead and one officer and 130 soldiers wounded. Among the wounded was their chaplain, Father William Fitzmaurice SJ, who, despite his wound, continued to care for the wounded at the dressing station established in L'Hospice after its capture. He was recommended for an immediate DSO but was awarded the MC. Among the honours were four Légion d'Honneur (Croix d'Officier) which the French high command sent to GOC 16th Division to award as he considered fit. Gen. Hickie awarded two to the Royal Irish, one to the Irish Fusiliers and one to the Leinsters. Doubtless the Inniskillings were content with 'Inniskilling Wood'. A rare tribute was paid to 16th Divisional Artillery Column, the men who kept the guns fed.

> Heavy work fell on 16th DAC. For more than a fortnight the personnel were constantly at work by day and night. They were often under heavy shell-fire and suffered many casualties, but the manner in which they carried out their duties was beyond all praise.[32]

Having been relieved on the night of 8–9 June, the brigades concentrated in Rossignol Wood. Four days later, on the 13th, 16th Division marched to the Merris area for training for the next offensive. On the 20th the division was transferred to the XIX Corps.

The death in battle of Maj. Willie Redmond MP, 'the Irish D'Artagnan', cast a shadow over his division for a while. His last speech in the House of Commons, delivered just a month before, was an appeal for immediate Home Rule and a direct appeal to Edward Carson, who was present, to enter into co-operation. Maj. Redmond's statesmanlike vision and gallantry had won widespread respect not least among his former political enemies.

> Willie Redmond also is dead. Aged fifty-four, he asked to be allowed to go over with his regiment. He should not have been there at all... How one's ideas change! And how one loathes the party politics that condone and even approve when his opponents revile such a man as this! I classify him with Stephen Gwynn and Harrison—all three MEN—Irish Nationalists, true, whom you and I in our Tory school were brought up to regard as anathema.[33]

Redmond had a special place in the hearts of his own regiment, especially its 6th Battalion, which numbered many from his own parliamentary constituency, especially the parish of Trinity Without in the city of Waterford.[34] He was picked up where he had fallen by stretcher-bearers of 36th Division and evacuated to their dressing station. The senior chaplain of 49 Brigade, Father Edmund Kelly, described the scene to Monsignor Ryan, Senior Catholic Chaplain to the Forces, in a letter.

> He received every possible kindness from the Ulster soldiers. In fact, an Englishman attached to the Ulster Division expressed some surprise at the extreme care which was taken of the poor Major, though no Irish soldier expected anything else, for after all, the Ulstermen are Irish too.[35]

There is a darker side to this tragedy. At Guillemont and Ginchy, Gen. Hickie had insisted that Redmond remain at divisional headquarters, considering him 'too old for the game'.[36] Following this, Redmond had received letters from Ireland accusing him of cowardice. Such an accusation requires some courage to make; significantly, all the writers preferred to remain anonymous. Nevertheless, Redmond was deeply hurt. For this reason, he requested Hickie to allow him to join his battalion for the Messines attack. At first, Hickie remained obdurate, but Redmond 'implored so insistently that at last the general gave way.'[37] Redmond was buried near the convent at Locre behind the military cemetery.

36TH DIVISION AT MESSINES, 1917

After the lessons of the Somme, 36th Division headquarters could hardly be blamed for studying the battle-plan with extra care and for insisting on repeated bombardments on certain sections until they were thoroughly satisfied.[38] Although there was a general feeling of quiet confidence among the troops waiting those final minutes, those who had been at the battle of Albert must surely have dwelt on the outcome of the attack. The newcomers to the division, attacking for the first time, also had their own special thoughts: 'What a memorable night it is just before one goes into action for the first time. What feelings and emotions absolutely indescribable surge up in one's brain. Happy the man not endowed with a vivid imagination.'[39]

When the mine volcano erupted in front of 8th Rifles, some of Lt. Witherow's men were standing, and were thrown to the ground. When the debris fell, 'the L/Cpl, one of my best section commanders, was killed by a stone'.[40] Disoriented by the effects of the gigantic eruption, for a time the platoons lost direction. 'In fact if we had not the German SOS lights to show us their positions... it might have been as easy to go right or left as ahead.'[41]

36th Division, the right division of IX Corps, had on its right 25th Division of II ANZAC Corps. Its objective was a line from Lumm Farm on the right to a railway cutting on the Wytschaete–Oosttaverne road east of Staenyzer Cabaret on the left. The attack was to be made by two brigades, 107 on the right and 109 on the left. A singular feature of Gen. Nugent's plan was the addition of a battalion of 'mopper-ups' between the attack waves of 107 and 109 Brigades, achieved by attaching a battalion of 108 Brigade to each.

As in 16th Division, the leading battalions had two companies up and two behind. At Red Line, the leading companies would pause and those in the second were to leap-frog and take the lead for the advance to Blue. Up to 'Blue Line', mopping up was the responsibility of the attached battalion. The follow-up battalions, having passed through on Blue Line, would cross the Green Line and halt on the Black, then mop up themselves, presumably because less resistance was expected there.

107 Brigade
First Wave. Right—8th Irish Fusiliers; left—9th Irish Rifles; mop-up battalion—12th Irish Rifles of 108 Brigade.
Second Wave. Right—10th Irish Rifles; left—15th Irish Rifles

109 Brigade
First Wave. Right—14th Irish Rifles; left—11th Inniskillings; mop-up battalion—11th Irish Rifles of 108 Brigade.
Second Wave. Right—9th Inniskillings: left—10th Inniskillings

Through the smoke, the first wave of infantry went forward, followed at twenty-five yard intervals by the second. The four enormous mine craters had to be skirted and platoon commanders were instructed to march on compass bearings to keep direction. Such were the effects of these colossal explosions, which to some might have represented a vision of hell, that there was no enemy resistance to the advance either in the front line or support trenches, where demoralised German survivors surrendered. On the front of the Ulster Division, only two enemy machine-guns opened fire, both against 109 Brigade. Lewis gunners and rifle-grenadiers of 11th Inniskillings silenced these. Apart from this, only the cratered ground and mass of shattered barbed wire impeded the advance of the Ulstermen to Red Line. Here the barrage paused for fifteen minutes, allowing the companies to leap-frog. Then, for the first time, serious resistance was encountered from the German machine-gunners who yet again earned their reputation for resolute courage. Two German machine-guns at Skip Point were handled with particular bravery. They continued firing until the position was bombed and rushed by 9th Rifles, helped by a bombing platoon of 14th Rifles. Over 150 prisoners were taken.[42]

The Blue Line was reached at 0450, on schedule. Here there was a halt of two hours and consolidation began. Moving forward, the second wave prepared to advance on Black. The barrage advanced at 0650 and the fresh troops followed it with dash. Little resistance was met until Green was behind them and they were almost on the Messines-Wytschaete road. Pick House resisted strongly, but was taken by co-ordinated attacks by Lewis gun teams and bombing sections. The Vickers gun teams had not yet come forward, but a captured machine-gun sprayed the position from a flank and the garrison was bombed into surrender. 9th Inniskillings were held up for a time by a determined machine-gun until an Inniskilling sergeant obtained the support of a tank by beating on its side with a grenade. Then, having attracted its attention, he guided the lumbering vehicle onto the enemy position. On the southern outskirts of Wytschaete, the Inniskillings joined hands with the Munsters.

Only on one sector had resistance been stubborn. On the extreme right of the 36th front about 200 yards short of the Messines-Wytschaete road, the right flank company of 15th Irish Rifles was fired on from two concrete pill boxes situated on both flanks. So strong were these positions that only a direct hit from a heavy gun or heavy mortar could put them out of action. Both were put out of action by platoon bombing attacks supported by Lewis guns. The company of 15th Rifles then advanced to the Black Line which was consolidated in strength by two 'mopping up' battalions of 108 Brigade. Precisely on time, 34 Brigade of 11th (Northern) Division, with artillery sections behind, passed through and gained its objective on Mauve Line.

After dark on 7 June, 108 Brigade relieved 107 and 109 Brigades by moving forward its remaining two battalions to reinforce the two mopping-up battalions already in line. There they entrenched until relieved the following afternoon, 8 June, by 32 Brigade of 11th Division. The last elements of 36th then withdrew to bivouac on the slopes of Kemmel Hill.

At celebratory dinners held by the various messes that June, the toast was 'The 16th and 36th Divisions', toasted of course in Irish whiskey. For the gains made in the offensive, the casualties were incredibly light:

16th Division	748 All ranks killed and wounded
36th Division	700 All ranks killed and wounded

On the left of the Kemmel-Wytschaete road just outside Wytschaete stands a Celtic cross in a simple plot near the British Commonwealth War Cemetery. On it is the inscription:

Dochum Glóire Dé agus Onóra na hÉireann
To the Glory of God and the Honour of Ireland

CHAPTER TWENTY-SIX

Third Ypres: 16th Division

THIRD BATTLE OF YPRES, JULY–NOVEMBER 1917

In the latter half of June 1917, 16th Division was transferred from Second Army to XIX Corps, Fifth Army. It was typical of Gen. Plumer that he inspected and took the salute of the brigades as they marched out of his area. Shortly after arrival, they were inspected by the new corps commander, Lt.-Gen. H.E. Watts. The period between Messines and Third Ypres was the most pleasant experienced by 16th Division on the Western Front. Although full of work, all had plenty of recreation, sports, gymkhanas and the occasional church parade. The two Jesuit chaplains of 48 Brigade, Fathers Francis Browne and Willie Doyle, had arranged a brigade church parade in St Omer cathedral. Brig. Ramsay, who was not a Catholic, and Gen. Hickie, who was, were to attend. At the last moment it was discovered that the date clashed with a major local event and Pontifical High Mass, causing both priests some worry, but in the event everything turned out very well: 'Our people are so punctual and the French so regardless of timetables that I was sure there would be confusion and delay. But it was not to be. Quietly and wonderfully quickly the Mass ended…'[1]

Father Willie gave the sermon and likened their service to that of the Irish Brigade in the service of France. 'Fighting for Ireland through another'.[2] He recalled to them that Daniel O'Connell had been a student at St Omer. The Dublin brigade, 2nd, 8th and 9th Dublins, loved it and suggested that Fr Doyle 'ought to get into Jim Larkin's shoes'.[3] Also present at Mass was a detachment of 6th Connaught Rangers who had been on a course. With them was Thomas B. Sheridan. Fifty years later he recalled: 'If the Ypres battle had been next morning and the weather was clement as it then was, we should not have had the dismal adventure of the end of the month and Fr Doyle would not have preached this as his last sermon, or died assisting wounded in the swamps round Frezenberg.'[4]

THIRD YPRES

Since the Arras battle, the Germans had altered their defensive tactics, relying on defence in depth. Long, continuous lines of trenches had given way to extremely strong, isolated strongpoints built by Russian prisoners and constructed of ferro-concrete. Small, mutually supporting pill boxes with numerous machine-guns, scattered throughout the forward defensive zone, were interspaced with larger fortresses, usually converted and moated farmhouses. All these were garrisoned by that most dedicated of soldiers, the German machine-gunner. The pill boxes could only be knocked out by the largest shells since they made small targets and were difficult to see; this, however, was very rarely achieved. First encountered at Messines, many had to be stormed by infantry, with Lewis gun and grenades, advancing heavily-laden across the battlefield. There, the demoralising effects of the gigantic mines had made the reduction of the strongpoints relatively easy. Behind these strongholds at a distance safe from all but long-range artillery, reserves of fresh troops were ready to counter-attack at the most opportune time. At Ypres, there were to be no great mines to rend the German front at Zero Hour, nor was there to be the painstaking attention to detail aimed at minimising casualties which typified Second Army planning.[5] On Haig's instructions, Gen. H. Gough and his Fifth Army headquarters had superseded that of Gen. Plumer's Second Army headquarters with responsibility for the coming offensive, although Plumer's staff reputedly 'knew every puddle in the Ypres salient.'[6]

The offensive opened on 31 July with an attack by 8th, 15th and 55th supported by 25th, 16th and 36th Divisions. Although gains were made, not all objectives were taken and the attack was to be renewed next day. That evening, heavy rain fell and the attack was postponed. The rain continued for about a month. Adverse weather seriously contributed to the failure of the British plan. Combined with shell-cratering, it created appalling battlefield conditions over which heavily-laden troops would have to drag themselves to come to grips with German strongpoints.

On the morning of 31 July, Gough and his four corps commanders considered the situation and decided that 'several adjustments' had to be made before Fifth Army attacked again.[7] Affecting 16th and 36th Divisions was the decision that XIX Corps would continue the attack on 4 August to capture the Green Line, an objective for Z-Day which had not been achieved. However, the attack was again postponed because of the weather until 14 August. Nevertheless, because of the pernicious policy of Fifth Army not to relieve troops in the line before an attack, the 16th and 36th Divisions were left there for two weeks under unrelenting bombardment and suffered heavy casualties even before the attack started. When it ultimately took place, decimated battalions, exhausted and mud-coated, were expected to advance behind a creeping barrage timed to be followed by fresh troops.[8] It was a policy inviting disaster.

On 23 July, the Irish brigades, headed by their pipes and drums, started for the front in line of route. Part of the journey was made by rail transport and the Connaught Rangers sang their favourite, 'My Irish Jaunting Car'.[9] Signs of the coming battle were all around them; every yard of roadside was covered with camps, dumps and transport. The roar of the bombardment was distinct and continuous; the roads were chock-a-block with vehicles of all kinds, all travelling towards the salient. On the night of 30–31 August, 16th Division moved forward into its reserve positions behind 15th Scottish. All night the roar of guns was incessant and the sky was continuously lit by gun-flashes. At dawn the battle opened. As they waited throughout the day, rumour of triumph and counter-rumour of disaster abounded. Finally, in the late afternoon came the good news—the attack everywhere had been successful and almost all first-day objectives gained. Evidence of the bad news was all around them: rain. The weather had broken.

Behind the infantry, about thirty artillery batteries moved forward in support. Working parties were demanded from the reserve divisions. 7th Leinsters were given the task of burying cable from battery positions around Ypres to Signals distribution points close to the front-line trenches for Forward Observation Posts in their sector. 11th Hampshire began repairing the roads for the artillery, especially the heavy guns. The Hampshires laboured in terrible conditions under shell-fire, filling craters, making detours, dragging guns into position. 2nd Dublins and 6th Rangers were detached to 55th Division as stretcher-bearers, searching the battlefield and bringing in the wounded over the muddy wasteland. 7th Irish Rifles and 7th/8th Irish Fusiliers were attached to 15th Scottish Division, holding their front line when the division attacked. The casualties sustained in these non-fighting tasks were not inconsiderable. The 7th Leinsters lost forty-four killed and wounded; the Hampshires thirty-three, including one wounded officer who insisted on remaining with his men and was awarded the MC.

Much of this work went on until the battalions actually went into the line. Despite the pressure of battle, other commanders remarked upon it. The general officer commanding 55th Division and its senior doctor, Col. H.S. Thurston, RAMC, both wrote to Gen. Hickie with thanks in appreciation of the self-sacrifice and devotion of the Irishmen to their wounded. The commanding officer of 9th Gordons wrote through his divisional commander to Gen. Hickie expressing their 'greatest admiration' for the Irish Fusiliers' help under shell-fire: 'Without their help, Gordon Road would never have been finished in time'.[9]

Their work was invaluable to the divisions they aided, but greatly increased the strain on troops about to carry out an assault.

On 1 August, 16th Division was in support to 15th Division. The original intention had been, when the 15th had gained their objectives, the Irish Division would pass through them and carry forward the attack. The Scots indeed reached their objective, but were heavily counter-attacked and forced back. On the night of 1–2 August, the Irish brigades prepared to enter the line. For two days they had bivouacked under groundsheets and laboured at diverse tasks in their supporting role. Having completed these, the men of the 16th returned to their concentration areas and got what rest they could. At dawn next day, leading elements went forward to the Frezenberg Ridge. It was a night of exhausting, unrelenting toil, making progress across the moon-like landscape pock-marked with linked shell-holes filled with water; every trench was knee-deep in watery mud.

16th Division assumed responsibility for the Frezenberg sector in the early hours of 2 August. At 0430, the battalions of all three brigades went into the line and held it for two weeks in conditions of misery which beggar description. In every battalion, hundreds were killed, wounded, gassed or overcome with trench fever and swollen feet. Units were relieved and rotated. But often the hardship of the journey out of and into the line outweighed the value of a few hours' rest.

Resupply, except of essential ammunition and water, was almost impossible. For the duration of each stay in the line, all had to subsist on whatever rations they had been able to carry forward. Evacuation of the wounded could only be achieved with utmost difficulty; many who might otherwise have survived died on the nightmare journey to the rear. Communication from company and battalion positions back to brigade could only be by 'runner'. Day and night these men, without hesitation, traversed the fire-swept mud; many were killed or wounded. Medical officers and orderlies performed their merciful duties with a cool courage matching that of their infantry comrades. One, Capt. G.D. Watkins, won the DSO for rescuing a Scottish soldier from inside a derelict tank which was lying on the Frezenberg-Zonnebeke road in full view of the enemy. Two devoted Irish chaplains were killed by shell-fire during the battle. Father Willie Doyle, Dublins, was killed instantly and Father Simon Knapp, 2nd Irish Guards, died of wounds in the Guards Division sector. Both priests were highly respected far beyond the bounds of the Catholic faith.

4 AUGUST: ADJUSTING THE LINE

On 4 August an attack was made 'to adjust the line' mentioned by Gough in his meeting with the corps commanders. The division advanced over Frezenberg ridge and entrenched on the Black Line. The battalions, already tired when they entered the line, were now practically exhausted. The wrecked lines were nearly all under water and with continuous shell-fire, little could be done to repair them. Father Doyle counted fifty shells passing over in sixty seconds: 'I have been through some hot stuff at Loos, and the Somme was warm enough for most of us, but neither of them could compare to the fierceness of the German fire here.'[11]

Chemical agents had been used at Ypres since April 1915 and most soldiers had become accustomed to the use of respirators. However at Third Ypres, the enemy introduced a new type, mustard gas: 'Little rest that night, for the Germans simply pelted us with gas... a gas which burns your hands and face, a beast of a thing which gives you all the delights of a rough sea voyage....'[12]

Conditions, which could hardly have become worse, gradually improved. Convoys of pack mules brought much-needed engineer stores to the

Frezenberg Ridge trenches which materially improved conditions. Despite the atrocious, miserable conditions, the Irishmen were in good spirits: 'But through all and in spite of all, the spirit of the men was excellent, and their behaviour could not have been excelled. Their only complaint was that they were not allowed to go through and complete the attack of the 31st.'[13]

An operation preliminary to the main attack was carried out by II Corps on 14 August. It failed everywhere. The only bright spot was on the Westhoek Ridge, where 2nd Royal Irish Rifles, after a short advance, rushed two intact strongpoints in Westhoek village. Apart from this, each temporary gain was lost to prompt and overwhelming German counter-attacks which were not broken up in their concentration areas by artillery.[14]

In their after-battle reports, brigade commanders protested at the weakness of the artillery barrages and the failure of spotting aircraft to detect German troop concentrations preparing counter-attacks. They were of the opinion that the allocation of one aircraft per corps was insufficient to effectively cover the front.[15]

After the battle of 31 July, Haig had told Gough: 'The next advance is to be made as soon as possible, but only after adequate bombardment and domination of hostile artillery.[16]

When the proposed attack was carried out, that dominance had not yet been achieved. Additional to this were the appalling ground conditions created by shelling and weather. One of 16th Divisional staff, going forward, observed and reported these to Gen. Hickie. He advised corps headquarters of the likelihood of failure because of them.[17] The corps commander responsible for the attack on the 14th, Lt.-Gen. Jacob, also asked for a postponement; this was refused.[18] Fifth Army headquarters was blinded to the reality of the situation by an obsession with keeping to a timetable, involving an amphibious landing scheduled to coincide with its offensive. Favourable tides necessary for this would not reoccur for a month.[19] In the event, this amphibious operation never took place.

BATTLE OF LANGEMARCK, 16 AUGUST 1917

Fifth Army attacked with three army corps, each with two divisions in line. XIX Corps attacked with 16th Division on the right, 36th Division on the left. It was a front dominated by massive defences overlooking the British line. Against it, the corps artillery had achieved little, except cratering the ground and creating a marsh. The artillery plan for XIX Corps was defective and lacked the detailed preparation of the Messines attack. Strongpoints which ought to have been knocked out or neutralised were untouched: 'Since the tactics of the day demanded a thorough fire plan, this was not given. The result was that many key points in the bombardment were not dealt with. On XIV and XVIII Corps fronts, the plan was better.'[20]

Gas to neutralise pill boxes was not included in the bombardment plan,[21] and although the weather was excellent, only one spotter aircraft directed artillery fire in XIX Corps area.[22] The lessons of the previous attack had not been learned.

The 16th and 36th Divisions were selected to lead the assault at Langemarck. They had been in the line for twelve days in the Hanebeek and Steenbeek valleys in exposed conditions. They were observed by the Germans in dominating positions under constant bombardment, gas attacks and incessant machine-gun fire from concrete emplacements. Casualties had reduced the fighting strength of both divisions by about one-third.[23] Those who survived were tired and mud-coated. Their weapons, particularly the Lewis guns upon which so much depended, were prone to jamming. Attack in the sense of bounding charges overrunning enemy positions was out of the question. It was to be a hard slog through mud, behind a barrage advancing at a rate of 100 yards in five minutes; this proved too fast!

Battalions attacked on a two-company frontage in four waves. The first objective was the Green Line, and the second the Dotted Green Line. Both lines had been designated objectives in the original 31 July offensive, but remained untaken. On reaching the first objective, the companies in the first two waves were to halt, and the third and fourth waves were to leap-frog and go on to the final objective. Support battalions were to advance and take over the Green Line. A supporting company was allocated to the leading two battalions on each brigade front as 'moppers-up'. Pill box strongpoints were targeted by specific platoons. Each machine-gun company sent forward four guns with the infantry; the remainder joined the barrage. So bad was the ground that Stokes mortars could not be taken forward. Engineer field companies and Pioneers were to consolidate on the objective.

Each division had its own artillery, plus that of another division, under the divisional commander Royal Artillery. The artillery, one gun to every twenty yards, provided a three-layer support barrage. First, directly in front of the infantry, was a creeping barrage similar to that at Messines. Four 18-pounder batteries fired a distant barrage, searching hidden ground and bombarding known strongpoints beyond the creeping barrage. Six 4.5-inch howitzer batteries fired a hundred yards ahead of the latter, resting on all known strongpoints and machine-gun emplacements. The pace of the barrage was a hundred yards in five minutes, with a pause of thirty-five minutes in front of the Green Line. Three German gas-shell counter-bombardments struck the British front prior to the attack, the last being on the night of 15–16 August. The British artillery did not use gas in reply, although gas laid on the known strongpoints would have helped to capture the enemy or put them out of action. One section of tanks supported each division, but so bad was the ground that the infantry realistically discounted the possibility of their getting through. The 16th Division operation order specifically warned the assault troops not to wait for tank support, but to press on to the objective. In the event, this order was proved right. Zero hour was at 0445.

16TH DIVISION, 16 AUGUST 1917

For the assault, Gen. Hickie deployed 48 Brigade on the right and 49 Brigade on the left. 47 Brigade, in reserve, had three of its battalions detached, one to each attacking brigade and one on carrying duties.

48 Brigade had the right attack, 9th Dublins with 7th Irish Rifles on their left, 2nd Dublins behind in support. Casualties in the preceding two weeks had reduced the battalions by half or more. 8th Dublins, reduced to a company, were attached to 2nd Dublins; their combined forces mustered only twenty officers and 378 men. To add weight to the attack, 1st Munsters was detached from 47 to 48 Brigade reserve holding the brigade line.

49 Brigade, the left attack, had 8th Inniskillings on the right and 7th Inniskillings on the left; 7th/8th Irish Fusiliers were in support, with 6th Royal Irish in reserve holding the brigade line. During the German pre-emptive gas bombardment on the evening before the battle, headquarters 49 Brigade was struck with gas shells. Brig. Leveson-Gower and most of his staff were gassed and evacuated. Lt.-Col. K.C. Weldon of 7th/8th Irish Fusiliers assumed command.[24] It was an inauspicious start.

On the evening of 15 August the assaulting battalions moved to their jumping-off positions along routes taped out by divisional engineers. Despite heavy shelling throughout the night along the Frezenberg Ridge, the battalions were in position on schedule. But the bombardment had taken further toll, which had the effect of reducing the numbers detailed as 'moppers-up'.

At 0445 the attack began. To reach the objectives the battalions would have to cross nearly a mile of open ground dotted with pill box machine-gun posts and strongpoints. Everywhere they were met by a withering blast of machine-gun fire. On the right, the 9th Dublin Fusiliers suffered badly, but incredibly reached the Green Line and found touch with a battalion of 23 Brigade, 8th Regular Division. But so weak were the mopping-up parties that the German machine-gunners were able to come out of their pill boxes, which had been bypassed, and fire into the backs of the Dublins. (The embrasures only faced to the front and flank.) Nevertheless two officers and ten men of 9th Dublins succeeded in reaching a point 100 yards from the objective. They were joined by the survivors of two platoons of 8th Dublins.

Three 7th Irish Rifle companies were held up by Fortress Potsdam: 'So strong were the pill boxes that their machine-guns actually maintained their fire as the barrage passed over them.'[25]

The right company of the Rifles worked its way up the railway line and cleared a machine-gun nest on the Green Line. They sent back thirty prisoners before the remnant of the company was brought to a halt by Potsdam. A few managed to keep up the barrage and crossed the Hanebeek stream going towards the final objective on the flank of 9th Dublins. A courageous handful reached the objective.[26]

The attack of 49 Brigade encountered opposition as fierce as 48 Brigade. 8th Inniskillings were held up by Fortress Borry Farm. The 7th/8th Irish Fusiliers advanced and joined the attack on Beck House and Borry Farm. They reported to battalion headquarters that the latter was holding up the entire right attack of the brigade. On the left, 7th Inniskillings stormed Ibernian Farm and Beck House and overran Delva Farm before being checked 400 yards from their objective, Hill 37. Having captured Beck House, 7th Inniskillings left it to the Royal Irish, which sent two platoons of D Company to occupy the place. 8th Inniskillings were almost annihilated by the resolute machine-gunners in Borry Farm, a concrete block house impervious to gunfire dominating the area.

On the left of 7th Inniskillings, a unit of 36th Division had not advanced and this flank was open. Although the left attack got forward as far as Delva Farm, enfilade fire from two exposed flanks made the position of the gallant 7th Inniskillings and the support company of 7th/8th Irish Fusiliers untenable. Heavy loss of officers and lack of communications between battalions led to confusion. Inter-communication was by runners who were often killed or wounded. This interdicted the passage of information and orders; the supporting troops were consequently misdirected, badly used or unused, and the fragmented battalions clinging onto their dearly won positions, unsupported, faced the inevitable German counter-attack.

A message was received from 8th Inniskillings that Borry Farm had not been mopped up and they were being sniped from there. Lt.-Col. Scott ordered D Company to attack the Farm and ordered B Company into the line, but 2/Lt. H. Wilson, OC D Company, reported that 7th Inniskillings had a company there; the order for the attack was cancelled.[27]

In modern battle, confusion, delay and delayed reaction are commonplace, but with real-time reporting by radio, mistakes can quickly be rectified. In the fire-swept mud at Ypres, fleeting opportunities, once gone, could never be regained. Mistakes once made were impossible to correct.

At about 0900, waves of fresh German infantry streamed over the crest of the Zonnebeke spur against the division; they were preceded by an intense artillery barrage described as 'crushing'. The German concentration had been undetected by air observation and unmolested by the British artillery: 'Although the morning was fine, no warning was given by air observation.'[28] On the right of 48 Brigade, 23 Brigade were bundled back. But the Dublins managed to hold their ground. The party of 7th Irish Rifles who had reached the objective on the flank of the Dublins were wiped out. 'A few may have been captured, but the majority must have been blotted out by the successive bombardments of each side. The last men west of Potsdam, mostly Dublins, fell back to our line at dusk.'[29]

The survivors of the attack managed to hold out all day in the positions they had taken. Not for the first time in the war, Irishmen refused to abandon a position they had won, but held on tenaciously. It was 2200 when the intrepid Dubliners finally retired into the darkness.[30]

7th Inniskillings, having overrun Ibernian and Delva farms, were finally stopped 400 yards from the summit of Hill 37, mainly by fire from the exposed right and left flanks. When the German counter-attack came, they held on resolutely until their exposed position became untenable and then withdrew to the original front line held by 2nd Royal Irish.

That night, 6th Connaught Rangers relieved 2nd Royal Irish holding the entire 49 Brigade sector, and 1st Munsters relieved 2nd Dublins in 48 Brigade trenches. Then began the work of evacuating hundreds of wounded to the Regimental Aid Posts on the reverse of Frezenberg Ridge. The stretcher parties were under shell-fire, in full view of the enemy until they crossed the ridge. Of all the many acts of gallantry performed that day, none exceeded that of L/Cpl. F.G. Room, a stretcher-bearer with 2nd Royal Irish. He worked untiringly throughout that dreadful day. Continually under fire, he brought in many wounded to the aid post who might otherwise have died. For his selfless and courageous devotion to the wounded under fire, he was later awarded the Victoria Cross.[31] Without detracting from Cpl. Room's bravery, it is recorded by regimental historians that all stretcher-bearers behaved with the utmost gallantry in terrible conditions of rain and knee-deep mud, under heavy and unrelenting shell-fire.[32] Wounded men, mainly Inniskillings who had attacked the previous morning, were being collected without pause from no man's land. After treatment, they were ferried back by the stretcher parties.

The tattered and scant remnants of 48 and 49 Brigades trudged slowly back to Vlamertinghe where they bivouacked until 18 August. There they were joined by 47 Brigade which held the line of 16th Division until relieved by 15th Scottish on 17–18 August. That afternoon, the division embussed from Vlamertinghe for Watou area. The artillery remained in the salient for a considerable time longer.

On 19 August, after baths and change of clothing, church parades were held, but the Dublin Brigade was without its loved and widely respected padre, Willie Doyle.

It was in this battle that Father Willie Doyle MC, chaplain of 8th Dublins, but known throughout the Irish and Ulster divisions for his saintliness, died. He died as he had lived for eighteen months on the Western Front, in no man's land, comforting the last moments of his lads. Let an Ulster Protestant speak of him. 'Father Doyle was a good deal among us. We couldn't possibly agree with his religious opinions, but we simply worshipped him for other things. He didn't know the meaning of fear, and he didn't know what bigotry was. He was as ready to risk his life to take a drop of water to a wounded Ulsterman as to assist men of his own faith and regiment. If he risked his life looking after Ulster Protestant soldiers once, he did it a hundred times in his last few days. The Ulstermen felt his loss more keenly than anybody and none were readier to show their marks of respect to the dead hero priest than were our Ulster Presbyterians. Father Doyle was a true Christian in every sense of the word, and a credit to any religious faith...'[33]

CHAPTER TWENTY-SEVEN

Third Ypres: 36th Division

THE MOVE FROM MESSINES TO YPRES

Before leaving Second Army, 36th Division remained in the Merris area for abut twelve days' training and resting. These days were remembered as the most pleasant ever spent in France. Trout fishing and sunbathing in lovely summer sunshine were the two favoured recreations. The rest period ended on a high note with a great gymkhana at Acquin on 23 August. Competitive games of all kinds were held and in the afternoon a divisional drag-hunt took place. Divisional Signals lent horses and even if hairy round the ankles, they nevertheless provided good sport for riders and spectators alike. Next day the division moved to Wizernes, coming under the command of XIX Corps, Fifth Army. Bussed in large brigade motor convoys, the division was in position between Watou and Poperinghe by 30 July.

IN THE LINE, 31 JULY–15 AUGUST

On the opening day of the offensive, the Ulstermen supported the Lancastrians of 55th Division by road making, casualty clearing and carrying supplies. All went well until the rain started. Then, in the rain and mud that night:

> The confusion was awful as the ground in the area had been badly cut up by our preliminary bombardment, and in the darkness, with the ever-watchful enemy shelling the road, it was difficult to find the way. The 55th Division retired en masse and some of the guides joined the fellows. Lt. Patterson of 8th Rifles—16 stone, went into the mud up to his waist and was difficult to extricate.[1]

On 2 August, leading elements of 36th began relieving the 55th Division on a single brigade frontage. First into the line was 108 Brigade and two battalions of 109 Brigade. On taking over the line, Gen. Nugent decided that, in view of the dreadful conditions, it might be held more lightly. He therefore withdrew two of the supporting battalions to the rear area camps, replacing them with companies of the supporting battalions of 107 Brigade. The six battalions which were to lead the assault on 16 August were to be saved as much as possible. The attack of the 36th was made by 108 Brigade on the right, 109 Brigade on the left, with 107 Brigade in reserve. Each was to attack with two battalions in front, one in support about 1000 yards behind and one in reserve, held back in the old British front and support lines.

THE BATTLE OF LANGEMARCK, 16 AUGUST

As in 16th Division, the enemy counter-barrage caught troops moving forward; the casualties included Lt.-Col. A.C. Pratt, CO 11th Inniskillings. At Zero Hour German artillery counter-bombarded the crowded British assembly trenches. Shells rained down, but this time there was little effect on the assaulting troops. At the same time, the enemy machine-guns opened fire from all the German strongpoints which appeared to have been unaffected by the bombardment. Great difficulty was experienced moving forward in the marshy conditions: 'The state of the ground, even had little opposition been met with, prevented the Infantry keeping up with the attack barrage.'[2] The wire had not been completely destroyed; and the lanes cut through, covered by German machine-guns, served only to canalise the Ulster infantry into killing grounds.

On the extreme right of 108 Brigade, 9th Irish Fusiliers attacked from the Pommern Redoubt pressed up across Hill 35, driving the Germans before them. On their left, the 13th Rifles advanced equally well. The position called Somme, one of the strongest forts on the front, was bypassed by the leading wave, to be reduced by a following wave. But the platoon detailed to take and hold it was unable to do so, although the rifle-grenade section tried to work around and take it in flank. The adjutant, Capt. Belt, made an attempt to dig in in front of the place with a handful of men, but he was wounded and made his way back to the front line. The failure to take or neutralise Somme adversely affected the right attack of 36th Division. Already both 9th Irish Fusiliers and 13th Rifles were forced back. In the struggle for Hill 36, Lt.-Col. Somerville, commanding 9th Irish Fusiliers, was mortally wounded.

Seeing the check to his battalion, the commanding officer of 13th Rifles, Lt.-Col. R.P. Maxwell, personally led his battalion headquarters party in a courageous last attempt to take Somme. Again flesh and blood was no match for concrete and machine-guns, and Maxwell was severely wounded. The right attack of 36th Division had made no progress; this affected the left attack of 16th Division.[3]

On the front of 109 Brigade, the flooded Steenbeek and an adjacent swamp slowed the advance, and fire from Pond Farm and Border House slowed the assault waves further. The leading battalions lost the barrage; nevertheless the left battalion managed to occupy Fortuin Hill 400 yards from the start line. The Ulstermen, struggling through the mud and halted by uncut wire, were cut down by the relentless machine-guns against which the survivors could not advance.[4]

On the right of 109 Brigade, 14th Irish Rifles came under fire from Pond Farm. A much reduced platoon under Lt. Ledlie attempted to rush the place but was beaten back. Ledlie covered it on three sides and sent back two messages to battalion for support; none came. The following waves had been caught in the German counter-barrage and suffered heavily.[5] Ledlie could do no more than mask Pond Farm and wait. At 0800, seeing that his position was hopeless, Ledlie withdrew his platoon 150 yards, covering his retirement with Lewis gun fire.

On the left, the 11th Inniskillings attack was met with unrelenting fire. Despite it, an officer and seven men somehow managed to keep up with the barrage and made a lodgment on the Green Line. There they held out all day, but so intense was the enfilade crossfire that no support could reach them. After dark the courageous handful, having held on all day without support, could do no more. They retired as best they could to the start-line.[6]

The reserve battalions of each brigade, the 12th Irish Rifles on the right and 10th Inniskillings on the left, had moved up to the Black Line (the original German front line and the jump-off for this attack). When the German counter-attack streamed across the St Julien spur at 0900, so serious did the situation look that officers prepared their men to hold the British front line. SOS rockets were sent up and an artillery barrage struck the enemy assault troops in the open and eventually halted them.

Gen. Nugent considered arranging a new barrage and renewing the attack in the afternoon in an attempt to take at least the Green Line to show some appreciable gains for the day. But he was dissuaded by reports from his brigadiers and staff officers, who made it clear that his troops 'were in no fit state for any such attempt.'[7] A high proportion of officers and NCOs were killed or wounded, the surviving men exhausted, the battalions shattered. Following this, Gen. Nugent resisted pressure from Corps for a renewed attack and ordered the relief of 108 and 109 Brigades by 107 Brigade that night. On the following night, 17–18 August, a brigade of the 61st Division relieved the 107th in the line and 36th Division withdrew from Ypres.

Casualties	2–15 August Killed, Wounded & Missing	16–18 August Killed, Wounded & Missing	Total
16th Division	107 Officers, 1957 ORs	125 Officers, 2042 ORs	4231
36th Division	70 Officers, 1500 ORs	74 Officers, 1941 ORs	3585
		Total	7816[8]

The losses were a severe setback for 16th and 36th Divisions. In the latter, it was the end of the original Ulster Volunteer Force Division. The failure of the offensive could be directly attributed to the length of time in the line, the casualties suffered before the attack took place, as well as the terrible ground over which the battle was fought. But most of all, it was the ferro-concrete emplacements manned by resolute German machine-gunners which the bombardment failed to destroy that broke the attack. These emplacements were exactly the same ones which caused the failure of the original attack on 31 July.

Historically, the British soldier has overcome both bad generalship and indifferent staff-work. What sets Third Ypres apart from any other battle on the Western Front was the inflexible persistence with which it was pursued in appalling conditions and despite dreadful casualties. Shell-torn ground, soaked by unceasing rain, reverted to a primeval swamp over which it was impossible to advance except on duckboards. Notwithstanding the conditions, it was the policy of Fifth Army to move divisions into the line for extended periods before an attack. Troops already exhausted by their travail had little possibility of capturing positions which had already proved almost impregnable. That some troops nevertheless managed to capture a few strongly defended enemy positions and advance to the objective can only be accounted extraordinary. The failure of others is readily understandable.

In his description of 36th Division's part in the battle of Langemarck, Cyril Falls for once fell from his high standards of historical scholarship. Having criticised 32nd Division for its failure to capture Thiepval and waspishly refuting 25th Division's claim to have taken a farm at Messines, he attempted to involve 16th Division in the failure of his own division to advance on that fatal day.

> On the right of the 36th Division, the 16th had at first made good progress, but a counter-attack drove its troops back to their original line. From 9.00 a.m. onwards, the troops fell back.[9]

With disingenuous ambiguity, Falls insinuates that 16th Division withdrew before the 36th; this was not the case. The brevity of Capt. Falls' description of the battle of Langemarck does little justice to the Ulstermen. It glosses over their stout-heartedness in terrible conditions, their suffering and death. Instead of open criticism of the commander and plan of attack (he was an official historian), he gave coded words of condemnation for the tragedy. However, in a later history of the battalions of the Royal Irish Rifles that served other than with 36th Division, Falls corrected this and gave full credit to units of 16th Division for their advance that tragic day.

On the evening of the 16th, in a letter to his wife, Gen. Nugent revealed his deep sorrow with direct honesty:

> It has been a truly terrible day. Worse than 1 July I am afraid. The whole division had been driven back with terrible losses. Our failure has involved the failure of the divisions on both sides of us and that is so bitter a pill. In July of last year, we did our work but failed because the Divisions on either flank failed us. This time it is our Ulster

Division which has failed the Army... I am heartbroken over it.[10]

Later, Nugent was somewhat mollified at hearing that the attack by divisions on other parts of the front had also been stopped.

> In spite of their dreadful losses, the survivors in the Irish battalions went forward to the assault with desperate valour on the morning of 16 August, surrounded the pill boxes, stormed them through blasts of machine-gun fire, and towards the end of the day small bodies of these men had gained a footing on the objectives which they had been asked to capture, but were then too weak to resist the German counter-attacks. The 7th/8th Royal Irish Fusiliers had been almost exterminated, the 9th Dublins lost fifteen officers out of seventeen, and sixty-six per cent of their men. The two Irish Divisions were broken to bits, and their brigadiers called it murder. They were violent in their denunciation of the 5th Army for having put their men into the attack after thirteen days of heavy shelling.[11]

These lines were written after the war by Sir Philip Gibbs. An eminent war correspondent, Gibbs was present on the Western Front at the time of the attack at Langemarck. Like many correspondents, he failed, for whatever reason, to report accurately the true prevailing conditions. Even had such reports not been published for security reasons, they would have drawn critical attention earlier to the abomination. Just as Ellis Ashmead-Bartlett and Keith Murdoch had at Gallipoli, or indeed Russell of the *Times* in the Crimea, Gibbs and other war correspondents failed at Third Ypres.

One of the staff of 16th Division had warned Gen. Hickie that the conditions were extremely unfavourable and the troops were unlikely to meet with success. Maj. Noel Holmes, Royal Irish, then DAAG at divisional headquarters, had made the journey to the front line without equipment except for belt and pistol. An all-round sportsman to international and army standard, he found the journey made him 'absolutely exhausted before reaching the front line'. Convinced the troops would not be able to 'go over the top'[12] in such conditions, Holmes reported to Gen. Hickie what he saw, and his opinion:

> I said to General Hickie that I don't think the men could do it. To which Hickie replied, 'I'm not going to mention your name, else they'll say what does that young pup know.' He telephoned somebody else who telephoned somebody else. I suppose it went to the top, but nothing was done.[13]

Despite the warning by Maj.-Gen. Hickie, and possibly others, nothing was done to cancel the ill-fated attack at Langemarck. The failure of Fifth Army's offensive between 31 July and 16 August began a series of abortive attacks in the Ypres Salient. Known to history as Third Ypres, they lasted until 20 November 1917. However, the whole series of battles is often called after a place where two costly attacks were made: Passchendaele.

Battle of Third Ypres: Outline of Operations, 31 July–10 November 1917

Pilckem Ridge	31 July–2 August
Langemarck	16–18 August
Menin Road Ridge	20–25 September
Polygon Wood	26 September–3 October
Broodseinde	4 October
Poelcappelle	9 October
Passchendaele I	12 October
Passchendaele II	26 October–10 November

Irish battalions, in divisions other than 16th or 36th, fought in almost all these battles.

General Headquarters, BEF, were well aware of the true state of affairs in Fifth Army. Staff 'liaison', which bypassed the chain of command, saw to that. In September, Gen. Kiggell, Chief of Staff at GHQ, reported to Sir Douglas Haig that some of Gough's subordinates (his corps commanders) 'do not always tell Gough their true opinions as regards their ability to carry out an operation.'[14] Haig was aware of the dissatisfaction within Fifth Army and its notoriety throughout the BEF. However, either out of loyalty to Gough or because he was in agreement with Gough's actions, Sir Douglas took no action until after the battle. On 17 December 1917, Haig recorded:

> I mentioned to Gough how many divisions hoped they would not be posted to Fifth Army to fight. This feeling I put down to his staff. I had not told him before as this might affect his self-confidence during the battle… It was of course a surprise to Gough.[15]

If divisions were reluctant to serve in Fifth Army, their operational ability could have been affected. It was Haig's duty to tell Gough without delay, so that Fifth Army headquarters staff could be put right. Haig owed his fighting troops no less. The official historian is critical of Field-Marshal Haig for superseding Gen. Plumer and Second Army headquarters, who were more aware of conditions in the salient.[16]

Sir Hubert Gough, scion of a distinguished Irish military family, was Haig's man and had to be supported. Moreover, Sir Douglas Haig was carrying through the policy of attrition initiated by Sir John French at

Festubert. Gen. Gough acquiesced in that policy and any subordinate commander who disagreed was sent home. The ultimate expression of that unhealthy dogma, 'dissent has no rights', responded to criticism by censorship instead of finding solutions to tactical problems. It aimed, not at victory but at maintaining military authority.

On a matter of conscience, Hubert Gough defied the government during the Ulster crisis (although he afterwards said he would have obeyed orders but was given a choice and chose to disobey).[17] During that succession of battles known as Third Ypres, Gough lacked that moral will necessary to tell Haig the truth about the situation. A halt to the battle after Langemarck would have saved Fifth Army from further senseless slaughter. The difference was, in 1914, Gough was supported (or egged on) by senior officers at the War Office and leaders of HM Opposition. In 1917, bearing the responsibility of army commander, Gough stood alone. It was easier to obey orders and describe it as loyal duty. The battle bled white the BEF, drove a deep wedge between government ministers and army commanders, and ultimately resulted in the greatest disaster ever suffered by British arms to that time.

There was another, longer lasting, consequence to Langemarck. Gen. Plumer, that most 'blimpish' looking and beloved of English generals, had at Messines used an Irish assault corps with resounding success. Irishman Hubert Gough destroyed that concept. With its destruction ended the hope that between Orange and Green factions, the friendship and esteem engendered by successful collaboration in France would endure after the war. That, for Ireland, was the real tragedy of Third Ypres.

1ST DUBLINS—29TH DIVISION, BROODSEINDE, 4 OCTOBER

On 4 October, 1st Dublins were under orders to join 16th Division. The 'old Dubs' as they were affectionately known in the 'Incomparable' Division, volunteered for a last 'line adjusting' operation before departing. It called for an advance of 1000 yards on a two-company frontage. The objectives included the formidable 'Chinese House' in the Langemarck sector.

> Under command of Maj. A. Moore DSO, they marched up to the line by companies singing Irish Republican songs, the band in camp speeding them off to the strains of 'When Ireland is a Nation'... The Dublins attacked with what Gen. Cheape calls 'extraordinary vigour'. The divisional commander is of the opinion that nothing could have stopped the Dublins that day.[18]

On the right of the Dublins, 4th Division were thrown back by a counter-attack. The Dublins had prepared for such an eventuality and a flank guard of two platoons with two machine-guns poured enfilade fire across the flank.

The Germans withdrew, allowing the flanking unit to reoccupy its position. The Dublins then pressed on to their objective, the swollen Broembeek. In the course of the attack, Sgt. Ockenden identified a machine-gun position holding up the advance. Rushing it, he killed all the crew except one, who ran. Ockenden, under fire from other German positions, chased him in full view of the battalion who cheered him on. Later that day, Ockenden single-handedly captured a farm and took sixteen prisoners. He was awarded the Victoria Cross. In gaining all their objectives, the cost to 1st Dublins was high, 340 all ranks killed and wounded. 1st Dublins, part of 29th Division since that division's foundation in 1915, had fought in it at Gallipoli, Somme, Arras and Ypres. The Dublins had helped make the 29th the 'Incomparable Division'. Such was the esteem in which they were held that 29th Division gave them a rousing send-off.[19]

PASSCHENDAELE RIDGE, 10 NOVEMBER 1917

The tragedy in the mud continued until November 1917 when, at the second battle of Passchendaele, the ridge and village of Passchendaele were pyrrhically won by 1st British Division and 1st Canadian Division. As 10th Dublins had been present at the closing action of the Somme battle, so Ireland was represented by 1st Munsters in the last action of Third Ypres.

With 1st Canadian division on its right, the 1st Division attacked on Passchendaele Ridge on a two-battalion frontage, with 1st South Wales Borderers on the right and 1st Munsters on the left. Both battalions reached the main ridge, but the Welsh veered off to the right and left a gap which the inevitable German counter-attack exploited.[20]

Following a nightmarish approach-march in darkness across a shell-torn swamp, the attack on Passchendaele Ridge began long before dawn. Void Farm, a strong German machine-gun position, offered stout resistance, but was carried by Capt. Batten-Poll VC, with part of C Company. All objectives were taken by 0645. With the exception of Void Farm, the German garrisons put up a poor fight; they surrendered and were despatched forthwith to the rear. All the Germans helped the Munster wounded back, their only escorts. The attack was a limited one but the crest, 800 yards away, seemed bare of defenders. Battalion headquarters had a signals detachment with a power buzzer (an early transmitter) and brigade headquarters was asked for permission to take the ridge. The Munsters had no sight of the Borderers, but the Canadians could be seen going forward. The British barrage was concentrated on the ridge and the village of Passchendaele beyond.[21]

After a delay, the order to advance was received and the Munsters went forward. The terrible ground split platoons into small parties struggling forward, some faster than others. Eventually a few parties were 400 yards from the crest when exhaustion forced a halt about 0730. By this time, many personal weapons were mud-jammed: 'In some groups there were as few as three rifles in working order, in others as few as one. Most of the Mills bombs had been used clearing out the pill boxes.'[22] At 0750, the Germans could be seen preparing a counter-attack. SOS rockets were sent up and a message sent by four carrier pigeons. The British guns responded at once, and their fire descended upon 1st Munsters; apparently brigade headquarters had not informed the artillery of the Munsters' position.

Led by the celebrated 'Cockchafers', the Germans counter-attacked. Fresh and full of fight, they found the open flank left by the South Wales Borderers. Pouring through, they took the Munsters in flank and rear. In front of Void Farm, Capt. Batten-Poll inspired the defence with his own fighting spirit, making the enemy pay for every yard. When the Germans got within bombing range, clods of pressed mud were thrown forward to look like a grenade attack. None exploded, of course, but in mud this sometimes happened with real ones. The ruse worked and the Germans fell back. On the exposed flank Lt. Horan held Veal Cottage until he was killed. Capt. Batten-Poll held Void Farm until it was overwhelmed at 0830. But A Company, firmly entrenched in a captured pill box, held fast and all efforts to dislodge it failed.[23]

When headquarters learned of the situation, a counter-attack of battalion remnants was organised, led by the adjutant and signals officer. Helped by covering fire from A Company in their pill box, the attack was pressed home and succeeded in capturing a strongpoint, Tournant Farm. Meanwhile, fragments of the battalion, scattered half way up the ridge, held out all day. Some managed to return that night, but almost all, many wounded, were taken prisoner before nightfall.

At Passchendaele, the Munsters were ultimately dependent upon runners to pass messages. Conspicuous in that devoted band was Pte. J. Murphy. When all communications were cut with brigade headquarters and five runners had already been killed, he carried a message through the barrage to brigade headquarters and returned through the barrage with confirmation of its receipt. He well deserved a bar to his Military Medal. Inevitably, Munster losses were heavy: 413 all ranks were killed, wounded or missing.[24]

THE DEATH OF LT.-COL. A.D. MURPHY, 2ND LEINSTERS

In 17 Brigade of 24th Division, 2nd Leinsters had attacked on 31 July, just less than 400 strong (or weak). At the end of the battle they emerged with barely 150 all ranks; some companies had no officers left alive. Nevertheless, with 1st Royal Fusiliers, they were the only unit of 24th Division to reach the Blue Line.

On 16 November, at the close of the Passchendaele battle, the Leinsters had what their historian describes as the saddest day of the war, with the death in action of their commanding officer, Lt.-Col. A.D. Murphy DSO MC. As a lieutenant and transport officer, he had arrived with the battalion in

1914. He continued to be known as 'Mr Murphy' by the old hands after he became a distinguished battalion commander in line for a brigade command. A chance shell hit an RAP when Murphy was visiting his wounded. Everyone in the building was killed or wounded.

Universally admired for his fearless courage and peerless leadership, modesty and sense of duty, Murphy had temporarily commanded a brigade and was in line for a permanent brigade command when he was struck down in early manhood—twenty-seven years. The regimental historian, with obvious feeling, described him as 'a brave officer, a just commander, a loyal comrade and an upright man.'[25]

Lt.-Col. Alfred Murphy was buried in Roisel Cemetery. Such was the regard in which Murphy was held that the corps commander, divisional commander and brigade commander attended his funeral, along with his entire battalion.

CHAPTER TWENTY-EIGHT

The Battle of Cambrai

THE BATTLE OF CAMBRAI, 20–22 NOVEMBER 1917

For over a year, far-sighted officers had been pressing the case of the tank to break the stalemated deadlock of trench warfare, with poor success. Used prematurely in penny-packets during the closing stages of the Somme battle and over unfavourable ground at Messines and Ypres, the new weapon had failed to achieve the hoped-for results; its lack of success had strengthened its opponents. Even the Germans were unimpressed and had devised artillery tactics to defeat it. In a bid to close the year with some success, Field-Marshal Haig once again turned to the tank.

Headquarters Tank Corps had developed tactics for the use of massed tanks. Early in August 1917, they had proposed an attack with limited objectives. This would be a tank raid in force to break into the Hindenburg Line, to overwhelm, destroy and demoralise, then retire. The tank pioneers saw it as a limited demonstration of their weapon's possibilities, and a model for future attacks. It would depend for success upon surprise based upon the tank weapon, with no preliminary bombardment. An alternative proposal was a major offensive on the Flesquières Ridge.

The British Expeditionary Force, bled white by losses at Ypres which had not been replaced, was further weakened by disastrous events in Italy which demanded the despatch there of five divisions. Sir Douglas Haig, with insufficient reserves to exploit success, nevertheless accepted the proposed major offensive with massed tanks and set Cambrai as the objective. Haig envisaged an assault against the Hindenburg position in the Cambrai area, by five divisions supported by tanks on a six-mile frontage.

To achieve surprise, instead of a preliminary bombardment, there was to be a rolling barrage commencing at Zero Hour. When the assault troops had achieved the break-in, five cavalry divisions were to follow through and exploit. Their role was to capture Bourlon Wood, encircle Cambrai and, for further exploitation, secure the crossing of the Sensée River ten miles northwards. A division on the left would begin rolling up the Hindenburg Line and capture Mœuvres. Two follow-up divisions would secure the ground and consolidate.

THE SUBSIDIARY ATTACK, CROISELLES

Simultaneous with the main operation, demonstrations with gas, smoke and artillery were planned for practically the whole British Front south of the River Scarpe. Subsidiary attacks were to be launched west of Cambrai between Bullencourt and Fontaine les Croiselles by 3rd and 16th Divisions. 3rd Division would attack on a one-brigade frontage and 16th Division with three brigades in line. The objective of this subsidiary operation was the capture of a 2000 yard section of the Tunnel Trench and Tunnel Support near Fontaine les Croiselles, without tanks. Tunnel Trench, about thirty feet underground, ran beneath the German trenches for about twelve miles; it was wired for demolition in the event of capture. Formerly the support trench to the Hindenburg Line, it had become the German front line. Part of its surface line, four pill boxes, were similar to those which had proved so formidable at Langemarck. Made of ferro-concrete and manned by German machine-gunners, they posed the main threat to the success of the operation. Nicknamed Jove, Mars, Vulcan and Juno, these pill boxes were targeted by specific companies. Another, Pluto, was in front of 3rd Division. The 3rd Division was to attack only with its centre, 9 Brigade. Its objective was an 800-yard stretch of Bovis Trench. 9 Brigade hoped to pinch out the gap in the attack between the centre of 3rd Division and the right of 16th Division, with the help of a dummy attack and smoke.

THE CAPTURE OF TUNNEL TRENCH, 20–21 NOVEMBER 1917

16th Division departed from the Ypres Salient and moved to a section of the old German Hindenburg Line captured by the Australians in the Arras offensive. They were excellent trenches, quite the best 16th had ever occupied. The Irish troops quickly announced their presence, and one raid by 7th Leinsters yielded valuable information about Tunnel Trench.[1] On their sector, the British had artillery and air domination and, out of the line, the Irish brigades enjoyed a pleasantly quiet period. It was a rest badly needed after the horror of Langemarck, and Gen. Hickie presented decorations won there. The staff captain of 47 Brigade, in a letter to his mother, wrote:

> It really is beautifully restful sitting here with the door wide open looking out onto the sunny square, with its groups of sunny-haired children and on the right the ugly old church with a birds' nest on the head of the figure of the crucifix. It is difficult to imagine there is a war anywhere.[2]

During October, company training, football and sport were the order of the day. Then, in great secrecy, briefings and practise attacks over model trenches took place during the week preceding the assault. These were repeated daily until all troops knew their precise part. It was essential, should the officers fall, that NCOs and men, knowing their tasks and objectives, could carry on. A final divisional practise attack on 17 November was attended by the corps commander.

It is commonplace for regimental historians, of all regiments and nationalities, to praise their men, especially after a successful battle. The commanding officer of one battalion of 16th Division is no less praising in a letter to his wife: 'It was very edifying to watch the officers and men preparing for the attack—all optimistic, full of confidence and cheery.'[3]

Surprise was paramount. There was to be no preliminary bombardment to warn the enemy and plough up the ground. Zero Hour was 0620. The barrage began punctually and remained on the German front line for four minutes. Only 18-pounders, 6-inch trench mortars, Stokes mortars and Vickers machine-guns were used, all from within divisional resources. No heavy artillery or tanks were involved. As the barrage fell upon the enemy, the assault companies left their trenches, each in two waves. At the same time the enemy artillery replied: 'By this time the usual inferno... had worked up to its full fury.'[4]

Part of the barrage was smoke, and this deceived the Germans on the surface into believing gas was being used. They donned respirators. Six minutes later the first line of attackers took Tunnel Trench against slight opposition. The second line then passed through and captured Tunnel Support four minutes later. The wiring company followed in parties of ten, each with a sapper. Forty minutes after the attack started, the new front was well wired with a belt of concertina wire, and the wiring and covering parties were withdrawn. Concurrently, communication trenches were rapidly dug by the supporting battalions and the divisional pioneers. Consolidation was achieved everywhere, except on the extreme right and left. There, heavy fighting was taking place. That on the right involving 6th Connaught Rangers was the most serious.

The brigade of 3rd Division attacked on a two-battalion frontage, 12th West Yorks and 1st Northumberland Fusiliers. The right battalion gained its objective; the left battalion had its left company driven back. This was to affect the right of 47 Brigade.

The right attack, 47 Brigade, 6th Connaught Rangers and 1st Munsters, advanced across the 300-400 yards of no man's land 'with great dash'. They arrived at Tunnel Trench and occupied it almost without casualties. To the troops, the objective was deceptively simple, a muddy ditch without duckboards. It had, in fact, been both wide and deep but had been destroyed by the bombardment. Some couldn't believe this was the objective until the actual tunnel was discovered.[5] Its entrance was masked by curtains and had long flights of steps leading down into darkness; some were defended by machine-guns firing upwards. Sentries were posted at tunnel entrances and parties were sent down armed with Mills bombs to clear the tunnel.

Tunnel Trench was found to be seven feet high by six feet wide, nearly thirty feet below the surface, with entrances at regular intervals about every twenty-five yards. It ran the full length of the surface trench. Spaced along the main passage-way were tiers of bunks. In numerous small side chambers were stores of food and ammunition; everywhere was lit by electric lighting. Dead and wounded from the grenades thrown down in the attack littered the place. So surprised was the German garrison that most surrendered after slight resistance.

The centre attack, 48 Brigade, 10th and 1st Dublins, swept forward so swiftly that the Germans were taken completely by surprise and surrendered immediately.

The left attack, 49 Brigade, 2nd Royal Irish and 7th/8th Royal Irish Fusiliers, achieved equal success, except on the extreme left. There, 7th/8th Irish Fusiliers attacked with two companies up and two in support. The left, B Company, suffered considerable loss when it was held up for nearly an hour by a machine-gun post. This delayed the attack and broke up the wiring parties, which postponed the front-line wiring until the second night. The remainder of the battalion attack went according to plan. Tunnel Trench and Tunnel Support were taken. Patrols went down and met a little opposition which was swiftly overcome.[5] Engineer detachments, following immediately behind, cleared the demolitions. Four times during the day, the Germans counter-attacked; each time rifle and Lewis guns, with artillery support, drove them off.

On the extreme right of 47 Brigade, the situation was more serious. As soon as Tunnel Trench was occupied, two companies of 6th Connaught Rangers closed on the pill boxes Jove and Mars and took them from the rear, as they had practised, and 152 prisoners were captured. The commander of A Company, Capt. C. Brett, established his headquarters in Jove. B Company, under Capt. T. Tuite MC, took all its objectives just as quickly and established its headquarters in Mars. An advance signal detachment established communications rearwards. Only on the boundary with 3rd Division did the enemy hold on to their trench. There, the Rangers established a flank guard. The German counter-attack began at 0710, inevitably, against the exposed right flank.

On the front of 3rd Division, Pluto was untaken. Fire from this enfiladed the Rangers and swept their rear, causing casualties to the support companies and preventing their movement. At the same time, enemy bombers appeared from a support tunnel which should have been demolished by this time, but the engineer detachment detailed to its destruction was blown up by a chance shot striking their own explosives. Under cover of machine-gun fire, strong enemy bombing parties advanced through the tunnel and the right of the Rangers became involved in savage fighting which lasted for several hours. In the fighting, the commander of the right flank platoon was wounded and all but two of his twenty-eight men killed or wounded. When A Company ran out of bombs, B Company sent over all theirs, but these in turn gave out. German grenades were collected from Tunnel Trench and well used.

> At a critical moment, one of the men, Private K. White, rushed close up to a traverse from behind which the enemy was bombing, and actually catching some of their bombs in the air, threw them back before they had exploded.[6]

Firing from open positions, the platoon Lewis guns returned fire but suffered heavily in the fire-fight. After an hour's fierce fighting, Capt. Brett was wounded; most of his men were casualties. The survivors refused to retire to the British front line, but held onto the exposed flank as a stop, falling back on B Company in Mars and 'yielding their ground only inch by inch and leaving a trail of dead behind them', carrying all their wounded as they withdrew.[7]

Jove was lost. By this time, no man's land was swept by German machine-gun fire. With great difficulty, three platoons of the supporting companies forced their way forward to support the two embattled companies. An explosive bullet severely wounded Capt. Tuite and although wounded himself, the company sergeant-major, CSM Morritt, carried his company commander across the fire-zone to safety. Morritt was later awarded the DCM. The situation was now desperate.

7th Leinsters, in support, moved into the old front line, freeing the two remaining Ranger companies to reinforce the remnant of A and B Companies in Tunnel Trench. Two Lewis guns were positioned to cover the Rangers' right. Because of the heavy fire, 11th Hampshires, constructing the communication trench at Jove Lane, were forced to sap forward under cover instead of digging in the open. Although the work was slow, the trench was completed and connected to Tunnel Trench. A firm defensive flank was formed along this sap soon after 1300 and the position was firmly consolidated.

Pluto, on 3rd Division front, was untaken and represented a continuing threat to the Irish. 7th Leinsters relieved the Rangers. Preparations were made to gain the section of Tunnel Trench on the boundary with 3rd Division which still lay in enemy hands. At the same time, the Leinsters were to force the enemy out of Jove, Vulcan and Pluto.

The final phase of the divisional operation started at 1900 on 23 November. Two parties from 7th Leinsters (Lt.-Col. Buckley), each of sixty-five men under Capt. V.J. Farrell MC attacked, captured and consolidated Jove and the untaken portion of Tunnel Trench. In a dashing and gallant action with comparatively light casualties, thirty-one enemy were taken prisoner and considerable equipment captured. More grim was the discovery of the carnage in the trenches around Jove where many of the Rangers' dead were found. One dead Ranger was locked in a death grip with a dead German, indicating the ferocity of the fighting.[8] Vulcan was discovered unoccupied and blown up. Pluto, now dangerously exposed, was vacated by its German garrison and blown up also. The operation was completely successful.

The highest casualty percentages in the Division during the attack were those of 6th Connaught Rangers. Of the 240 officers and men in the assault companies, thirty-four men were killed, three officers and 109 wounded, almost all in the fight to hold the exposed flank.

It was a brilliantly planned divisional operation, executed with boldness and dash, which kept casualties to a minimum. Described by the regimental historian, 'this swift and successful operation by the 16th Division was a model of attack with limited objective'.[9] The enemy 470th and 471st Infantry Regiments (the equivalent of two British brigades) were almost completely destroyed and 635 prisoners were taken. 'Crowds of Fritz prisoners, altogether a "grand success". The Bocheman has had one of the worst jolts of his military career. It was an absolute surprise for him.'[10]

The exploits of 16th Division, which a few days earlier would have been hailed in Parliament as a major success, were overshadowed by events taking place at Cambrai. For this reason, 16th Division's success was largely overlooked. After the war, the Honours Award Committee decided that 16th Division was outside the territorial boundary for the 'Cambrai' honour. The regular 3rd Division on its right, which had one brigade in the operation and had partially failed to achieve the objective, was nevertheless so honoured. The Irish might be forgiven for complaining at the lack of recognition for their exploits.

Immediately after the operation 47 Brigade said good-bye to Brig. Pereira, known to his brigade as 'Hoppy', a soldier nickname 'given to one we always admired'.[11] He handed over his command to Brig. Gregorie, late of the Royal Irish. Stout-hearted Pereira had been too frank with his opinions on the failure of 3rd Division and was relieved of his command.

> My dear old general has been sent home for good. He had a little misunderstanding with the 'powers that be' and was sent home. I am absolutely cut-up. One couldn't help loving the gallant old man, the men will be heartbroken.[12]

Brig. Pereira was then fifty-three years of age and had commanded his brigade for two years. He was universally admired. A commander, especially one so beloved of his officers and men, can become over-protective. In military operations, this can be burdensome, and finally, however sad and regretful the occasion, that commander is best relieved and rested.

40th Division replaced 16th in the line on the evening of 2 December and was transferred to the Ronssoy-Lempire sector, a sector on the flank of the German counterstroke. There it remained from 3 December until the fateful 21 March 1918. Its departure from VI Corps was recognised in a most fitting way by the corps commander.

I desire to place on record the good service of the 16th (Irish) Division which is about to leave the VI Corps after serving with it for 3 1/2 months.

The work of the Division, both in the trenches and behind the Line, has been admirable and might well serve as a model of how such duties should be performed.

In carrying out the capture of the German trenches on the 20th November and their rapid consolidation—an exploit which had defeated the efforts of the other Divisions—the Division showed once again what a splendid fighting machine it is.

It is with great regret that I am forced to part with the Irish Division. I desire to express to Major-General Hickie and all ranks under him my warmest wishes for their future welfare and the hope that I may at another time be so fortunate as to have the Irish Division under my command.

Sgd (Haldane) Lt.-Gen.[13]

36TH DIVISION, YPRES TO CAMBRAI

Following their relief at Langemarck, the 36th was transferred to IV Corps and, after four days reorganising and cleaning, moved to a rest area near Bapaume. The country behind the lines was rolling downs, well watered and thickly wooded. The wood still provided good cover. It was totally devoid of civilians. After the mud of the Ypres Salient, it was remembered as the most pleasant spot the division had ever occupied. Here they were joined by 1st Royal Irish Fusiliers, the first of many such transfers. This was described as 'highly significant, in altering the character of the Ulster Division.'[14] The towns, villages and townlands of rural Ireland could give no more; recruiting had dried up. To keep the battalions of both 16th and 36th Divisions up to strength, it was necessary to post in regular battalions, bringing them to establishment by absorbing their 'Service' battalions where necessary. It marked the end of the Ulster Volunteer Force Division after twenty months' operational duty in the front line.

Troops from elsewhere also poured in. 300 troopers from the North Irish Horse were posted to the 9th Irish Fusiliers, which became 9th (North Irish Horse) Battalion of that regiment. The 8th and 9th Royal Irish Rifles were amalgamated and became 8th/9th Royal Irish Rifles. The regular 2nd Royal Irish Rifles was transferred from 25th Division to the 36th. The 7th Royal Irish Rifles, transferred from 16th Division, was disbanded and its personnel posted to 2nd Royal Irish Rifles. Not all moves to 36th Division were welcome. One officer of 1st Royal Irish Fusiliers on the staff of 33rd Division wrote, 'The 87th are ordered off to join the Ulstermen and they are all sick about it.'[15]

Between 28–30 August, 36th Division relieved the 9th Scottish in the Cambrai sector of the line, manned with all three brigades in line. The Front was along the half-completed Canal du Nord. Although dry in summer, it was deep and proved a considerable obstacle before the Hindenburg system. In the divisional area, two spoil heaps about sixty feet high were of tactical importance. One, north of the divisional sector, was occupied by the Germans and could sweep 109 Brigade trenches with machine-gun fire. In the southern sector another, Yorkshire Bank, was manned by Ulstermen. Soon, by aggressive patrolling, the 36th dominated no man's land. But the Germans retaliated. Under cover of a box barrage, they raided 1st Irish Fusiliers on 18 November, just two days before the attack, and took six prisoners. Evidently little real information was gained from the Fusiliers. On the night of 19 November, the assaulting Allied troops and tanks were ready.

During the period of trench warfare before the Cambrai offensive, 12th Rifles suffered a sad loss when their chaplain, Rev. Alexander Stuart, was killed near the RAP. A shell-burst on the parapet killed him instantly. Although only ten days with the battalion, Rev. Stuart had obviously made a deep impact on the unit, for the war diary commented: 'His death caused great sorrow throughout the battalion.'

CAMBRAI, NOVEMBER 1917

Third Army, Gen. the Hon. Sir Julian Byng, with four corps and reinforced by the Cavalry Corps, was responsible for mounting the operation to gain Cambrai. The offensive would be carried out by the two centre corps, III on the right with three divisions, 12th, 20th and 29th. The IV Corps would be on the left, with 51st and 62nd. In addition, GHQ reinforced Byng with a further corps, V Corps. Its two infantry divisions were to occupy and consolidate ground captured by the cavalry. The two remaining divisions of IV Corps, 36th and 56th London, were to hold the line. One brigade of 36th Division was involved in the offensive. Its task was to roll up the Hindenburg Line westwards and capture Mœuvres. Brig. Ricardo's 109 Brigade was chosen for this task.

The Hindenburg defences, as formidable as German military engineering skill could devise, were built by the forced labour of thousands of Russian prisoners. It consisted of a lightly manned 'forward zone' not less than 1000 metres deep. On the forward edge of the 'battle zone', covered by a wire apron 100 yards deep, was the main defensive trench. About 500 yards behind was a support system similarly wired. Behind this, at 2000 yards, was a complete replica—the Hindenburg Support Line. A third system was in the course of construction 3000 metres behind on the rear edge of the battle area. Strongpoints armed with machine-guns and field artillery dotted the area of the two lines. The German High Command could be forgiven for considering impregnable what they called Siegfried Stellung I, II and III. To meet the emerging British tank threat, German field commanders had practised new tactics designed to separate infantry from its armoured support.

As on the Somme, there was considerable preparatory work and again 36th Division was fully employed on accommodation and road construction. Camouflaged hutments were crammed into Havrincourt Wood; road building was carried out by day and night. Weather conditions were favourable, dry with ground mist persisting throughout the day. A few days before Zero Hour, the additional divisions and tanks moved into the area and the 109 Brigade began training for its role. The remaining brigades relieved 51st and 62nd Divisions, who retired from the line to train for the coming offensive.

The offensive on Cambrai was mounted in three phases. A surprise infantry attack would be led by tanks and supported by an unregistered artillery barrage with no preliminary bombardment. Its aim was breaching the Hindenburg Line and capturing the canal crossings. This was to open the way for exploitation in the next phase. The second phase was the advance of the Cavalry Corps to isolate Cambrai and the capture of Bourlon by IV Corps. Third phase involved the clearance of Cambrai and the surrounding area. The IV Corps' objective was the Bapaume-Cambrai road, the high ground crowned by Bourlon Wood and Bourlon village.

The 107 and 108 Brigades were to act as flank guards, while 109 Brigade captured German trenches between the Canal du Nord and the Bapaume-Cambrai road, including a vital bridge over the canal. Its final objective was Mœuvres.

109 Brigade was supported by the complete divisional artillery and one army artillery brigade. Brig. Ricardo decided to take the northern spoil heap and use this to dominate the German trenches. Covered by machine-guns on the heap, the assault battalions would clear the enemy trenches in a 'bombing action'. Brig. Ricardo, concerned lest this might slow down the rate of advance, decided to use Lewis gun-teams co-operating with the bombers. It was a tactic which had been successfully developed by the Canadians on Vimy Ridge.

On 19 November a mass of 380 tanks were 1000 yards from the German line. For the final approach, the noise of their advance was covered by sustained machine-gun fire. In Havrincourt Wood, the guns stood almost wheel-to wheel. At 0630 on 20 November the offensive at Cambrai began.

Surprise was complete. A torrent of fire closely followed by massed tanks flattened the huge wire apron. Behind the tanks, columns of infantry followed hard. Fascines, huge bundles of wood, were dropped into the trenches and the tanks advanced over them. Demoralised Germans surrendered in droves. Some gallant individual resistance was met, but there was no counter-barrage to support the defence. Before 0800, the first objectives, including the villages of Havrincourt, Ribécourt, Covillet Wood and the front system of the Hindenburg defences west of the canal, had been completely taken.

After a pause of thirty minutes to allow a pass through of troops, the fresh advance began. Only at one point was the tank attack defeated. Maj.-Gen. Harper of the 51st had insisted upon using his own tactics, and not those developed by the Tank Corps. This held the infantry 200 yards back from the tanks; it suited the German anti-tank doctrine and was chiefly responsible for the failure of 51st Division. On the outskirts of Flesquières, when the tanks breasted a rise, they were confronted by German Artillery. Thirty-nine tanks were destroyed before the infantry could engage the gun-crews. With the tanks destroyed, German machine-guns halted the Highlanders.

The assault of 109 Brigade on the Spoil Heap went well. A battery of 4-inch mortars firing 'termite' incendiary bombs joined the four-minute bombardment seconds before the 10th Inniskillings charged home and took the heap. There was little resistance following the demoralising effects of the incendiary shelling. Having gained an entry, 10th Inniskillings pressed the attack home. About a mile farther north, a company of 14th Rifles, under cover of the barrage, had also forced an entry to a communication trench on the Demicourt-Flesquières road. 10th Inniskillings reached their second objective at 0930.

With entry gained at the Spoil Heap or Hill 90 by 10th Inniskillings, 9th Inniskillings now moved in for the clearance. The great width of the Hindenburg trenches aided the attack and there was no congestion. The pass-through accomplished, 9th Inniskillings began the systematic clearance of trenches as rehearsed. Sentries were positioned at dug-out entrances and left for mopper-ups to clear. When a dug-out was cleared a notice, 'Cleared', was left to avoid duplication of effort. A platoon of the 9th entered the dry bed of the canal and advanced along it, moving behind the trench-clearing operation. Some machine-guns in craters on the Demicourt-Graincourt road caused trouble, but the right flank companies pushed on and gradually the machine-guns were overcome.

11th Inniskillings moved in for the third and final stage of the attack and met stronger resistance. On the right German bombers held up their advance for a time, but rifle-grenadiers cleared them out and the advance resumed. At 1530, 11th Inniskillings reached their objective on the Cambrai-Bapaume road and consolidated about 1500 yards from the brigade's final objective. But the Germans had demolished the vital bridge across the canal. Ricardo's plan was efficient and methodical, but gave little scope to native dash. The 'steadiness' which he liked slowed the rate of advance and gave the Germans time to recover.[16]

Left of the Inniskillings, 56th Division advanced north of the Cambrai-Bapaume road, while on their right, 62nd Division worked up the Hindenburg support system with complete success and captured Graincourt at 1330. However, 51st Division was still held at Flesquières. Its failure to advance threatened the success of the entire operation. Only the evacuation of the village by the enemy in the early hours of 21 November allowed the Highlanders to advance again. But the delay was subsequently to prove serious.

To the south, III Corps had achieved considerable success. 6th and 29th Regular Divisions had taken Marcoing and southern Masnières and reached Noyelles. However, on the extreme right of the Corps, 20th Division had been unable to gain the canal bank and the Germans were able to hold an important bridgehead on the St Quentin Canal. Most serious was the total failure of the Cavalry Corps to break through. Gen. Byng had no reserves, and the troops would have to rest before continuing the offensive. This would lose him the element of surprise.

At dawn on the second day, the 51st occupied Flesquières and pressed on up the Graincourt-Marcoing Road where it positioned itself by 1100 hours. Several guns were taken in Orival Wood. After strong resistance, Cantaing was captured by 2 Cavalry Brigade, supported by elements of the 51st. Late in the afternoon, Fontaine Notre Dame on the Cambrai road was also captured. On their left, the 62nd Division had advanced well. Anneux and Anneux Church, after stiff fighting, were taken. However, in late afternoon, the assault on Bourlon Wood by both divisions failed in the face of German machine-gun fire. This was critical. The enemy held high ground which dominated all the British gains in that area.

Meanwhile, the attack of 109 Brigade continued along the Canal du Nord towards Mœuvres. 9th Inniskillings, attacking west of the canal, reached the point 1000 yards north of the Cambrai road, but were halted by heavy machine-gun fire from Lock 5 across the canal. East of the canal, the 14th Rifles and 10th Inniskillings resumed the attack. Despite stiffening opposition they reached the outskirts of Mœuvres, but heavy machine-gun fire drove the Ulstermen back. The final objective at Mœuvres was untaken.

At the end of what was to be a two-day battle, Bourlon Wood and village on its commanding heights, the outstanding tactical features in the area, were untaken. The tanks (both vehicles and crews) which had mainly been responsible for the early success had reached their limit. Crucially, the absence of reserves to exploit the success of Day One and Day Two was to have serious consequences. In battle, the moment of opportunity is fleeting. FM Haig had forgotten the main lesson of his Loos battle: hold reserves sufficiently forward to exploit success immediately.

The Germans sent reserves to seal the breach. GHQ, realising for the first time the potential for success, belatedly rushed reserves to the scene. It was a race which the German staff won. The Guards and 40th Divisions, intended to occupy ground after capture, were now tasked with capturing Bourlon Wood, Bourlon and Fontaine.

On the night of 22–23 November, 109 Brigade was relieved. To capture Mœuvres, Gen. Nugent planned an attack astride the Canal du Nord on a two-brigade frontage.

East of the Canal, two battalions of 107 Brigade were to clear the Hindenburg support system east of Mœuvres. Two battalions of 108 Brigade were to attack west of the canal and capture Mœuvres. A barrage fired by 36th Divisional Artillery, reinforced with an army field artillery brigade and five heavy batteries, was to begin at 1100.

The 36th attacked as planned at 1100 after a forty-minute bombardment. East of the canal, the 15th Rifles advanced against stiff opposition up the Hindenburg support trenches. They gained 500 yards in hand-to-hand fighting and reached their objective. Then 10th Rifles leap-frogged, ran into a block and were stopped. At dusk the survivors charged with bayonets but were driven back.

The attack of 108 Brigade, west of the canal, fared better. 12th Rifles attacked Mœuvres with three companies and gained entry into the village defences. One company worked around west of the village while the centre company cleared the village. At this critical stage, the Germans counter-attacked in regimental strength. Col. Goodwin of 12th Rifles called for support. 9th Rifles were sent forward, but before they could get through, 12th Rifles had already retired.

Exploitation of the initial break-in by capturing Cambrai faded, and with the mass of Bourlon Wood and village dominating them, the newly-won positions were vulnerable. To secure his gains, Haig was forced to continue the attack and therefore committed more reserves. Meanwhile, the weather changed for the worse, becoming colder; the rain changed to snow.

In a continuation of the battle, the IV Corps was ordered to retake Fontaine and secure Bourlon Wood and village. Simultaneously, the battle to extend the left was to continue. This time, in addition to its artillery support, 36th Division was given sixteen tanks which were attached to 107 Brigade. The final objective was a line from the canal at Lock 4 to Quarry Wood.

The attack of 107 Brigade was hastily organised because Brig. Withycombe could not issue orders until 0830 (the tank officers could not be found).[17] In the attack, because the Ulstermen had no training with tanks as other divisions had, the German anti-tank tactics were successful and the attack failed when 15th Rifles and its tanks ran into stiff opposition. In the only gain of the day, Lock 5 and Round Trench were taken by 8th Rifles, supported by a tank in spite of heavy enemy artillery fire.

Of that day's fighting, Gen. Nugent wrote:

> We had a hard day's fighting yesterday and made very little progress. On my left I have been held up by machine-guns and uncut wire round the village of Moeuvres which we have been trying to take all day but we could not get in. Tanks must be used in large numbers or not at all.[18]

The two leading battalions of 108 Brigade made little progress until 2nd Irish Rifles, newcomers to the division, were brought up from support and showed their mettle. Their charge swept the Germans out of three-quarters of Mœuvres and captured four machine-guns. Because the Hindenburg system on each side of the village remained untaken, the village was untenable. At dusk all withdrew to the southern edge of Mœuvres. That night, 23–24 November, 108 Brigade was relieved by 109 Brigade. 36th Division was relieved the following day. At the same time, 51st Division was relieved by the Guards Division, and 1st and 2nd Irish Guards entered the battle.

The Guards Division watched the opening battle develop, waiting at two hours' notice for their turn, which came on 23 November. The Division advanced to relieve the Highland Division before Fontaine Notre Dame where the ridge dominated all the British gains in that area. In an attempt to secure the ridge, Fontaine and Bourlon Wood were attacked by 2 Guards Brigade (2nd Irish Guards) on 27 November. The regimental historian described the action with the succinct, forceful prose of the father who had lost his only son in that same battalion at Loos in a similar attack.

> They did so attack; they were cut to pieces with machine-gun fire in the advance; they were shelled out of Bourlon Wood; they were counter-attacked by heavy reinforcements of the enemy; they had no reinforcements; they fell back on Fontaine village in the evening; they withdrew from it in the darkness and fell back on La Justice.[19]

In that heroic attack on a position which could have been gained on Day One had the divisional commander listened to tank experts, 2nd Irish Guards lost just ninety officers and men killed or died of wounds and nearly 300 wounded.[20]

29TH DIVISION: 1ST INNISKILLINGS

On the opening day of the battle, 1st Inniskillings followed in support during the attack on the canal. Well commanded by Lt.-Col. Sherwood-Kelly, 1st Inniskillings overcame resistance on the northern side of the canal.

The battalion, without tank support, then attacked a force of motor machine-guns at the top of a long slope leading to Cambrai. The battalion advanced by alternate company rushes, covering each other as they worked forward by fire and movement, until stopped by a wide belt of barbed wire. Undaunted by enemy machine-gun fire, the Inniskilling wire cutters clipped their way through. The attack companies followed and under covering fire stormed the enemy position.[21] For his outstanding and courageous personal leadership in the action, Sherwood-Kelly was awarded the Victoria Cross. Although a very good commanding officer, he was not popular with the Inniskillings: 'He didn't understand them, possibly because he was a South African, he didn't know them, but he was a very gallant man.'[22]

On the morning of 30 November a lightning German counterstroke struck the north and south of the British salient in an effort to pinch it out. Without advance warning of their intentions by preliminary bombardment, the Germans delivered a short hurricane bombardment of mixed high-explosives, gas and smoke. In the southern sector of the salient, assault infantry probed the British defences, found weak areas, infiltrated through and followed up with infantry in strength. They swept over trenches and gun-lines before the British had time to realise what was happening. Gonnelieu and Villers Guislain were captured and Gouzeaucourt was penetrated. In the northern sector, the Germans attacked in orthodox linear formation and were everywhere repulsed.

In the south, only one division held firm. The 29th Division, true to its Gallipoli tradition, held its ground with stubborn tenacity. But eventually, on the night of 3–4 December, the entire division was ordered to retire west of the St Quentin Canal to shorten the line.

At the opening of the enemy counterstroke, the Guards Division was in reserve when the line cracked. Attached to III Corps, they advanced to recover lost ground against the wreck of disaster. Nearing the enemy, they passed Labour Corps men who joined the advancing guardsmen armed only with picks and shovels.[23] 3 Guards Brigade advanced to retake Gouzeaucourt with astonishing steadiness and majestic resolution.

> They halted and fixed bayonets just outside Gouzeaucourt Wood, the Irish on the left of the line, their right on the Metz-Gouzeaucourt road, the 3rd Coldstream in the centre, the 2nd Coldstreams on the right, the 2nd Grenadiers in reserve in Gouzeaucourt Wood itself. They were shelled as they marched to the Wood... They came under machine-gun fire from the village... As they swept down the last slope to Gouzeaucourt the machine-gun fire from the village grew hotter.[24]

1st Irish Guards overran the village and advanced to the slope outside. There they dug in for the night. For a time, their left flank was in the air until

1 Guards Brigade came up on that side. Touch was gained with 4th Grenadiers and next morning they moved into reserve. Later, they returned to the line to relieve 2nd Scots Guards and half 1st Grenadiers. Without greatcoats or blankets in bitter weather, they stoically endured great hardship.[25] Their light dress would shortly be a decided advantage when rapid movement was necessary.

A strong German attack out of Gonnelieu and along the trench systems began at dawn on 5 December under cover of a heavy mixed barrage. A trench block was blown down and the Irish were assaulted by heavily armed troops; several trench bays were lost. The Irish recovered and, lightly clothed, they jumped out of the trench into the open. They lined the trench, now jammed with heavily-equipped Germans, and poured fire and grenades down on the tightly-packed mass. At the same time, an attempted attack straight out of Gonnelieu was driven back by rifle and machine-gun fire. In addition to suffering the guardsmen's fire, in their retreat the enemy were 'heavily bombed by their own side'.[26] In the action, 1st Irish Guards lost over fifty officers and men killed or died of wounds and some 150 wounded.[27] So successful was the German advance that much of the area captured in the opening days now had to be given up. On 3 December, GHQ decided to withdraw from exposed areas of the salient. Bourlon Wood, Cantaing, Noyelles, Graincourt and Marcoing were all evacuated. In his after-battle report Haig assumed the blame for the failure. But he also sacked some commanders.

On the opening day of the German attack, advance parties from 36th Division were happily fixing billeting areas in the Arras area. The units of the division were moving into the sector when recall orders arrived. 36th Division was to resume its place in the line under III Corps from 4 December. Late on 3 December, 108 Brigade came under command of 61st Division near Beaucamp. It was followed next day by 107 Brigade. On the following nights the division entered the line by relieving brigades of 61st and 29th Division.

61st Division was relieved in the middle of a battle for Welsh Ridge. First to arrive during the afternoon was a company of 9th Inniskillings. A heavy bombardment rained down in support of the enemy bombing up the Hindenburg system. The situation was critical. Exhausted remnants of 61st Division were on the point of complete collapse, and their dead and wounded crammed the trenches. The leading Inniskilling platoon rushed along the front and formed a stop line in the Hindenburg support trench. With few grenades, they opened rapid fire and halted three enemy attacks against the Inniskilling stop. Another attempt up the support trenches was also repulsed. That night, a supply of grenades was brought up. With these, 9th Inniskillings counter-attacked, helped by a platoon of 14th Rifles.

The attack was at first successful, but the Germans rallied. Outflanking them, they forced back the Inniskillings. Lt. Emerson, wounded by shrapnel, fought on heroically with a few men and for a time held off the bombers, but eventually he too had to fall back. Then rallying the remains of his company, Emerson attacked again and forced the enemy back along one hundred yards of trench line before he fell mortally wounded. Later he was awarded the Victoria Cross. So great were the losses of 9th Inniskillings in fierce fighting that they had to be relieved by 11th Inniskillings.[28]

The front stabilised on 7 December. Enemy attempts to concentrate were broken up with artillery fire. The brigades of the 36th consolidated their positions and settled down once again to a war of attrition. Shelling increased, aircraft straffing and area bombing were carried out day and night. But physical endurance has a limit and by mid December it became obvious that the infantry had reached it.

In the period of a month, 36th Division had been in offensive action for nearly a week, had marched and counter-marched in appalling weather. Then, flung into a desperate trench battle at no notice, it had withstood repeated counter-attacks. The physical condition of its troops had become so low that 'medical services submitted a strong report which was supported by the GOC.'[29] The Ulstermen were relieved during a blizzard on 14 December. Although the 'butcher's bill' had not been as high as at Langemarck, the battle of Cambrai was the starkest period 36th Division had endured since arriving in France.

Casualties: 20 November–8 December 1917[30]

	KIA/DOW	Wounded	Missing	Total
16th Division	159	713	21	893*
36th Division	320	1163	151	1634*

*Not including those evacuated through illness

CHAPTER TWENTY-NINE

Palestine:
Third Battle of Gaza

PALESTINE, 1917–18

At the end of June 1917, Gen. Sir Edmund Allenby, who had once been a Squadron Leader of the Inniskilling Dragoons and Commanding Officer of the Royal Irish Lancers, had relinquished command of Third Army in France and assumed that of the Egyptian Expeditionary Force. His remit from the Premier, Lloyd George, was to provide a suitable Christmas present for the British Empire, Jerusalem. Allenby's arrival at his new headquarters with a spare major-general in tow (Maj.-Gen. John Shea, first commissioned into the Royal Irish) caused not a little unease among senior officers of his new command. This unease seemed fully justified in their eyes when the new commander moved his headquarters from the pleasant watering-holes of Cairo three hundred miles eastwards, to the front in dry Sinai. There, without distraction, his staff began planning a stroke to deliver Lloyd George's Christmas present.

Twice had the Expeditionary Force failed against the Turkish defenders of Palestine, once by ill-preparedness and once by ill-luck. Now the army, seasoned veterans but dispirited and disillusioned like the Army of Italy in 1796 and the Army of the Potomac in 1864, awaited a new general with cynical curiosity and little expectation of success. What they knew of Allenby was conveyed by rumour and his army nickname 'the Bull'. In one respect they were right. On his first morning, by flinging his 'in tray', filled with administrative trivia, into a corner of his office, he demonstrated forcefully to his general staff where his priorities lay.[1] Then, a rampaging bull-like tour of his scattered command left vivid impressions and galvanised staff and soldiers alike, leaving behind new hope and inspiration.

> Stories began to circulate about him. The best being, on his way to the line in Palestine he saw beer being unloaded at Kantara. He ordered it reloaded and sent to the Front. True or false, it sent morale soaring. I do know that after Allenby took over, canteens began to be established. A thing which had never before happened.[2]

As a result of his own appreciation of the situation and advice from senior commanders, Allenby communicated his outline plan to London for approval and with it his requests for additional troops. The War Cabinet approved. As result the 10th (Irish) and 60th (London) Divisions were despatched from Salonika to Egypt.

10th Division embarked on a fleet of hired transports between the first and third weeks of September 1917. By the end of the third week, the entire division was concentrated in the area of Ismailia on the edge of the Suez Canal by Lake Timsah. At Moascar Garrison north-east of the town, the leading battalions of each brigade had established tented camps in 'Lines' surrounded by rush matting screens. Here they spent ten days training and re-equipping before marching to El Kantara, the railhead of the cross-Sinai railway, which was reached on 30 September en route to Palestine.

All the brigadiers inspected their units before embarkation at Salonika, but none more rigorously than Brig. Vandeleur, or 'Vandy, our excitable little brigadier'[3] to his 29 Brigade. Vandeleur insisted on his men being turned out to the 'ninety-nines'. The day after arrival in Egypt, 'Vandy' again inspected his battalions. In one, the second man he inspected had part of the embarkation label still attached to the butt of his rifle; that battalion was marched off forthwith to be re-inspected the following day.[4] History does not relate what happened to the unfortunate soldier.

On its arrival in Egypt from Macedonia, the 10th was not medically fit; 3000 men were in hospital with malaria.[5] In fact, the Army Medical Services advised Allenby that the divisions should have a prolonged rest before being committed to active operations. The future FM Lord Wavell wrote:

> The 10th Irish Division, when it arrived from Salonika, in the middle of September, presented another problem for decision [by Allenby]. It had suffered much from malaria in the Struma valley, and the medical authorities advised Allenby that it should have a three months' rest before being used for any operations. Allenby went and inspected the division for himself, and liked its look. He cross-questioned Longley, who had served under him in France, on the fitness of his men to march and fight; and thereupon rejected the advice of the doctors, and trusted to his own judgment that the division could do its job. His judgment was fully justified by events; the division stood up to the hard work of the campaign without undue sickness. Allenby's decision was probably also based on psychology; he knew that to leave an Irish division at rest when fighting was toward was likely to be destructive of its morale and discipline.[6]

Typically, Allenby's inspection was informal. Doing every unit of the division in its own lines, the men paraded in front of their tents. He left a vivid impression on all ranks. One officer of 1st Leinsters wrote:

> General Allenby inspected our division, in one bite so to speak... he gave us twenty minutes and left us with the impression here was a

man to serve under; for he didn't waste one iota of time in pointless criticisms; he inspected the men rather than his reserve ration. From that moment he won the confidence of at least one battalion.[7]

Ismailia was too great a temptation for the troops long absent from reasonable rest and recreation facilities and the ANZAC police had an even rougher time with the Irishmen than their own turbulent 'Diggers'; two policemen were thrown into the canal.[8] The officers were offered the hospitality of the French Club and enjoyed cuisine the like of which they had not tasted for years. There, the divisional band played several times during their short stay, Moore's melodies possibly. The climate delighted them, with its hot days and cool nights and, because of tight anti-malarial control, an absence of mosquitoes. In such surroundings the division's health rapidly improved.[9]

Training began on 17 September and continued until the 27th. A major boxing tournament was held to divert the men from the ANZAC police perhaps. Then on 29 September, 10th Division departed Ismailia for El Kantara. The battalions paraded by brigades and were led out of the town by the divisional band. In 29 Brigade, 6th Leinsters followed its senior battalion, the 1st. However the commands given were quite different. The commanding officer of the 1st Battalion shouted, '1st Battalion, Royal Canadians, quick march'. Such is unit pride that Col. Craske, the veteran commander of its sister battalion and noted throughout the regiment for his individuality, ordered, '6th Battalion, Leinster Regiment, quick march'.[10] Both orders were perfectly correct. However, the 6th, with such elements as the Royal Meath Militia in its ranks, was historically senior to the 'Old Hundredth' and was without foreign connection.

On the outskirts of Ismailia, Brig. Vandeleur waited with his staff to take the salute of his brigade. The leading battalion gave 'Eyes Right' and the salute was replied to by the Garrison Assistant Provost Marshal who was supervising traffic control nearby.[11] He was later interviewed by the discommoded brigadier, who never failed to live up to his reputation. His brigade must have regarded it as a fitting farewell to Ismailia.

Marching by way of El Firdan and El Ballah, between the railway and canal, the battalions reached El Kantara that evening, where most took the opportunity to swim in the canal. El Kantara, an ancient crossing over the salt-marshes thereabouts, was said to have been used by the Holy Family fleeing from Herod. A great and much appreciated addition to the division's transport were motor lorries fitted as field kitchens. Each battalion could cook on the line of march, enabling hot dinners to be taken during a break on the route. It would have been a brave medical officer who suggested this was unhealthy in the tropics. The officers' mess vehicles went ahead and dinner for the officers was ready shortly after the battalions' arrival.

Gen. Sir A. Murray, Regimental Colonel, Royal Inniskilling Fusiliers, and previous CinC MEF, was one of the greatest administrators in the army, but an unlucky commander. Following a defeat of the Turks at Romani in 1916, during the winter of 1916–17 he had pushed them back to Gaza. Murray's army advanced building a railway behind it. But at Gaza, Murray suffered a repulse. Later he suffered a second and bloodier reverse. As a result of this, he was relieved of his command and replaced by Allenby. The Front extended from the sea at Gaza to east of Beersheba. Allenby reorganised his army into three corps: XX Corps, XXI Corps and Desert Mounted Corps. The first was under Lt.-Gen. Sir Philip Chetwode; the second under Irishman Lt.-Gen. Sir Edward Bulfin (born at Rathfarnham, Co. Dublin, he was educated at Stonyhurst and Trinity College, Dublin); and the last by Australian Lt.-Gen. Sir Henry 'Light Horse Harry' Chauvel. One 'out-of-depth' general was sent home, and Gen. Shea was given command of 60th (London) Division when Bulfin was promoted.

Allenby's plan for what was to become known as Third Gaza was based on concentration and deception. He would concentrate on the right, having induced the enemy to believe he was threatened from the left, the obvious seaward axis of advance. The main problems were transport and water. The desert tracks of Sinai were unsuitable for wheeled vehicles; animal transport would therefore have to be used, a situation which further increased the water problem. In the event, 30,000 camels were employed to carry water and transport the force. But these could only supply the striking force for the march to Beersheba. Operations beyond there depended upon its excellent wells being captured intact.

The Beersheba attack, the opening act of the offensive, was eventually fixed for 31 October 1917, following a three-day bombardment of Gaza.

On 2 October, 5th Royal Irish (Pioneers) was railed to Rafa, where they spent a fortnight marching, training and doing gas drills to become acclimatised. On the 15th, they started for Sheik Nuran and arrived there next day. There they were split up by companies, developing water supplies, making roads and building divisional camps for 53rd, 60th and 74th Divisions. For the next two months, Lt.-Col. Grogan's battalion of artisans was detached from the 10th to improve road communications for Sir Edward Bulfin's XXI Corps. Bulfin, although without Chetwode's brilliance, was invariably called upon by Allenby when, to use a Wellingtonian expression, 'hard pounding' was necessary.[12]

During a short stay at El Kantara, the base camp for the expeditionary force, battalions deposited base kit, drew the final items of war establishment, arms, ammunition and equipment, loaded stores onto railway wagons. Then, in long freight trains, they departed during the cool early hours of the morning on a journey of between two and three hours. The 10th detrained at Rafa, the Egyptian Expeditionary Force headquarters and railhead. It was five miles from the sea and bathing was allowed. This quickly became the chief recreation.

Allenby had designated 10th Division as his army reserve and intended to use it in support of Chetwode. Chetwode, under whom 10th Division was to serve, was currently planning his corps battle. In a discussion paper to his divisional commanders, he made his objective clear, but warned them: 'GOCs will clearly understand that the above is only a rough outline of what I think may happen. The only thing that will not alter is my determination to find the enemy flank if manoeuvre or fighting can give it to me...'[13]

Training began in the expectation that the division would at last operate as a complete formation in a mobile role. The detail of breaking camp, loading animals, moving and setting up again, was practised more than ever before. This time emphasis was on the organisation of brigade camps, in which battalions were in closed locations. Each was responsible for establishing its own bivouac areas, especially latrines, cooking areas, and transport line, with special attention to camels. Brigadiers paid close attention to the alignment of tents, cleanliness of cooking areas and general hygiene. On the march in Sinai, water discipline was enforced. There were no threats or punishment. A man could drink his water on the march, but later, in the evening, when water was collected from each man for a 'brew up', those with no water got no tea. All soon learned to retain enough in their bottles.[14] But not all was well, as many former cases of malaria lapsed and fell ill. Many had to be evacuated and some battalions were reduced to two or three companies. However, reinforcement drafts also began to arrive, among whom were a new phenomenon to the battalions, conscripts from England.

An essential element of battle-logistics in the Middle East is water. Neglecting to provide adequately for this at Suvla was a major contributing factor to the failure. Gen. Sir Archibald Murray, Allenby's predecessor, had not only built a strategic railway from Egypt, but also had set in motion the construction of a water pipeline across the Sinai. This was now completed. However it was a beginning, not an end, to the water distribution problem. A total of 30,000 camels were employed to transport water from the pump-head to the battle formations; two infantry battalions were detailed to replenish the water containers, fanatis (a local term for a camel-carried water container), and control the watering points. Two fanatis, each containing fifteen gallons, were carried by pack animals. All water was to be treated with bisulphate as a safeguard against cholera.[15] For the period of the Third Battle of Gaza, 1st and 6th Leinsters were detailed for this vital task in XX Corps. They operated from El Shellal, El Imara and finally from Karm, filling 34,000 fanatis. When the vital Beersheba wells were captured, they pushed up to that place and worked day and night to keep the troops supplied. On the second day after Beersheba fell, the Leinstermen worked in choking dust to keep the constant stream of water-laden camels moving up to the front. Thousands of thirst-maddened horses from the Desert Mounted Corps were watered. For twenty-four days, the Leinsters battalions performed this vital duty day and night.

Two of the three wells at Beersheba were destroyed by the retreating Turks. One working trough for thirty horses was all that was available, with mounts for an entire cavalry regiment waiting in nearby enclosures. There was great difficulty in lining up the thirst-crazed horses that had not been watered for three to four days. Mad with thirst, some animals tried to get their entire bodies into a foot-wide trough. 'All drank for ten minutes like beasts hysterical.'[16] Eventually the two Leinster battalions were relieved on 6 November and rejoined the division. Inglorious work perhaps, but had such attention to detail been given to the Suvla operation, the history of that campaign would have been different.

THE THIRD BATTLE OF GAZA

When it came, the battle consisted of a succession of blows alternating at either end of the Turkish line, some twenty-five miles apart. The initial bombardment by naval gun-fire and land artillery was intended to fix the Turks to Gaza, in the belief that this was to be the Allied main objective. On the fourth day, a direct assault on Beersheba by Chetwode's XX Corps was timed to coincide with a wide right-flank turning movement by the Desert Mounted Corps. Its principal objective was the vital wells north of the town. Although Chauvel's horsemen were delayed by a stubborn Turkish stand, a mad hair-raising cavalry charge by Australian Light Horse and English Yeomanry from the Shires carried the wells before they could all be blown up. Two days later, an attack on Gaza by Bulfin's XXI Corps captured the greater portion of its defences. This was followed by another blow on the right-centre of the Turkish line at Hureira. The spirited dash of the infantry and the superb élan of the cavalry won the battle with comparatively light casualties.

Such is the brief outline of a notable victory which brought Allenby's army to the gates of Jerusalem. None of this could have happened without first concentrating secretly at the decisive point, with adequate reserves close at hand, while convincing the Turkish commander that the bulk of Allenby's forces were elsewhere and, most importantly, by good logistical support, including elaborate watering arrangement.

10TH DIVISION AT HUREIRA, 6–7 NOVEMBER 1917

10th Division marched on the night of 28–29 October from Rafa to Kemp Station. Then on the night of 29-30 October they moved from Kemp Station to Shellal, the central position of Wadi Ghuzze. They were under strict orders to remain concealed from Turkish observation. On the final day, 10th Division advanced with 60th and 74th divisions and Yeomanry Mounted Divisions in artillery formation. The assault on Beersheba took place on 31 October 1917 after a final night march in which 40,000 troops marched faultlessly to contact with 5000 Turks. Gallipoli, in time, distance and professional skill of both commanders and men, seemed eons away. After an artillery bombardment, 60th and 74th with 10th in reserve, swept over the Turkish positions in triumph and remained south of the town until Chauvel's horsemen had secured the wells. By evening that day, Beersheba was in Allied hands.

It is axiomatic that operational plans are viable only until the first shot of the battle, and thereafter have to be amended (or massaged) to meet changing situations. Failure to observe this rule was Hubert Gough's weakness at Third Ypres. A situation arose at Beersheba which was to demonstrate that Allenby, and Chetwode, had the flexibility of mind which is the mark of great commanders.

The second blow against Gaza on the night of 1–2 November maintained the pressure and kept the enemy off balance. But the advent of the annual Khamsin winds raised a duststorm at Beersheba, increasing the water problem 'which even the staff's elaborate preparations for watering could not completely avoid'.[17]

Following the taking of Beersheba, the second phase of Chetwode's offensive was the assault on the Hureira positions between Gaza and Beersheba, where the Turks were still holding out in strong earthwork redoubts. It had been the commanders' intention that no more than two days would be allowed for preparation and approach to the next objective. Hureira would be assaulted on 4 November, allowing the enemy no respite. However adverse weather, the water problem and an unexpected strong stand by the Turks in the mountains north of Beersheba, at Khuweilfe, momentarily fixed the attention of the staff away from the primary objective. To support the Desert Mounted Corps, one of Chetwode's infantry divisions had to be deployed to overcome Khuweilfe. In the stifling heat of a duststorm, men and animals became exhausted. Chauvel's corps was unable to cut off the Turkish retreat and Chetwode's redeployment against Hureira was delayed. When Allenby at GHQ was told this, he motored at once to XX Corps headquarters to confront Chetwode, ready to provide motivation by will-power should this be necessary. However, notwithstanding his natural impulse to force the operation through, Allenby accepted the reasoning of XX Corps' commander and staff, and the assault of the Turkish redoubts was arranged for 6 November.[18]

The move forward of 10th Division to Beit Abu Taha began at 0945 on 5 November; they arrived at midday after a march in a sandstorm. That evening, the battalions crossed their start lines at 1900 hours, reaching their final assault positions at 2330. In that night-move, all brigades made a successful night march on a compass bearing, successful, that is, except for 29 Brigade headquarters, which was held up by a deep wadi. It is recorded that the temperature of the brigadier soared, but all arrived in time for the battle.[19] On the morning of 6 November, the assault on the Turkish line began.

THE CAPTURE OF THE SHERIA AND RUSHDI POSITIONS

The Turkish redoubts situated on a great open plain presented conflicting factors which rendered an attack difficult from any but a frontal assault, with all its inherent risks. Chetwode positioned 74th Division on the right, 60th in the centre and 10th on the left. 74th was to attack first and roll up the left flank of the Turkish trench system and gain ground up to the railway line. When this was taken, 60th and 10th were to commence their attack; 60th Division attacked with two brigades up, 10th with one.

The two battalions of Inniskillings and the two of Irish Fusiliers in 31 Brigade would lead the assault. The Royal Irish, Munsters and Dublins of 30 Brigade were in support to go through and hold the position in case of a counter-attack; 29 Brigade was in reserve. Brig. Morris, commanding 31 Brigade, had placed 5th Irish Fusiliers on the right supported by their 2nd Battalion, with the two Inniskillings battalions echeloned on the left. The 10th Division artillery concentrated on the enemy's trenches and on wire cutting. Each battery was to cut two ten-yard gaps in the wire.

On 6 November, Chetwode unleashed his corps. 74th, a dismounted Yeomanry Division (it had as its divisional sign a broken spur), forced home its assault well and carried its objective ahead of schedule. Two brigades of John Shea's 60th London followed fast. Brig. Morris, well up with his brigade, did not wait for Gen. Longley's order but released 31 Brigade as soon as it became obvious he could do so. The vast open plain, the mass of horse, foot and guns, was reminiscent of the bygone age of warfare. One officer with 1st Royal Irish, struck by its almost theatrical atmosphere, wrote home: 'It was like the Royal Tournament. The best sight was our artillery changing position. The battery would gallop into the open, then take up its new position, unharness the horses, which galloped back under cover.'[20]

The infantry battalions likewise added to the military spectacular, going forward steadily in artillery formation. On reaching the enemy positions, after a brief fire fight, the Irish closed with their bayonets. The enemy took to their heels, falling back to the stronger Hureira Redoubt.

> The heavy wire of the main Kauwukah position had to be methodically cut before the attack could be launched. To reach its object, the 10th (Irish) Division had to cross a perfectly flat plain, two miles wide, which was swept from end to end by enemy guns of all calibres and by machine-guns and rifle fire. The advance of this grand division marching across the fire-swept plain as steadily as though on parade was a sight never to be forgotten by those who were privileged to see it.[21]

Chetwode entrusted the last phase of the battle to 10th Irish. This was the capture of Hureira Redoubt on the Gaza-Beersheba road, widening the breach in the enemy's line. Gen. Longley again gave the 'place of honour' to

31 Brigade, which attacked on 7 November. 29 Brigade was in support and 30 Brigade in reserve. For his artillery, Longley was allocated 68 Brigade, RFA, with one additional howitzer battery, C/268. This time there were fewer galloping horses: 'However, the horses of this last were away watering and could only be brought into action by using the pack mules of 5th Irish Fusiliers.'[22]

The enemy defences were strong, wired and manned for all-around defence. They had a garrison of about 200 men with thirty machine-guns. The artillery would bombard before the attack, but because of a lack of communications between the forward troops and the battery positions, the final Irish assault had to be made without fire support over open ground. Luckily, the Turkish artillery fire was inaccurate, although heavy and sustained machine-gun fire struck 2nd Irish Fusiliers, two companies of 5th Irish Fusiliers and 6th Inniskillings. Three hundred yards from the position, the attackers went to ground. The Fusilier support company worked its way around to the left, while the Inniskillings did the same on the right where they captured an enemy trench north of a wadi. The Turkish garrison, threatened on both flanks with encirclement, retreated when the Irish Fusiliers assaulted the redoubt. Twenty-eight prisoners and four large trench mortars were captured. Gen. Longley rode forward to a position to congratulate the victors. As he rode off, two enemy guns just north of the position opened fire on him before the Inniskillings were able to capture them.

The infantry of 29 Brigade crowded onto a slight hill to watch the assault and cheer the 'Faughs'. No doubt the sight of their general under fire caused a certain hilarity, which would have turned instantly to grief had he been hit.[23] But their cheers didn't last long. Outlined on the skyline, they too drew Turkish fire, which wounded a few Connaught Rangers and mules. Next morning, 29 Brigade went through 31 Brigade and occupied the captured trenches. The Turks were in full retreat and the forward battalions were able to establish an outpost line unmolested. 1st Leinsters, relieving the Irish Fusiliers inside the redoubt, were surprised when they actually found water flowing in a wadi. All who inspected the redoubt marvelled at its cunning siting and strength, with elaborate dug-outs and trenches ten feet deep.[24] Considering the strength of the place, the Allied casualties were extraordinarily light: two officers and twenty-one other ranks killed, and five officers and ninety-four soldiers wounded. These surprisingly low casualties say much for the battlecraft and tactics developed since the same battalions assaulted Kiretch Tepe Sirt.

Hureira was the last attack of Chetwode's corps during the offensive. While it took place, Bulfin's attack was renewed in the Gaza sector. The town was captured and the Turks forced to retire from almost the whole of their positions. On 10 November the Irish concentrated at Karm under Allenby's hand. On their way, they picked up abandoned Turkish guns as booty before moving to Deir el Belah on the 17th.

The officers of the Irish battalions observed, curiously, that their troops always found marches away from the front more trying than when marching into action. On the withdrawal from Hureira Redoubt, 1st Leinsters marched to Karm about ten miles across the desert and found it 'very trying, while their forced march to Beersheba and then to Hureira [was] nothing by comparison.'[25] Because of the drying up of reinforcements from Ireland, and recurring malaria, both Leinster battalions were down to two companies, but a newly arrived draft of ninety-four men arrived, enabling the 1st Battalion to re-form in three companies.

Meanwhile, XXI Corps drove the Turks northwards along the coastal plain until 13 November, when a wheel to the eastward commenced: 'The pursuit was a very fine effort and Bulfin constantly outflanked the enemy by the sea and drove them from position to position until he reached and took Jaffa. When our left reached Jaffa, Allenby allowed the Turks no time to mount resistance on the Jaffa-Jerusalem road, in the mountains.'[26]

Bulfin's corps pursued the Turks along the Philistia plain close to the sea, turning the Turkish flanks at the mouths of the great wadis which in November were dry. Further inland, elements of the Mounted Corps reached Ramleh. On 16 November Jaffa was occupied and the Turkish forces were broken up, their Eighth Army having been driven to the north. The Turkish Seventh Army in the Judean Hills posed a threat to Bulfin's communications. 10th Division in army reserve guarded against this possibility. Allenby's next phase was to halt his left while allowing the right to advance towards Jerusalem. Not wishing to fight in the area of the Holy City, he prepared the left for another stroke. For this he switched his reserve, 10th Irish, to the left, thus enabling Bulfin to regroup for his next objective—Jerusalem.

CHAPTER THIRTY

The Capture and Defence of Jerusalem

PALESTINE, 1918

10th Division marched from Karm to Gaza. On 1 December they advanced into the line occupied by Bulfin's XXI Corps. 30 Brigade relieved part of 52nd Lowland Division. The following night, 29 and 31 Brigades took over from two brigades of the 74th Division. One of the problems facing the Irish was that the inhabitants of the villages in the area were trading information for immunity from shell-fire from the Turks. One battalion, 6th Leinsters, discovered this and ended the trade agreement. The villagers then had to endure occasional shelling from their fellow Muslims.[1]

When XXI Corps reached Jaffa, Bulfin allowed the Turks no time to mount resistance on the Jaffa-Jerusalem road in the mountains. Holding the left flank with minimum forces, XXI Corps swung east with two infantry divisions (relieved by 10th Division) and the remainder of the cavalry. They forced the Turks back in one rush through the mountains to a line about seven miles from Jerusalem. The difficulties were considerable. Only one bad road existed; this had to be improved. Others had to be made up almost precipitous mountains for the artillery and supplies. Once again, 5th Royal Irish were called for road-building in preparation for the next phase.

Allenby was concerned to avoid fighting around the Holy City. Judging the moment to be right on 8 December, he struck from the west and south. 60th and 74th Divisions from the west and 53rd Welsh Division, advancing from Hebron, passed through Bethlehem and formed a line two and a half miles south of the city. During the night, the Turks retired north and northeast from Jerusalem and next morning the city surrendered to the British. The mayor, having difficulty finding someone to accept the keys of the city, finally surrendered them to the Irishman Maj.-Gen. John Shea.

On 11 December, Gen. Allenby, followed by representatives of the Allied nations, made his formal entry into Jerusalem. Historic Jaffa gate, after years of disuse, was opened for his entry. Unlike the Kaiser, who on a state visit before the war had entered on a white Arab charger, Allenby entered and left the city on foot out of deference, as all pilgrims had for centuries. Near the gate, at the entrance to the Citadel and below the Tower of David, a proclamation was read in seven languages, announcing that order would be maintained and that the hallowed sites of all religions would be preserved for the free use of worshippers. No flags were displayed, and representatives of all allied forces, including a detachment from the Irish Division, were present.

With the capture of Jerusalem, Bulfin side-stepped once more onto the coastal plain, while Chetwode's corps advanced to positions around the city. Again it was Bulfin's corps which struck first. On the coastal plain sector, the Turks were driven from the line of the River Auja by 52nd Division. The Lowlanders, attacking on 20 December, bounced the enemy out of their positions. Once the River Auja, the only natural barrier on the plain, had been crossed, the Turks retired north of Jaffa. Allenby's whole line from Jaffa to Jerusalem was advanced about ten miles. His right extended about five miles eastwards towards the Jordan valley.

Christmas 1917 in the Holy Land was the most bleak the men of the 10th had ever had. They were situated in the area of Beit Sira, an Arab village twenty-five miles north-west of Jerusalem. Poor roads and bad weather delayed supplies and all were on half rations: 'Terrible rain on Christmas day, bully beef and a cup of rum.'[2] It was not a Merry Christmas, although all spare regimental transport had been sent back to an Expeditionary Forces Canteen depot for supplies. Only one battalion opted for all the beer its transport could carry. When loaded, this would only provide a bottle per man. The other battalions loaded completely with food, cigarettes and tobacco.[3] Nevertheless it was generally a miserable Christmas. Many, however, may have consoled themselves with the thought of being close to the beginning of 'the Word' of their faith.

Needing more room to secure his front before Jerusalem, Allenby had intended opening a new offensive with XX Corps to coincide with Bulfin's attack. Incessant rain turned the black cotton soil of the coastal plain into a morass and prevented even camel transport and supply movement. The attack was delayed until 27 December. Then, XX Corps was to attack with 60th Division on the right, 74th in the centre and 10th on the left. 60th was to advance along an axis of the Nablus road, while 10th was to attack towards the north-east, pushing back the enemy's right flank and rear, which was aimed high up the Nablus road.

At midnight on 26 December, the Turks pre-empted Chetwode's stroke and began a counter-offensive in great strength against 60th Division. In severe fighting, they drove the Londoners from some of their forward positions. After a bloody struggle throughout 27 December, the Turks were repulsed with difficulty. Chetwode used the preparations of his strike to relieve pressure on the 60th. Maintaining only light contact with Bulfin's corps, 10th Division secured the left and, with elements of 74th Division, pushed forward on 27 December.

In the operations at Deir Ibzia, or the Defence of Jerusalem, for the first time in its three-year history 10th Irish Division attacked as a complete formation under its own divisional commander. It is not difficult to imagine the deep frustration and bitter disappointment felt by Lt.-Gen. Sir Bryan Mahon and Maj.-Gen. John Langley in those intervening years.

In Chetwode's plan, one brigade of 74th Division was the right attack with its objective the eastern end of Zeitun ridge. 10th Division formed the centre and left attack. Its mission was to gain the Kereina Ridge and to form a long defensive flank facing northward, where only a thin cavalry screen guarded its flank in the rugged Judean Hills. It had the greatest distance and the most difficult country to cover.

The operation was in two phases. The attack of the 10th was carried out in two groups; the centre group, 31 Brigade, had as its objective the Kereina Ridge. Left group, consisting of 29 and 30 Brigades under Brig. Vandeleur, was to advance between Wadi Sad and 'Ain Arik and form a long defence flankguard. For the second phase, the final objective was a line of high ground beyond the village of Beitunye to the hill of Abu el 'Ainein. For contingency purposes, Chetwode attached two battalions of 74th Division to Gen. Longley.

It was a country of rugged terrain, with no roads and few tracks. High, boulder-covered hills rising to over 2000 feet were intersected with deep ravines or wadis. The mean height was not less than 1300 feet.

On Boxing Day, St Stephen's Day to the Irishmen, 10th Division attacked Zeitun Ridge. A strong position, the ridge was protected by deep, steep-walled wadis. In front of the Irish battalions, the ground rose steeply to the ridge. The Turkish defences were covered by considerable numbers of machine-guns. A formidable position, the veterans of Gallipoli remembered how the Turks had defended such positions, and might well have felt some trepidation. Adding to the risk was the country over which the artillery must cross if the division was to have artillery support. One track up the Kereina Ridge could be used, but only if it was improved. It was a formidable task for both Commander Royal Artillery and Commander Royal Engineers.

The left attack began as dawn was breaking at 0545. Lewis gun sections worked forward, engaging the Turkish positions while the infantry platoons advanced in short rushes. 1st Leinsters knocked out six machine-gun posts on their section of front. A forward liaison officer and his batman, seeing one Turkish machine-gun open up close by, took it out themselves. The Leinsters retained two captured Maxim guns; later they trained crews and used them effectively thereafter.[4] By 0900, the enemy positions on their objective, 'the Hump', had been carried.

On the left of 1st Leinsters, 5th Connaught Rangers was held up by machine-gun fire from the Hump and lack of artillery support to deal with them. Signals had run out of telephone cable for a telephone line between the artillery forward observation officer and the gun-battery positions. Half an hour later, with communications connected, the divisional artillery put the machine-guns out of action. The advance continued until held up by a deep defile which was heavily defended. Col. V.M. Scully ordered his machine-guns to sweep the ridges and rifle fire was opened from the hastily-built stone breastworks (sangars). Under its cover, two companies crossed the gorge and stormed the ridge; covering fire was maintained over their heads for as long as possible. As the Rangers charged home, the enemy fled.

6th Leinsters, between 1st Leinsters and 5th Rangers, were held up at Shabuny. The Rangers and 1st Leinsters, from their newly-won positions, poured enfilade fire into the Turkish position. Sending scouting patrols out, they discovered Shabuny had been vacated. 6th Leinsters were able to occupy it without fighting. On the other flank of the Rangers, the 6th Rifles had been held up in a way similar to the Rangers. They were also relieved when a fighting patrol of the Rangers infiltrated around the flank, threatened the enemy rear and forced the machine-guns back, allowing the Rifles to advance. 30 Brigade now went through 29 Brigade and the advance continued at considerable speed, considering the rugged terrain and the Turkish machine-gun fire. It could only have been achieved by the closest co-operation between units of all arms, infantry, artillery and engineers.

On the right, 6th Munsters continued the advance against the right of Shamrock Hill, supported by covering fire from 6th Leinsters. At the same time 7th Dublins went through 1st Leinsters to assault the left of Shamrock Hill. The Turks fled before them. During the advance on the 27th, a scouting patrol of 1st Royal Irish carried a Turkish machine-gun post at the point of the bayonet. Normally a foolhardy operation, it succeeded because 2/Lt. M. Fitzgerald handled his platoon particularly well and drove the Turks off positions which could enfilade the advancing line.[5]

A notable feature of the operation was the way in which the battalions supported each other. No senseless frontal attacks against machine-guns were made. They probed for weak spots, infiltrated and took the enemy from the flank and rear. Where a frontal assault had to be made, it was carried out under cover of heavy covering fire. Good tactics based on fire and movement were able to maintain the attack momentum with comparatively light casualties. Skill in battle was now successfully added to the Irish dash.

The 31 Brigade under Brig. Morris, 6th Inniskillings on the left, captured Kereina Peak by 0830 hours. During that fight, one of the battalion stretcher-bearers, Fus. James Duffy, went forward under fire and attended two wounded men. Then, while under Turkish fire, he carried both to safety. It was an act of supreme courage for which he was later decorated with the Victoria Cross. 6th Inniskillings halted and secured both flanks. 5th Inniskillings assaulted and captured the Hog's Back, a feature 2300 feet high. This was an important position from which Turkish observers had been able to give their artillery good target-spotting of the Kereina track where the engineers and pioneers were working. 5th Irish Fusiliers passed through the Inniskillings and pushed forward along the ridge until they came in line with the brigade of 74th Division. The first phase was ended successfully.

That night, Gen. Chetwode might well have reviewed his situation with satisfaction. On the extreme right, 60th Division had flung back the Turkish offensive. In the centre and left, his own attack was successful, so it was tempting to leave it to 10th Division to envelop the Turks. He realised, however, that the extremely difficult ground over which the 10th were operating would slow their advance. Pressure was also off the 60th. Again exercising his flexibility of mind, Chetwode ordered Shea's division to counter-attack. The Londoners would drive the Turks along the axis of the Nablus road in accordance with the original plan.[6]

Next day, 28 December, the rain stopped and the sun warmed the soldiers. 30 and 31 Brigades pushed on into the rugged hills, driving the Turks before them. Forced back from ridge to ridge, the Turks were not allowed the opportunity to make a stand. Exhausted but triumphant, 29 Brigade moved into support. 6th Irish Rifles, the flank guard on the extreme left, found touch with the Australian Mounted Division. 6th Munsters captured Abu el 'Ainein and the Khan Rubin ridge, while 31 Brigade in the centre seized Kefr Shiyan. 60th Division found the Turks exhausted and dispirited. Because of pressure by 74th and 10th Divisions, the Turks opposite 60th Division had had little support since 26 December. Allowing the Turks no rest, Shea's division of Londoners pushed them northwards along the Nablus road a distance of about fifteen miles. Allenby then gave orders for the 10th and 74th Divisions to consolidate their positions, while 60th prepared to extend the front into the Jordan valley in co-operation with the Desert Mounted Corps. Seen through the eyes of a platoon commander it was a brisk affair.

> Right well did they do their job. Indeed the dash and spirit shown by the Irishmen in their advance over these steep and boulder-strewn ridges and hills could not have been bettered; and, ably supported by our artillery, the end of the day saw us in possession of all our objectives along the entire front. Next day, 10th Division continued its advance with the same dash. By the evening of 28 December, most of the Infantry of 10th Division were in a position to act against the Turks on the Nablus road, who were already within shell-fire of the artillery. The Turkish attack was turned into a rout.[7]

When Lt. Shelbeck-Smith left 10th Division to join an Indian regiment he wrote: 'I can only say that... the men with whom I had the honour to serve, the more I saw of them the more did I learn to respect them as really fine fellows.'[8]

At the close of the December operations, Allenby's army, although elated by its success in the preceding two months, was tired by the sheer physical efforts of operating in difficult country, apart from fighting. It badly needed rest, regrouping, and time to allow the support services to catch up. The water-flooded coastal plain added to supply difficulties. London, which had been cautiously hanging onto Allenby's coat-tails after Beersheba, now urged him forward. Acting on his own counsel, Allenby heeded neither curb nor spur.

After its work in Sinai, Lt.-Col. Grogan's 5th Royal Irish concentrated on 4 December and rejoined 10th Division. Throughout December, roadwork continued, this time for its own division during the crucial battle for the defence of Jerusalem and the counterstroke after it. Without good roads the artillery could not have been brought up to its support. Long after 10th Division had departed from the Holy Land, many roads north of Jerusalem bore Irish names in their memory. During the operations of 27–28 December, only very hard work by the divisional engineer field companies and Pioneers opened up the roads. Without them, the artillery could not have moved forward in support of the infantry. Had artillery support not been available casualties would undoubtedly have been heavy. So greatly was this recognised that at the end of December on the conclusion of the operation, Gen. Longley congratulated the Pioneers in a letter to its commanding officer, Lt.-Col. Grogan DSO.

> The GOC sends his grateful thanks to you and your battalion for the masterly and rapid manner in which you opened up communications, with which today's operations would have met with far less success.
>
> (Sd) H.F. Salt Lieut Colonel
> GS 10th Division. December 27 1917.[9]

On 10 January 1918, a patrol of 1st Royal Irish blundered within fifty yards of a concealed Turkish post and was caught unawares. The Turks opened fire and attempted to cut them off. In the hasty withdrawal, one man fell from a rock and broke his ankle. The patrol commander, Cpl. Walsh, picked him up under fire and carried him to safety. For this act of gallantry he was subsequently awarded the DCM.[10] Two weeks later, Cpl. J. McCarthy, also of the 1st Royal Irish, was cleaning a grenade and ignited its fuse. Realising he could not get rid of it without endangering others, Cpl. McCarthy, in a supreme act of self-sacrifice, held the grenade in both his hands close to his body. The grenade exploded, killing himself and wounding four men. The King made the posthumous award of the Albert Medal in Gold for his gallantry. The Albert Medal in Gold is now known as the George Cross.[11]

BATTLE OF TELL 'ASUR, 9–12 MARCH 1918

In the latter half of February 1918, the British advanced eastwards, capturing Jericho and driving the Turks across the Jordan. During the beginning of March, the 53rd, 74th and 10th Divisions carried the right and right-centre of the British line forward about eight miles. On 9 March a general offensive began in which 10th Division gained the battle honour *Tell 'Asur,* in breaking the Turkish line at that place.

10th Division operated in two groups. The 30 and 31 Brigades, less a battalion of each in divisional reserve, was the right attack force, and 29 Brigade was the left attack. Each was supported by a brigade of artillery with a heavy battery for divisional counter-battery and bombardment fire. This time, the division operated in an area of cultivated, high, rolling hills and deep valleys. The dominating features were Sheir Kalrawani (2704 feet) and 'Atara (2742 feet). Across the front of 30 and 31 Brigades, Wadi el Jib, a deep boulder-strewn depression, presented a formidable obstacle.

The first objective of the right attack was the high ground between the villages of 'Atara and 'Ajul, which commanded the crossings of Wadi el Jib. That of the left attack was a line from Deir es Sudan to Nabi Salih.

The advance was delayed by dense fog and the troops did not cross the start line until 0630. But when they did, the attack was carried out with great speed. On the front of 31 Brigade, 2nd Irish Fusiliers captured Sheir Kalrawani, south-west of 'Atara. 5th Irish Fusiliers carried on the attack and took 'Atara by 0930. At the same time 30 Brigade had captured the Kalrawani Ridge, 2276 feet high.

On the left, 29 Brigade acting in concert with 232 Brigade, was tasked with the capture of Khan Rashiniyeh Plateau, Deir en Nidham, Umm Suffa Ridge and Deir es Sudan. 1st Leinsters and 6th Irish Rifles were to secure Umm Suffa and cover 6th Leinsters, taking the ridge through Deir en Nidham. All battalions secured their objectives in fine style and 1st Leinsters drove off a counter-attack. 6th Leinsters, however, met more opposition which was overcome by their six machine-guns, two Maxims over establishment. By 1100, 1st Leinsters had occupied Umm Suffa; by 1600 its patrols had reached Deir es Sudan.

Because of the rugged terrain, the artillery, in order to advance three miles, had to make a long detour of twenty miles to support the second day's operation. The last eight miles of this detour were on a track which that morning had scarcely existed. Its improvement in the required time was a fine achievement by the Royal Engineer field companies and 5th Royal Irish.[12]

The action on 10 March was notable for the severity of the struggle on the front of 1st Royal Irish. On the right, 31 Brigade forced the passage of the Wadi el Jib and seized the lower slopes of the hill which formed the main defence of Gilgal.

In the centre, the struggle was particularly severe. 30 Brigade having taken the Kalrawani Ridge on the 9th, 1st Royal Irish were ordered to reach Wadi el Jib by dawn the next day, the 10th. At 0130 Maj. Anderson, commanding the two leading companies and having neared the objective, reported by telephone that the route he had used to the wadi was bad and took nearly seven hours to traverse. He recommended the battalion should use a different route. Acting on the report, Lt.-Col. Graham decided to move his remaining half-battalion as quickly as possible and started at 0315.

The going was slow, and Graham with half C Company had only cleared the northern slopes of 'Atara hill by dawn. Directly the enemy saw the rear of the column, they opened machine-gun fire. Fire intensified as the light improved and more Turkish positions came into action. Enfiladed from both flanks, the Royal Irish took whatever cover it could find. Meanwhile, its two leading companies had attacked the objective but were held up by a rock face. Signal cables had run out and artillery support could not be demanded. A counter-attack by the Turks drove off the leaders and killed or wounded half D Company including its OC, Capt. Jeremiah O'Brien. D Company fell back on its support company. Under command of Maj. H. Anderson MC, the remnant of B and D companies held the Turks. When the Allied artillery opened fire, the Turks retired to their positions on the crest. The two Royal Irish Companies then gained the ridge crest and charged the Turkish position. The Turks stood firm, poured fire into the attackers and stopped the attack. In this, the second company commander, Capt. E. Faithfull, was killed.[13]

Col. Graham, receiving reports from returning wounded of the check to his two leading companies, gathered whatever men he could and advanced to their support. Communication with 30 Brigade headquarters was established and Brig. Greer ordered Graham to reorganise and wait. Greer ordered a company of 6th Dublins to reinforce the Royal Irish and arranged an attack for 1530 which would include artillery and machine-gun support. At 1530, Graham, with 125 men and assisted by 180 men of 6th Dublins, attacked under cover of artillery and machine-gun fire. The climb of the steep northern slopes of the Jib was stiff and the summit was not reached until 1715. Graham's forces pressed home the attack and as they did so, the Turks rose and fled.

This action, although severe, was typical of the fighting. The Royal Irish suffered three officers and twenty-two men killed and five officers and eighty-three men wounded. Maj. H. Anderson was awarded the DSO. Two MCs and a Croix de Guerre were also awarded to the battalion.[14]

The two company commanders who were killed, Capt. J. O'Brien and Capt. E. Faithfull, were buried with their men on the hilltop they had won. In a letter to Capt. Faithfull's sister, Lt. F.G. Smith wrote:

> We scrambled up knowing our only chance was to get as near the top as possible before dawn. We got to within 100 yards of the top when we found ourselves held up by immense boulders with only a space here and there for one to get over at a time. This was slow progress and dawn found us sixty yards from the top, with the crest of the hill black with Turks and bristling with machine-guns. We had no casualties up

to this, but here we had a good few killed and wounded by bombs. We built up a firing line and a general battle ensued. Machine-gun, rifle and bombs coming into action. We gained fire superiority and then charged the hill. It was at this stage that poor Eric was knocked out at about 7.00. He was charging a sangar when he was hit three times in the chest by machine-gun fire.[15]

In his last letter to his sister, Capt. Faithfull had written, 'You have no idea what attack means here, quite different from flat Flanders... The countryside is now beginning to look lovely with all the wild flowers in bloom, like a summer's day at home—perhaps fishing.'[16]

On the left, 5th Connaught Rangers passed through the Leinsters and attacked Nebi Salih, covered by 6th Leinsters and four guns of 29th Machine-gun Company. The machine-gunners maintained a steady fire on the heights near the village. The advance of the Rangers was rapid and successful. By 0630, the first objective at Nebi Salih was gained and at 0700, the village and heights were captured with slight opposition; only three soldiers were wounded. At the same time, 6th Irish Rifles went through to take the Arura Ridge near Shere Redwan. In a frontal attack, they suffered heavy casualties against a position guarded by superbly-sited machine-guns manned by Germans. Sixty men were killed, at least twice that number wounded.[17] The Rangers made an outflanking movement against the enemy position; helped by this, the Rifles gained their objective.[18]

On 12 March, the Rangers at Nebi Salih were attacked shortly after dawn by a mixed force of Germans and Turks, who were driven off by Lewis gun and rifle fire. Having failed in front, the enemy attempted to turn each flank in turn, but all attacks were repulsed. Eventually giving up, the Turks and Germans withdrew, but were punished severely in retiring across open ground. On the right, 1st Leinsters advanced against little opposition to its final objective in front of Deir es Sudan. At this point, the line was consolidated and work began on the improvement of the rough tracks throughout the divisional area.

It is interesting to note that throughout this operation, notwithstanding the ruggedness of the terrain, the Divisional Signal Company was able to maintain telephone communication from division headquarters through brigade to battalion command posts, and from there even to forward observation posts (although they ran out of cable at critical times).

During January, February and March 1918, the divisional engineers and 5th Royal Irish worked constructing roads, culverts and bridges, assisted from time to time by details from other battalions. The roads were steadily pushed northwards and contributed in no small way to the success of the campaign. For long afterwards, their Irish names showed the passage of 10th Division. One in particular, Irish Road, went from the junction of he Jerusalem-Nablus road to the coastal plain.[19]

That year in Palestine, St Patrick's Day was wet, but not in the traditional festive way. The division was in the line and only companies of each battalion could be spared for the traditional celebrations. They attended Mass and spent the remainder of the day in whatever shelter the villages offered, drying their clothing before fires. On the following days, the weather brightened. Turkish patrol activity increased and occasional skirmishes took place. On 20 March HRH the Duke of Connaught visited the 10th Division. Detachments from all the battalions attended a parade at which many officers and men were decorated.

In this period, 1st Leinsters barely escaped the famous wrath of the commander in chief, Gen. Allenby, who showed considerable concern for the antiquities and the environment of Palestine, had issued orders against cutting down trees. When he made a surprise visit to 10th Divisional area, the usual warning, 'The Bull is loose,'[20] reached the Leinsters barely in time for them to conceal the stumps of two fine cedars of Lebanon. Fearing the wrath of Allenby, which was greater than that of the Almighty, these stumps became graves, complete with crosses of two unknown Australian soldiers. Seeing them, Allenby shortly afterwards issued orders against the casual interment of dead soldiers. [21]

At the end of April, the ration strength of most battalions was much below establishment. The battalions had an average fighting strength of about twenty officers and 480 men. Some battalions were reduced to two or three companies. But in this, it was generally no worse than most other divisions, either in Palestine or on the Western Front, before the reorganisation into nine-battalion divisions.

As a result of the German March offensive on the Western Front, Allenby was forced to despatch to France two complete infantry divisions and the infantry strength of two more, plus several brigades of artillery and machine-gun companies. In all divisions except one, the departing battalions were replaced by Indian Army infantry battalions, made up of mainly young and inexperienced soldiers. The 10th Division from this time ceased to be 'Irish'.

CHAPTER THIRTY-ONE

The Fifth Army, March 1918

For the first time since April 1915, the British Expeditionary Force stood on the defensive and was about to enter its gravest period since 31 October 1914. Starved of replacements by a government which saw this denial as the only effective way of curbing the offensive ardour of its generals, Prime Minister Lloyd George had lost confidence, not in the army but in its commanders. Serious disagreement between the Chief of the Imperial General Staff (CIGS) and the PM on the conduct of the war, the allocation of large numbers of trained soldiers accumulated in the Training Reserve in Britain, and the formation of a General Reserve in France, brought matters to a head. Neglecting to inform the incumbent CIGS, Gen. Sir William Robertson, the government announced his resignation and replacement by Gen. Sir Henry Wilson. Wilson had been sent home from France; Pétain refused to have him at his headquarters and FM Haig was unwilling to find employment for him with the BEF. When told of the government's intention, Haig reacted instantly: 'The CinC at once mentioned the distrust in which General Wilson was held by the army.'[1] Nevertheless Lloyd George persisted, and Wilson, previously a firm 'Easterner' to Lloyd George, shortly became a 'Westerner', a sudden change of heart which surprised none who knew Henry Wilson.

Despite a serious manpower shortage in the BEF, and under the threat of resignation from the French Prime Minister, the Supreme War Council ordered FM Haig to take over an additional twenty-eight mile sector of front from the French in January 1918. The protestations of the CinC, BEF being over-ruled, the new sector was allocated to Fifth Army (Gen. Sir Hubert Gough).

After Passchendaele, Fifth Army was in reserve, resting its shattered corps when the news of the relocations arrived. In the first regrouping phase, Fifth Army took over the two right corps of Third Army, an additional twelve miles of frontage, making Gough's proposed front about forty-two miles. By 30 January the new sector had been taken over. The order of battle from right to left was Fifth, Third, First and Second Armies. HQ Second Army had just returned from Italy and Fourth Army had temporarily ceased to exist.

Fifth Army's order of battle and frontage

III Corps—Lt.-Gen. Sir R.H.K. Butler, 27,000 yards
58th, 18th, 14th, 2nd Cavalry and 3rd Cavalry Divisions

XVIII Corps—Lt.-Gen. Sir I. Maxse, 16,000 yards
36th, 30th and 61st Divisions

XIX Corps—Lt.-Gen. Sir H.E. Watts, 12,000 yards
24th and 66th Divisions

VII Corps—Lt.-Gen. W.N. Congreve VC, 15,000 yards
16th, 21st and 9th Divisions

In reserve—39th Division
Later, behind Fifth Army, in GHQ Reserve—20th, 8th and 50th
Divisions

At the end of 1917, intelligence estimated that the Germans would acquire a substantial superiority on the Western Front by transferring fifty divisions and thousands of guns from Russia. This was generally accepted by the Allied commanders, although precise numbers and ready-for-action dates were in dispute. Henry Wilson estimated the maximum number of enemy divisions would not be ready until late May. That they planned a massive blow against the Allied line before the arrival of American reinforcements none doubted. As usual, the essentials of the German plan, its strength, time and place of assault were unknown. To meet the threat, GHQ issued orders for strengthening defensive positions. Based on the German defensive system, there were to be three zones: Forward Zone, the existing front-line system with its support and reserve trenches; Battle Zone, about one to three miles from the front line and itself about 2000 to 3000 yards deep; and Rear Zone, four to eight miles behind the Battle Zone. However, unlike the Germans who had constructed their defence lines over a period of years, the British had only weeks to do so. It had to be accepted that, in the event of a serious German attack, the battalions manning the Forward Zone would be lost.[2]

By order of the War Cabinet, a reorganisation took place of all British divisions in France which further increased the strain on front-line battalions. The division infantry establishment was reduced from twelve to nine battalions by removing one battalion from each brigade. Many 'Service' battalions were disbanded and their personnel used to bring other battalions to strength. Where a surplus remained, 'entrenching battalions' were formed. Rear areas were trawled and the catch posted to front-line units. One battalion in 36th Division, 1st Irish Fusiliers, received fifty Army Service

Corps bakers.[3] While this reorganisation made brigades and divisions more compact and easier to command, it further reduced the number of troops manning the front line. Because of the demands made for extra-regimental employment at brigade and divisional headquarters, providing 'Defence Companies' (usually employed as batmen, grooms, postmen, runners) the average bayonet strength of battalions was 600.[4] Most of the replacement drafts from England were returned wounded; some had been wounded several times. At the same time, tens of thousands of trained men who had never been in action were retained there.[5] Battalions, which even in the trying winter of 1914–15 had been relieved every forty-eight hours, now had to man the front line for extended periods. On the eve of the German offensive, 2nd Dublins had been in the line for forty days, 1st Munsters forty-three days, and the 6th Rangers had just been relieved after twenty-four days. Even those out of the line, 'resting', had to work long hours improving defences.

Shortly after his arrival, Gough inspected the new sector and found it wanting. For over a year, it had been quiet and its defences were very neglected. Only what was now to be the Forward Zone could be considered in a state of partial readiness. When the Germans eventually attacked, the Allied Battle Zone defences were still far from complete; on the Rear Zone, little work was done beyond marking out the line. Much of the available labour was directed to the gigantic task of implementing GHQ's orders for the construction of defences. But in addition to this, the rear-area logistical infrastructure had to be constructed, along with new supply depots, ammunition dumps and camps. Access roads and railway spurs were made or improved and communications cables buried. More labour battalions eventually arrived. In six weeks, the total labour force rose from 17,400 to 48,000. But the task was still too great to complete before the German offensive.

With labour in short supply, all support arms competed for whatever was available to improve their aspect of battle preparations; none were satisfied. In addition to the needs of teeth and supporting troops were those of the services, especially the medical services. The Fifth Army Director of Medical Services[6] considered VII Corps unwise in situating the bulk of its medical services dangerously forward at Tincourt in the Cologne Valley. The DMS felt there would be no time and no transport to evacuate wounded from there in a general withdrawal. ADMS VII Corps, however, based assumptions upon being able to use ammunition and supply vehicles returning empty from the ordnance depot at nearby Hamel for the carriage of the wounded to the rear. The matter was still unresolved when the blow fell.[7] The fears of the DMS were fully justified by events.

Intelligence reports indicated to Fifth Army that the Germans were preparing an attack in their area. A German general, von Hutier, noted for mounting successful assaults in Russia, was now opposite them. Gough lost little time informing GHQ of his fears in a long letter dated 1 February 1918. It began: 'The German Eighteenth Army, under General von Hutier, who was so successful at Riga, has been interpolated opposite my front.'[8] Gough warned GHQ of German engineer work, indicating a massive build-up, including additional crossings of the St Quentin-Cambrai Canal and airfields. A blasé reply from GHQ gave little comfort: 'Of the Fifth Army front, the southern twelve miles are unlikely to be the scene of a serious hostile attack'. But significantly, it went on to say, 'it is for consideration whether our main resistance in the Fifth Army area should not be made behind the line of the River Somme.'[9]

Amplifying this last statement, GHQ instructed Gough, on 9 February, 'it may well be desirable to fall back to the rearguard defences of Péronne and the Somme'.[10] The communication then continued with 'considerations' upon Gough's rearguard defences, listing their assessment of the priorities. The protection of the crossing at Péronne secured by a bridgehead and constructing defences on the line of the Somme 'was paramount'.[11] GHQ assumptions appear to have allowed for several months' preparation against the expected attack. Gough, in fact, had a mere six weeks. It would have helped relieve Gough's army if GHQ's reserve divisions in the Fifth Army area had deployed on the line of the Somme, twelve miles behind the existing front line, and if it had commenced its fortifications at this time.

Haig, looking at the overall situation, considered his Flanders front more important than the southern sectors because he had very little space for manoeuvre to safeguard the vital Channel ports. But having visited Fifth Army, three more divisions were released to Gough. The total Allied force available to man forty miles was now eleven divisions and the cavalry corps, equivalent in rifles to about an infantry division.

It was on this visit to Fifth Army that Haig said, 'Well, Hubert, one can't fight without men'.[12] Gen. Gough had every reason to agree. But when on 18 March Gough moved his reserve, 2nd Cavalry Division and 39th Division, closer to the line and requested permission from GHQ to move 20th and 50th Divisions (of GHQ's reserve) forward, he was mildly rebuked by the Chief of Staff about thirty-six hours before the start of the German offensive and told 'that it was not sound to move reserves before the situation was clear'.[13] Nothing so infuriates a front-line commander facing imminent attack as inane clucking noises from headquarters.

German intentions for the coming battle were massive in scope. Seventeenth Army's twenty-five divisions (von Below) were to capture Arras, the pivot of the plan, and take Flesquières by divergent attack from the north. Second Army's twenty-one divisions (von der Marwitz) were to break through the British line and capture Flesquières by divergent attack from the south. Then, with the left of Second Army, they would strike north and drive the British Expeditionary Force into the sea. Eighteenth Army's twenty-five divisions (von Hutier) would attack each side of St Quentin, break the British line, cross the Somme and the Crozat Canal and advance westwards with no daily limit. Their objective was to divide the British and French armies.

This vast German army was supported by 1755 batteries of field, heavy and super-heavy guns and 3532 heavy mortars. With extraordinary efficiency, the concentration was fully completed on schedule. Ammunition stocks were positioned by 15 March; supporting artillery placed between 11th and 19th and ready on the 20th. Sixty fresh divisions were moved up on the 16th. They rested on 18–19 March and made final preparations on the 19th and 20th. Strategic and tactical surprise being deemed essential, an elaborate deception and camouflage plan was put into operation which succeeded in holding French and British reserves in other areas until long after the attack was launched.

The German offensive against the British Front opened at 0430 on Thursday 21 March, with a five-hour bombardment of unprecedented ferocity, even by 1917 standards. This was planned to destroy not only the defences but also disrupt communications to a depth of 15,000 yards. Using 10,005 guns and heavy mortars along the threatened front, the Germans first swamped the British line with a deadly mixture of chlorine, mustard and tear gas, which reached far into rear areas. Everywhere Allied troops were forced into their respirators for several hours. The gas was followed by high explosive shells which rained on trenches, battery positions, camps, depots, headquarters, crossroads, roads, railways and communication sites. Mortar fire flattened forward defensive wire belts. Movement on the British front was severely interrupted. Prolonged wearing of respirators caused claustrophobic sensations; coupled with the deafening noise of the barrage, this induced some disorientation. Horses, upon which artillery greatly depended for movement, had to be protected, and their nose-bag type of respirator caused panic and terror, adding to the confusion. Shell-fire slaughtered men and horses. Transport and artillery movement were severely restricted.

Communications were cut, so all units and formations fought blind. Even signal rockets were ineffective because of fog. Little artillery support could be given to the hard-pressed infantry.

> Previous experience had been sufficiently decisive to make all signal personnel absolutely certain that, when the attack came, the first thing that would happen would be the failure of line communication all along the front. No one, however, could have foreseen the completeness with which that prophecy would come true. The work of the German artillery was to be far in advance of anything previously achieved.[14]

The German assault divisions, which had been practising their tactics for months, were closed up, all moving forward simultaneously. Reserve formations came under combat commanders once they entered his zone. It was no coincidence that in many places the heaviest attacks were directed against British corps boundaries, the weakest points. The German attack was launched in a thick fog which was caused by a warm March day on the 20th, following a wet one on the 19th, which greatly aided the Germans. By the evening of Day One, British Fifth Army Forward Zone and a great part of the Battle Zone had been over-run. Losses to the enemy were great, but not as heavy as had been expected because fog masked their movement and restricted the fields of fire for machine-guns, 'many of our posts being annihilated by the artillery fire before a single German appeared, and many others losing a large proportion of their effectives.'[15]

Shortly after midday, the fog had lifted sufficiently for Allied aeroplanes to take off. Shortly afterwards, they reported masses of Germans moving forward; roads ten to fifteen miles behind their lines were 'packed with troops': 'I spoke on the telephone to all the four corps commanders during the early afternoon, and told them that our policy was to fight a delaying action, holding up the enemy as long as possible, without involving the troops in a decisive struggle to hold any one position.'[16]

Gough's last-minute instructions to his corps commanders indicate a lack of formal policy relative to the conduct of operations on Fifth Army front. That the army commander should have to telephone such a last-minute order, followed by signal confirmation, shows a lack of rapport and clear understanding about the nature of the imminent battle. In view of the exchange of letters between Gough and GHQ, followed by a discussion with the CinC, the need for such a last-minute declaration of policy is incomprehensible.

THE SECOND BATTLE OF THE SOMME, 21 MARCH–5 APRIL 1918

By evening on 21 March, the situation on the Fifth Army front became clear. On the III Corps' front, 14th Division, which had been concentrated forward, was roughly handled and driven back a considerable distance, threatening the security of its flanks of 36th and 18th Divisions. Gough confirmed Gen. Butler's decision to move III Corps behind the Crozat Canal, and 3rd Cavalry Division was sent to reinforce Butler from army reserve.

Within XVIII Corps, all three divisions had lost their Forward Zone but held the forward edge of the Battle Zone. The units in the forward area, however, were completely lost. The corps' right flank was threatened by the retirement of III Corps and the loss of Essigny, and the left flank by the loss of Maissemby. The corps commander, Gen. Maxse, was ordered to hold as long as possible but to conform with the movement of his flanks.

Watt's XIX Corps, the smallest corps, had both its flanks flung back to the rear edge of the Battle Zone, but its centre held on the forward edge. Maissemby on the right and Templeux on the left were lost, but in the centre Le Verguier was held. A cavalry division from army reserve had been committed to Gen. Watts. A reinforcement division from GHQ reserve was ordered forward, but would not arrive until the morning of 22 March.

Congreve's VII Corps had held the Battle Zone everywhere except at the extreme right where Ronssoy was lost. Epéhy, key to the Flesquières salient, had held. His left, against the salient, had been only lightly attacked. An army reserve division was committed to cover the Cologne Valley at the junction of XIX and VII Corps.

It took GHQ some time before they realised the gravity of Gough's position. This was possibly because of initial over-optimistic chords struck by Fifth Army, mistakenly making a *sang-froid* pose instead of accurate military judgments.[17] When Gough spoke to Gen. Lawrence, the Chief of the General Staff, on the telephone that evening and outlined the situation after the day's battle, he expressed his fears for the morrow and succeeding days, and received bland reassurances in reply. Understandably, Gough's anxiety was only increased by Lawrence. Gough wanted immediate reinforcements, not asinine, soothing noises.

> Lawrence did not seem to grasp the seriousness of the situation; he thought that 'the Germans would not come on again the next day'. 'After the severe losses they suffered,' he thought that they 'would be busy clearing the battlefield, collecting their wounded, reorganising and resting their tired troops.' I disagreed emphatically but failed to make much impression.[18]

Sir Hubert found himself at the receiving end of the same obtuseness which his own corps and divisional commanders had experienced at Passchendaele.

CHAPTER THIRTY-TWO

The March Offensive: 36th Division, St Quentin, 12 January–22 March 1918

The divisional front opposite St Quentin ran from Sphinx Wood to the St Quentin-Roisel railway line, about 6000 yards. It was 'a quiet front and not uncomfortable'.[1] Later, the front held was reduced on the right flank to the St Quentin Canal.

The losses of 1917 and the continued lack of replacements from Ireland meant that 36th Division was seriously under-strength. It was only partially relieved by the general reorganisation of the BEF. To bring its manning levels to establishment, it was necessary to transfer to the 36th all regular battalions of the Ulster-based regiments—1st and 2nd Royal Inniskilling Fusiliers, 1st Royal Irish Fusiliers and 1st Royal Irish Rifles. This would be in addition to the regular and service battalions already posted in. The 10th and 11th Inniskillings and the 8th/9th, 10th and 11th/13th Irish Rifles were disbanded.[2] The dismemberment of these units, although necessary, could only have brought heartache to all concerned.

Following its reorganisation, the order of battle was:

107 Brigade	108 Brigade	109 Brigade
1st R. Irish Rifles	12th R. Irish Rifles	1st R. Inniskilling Fusiliers
2nd R. Irish Rifles	1st R. Irish Fusiliers	2nd R. Inniskilling Fusiliers
15th R. Irish Rifles	9th R. Irish Fusiliers	9th R. Inniskilling Fusiliers

Divisional Pioneers: 16th Royal Irish Rifles (Pioneers)

The reorganisation meant a fundamental change in the character of the division. The original 36th, composed largely of the Ulster Volunteer Force and mainly Ulster-Scot,[3] had been killed, wounded or taken prisoner in the battles of 1916 and 1917. The regular battalions were recruited from the whole spectrum of Ireland's religious and political spheres. If some of them were unhappy at being posted to the 36th, the surviving original Ulster Volunteer Force men were not altogether happy with the newcomers. An officer of 8th Royal Irish Rifles reflected afterwards: 'That day, the 6th February, I will always remember as one of the most depressing that I have ever come through… We were such a happy crowd that it is difficult to realise the feeling of depression that settled down on everyone at the prospect of parting.'[4]

On arrival in his new battalion, the regular 2nd Royal Irish Rifles, he felt unwelcome: 'We were looked upon as strangers by most of the officers who were not originally Ulster Division officers at all and who were not inclined to look at things from an Ulster point of view.'[5]

In reality, of course, the Ulster Division had become more representative of all the people and views of Ulster than at any time previously. Illustrating the change, and harmony, were two occurrences in March. On St Patrick's Day, Mass was celebrated and shamrock distributed throughout the division. At the same time, the adjutant of 15th Irish Rifles requested the Senior Chaplain 107 Brigade, Father Henry Gill SJ, DSO MC, chaplain to 2nd Royal Irish Rifles since 1914, to conduct a burial service.[6] Before Cambrai, such events would have been unthinkable.

THE FRONT OF 36TH DIVISION

The divisional front was well suited for defence, a series of ridges and valleys running roughly parallel with the front. On the first ridge was the edge of the Forward Zone, on which also rested the German outpost line. Behind was the deep Grugies Valley, which was studded with machine-guns, rising to another ridge on which stood a line of redoubts. From the right were Jeanne d'Arc, Racecourse and Boadicea Redoubts. On a third, slighter, ridge was the second line of redoubts of the Battle Zone, some six thousand yards behind the front edge of the Forward Zone.

The divisional front ran east-west across the southern suburbs of St Quentin. On the right and left flank of the 36th, the front took a northerly turn around St Quentin. An enemy would therefore have to penetrate deep into flanking formations to outflank the division.

All of the works in the Battle Zone were constructed from scratch. These were, from the right, Station, Quarry and Ricardo redoubts. Many of the trenches were no more than eighteen inches deep, on the principle that when the time came, those who would shelter there would deepen the trench themselves. Because of the spacing and ground, none of the positions were mutually supporting; all could simply be bypassed, cut off and assaulted in isolation. Gen. Maxse, the corps commander, made it clear to his troops that once attacked, the outpost line was to fall back on the line of redoubts and the redoubts would have to hold out for up to forty-eight hours until a counter-attack relieved them. Artillery was to deny the ground between the line of redoubts.

Their right flank neighbours gave the Ulstermen cause for concern. Irish officers noticed that their neighbouring division on that flank, 14th Light Division, were massed in the forward areas and not deployed in depth. When representations were made through Corps to Fifth Army headquarters, a reply was to sort it out themselves.[7]

Early in March 1915, Sir Douglas Haig, while inspecting Fifth Army front, visited 36th Division. In conversation with Gen. Nugent, he was fulsome in his praise. Oliver Nugent, possibly remembering that William Hickie had left the 16th Division shortly before, shrewdly observed:

> I have a suspicion that he [Haig] meant it as a farewell and that my days in command of a Division out here are numbered. The new Chief of the Staff was with him, Lawrence. I spoke to him and said I hoped I should not be one of the officers to have to go home. He did not say I was going to be one of these, but said it was necessary to give promotion to younger men and that it was decided that a number of the older Divisional Commanders were to go home and command Divisions at home... I feel I am to be one of them.[8]

All through March, constant reports were being received of an enemy build-up opposite Fifth Army. There was much noise at night as well as daylight sighting of German officers with maps studying the ground. The daily-expected attack was not awaited with confidence: 'The prayer of each battalion was that they might not be in the front line when the day arrived.'[9] On the 20th, two German deserters brought word of impending assault, massed mortars and artillery. St Quentin was packed with waiting troops. 61st Division raided on the night of 20–21 March, and took a prisoner who said an attack was to be launched the following morning. As a result, corps launched a pre-emptive artillery barrage from 0230–0300, sending heavy rolling barrages searching dead ground and likely concentration areas.

That morning, the divisional deployment was:

	Forward Zone	Battle Zone	Reserve
Right			
108 Bde	12th R. Irish Rifles	1st R. Irish Fusiliers	9th R. Irish Fusiliers
Centre			
107 Bde	15th R. Irish Rifles	1st R. Irish Rifles	2nd R. Irish Rifles
Left			
109 Bde	2nd R.Inniskilling F.	1st R. Inniskilling F.	9th R. Inniskilling F.

On the night of 17 March many of the British batteries moved location, which proved fortuitous. On the morning of 21 March the entire area was mist-covered when, with an earth-shaking crash, the German hurricane bombardment began. Hundreds of guns and mortars rained shells and bombs on the lines of forward defences. High explosive was mixed with gas and smoke. At the same time heavy guns searched out the rear areas, particularly the canal crossings. Heavy fire was directed on the redoubts, and the bombardment saturated the old battery positions; only their timely move had saved them from total destruction. Morning mist added to the confusion. At 0500 it was impossible to see ten yards, and visibility remained poor until the afternoon. Five minutes after the commencement of the bombardment the order 'man battle stations' was given. It was hardly necessary.

Using infiltration tactics so successfully tried during the counterstroke at Cambrai, the German initial assault waves avoided the known keeps and redoubts of the Zone of Resistance. Bypassing them, they pressed into the Battle Zone, which was still covered by the mist. Although it was heavily attacked in front, the main thrust of the German attack was not through St Quentin onto the front of the 36th, but to its right flank division, the 14th Light. Nevertheless, the enemy assault was made in such strength and determination that the scattered posts of the Forward Zone, taken in front and flank, were overwhelmed in the mist before they realised the enemy were upon them.[10] By noon the redoubts in the Forward Zone had been cut off and fallen, but certain isolated posts fought on gallantly. On the right of the Line of Resistance, C Company, 12th Irish Rifles, resisted strongly throughout the day. The company commander, Capt. L.J. Johnston, led his men forward to its battle position. On the way they destroyed a German patrol. Ominously, its presence indicated to Johnston that the Germans had broken through into the Battle Zone. By 1100, the strongpoints held by A and D Companies were captured. Johnston's company held its position in Foucard Trench for four hours. At times the enemy gained entry and were expelled in bitter hand to hand fighting. An attempt to use a flame-thrower against them at midday was scotched in flames.

Shortly afterwards, the fog suddenly lifted and it became obvious to C Company what progress the enemy had made. From their positions, Johnston's men could see Germans swarming about Jeanne d'Arc Redoubt (which held B Company and battalion headquarters) about a mile to their rear. Further to the right, German cavalry could be seen advancing through positions which ought to have been held by 14th Division. Then, astounded, they watched a column of German transport appear, three hundred yards long, moving steadily down the St Quentin-La Fere road within easy range. Undaunted by the realisation that their own position was now perilous, they struck hard at the enemy with Lewis guns and rifles. In minutes the column of horses and men was a mass of destruction.[11]

The Germans reacted swiftly and attacked the company from both flanks. The company commander ordered a withdrawal to Lejeune Trench 500 yards behind. The enemy followed up fiercely and with great courage, a single German with bayonet fixed charged the position![12] This incident clearly demonstrated the offensive spirit of the attackers. C Company was joined by the battalion forward headquarters from Le Pontchu Quarry. Numbering nearly 120 men, it fought on resolutely. In mid-afternoon, a German company appeared marching along in fours. Fire was held until the last moment. Then concentrated rapid fire annihilated the enemy.

Surrounded, the end for C Company and for Johnston's men came quickly about 1600 when a tank appeared down the main road, taking the trench in enfilade with machine-gun fire while a battalion attacked their front. Their position was hopeless and Johnston, to save his remaining men, about 100 including many wounded, from useless slaughter, surrendered. His was the most courageous stand that day. After the war, when his exploit became known, Johnston was deservedly awarded the Military Cross.[13]

It must be said that an analysis of the death casualties shows that the resistance of all other elements of the battalion was not as resolute as that of C Company: 'They surrounded us, the whole battalion was made prisoners. I vividly remember smashing my rifle and throwing the bolt away.'[14] Total killed and died of wounds of 12th Rifles were four officers and thirty-five men. Many of these must have been suffered by the gallant C Company.

By 1200, the Germans had captured the entire Forward Zone, except the area dominated by C Company, and were attacking the Battle Zone. Shortly after noon, divisional artillery units began preparing to withdraw. The 173 Brigade RFA was forced to abandon its guns, but removed the breech blocks before doing so. In the centre, 107 Brigade reported the enemy was in Contescourt.[15] A company of 2nd Rifles attempted to recover the position there, but was repulsed. When the mist cleared, the defensive machine-guns in the Battle Zone at last became effective. On the left, 30th Division was also holding its Battle Zone, but on the right the 14th Division had already been flung back with the loss of Essigny.

This loss was grave. Deployed as it was in the Somme Valley, the presence of the enemy on dominating heights on the flanks of 36th Division made its position precarious.[16] About midday, with the clearing of the fog, the seriousness of the position became apparent to divisional headquarters. The enemy, penetrating deep into 14th Division's Battle Zone, had captured Essigny and were now threatening the entire right of 36th. By 1300, the front of 108 Brigade was turned. Divisional signals had restored line communications with Station Redoubt and headquarters 1st Irish Rifles reported fierce fighting in progress. They confirmed the withdrawal of 41 Brigade on its right. In the centre sector of Racecourse Redoubt, repeated German attacks were beaten off by the courage and determination of the local commander, 2/Lt. E. de Wind, until he was killed. His citation for the Victoria Cross tells of his heroism.

> For most conspicuous bravery and self-sacrifice on 21 March 1918, at the Racecourse Redoubt near Grugies. For seven hours he held this important post, and, though twice wounded and practically single-handed, he maintained his position till another section could be got to his help. On two occasions, with two NCOs only, he got out on top, under heavy machine-gun and rifle fire, and cleared the enemy out of the trench, killing many. He continued to repel attack after attack until

he was mortally wounded and collapsed. His valour, self-sacrifice and example were of the highest order.[17]

Station Redoubt were still holding at 1430, but the enemy south of Essigny had advanced to a depth of 3000 yards behind the front of 14th Division's Battle Zone. Brig. Griffith ordered his reserve battalion, 9th Irish Fusiliers, to the rear of Essigny with orders to prevent the enemy from turning the right flank. 1st Inniskillings were holding well on the left of the division, so Gen. Nugent moved 9th Inniskillings from the left to the right flank to support 9th Irish Fusiliers. By 1700, 9th Inniskillings were in position east of Station Redoubt behind the railway line. Their commanding officer, Col. Peacocke, reported that 41 Brigade (14th Division) were still holding on. The position on the right had stabilised.

Fighting took place all across the divisional front throughout the afternoon and confirmation was eventually received of the fall of the redoubts in the Forward Zone, with its three battalions completely lost. The 61 Brigade (20th Division) was placed under command of 36th and was ordered to man the St Simon defences, an arc covering the hairpin bend in the Canal de St Quentin.

North of the Somme Valley, up to 1400, there was no penetration of any part of the Battle Zone held by the 30th and 61st Divisions. When the fog lifted, the enemy changed tactics and tried to work up the trenches by bombing. In places where the defences proved strong, enemy attacks against the 61st Division stopped. When the Germans broke through XIX Corps' right in the Omignon Valley, 61st Division threw back a defensive flank and retained a firm hold of its position. At 1400, practically the whole of the XVIII Corps Battle Zone still held. The 20th Division was taken by Gen. Gough from GHQ reserve and was placed at Gen. Maxse's disposal at 1300.

The Battle Zone of XIX Corps lay on ground very favourable for defence, a sea of low ridges and shallow depressions between the valleys of the Omignon and the Cologne rivers. But in the fog, the Germans were able to overwhelm the Forward Zone, breaking into the Battle Zone and making significant successes on each flank.

It became clear that a complete breakthrough had occurred on the extreme right of Fifth Army, affecting the whole of III Corps. Gen. Gough toured the front visiting his corps commanders, seeing and hearing for himself. Acting on this, Gough placed 20th Division at Maxse's disposal. Its 61 Brigade was ordered to support the 36th Division, making up for the loss of three battalions in the Forward Zone. Gough also ordered all divisions south of the Somme to withdraw to the Crozat Canal. This meant that, although it still held its Battle Zone, the 36th would have to conform to the movement of III Corps and withdraw behind the Somme-Crozat Canal. The remainder of XVIII Corps, helped by 20th Division, remained in its original position.[18]

That night beginning at about 2230, using 1st Inniskillings as a pivot, Gen.

Nugent swung his division back behind the canal. 61 Brigade was ordered to withdraw across the canal, keeping in touch with 14th Division. The Germans held back while the withdrawal took place and it was completed before dawn on 22 March. Serious losses had been sustained. In addition to losing three battalions of the Forward Zone, the three battalions in the Battle Zone were reduced to 250 men each; only the three reserve battalions were at reasonable strength.[19] The fighting strength of the division now numbered less than 3000 men. Additional to the infantry losses were the casualties suffered by the artillery. Many guns had been lost in the withdrawal. To replace them, two batteries of 91 Brigade of 20th Division and 232 Siege Battery were placed under command.

The early hours of 22 March passed quietly; like the preceding day it was misty. 1st Inniskillings were attacked and retired on the Ricardo Redoubt. They were ordered to hold this line, covering the withdrawal of the 36th. They did so with tenacity.

> The 1st Battalion the Inniskilling Fusiliers are the heroes of this Division. They are one of the regular battalions. Their duty was to hold a redoubt in the line and they held it to the end. No man came back from it. They beat back twelve different attacks made by the 1st Guard Division of the Prussians. They were ordered to hold this line and they held it to the end. It is a great and gallant story.[20]

In their splendid stand, 1st Inniskillings lost four officers and eighty-two men killed or died of wounds. It was the greatest loss suffered by a battalion of the Ulster Division on 21–22 March.

9th Inniskillings was compelled to fight a rearguard action back to the Happencourt-Fluquieres Line, where they linked with troops of 60th Brigade. On the right, the Canal Line held although the enemy had brought up gun batteries, trench mortars and machine-guns under cover of the mist and was bombarding it heavily. Rfn. Albert Wilson of 9th Rifles was cut off at the canal and taken prisoner. A German officer greeted him in good English with the words, 'It's a long way to Tipperary, Mac.' Before he was sent to the rear, Wilson and the other prisoners were made to bury German dead (he was pleased to note there were many of them). But he was somewhat repelled by being made to first strip them of their uniforms and boots for salvage.[21]

Suddenly, at midday on 22 March, commander XVIII Corps ordered a withdrawal behind the Somme. It was said to have been caused by a misunderstanding between Maxse and Gough.[22] The effect was a withdrawal, in daylight across a distance of eight to nine miles, which was only accomplished by severe fighting.

When Gough was told of this order, he directed that XVIII Corps rearguards should delay the enemy as long as possible, maintaining contact with the right of XIX Corps. This order was not passed on to the divisions concerned and all fell back as directed by the corps commander.[23] Two entrenching battalions were sent rearwards to occupy and entrench the line of the Somme, and details of engineers and men from the corps' reinforcement holding unit and corps' schools were ordered to man it. 36th Division was ordered to withdraw and to hold a front from the junction with III Corps on the Crozat Canal to Sommette Eaucourt, remaining in touch with 30th Division.

During the withdrawal, the stand of 1st Inniskillings in Ricardo Redoubt delayed the enemy and allowed 36th Division to retire to the Green Line almost unmolested, except for machine-gunning by two German aircraft. But the other two divisions, 30th and 61st, were not so fortunate and took severe casualties when they fell back across open country. Maxse's precipitate withdrawal also had severe consequences for the northern corps. XIX Corps had its right flank uncovered for a distance of three miles, which forced its commander, Gen. Watts, to move his only reserve division to cover it. This left him without adequate reserves when the enemy attacked in strength down the Cologne Valley at the junction of XIX and VII Corps, where 16th Division was.

Gen. Maxse's order also had a disheartening effect on his troops, who failed to see the reason for the withdrawal on their front. In the absence of positive information, all suspected disaster had befallen elsewhere because on their own front, once they disengaged, rearguards were engaged only by German patrols.[24] Maxse's similar action, when commanding 1 Guards Brigade in 1914, had left 2nd Munsters standing alone at Etreux.

All road bridges across the Somme in their area had been prepared for demolition by 36th Division's 121st and 150th Field Companies, and these were blown once it was thought all troops had crossed. On one bridge at Tugny, covered by 150th Field Company RE, the time-fuse failed just as the enemy approached the bridge. To save it from capture, Lt. C.L. Knox, RE, rushed forward as the enemy were actually advancing on the main bridge. Climbing under the steel frame, he placed an instantaneous fuse in position and ignited it himself. His death seemed certain to all who watched, but in the explosion he miraculously escaped unscathed. Hardly surprisingly for such an act of cool heroism, he was later awarded the Victoria Cross. But in the confusion, a rearguard of three platoons left on the wrong side of the canal was captured. The withdrawal of the brigades of 36th Division was complete at 2300 when the last troops passed through Pithon.

108 Brigade took over the defence of the canal bank from left of 7th DCLI to Sommette-Eaucourt, taking under command 21st Entrenching Battalion. 107 Brigade moved to Eaucourt and Cugny, with 109 Brigade moving to Brouchy in support. No touch could be obtained with 30th Division on the left. Effectively, both flanks of 36th Division were open.

At 0200 on 23 March, 36th Division, with attached troops, held a line of canals from a mile and a half north-west of Jassy to a mile west of Sommette-Eaucourt, a distance totalling about five miles. Manning it were, from right to left: 61 Brigade; 7th SLI, 7th DCLI, with 12th King's in support. This was in essence the only properly organised subordinate formation in the division.

Divisional headquarters had withdrawn to Freniches, and its attenuated brigades had to be drastically reorganised to form effective fighting units.

When reorganised the composition of each brigade was:

108 Brigade: The remnants of 12th Rifles, 9th Irish Fusiliers, 1st Irish Fusiliers, 21st Entrenching Battalion and a Composite Unit of details from support troops.

109 Brigade: 9th Inniskillings and the remnants of 1st and 2nd Inniskillings.

107 Brigade: 2nd Irish Rifles, and the remnants of 1st and 15th Irish Rifles.

The Pioneer Battalion, 16th Rifles, was at Sommette-Eaucourt working on defences. The 36th Machine-Gun Battalion had been destroyed. Its few surviving machine-gun detachments were distributed between the brigades.

The attached artillery was ordered to rejoin its own division. This left 36th Division to depend on the remnants of its own Divisional Artillery for support. So reduced was this by losses that the remaining gun sections had to be reorganised into two artillery groups named after their commanders.

Erskine Group. Three composite batteries were formed from the survivors of two field artillery brigades and were positioned on the right around Aubigny.

Ely Group. Was composed of elements of five field artillery batteries and one gun section of B Battery 232 Army Brigade. The Group was positioned on the left near Brouchy. All the heavy artillery had withdrawn out of range.

During the afternoon of 22 March, engineers of 36th Division took over from XVIII Corps the responsibility for demolishing the bridges in Ham and along the river and canal to Ollezy. All were destroyed except the vital railway bridge at Pithon near Ham, which had not been prepared for demolition by the French railway authorities whose responsibility it was. French railway troops did all the damage possible with insufficient explosives, and a small party of 121st Field Company was subsequently despatched to destroy it 'by whatever means possible'. But explosives could not be supplied and the party were never heard of again. From German sources, it was discovered after the war that the bridge was almost intact when captured by No. 3 Foot Guard Regiment. However, they reported being held up by heavy fire until 1100.[25] From this, it would appear that the Ulstermen, unable to destroy the bridge, defended it heroically until all were killed. Once carried, the bridge was quickly repaired by German engineers and their infantry and artillery poured across the Somme.

CHAPTER THIRTY-THREE

The March Offensive: 16th Division

16TH DIVISION, 1918

Following the reorganisation of 16th Division the order of battle was:

47 Brigade	48 Brigade	49 Brigade
6th Connaught Rangers	2nd R. Munster Fusiliers	2nd R. Irish
2nd Leinster Regiment	1st R. Dublin Fusiliers	7th (SIH) R. Irish
1st R. Munster Fusiliers	2nd R. Dublin Fusiliers	7th/8th R. Inniskilling Fusiliers

Divisional Pioneers: 11th R. Hampshire Regiment (P)

Only four New Army battalions remained: the others were disbanded and their men posted to regular battalions, enabling them to retain their essential Irish character. Two battalions, 7th Royal Irish Rifles and 7th/8th Royal Irish Fusiliers, about 1000 men, had been posted to 36th Division.

At the same time as the reorganisation occurred, Maj.-Gen. W.B. Hickie, who had commanded the division in France for over two years, fell ill on 10 February 1915 and Brig. Ramsay took over temporary command. A new commander, Maj.-Gen. C.P.A. Hull, was appointed on 23 February.

The front, extending from the left of 66th Division in the Cologne Valley for 5000 yards to the boundary with 21st Division south of Epéhy, was a pronounced salient. The Forward Zone was narrow, less than 2000 yards, with re-entrants between the spurs of the ridge. It consisted of a well-wired outpost line with strongpoints and numerous machine-gun posts, upon which its strength heavily depended. The forward edge of 16th Division's Battle Zone ran along the crest of a ridge on which stood Ronssoy, Lempire and Epéhy. Two trench lines, almost continuous, ran along the forward edge of the Battle Zone on each side of the Epéhy-Lempire road; these were Red Line (or forward line) and Yellow Line. The straggling villages of Ronssoy-Lempire were wired and entrenched as one defended area. A switch (lateral trench) south of Ronssoy was intended to provide complete flank defence for the zone, but in places only a single belt of wire protected it. Behind the Yellow Line, the ground sloped down two miles to the Brown Line in front of St Emilie on the rear boundary of the Battle Zone. The Brown Line was well wired and entrenched. However, a third line of defence, the Green Line, was wired but the trench line was only marked.

Corps HQ ordered that, in case of attack, the posts in the front line were to retire, but the strongpoints and defended areas were to hold out to the last. A major limiting factor, however, was the inability of units to fully garrison the posts and switches since the reduction of the divisional establishment.

At the opening of the German March offensive, the division was deployed with two brigades in line and one in corps reserve. Because of ground configuration, the two brigades were concentrated on the Ronssoy Ridge. 49 Brigade on the right had two battalions in the Forward Zone and one in the Battle Zone; 48 Brigade had three battalions in line, each with two companies in the Forward Zone and two companies in the Battle Zone. The third brigade was held back in corps reserve. The divisional reserve was the three companies of the pioneer battalion.

Forward Zone	Battle Zone
49 Brigade—2nd Royal Irish, 7th Royal Irish	7th/8th Inniskilling Fusiliers
48 Brigade—Two companies each of	Two companies each of
2nd Dublins, 1st Dublins, 2nd Munsters	

Divisional reserve—11th Hampshire (P)
Corps reserve—47 Brigade 6th C. Rangers, 7th Leinsters, 1st Munsters

The brigade held in corps reserve was so far behind the front that, in the opinion of the divisional commander, it could not respond quickly to render timely assistance in case of an attack.[1]

Forward concentration, contrary to the principles of defence in depth, was made on the express order of the corps commander, Gen. Congreve. Gen. Hull protested over Congreve's head to Fifth Army commander, who visited 16th Division to resolve the difference. The Divisional Machine-Gun Officer, Maj. K.S. Mason, describes the scene.

General Gough arrived on the morning of 14 March and stayed until after tea… I was present at lunch time and for part of the discussion and had to show General Gough my map of the M-G positions in the front system. General Gough would not agree to any alteration in the disposition of the troops, but promised to discuss with GHQ the question of moving forward the division in reserve.[2]

Defending the existing deployment, Gough proclaimed: 'The Germans are not going to break my line.'[3] It was not best calculated to inspire confidence at a divisional headquarters facing imminent attack. The effect of Gough's visit was to leave behind an air of gloomy pessimism at HQ 16th Division.[4]

A British sector awaiting an attack had not been so thinly manned since the first battle of Ypres. Since then, the size and weight of enemy artillery had vastly increased. Elements of a total of five German divisions were opposite two Irish brigades. From this it was deduced that 16th Division was astride the main German thrust line.[5] It was the German intention to pinch out the Flesquières salient by a convergent attack north and south of the bulge, with only subsidiary holding attacks on the salient itself which was drenched with mustard gas during the offensive. The main southern thrust would strike at the corps junction of 16th and 66th Divisions. There, because of the ground configuration, a co-ordinated defensive line was difficult.[6] Four enemy divisions were massed to breach the British defences at the corps boundary, wheel north and roll up the British line like a tidal wave swamping sea defences.

Across 16th Division's front the night was fine. There was little or no wind and a slight haze which developed into thick fog towards dawn. Visibility was generally reduced to twenty or thirty yards, and in places not more than ten yards. Troops manning the Red Line reported that their own wire could not be seen.[7] Shortly after the bombardment started, gas was detected and respirators worn. By 0630, nearly all telephone cables were cut between brigade and battalion headquarters, from battalions to support artillery, and to flanking battalions. Command and control along the front became deaf and dumb as well as blind. At 0630, the enemy barrage intensified. A ferocious bombardment by heavy trench mortars, directed against the front-line wire and observation posts and strongpoints, continued until 0900 when the assault began.[8] Defensive wire was flattened and most remaining cable cut. Trenches and dug-outs were destroyed, their garrisons mostly killed or wounded. When the enemy deemed the front sufficiently softened up, infantry attacks were launched up the valleys leading to the ridge from the Schelde valley. In the last phase of the bombardment, all surviving cable between Irish companies and platoons was badly cut or completely destroyed. No help could be summoned. Thick fog rendered ineffective the elaborate machine-gun cross-fire of sixty-four machine-guns in the defence system. Grenades at ten yards were more deadly, and this became the main enemy assault weapon.

With considerable battlecraft, the Germans infiltrated between the posts, surrounded them, and after a hail of grenades, rushed and captured them by weight of numbers. One by one the posts were picked off. Because the division's Forward Zone lacked depth in most cases, the enemy was upon them before the defenders could rally to resist. Those who could fired their SOS signal rockets, but in the fog these were unseen.

DEFENCE OF THE ZONES, 49 BRIGADE

Three battalions of the two oldest Irish regiments faced the main weight of the German flank attack. 2nd and 7th Royal Irish were on the extreme right of the divisional line; behind them, 7th/8th Royal Inniskilling Fusiliers defended Ronssoy.

The Royal Irish companies moved to battle positions at about 0400 on 21 March and were caught in the barrage. Two forward companies of 7th Royal Irish suffered badly. One was annihilated; only one badly-wounded officer, 2/Lt. P.J. Gibson DCM, and a few men got through. Half of the other company was killed or wounded. Despite this crushing loss, posts at Z Copse, Queuchettes Wood and Basse Boulogne resisted fiercely. Pte. R. Barry single-handedly captured a German machine-gun; Sgt. Rudge and Pte. Brown attacked an enemy machine-gun with grenades and silenced it (all were awarded the Military Medal after the war). Later, Sgt. Rudge was killed in the last-ditch defence of his post. With the assistance of a platoon of 2nd Royal Irish under command of 2/Lt. J.M. Terry, Z Copse held out until almost 1500 and was the last post taken in 48 Brigade Forward Zone. By 1030, the enemy had arrived in front of the Red Line and had broken through on the right. D Company headquarters at Basse Boulogne South was attacked at about 1030, but it held out until 1145.[9]

B Company, defending the main battle zone on the boundary with 66th Division, was attacked from the right flank and right rear, indicating that its flank was turned. Capt. A.V. Bridge decided to move his company remnant back through Ronssoy village and gain touch with the flanks. He had led his men back through the Inniskillings who were defending a trench between Ronssoy Wood and Ronssoy village to a position in the sunken road west of Ronssoy. During its fighting retirement, Bridge's company lost officers and men along the way. Lt. Dignan fell in Ronssoy village, but most casualties occurred in Ronssoy Wood where Capt. Fogarty and 2/Lt. Jones were killed and Lt. McGoey wounded. When the officers fell, the NCOs carried on. One, L/Cpl. McMasters, showed great initiative and leadership. He collected some men and counter-attacked along the sunken road and for a time drove back the enemy.[10] The company again retired and in the evening joined 6th Connaught Rangers and fell back with them.[11]

When the Germans reached the Red Line at about 1030, Lt.-Col. F. Call ordered the abandonment of the battalion headquarters dug-out. Leaving his adjutant behind to destroy the documents, Lt.-Col. Call gathered up his headquarters staff, the RSM, clerks, signallers and runners and fifteen of a defence section, about thirty in all, and led them into Rose trench, still held by a platoon of 2nd Royal Irish.

> By 1130 am, the mist was beginning to clear, so Colonel Call ordered the three SOS mortar signals fired. These were apparently seen and a few rounds were fired by our artillery against the enemy in front. By noon the houses of Lempire became visible and shortly afterwards the enemy were seen advancing into the village (Ronssoy) by the Tombois road and around the north of it.[12]

Shortly after midday, a message was sent by two runners to brigade headquarters. One runner, Pte. Henning, not only delivered it, but returned through enemy fire to battalion headquarters. He was later decorated with the Military Medal.

Although enveloped on both flanks, Col. Call and his little force held their position. Bombing blocks were formed on their right and left. With one Lewis gun and grenades, they held off the enemy until nearly 1600. RSM G.H. Floater DCM was shot in the face, but continued to encourage his men and 'set a fine example'.[13] When the grenades ran out, and under machine-gun fire from both flanks, the end came when the Germans rushed the position and captured the survivors at nearly 1600: 'Although the situation had obviously been desperate since 1 pm, yet the men of the South Irish Horse and 2nd battalion continued to fight as long as it was possible to do so.'[14]

The casualties of 7th Royal Irish speak for themselves. Not counting the wounded, ninety-one all ranks were dead or dying.[15]

Few remained in 7th/8th Inniskillings, the last Ulster battalion in 16th Division, of the two battalions formed at Tipperary in 1914. Of the original 'Fighting Seventh', only one officer and twenty-one NCOs and men were left. It is unlikely that many more of the 8th Battalion survived. But their spirit was undiminished. With 11th Hampshires and 6th Connaught Rangers, they were the last of the original 16th Division.

The battalion was enveloped from right flank and rear by assault troops climbing the hill from the Cologne Valley, and the single flanking wire belt was no doubt flattened. After severe fighting with heavy casualties, battalion headquarters attempted to fight their way out. The commanding officer, Lt.-Col. Walkey, was wounded; the adjutant, Capt. A.H. Robbins and the battalion signal officer, Lt. W.A. Wilkinson, were killed. The second-in-command, Maj. Parr DSO MC, was captured. Four company officers were also killed and most of the remainder were wounded and captured.[16] In six hours from the commencement of the bombardment to the fall of the position, such was the intensity of the fighting that ninety-five Inniskilling Fusiliers were killed or died of wounds; hundreds were wounded.[17] No company officer came out of the battle. Only the Intelligence Officer, Lt. J.R. McIlroy MC, succeeded in escaping from the village and was later wounded. A post in the wireless station held out until 1700. Ronssoy was captured over the bodies of its Inniskilling defenders. No decorations were awarded for the defence of Ronssoy, probably because no company officers were left to tell the story and write the citations.[18]

While Ronssoy was being captured from the south, a severe struggle was raging in and around Lempire, an extension of Ronssoy. The front line of the Battle Zone formed a sharp salient round Lempire, so that the garrison (2nd Royal Irish), exposed to attack on three sides, was eventually cut off by the fall of Ronssoy and the wood nearby. After a desperate fight, most of the battalion was killed, wounded and captured. The enemy, however, was not able to establish himself in Lempire until towards 1400. Even then, some posts in and around the village held out until a much later hour: '2nd Royal Irish Regiment isolated in Lempire completely surrounded, it held on with great tenacity till 2 pm against overwhelming assaults.'[19]

A single officer linked the original battalion of 1914 with the one which now faced the enemy at Lempire; he was Maj. M.C.C. Harrison MC. As Lt. Harrison, he had been adjutant in 1914. Badly wounded and captured at Le Pilly, after repeated attempts he had finally succeeded in escaping from the First World War equivalent of Colditz. He managed to cross into Holland and eventually returned home late in 1917. Rejoining the battalion in December, he was second in command.

Shortly after the barrage ceased, rifle fire close to battalion headquarters announced the arrival of the enemy. Lt.-Col. Scott ordered his headquarters personnel to man Rose Trench, a forward trench on the Red Line at the tip of the Lempire defences. At 1000, some Germans reached the position, but were repulsed with bombs and rifle fire. On the left, the reserve company was in touch with 2nd Dublins. The Germans broke through on the right and occupied a position between Rose Trench and Lempire defences. The Germans also broke through the Dublins on the left. Rose Trench became untenable and when ammunition began to run out, the Royal Irish withdrew to Irish Trench. This was well stocked with ammunition and fighting continued. Lt.-Col. Scott was killed and the remnant came under incessant attack at 1415. Bombed on one flank and swept by machine-gun fire from the other, the survivors fell back through the village towards St Emilie, gathering others as they went. But on emerging from Lempire, they discovered themselves surrounded. Under Maj. Harrison, the remnant of 2nd Royal Irish refused to surrender and held out until a counter-attack relieved them in the evening. The 2nd Royal Irish had eighty-eight officers and men dead or dying in the trenches around Lempire when it was overrun. One of its platoons held out longer. At 1245 a platoon which had been driven out of Thistle Trench joined 7th Royal Irish and took up the post on their left near the wireless station in Ronssoy, which actually held out until early on 22 March.

> Until 8.30 pm, many hours after they had been surrounded, wireless and power buzzer messages were received from isolated strongholds which were invested by the enemy. Such messages afforded valuable information to the higher command as to the situation in the forward positions which were still holding out. Prisoners since repatriated have told how the wireless sets, by enabling them to keep touch with their more fortunate comrades, put heart into defenders who felt they were in a hopeless position and encouraged them to fight to the last. The stubborn resistance of these isolated parties did much to embarrass the

German advance and thus to steady the retreat of the shattered Divisions endeavouring to withstand the impetuous rush of immensely superior forces.[20]

THE LEFT SECTOR, 48 BRIGADE

48 Brigade held the line from Lempire up to the divisional boundary, with 21st Division east of Epéhy. All its battalions were in the front line. On the right, 2nd Dublins' outpost line was overwhelmed in the bombardment and covered by the mist. It was not until the enemy attacked Rose Trench and Ridge Reserve on the Red Line north that HQ 2nd Dublins knew it was in contact.[21] Close-quarter fighting began and the enemy was repulsed.

Reinforced, the Germans renewed the attack at 1000 and succeeded in gaining a footing in Ridge Reserve. A platoon counter-attack dislodged them but not without loss; '2/Lt. Quigley and twenty men rushed forward to deal with an enemy machine-gun which was giving trouble; this was destroyed, but Quigley was killed when withdrawing.'[22]

For two hours of desperate fighting, bombing parties pushed along Ridge Reserve, driving the enemy before them. At the same time, a few men of C Company, cut off by the entry of the Germans into Ronssoy, formed a stop line and gallantly fought on and held that quarter until the afternoon.

Shortly after midday, the Ronssoy-Epéhy road, running between Ridge Reserve and Ridge Support, was swept by enfilade machine-gun fire. A little later, machine-gun fire came from the right rear. In the mistaken belief that this was friendly fire, a runner who was sent to warn the machine-gunners discovered they were Germans. With the fall of Ronssoy, German assault troops, heavily reinforced by succeeding waves of assault divisions, pushed up through the Cologne Valley, swept around the village and took the Dublins in flank. When the mist lifted about midday, the Dubliners could see parties of Royal Irish and Inniskillings withdrawing through Ronssoy towards St Emilie. Throwing back their right, they formed a flank guard. On the other flank, a heavy German attack had broken through 1st Dublins. With this came another barrage of 'heavy stuff' directed so as to cut off Ronssoy and Lempire from support.

> Matters now began to look very serious; the enemy showed in considerable numbers on the western outskirts of Ronssoy and Ronssoy Wood. Thus overlooking the position of the Battalion, and it was evident that the Germans were receiving substantial reinforcement by the east of Ronssoy over ground not covered by British machine-gun and rifle fire.[23]

Maj. Wheeler, the acting commanding officer, ordered a retirement on the Brown Line when it became obvious that the Germans had broken through on both flanks and that his remnant was in danger of being surrounded. On reaching the Brown Line, 2nd Dublins mustered seven officers and 200 officers and men.[24] A total of 106 all ranks of 2nd Dublins were killed or died of wounds[25] holding the right flanks of its brigade. From the numbers which fought their way out, obviously few unwounded 2nd Dublins could have been taken prisoner.

Under command of Maj. J.P. Hunt, 1st Dublins succeeded in holding the front centre of 48 Brigade throughout the early attacks. Between 1045 and 1100, Z and W Companies reported intensive German attacks which were held on the Red Line until close to 1130. X Company sent two platoons to reinforce W Company and two platoons to help Y Company. Under cover of the hurricane barrage, the enemy attacked the centre in overwhelming strength and broke through, gaining a footing on the Lempire–Epéhy road.

Brigade headquarters ordered Hunt to hold on as long as possible to protect the flank of the Munsters. Communications between the companies and battalion headquarters were cut, and the only indication of battle were streams of wounded and runners indicating the men in the front line were very hard pressed. 'But at the same moment, a very noble message came in from Captain Letchworth, commanding "Y" Company, that he was surrounded but would hold on to the end.'[26] At 1350, Brig. Ramsay ordered the battalion remnant back to the railway embankment south-east of the St Emilie–Malassise road to protect the right flank of the Munsters. This was done and the position held out until nearly 1700 when they fell back through the Leicestershire Regiment and joined the brigade on the Brown Line that evening. Some Vickers machine-gun detachments remained with the Leicesters and fought with them until the evening of the 22nd in the defence of Epéhy. The losses to 1st Dublins were fifty-two all ranks killed. These were the lightest death casualty figures of the division on 21 March. 49 Brigade and 2nd Dublins had blunted the main spearhead of the German flank attack. In the afternoon, a railway embankment on the St Emilie-Epéhy railway marked the extent of German penetration in the battle zone until 1700. 'The Munsters holding the hill south of Epéhy fought on until 5 pm and then the remnants fell back into the village and played a gallant part in its defence until it eventually fell next day.'[27] Commanded by Lt.-Col. H.R.H. Ireland (Leinster Regiment), 2nd Munsters held the extreme left of the division. With a total strength of 629 and a trench strength of 500, they fought off the enemy until nightfall.

The defenders of Malassise Farm dominating Deelish Valley held up the German advance. When the mist lifted, its defenders could see a German artillery column advancing along Malassise road up the valley. Devastating rifle and Lewis gun fire destroyed its animals and drivers.[28]

Heavy infantry attacks, co-ordinated with straffing by low-flying aircraft, overcame Malassise Farm. Lt. P.L. Cahill led A Company in a counter-attack which retook the position, but it was lost again shortly afterwards. In heavy fighting, strongpoints in Room Trench were also captured. The platoon commander, 2/Lt. Mehegan, was killed; the whole of his A Company platoon were killed or wounded.[29]

When the farm fell, the enemy bombed up Ridge Reserve Trench behind the farm with trench-mortars. Capt. Chandler MC 'fought a magnificent action'[30] and held Ridge Reserve until 1700. Although the left of the battalion was holding, the right flank was open and it was only a matter of time before this was turned.

By midday, the Munsters were isolated. 1st Dublins had retired either on the Brown Line or the railway embankment and were out of touch. Two German aircraft were brought down by Lewis gun and rifle fire. The commanding officer was mortally wounded early in the battle and evacuated. Maj. M.M. Hartigan DSO assumed command. About 1600, a very heavy bombardment struck the battalion area which cut line communications. The last message from Brig. Ramsay was received at 1630. Capt. Chandler reported to battalion headquarters at 1800 and was ordered by Maj. Hartigan 'to hold on and well he did it'.[31] About this time, a report was received at battalion headquarters in its deep dug-out that stretcher-bearers with wounded had been intercepted by the enemy two miles to the rear and ordered back. The headquarters staff emerged from the shelter just in time to repel Germans attacking from the rear. In this engagement, three prisoners were taken.[32]

The end now came quickly for headquarters, 2nd Munsters. Maj. Hartigan became separated and was captured. RSM Ring took charge of the headquarters party and in the darkness led them to St Emilie, where they arrived at 2000, still with their three prisoners.

Meanwhile, Capt. Chandler, Lt. McKeown, 2/Lt. Ardagh and about fifty fusiliers had retired from Ridge Support Trench to a position in a railway cutting south-east of Epéhy where they were holding on. All efforts to dislodge them had failed at dusk when the enemy attacks ceased. At about 0400 on the 22nd, Chandler's men withdrew in small parties covered by the morning mist and crossed the Brown Line. They rejoined the battalion remnant at Tincourt, arriving at about 1200, the last remnant party to arrive. A total of seventy all ranks, including the commanding officer, had died or were mortally wounded.[33]

Reinforcements

The German onrush had swept up the Cologne Valley and by 1000 had taken Templeux Quarries, deep in 66th Division sector. The defences of Ronssoy, crushed from flank and rear, had fallen. The aim of the Germans was to roll up the British front, pinch out the Flesquières Salient and drive on to the sea. 16th Division was crushed by a bombardment of unprecedented ferocity and swamped by overwhelming numbers coming ghost-like out of dense mist.

Nevertheless, the Irish infantry held the German flood surging towards Epéhy, the bastion to the Flesquières salient. By the time it reached the flank defences of Epéhy in late afternoon, the mist had cleared. The defenders were ready and the German onrush, sapped of its drive in the fight to overcome 49 Brigade and 2nd Dublins, was stopped.

That vicious forward deployment destroyed two brigades in their original positions. Liddell Hart, commenting on similar defensive deployment on the Chemin des Dames in a later attack, criticised the French General Duchêne:

> This general, indeed, bears a still heavier responsibility, for he insisted on the adoption of the long-exploded and wasteful system of massing the infantry of the defence in the forward positions. Besides giving the enemy guns a crowded and helpless target, this method ensured that once the German guns had made a bloated meal of this luckless cannon-fodder, the German infantry would find practically no local reserves to oppose their progress through the rear zones.[34]

Of Gen. Congreve's similar deployment of 16th Division, he says nothing.

When the German attack smashed through on the right, the only hope was to quickly seal off the breach with reserves. However, in addition to inviting the destruction of two brigades, holding 47 Brigade in corps reserve meant that once the crust of Battle Zone was broken into, there was little behind to fill the breach. For this a strong reserve was essential to plug the hole and at the same time garrison the Brown Line. But only one battalion, 1st Munsters, was in position on the Brown Line. It was released to the division at 1200.

A second battalion of 47 Brigade, 6th Connaught Rangers, was given a warning order to move from Villers Faucon to St Emilie at 1200, and 2nd Leinsters were released at 1355.[35] Both battalions were shortly afterwards moving to the Brown Line as quickly as enemy shelling allowed. In addition, 39th Division, released from GHQ reserve, moved at 1235. It was placed at the disposal of VII Corps and two battalions of 116 Brigade and two artillery brigades were designated to reinforce 16th Division. But they were six miles from the battlefield at 1400,[36] and were already too late to influence the outcome of that day's battle.

CHAPTER THIRTY-FOUR

The German Offensive, March 1918

THE COUNTER-ATTACK OF 6TH CONNAUGHT RANGERS AT ST EMILIE

6th Connaught Rangers received orders to move at midday.[1] As they marched out thirty minutes later, Lt.-Col. Feilding took the salute of his battalion on the outskirts of Villers Faucon. He called out a personal farewell to each company commander and shouted 'Good luck' to every platoon as the battalion marched past.[2] On the line of march, the destruction and confusion caused by the German bombardment was much in evidence. Shells fell thickly along the route and there were several casualties before the Rangers reached the Brown Line. On the way, two large 12-inch railway howitzers were seen, disabled by direct hits. 16th Divisional Artillery was under heavy German artillery attack and batteries of 18-pounders with their horse teams were destroyed trying to get their guns away.[3] At St Emilie, Feilding reported to HQ 49 Brigade and received orders.

Brig. Leveson-Gower, acting in accordance with his standing orders, ordered a counter-attack to retake Ronssoy. It would be carried out by 6th Connaught Rangers and 1st Munsters, supported by two tanks. Feilding departed to carry out his orders. Later, 16th Divisional Headquarters cancelled the counter-attack, and 49 Brigade sent a counter-order to 1st Munsters and 6th Connaught Rangers. The Munsters received the counter-order; the Rangers did not. The scene was set for a classic military tragedy.

At 1545, 6th Connaught Rangers, unaware that they were attacking in complete isolation without artillery support or tanks, began their advance. It was probably the only attack carried out by either Third or Fifth Army on 21 March.

They moved in orthodox formation on a two-company frontage. With one behind in support and a fourth coming up the rear in reserve, the battalion advanced on its 'forlorn hope'—a desperate enterprise.

The ground to the left of the St Emilie–Ronssoy road slopes upwards towards Ronssoy Wood on a spur and is devoid of cover. On the left, close to the edge of the ridge, was the remnant of a lateral wire belt. In front was a parallel wire belt, behind which was Ronssoy Wood, already in enemy hands. A more exposed area in which to deliver an attack in broad daylight would be difficult to find.

With that headlong gallantry usually associated with a Ranger attack, the two leading companies forced their way forward in the face of intense enemy fire. Although practically annihilated, a remnant of the company succeeded in gaining the sunken road bounding the western edge of Ronssoy Wood. Capt. Crofton was killed leading A Company. His second-in-command, Lt. Cummins, succeeded him but was also killed. Their men fell around them. D Company fared little better. Capt. Wickham was killed; Lt. A. Robbins who succeeded him was wounded and taken prisoner. Leading the reserve, C Company, Capt. Norman could see troops lining the factory ridge on his right front and mistook them for 1st Munsters. Not until their fire took the battalion in enfilade did he realise the awful truth of their situation. This was hammered home by the sight of the enemy advancing along the Ronssoy-St Emilie road, apparently trying to turn the right flank of D Company. Norman, appreciating the gravity of the situation, got his company into a defensive flank along the Ronssoy-St Emilie road. As he did so, a hail of fire struck his men. Norman was hit three times and fell; the last officer in his company was hit within minutes. The survivors of C Company, together with the 'scanty remainder' of A and D Companies, fell back to the Brown Line.[4]

Despite their terrible losses, the survivors of the leading companies courageously forced their way forward and reached Ronssoy Wood. Once there, they found themselves attacked by Germans on all sides. Hard pressed to defend themselves, they were soon out of ammunition, surrounded, and in most cases leaderless. Faced with a stark choice of surrender or useless death, they surrendered. Their experience is probably epitomised by that of No. 12 Platoon. Going forward by rushes—fire and movement—a handful led by 2/Lt. H.E.F Hall reached the sunken road near Ronssoy Wood: 'On reaching our objective, we regrouped and blazed away, all the time under heavy fire.' After a time, Hall was moving position when a voice ordered him to halt. He looked behind and saw a German officer with a group of enemy infantry. The officer was 'wearing white gloves. He ordered me to halt and in faultless English told me if we laid down our arms we would be properly treated and brought safely to the rear. With our ammo gone it would be pointless to show further resistance.'[9]

The counter-attack of the Connaught Rangers had been in the tradition of those at Second Ypres, against which regular battalion commanders had protested at their senselessness—attacks about which French officers, like their Crimean counterparts, had said, 'C'est magnifique, mais ce n'est pas la guerre.'

However, the valour of the Rangers achieved something. Maj. M.C.C. Harrison MC, faced with the prospect of again becoming captive, understandably fought desperately to evade it.

On 21 March, 1918, we (2nd Royal Irish) were in the frontline trenches of the Fifth Army and spent most of that day behind the German lines. A desperate counter-attack by the Connaught Rangers in the evening enabled me with the remnants of the battalion to evade captivity and take part in the great retreat.[6]

In a few minutes, the Rangers had lost eighty-four all ranks killed.[7] Almost every remaining company officer and hundreds of NCOs and men were wounded. For a time, the battalion was reduced to a remnant of between thirty and forty riflemen, Headquarters Company, transport, Quartermasters details and clerks. Lt.-Col. Feilding, who had come through unscathed, reported to Brig. Leveson-Gower at 49 Brigade headquarters in a dug-out under Château St Emilie. Here he learned for the first time that the counter-attack had been cancelled. He later described the meeting in a letter to his wife: 'The Brigadier looked up and said "I hope you will not think hardly of me." There was no answer to this. At least no civil answer.'[8] It was the epitaph of a fine battalion destroyed to no purpose.

16TH DIVISION ARTILLERY

Part of the German plan was to neutralise the Fifth Army artillery at the beginning of the offensive.[9] Like the infantry, the gunners were first forced into respirators by gas, then subjected to intense high-explosive fire at selected times. The story of one battery describes their battle.

B Battery, 180 Brigade, was positioned about 100 yards in front of the ruined château on the eastern outskirts of St Emilie. Between 1100 and 1130, the bombardment was particularly intense. It seemed to the battery commander that about twelve shells, 'pip-squeaks, 4.2's and 5.9's',[10] were descending together unceasingly. All straddled his position, then having lasted seven hours, the bombardment ceased at 1130. During this time, the battery wagons had arrived, but so intense was the fire they were ordered away. One was destroyed with its horse-team, the driver badly wounded. A battery officer was wounded but continued at duty. The wagons returned about 1300, shortly after a warning order to move had arrived by runner. About 1400, the order to retire was given and the battery withdrew by sections. The last section fell back at 1430, under intermittent shelling.

One of the last guns of 180 Brigade going off was struck and put out of action; it was the second out of six to be knocked out. Both damaged guns were sent off to the Artillery Field Park at Hamel for replacement. About 1600, the remaining four guns were again in action from a prepared position between St Emilie and Villers Faucon. From there, battery wagons returned under fire to St Emilie and brought away as much kit and stores as possible. All the while the roads were being straffed by German aircraft and under bombardment by heavy guns (at least 11-inch).[11] Shortly afterwards, a warning order was received to move to new positions in defence of the Brown Line. An advance party was sent there to lay out lines of fire and erect aiming posts. With this done, should the battery arrive after dark, it could be brought into action without loss of time.

Orders to retire arrived about 1900. The battery moved in darkness by cross-country tracks to a position near Roisel. Within an hour, they had sent an 'in action' message to brigade headquarters.[12]

> Late in the evening the Brigade Signalling Officer put us into telephone communication with Brigade Headquarters, which were at Marquaix, and we received orders to stop firing. The men had some tea and settled down for the night beside the guns. The officers had some food, and I believe we all had several hours sleep.
>
> I still had with me at the gun line Lt. A.B. Weeks and 2/Lt. W Wimbury; the remaining officers were at the waggon lines. Captain Archbutt took all our ammunition waggons to the dump at Hamel, where he found a scene of great confusion, as many batteries were clamouring for ammunition at the same time. It was past 2 o'clock in the morning before he succeeded in getting his waggons refilled ...[13]

A second battery had been in action close by. One of its guns had been hit badly and could not be taken off. Of the four officers, one was killed and one wounded; several NCOs and men were casualties. The battery retired all its remaining guns but lost its stores. Another battery had four guns put out of action in the bombardment.

> 'C' Battery had been in action on the right of the St Emilie-Ronssoy road, and had had four guns hit during the bombardment; they had then come under machine-gun fire and had been unable to withdraw any guns at all. The Major (Ormond Steven, MC) had fired the remaining undamaged gun as long as possible and had then armed his men with rifles and had withdrawn them to an infantry trench, remaining there till he received an order from the Brigade Commander to withdraw.
>
> 'D' Battery had been in action close to Ronssoy Wood, and had also had a bad time, but I think succeeded in withdrawing four out of five howitzers.[14]

In 177 Brigade RFA, the artillery battle was very similar to that of 180 Brigade. Because of casualties in the early bombardment, command of D Battery devolved upon 2/Lt. Trorey. The battery was in action firing in response to SOS signals when they were attacked by German infantry arriving from the right flank: 'The guns were in pits and could not be switched around, nor was there time to run them out into the open. The guns of the right flank section were destroyed. The gunners gave covering fire with small arms while the left section was run out into the open and swung onto the enemy at point-blank range.'[15]

Lt. Trorey, the surviving officer, manned a Lewis gun with a bombardier and killed many Germans until the bombardier was killed and the officer wounded. With the Germans only 100 yards from the gun-pit, Trorey ordered the guns disabled and his men to retire. He himself could not move: 'Some men who tried to help him were shot down, so he ordered them to retire and join some infantry to the rear and this gallant officer was captured...'[16]

This did not end the efforts of the gunners to save their precious weapons. It was now the turn of the drivers. Mounted postillion-like on the near horse of six-horse gun-teams and lashing them into furious action, they galloped forward: 'Determined to save the guns, the teams thundered up straight into German machine-gun fire; seven out of eighteen drivers died instantly but the rest galloped towards the guns, only to find the Germans on them in strength and they were forced to retire.'[17]

It is apparent from these two reports that fire was returned by the gunners—despite the confusion of an intense bombardment of high explosives and gas, teams of terrified horses on the point of stampede, wounded men, damaged guns, and disrupted communications. When orders to retire came, the gun sections withdraw to pre-selected sites, taking damaged guns with them. Communications between the battery positions and brigade (regimental) headquarters were restored and gun-fire resumed. Damaged guns were despatched to Ordnance in the expectation of replacements and a resupply of ammunition obtained during the night for the battle next day. Where guns were damaged and could not be withdrawn, the gunners took their place in the defensive line alongside the infantry, while others guarded the undamaged guns to the last man. Gunners regarded their guns as 'Colours'; to lose them is dishonourable. At St Emilie on 21 March 1918, no accusing finger could be levelled at the artillery of 16th Division.

Although engaged in a ferocious battle, confusion there may have been, but it appears to have been without panic. The military system continued to function and all ranks carried out their duties resolutely. A further example of the continuation of an orderly system is the story of the kit of Lt. Seymour Jourdain, 6th Connaught Rangers. A staff 'learner' at 16th Division headquarters, he was on leave at the time of the breakthrough. Recalled from leave, he was then stuck for three weeks at Le Havre. When he finally got back to divisional headquarters, he found his kit completely intact.[18] It had been packed and moved sixty miles along with the headquarters, during a period of such turmoil not experienced by the BEF since the retreat from Mons. Seymour's story does not suggest a panic withdrawal, or a breakdown of administration.

DEFENCE OF THE BROWN LINE

On the evening of 21 March, the Brown Line on the rear edge of the Battle Zone became 16th Division's main defence line. It had two advantages over the previous positions. There was a continuous line, and the soldiers were already in position, with no necessity to move under shell-fire to 'man battle positions'. Men would fight where they stood.[19] However, far too few were left to man the line.

The remnants of the broken battalions from the Battle Zone were directed to Tincourt where reorganisation was taking place. The Brown Line was held by 47 Brigade: the remnant of 6th Connaught Rangers, 2nd Leinsters, 1st Munsters, 11th Hampshire (P) and details of engineers, signals and police. That evening, several attacks on the line were repulsed, but eventually the enemy broke off the engagement and lapsed into silence. They were also reorganising for the resumption of the battle on the morrow.

> Successful though the Germans had been in over-running our forward defences, the stubborn fight the Third and Fifth Armies had put up, despite the fog, and other disadvantages, had been far from unsuccessful. German casualties had been heavy and their progress less than they had confidently reckoned upon. Had more adequate reserves been available the Fifth Army might have held the German advance well east of the Somme, but the heavy losses suffered, largely through fog, by the defenders of the forward lines had left several Divisions too weak to have much chance of making a successful defence of the battle and rear Zones, let alone to counter-attack. The Sixteenth, for instance, had only the 11th Hampshire and two battalions of the 47th Brigade intact for this purpose.[20]

On 22 March stand-to was at 0230. From three enemy prisoners (an officer and two soldiers) brought in by a patrol of 2nd Leinsters, it was learned that an attack was to be expected later that morning.[21] Barely had the information been passed to brigade headquarters than the German attack began. Under cover of another heavy bombardment, and helped again by fog, the enemy advanced, but the Allied line was stubbornly held. Between 0700 and 1200, five separate attacks were repulsed with heavy losses by the centre and left of the divisional front. On the right, however, the situation was critical. A German thrust down the Cologne Valley had pushed 66th Division back, exposing the right of 2nd Leinsters which had taken in enfilade and had suffered heavy casualties. A counter-attack by 66th Division to regain their lost ground came too late to help the Leinsters[22] who were forced back 500 yards.

To avoid disaster to his division, Maj.-Gen. Hull, 'with the concurrence of the corps commander, and in accordance with the Fifth Army policy,'[23] gave clear orders to his brigades to retire to the Green Line. Although closely engaged, all units withdrew to successive lines, first on the Roisel-Epéhy railway line cutting, then on the high ground west of Villers Faucon. The Green Line between Hamel and Tincourt was reached by all units around 1600 'in an orderly in-hand fashion'.[24] In the usual way of withdrawals, however, some units did not receive the order and were cut off. One company of 1st Munsters and 13th Sussex (of 116 Brigade which had come forward in support), together with the remnant of 6th Connaught Rangers, did not get the message to retire. After repulsing repeated attacks they were surrounded by 1600. Out of ammunition, some of the survivors attempted to break out and were shot down. The remainder surrendered. 'The order to retire did not reach the troops which were in the line.'[25]

At about 1100 on 22 March, Capt. R.T. Roussel, Connaught Rangers, realised that his own men and detachments of Munsters and Sussex, astride the St Emilie-Ronssoy road on the Brown Line, were cut off. Having conferred with Lt. Cahill of the Munsters, it was decided to hold their position. Roussel, with the Sussex and Connaughts, faced north and east, while the Munsters faced south and west. They must have known their situation was hopeless, yet they resolutely faced the enemy and held onto an impossible position for a further six hours.

> As expected, we were soon surrounded, and all runners between Cahill's party and mine were killed. The enemy tried to dislodge us by TM and MG fire. Our fire held back his infantry. At 1530 we ran out of ammunition, so destroyed everything that might be of value to the enemy. After this the enemy stood up several times and beckoned to us but would not come to close quarters. At sunset we still had nine men able to stand, but as they were very weak and quite defenceless and would soon be uselessly put to death, I consented to give them their liberty and three men surrendered, whereat the enemy rushed up to us, and holding us up with rifles and egg bombs ordered us to go east. There was no other course than to comply. I saw no foul play. I would like to add that Act. Capt. Leader, Connaught Rangers, did excellent service on the morning of 22 March despite three wounds received the previous day.[26]

The Irish under Cahill and Roussel and the unknown men of Sussex sacrificed themselves so that 16th Division might have time to form a defensive line to the rear. It was what in bygone days was described as 'a beau geste'.

Congreve's VII Corps and Watts's XIX Corps were holding the Green Line on the night of 22–23 March. However, whatever their troops did to delay the enemy was of no avail. Events occurring farther south would dictate the morrow's battle because, 'through an unfortunate misunderstanding, a Corps further to the right retired sooner and further than General Gough intended'.[27]

This was, of course the retirement of Maxse's XVIII Corps which had retired in a single day from the Battle Zone to behind the Somme.

16TH DIVISION'S ACHIEVEMENT ON 21 MARCH 1918

The 16th Division was savaged by the decision of VII Corps' commander to position two of its three brigades in the Forward Zone, thus inviting destruction. Its third, 47 Brigade, which ought to have been able to cover their withdrawal in a delaying action, was held back in Corps Reserve for too long. The release of the battalions of 47 Brigade from VII Corps reserve was too late to affect the outcome of 16th Division's defence of its Battle Zone. This was contrary to Fifth Army policy, that once the order 'man battle positions' was given, 'there should be no delay or hitch moving units, thus held back, into the defences assigned to them'.[28] In moving forward, two reserve battalions were exposed to casualties and delay by German shell-fire expressly directed to interdict such moves. Finally, the rushed deployment of 6th Connaught Rangers contributed to its destruction.

Yet, despite these handicaps, unquestionably the infantry and supporting arms of 16th Division resisted fiercely. Against the main thrust of the German offensive on 21 March 1918, the Irish Division contributed greatly in denying the enemy quick victory at Epéhy. The successful defence of Epéhy saved the British divisions in the Flesquières salient.

But the cost in doing this was high. 16th Divisions casualties on 21–22 March 1918, in infantry alone, were:

Killed and died of wounds, all ranks	749[29]
Wounded (estimated at a ratio of 3 : 1)	2247
Total	2996

The average rifle strength of battalions was 600.[30] From this, the estimated front-line infantry strength of the division can be calculated at 5400. Casualties were more than fifty-five per cent of the infantry engaged. From the strength of battalion remnants on 22 March, it can be estimated that most of the prisoners taken on 21 March were wounded.

CHAPTER THIRTY-FIVE

The Great Retreat: 36th Division, 23–30 March 1918

During the early hours of Saturday 23 March 1918, XVIII Corps had established a defensive line along the Somme north and south of Ham. 36th Division, on the right, was in touch with 14th Division of III Corps on the Crozat Canal to its right and 20th Division to its left. Gen. Maxse, without a warning order, had needlessly ordered his corps to withdraw from the front of its Battle Zone to behind the Somme in a single day. In doing so, it had suffered heavy casualties without adequately delaying the Germans, destroying a vital railway bridge or preparing the Somme defences. By his actions, Maxse initiated a chain-reaction which adversely affected the entire Fifth Army front north of the Somme.

At 0700 on the morning of 23 March, the troops holding Ham on the left of the 36th were forced back. Although a battalion of the King's Regiment defended the bridgehead for several hours afterwards, the Germans were able to force the canal by 1200. 21st Entrenching Battalion formed a defensive flank but were driven back on the railway at 1030. There, reinforced by a company of 9th Inniskillings, they made a stand. By this time, an enemy Guards Regiment had captured the Pithon railway bridge and was advancing. The combined German attack from Ham and Pithon forced the defenders back on Aubigny, which was held by the remnant of 9th Inniskillings. The enemy captured Aubigny, but Capt. G.J. Bruce, Brigade Major 109 Brigade, rode forward, rallied the retreating men and restored the local situation by a counter-attack. But it was impossible to recapture the lost bridges and eventually the little force had to retire. The enemy gave no further trouble in this sector until late afternoon.[1]

The real danger appeared on the right flank, when the enemy forced back 14th Division at Jassy and established a crossing of the canal at 0330. By midday they had advanced to Martel, deep into the left of 14th Division.

At this time, the only real cohesive formation remaining under command of 36th Division was 61 Brigade of 20th Division. It was stationed on the right, between 14th Division and 36th Division. Now in a difficult situation, its commander, Brig. Cochrane, established a defensive flank towards Jassy and held it until mid afternoon when he was ordered to retire. When Cochrane ordered a withdrawal at 1630, his battalions were heavily engaged. Although the Cornwall Light Infantry managed to fight its way clear, the 7th Somerset Light Infantry were held to their positions. They fought until their ammunition was exhausted. Then three companies surrendered, leaving only one company and battalion headquarters.

The remnant of 107 Brigade moved to the right at 1045. 2nd Irish Rifles defended a line east of Cugny and gained touch with troops of 14th Division. But the Rifles were exposed when that division retired, leaving only a rearguard. The handful of 1st Irish Rifles were moved quickly alongside its sister battalion with orders to hold. Dismounted French dragoons and later 13th Entrenching Battalion came alongside to help. Together they managed to hold the position until nightfall against the regiments of Prussian Guards.

Meanwhile, 108 Brigade had withdrawn with 61 Brigade to the railway and had formed a defensive flank towards the left. 109 Brigade was forced back by Prussian Guards pouring across the railway bridge at Pithon. Aubigny, Eaucourt and Brouchy were lost. The front of 36th Division was now a narrow salient resembling a thick-stemmed mushroom. The enemy was brought to a halt in the immediate vicinity and fighting raged well into darkness. The Germans were held until 13th Entrenching Battalion, positioned between 1st and 2nd Irish Rifles, gave way. Then, alert to such weakness, the Germans attempted to exploit the gap, but the Irish Rifles fought tenaciously, clinging to their position until nearly 2200. Then the officers of two Prussian Grenadier regiments made personal appeals to their men. Responding to this, the Grenadiers made a last effort. Breaking through the Irish lines, they captured Cugny.[2]

Gen. Nugent refused to be forced back further. 61 Brigade, holding the tip of the salient, was ordered to hold on 'at all cost'. The Cornish and Somerset men formed three sides of a square. Under Lt.-Col. H. Burges Short of SLI, they beat off all attacks until next day. Then the west-countrymen only retired when ordered to do so.

During the night, a composite battalion was formed under Maj. Knox consisting of broken units and men returned from courses. Its companies were commanded by Capt. C. Drummond, Gen. Nugent's ADC, and Capt. W. Smyth, RE, from divisional staff. Only a scratch force, nevertheless it bravely attempted a counter-attack to recapture Aubigny but was unsuccessful. It then took up a position on the left of 9th Inniskillings in 109 Brigade. The men in the trenches got whatever rest they could while divisional headquarters wrestled with the task of re-organisation. Desperate measures were taken to reinforce the line. Clerks, orderlies, cooks, batmen, all suddenly found themselves holding a rifle. They were supported by two batteries from 91 Brigade RFA, attached from 20th Division. At times the gunners fired over open sights.[3] Somehow the line held and 36th Division retained its dangerous salient.

The stand of the 36th gave time for a line to be formed behind, manned by French 9th and 10th Divisions, with remnants of 14th Division on their right. Behind them were two further French divisions, with 30th and 20th Divisions of XVIII Corps.

On the morning of 24 March, the front of Gen. Maxse's corps was oddly shaped. 36th Division held its salient and two brigades of 20th Division still held the line of the Somme on the left of the corps. But in the centre, 30th Division had been forced back and a deep wedge had been driven between it and 36th Division.

Fog again blanketed the front and the enemy, unsure of the position of 36th Division, delayed renewing its attack. But when the German assault began about 0900, the position of 61 Brigade became untenable and it withdrew, taking with it 109 Brigade. Both brigades fell back onto the newly formed French line. That too broke and, with 36th Division, was forced back on Villeselve. The order to retire failed to reach the remnant of 2nd Irish Rifles who, when their ammunition was exhausted, fixed bayonets and charged. Of the four remaining officers, two were killed. The remnant of the battalion, about 150, surrendered.[4]

Some remnants of 2nd Rifles, with a 'gathering up' of Pioneers, butchers, ASC men and other details under Lt.-Col. Peacocke of 9th Inniskillings, counter-attacked with little hope of success and were forced back: 'Several men were wounded, but it was impossible in the circumstances to render any help. That would be close in a short time by the advancing enemy. It will always be a miracle to me how any of us survived that retreat, the retirement was now chaotic and everyone was now mixed up.'[5] Across the front, retirement was general. The more resolute leaders gathered men around them and fell back fighting dourly as long as their ammunition lasted. One such band was led by Lt. Witherow of 2nd Rifles, supported by a section of machine-guns. For a time they succeeded in fighting off the enemy, but eventually were outflanked and in danger of being cut off. Realising his danger, Witherow arranged a further withdrawal: 'I first got the wounded away before the danger got so acute and then I gave orders to the nervy machine-gun officer that he should retire to a hedge and cover our retirement. He was delighted to be off, but that was the last I saw of him.'[6]

Witherow led his men back through a village to be confronted by a mounted staff officer: 'A staff officer rode up and implored us to defend the village, but I told him we were very short of ammunition... The officer spurred his charger and disappeared.'[7] Eventually the young officer found a remnant of his battalion, the adjutant and twenty-five men. Marching together to Avricourt, they found their brigade and 'marched into a field and prepared food'. This last comment by Witherow is interesting. Inexperienced soldiers or totally exhausted troops flop down immediately and sleep; veterans, realising the importance of keeping up their strength, eat before sleep, not knowing what dawn might bring. So dangerous was the situation during that day's fighting that a brigade of 3rd Cavalry Division actually charged to relieve the 36th at a critical moment. As the cavalry charged, the remnants of 1st and 9th Battalions of the Royal Irish Fusiliers, their fighting spirit unbroken, rose up cheering. They charged the enemy and took about 150 prisoners. [8]

French reserves were now reaching the line in strength, but were without artillery and had only limited ammunition. That night at 2300, 36th Division came under orders of the French 62nd Division. Its remaining two artillery groups were divided between 9th and 62nd Divisions; Erskine Group was under 9th Division, and Ely and Potter (61 Brigade) Groups with the 62nd Division. Early on the morning of 25 March, 36th Division moved behind the French into reserve for much-needed rest, and 61 Brigade was ordered to return to its own division.

36th Division, reduced to little more than a cadre, rested several hours at Avricourt before moving on to a concentration area close to the River Avre. They arrived in the early hours of 26 March. Last to arrive was 1st Irish Fusiliers who got in at 0200 and had six hours' sleep. Its accommodation requirements were less than at any other time since its formation. The brigades were skeletal.

107 Brigade—Remnants of 1st and 2nd Irish Rifles, about the strength of a large platoon; 16th Irish Rifles (Pioneers); 121st Field Company RE and 21st Entrenching Battalion. It was divided into three groups. The largest, under Lt.-Col. McCarthy-O'Leary of the Royal Irish Fusiliers, was composed of the remnant of three Irish Rifle battalions.

108 Brigade—9th Irish Fusiliers and 122nd Field Company RE

109 Brigade—Remnant of 1st and 2nd Inniskillings[9]

Although the Ulster Division was, in the words of the official historian, 'only a cadre',[10] some of its old covenanting spirit remained.

> The padre of the Battalion (Fr Henry Gill SJ) who had been with the regiment since the beginning of the war was now with us. He was a fine-looking priest of middle age and very distinguished looking. He was a great help to us on the retreat because of the respect [with which] French people treated him. He could get any billet he wanted in a village because the inhabitants were only too glad to have a priest in their house, both for his own sake and for the fact that his presence would be a guarantee that the property would be respected. I had some very interesting arguments with his reverence, who had the DSO.[11]

On 26 March 1918, Gen. Foch was created 'Generalissimo' and his appointment was generally welcomed. Gen. Fayolle was placed in command of all French and British troops between the Oise and the Somme. The French held eighteen miles, the British nineteen. The line held was continuous, except for a gap between both armies extending from the French left at Roye and the right of XIX Corps at Fransart held by 61 Brigade. The remnant of Maxse's corps was ordered to fill this gap. But XVIII Corps was without artillery; the entire Corps artillery was retained by the French.[12]

Gen. Nugent received orders to hold a line north of the Avre between L'Echelle-St Aurin on the Avre, just west of Roye and behind Andechy to just south of the Amiens-Roye road. It was part of a line between the French and 30th Division protecting the Amiens-Montdidier railway.[13] In a cluster of little villages on the line of Avre within the triangle Moreuil-Roye-Montdidier, the 36th fought its last action as an 'Ulster' division. Thereafter it retained the title, but such were its grave losses in the March battles that its highly distinctive volunteer ethos became drowned in a flood of conscripts.

108 Brigade was late into position, possibly because its units arrived in the early hours of the morning after a very long march. This delay allowed the Germans to reach Andechy, and when the Irish Fusiliers attempted to reach that place, they were driven back by enemy machine-gun fire. A unit of 30th Division had also fallen back to about a mile from Bouchoir. Eventually the division established a line between Guerbigny, through Erches, to just south of Bouchoir.[13] The 109 Brigade was on the right, 108 in the centre and 107 on the left.

In the north, following the retirement of 30th Division to Bouchoir, 122nd Field Company formed a left flankguard. With Lewis gun fire, it succeeded in driving back repeated German turning movements. An old French line on the Erches-Bouchoir road still had some trenches with wire in front and Nugent ordered 107 Brigade to hold it. The brigade was in position by 1600, so when the Germans arrived they were halted by small-arms fire. The Germans, knowing their opponents were without artillery, took risks they could not otherwise have dared and repeatedly presented superb targets. They brought forward some artillery of their own and at dusk bombarded Erches, forcing Headquarters 108 Brigade into the surrounding fields where Brig. Griffiths was wounded. This was immediately followed by an attack in strength and by 2000, the enemy was in Erches, driving a deep wedge into the division.

During the action, a serious loss occurred when a motor car with the GSO1 of the divisional staff drove into a German patrol and its occupants were captured.[14] They included Col. Place, the CO of 1st Irish Fusiliers, Lt.-Col. Furnell, and A/CO of 9th Irish Fusiliers Major Brew, all of whom were returning from a conference.

When 108 Brigade headquarters was cut off and almost captured, its units formed a line west of Erches and placed themselves under Headquarter 109 Brigade. Lt.-Col. S.U.L. Clements DSO took over command of the Irish Fusiliers and was told by the brigade major of 109 Brigade that their position at Andechy had to held for twenty-four hours. That night there was considerable confusion and heavy shell-fire, and the supply services failed for the first time. The fighting troops received no ammunition, rations or water. The pitiful remnant of 36th Division, split up but still defiant, fought on independently.

At dawn next morning, the Germans attacked. On the right of the Ulstermen, south of the Avre, the French withdrew. To save itself and its units from being trapped, HQ 109 Brigade ordered all units to cross the River Avre. Having crossed, the units and HQ 109 Brigade retired with the French. Guerbigny was captured immediately, leaving the Irish Fusiliers near Erches isolated. A message to their commanding officer, Lt.-Col. Clements, telling him of the withdrawal, failed to reach him.[15]

They held out until 1120 that day before they were overwhelmed; 'only one officer and nineteen other ranks got away'.[16] North of Erches, a handful of men with a machine-gun was attacked at dawn.[17] Under Capt. Walker of 36th Machine-gun Battalion, the last machine-gun with 107 Brigade was brought into action and the Germans were stopped. Walker withdrew his little force north-westwards. Nearby, the remnants of 15th Irish Rifles held on until their trenches were blown in before midday. Then the company commander, Capt. Miller, withdrew his little group towards Arvillers. On the way, contact was made with the remnant of 1st and 2nd Irish Rifles. Lt.-Col. McCarthy-O'Leary, whose indomitable spirit through the battle and retirement had inspired his men, was wounded a second time and evacuated. Combined, the three battalion remnants, numbering half a company strength, fell back on Arvillers.

Behind the steadfast Fusiliers at Erches and the Rifles at Arvillers, Brig. Withycombe ordered a retirement of about a mile to Hangest-en-Santerre. From there, 107 Brigade retired on the division headquarters at Sourdon, fifteen miles to the rear. The Rifles, three officers and sixty riflemen, held their position at Arvillers until the morning of 28 March and were then relieved by the French. They were the last troops of 36th Division to come out of the Battle of St Quentin. They marched to join the division at Sourdon. It was described as 'a long, trying march.'[18]

Now out of the line, the 36th Division marched to Saleux south of Amiens. The exhausted remnants entrained for Eu via Gamaches on the Channel coast. The Ulster Division, on arrival in France, needed a fleet of trains to move them to the Somme area; now, only one was required to take them away.[19] 'I doubt if the whole Division could produce more than the equivalent of a full battalion. It has been the worst battle of the war, as far as we are concerned.'[20]

CHAPTER THIRTY-SIX

The Great Retreat: 16th Division, 23 March–5 April 1918

16TH DIVISION'S RETREAT

On the morning of 23 March the left of XIX Corps was about two miles to the rear of 16th Division. 'Fortunately, the enemy did not realise this circumstance soon enough to take advantage.'[1] About 0440, Gen. Watts telephoned Gen. Congreve and informed him that he had been ordered by Gough to retire behind the Somme. Congreve pointed out that this would leave his troops exposed to daylight retirement with an exposed flank. 'To this Lt.-Gen. Watts replied that the retirement of the XIX Corps behind the Somme was a matter of necessity.'[2] In the morning mist of 23 March, between 0600 and 0700, 16th Division slipped away quietly. Between 1000 and 1100 they were digging in on a new position from Doingt to Bois des Flacques, a front of 2000 yards. Behind them, the enemy had begun a heavy and futile bombardment of the Green Line at 0720. 39th Division came up on the left and extended the line to Bussu. 9th Division, farther north, was hotly engaged and inflicted heavy casualties on the enemy before retiring behind the Canal du Nord.

During the previous night, the now weak 16th Division had reorganised into composite battalions under original brigade headquarters. They included the Engineer Field Companies, divisional Pioneers and an entrenching battalion (formed from surplus men from the divisional battalions after the reorganisation of February). 11th Hampshire had won the respect of the Irishmen for their courageous hard work under fire in all their battles of 1916 and 1917. They were now to demonstrate their fighting ability. They were ably led by Lt.-Col. B.E. Crockett DSO, 'a sensible very level-headed ex-regular officer'.[3]

47 Brigade consisted of two decimated battalions, 1st Munsters and 2nd Leinsters with the remnants of 6th Connaught Rangers. In 48 Brigade were the remnants of 1st and 2nd Dublins and 2nd Munsters; along with 157 Field Company RE and 11th Hampshires (P), 49 Brigade consisted of a composite two-company battalion comprising remnants of 2nd and 7th Royal Irish and 7th/8th Inniskillings under Maj. M.C.C Harrison, and 17th Entrenching Battalion.

16th and 39th Divisions were covering the important communications and logistics centre of Péronne, which was being evacuated. Behind the front appeared scenes which were most depressing to fighting troops—a fleeing civilian population. Massed refugee columns appeared on the roads as French people fled with whatever few possessions they could carry. The army was also evacuating the town, and stores dumps were being cleared. Yet despite the chaos in the narrow streets of the provincial town, efficient traffic control managed to keep the congested mass moving freely. When it later became obvious that the stores could not be moved before capture, they were torched, 'even those of the Expeditionary Force Canteen had to be set on fire'.[4]

Added to this was the problem of evacuating the wounded. The after-battle report of 16th Division makes clear that 'the touch between motor ambulance convoys and field ambulances was defective, which caused the long distances which usually existed between casualty and clearing station and main dressing station to be an embarrassment to divisional ambulances which were badly overworked'.[5] The experience of one badly-wounded officer is perhaps typical. The second-in-command of 6th Connaught Rangers, Maj. Raynesford, was seriously wounded. While a Lewis gun team gave covering fire, Raynesford was carried away on a groundsheet with a Ranger at each corner.[6] Eventually he reached Lucknow Casualty Clearing Station at Péronne where there were 2500 stretcher cases awaiting treatment, although it was only equipped for 600.[7] Raynesford was lucky to have devoted men who were prepared to take him back for immediate treatment. 'It's all right, sir, you can trust us to get him out,' the litter-bearers assured the commanding officer.[8] And they did. It was because of the loyalty of such men that somehow the medical services, using hospital trains, succeeded in evacuating all wounded handed into their care.[9] Nevertheless, the suffering of the wounded can be well imagined. During the action in which Raynesford was wounded, Feilding gave the command to his depleted battalion, 'Connaught Rangers, advance'.[10] Although they only advanced fifty yards, 'it gave us a feeling of exhilaration, perhaps the only 5th Army unit to advance that day'.[11]

From about 1130, the new VII Corps positions came under artillery fire; an hour later enemy infantry began probing attacks. The commanders of 16th and 39th Divisions, Generals Hull and Feetham, made arrangements for a withdrawal in mutual agreement after consultations with their brigadiers. To cover this, 1st Dublins were armed with six machine-guns and positioned on high ground south-west of Doingt in the Cologne Valley. The Germans attacked at 1300, and 16th and 39th Divisions were ordered to retire. Covered by the machine-guns of the Dublins, 'a particularly fine rearguard action [was] fought by the 157th Field Company RE and the 11/Hampshire (Pioneers).'[12]

For a time the German advance was checked and the division was able to retire through the southern part of Péronne by the Bristol Bridge. One brigade was left east of the river, guarding the bridgehead and in touch with 66th Division. The other two dug in behind the river west of Biaches.[13] That night, 16th Division was ordered into reserve at Cappy on the Somme, seven miles west of Biaches. Later the rearguard brigade retired unmolested and the Somme bridges were blown.

At dawn on 24 March, Palm Sunday 1918, Fifth Army had retired everywhere. The III Corps, which had been driven from its position on the Crozat Canal, had been almost entirely relieved by French troops. Elsewhere, Fifth Army had retired behind the Somme from Ham to Biaches opposite Péronne and on to Clery, a distance of over twenty miles. However, Gen. Gough lacked sufficient troops to hold this line securely throughout its entire length. Moreover, several important crossings were under French railway control for demolition, but had been neglected. At dawn on the 24th, VII Corps was in contact with XIX Corps, but to the north, a gap opened between VII and V Corps was widening. In addition to this difficulty, VII Corps was now divided by the Somme.

At Péronne the course of the River Somme makes a bend from its north-south line, behind which the British had withdrawn, to a general east-west direction. The 16th and 39th Divisions were to its south, and the 21st and 9th to the north. Command of his corps in these divided circumstances was difficult for Gen. Congreve.

In the absence of reinforcements, each corps trawled vigorously its own resources and mustered scratch units. In VII Corps this was 'Hunt's Force', under newly promoted Lt.-Col. J.P. Hunt, 9th Dublins. Built around cadres from VII Corps Reinforcement Training Camp, it consisted of eight battalions, comprising 39th Division details; 24th Entrenching Battalion; two battalions of corps reinforcements; VII Corps school of instruction and a company of engineers; two battalions of men recalled from leave.[14] Many, especially those from holding units, were mere recruits and the force had few automatic weapons except those salvaged from derelict tanks and manned by their crews. Despite these shortcomings, the force won a considerable fighting reputation.

On the night of 24–25 March, GHQ ordered 16th and 39th Divisions to come under command of XIX Corps (Gen. Watts). The remainder of VII Corps, north of the Somme, under its own corps headquarters, was to be transferred to Third Army. The order was effective from 0400 on the 25th. An hour earlier, at 0300, Fifth Army had passed from the command of Sir Douglas Haig to that of the French general, Fayolle. A counter-attack was arranged to regain the line of the Somme to the south; Gen. Watts was confident of success. However, the French first postponed Zero Hour, then withdrew without fighting. It upset Watts' plan of battle and ultimately contributed to the complete loss of the Somme.[15]

Palm Sunday dawned in heavy mist. It had been a cold, miserable night for troops as well as refugees. During the previous evening, 16th Division were 'expressly ordered' to line the Somme from Bray to Cérisy, a distance of four miles, facing *south* to prevent the enemy from cutting in behind 39th

Division. In the event, this order was ignored and the direct opposite was put into effect. On the front immediately south of the Somme, the enemy halted in the face of 39th Division, with 16th Division in echelon behind. However, north of the Somme, on the front of VII Corps, the situation had become critical. In a day of confused fighting, VII Corps was forced back several miles. The right of 21st Division retreated to Cérisy, uncovering the left of XIX Corps.

The units of 16th Division, facing north to protect their exposed flank, helped 21st Division by firing across the river and enfilading the advancing Germans. That day they also collected twenty guns from Fifth Army Gun Park, a welcome addition for the gunners; some Lewis guns which were distributed to the brigades. Gradually, after years of trench warfare, the units, although only remnants, were becoming accustomed to fighting in the open and were giving a good account of themselves.

Although fiercely attacked on the Somme line, XIX Corps initially held its own. However, its right flank was exposed by the retirement of XVIII Corps and its left was uncovered by the retirement of VII Corps. Watts was in a dangerous position. He decided to abandon the Somme and retire to a line Hattencourt-Chaulnes-Ablaincourt-Estrées-Frise, which had hastily been prepared. At 1615, orders were given for a withdrawal after dark. Prior to this, Watts took the precaution of warning his divisional commanders that, in the event of being hard pressed on the 26th, they should fall back on the Rouvroy-Proyart-Froissy line. At the same time, Watts sent a strong force of engineers and pioneers back to prepare that line. The XIX Corps was now the only corps of Fifth Army still in the line.[16]

Throughout 26 March, 16th Division guarded the line of the Somme, north of which as far back as Bray was held by the enemy. All the divisional engineers, pioneers and a working party of 800 infantrymen had been sent back at 0800 to prepare its portion of the new line from Proyart to Froissy.[17] Soon after 1300, 47 Brigade moved to the right of a new line. At the same time, orders were given for the Somme bridges to be prepared for demolition. When XIX Corps headquarters ordered the retirement at 1000 hours, 48 and 49 Brigades were ready; by 1430, the whole division had retired to the new line. That afternoon, the enemy advanced to attack the centre, but the fire of the divisional artillery and small-arms fire brought the attack to a standstill. During the evening, the left was attacked from across the Somme, which had again been opened by a further withdrawal of VII Corps to Bussy les Daours. To cover this, 49 Brigade and part of 48 Brigade swung back to face the threatened area. 11th Hampshire filled a gap in the line and the front remained unbroken. But farther back, only 16th Divisional engineers covered the Somme bridges.[18]

With his left completely in the air, Gen. Watts ordered the destruction of all the remaining Somme bridges as far west as Cérisy and appealed to the Army Commander for help. In response, Gough sent a Canadian motorised machine-gun battery and a composite battalion to protect the area. Under cover of this demolition guard, the engineers of 16th and 39th Divisions successfully demolished the bridges.

Gough then decided the time had come for a determined stand. Amiens, a communications centre essential to the conjunction of the British and French armies, had to be held if the German plan to divide the British and French was to be defeated. On the night of 25–26 March, Fifth Army staff began planning the defence of Amiens. The 'Amiens Defence Line', an old French line dating from 1915, was partially extant. Fifteen miles in advance of the city and three miles from Villers Brettoneux, its frontage extended for eight miles. Maj.-Gen. P.G. Grant, Chief Royal Engineers, Fifth Army, collected a force of nearly three thousand men during the 26th and set them to work. That evening, Maj.-Gen. G.G.S. Carey arrived and assumed command of the scratch force working there; it was thereafter called 'Carey's Force'. Mainly engineer troops of all disciplines, it also included 500 American and 400 Canadian engineers.[19]

THE BATTLE OF ROSIÈRES, 27 MARCH 1918

16th Division had been in action continuously since the morning of 21 March. Despite terrible fighting against overwhelming force, it maintained its organisation and discipline regardless of the chaos around it. It held a united front against the enemy and retired only in concert with the formations on its flanks. Although it was to see more fighting before being finally withdrawn from the line at the end of the German offensive, on 27–28 March the 16th fought almost its last major action as an Irish division—the battle of Rosières.

Fought between Rouvroy and the Somme, Rosières was as severe as any defensive battle of 1914–15. Fighting with desperate courage against great odds, the dour stand of XIX Corps, although unable to halt the German offensive, sapped the enemy's strength to such an extent that it was later unable to muster sufficient force to break the last British defence line before Amiens.

Comparing Watts' stand with that of Wellington at Waterloo, the official historian declared that Watts and his men 'fought on the 27th March on a wider front, for a longer time and against heavier odds than did the Duke on the 18th June 1815.'[20]

The Germans attacked with eleven divisions, and Watts was ordered to maintain the line at all costs until the arrival of French reinforcements. His chief dangers existed on his flanks, the southern held by Maxse's very weak corps and the northern flank, where Third Army had retired six miles behind his left on the Somme.

To protect the northern flank, 16th Division was broken back in echelon. Inevitably this weakened its front. Only 47 Brigade, covering Proyart, was in the main line; 48 and 49 Brigades were deployed to its left rear leaving a large gap between each. 47 Brigade held a wide frontage with scattered forces. With poor communications, it was difficult to control from brigade headquarters at Morcourt. 1st Munster on the left, Connaught Rangers in the centre and 2nd Leinsters on the right were in touch with the Hertfordshires of 118 Brigade. Behind the line of 16th Division, Germans forced a crossing of the river line. Compelled to evacuate Morcourt, headquarters 47 Brigade lost contact with its battalions.

At about 0700, the enemy in front of 47 Brigade were seen preparing to attack. An hour later, 4th Guards Division advanced against Proyart. Their frontal assault was repulsed with heavy loss. But reinforced by infantry brought up in motor lorries, they worked round the open flank of the brigade and by 1000 had forced the line. 47 Brigade withdrew, the greater part joining the 39th Division on its right flank. Because the front was so wide, elements of the brigade split into three main groups under command of Lt.-Col. R. Kane (Munsters), Lt.-Col. R. Feilding (6th Connaught Rangers) and the third under Lt.-Col. K.C. Weldon (7th Leinsters).

While the first two 'composite battalions' withdrew south-westwards and fought with 39th Division, two companies of 2nd Leinsters, although separated, clung to the advancing Germans and fought a tenacious delaying action. When all their officers were killed or wounded, with the sole exception of the commanding officer, they marched out at the end of the battle under their regimental sergeant-major. One company commander, Capt. Webster, was killed. The other, Capt. McCann MC, was seriously wounded and evacuated (he was later awarded a bar to the MC). Later, he said of his company, 'The men fought like heroes. I was never so proud in my life before of being a Leinster.[21] A young officer recently joined who had been wounded, spoke with feeling when he said: 'R.S.M. Knight is one of the bravest gentlemen that ever wore the King's uniform. His behaviour was priceless throughout and he knows not the word "fear". He is simply adored by all ranks.'[22] Since 21 March, the Leinster officers had seven killed, eighteen wounded and five prisoners. Two officers survived unwounded.

FEILDING'S GROUP

The element under command of Lt.-Col. Kane continued holding a sector on the right of 39th Division and took part in the fighting around Harbonnières and Vauvillers until 29 March. The party under command of Lt.-Col. Feilding, 6th Rangers and 1st Munsters, fell back, collecting stragglers from other regiments as they went. With these additions, the strength built up to 400 all ranks. Feilding reported to Brig. Bellingham commanding 118 Brigade, late of 8th Dublins (both had commanded battalions at Ginchy). Feilding's force was added to 118 Brigade and ordered to hold three lines of old trenches crossing the main Amiens road. Feilding's men repelled repeated attacks at Raincourt and Framerville. Then a counter-attack force from 8th Division was brought up in lorries. These fresh companies finally checked the German attack and they began to fall back. As they retired, the enemy offered good targets for the Rangers and Munsters. Lt.-Col. Feilding ran forward to direct one Lewis gun himself. He tripped and, falling badly, was seriously injured and had to be evacuated. Maj. G.W. Nightingale of the Munsters assumed command.

The Irish held their position with 118 Brigade that night against mounting German pressure. Watts sought permission for his Corps to retire, but Gough was forced to wait until Foch could be got out of bed before permission was granted. As a result of the delay, Watts had to disengage in daylight. Early the following day, Brig. Bellingham's brigade was surrounded. Although the Rangers and Munsters succeeded in fighting their way out, it was at the cost of abandoning the wounded. In the retirement, Bellingham and his brigade major were captured.[23]

At Caix, the two elements of 47 Brigade were united, having fought on different flanks of 39th Division. The joint force, commanded by Lt.-Col. Kane, retired through the French south-westwards to Démounin. After an extraordinary chapter of adventures, Kane reported to Maj.-Gen. Daly of 24th Division (the right flank division of XIX Corps). Given rations by 24th Division, they made their way to Aubigny next day and reported to 16th Division on the evening of the 30th.[24]

Following the disintegration of 47 Brigade, 48 and 49 Brigades were subjected to continuous artillery and machine-gun fire from north of the Somme. They were attacked in front by the reinforced German 4th Guards Division. In stubborn fighting, they held their position until 1400. Then, after consultation between the brigade commanders, the battalions were ordered to retire about two miles to the spur west of Morcourt. Three battalions on the left received the order and withdrew; the three on the right did not receive the order and held on. As the units fell back, they came under heavy fire from the northern bank of the Somme and from their rear. It became evident that the enemy had crossed the Somme behind 16th Division. Three battalions from the German 1st Division had forced a passage despite determined resistance by a 16th Division engineer field company of only eighty men.[25]

These eighty divisional engineers ought to have been reinforced by a unit despatched from Carey's Force detailed to defend the crossing, but it had not arrived in time. By good fortune, the enemy did not press the attack home because the three battalions left in the line had delayed the German 4th Guards Division by their 'stout conduct'.[26] The withdrawal of the main elements of 48 and 49 Brigades was well supported by the divisional artillery. Additionally, 11th Hampshire formed a defensive flank and the divisional engineers maintained a stop line. All this succeeded in checking the enemy's advance as three battalions withdrew. Then, a counter-attack organised by Capt. G. Peirson, brigade major 48 Brigade, drove back the enemy before retiring at dusk through the Hampshires and engineers to Carey's Force. The 'Amiens Defence Line' became the main line of resistance behind which the remnants of 16th Division were ordered into support and reserve between Hamel and Fouilloy.

BREAK-OUT BY NIGHT

The three battalions of 48 and 49 Brigades which remained in the line at Proyart, each of little more than company strength, were 2nd Dublins, 2nd Munsters and remnants of two battalions of Royal Irish and Inniskillings. For six hours they repulsed all attacks[27] and with rifle and Lewis gun fire caught three enemy guns in an exposed position and put them out of action.[28] At one point, such was their indomitable spirit that a counter-attack was made by a tiny band of Munstermen. They included 2/Lt. C. O'Callaghan with a section of seven men under Cpl. Gallagher. RSM John Ring added to the legends surrounding him by joining them. 'The counter-attack proceeded in full view of the battalion, a couple of hundred yards away across a valley. The men dashed into one side of a copse, and after a short interval the Germans began bolting from the far side on the top of the ridge, and Regimental Sergeant-Major Ring could be seen shooting at them as they ran.'[29]

The Irishmen's 'stout conduct' had held up the advance of the German 4th Guards Division. Although the last orders to Maj. Wheeler were quite clear—give no ground and fight to the last—that evening it was obvious they were completely surrounded. There was little point in holding their position and surrendering when they were out of ammunition. Wheeler of the Dublins, Monson-Rye of the Munsters and Harrison of the Royal Irish agreed to withdraw at dusk.

The retirement began at 2000. Shaded by darkness, the remnants of the four battalions filed as quietly as possible out of the trenches. The Munsters left a Lewis-gunner behind with orders to fire occasionally until 2200, then withdraw. In January 1920 the steadfastness of this man, Cpl. Padfield, was recognised by the award of the Military Medal.[30]

About 400 strong, the column marched to the Somme. The intention was to cross to the northern side of the river in the mistaken belief that there lay safety. The Dublins led, followed by the Munsters, then the Royal Irish. Capt. Sitt, the adjutant of the Dublins and a German-speaker, went forward and discovered the countersign. The column made its way through burning Morcourt to the Cérisy bridge. Approaching this, Maj. Wheeler of the Dublins called for his batman, Fus. Byrne, the divisional heavyweight champion:

> I called him up and had him placed in the leading section of fours *without his rifle!* He knew without being told what he was likely to have to do. When all was ready we moved off, Captain Sitt and I leading. The Germans showed no sign of suspecting anything until we were within some fifteen yards of them when they challenged. We

immediately rushed forward. Fusilier Byrne knocked out two Boches with a right and left; a couple of revolver shots accounted for two more, and so completely had we taken this picquet by surprise that the remaining Germans made themselves scarce.[31]

Like good soldiers, they marched towards the sound of gunfire, and eventually reached Sailly-Lorette. There, fierce hand-to-hand fighting took place with another enemy picquet in which all the enemy were killed or wounded, but not without loss to the Dublins. Marching on quickly, they eventually reached Bois de Hamel in the British lines at 0200 on 28 March and immediately fell into exhausted sleep. Having fought all day against a German guards division and halted it, they had then marched twelve miles through German lines, fighting several times on the way. About 200 all ranks reached safety. Among those lost on the way out was the brave 2/Lt. O'Callaghan of the Munsters who had led the counter-attack earlier that day.[32]

Elsewhere on the front of XIX Corps, the fighting had been heavy and stubborn. The withdrawal of 47 Brigade was serious to its flanking division. The 39th Division had to conform and form a defensive flank towards Morcourt. Watts managed to scrape together a counter-attack force to restore the position on the front of 39th and 66th Divisions. Throughout the day, heavy fighting took place all along the line. On the right, 24th Division lost some trenches but recovered them by a counter-attack. The 8th Division, recently arrived from GHQ reserve and almost the only intact division present, succeeded in holding its front at Rosières. The 50th Division lost Vauvillers, although counter-attacking recovered it. But when the enemy attacked again, that division had to retire when its troops ran out of ammunition. 66th Division, effectively reduced to one weak brigade, had held its position until late afternoon. Then it retired with 50th Division to Harbonnières.

The Defence of Amiens, 28 March–5 April 1918

German pressure continued. There was little rest for the exhausted troops of 48 Brigade who had fought their way through the German lines. With the rest of 16th Division, they were rushed into the line on the left of Carey's Force to repulse a strong attack on Hamel.[33] At the same time, 61st Division arrived from the disbanded XVIII Corps and counter-attacked Lamotte but were repulsed.[34]

Fifth Army was now in effect only XIX Corps since III Corps was with the French. XVIII Corps was disbanded and VII Corps was with Third Army; 66th, 39th and 61st Divisions were in the line with 20th in close support, and 16th Division and 1st Cavalry Division were on the left of Carey's Force. 16th Division was reduced to a single brigade made up of a 48 Brigade composite battalion, 49 Brigade composite battalion, 11th Hampshire Regiment and the engineer battalion.

Gen. Rawlinson had taken over command and Fourth Army staff were arriving to take over from staff of Fifth Army. Rawlinson immediately wrote to Foch, expressing his concern, and doubted that XIX Corps could hold the line any longer.[35] But he received as little help from the French as Gough had. Rawlinson may have judged the state of his front-line troops by the hordes of stragglers, 'mainly Labour Corps and transport troops',[36] who flocked to the rear spreading despondency. He was to find that the resolution of fighting troops was unimpaired, as the Germans were discovering.

30 MARCH 1918: THE LAST MAJOR GERMAN ATTACK

As a result of the outflanking move across the Somme, XIX Corps, which had been holding east of Harbonnières and at Rosières, was forced back almost in line with Carey's Force. The Germans paused on the 29th and launched their final great attack on Fifth Army on 30 March. After a bombardment, the enemy assaulted the line and gained a footing at one place. Units of 16th Division, which had been held as the counterstroke force, were rushed forward. Charging together, 2nd Munsters and 2nd Dublins met the Germans and expelled them in fierce hand-to-hand fighting, although suffering heavy casualties themselves. Capt. Challender MC of 2nd Munsters, who had performed so well on 21 March, was killed.

On 31 March (Easter Sunday), 16th Division concentrated at Aubigny, and 47 Brigade re-formed as a composite battalion. Lt.-Col. A.J. Digan DSO assumed command of 6th Connaught Rangers; it had a strength of five officers and about 150 other ranks. 1st Munsters was led by Lt.-Col. R. Kane, with eight officers and 230 other ranks. In 2nd Leinsters were Lt.-Col. K.C. Weldon, two officers, the RSM and thirty-nine other ranks. Together they formed 47 Brigade composite battalion, with fifteen officers and 420 other ranks. There was little further fighting that day. The Germans were temporarily checked and, as exhausted as the British, they halted until fresh troops could be brought up. 47 Brigade composite battalion went into the line at Hamelet early on the morning of 2 April during the last German attack which it helped repel.

On 4 April, the last day of the battle of Second Somme, 16th Divisional Artillery particularly distinguished itself when massed artillery broke the last German attack of the March offensive.

> 'C' and 'D' Batteries of 177 Brigade caught the enemy in enfilade and broke them up in one of the great artillery actions of the war. All attempts to advance were stopped largely by artillery fire; the guns remained in action although the Germans came within 1500 yards of them. Some guns of 16th Division were indeed taken forward to the crest and fired over open sights with great effect.[37]

It was just retribution for the bombardment their division had taken from massed German artillery on 21 March. Although the 16th Division's headquarters and the brigade headquarters withdrew for organisation, its infantry remnant became part of 'Whitmore's Cosmopolitan Force' and held the northern sector of the Amiens defence line near the Somme until 5 April 1918.[38] Then, having been in action continuously for over two weeks, the last elements of 16th Division's infantry were finally relieved and returned to their division. The 16th Divisional Artillery remained in the line continuously until September 1918.

The survivors of 16th Division had taken part in the resistance to the great German March Offensive from beginning to end. They had suffered a crushing defeat on 21 March while holding a line which lacked depth, with inadequate forces and scant reserves. During a long retreat with few reinforcements and little rest, they maintained an unbroken front against a vastly superior enemy. After ten days of fierce fighting, they took part in the battle which brought the German offensive to a halt without having achieved its objective. It was a fine achievement. It ill-deserved that often quoted entry in the diary of FM Haig for 22 March 1918.

> Our 16th (Irish) Division which was on the right of 7th Corps and lost Ronssoy, is said not to be so full of fight as the others. In fact certain Irish units did very badly and gave way immediately the enemy showed.

Of course the entry began:

> All reports show our men in great spirits. All speak of the wonderful targets they had to fire at yesterday.[39]

Placing the two reports together in the light of the evidence, which ought to have been known then (heavy mist for example), it is difficult to know where precisely the Commander-in-Chief got his information; indeed it calls into question his evaluation of that information.

CASUALTIES IN THE IRISH DIVISIONS, 21 MARCH–5 APRIL 1918
The losses to the Irish divisions had been exceedingly heavy. Indeed they have never been accurately computed. The figures given in the official history from contemporary records are:

	Officers			Other Ranks			
	Killed	Wounded	Missing	Killed	Wounded	Missing	Total
16th Div.	29	104	144	369	1327	5176	7149
36th Div.	31	96	185	179	1159	4458	6109[40]

The heading 'missing' is often a euphemism for prisoners, as distinct from 'missing believed killed'. However, an analysis based on dead casualties, listed in *Officers Died* and *Soldiers Died*, gives more comprehensive data. By using a ratio of 3-to-1 (three wounded to every one killed), reasonably accurate numbers of wounded and prisoners can be obtained. It must be borne in mind that, although thousands of wounded were evacuated, many had to be left on the battlefield; medical officers and chaplains often remained with them. This was the case with Lt. O.L. Milburn, RAMC, and Father Duggan of 48 Brigade, Father Fitzmaurice of 49 Brigade, and the unnamed Anglican chaplain at St Emilie.

Casualties: Officers and Other Ranks Combined

	Killed	Wounded	Total	Unaccounted for	Totals
16th Div.	1085	3255	4340	2095	6435*
36th Div.	916	2748	3664	2445	6109
Totals	2001	6003	8004	4540	12,544

* The difference is 10% returned stragglers.[41]

Support troops' casualties have to be deducted from the 'Unaccounted for'. It is known that 16th and 36th machine-gun battalions were destroyed, about 300 casualties each. The engineer and artillery casualties were heavy, but exact casualty figures are largely unknown. However, 180 Brigade RFA, 16th Divisional artillery, recorded its casualties in the war diary. Between 21 March and 4 April 1918 these had 20 killed, 99 wounded or gassed, and 8 missing; total: 127, or approximately 25 per cent. Some wounded probably died subsequently. 177 Brigade RFA, more exposed on 21 March, suffered no less. The engineers fought as infantry. It can be estimated that each division had not less than 700 casualties among its 2500 support troops and had about 50 service troop casualties. From this it is deduced that the number of unwounded prisoners from the total 'missing' in the official history was probably about 1045 and 1400 for 16th and 36th Divisions, respectively.

Gen. Gough is Relieved

Gen. Sir Hubert Gough had never been forgiven by certain elements of the government for his part in the Curragh 'Mutiny' of 1914. Indeed that event caused a rift between the Liberal government and the army command which the emergency of war never completely healed. Gough became the scapegoat for the March disaster. Gen. Sir Henry Wilson and the new Secretary of State for War, Lord Milner, had been those chiefly responsible for using Hubert Gough as the opposition's cat's-paw during the Curragh 'Mutiny'. They were now among the first to counsel his removal. Gen. Gough and the staff of Fifth Army headquarters were relieved by Sir Henry Rawlinson and his Fourth Army staff on 29 March 1918. Within a week, Gough was ordered home. To his credit, Sir Douglas Haig resisted this and offered to resign instead. Haig outlined the disadvantages which Gough had to contend with: inadequate forces in line, lack of reserves and insufficient time to prepare the line taken over from the French. But since this would reflect on the government itself, it was a reasoning which was hardly likely to be accepted by astute politicians. Haig was retained. Henry Wilson advised Lloyd George that 'they would not get anyone to fight a defensive battle better than Haig, and that the time to get rid of him was when the German attack was over.'[42] It was Henry Wilson at his most cynical.

It has to be said that the British Expeditionary Force probably echoed the sentiments of Maj.-Gen. Oliver Nugent, who wrote on 29 March: 'Gough has gone home or at any rate has been relieved from command of 5th Army. If it had only been six months earlier…'[43]

Not content with sacking Gough, the number of his army was changed and it became Fourth Army. This gave rise to the spurious report that Fifth Army had been destroyed. It was the final insult to fighting soldiers. In that curious soldierly spirit of loyalty which is sometimes misunderstood, after the war Fifth Army veterans showed their sympathy to Gough and pride in their own achievement by forming a 'Fifth Army Association'. For nearly fifty years after the events outlined above, survivors marched proudly in Dublin and Belfast under their 'Fifth Army' banner at Remembrance Day parades.

THE OFFICIAL SUMMARY

The official historian summarised the battle eloquently, and shot the canard about 16th Division raised in the diary of FM Haig on 22 March 1918.

> The Fifth Army had grown smaller owing to casualties; it bent, but never broke; and its components all remained in being. The legend that certain of the Fifth Army failed is no more true than that the army as a whole failed until duly relieved… Spread out over a front too long for its strength; crushed and poisoned by a bombardment the intensity, if not the duration, of which was never experienced before or after 1914–18; assaulted and pursued by a numerically superior and specially trained enemy, the officers and men of the Fifth Army carried out a most difficult retirement, as planned by Gen. Gough, without even being morally defeated and without losing heart.[44]

It should be a matter of pride to the Irish people that two of the eleven infantry divisions which comprised Fifth Army on 21 March 1918 were largely of their nation.

CHAPTER THIRTY-SEVEN

Backs to the Wall,
9–29 April 1918

THE LYS OFFENSIVE, 9–29 APRIL 1918

On the morning of 9 April 1918, a bombardment which rivalled in intensity that of 21 March broke out from Lens to Armentières. Parts of Second and First Armies were overwhelmed. Aided by mist, forty-two German divisions assaulted and broke the British line from Wytschaete to Givenchy. It was achieved with the same crushing rapidity with which Third and Fifth Armies were broken in March.

Ploegsteert, Bailleul, Estaires, Neuve Chapelle, Armentières—names made immortal by the blood of countless men in over three years—were lost in as many days. Eight British and two Portuguese divisions were shattered. In the north, only that part of Messines Ridge held by 9th Scottish, and in the south at Givenchy and Festubert by 55th Lancashire, was firm resistance offered. The Lancastrians held tight to their positions. Part of 19th Division was forced back from Messines, but the Scots, throwing back their right flank, managed to hold on to Wytschaete.

In this hour of crisis, Douglas Haig, usually tongue-tied with his troops, published a stirring 'order of the day' to his armies on 12 April: 'With our backs to the wall and believing in the justice of our cause, each one of us must fight on to the end.'[1] Haig, well-served by the army's Chief of Intelligence, Maj.-Gen. Sir G. MacDonagh, had precisely forecasted the location of the second German offensive astride the Lys. But with impenetrable arrogance, the French CinC, Gen. Pétain, dismissed Haig's logic, convinced that the next German blow was aimed at him: the German deception plan had succeeded! Pétain's tardiness in committing French reserves to Fifth Army support, notwithstanding his agreement with Haig, confirmed the opinion of the Germans: the French would not rush to the aid of their ally. This time, Pétain's reluctance was belatedly overruled peremptorily by Marshal Foch.

HAZEBROUCK—THE IRISH GUARDS

Near Villers Brulin on 9 April, 4 Guards Brigade were recovering and resting from heavy fighting on the Arras front when news came that the line had broken. Despatched on 10 April, 2nd Irish Guards moved to Vieux-Berquin in the Vierhoek area in front of Hazebrouck, where the Germans had broken through the line of 15th Scottish. In one of the staunchest brigade defence actions of the war, 4 Guards Brigade, Grenadiers, Coldstreams, Scots and Irish held up to the German thrust for four days. On 14 April they were relieved by 1st Australian Division. But the cost was high. 2nd Irish Guards lost eighty-five officers, NCOs and guardsmen killed or died of wounds and 126 officers, NCOs and guardsmen wounded. One officer and thirty-seven guardsmen, mostly wounded, were captured.[2]

108 Brigade—Kemmel and Wulverghem, 10–18 April

36th Division remained on the coast just long enough to reorganise its shattered battalions by absorbing entrenching battalions. A flood of replacements poured in. Mostly conscripts, boys of eighteen and nineteen, they were nevertheless all good material, and English. Save only in name, the 36th was no more an Ulster Division. (This was not unusual. 50th Division, almost half Irish, was still called 'Northumbrian'; 66th, with a South African and Irish brigade, retained its 'East Lancashire' title.) In a short time, these youngsters would be put to a severe test against seasoned veterans from the Eastern Front; those that survived would emerge with considerable distinction as soldiers.[3]

Divisional headquarters was established near Poperinghe. On the night of 6–7 April, 107 Brigade took over a support line from 1st Division, with 109 Brigade in support. 108 Brigade was held in II Corps reserve. When the German Lys offensive began, 108 received orders on 10 April to move quickly to Kemmel. Buses carrying the brigade's personnel arrived there at 1600 and came under command of 19th Division. This division, with 9th Scottish, was fighting desperately on Messines Ridge

Unlike Fifth Army battalions dispersed in their 'birdcages' on an inadequately manned line, Second and First Armies held a continuous front line in old British defences. Despite these advantages, however, the Germans broke through in many places, again attacking under cover of mist. At Messines, a brigade of 19th Division had been badly cut up and pushed back out of the village and off the ridge; another brigade suffered heavy losses but held on. Part of 19th had held their positions and the Scots clung grimly to Wytschaete until reinforcements secured it. That night, Brig. Griffith was ordered to move his brigade up to Messines Ridge, supporting the South African Brigade of 9th Division. 1st and 9th Irish Fusiliers took over positions on the Messines–Wytschaete road, with 12th Irish Rifles in support on the Spanbroek Ridge. In heavy fighting, the South Africans and 1st Irish Fusiliers were pushed back. Rallying, they counter-attacked and recaptured the position. Resisting resolutely, the raw young soldiers repulsed another enemy attack with the help of two companies of 12th Irish Rifles. The Fusiliers suffered heavy casualties and had to be withdrawn. So grievous were the losses of 1st Irish Fusiliers that later that night, they reorganised into a company and were attached to their 9th Battalion. 19th Division and the remnant of 108 Brigade fell back on Wulverghem, but 9th Scottish Division formed a defensive flank and clung with dour tenacity onto Wytschaete.

The British line, four miles long from Nieppe to the forward slopes of Neuve Église and on to the Wulverghem spur, was held by IX Corps. It was a mixture of tired and broken divisions, brigades and battalions who held their positions against four German divisions.[4] For three vital days, 108 Brigade took part in heavy fighting. At times their lines were broken and then restored only by desperate counter-attacks led personally by their commanding officers, Lt.-Col. P.E. Kelly, 1st Irish Fusiliers and Maj. H. Waring, 12th Irish Rifles. With only breaks for a few hours' sleep, both battalions fought on until compelled to retire west of Wulverghem. Here their line was again broken and in a desperate counter-attack, Maj. Waring was killed and the remnants of the brigade were again forced back. In the early hours of 13 April the fragments of these three battalions were relieved. But not for long.

After a short rest, the remnants of 108 Brigade, about 400 strong, were mustered into a composite battalion under Lt.-Col. Kelly and deployed behind Kemmel Hill. There they remained throughout the 17th and 18th under almost unrelenting shell-fire. On the evening of the 18th, French troops took over part of the line and the British withdrew. For the second time in a month, 108 Brigade had been very nearly annihilated. Its survivors rejoined 36th Division.[5]

The German attacks against Second Army continued until 30 April, but the crisis had passed. The failure to penetrate the northern sectors of the British front ended the German offensive against the British armies. Ludendorff's great gamble had failed in the face of the stubborn courage of the BEF, which for forty days withstood, almost alone, the whole might of the German attack.

For six weeks, 36th Division rested, reorganised and retrained. Maj.-Gen. Clifford Coffin VC DSO replaced Gen. Nugent as GOC and Brigs. E.J. de S. Thorpe DSO and E. Vaughan DSO replaced Withycombe and Griffith in 107 Brigade and 108 Brigade, respectively. Gen. Coffin, late RE, had won his VC at Ypres and had a reputation for bravery and vigour. He had recently commanded a brigade in Fifth Army's fighting retreat with distinction.

Gen. Nugent assumed the appointment of GOC for the Boulogne Base Area. On the other side of the English Channel was Gen. Hickie, GOC Dover Area.

THE END OF 16TH IRISH DIVISION
When 16th Division was relieved in the line on 3 April, it left its machine-guns and artillery to cover 14th Division. Both divisions were the last of the original Fifth Army to be relieved and were reduced to training cadres for newly-arrived United States Army divisions. During May and June 1918,

16th Division training cadres trained 4th and 80th Divisions before they were committed to battle. (4th Division of the Army of the United States subsequently earned the sobriquet 'Rock of the Marne Division', which they still proudly carry.)

Brig. F.W. Ramsay was rewarded for his fine performance in command of 48 Brigade during the March battle by promotion to major-general and command of a division. It was also official recognition of his brigade's excellent behaviour on many occasions during the battle. In June, 16th Division, less its artillery which remained in the line, returned to Aldershot for refitting and reconstitution by filling up with B1 category conscripts from the Training Reserve. By this time, the 16th had lost all its Irish battalions and only 11th Hampshire remained of its original fighting formations. 5th Royal Irish Fusiliers joined the division from Palestine and became the sole Irish link, but the majority of its Irishmen had first been transferred to 36th Division. The reconstituted 16th Division returned to France at the beginning of August 1918 and was attached to I Corps of Fifth Army (Sir W. Birdwood) and took part in the final advance to victory in Artois and Flanders.

The 6th Connaught Rangers was disbanded and its personnel posted to 2nd Leinsters. It was particularly distressing to the Rangers: 'It seemed to us a very harsh decision. But unfortunately we had no senior officers to speak up for us, and seemingly no friends in high places.'[6] Considering the gallantry of this fine battalion, it was a harsh decision. It also meant that, until the return of 5th Connaught Rangers from Palestine, there was no battalion representing the regiment on the Western Front.

At the end of May 1918, the 10th Division's battalions arrived in France and the process of reconstruction and retraining began. 2nd Dublins under command of Lt.-Col. K.C. Weldon left 48 Brigade and joined 94 Brigade at Requinghem. There it was joined by 7th Dublins which it absorbed; 6th Munsters was absorbed by 2nd Munsters.

Most men in the returned units were suffering from the effects of malaria. The BEF Medical Services had no concept of the amount of quinine necessary for their treatment until all the returned units were inspected by Sir Ronald Ross, an eminent specialist. A period of treatment and convalescence was ordered before the battalions entered the line. Sadly, the hope that a return to Europe would see the granting of home leave was ill-founded. Not until long after they had returned to the Western Front would these men, who had been abroad for over three years, be allowed home leave.

The battalions of 10th and 16th Divisions were distributed to other divisions on the Western Front.

29th Division	*30th Division*	*50th Division*	*57th Division*	*63rd Naval Division*	*66th Division*
2nd Leinsters	7th R. Irish	5th R. Irish	1st Munsters	2nd R. Irish	5th Inn. Fus.
1st Dublins	7th/8th Inn. Fus.	6th Inn. Fus.			5th CR
		2nd Munsters			6th Leinsters
		2nd Dublins			6th Dublins

Two new line battalions, 8th Royal Irish and 13th Inniskillings, were formed from B1 category men of Irish garrison and reserve battalions; both went to 40th Division and served throughout the advance to victory. They were the last Irish Service battalions raised in the war.

The battalions of 10th Division which returned to the Western Front were still largely Irish in character. After Gallipoli, they had been absent from the main killing grounds of the war. With the returned wounded, they were at effective strength comparable to Western Front standards. Moreover, their personnel were seasoned veterans. Reorganising the Irish regular battalions necessitated absorbing several 'Service' units, but with this done, nine Irish New Army battalions remained. Sufficient New Army battalions therefore existed to re-form the 16th as an Irish division.

It is possible that the Army Medical Services considered it inadvisable to concentrate so many battalions infected with malaria. However, although in different divisions, all were later in close operational proximity and all the battalions appear to have borne well the rigours of the final campaign. During this, evidence that malaria did not affect their fighting spirit can be amply shown. Even without the malaria-affected battalions, sufficient Irish regular infantry units existed to make the Irish Division viable. Which leaves the question: Why did the War Office not reconstitute 16th Division as an Irish formation?

Suspicion must exist that disbanding the Irish division was for reasons other than the old British military one of providing Celtic leavening, the traditional 'mix', to several divisions. Against this possible reason other values have to be weighed. The Australian and Canadian Corps proved the worth of homogeneous formations which, when kept together as a corps, had an incomparable team spirit. To this extent the official historian declared that the day of the traditional mix, long favoured by the army since Wellington spoke in its favour, was over.[7] Therefore, the addition of some of 10th Division's battalions to 16th and 36th Divisions could have rejuvenated both for the final advance to victory, which they could have made together. It was not tried, and the closest thing there was to an Irish Corps in 1918 was the operation together of 50th and 66th Divisions in XIII Corps, which spearheaded Fourth Army in the advance to victory during the last one hundred days.

The most likely explanation of the demise of the 'Irish' division is that it was done as an act of policy by the War Office. They instructed GHQ as to which battalions were to be disbanded, and where decimated divisions were to be reconstituted. In 1918, the Irish had few friends at Whitehall and Sir Henry Wilson, that implacable foe of Irish Catholic Nationalism, was Chief of the Imperial General Staff (CIGS) ('He hated Papists and Irish patriots').[8] It is inconceivable that he, with the Adjutant General, Sir C.F.N. Macready, would not have been part of that decision, in which case the result was a foregone conclusion.

The Continuation of the German Offensive

In the wake of two costly attempts to drive the British into the sea, Ludendorff turned against the French on the Aisne front in May 1918. On 27 May, the Germans smashed through at the Chemin des Dames between Rheims and Soissons. They reached the Marne where the Americans, at Château Thierry, helped stem the offensive. As a result of this misfortune, the French better understood the nature of the British defeats. Thereafter they were less reluctant to cooperate as allies.

> The misfortunes of the Battle of the Chemin des Dames had the remarkable effect of improving the relations between the British and French armies. After a surprise so glaring and a retreat of twenty kilometres in a single day—the record of all battles on the Western Front—the French were in no position to maintain the airs of superiority which they had been unable to conceal from the Italians after Caporetto or altogether from the British after 21 March.[9]

The last major effort of the *Kaiserschlacht* (Emperor Battle) took place on 6 July on both sides of Rheims and was stopped by the 15th. German gains in three months of supreme effort represented a great salient, containing the devastated area they had created in 1917 before retiring to the Hindenburg Line. They failed to achieve their objectives. Instead of breaking, the Allies were strengthened by the creation of a unified command structure under Marshal Foch. Under his direction, a series of counter-strikes began. First, south of the Somme, Mangin's army concentrated over three hundred Renault tanks in the forest of Villers-Cotterêts and, using the Cambrai tactics of no preparatory bombardment, launched a counter-attack west of the Marne salient. This was followed by another attack from the east. Only skilful handling extricated Prince Rupprecht's army from its dangerous cul de sac.

The massive German effort was almost at its last gasp. Tactically their attacks succeeded, but strategically the offensive failed in its original intention of dividing the Allies and destroying the BEF. Moreover, by consuming vast quantities of men and material, the *Kaiserschlacht* destroyed the ability of the German army to prolong the war and to achieve a stalemate compromise in 1919.

Soissons was recaptured on 2 August, and the striking success of the Allied counter-offensive south of the Aisne completely altered the military situation. The bulk of the German reserves had been used up and the US army was growing rapidly. The BEF, reinforced with the return of troops from Italy, Salonika and Palestine, in addition to those which poured from the Training Reserve in Britain, was preparing to take the offensive.

At the end of July, as the preparations for his offensive were nearing completion, Field-Marshal Haig received from Chief of the General Staff, Sir Henry Wilson, a thirty-three page memorandum dated 25 July 1918 and entitled 'British Military Policy 1918–19'. Wilson envisaged the final offensive taking place in July 1919, because 'it would be unwise to defer the attempt to gain a decisive victory until 1920'. Two months before Gen. Allenby had annihilated two Turkish armies at Megiddo, the CIGS concluded his memorandum by recommending that nothing should be done in Palestine except consolidation.

The comments of Allenby, 'the Bull', are not recorded. Sir Douglas Haig was characteristically laconic: 'Lots of words! and little else.'[10] Wilson's war appreciation of 1918–19, in its misjudgment, is matched only by his 1914 assessment of Kitchener's New Armies.

After skilful preparations, Haig launched his attack at Amiens on 8 August. Fourth Army won a decisive victory. It was, in the words of Ludendorff, the 'black day of the German army'. Attacking from the last line held by the remnants of Fifth Army in early April, Fourth Army broke into the German line using spearheads of tanks, armoured cars and cavalry which caused havoc behind the enemy lines. These thrusts were followed hard by the Australian and Canadian Corps. Only against the Somme was the advance slow because the Allied corps north of it had failed to advance. As a result, the Germans enfiladed across the river in exactly the same way as they had against 16th Division when Third Army fell back on its northern flank.

With the arrival of American divisions, the Allies at last had adequate reserves. Foch directed a succession of unrelenting blows on the Germans along the entire American, British and French sectors. The Germans, given no time to pause or rest, were without sufficient reserves to repel all attacks. Amiens was followed by the Battle of Albert. This was overlapped and continued by the battles of the Scarpe, Péronne and Epéhy. By early September, the Germans had lost all their gains.

The 2nd Royal Irish in 63rd Naval Division took part in the Battle of Albert (21–25 August). It was a continuation of the success gained at Amiens. With their brigade, they captured Achiet le Grand and advanced along the Albert-Bapaume road where Royal Irish were driven back by a fierce attack by a Bavarian regiment. However, they dug in and repulsed a second attack and captured a complete machine-gun company of eight officers and 100 men and ten machine-guns. During the battle, 2nd Royal Irish lost 329 all ranks killed or wounded.[11] The Naval Division was then transferred to XVII Corps in Fourth Army, in time for the first attack on the Hindenburg Line at Drocourt-Quéant.

On 1 September, Péronne was recaptured and the Germans fell back to the Hindenburg Line, with Fourth Army in hot pursuit. Allowing the enemy no time to recover, the attack was renewed the following day. XVII Corps, 57th and 63rd Divisions (1st Munsters and 2nd Royal Irish) were without tanks and could have no possibility of success against the Hindenburg position at Quéant. On the same day, the Canadian Corps of First Army, well supported by tanks, stormed the elaborate system of wire, trenches and strongpoints of the line in hard fighting.

57th Division, which had gone into First Army sector, advanced behind the Canadians and the tanks. Then 57th Division passed through and turned southwards, rolling up the German front (across the front of its own corps) to assist a breakthrough on Fourth Army front. In this manoeuvre, 1st Munsters particularly distinguished itself by pushing forward 1000 yards in advance of its objective.[12] This enabled 52nd Lowland Division to carry the Hindenburg Support Line up to their objective.

Following the success of 57th Division, 63rd Division passed through, led by 2nd Royal Irish and a marine battalion. Because all available artillery was supporting the 52nd and 57th Divisions, their attack was unsupported except by their own infantry weapons. Consequently, despite hard fighting, they were checked by the as yet untaken Hindenburg Support Line. Reinforced by Anson Battalion and despite the fire, all three units reached their objective. The villages of Quéant and Pronville which had stood defiant for so long were at last captured. Shortly afterwards, 57th and 63rd Divisions withdrew for rest and training.

SECOND ARMY—THE REBOUND, 4 AUGUST–7 SEPTEMBER

The resounding success of the Battle of Amiens opened a succession of battles which gave the Germans little respite. With dwindling reserves, they were given no time to use these strategically, but were forced to deploy them piecemeal along the entire front. Spearheaded by tanks, the Allied armies repeatedly broke into the enemy front and outflanked the Germans, forcing them back. Their most decisive defeat occurred when the Hindenburg Line was massively smashed by British Fourth Army. Thereafter the German front crumbled.

As a result of the successful offensives south of the Aisne from early to mid August, the Germans in Flanders had been retiring to shorten their line. The British Second Army and the reconstituted Fifth Army began offensive operations to hasten and harass their withdrawal. The opening phase of this was for 29th Division to conduct aggressive patrolling. During one fighting patrol, a very young soldier of 1st Dublins was cut off, lost his way and got behind German lines. Repeatedly challenged and pursued by the Germans, he evaded capture and made his way into the lines of 1st Middlesex a mile farther south. Having given them much valuable information, the soldier reported back to his battalion with a note of explanation from a Middlesex officer: 'This boy—for he was only seventeen—was complimented by Brig.-Gen. Cheape, particularly for having stuck to his rifle throughout, and was recommended for and received the Military Medal.'[13] Regrettably, the regimental historian does not give the youth's name.

The Outtersteen Ridge was retaken on 18 August by 9th Scottish Division, supported by artillery of 29th and 36th Divisions (XV Corps). This, coming on top of the offensives by First, Third and Fourth Armies, forced the Germans in front of Second and Fifth Armies into further withdrawals. In a continuation of the advance of the Allied line, Second Army began operations on 1 September to pinch out the Lys salient. A major part in this offensive was played by 29th Division (2nd Leinsters and 1st Dublins), 30th Division (7th Royal Irish and 7th/8th Inniskillings) and 36th Division. In the advance, severe resistance was put up by German machine-gun rearguards. Strongpoints were methodically attacked and captured one by one.

Rarely did the British line actually come up with the retreating Germans, except at Neuve Église and Ploegsteert. 2nd Leinsters captured Hill 63, an important tactical feature. At Ploegsteert village on 4 September, 1st Dublins captured the place against a strong German rearguard in a stiff fight. Two platoons under Lts. O'Donnell and McNulty suffered heavy casualties. Lt. McNulty and twenty-three men were killed and over ninety officers and men wounded, against 170 German prisoners and four captured field guns.[14]

On the left, the 30th Division (7th Royal Irish and 7th/8th Inniskillings) had taken Wulverghem on 3 September, but resistance stiffened as the front narrowed. A brigade of 29th Division relieved the 31st Division for an assault on Hill 63. Then, while 2nd Leinsters of 29th Division assaulted and captured Hill 63, 36th Division advanced steadily behind a creeping barrage, following the retreating Germans until they reached their old front line of 1915. Several attacks and counter-attacks proved the enemy were prepared to resist strongly on this line and 36th Division dug in. The objectives of its limited offensive being achieved, GHQ switched the weight of Second Army to its northern sector, the Ypres salient. It was to this area that 29th and 36th Divisions were moved for their final major battle.

CHAPTER THIRTY-EIGHT

Victory in Palestine,
September–October 1918

MESOPOTAMIA, 10 JANUARY 1916–3 APRIL 1918
When the Indian Corps left France at the end of 1915, it had been the War Office's intention to send it to Egypt. But Gen. Townshend's check at Ctesiphon and the siege of Kut al Amara (December 1915) changed the plan and the Indian Corps went to Mesopotamia. Because of the urgency of the situation there, all units as they arrived at Basra were rushed up the River Tigris towards Kut al Amara. In many cases, they left without transport or medical services and inevitably suffered as a result. It is hardly surprising that their advance was checked. The Rangers arrived at Basra on 10 January 1916 and took part in the mishandled attempted relief of Kut. In the action at Umm al Hanna, they marched in blinding rain straight into Turkish fire through a mêlée of disorganised Indian units. There they lost 285 officers and men killed and wounded, including the commanding officer, Lt.-Col. Murray, who was among the wounded. Maj. W.A. Hamilton assumed command of 1st Connaught Rangers and held it until the end of the war. In the retirement following the failure of Kut's relief, the Connaught Rangers distinguished itself at Thorny Nullah during the action of Abu Roman.

The pursuing Turks had occupied trenches at Abu Roman and a night counter-attack was ordered. The Rangers, with three companies in front and one in reserve, advanced on the Thorny Nullah trenches in open order. A very heavy but wild and inaccurate fire suddenly opened as they neared the enemy. Without checking, the battalion pushed on. In the dark Thorny Nullah was missed and although realising they had overshot the objective, the battalion continued its advance and eventually reached the Abu Roman trenches, the main Turkish line. Undeterred, the Rangers charged and 'a very hot fight ensued at the point of the bayonet'.

> The encounter was sharp and decisive and resulted in the Turks being cleared out of the greater part of the position, a large number being killed and upwards of sixty, including two officers, made prisoner.[1]

By this time, the Turks had withdrawn from Thorny Nullah and at dawn it was occupied by the Rangers. Over seventy Rangers were lost in this minor operation. And if the battalion got no marks for night navigation, the enemy got a severe jolt and the objective was captured.

In the following two years, 1st Connaught Rangers fought throughout this backwater campaign in 'Mespot'. Wounds festered easily in the torrid heat, where the army suffered almost every possible disease, especially malaria. In the desert summer and winter, they alternately baked and froze. In addition to the action at Hanna and Abu Roman, they fought at Dubailah, Beit Aeissa and Mohamed Abdul Hassan and in numerous trench raids.

Eventually in 1918, the battalion left Basra for Palestine and disembarked at Suez on 15 April. They then went into camp at Moascar where they remained until 9 May. After re-equipping at El Kantara, the battalion entrained for Ludd, the railhead and base on the western flank of the British line. On the way they were delighted to see names indicating the presence of their Service battalion: 'Ranger Corner' and 'Connaught Road'.[2] After the inevitable period at road-making and repair, training and patrolling, 19 September saw the Rangers with 7 Brigade of 3rd Indian Division facing the Turkish Eighth Army on the Plain of Sharon.

PALESTINE 1918: THE INDIANISATION OF 10TH DIVISION

Following the completion of Indianisation, 10th Division's organisation and order of battle was:

> Maj.-Gen. J.R. Longley remained as GOC, and the divisional and brigade staffs remained the same. Brig. C.L. Smith assumed command of 29 Brigade from Brig. Vandaleur, who departed with the main body of battalions.

29 Brigade	*30 Brigade*	*31 Brigade*
1st Leinster Regiment	1st R. Irish Regiment	2nd R. Irish Fusiliers
1st/54th Sikhs	38th Dogras	2nd/42nd Deoli
1st/101st Grenadiers	46th Punjabis	74th Punjabis
2nd/151st Infantry	1st Kashmir Rifles	2nd/101st Grenadiers

> *Divisional Troops*
> 424 Battery RA
> 3rd Sappers and Miners RE
> Pioneers 2nd/155th Inf. (Pioneers)
> RAMC
> 154 Combined Field Ambulance
> 165 Combined Field Ambulance
> 166 Combined Field Ambulance

10th Battalion, Machine-Gun Corps, was formed from the three machine-gun companies. 6th Royal Irish Rifles, crippled by its Tell 'Asur losses, was disbanded and its troops posted to the three battalions remaining with the

10th. The surplus units of 10th Division—nine infantry battalions, its artillery, engineer field companies and field ambulances—left for France. Together the units were sufficient to provide the infantry and support arms for a BEF division.

10th Division was now facing strong Turkish defences along the Furkah Ridge which overlooked the entire XX Corps front. Patrolling began and soon the Turks began to show evidence of 'wind', opening fire blindly at the slightest provocation day or night. But successful aggression was not all one-sided, and an advanced and isolated platoon of the Leinsters was attacked and wiped out before support could reach it. In this period, the divisional artillery reached a high level of co-operating efficiency with the infantry in response to its Forward Observation Officers both in time and accuracy.

THE CLASSIC NIGHT RAID OF 1ST LEINSTER REGIMENT

> On August 12, a night raid on a large scale was carried out by the 10th Division against the Turkish defences just west of the Nablus road. It was well planned and executed and resulted in the capture of nearly 250 prisoners and fourteen machine-guns, as well as inflicting heavy loss on the enemy. The losses of the raiding brigade were only just over a hundred.[3]

In mid July, to test the newly-arrived Indian battalions, 10th Division was chosen to carry out a large-scale night raid west of the Nablus road on a frontage of four thousand yards. The tactical objective was the Turkish trenches on the Ghurabeh Ridge where the enemy defences were very strong. Wire in places was sixteen feet thick and very high. Good trenches were cut into solid rock, with many tunnelled shell-proof dug-outs five feet by twenty-five feet long. Their German and Austrian machine-gunners were well concealed with good cover and excellent fields of fire. Their garrison was numerous. To carry out this night raid, Gen. Longley selected 29 Brigade, 1st/54th Sikhs on the right, 1st/101st Grenadiers on the left; a wing of 1st Leinsters was to operate on each flank. With memories of Gallipoli, the Leinsters considered it might be 'the very devil to attack'[4] and prepared accordingly.

Success was important for the morale of the young Indian troops. Nothing was left to chance. Staff planning at divisional and brigade levels was meticulous and considerable special training was carried out. Thick felt pads were nailed to boots to deaden the noise of hob-nails on rocks. To cross the wide enemy wire belt, all platoons carried long bamboo ladders covered with matting. The Leinsters built a replica of the enemy positions on which TEWTs (tactical exercises without troops) were carried out. After this units were briefed on their role. Unluckily, just before Z Day, 12 August 1918, a bad bout of recurrent malaria struck 1st Leinsters; however, 'on the day' every man was on parade.

Before the attack, linesmen of 10th Division Signal Company crept out one thousand yards into no man's land where they laid telephone cable. A heavy concentration of artillery, including the neighbouring divisions' and the corps ' own heavy artillery, was put at the disposal of the brigade doing the raid. The Irish battalion was divided into two wings; A and B Companies under Capt. T.D. Murray were on the right, with C and D under Capt. Cavendish on the left. There was a moment's confusion on the right wing where the Sikhs deployed at the double in pitch dark and lost touch with the Leinsters. However, Capt. Murray led his men towards the loudest noise, which proved a successful if elementary ploy. On the left, Capt. Cavendish led his men behind the Grenadiers down a narrow path to the assembly point, but because of the slowness of the Indian troops, they arrive fifteen minutes after Zero Hour. This resulted in a rush deployment in which one platoon and the Signal section lost their way. The left came under shell-fire. The platoons instantly scattered for cover, losing precious time. Like all young troops under shell-fire for the first time, the Indians had a tendency to scatter at every shell-burst, which lost time. Eventually, with encouragement from the Leinsters no doubt, they learned to accept it philosophically. The Allied guns laid down a heavy concentrated barrage on the Turkish positions, and although it caused few casualties in the well-protected positions, the moral effect on both enemy and attackers was great.

Under cover of the bombardment, the infantry gained the enemy positions with few casualties. After the brigade had established itself in sharp fighting, 1st Leinsters rolled up the front from each wing in the face of stiff opposition. Notwithstanding the courage of the Turks, the operation was a complete success. Fourteen machine-guns were captured, and although only 239 Turkish prisoners were brought in, a large number of the enemy were killed or wounded in their positions. More importantly from a military aspect, the Indian battalions had given a good account of themselves and learned valuable lessons. It is an indicator of what might have happened at Suvla had Gen. Hamilton used his veteran regular battalions of 29th Division to stiffen the New Army brigades.

In the course of the action, the Leinsters had the heaviest casualties: one officer and three soldiers killed and two officers and twenty-five soldiers wounded. One, Pte. Flanagan, although wounded in the ankle early during the action, carried on without reporting his wound and accounted for many of the enemy. He was awarded the DCM.[5] After the war, this minor operation was studied as the modern classic raid in strength.

THE BATTLE OF MEGIDDO/NABLUS

Gen. Allenby planned nothing less than the complete destruction of Seventh and Eighth Turkish Armies. It was a relentless pursuit the like of which was not seen by any other army in the Great War. It featured three essentials required for complete military success: deception of the enemy as to the aim, concentration at the decisive point, and relentless pursuit of a defeated army. It was in two phases. First, 35,000 infantry would attack on the left upon a frontage of fifteen miles supported by 400 guns. Having broken enemy resistance, 9000 cavalry would pass through to harry the retreating enemy to its front and, in a wide turning movement, descend far in the right rear of the Turkish army. In the second phase, 20,000 infantry and 3000 cavalry supported by 130 guns, on a front of fifty miles, would break through the Turkish line and, bypassing the front-line troops, would force the Turks into the arms of the cavalry.

But first, Allenby deceived the Turkish command into believing his intention was to attack on the right.

> New camps were pitched in the Jordan Valley and additional bridges thrown across the Jordan. Fifteen thousand dummy horses, made of canvas, filled the horse lines; and sleighs drawn by mules raised clouds of dust at the times when the canvas horses should have been going to water. Battalions marched ostentatiously down to the valley by day and returned by lorries at night. Wireless traffic was continued from Desert Mounted Corps headquarters near Jericho long after the headquarters and nearly all the troops had been transferred to the other flank.[6]

For the first phase, Allenby tasked Sir Edward Bulfin's XXI Corps with breaking into the Turkish line on the coastal plain and opening a way for the Desert Mounted Corps.

The moon had set thirty-five minutes earlier when Bulfin's corps attacked at 0430 on 19 September. There was no preliminary bombardment. The guns opened a seventeen-minute barrage with three hundred guns firing together. 60-pounders and heavy howitzers rained fire on enemy batteries; 18-pounder field guns and light howitzers were trained on the enemy trenches and wire. Before the Turks were prepared, the attackers were upon them with bombs and bayonets. Surprise was complete. In front of 3rd Indian Division, there was negligible resistance.

At 0400, the Rangers advanced from their positions about 200 yards to the start line and formed up along a front of 300 yards behind 27th Punjabis on the brigade left. The instant the first guns fired, the Rangers sprang forward and were almost into the Turkish lines before the enemy fired. They were well inside enemy lines within the first fifteen minutes. The first objective was gained with little difficulty. Skilful tactics in co-operation with the Punjabis and artillery gained the second by 0600, despite stubborn resistance on the part of the Turks. Without pausing to relish their little victory, the Rangers continued their advance. Moving through Kefar Saba, they were in

Kalkilieh Wood by 0900. 8 Brigade went through and led the way along Wadi Azzun. They rested that night, having achieved their objectives and captured three officers and 342 soldiers. Their own casualties were just over fifty all ranks killed and wounded.

Next day, progress slowed as the enemy recovered and fought a stubborn rearguard action with machine-guns. A large number of Turkish ammunition wagons and a German field hospital were captured a little after noon. Following this the force halted for about four hours in the heat of the day to rest and regroup. That evening in a wide turning movement, 7 Brigade passed through 8 Brigade and with the Rangers in the lead. They captured a section of road running north from Kefar Haris to El Funduk and formed a roadblock across the enemy's line of retreat. But hearing a distant rumble of vehicles from the north, it was realised that they had just missed a retreating Turkish column.

Lt.-Col. Hamilton reacted quickly. One company was left to man the roadblock. Removing their packs for speed, the remaining three companies set out in pursuit. Within fifteen minutes they came up with a Turkish artillery column and captured it with great dash but little firing. As they charged among the rear vehicles, the enemy drivers cut the traces and galloped off, leaving behind four 77 mm guns, two other field guns and two machine-guns. Four German artillerymen, sixteen Turks and upwards of 150 wagons laden with ammunition and other supplies together with 270 animals were also taken. So surprised had the enemy been that the incredible capture was achieved without a casualty. Subsequently, four of the German guns were requested as trophies for each of the battalions represented there—1st Battalion together with its 2nd, 3rd and 4th militia battalions.[7]

In the folklore of the battalion, that night became the 'Night of the Soup'.[8] Among the booty taken were several German 'Goulash Kanonen'. These, filled with excellent soup, were perhaps the most welcome of trophies to the hungry Rangers. After a night's rest at El Funduk, the battalion moved out at the head of 7 Brigade at 0700 (having taken the precaution of painting the battalion title on the captured guns). Marching to intercept the retreat of Turkish Seventh Army, they moved eastwards through the hills in the direction of Nablus. After much marching and rounding up of prisoners, the Rangers entered the littered streets of Nazareth at noon on 25 September. Nazareth, former GHQ of Turkish German command in Palestine, was littered with broken-down motor vehicles and dead Turks. Lt.-Col. Hamilton took over the government of the town from 27 September 1918. It was a fitting place for 1st Connaught Rangers to end their long crusade, which had begun in India almost exactly four years previously.

In a post-battle anti-climax, the Rangers suffered considerable sickness, chiefly malaria, and their strength dropped to 584. The battle of Megiddo became their last action before being reduced to cadre by demobilisation. Following the armistice, the cadre remnant embarked for Dover where 1st

Connaught Rangers was reconstituted in 1919.

THE BATTLE OF NABLUS

On 9 September, Maj.-Gen. Sir L. Bols, the army chief of staff, wrote to Gen. Chetwode, commanding XX Corps:

> In view of the long marches which you have to make and the necessity of conserving your full strength to carry out the important role assigned to you in the enemy's rear, you must on no account allow your troops to be drawn into an infantry fight... The actions of your troops must be characterised by the greatest vigour and rapidity.[9]

With these words, Chetwode's XX Corps was committed to an operation which Allenby planned not only to clear the Turkish army out of Palestine but also to pursue it to destruction. 10th Division was widely separated and extended in the Judean Hills. The other division in the corps was the 53rd Division which until recently had been 'Welsh' and like the 10th was 'Indianised'. Chetwode's two divisions were operating against four understrength Turkish ones. The objective of the 10th was the Furkah Ridge. No move could be made until the success of Bulfin's Corps was known.

One of Gen. Longley's problems was holding his men in readiness near the front and keeping them relatively fresh preparatory to their long advance. Their objective, Nablus, was twenty miles deep in enemy territory. Depending as he was on Bulfin's movements, Longley could not forecast exactly when he might receive orders to attack. He had a time bracket of twelve to thirty-six hours to work on. Longley solved this by concentrating well forward and dumping supplies sufficient for five days as near the front as possible.[10] The movement of Army Service Corps lorries bringing the supplies forward was drowned with artillery fire.[11] Miscellaneous replacements from the corps' reinforcement unit under command of Capt. Murray of 1st Leinsters took over a portion of the line, thus relieving one battalion.[12] Other battalions in the brigades were relieved in a similar way. 29 Brigade was to make the first breach and 31 Brigade was to extend it. 30 Brigade was to exploit success, but its first mission entailed hard work. A road in enemy territory, identified as being essential to the advance, had to be repaired immediately after its capture. 1st Royal Irish and half 30 Brigade engineer field company were tasked with this.[13]

At noon on 19 September, Gen. Longley received the order to attack that night. 10th Division launched its attack at 1945 and found the enemy's new line of defence well organised and strongly held. 29 Brigade advanced with great determination. 1st Leinsters on the right and 2nd/151st Infantry on the left met dogged resistance from German troops almost from the first, but made steady progress. On the right, 1st Leinsters also met stiff opposition from German troops and brought forward its support company. The advance slowed, then lost the barrage, but co-operation with the artillery was such that it was easily brought back and the advance continued. The objective was carried with a bayonet charge.[14] Despite the delay caused by German resistance, all objectives were gained by 0200 on 20 September. 1st Leinsters captured the trenches covering Furkah, and an Indian company took the village of Furkah itself. The 101st Grenadiers then passed through to fight their way to the second day's objective.

Over Furkah Ridge, 101st Grenadiers got into difficulties, and two companies of Leinstermen went forward to help. The remainder of the battalion, in support, provided water-supply detachments. That evening, Gen. Longley, feeling the enemy was breaking, ordered an immediate advance. About 2240, the orders reached HQ 29 Brigade which sent out a warning order to its battalions. At 2330, the Leinsters reached the concentration area; at midnight 29 Brigade marched. The aim was to secure the Nablus crossroads before daylight. The axis of advance was Iskaka, Yasuf, Kuzah, Huwarah, the heights north of Nablus, and Shechem.

The German commanders of the Turkish armies, knowing a disaster had occurred on Bulfin's front—the Plain of Sharon—had pre-empted Chetwode's stroke and had fallen back on a natural strong position from Iskaka, to the wooded hills around Kefar Haris. This was done on the night of 19–20 September. 10th Division had to follow hard to allow the Turkish command no time to form a new line.[15]

In the opening minutes of 21 September, the Leinsters led what was to be a brigade dash. Leading were three mounted officers, Lt.-Col. Wildblood, a company commander and the adjutant. Behind came one platoon as an advance guard, then the brigade. The march was a stiff one, but by 0400 the Nablus-Jerusalem road was reached and the brigade closed up. 30 Brigade then passed through. In daylight, one Leinster company pushed forward to Huwara and 69th Battery opened fire on the crossroads east of Nablus, the junction of the Nablus–Jerusalem and Damascus roads. At Huwara, which had been bypassed by 30 Brigade, some thirty-six prisoners were taken.[16]

31 Brigade, delayed by the final work on the new road, moved two hours behind 29 Brigade. After a fine start, the brigade was stopped dead by fire from high ground. Because of the close wooded country, the exact position of the enemy could not be located. Repeated attacks by 101st Grenadiers and 2nd/42nd Deolis reached the wooded hills east of Haris and south of Kefar Haris, but they were stopped by machine-gun fire and lost over 150 men. Two field artillery brigades were brought into action and a dashing assault by 54th Sikhs of 29 Brigade through the Grenadiers and Deolis broke through.

As the Sikhs attacked, 2nd Irish Fusiliers attacked Kefar Haris from the west. Commanding the battalion, Maj. A.H. Caldecott told his men: 'If they moved fast they might not get killed, but if they moved slowly they certainly would be'.[17] On the command, the Fusiliers charged down the hillside and up the other slope, with few casualties. Their final charge carried them into Kefar Haris with no loss. The Turkish line had again been broken.

That evening, Chetwode ordered the 53rd Division to advance, with the 10th going all out for Nablus. Speaking to both divisional commanders by telephone, Chetwode steeled them against regard for the fatigue of the men. The victory was to be exploited fully.[18]

While the infantry attacked the Turkish front, the airmen of the Royal Air Force and the Royal Australian Air Force carried out a series of morally devastating attacks on the retreating German and Turkish artillery and transport columns. One column caught in Wadi el Far'a was annihilated. The airmen, using light bombs and machine-guns, straffed mercilessly. Over 100 guns, fifty trucks and nearly one hundred carts of all descriptions were later found in chaos. Ammunition, stores and food were scattered in utmost confusion. At the same time, the Desert Mounted Corps had passed through Bulfin's Corps, reached El 'Affule and Beisan and blocked the roads leading northwards.[19]

Shortly before midnight on the night of 20–21 September 1918, the final effort to secure Nablus began. The hardest task was allotted to Brig. Greer's 30 Brigade, already wearied by its efforts in repairing the road. Having passed through 29 Brigade, 30 Brigade started at 0200, with 1st Royal Irish on the right and 38th Dogras on the left, followed by 1st Kashmir Rifles and 46th Punjabis. The brigade passed through during the early morning and moved in artillery formation, columns of half companies at 150-pace intervals. Through the wide valley south of Nablus they advanced, ignoring hostile machine-gun fire at Huwara. They left this for 29 Brigade to deal with and pressed rapidly on until the village of Rajib was found to be strongly held by the enemy. A short, sharp fire-fight ended with a bayonet charge and Rajib was in the hands of the Royal Irish. A Yeomanry squadron arrived, and after being briefed by Maj. Anderson, it galloped forward just in time to capture the surviving enemy.[20] 30 Brigade reached the Damascus road a few miles north of Nablus at 1720 on the evening of 21 September. None of the battalions of the 10th had been able to rest for more than six hours in the past forty-eight. Allenby drove up to the 1st Royal Irish in the lead of 30 Brigade that day and urged them to keep going despite their exhaustion. Willingly, the men responded in a most remarkable way to the personal touch by their Commander-in-Chief and reached a position on the line Kefar Kus–Nebi Belam–Azmud. In thirteen hours they had covered twenty-one miles of rough going and fought a victorious action. Nablus was captured by sweat and guts rather than by blood. Also demonstrated was an inspiring display of leadership and moral courage on the part of Gen. Longley who rode among his troops, congratulating and exhorting when and where necessary.

So swift had been the advance of the Irish and Indians that when Sir Philip Chetwode received a message reporting the arrival of 10th Division at Nablus crossroads, he refused to believe it until told that it came from Gen. Longley personally.[21]

The 10th Division had captured 1223 prisoners and had suffered about 800 casualties in the course of two days' continuous fighting and marching amid the craggy hills and deep gulleys of Mount Ephraim. Its final efforts had been magnificent and in particular the march on Nablus deserves an honourable place in our military records. The Royal Irish and 1/Kashmir Rifles of the 30th Brigade had spent the whole night of the 19th with pick and shovel on the Wadi el Mutwy road, and in forty-eight hours, individual men cannot have had more than five or six [hours] of uneasy sleep, snatched at intervals. In the last few miles it was only the driving force from above, through divisional commander, brigadier, and battalion commanders, and their own resolution, aided by the inspiration of victory, which had kept them on their feet.[22]

By the evening of 21 September the Turkish Seventh and Eighth armies had been destroyed. It was the complete victory which German generals, inspired by Hanibal's at Cannae, had dreamt of for themselves for years before the war, but had never achieved.

After the battle, the number of prisoners was so great that their accommodation, feeding and evacuation gave major problems to the victors. Few can have been more surprising than one which was presented to 1st Leinsters by a German nursing sister. This lady insisted upon, and received from the bemused Irish, two fanatis of water and a lorry in which to carry about twenty of their worst wounded. But just as the vehicle was about to leave, the Germans realised they had a badly wounded Turk in their midst and insisted upon his removal. It couldn't help but leave a bad impression on the Irish. Later the Leinsters also provided guards to protect the Austrians and Germans from the Turks.[23]

Meanwhile, Chauvel's cavalry had pressed northwards. By the evening of 24 September Haifa and Acre were captured, and Damascus fell on the 30th. The 7th Indian Division left Haifa on 1 October; by the 8th they had reached Beirut and by 18 October, Tripoli. Before the end of October, the cavalry had captured Aleppo and cut the Baghdad railway. The country was eventually occupied to a line running east from Alexandretta. The war in the Near East was over.

After the capture of Nablus, 10th Division spent nearly a month salvaging the wreckage of the battlefield and undergoing training. At Sarafand, three miles west of Lydda in mid November, the 'Old Namurers', the 'Faugh-a-Ballaghs' and the 'Old Hundredth' celebrated the end of the war. 10th Division was nearing the end of its service. The war in Europe had also ended. The crusade was over. Beginning on 19 November, the units were railed from Ludd to Cairo, stopping a few days en route at Kantara for de-equipping. By early December, the division was concentrated in the Cairo area. Sir Edmund Allenby inspected 10th Division and in a short address, expressed his appreciation of their turn-out and thanked them for the splendid work performed during the advance through Palestine. It was their last parade.[24]

During the Great War, the 10th (Irish) Division lost 9363 killed, wounded, and missing.[25] But it has to be said that 'missing' was very often a euphemism for prisoner-of-war. It occurred very rarely in the battles of the 10th, and indeed in all other divisions which fought away from the Western Front. Most casualties were killed or wounded in action. Those who suffered and died from disease, in Gallipoli, Macedonia, Palestine—and long afterwards—were not included.

Bringing Turkey into the war on the side of the Central Powers was a master-stroke for German diplomatic *realpolitik,* made relatively easy by a certain British arrogance. This was particularly relative to two battle-cruisers made in Britain for Turkey. They were on the point of being delivered when they were commandeered on the orders of Winston Churchill. Germany made Turkey her surrogate and forced Britain to operate simultaneously on three fronts in the Near East—Mesopotamia to protect the oil fields which were essential to Britain's war economy; Egypt and Palestine to protect the Suez Canal; and Gallipoli. The failure of the Gallipoli operation made a Macedonian campaign necessary. The misfortune of some of these overseas subsidiary operations, notwithstanding their ultimate success, cost Britain dear in lost prestige. They tied down over one and a half million men and the British Empire lost 350,000 killed in action, dead of disease and wounded. Additionally there was the huge expenditure of money, the waste of mountains of matériel and the vast shipping space used to move it across thousands of miles. It was a terrible price.[26]

CHAPTER THIRTY-NINE

The Last Phase,
September–November 1918

Tout le Monde à la Bataille.—Foch

SECOND ARMY: FOURTH BATTLE OF YPRES, 28 SEPTEMBER 1918

In the Ypres salient, the attack as usual began in pouring rain. The II Corps attacked after a five-minute bombardment behind a smoke-filled creeping barrage. The troops, British and Belgian, went forward with dash and determination. 9th Scottish took Frezenberg Ridge and 29th Division captured Gheluvelt. The Belgians were into Zonnebeke.

29th Division advanced astride the Menin road; 86 Brigade with 1st Dublins were in the van, while 88 Brigade with 2nd Leinsters were in support. The eagerness of the Dublins and some of the guns firing short caused some casualties from their own artillery barrage, but it had been successful in breaking enemy resistance. The third objective was reached and the German line broken for the loss to the Dublins of 126 killed and wounded.[1]

The pipers of 2nd Leinsters, in saffron kilts, marched in fours along the Menin road with the companies on each side.

> Throughout our advance to Hooge enemy shelling was spasmodic; the only real shell-fire was just before we got to Leinster Farm, but the Menin road and the Roulers railway got heavily shelled... Through the mist we caught glimpses of the pipers in fours on the Menin road marching parallel with us. We closed in with them near Birr Crossroads and caught the strains of 'Brian Boru'.[2]

Very few survived of those who fought during the terrible winter and spring of 1914–15, who defeated the German onslaught at heavy cost. Now, in the early morning mist and the rain which always seemed to accompany a British operation in the salient, the Leinsters advanced resolutely to the music of the war pipes despite the difficulties of the terrain.

> It was raining steadily in our faces as we moved up the rise of that desolate and shell-ravaged region, not even the rank grass was to be seen on that denuded ridge—just mud, brown, clinging mud and pitted everywhere with slate-coloured shell-holes overlapping themselves in the water-logged area. The company arrived on the

> commanding ridge at Hooge before its allotted time... We were all very
> wet, most of us had been bogged up to our knees, struggling through the
> liquid mud... Battalion Headquarters arrived with the pipers, who had
> practically blown themselves to a standstill with only one wounded.[3]

Everyone in the ranks knew the cost of holding this stretch of line, and the
price they themselves had paid just twelve months previously in attempting
to reach the tragic ridges they were now marching over with such
confidence. Confidence of the outcome, yes, but only the foolish or
insensitive was without fear. One young officer, fresh from home, confided
in his diary: 'They shelled the roads and also used a lot of mustard gas.
However I am in God's hands and must pray to Him. I know that of myself I
am mortally afraid but He will give me strength.'[4]

Responding quickly to the situation, II Corps ordered 36th Division
forward without its artillery, which would follow. The brigades moved in
echelon, and 109 Brigade entered the line on 28 September between the 9th
and 29th Divisions. Its objective was Terhand. Passing through the Scots, the
Inniskilling brigade had 2nd Battalion on the right and the 9th on the left,
with the 1st Battalion in support. The enemy machine-guns were attacked
with great élan; they were often put out of action by rifle fire alone. The
Germans were now feeling the effects of not having their concrete pill boxes.
One after another, the objectives were taken with comparative ease. By
evening, Terhand fell to 2nd Inniskillings; Vijfwegen fell to the 9th. That
night, 108 Brigade moved up in support of 109, with orders to pass through
at dawn next morning.

The next objective was the Menin-Roulers road from Kezelberg,
northwards. Central to the German defensive line in the area was Hill 41,
sixty feet above the surrounding country. Capped by a farmhouse and
outbuildings strengthened with concrete in the usual way, it was very
strong. Without artillery, the attacks by 12th and 1st Irish Rifles were
repulsed, although elsewhere the advance had kept pace with 9th and 29th
Divisions. The Germans were holding the line in strength and launched a
counter-attack:

> From an observation post about 100 yards behind his front line, Lt.-Col.
> Smyth saw the Germans collect troops for a great counterstrike and the
> King's Own Scottish Borderers were bracing themselves for a desperate
> resistance at Manhattan Farm when the timely arrival of 1st Inniskilling
> Fusiliers, who made a most heroic attack on Hill 41 from the north,
> scared the enemy solely to defence. Though the Inniskillings failed to
> take the hill, their plucky effort probably saved the KOSB. This excited
> the admiration of the Scots. The General Officer Commanding wrote to
> 36th Division expressing admiration and thanks of the men of 9th
> Scottish.[5]

In the operations to take Hill 41, Capt. N.A. Bruce DSO, one of the last officers of the original division, was killed in the bombardment which preceded a successful attack the following morning.[6]

THIRD ARMY: SECOND BATTLE OF CAMBRAI, 27 SEPTEMBER–5 OCTOBER 1918

After their break into the Drocourt-Quéant line during mid September, the 57th and 63rd Divisions underwent a series of training exercises in open warfare in preparation for the next operation. The British preparations to capture Cambrai were pre-empted by a German withdrawal. But it resulted in several Third Army objectives being gained without fighting. 63rd Naval Division led the assault on Cambrai. Having gained the first objective, the Hindenburg Support Line, the Royal Irish with Hawke Battalion captured Havrincourt. 57th Division passed through and, following a series of operations around Cantaing, 1st Munsters captured Lock 5 (which had been captured by the Ulster Division nearly a year before in the Cambrai offensive). Next day at dawn, Cantaing was taken and by midday on 29 September, 57th Division had cleared the Marcoing line from the Bapaume–Cambrai road to the Schelde Canal. In a last attack towards the southern suburbs of Cambrai, 1st Munsters with 8th King's encircled and captured Proville. This was despite the enemy 'making a desperate attempt to retain possession of Cambrai, and hold on to what remained of the line of the canal'.[7]

FOURTH ARMY: BATTLE OF THE BEAUREVOIR LINE

The climax of the battles of 1918 was reached on the front of Fourth Army. To them went the responsibility for breaching the group of defences known as the Hindenburg Line, and theirs was the principal role in the advance to victory. Haig had expected the advance of First and Third Armies to materially assist its attack, but this did not materialise. On the fronts of First and Third Armies, stiff opposition on the Canal du Nord, Schelde Canal and Sensée Canal had slowed their advance.

At Le Catelet on 4 October, XIII Corps had 50th Division in front (5th Royal Irish, 6th Inniskillings, 2nd Munsters, 2nd Dublins), with 25th Division in support and 66th Division (5th Inniskillings, 5th Rangers) in reserve. Its objectives were Prospect Hill, Gouy and Le Catelet, all strong positions in the Beaurevoir sector of the Hindenburg defences. The attack was supported by thirteen artillery brigades. In the hilly country, 151 Brigade met considerable opposition, especially from Gouy, and the leading companies of 6th Inniskillings under Maj. G. Greville suffered severely. At the end of the battle, two companies could only muster thirty fusiliers each.[8] In their advance on Prospect Hill, 6th Inniskillings came under very heavy enfilading fire from Gouy. To suppress this and continue their advance was impossible, so the Inniskillings engaged the enemy on their flank. While 6th

Inniskillings engaged the enemy, 1st King's Own Yorkshire Light Infantry, who were immediately behind, seized the opportunity to storm the hill. Two German divisions were defending the area.[9] They put up a stout resistance in the houses and cellars of Gouy and Le Catelet and the hills surrounding them. Grim close-quarter fighting took place before the enemy were all driven out or captured by the remnant of the Inniskillings and 4th King's Royal Rifle Corps.[10]

At the same time, while 2nd Dublins were taking a position west of Le Catelet, a determined counter-attack by five German battalions recaptured Le Catelet, but the rest of the line was held. Fourth Army had achieved a particularly fine tactical success against stern resistance. But because of the heavy resistance against Third Army, Fourth Army had to continue the pressure. On the following day, the attack was renewed; 25th Division was to attack Beaurevoir on the right, while 50th Division was to retake Le Catelet. Part of the leading brigade of 25th Division failed to arrive on time and a disjointed attack against Beaurevoir failed. On the left, 50th Division (2nd Dublins, 3rd Royal Fusiliers and 2nd Munsters advanced in line under cover of eleven artillery brigades, and the 2nd Munsters fought their way into Le Catelet.[11] When the Munsters became scattered and were held up by two machine-gun pill boxes, Lt.-Col. Tonson-Rye blew his hunting horn to rally his men: 'Munsters came from all directions, and, taken in front and rear, both posts were captured after a sharp and bitter struggle.'[12]

On the third day of the battle, while 25th Division again assaulted Beaurevoir, 50th Division advanced across the St Quentin Canal and established a line east of it which enabled the right division of Third Army to advance. By the end of 5 October, the first phase of the battle had been won. In three days' severe fighting, 50th and 25th Divisions had engaged double that number of German divisions who had made a desperate bid to hold this important line intact.[13]

But the German line was still unbroken. On 6 October, 150 Brigade forced an entry into the Beaurevoir Line and, although they failed to widen the breach, they succeeded in penetrating as far as the inner wire. 149 Brigade relieved 150 Brigade on the 7th and twice assaulted unsuccessfully. 151 Brigade was then brought up and the Beaurevoir line was taken in the early hours of 8 October under cover of a heavy barrage. The hard-fighting 50th was then withdrawn into reserve. The advance of 50th Division towards Le Catelet took the Dublins and Munsters across ground held by these same battalions in the March offensive just over six months before. For 5th Royal Irish and 6th Inniskillings, it was their first battle on the Western Front.

THIRD ARMY: BATTLE OF CAMBRAI

At 0420 on 8 October massed British guns of eleven artillery brigades opened up on the front of XVII Corps. The corps was tasked with encircling Cambrai on the southern side, forcing its evacuation. The main attacking force was

63rd and 57th Divisions. After ten minutes' bombardment, 2nd Royal Irish, supported by a tank, advanced behind the barrage. The enemy resistance was mainly machine-gun fire and this was overcome chiefly by skilful fire and movement. All the battalion objectives were reached by 0600, with numerous prisoners taken and three field guns, two trench mortars plus many machine-guns captured. The Marine battalion helped by Anson reached their objectives by 0800 and the line was secured. Enemy counter-attacks supported by a tank were repulsed, the tank being knocked out by a captured anti-tank gun under command of Lt. McCarthy-Barry.[14] 57th Division co-operated with the Naval Division in an attack under cover of smoke, and on the following morning, 9 September, patrols of 1st Munsters penetrated into the town and found it deserted of Germans. After this, their division was withdrawn and went into rest and intensive training, followed by brigade sports. The days of leaving units in the line until they disintegrated had mercifully passed. The 57th Division was transferred to the La Bassée front and was 'in' at the reoccupation of Lille. 1st Munsters provided a Guard of Honour for M. Poincaré, President of the French Republic.[15] About the same time, Lt.-Gen. Sir Bryan Mahon was appointed Military Governor of Lille.

Fourth Army: Breaking the Hindenburg Line

The attack on 8 October by the right division of Third Army woke up the German artillery, and their counter-bombardment caught 66th Division in the act of assembling and cut them up. The enemy attack was strongly supported by artillery, tanks and aircraft dropping 40 lbs phosphorus bombs in the rear areas.[16]

66th Division's leading battalions experienced stubborn resistance on their front and from flank positions not yet taken, mainly from skilfully handled machine-guns in good positions. The 5th Inniskillings and 6th Dublins, with the help of five tanks, had captured the strongpoint, Marliches Farm, and six field guns by 0730.[17] The Dublins then took a fortified farm and captured 113 men, including two officers. One field gun and forty-nine machine-guns were also taken.[18] Heavy shell-fire drove the Dublins out of the position and this was immediately followed by a strong counter-attack which was driven back by rapid fire. Repeated attacks to retake the farm failed, even after two tanks came forward to help. Later the 38th Division of Third Army came up on the left and, helped by their attack at 1130, the Dublins recaptured the farm. The 'farms' were, of course, farm buildings reinforced with concrete and armed with machine-guns which had been turned into miniature fortresses.

Elsewhere the attack continued. The 5th Connaught Rangers and 9th Manchester attacked Serain from north and south and captured the village. In this and several days' fighting, 5th Connaught Rangers took a total of eighteen enemy guns of all calibres, three 8-inch, ten field guns, one anti-tank and four high-velocity guns.[19] One young officer who was later ordained and became a bishop recalled:

> We attacked supported by a couple of tanks, and right ahead of us, were German field guns firing at point blank range. Our tanks backed out of range right away, and we got it in the neck. However, the guns were captured and then Bond was wounded, and I took over 'C' Company.
>
> I remember we were ordered not to go through the village, but around it, for it was a machine-gun nest. However, Lt. J.J. Walsh went right ahead, and although I shouted to him, he did not seem to hear. Shortly after that I received a machine-gun bullet in the arm, but not so bad that I could not carry on. Then an orderly came to tell me that 'poor Mr Walsh was killed'. When we did go through the village I saw him lying there with three or four others, and only a couple of nights before in the Hindenburg Line, J.J. sang in his beautiful voice, the song 'When you come to the end of a perfect day'.[20]

Once the elaborate fixed positions of the Hindenburg Line were broken into, despite the best efforts of its machine-gunners, the defences hastily built by the Germans were repeatedly smashed just as the defences of the Fifth Army had been in March. The difference this time was that the Germans did not attempt to made a determined stand with the same resolution as the Fifth Army had before Amiens or the Second Army at Messines and Kemmel.

In this stage of the fighting, the veterans from 10th Division demonstrated their prowess, and although they were not completely fit, their battlecraft in open warfare 'was supreme.'[21] 'The change to open warfare once more was extraordinarily exhilarating; an advance of thirteen miles in two days was an experience the battalion had not undergone since 1914. Heavy losses and exhaustion were quickly forgotten, and it was felt that at long last the decisive stage had been reached.'[22]

Throughout its advance, Fourth Army was well supported by tanks, especially Whippets and Mark Vs. But each time the cavalry attempted to pass through to exploit success, it was driven back by machine-gun fire. The cavalry commander, Lt.-Gen. Sir T. McM. Kavanagh, told Gen. Rawlinson that it 'was impossible… without hard fighting'. It would take a wide break in the German defences for a cavalry corps to pass through; anything less could quickly be sealed off by a few machine-guns.[23] Meanwhile, it was left to the infantry to spearhead the advance.

> We advanced, sometimes in front in open order, sometimes behind in artillery formation, through fields and mud, streams and lanes and

more or less intact villages—Maretz, Mauroil, Reumont—always under shell-fire which was sometimes light and sometimes intense, running into enemy outposts and machine-gun nests and strong points which, of course, we knew nothing about till they opened fire on us, and as we went, the roads and crossroads, which had been mined, blew up, and artillery support became less and less.[24]

Had Hubert Gough not been promoted to command Fifth Army, the course of the war in 1917–18 would have been vastly different. This was seen not least in the handling of the Cavalry Corps. Under his switch and spur, at Cambrai and during the advance to victory, the actions of the Cavalry Corps would have been more decisive.

FOURTH ARMY: THE BATTLE OF THE SELLE, 17–25 OCTOBER 1918
During the advance to Le Cateau on 16 October, 5th Connaught Rangers distinguished themselves on the evening before the general assault. The battalion forced an entry into the town ahead of other units of the two assault divisions. But because of their exposed situation they were ordered to withdraw. The Rangers did so, but not before they had caused some consternation to the occupying garrison.

> The assault was delivered at 5.00 pm, by 5th Connaught Rangers on the right and 18th King's on their left. The Rangers rushed the town with great gallantry and a considerable number of the Rangers succeeded in establishing themselves in a deep railway cutting which ran in a gentle curve round the eastern outskirts of the town. As both flanks were exposed, it was withdrawn during the night and held the line of the Selle where it passes through the town.[25]

XIII Corps was now to force the Selle in the St Souplet-to-Le Cateau sector. Its 50th and 66th Divisions were the right and left prongs of a converging attack. The Selle was regarded by the Germans as vital to their defensive position on the Western Front, especially as a bargaining counter at the armistice negotiations. Orders were issued by the German High Command that it was to be held 'at all costs'. Le Cateau was central to that order.[26]

The Selle, in a deep valley with bare ridges rising up each side, is a winding, sluggish and moat-like stream, four to five feet deep and twelve to twenty feet wide. Some 300 yards behind it was a railway embankment. A defended river crossing, never an easy operation, is doubly difficult at night, but it presents the greatest opportunity for success. This particular plan was a complicated one, and the operation was mounted in three phases:
First. Three battalions of 151 Brigade, having formed up in depth on a

two-company frontage, were to cross north of St Souplet (on bridges constructed by 5th Royal Irish under the divisional engineers), capture the railway embankment to its front and fan out on either side. The left battalion, on crossing, was to wheel left, roll up the enemy defences along the railway line, and capture the buildings and sheds of Le Cateau station, the railway triangle.

Second. 149 Brigade, with two battalions using the same crossings and a demolished bridge at St Benin, were to pass through the railway embankment and capture the ridge 1200 yards behind. Its third battalion was to cross immediately behind and follow the railway into the railway triangle, reinforcing the first battalion there. At the same time, the South African Brigade of 66th Division acting in conjunction was to cross north of the town and link up with 149 Brigade north of the railway triangle.

Third. 150 Brigade was to pass through 149 Brigade on the ridge and capture Bazeul. At the same time, the South Africans were to swing forward on the right and connect with 149 Brigade on the ridge. 198 Brigade of 66th Division were to 'mop up' Le Cateau. Luckily the southern ridge overlooking Le Cateau and the Selle was exceptionally suited for artillery and machine-gun support.

During the night, covered by a thick mist, 5th Royal Irish worked forward a total of fourteen duckboard and floating bridges, closely followed by the infantry. Five minutes before Zero on 17 October 1918, the Irish and Sappers had already got five duckboards across the river. When the barrage of three artillery brigades and ninety-six machine-guns opened, the remaining nine bridges were constructed within fifteen minutes; in seven minutes more, the infantry were crossing without a casualty.[27] Although the actual crossing was achieved without loss, the two battalions on the railway embankment had to overcome fierce resistance and a thirty-yard belt of wire before gaining the railway. From there they were only able to advance 400 yards at most. 6th Inniskillings, the left battalion, crossed on time and, against fierce opposition from the alerted Germans, they reached the railway. There, the Germans fought so stubbornly that the Inniskillings sent for support by 13th Black Watch.[28]

Eleven Allied tanks crossed the river on 'cribs' (steel cage-like fascines), but on account of the mist and noise of battle they were unable to co-operate properly and it was some time before they could help on the railway line. The crossing of 149 Brigade was slow because 2nd Dublins, masked by 13th Black Watch going to the aid of the Inniskillings, waited until they cleared its front.

The fog, at first an aid in the crossing, was now a hindrance. Positions could not be fixed and machine-gun covering fire from the heights could not be directed.[29] A confused fight began. The Inniskillings, aided by the Black Watch, working along the railway and after severe fighting reached the strongly-held railway station. The planned attack of 50th Division had failed and its brigades were hopelessly mixed. The GOC reorganised his battalions into three groups, with each brigadier commanding the three battalions closest to him, whatever their original brigade. Then an attack was arranged preceded by a bombardment of the railway triangle from 1530–1630.[30] In the meantime, 66th Division could expect no help.

The attack of 66th Division had less distance to cover and started at 0805. But an earlier attack was made to coincide with 50th Division in which the greater part of 5th Connaught Rangers fought their way into the town, although several parties were held up until 1100. The commanding officer, Lt.-Col. Scully, was wounded just before the assault, but gallantly led the attack.[31]

The South Africans had also run into trouble against thick barbed wire uncut by the bombardment. By mid morning they had reached the intermediate position. The Irish had successfully broken into Le Cateau town, but 6th Dublins discovered that instead of a 'mopping up' operation they had a tough nut to crack open with its maze of streets; instead of two companies, it had to deploy the entire battalion for the task.[32]

Despite stiff resistance, the whole of Le Cateau was in the hands of the Irish by 1800, with the exception of the Faubourg de Landrecies in the eastern outskirts. Fighting continued throughout the night in the railway triangle. Elsewhere, the battle died down as the battalions prepared for the renewal on the morrow.

Next day, after a short bombardment, 50th Division attacked at 0530 and gained the ridge, and much else. The group, consisting of 2nd Munsters, 2nd Dublins and 1st King's Own Yorkshire Light Infantry, marching on compass-bearing in fog, completely surprised the German defences. Machine-guns and hundreds of prisoners were captured, and at one place a steaming hot breakfast 'which was not wasted'.[33]

> At 6.30 the fog gradually thinned and finally disappeared, leaving the Battalion [2nd Munsters] advancing over a rolling plain. There was every proof that the attack was a complete surprise. Hurriedly abandoned dug-outs, machine-gun emplacements, trench mortars, and equipment of all kinds were found all over the battlefield.[34]

It was a reversal of the experience of 21 March. A company of 2nd Munsters which had all its officers dead or wounded, unrestrained, carried on the attack and captured Basuel 1200 yards beyond the objective, but they were forced out by their own barrage.

Sgt. H.A. Curtis of the Dublins, who as Cpl. Curtis had served with 7th Dublins in Macedonia, gave a remarkable display of bravery and initiative which earned him the Victoria Cross. Curtis, locating a machine-gun post, got covering fire from his platoon. He then outflanked the position and bombed it into surrender: 'Sergeant Curtis was always in the lead. Eventually he came up with a stationary train load of German troops, shot the driver and virtually captured the train load of troops before his men joined him.'[35] Among the booty captured by the Dublins was an entire battery of guns, complete with horse-teams. Later Sgt. Downie, who had won the Victoria Cross earlier in the war, was posted back to his old company and platoon, the same one as Curtis. To have two men holding that coveted decoration in the same platoon must surely have been unique. The 2nd Dublins had returned victorious to Le Cateau, the scene of their first action of the war. Alongside them were 5th and 6th Inniskillings, representing their 2nd Battalion which had fought alongside the Dublins in that battle. It would be too much to expect any Dubliner who had fought there in '14 to be present in 1918.

The Inniskillings and Black Watch cleared up the whole of the railway triangle and fought their way slowly up the railway. They gained touch with 198 Brigade which secured the remaining Faubourg and the ridge.

25th Division leap-frogged the 50th, occupied Basuel, and advanced to the line of exploitation in preparation for the next phase.[36]

SECOND ARMY: COURTRAI AND THE PASSAGE OF THE LYS, 14–15 OCTOBER 1918
GHQ Intelligence reports had indicated to Gen. Plumer that German evacuation on his front was 'well advanced', promising an early retirement to the Schelde. Possibly it was co-ordinated with a retirement from Lille as a result of the advance of Fourth, Third and First armies. Accordingly, Sir Herbert Plumer issued orders to his three corps to advance to the Lys and to hustle the Germans out of Lille. He warned corps commanders that, given the opportunity, they should be prepared to cross the Lys.

Zero Hour was fixed for 0535 on 14 October. There would be no preparatory bombardment. Under cover of a creeping barrage, 29th Division (2nd Leinsters and 1st Dublins), 40th Division (8th Royal Irish and 13th Inniskillings) and 36th Division, with seven other divisions of Second Army, began their advance eastwards towards the Lys and achieved considerable success on the first day. In the opening phase, there was little resistance. In fact the Germans were standing with their kit, ready to march away as prisoners. However their resistance increased in the afternoon.[37]

The II Corps had as its first-day objective the Courtrai-Roulers railway. However, all three divisions were delayed by wide wire belts and gas shelling. In 36th Division, 108 and 109 Brigades led II Corps' attack. At first, all went well but about midday, 15th Irish Rifles were checked by machine-gun fire until they were reinforced by 1st Irish Rifles. The attack resumed and by midnight the lead brigade was about 300 yards from the strongly-held village of Gulleghem.

After a good start the 29th Division was eventually held up about a mile short of its final objective, the railway embankment, by serious resistance on the Steenbeek road. In stiff fighting, 2nd Leinsters particularly distinguished itself; two in particular, Sgt. John O'Neill MM and Pte. Martin Moffat, won individual renown. Close to Moorsele, O'Neill's company was held up by two machine-guns and a battery of guns firing over open sights. Leading a section attack, O'Neill charged the battery and captured four guns, two machine-guns and sixteen prisoners. Near Ledeghem, Martin Moffat, who until April had been a Connaught Ranger (he came from Sligo), came under heavy fire from a fortified house while advancing with his section. Alone, Moffat charged the house under a hail of fire, tossed grenades through the front apertures, ran to the rear, kicked in the door and stormed the house singlehandedly. In clearing the house, he killed two and captured thirty. For his valour and initiative, Martin Moffat was awarded the Victoria Cross.

Elsewhere on Second Army front, there was a significant development. On the extreme right in XV Corps sector, in front of 14th Division, Comines appeared to have been evacuated. Second Army operational orders for 15 October instructed corps to keep contact with the enemy and to establish bridgeheads on the Lys, but 'without undue loss'. It was a typical 'Daddy' Plumer rider.[38]

A brigade of 14th Division began the Lys crossing at 0435 from both sides of the village of Comines after five minutes' bombardment. By the afternoon of 15 October, they had extended the bridgehead deeply. On the right, 121 Brigade of 40th Division crossed the Lys in two places. At 0830, 6th Cheshire crossed. But at 0530, 8th Royal Irish had already crossed at Houplines on the extreme right. Having crossed, 8th Royal Irish sent patrols against the German trenches where they met strong resistance. Artillery support was called for and after eleven hours' fighting, the battalion had advanced the bridgehead a mile across the Lys.

On 15 October, the II Corps had as its objective the River Lys, but opposition on the front of 35th Division slowed the advance. In 36th Division's sector, 1st Irish Rifles and 2nd Inniskillings, following a very effective barrage on Gulleghem, swept resistance aside. By midday, they were on a line east of the village. 9th Inniskillings passed through unopposed and captured Heule. They almost gained the line of the Lys, but heavy machine-gun fire forced them to halt. 2nd Inniskillings called for artillery support which silenced the enemy and all three battalions halted on the Courtrai-Roulers railway embankment.

At dawn the next day, 16 October, 108 Brigade assumed the lead and established itself on the Lys. 107 Brigade were then to go through them and establish a bridgehead. Patrols of the latter were sent forward to reconnoitre the crossings. There were scenes of great enthusiasm in Courtrai when its citizens met the advancing troops. However, the Germans had not evacuated Courtrai completely, and at the quays a hail of fire met the troops: 'The 9th and 29th Divisions agreed to cross simultaneously, but 36th Division decided to cross earlier.'[39]

Brig. Vaughan decided to force the passage in daylight. The 122nd Field Company brought forward its pontoons, and under cover of smoke and machine-gun fire, the river crossing began at 1400. The first pontoon of assault troops crossed without a casualty. A second boatload followed and in a remarkably short time, infantry were crossing a footbridge. A company of machine-guns crossed and established a bridgehead and held off the enemy infantry. However German guns were more successful. Having ranged on the bridge and found its positions, heavy fire rained upon it and destroyed it with heavy casualties to the engineers. Considerable damage was also done to the town. Corps headquarters decided to save Courtrai from further damage and that night, the bridgehead troops safely withdrew. 123 Brigade of 41st Division relieved 107 Brigade.

THE ADVANCE TO FINAL VICTORY: 18 OCTOBER–11 NOVEMBER 1918

It was planned to bounce the Lys on a wide front on the night of 19–20 October. The II Corps attacked with 29th Division on the right, 9th in the centre and 36th on the left. 36th Division, now on the extreme left of Second Army, had the French 164th Division on its left. The Lys at this point was some 100 feet wide and lightly defended. The plan was to ferry a battalion of 109 Brigade across the river at dusk on 19 October. They had orders to push forward to the main Courtrai-Ghent road on a front of about 1000 yards and to hold the bridgehead. Another battalion would cross on the left and form a flank guard. Two machine-gun companies were to accompany.

The 9th Inniskillings were all over the Lys by 2000, but heavy machine-gun fire held them up; nevertheless they succeeded in establishing a bridgehead. Meanwhile, 121st Field Company's bridge was delayed when it was discovered that the river was wider at this point than expected; an additional pontoon had to be brought up. Despite this, the bridge was competed at 2200, just as the platoons of the second battalion arrived.

1st Inniskillings had been allowed just four hours for its part in the operation. They were to cross the river, assemble on the distant bank, move to the left behind 9th Inniskillings and take a cluster of four villages—Desselghem, Spriete, Straete and Dries. The crossing and movement to the objectives went according to plan. The first two villages were carried with great dash; the third, Straete, fell after some stiff fighting. But on the right, the flank company could only get into the outskirts of Dries; there it established its position and consolidated. On schedule at 0200, 107 Brigade crossed. 15th Irish Rifles went first and relieved 9th Inniskilling, followed by 1st Irish Rifles. On the right flank, 9th Division had also crossed.

The attack to enlarge the bridgehead began at dawn on 20 October. Beveren on the left of the line was quickly taken with the aid of a battalion of

9th Division. Here the defensive machine-gun fire had been heavy and 15th Irish Rifles had many casualties, including the commanding officer, Lt.-Col. B.Y. Jones DSO. Despite this, the battalion reached the main Courtrai-Ghent-Antwerp road by 0800 and at 0900 the leading troops were astride the Deerlyck road. The corps' bridgehead extending to $2^1/_2$ miles over the Lys was secure. However, Dries was still untaken.

There was little advance on the 21st and heavy fighting took place around Dries before it finally fell. Although it had been said that the Germans were not the Jerry of old, neither were the British the same enthusiastic amateurs of the Somme. There was no rushing machine-gun positions this time. The German garrison of Dries resolutely held out for over thirty-six hours before it was finally overcome. After a stiff fight between 2nd Irish Rifles and a Prussian battalion, the advance began and Heirweg, Vossenhoek and Hutteghem were taken. They were the last objectives of 36th Division. On the night of 26–27 October, 34th Division relieved the 36th. As they rested and reorganised near Tourcoing, news arrived of the Armistice. In the Ulster Division there was little outward jubilation, 'only quiet relief, and deep satisfaction'.[40] The young men who joined the surviving veterans in April had worthily upheld the tradition of dash established by 36th (Ulster) Division at Thiepval. It was no mean achievement.

FOURTH ARMY: FORÊT DE MORMAL, 5–7 NOVEMBER 1918
Fourth Army's last operation of the war, forcing a passage of the Sambre and Oise canal and securing a footing in the Forêt de Mormal, was conducted with two corps, IX on the right and XIII on the left.

50th Division had 149 Brigade (2nd Munsters and 2nd Dublins) on the right opposite enclosed country beyond which lay the army objective, the canal. On the left, 150 Brigade had 6th Inniskillings attached for the operation. It was tasked with traversing the southern extremity of the forest to a depth of 5000 yards in thickly wooded country strongly held with many machine-guns. It was to be their last operation of the war, and was conducted with considerable 'offensive spirit' in which its Irish battalions played a leading part. In the opening phase, a tank crew was overcome by gas and put out of action. Then, unlikely as it may seem, the tank was manned by a volunteer scratch crew of 2nd Dublins 'which caught up the infantry at 8.50 am and did good service'.[41] 'The advance was rapid... treading on the heels of the retiring enemy, who in several instances turned and fired standing at their pursuers. The inhabitants welcomed the men with open arms, heaping food of all kinds on them...'[42]

Near the village of Jean Ledoux, the Munsters captured a field gun and several machine-guns. In the vicinity of St Rémy the battalion paused to allow the troops on either flank to catch up. When it advanced again, the Germans had retreated from the village. Commanding the leading company was Capt. Dodds who had been with the regiment at Gallipoli, Salonika, Palestine and now France. He was killed by shell-fire during the closing phase of what was the last battle the Munsters fought.[43] In the same action, when the attacking battalions of 149 Brigade were temporarily checked, 2nd Dublins captured a dominating position overlooking Landrecies and enfiladed the Sambre Canal. Two companies under Capt. Barry and Lt. Morris captured the position, a battery of 4.2-inch howitzers, three field guns and three machine-guns.[44] By dusk, 149 Brigade held the canal to a depth of $2^1/_2$ miles. All organised resistance on their part of the line appeared to be at an end.

As 50th Division advanced, so did its Pioneer Battalion, 5th Royal Irish. For them there was no glory, only endless toil, often under shell-fire, remaking roads and building bridges without which the rapid advance could not be sustained. It was a task they knew supremely well. They followed the advance by way of Maretz, Le Cateau and Noyelles to Semousies. There they arrived on 10 November and halted.

The end of the war on the front of these particular battalions of Dublins, Munsters, Connaught Rangers, Inniskillings and Royal Irish is noteworthy as a demonstration of the tenacity of the German machine-gunners. Warned during early morning that hostilities were to cease at 1100, 50th and 66th Divisions held their positions. On their front, German machine-gun fire continued all morning until about three minutes to eleven when it ceased, but not for long: 'At two minutes to 11 a machine-gun, about 200 yards from our leading troops, fired off a complete belt without a pause. A single machine-gunner was then seen to stand up beside his weapon, take off his helmet, bow, and turning about, walked slowly to the rear. Then all was silence.'[45]

The battalions of 10th Division had reached the limit of their advance in a long crusade. Theirs had been a tortuous route: Gallipoli, Serbia, Bulgaria, Egypt, Palestine, France and finally Flanders. It was fitting that one of their battalions should be uniquely honoured. At Huy in Belgium, news reached 5th Connaught Rangers that it had been given the singular honour of becoming a regular battalion; it was ordered to change its number to 2nd Battalion of the regiment in recognition of its service. A parade scene took place which had only been enacted once previously, in 1660, when Monck's Regiment of Foot became the Coldstream Guards after the Restoration. The battalion was ordered '5th Connaught Rangers, ground arms.' When this had been done, the next order was '2nd Connaught Rangers, take-up arms.'[46] After nearly four years in Limbo, the old 97th was resurrected.

FIRST ARMY: MONS, NOVEMBER 1918
Having marched and bussed, 2nd Royal Irish of 63rd Division, under command of Lt.-Col. M.C.C. Harrison DSO MC, were at Nouvelles in the

vicinity of Mons at midday on 10 November. The Royal Irish took up the pursuit on a two-company frontage without artillery support. An hour later, the leading companies were checked by heavy machine-guns in defilade and enfilade positions. Three separate attempts to advance were driven back by German artillery and machine-gun fire. The Irish then fixed the Germans to their position, while Anson Battalion succeeded in forcing a passage of the river and railway. Supported by two Royal Irish reserve companies, they captured the brigade's first objective. Both battalions then halted on the captured position, waiting for artillery to support their attack by nightfall.

At 1800, under cover of a barrage, the battalion advanced and by 2000 all objectives were captured. Nevertheless the battalion continued advancing. At midnight, patrols entered St Symphorien and found it deserted by the enemy. Two machine-guns abandoned at a railway embankment were taken. At 1100 on 11 November the Royal Irish reached Spiennes south of Mons where, just over four years before, Lt. M.C.C Harrison, the brigade billeting officer, had taken over command of A Company at the first battle of Mons. Six officers and 200 men of 2nd Royal Irish took part in the official entry into the town on 15 November.[47] Few had fought throughout the war with more courageous tenacity than that of its commanding officer.

SECOND ARMY, 29TH DIVISION
The Germans had been expected to defend the line of the Schelde vigorously, so all divisions were surprised at the unexpected ease with which they crossed. 40th Division (8th Royal Irish and 13th Inniskilling) was fired on by only three machine-guns in their passage. In the sector of 30th Division (7th [SIH] Royal Irish and 7th/8th Inniskillings), four footbridges were constructed during the night of 8–9 November and the division crossed unopposed.

In their passage of the Lys on 19–20 October, 2nd Leinsters had again seen stiff fighting and Sgt. O'Neill once again distinguished himself. With only one man, he charged a company position supported by a machine-gun, capturing the gun and about 100 enemy. For his gallantry and leadership on this occasion and on 14 October at Moorsele, O'Neill was awarded the Victoria Cross.

2nd Leinsters crossed the water lines of both the Schelde and Le Grand Courant on the night of 8–9 November. By dawn they were in Espinois, where they were told the Germans had left the previous evening.[48] 2nd Leinsters ended the war in typical 'Forty-Ten' style: 'While we were on the march the Brigadier had galloped up and yelled out: "The war is over! The Kaiser has abdicated!" We were typically Irish, and never cheered except under adverse conditions, such as shell-fire and rain. Somewhat crestfallen, the brigadier rode slowly off to communicate his glad tidings to an English battalion who, no doubt, took the news in a different way.'[49]

FIFTH ARMY, 16TH DIVISION

Sandwiched between Second and First Armies, the re-formed Fifth Army advanced each side of Tournai. 16th Division had returned to the Western Front in August, and in September its own artillery which since March had never left the front line, rejoined. The reconstituted 16th Division (Maj.-Gen. A.B. Ritchie) had 5th Royal Irish Fusiliers as the only Irish representative. 11th Hampshire was the only original battalion. From 1–4 October, the division had taken part in the pursuit to the Haute-Deule Canal, then the pursuit to the Schelde during which 47 Brigade took the strongpoint of Annœulin and captured Phalempin. At the end of October, 16th and 15th Divisions pushed forward and gained the banks of the Schelde on either side of Tournai, with the exception of German bridgeheads covering Antoing and Tournai. For the next week, Fifth Army were content to watch and threaten with vigorous patrolling. During the night of 7–8 November, a patrol of 5th Irish Fusiliers found the Germans had evacuated the bridgehead west of Antoing. In the morning, fighting patrols which were attempting to cross the river were held up by machine-guns firing from Antoing.[50]

That evening, Antoing was outflanked by the other battalions of the brigade on bridges constructed by 11th Hampshires (at the cost of a man drowned and another wounded). Near Antoing, 5th Royal Irish Fusiliers crossed and climbed the gentle rise from the Schelde where, on 11 May 1745, Marshal Saxe had positioned his reserve, the battalions of the Irish Brigade.[51] Having captured Antoing, 16th Division was ordered to halt. On 11 November 1918 they lay upon the battlefield of Fontenoy. Had they been allowed to remain with their division, the almost knightly romantics of 16th (Irish) Division, who believed they had inherited not only the traditions of their regiments but those of the Wild Geese as well, would have rejoiced in that extraordinary coincidence.

> Then lift the flag of the last Crusade!
> And fill the ranks of the last Brigade!
> March on to the fields where the world's re-made,
> And the ancient Dreams come true!

> T.M. Kettle KC, Lieutenant, 9th Battalion, Royal Dublin Fusiliers.

Epilogue

Four selected divisions occupied part of Germany before Christmas—the Guards, the 29th Regular, 15th (Scottish) and 1st Canadian Divisions. The Irish Guards crossed the frontier with their pipers playing 'St Patrick's Day',[1] while the pipers of the Leinster Regiment played 'Come Back to Erin'.[2] However, it was on the Rhine that a triumphal crossing was staged. The Canadians, Scots and Regulars were to cross Rhine bridges simultaneously. The Scots marched to 'Scotland the Brave' across a bridge of boats at Mülheim. At Cologne the Regulars, led by the fusilier battalions of 86 Brigade, which included 1st Dublins, marched to 'The British Grenadiers'. Behind them in 88 Brigade the pipers of the effervescent Leinsters, their saffron kilts making a splash of colour, played the rollicking 'Paddy Maginty's Goat'.[3] Later, the Guards Division made its imposing entry. And as the Irish Guards swung into the Hohenzollern Ring, fittingly, their pipers played 'Brian Boru'.[4]

The German army marched back to its homeland, claiming it had been undefeated in the field but 'stabbed in the back' by the Naval Mutiny and defeatist elements in the German government. It was given a hero's welcome by a war-weary people glad the trial had ended. In what has come to be known as the 'policy of evasion', the British government turned its back on Europe, with disastrous consequences for Europe and, ultimately, the world. The focus of British attention was Ireland, India and the retention of imperial power. At the Paris Conference, British statesmen, dazzled by the mirage of an imperial vision, neglected to negotiate a lasting settlement. Castlereagh and Wellington, concluding the Napoleonic Wars at the Congress of Vienna, had wider vision; their arrangement of balances maintained a general, if precarious, peace in Western Europe for fifty years.

Given different circumstances, such as a successful outcome to the Irish Convention of 1917–18, swayed by men of the 16th and 36th Divisions standing together, it might have been unnecessary to present an Irish case at the Paris Conference. But had it been thought desirable to do so, the advocacy of Tom Kettle KC and the passionate eloquence of Willie Redmond MP, enhanced by the mud of the trenches, would have achieved more for Irish nationalism than was actually won. Alas, their eloquence had been silenced for ever in a successful crusade which left *their* dreams unfulfilled.

Gen. Sir William Hickie declined command of the Murmansk expedition against the Russian 'Reds' on the grounds that 'it was not a fair show';[5] he retired and became a senator in the first Irish parliament, one of five senior officers to do so, the others being Gen. Sir Bryan Mahon, Brig.-Gen. Sir Edward Bellingham, Col. the Earl of Granard, and Lt.-Col. the Macgillycuddy of the Reeks. Gen. Sir Oliver Nugent, after an appointment in India, retired to Mount Nugent, Co. Cavan. Some ex-soldiers, such as Lt. Emmet Dalton MC, joined the Irish revolutionary movement and after the Treaty helped form the Irish National Army. One, Maj. C.B. O'Connor DSO MC Croix de Guerre,* was appointed Principal Private Secretary to the Minister for Defence of the new state.[8] FM Sir Henry Wilson was assassinated in 1922 by two discharged soldiers, a former Irish Guardsman and an ex-Munster Fusilier. Gen. Sir Hubert Gough, outliving all his contemporaries, died in 1963. He had accepted dismissal with such dignity that leading British politicians, including Lloyd George, conceded in the late 1930s that Gough's treatment had been unjust.

After the war a committee headed by FM Earl Ypres (formerly Sir John French) conceived the Irish National Memorial Garden at Islandbridge, Dublin. It was constructed, with the full co-operation of successive Irish governments, to a design by Sir Edwin Lutyens and contains the memorial record of the 49,400 Irishmen who gave their lives in Irish regiments during the Great War.[6]

Most Irish ex-soldiers retired into historical oblivion.

> Many of the younger generation had volunteered for service in France since the outbreak of World War I. The death roll from the front read out for prayers at the College is one of the most quoted memories by students of these years.
>
> A day came when it was unpopular to pay tribute to the idealism and generosity of these young men who risked their lives fighting, as they believed, for the preservation of democracy; but in recent years a more correct perspective allows us to judge them in their historical context.[7]

For overlong those gallant Irishmen, of all creeds, affiliations and class, who writ large their country's name in the years 1914–18, have been written out of history. As Europe moves towards greater union, let them therefore be properly judged in the wider context of European history. They deserve no less.

---

* In 1984 Maj. O'Connor's medals were presented to the museum of his regiment, the Loyal North Lancashires. The presentation was made by his niece, Mrs Vera de Valera, daughter-in-law of the late President de Valera.

References

ABBREVIATIONS
ABR   after-battle report
DNB   *Dictionary of National Biography*
JAD   Jesuit Archives, Dublin
LC   Liddle Collection, University of Leeds
MP(ADA)   Maher Papers, Archdiocese of Dublin Archives
OO   Operation Order
PRO   Public Record Office
PRONI   Public Record Office of Northern Ireland
Statistics   *Statistics of the Military Effort of the British Empire
             During the GreatWar*, London: HMSO 1922
UPM   Unpublished memoirs
WD   War Diary

CHAPTER 1: ARMY MOBILISATION AND EXPANSION, AUGUST 1914 (P.1–8)
1. Gen. Sir David Fraser. *Alanbrooke*. London: Collins, 38.
2. Sir George Arthur. *Life of Lord Kitchener*. 3 vols., London: Macmillan 1920, vol. 3, 9.
3. Brig.-Gen. Sir James Edmonds. *Military Operations: France and Belgium, 1914–1918*, 16 vols., London: HMSO 1922–49, vol. 3, 260.
4. Arthur, vol. 3, 308.
5. Brig, Sir John Muirhead. UPM.
6. Arthur, vol. 3, 310.
7. Maj.-Gen. Sir C.E. Callwell. *Life and Diary of Field-Marshal Sir Henry Wilson*. 2 vols., London: Cassell 1927, vol. 2, 178.
8. Fraser, 38.
9. Lt.-Col. F.E. Whitton. *The History of the Prince of Wales's Leinster Regiment*. 2 vols., Aldershot: Gale and Polden, vol. 2, 5.
10. Ibid., 6.
11. Ibid., 10.
12. Brig.-Gen. S. Geoghegan. *Campaigns and History of the Royal Irish Regiment*. 2 vols., Edinburgh: Blackwood 1927, vol. 2, 8.
13. Ibid.
14. Whitton, vol. 2, 12.
15. Capt. F.C. Hitchcock. *Stand-To: a Diary of the Trenches*. London: Hurst and Blackett 1937, 140.
16. Col. H.F. Stonham. Papers. LC.

CHAPTER 2: IRELAND RESPONDS (P.9-16)

1. George H. Cassar. *Kitchener: Architect of Victory*. London: William Kimber 1977, 218.

2. Capt. C. Falls. *The History of the 36th Ulster Division*. Belfast: M'Caw, Stevenson and Orr 1922, 3.

3. A.F. Becke. *The Order of Battle of Divisions*: parts 1 to 3b. London: HMSO, part 3b, 67.

4. Falls, *36th Div.*, 7–8.

5. Gen. Sir A. Godley. *The Life of an Irish Soldier*. London: John Murray 1939, 215.

6. H. Hanna. *The Pals at Suvla: D Company, the 7th Royal Dublin Fusiliers*. Dublin: Ponsonby 1916, 13–16.

7. H. de Montmorency. *Sword and Stirrup*. London: G. Bell and Sons 1936, 245.

8. Rudyard Kipling. *The Irish Guards in the Great War*. 2 vols., London: Macmillan 1923, vol. 1, 70.

9. Capt. C. Falls. *The History of the First Seven Battalions of the Royal Irish Rifles*. Aldershot : Gale and Polden 1925, 186.

10. Brig.-Gen. A.R. Burrowes. *The 1st Bn the Faugh-A-Ballaghs in the Great War*. Aldershot: Gale and Polden, 177.

11. Maj. B. Cooper. *The Tenth Irish Division in Gallipoli*. London: Herbert Jenkins 1918, 252–4.

12. Peter Simkins. *Kitchener's Armies: the Raising of the New Armies, 1914–1916*. Manchester: Manchester University Press 1988, 70.

13. War Office. *Soldiers Died In the Great War*. London: HMSO 1922, parts 1–80.

14. Falls, *36th Div.*, 5.

15. Brig.-Gen. F.P. Crozier. *A Brass Hat in No Man's Land*. London: Jonathan Cape 1930, 45.

16. Trimble Press. *Story of the 6th Service Battalion, the Royal Inniskilling Fusiliers*. Enniskillen 1919, 9. (No attributable author.)

17. Falls, *36th Div.*, 9.

18. D. Gwynn. *Life of John Redmond*. London: Harrap 1932, 405.

19. Maj. G.A.C. Walker. *The Book of the 7th Royal Inniskilling Fusiliers*. Dublin: Brindley 1920, 9.

20 De Montmorency, 243.

21. Kipling, vol. 2, 233.

22. Gwynn, 402–9.

23. Crozier, *Brass Hat*, 45.

24. Cooper, 65.

25. Capt. B.W. Williams. *Raising and Training the New Armies*. London: Constable 1918, 76–8.

26. Arthur, vol. 3, 267–8.

27. Edmonds, 1918, vol. 5, 498.

28. Ibid.

29. Becke, part 3a, 68.

30. De Montmorency, 248.

CHAPTER 3: THE BEF AT MONS AND LE CATEAU, 23–26 AUGUST 1914 (P.17-27)
1. Arthur, vol. 3, 22.
2. Ibid., 23.
3. John Lucy. *There's a Devil in the Drum*. London: Faber and Faber 1938, 111.
4. Geoghegan, vol. 2, 11.
5. Edmonds, 1914, vol. 1, 74.
6. Geoghegan, vol. 2, 15.
7. Ibid., 12.
8. Lucy, 112.
9. Ibid., 114.
10. Ibid.
11. Edmonds, 1914, vol. 1, 11.
12. Lt.-Col. H.F.N. Jourdain. *History of the Connaught Rangers*. 3 vols., Whitehall: Royal United Service Institution 1924–1928, vol. 2, 404–5.
13. Ibid.
14. Ibid.
15. Ibid.
16. Ibid., 410.
17. Ibid.
18. Col. H.N. Thompson. 'An account of my capture and experiences in Germany,' *RAMC Journal*, 1915.
19. Ibid.
20. Jourdain, vol. 2, 418.
21. Lucy, 130.
22. Gen. Sir Martin Farndale. *The Royal Artillery, 1914–1918*. Royal Artillery Institute 1986, 51.
23. Edmonds, 1914, vol. 1, 164.
24. Geoghegan, vol. 2, 18.
25. Ibid., 17.
26. Maj. R.E. Priestly. *The Signal Service in the European War*. Chatham: Institute of Royal Engineers and Signals Association 1921, 20.
27. Geoghegan, vol. 2, 18.
28. Lucy, 144. 'He had, I think, Grádh for the Irish.' Op. cit.
29. Ibid., 126.

CHAPTER 4: THE RETREAT FROM MONS AND THE ADVANCE TO THE AISNE, AUGUST–SEPTEMBER 1914 (P.28-40)
1. Lt.-Col. H.S. Jervis. *The 2nd Munsters in France*. Aldershot: Gale and Polden 1922, 2.
2. Ibid.
3. Ibid., 3.
4. Ibid.
5. Ibid., 4.

6. Capt. S. McCance. *The History of the Royal Munster Fusiliers.* 2 vols., Aldershot: Gale and Polden 1927, vol. 2, 112.

7. Ibid., 116.

8. Ibid.

9. Jervis, 5.

10. Ibid.

11. Ibid.

12. The father and grandfather of Capt. Jervis had been officers of the same regiment.

13. Jervis, 6.

14. Edmonds, 1914, vol. 1, 212.

15. Army List, 1915. In the Army List, December 1918, RSM P. Cullinan, 2nd Munsters, is shown as the army's senior warrant officer.

16. Thompson.

17. Jervis, 6.

18. Mrs L. Rickard. *Story of the Munsters at Etreux, Festubert, Rue de Bois and Hulluch.* London: Hodder and Stoughton 1918, 14.

19. McCance, vol. 2, 112.

20. Rickard, 15.

21. Jervis, 6.

22. Edmonds, 1914, vol. 1, 212–3.

23. Thompson.

24. Ibid.

25. Ibid.

26. McCance, vol. 2, 119.

27. Ibid.

28. Jervis, 37.

29. Ibid., 7.

30. McCance, vol. 2, 207.

31. Quoted by McCance, vol. 2, 119.

32. Jourdain, vol. 2, 420.

33. Geoghegan, vol. 2, 21.

34. Jourdain, vol. 2, 422.

35. Ibid., vol. 1, 452.

36. Kipling, vol. 1, 14.

37. Ibid., 17.

38. Jourdain, vol. 2, 426–7.

39. Kipling, vol. 1, 17.

40. 2nd Irish Rifles, WD, and *Soldiers Died*, part 67.

41. Whitton, vol. 2, 17.

42. Ibid., 20.

43. Ibid., 22.

44. Ibid., 29.

CHAPTER 5: LA BASSÉE, 10–31 OCTOBER 1914 (P.41-51)

1. Edmonds, 1914, vol. 2, 76.
2. Maj. M.C.C. Harrison and Capt. H.A. Cartwright. *Within Four Walls*. Penguin 1940, 11.
3. Geoghegan, vol. 2, 25.
4. Ibid., 26.
5. Harrison, 11.
6. Geoghegan, vol. 2, 27.
7. Edmonds, 1914, vol. 2, 85–6.
8. Ibid.
9. Geoghegan, vol. 2, 27.
10. Lt. Matens, 56th Regiment, quoted by Geoghegan, vol. 2, 27.
11. Edmonds, 1914, vol. 2, 85–6.
12. Harrison, 11.
13. Edmonds, 1914, vol. 2, 88–9.
14. Lucy, 247–8.
15. Ibid.
16. Ibid., 236.
17. Harrison, 12.
18. Ibid., 13.
19. Ibid., 14.
20. Ibid.
21. Ibid.
22. Ibid.
23. Prof. Dr M. Kirschener [senior surgeon of the reserve, 3rd Bavarian Army Corps], 'Remarks on the action of the regular infantry bullet and of the dumdum bullet on the human body' [translated from the *Münchener Medizinische Wochenschrift*, 29 Dec. 1914], *RAMC Journal*, 1915.
24. Ibid.
25. Ibid.
26. Whitton, vol. 2, 40.
27. Hitchcock, 276. The watch was returned to the house of Hesse after the war. The doctor, Capt. Charles P. O'Brien-Butler, was killed in action before the end of the month. Op. cit.; *Officers Died*.
28. Whitton, vol. 2, 52.
29. Ibid., 56.
30. Ibid., 57.
31. Edmonds, 1914, vol. 2, 111.
32. Capt. Robert Parker. *Memoirs of the Most Remarkable Transactions*. London 1741 (reprinted 1968), 8.
33. Edmonds, 1914, vol. 2, 113.
34. Whitton, vol. 2, 65–6.
35. Hitchcock, 261.
36. Ibid., 37.
37. Edmonds, 1914, vol. 2, 140, n. 1.

CHAPTER 6: FIRST YPRES (P.52-63)

1. Kipling, vol. 1, 35.
2. Ibid.
3. Edmonds, 1914, vol. 2, 386.
4. Fr F. Peal SJ. *War Jottings*. Calcutta 1916; quoted by Jourdain, vol. 1, 437.
5. Edmonds, 1914, vol. 2, 386.
6. Kipling, vol. 1, 38.
7. Ibid., 43.
8. Edmonds, 1914, vol. 2, 340.
9. Jourdain, vol. 1, 437–8.
10. Ibid., 439.
11. Ibid.
12. Edmonds, 1914, vol. 2, 355.
13. Edmonds, 1914, vol. 2, 355, quoting '3,000 kilometres mit der Garde-Kavallerie' by Hofprediger Dr Vogel, 210.
14. Edmonds, 1914, vol. 2, 354.
15. Ibid., 420.
16. Ibid., 396.
17. McCance, vol. 2, 121.
18. Lucy, 280.
19. Gerald Achilles Burgoyne. *The Burgoyne Diaries*. London: Harmsworth, 2.
20. Crozier, *Brass Hat*, 23–4.
21. Edmonds, 1914, vol. 2, 354.
22. McCance, vol. 2, 122.
23. Jourdain, vol. 2, 438.
24. Falls, *Irish Rifles*, 23.
25. Lucy, 289.
26. War Office. *Officers Died in the Great War*. London: HMSO 1922; and *Soldiers Died*.
27. McCance, vol. 2, 122.
28. *Officers Died* and *Soldiers Died*.
29. Sir John Willcocks. *With the Indians in France*. London: Constable 1920, 89–90. At Orléans on the journey to the front, Willcocks had delivered a blistering rebuke to the Rangers on 'a certain matter'. As Gen. Willcocks left the parade an unmistakable Irish voice called, 'Three cheers for the general.' A French liaison officer hearing the cheers said, 'I suppose the general is telling them something they like.' Op. cit., 252.
30. Jourdain, vol. 1, 450–1.
31. B.H. Liddell Hart. *History of the First World War*. London: Book Club Associates, 111.
32. *Officers Died* and *Soldiers Died*.

CHAPTER 7: 1915: WINTER IN THE TRENCHES (P.64-72)

1. Edmonds, 1915, vol. 3, 21.

2. McCance, vol. 2, 124.

3. Ibid., 126.

4. Whitton, vol. 2, 81.

5. Burgoyne, 25.

6. Edmonds, 1915, vol. 3, 23.

7. Whitton, vol. 2, 104.

8. Ibid., 103.

9. Ibid., 104.

10. Edmonds, 1915, vol. 3, 7.

11. Whitton, vol. 2, 105.

12. Lt. J.G. Bland, 2nd Royal Irish Rifles. Correspondence, LC.

13. Edmonds, 1915, vol. 3, 12.

14. Hitchcock, 164.

15. Kipling, vol. 1, 274.

16. Lucy, 312.

17. Kipling, vol. 1, 99.

18. McCance, vol. 2, 207.

19. Bland.

20. Maj.-Gen. Sir John Capper. Foreword to Hitchcock, 7–8.

21. Burgoyne, 56–7.

22. Whitton, vol. 2, 112.

23. Quoted in McCance, vol. 2,126.

24. Edmonds, 1915, vol. 3, 30.

25. Hitchcock, 140.

26. Whitton, vol. 2, 116.

27. Geoghegan, vol. 2, 76.

28. Lucy, 331–2.

CHAPTER 8: 1915: THE SPRING BATTLES (P.73-86)

1. Edmonds, 1915, vol. 3, 224.

2. Ibid., 230.

3. Brig. W. Carden-Roe, Royal Irish Fusiliers. Memoirs, LC.

4. Edmonds, 1915, vol. 3, 242.

5. Ibid., 243.

6. Col. H.C. Whylly. *Crown and Company: 2nd Royal Dublin Fusiliers*. 2 vols., Aldershot: Gale and Polden, vol. 2, 40.

7. Whylly, *Crown and Company*, vol. 2, 41.

8. S.P. Kerr. *What the Irish Regiments Have Done*. London: Unwin 1916 (2nd imp.), 115.

9. Carden-Roe.

10. Fr Frederick Beal SJ [chaplain, 1st Connaught Rangers]. *War Jottings*. Calcutta: Catholic Orphan Press 1916, 54.

11. Edmonds, 1915, vol. 3, 259.

12. Willcocks, 253.

13. Edmonds, 1915, vol. 3, 259.

14. Whylly, *Crown and Company*, vol. 2, 43.

15. Ibid., 45.

16. Edmonds, 1915, vol. 3, 352.

17. The casualty figures have been computed from Whylly, *Crown and Company*, vol. 2, 50–1; *Officers Died*; and *Soldiers Died*.

18. Whylly, *Crown and Company*, vol. 2, 50.

19. Burrowes, 42.

20. Edmonds, 1915, vol. 3, 353.

21. Fr Francis Gleeson, chaplain, 2nd Royal Munster Fusiliers. Diary, MP (ADA). (For the origin of the Munster flags see Jervis, 18.)

22. Gleeson.

23. Ibid. The scene was well captured on canvas by Fortunino Matania from a description obtained by Mrs Rickard. The original painting was presented to the Royal Army Chaplains' Department (RC) by Maj. Henry Harris, author of *The Irish Regiments in the First World War*. Informant: Mgr John Moran, former Principal Roman Catholic Chaplain (Army).

24. Jervis, 19.

25. Ibid. The leader of the Munster company was Lt. T. Price. He was wounded three times and taken prisoner. His award for achieving the near-impossible was a Mention in Despatches. In the opinion of H.S. Jervis, 'his services received inadequate recognition.' Op. cit.

26. Fraser, 67.

27. Jervis, 20.

28. Jourdain, vol. 1, 456.

29. Edmonds, 1915, vol. 4, 22–3.

30. Ibid., 52.

31. Ibid., 72.

CHAPTER 9: RAISING AND TRAINING 10TH DIVISION (P.87-99)

1. Becke, part 3a, 17. On the relationship between nationalist and unionist in 10th Division, the divisional historian wrote: 'Once we tacitly agreed to let the past be buried, we found thousands of points on which we agreed.' Cooper, 212.

2. Cooper, 5, and *DNB*.

3. Ibid., 10.

4. Ibid., 11.

5. Ibid., 15.

6. Ibid., 15.

7. Maj. Terence Vershoyle, 5th Royal Inniskilling Fusiliers. Memoirs, LC.

8. Hanna, 58.

9. *Soldiers Died*.

10. W.S. Cowland. *10th and 12th Battalions the Hampshire Regiment*. Winchester: Warren 1930, 27.

11. Ibid., 28.

12. Sgt. J.C. Dart, 10th Division Signal Company RE. Memoirs, LC.
13. Ibid.
14. Capt. D. Campbell, 6th Royal Irish Rifles. Memoirs, LC. After the war Capt. Campbell became the resident engineer to the Irish National War Memorial. According to its history he was 'tactful in administration, efficient in management and unwearying in his devotion to his task.'
15. Ibid.
16. Vershoyle.
17. Ibid.
18. Ibid.
19. Ibid.
20. Ibid.
21. Ibid.
22. Campbell.
23. Hanna, 30.
24. Ibid., 30.
25. Mrs M. Brien: conversation with author.
26. *Irish Times*, 1 May 1915.
27. P.F. Edwards, staff, Custom House, Dublin, 1921: conversation with author.
28. Hanna, 33.
29. Ibid., 32.
30. Cooper, 25.
31. Campbell.
32. Dart.
33. Hanna, 37.
34. Cooper, 28.
35. Ibid., 29.
36. Ibid.
37. Quoted by Cooper, 29–30.
38. Cooper, 33.
39. Vershoyle.
40. Jourdain, vol. 3, 563. The battalions of 10th Division left Basingstoke singing 'God Save Ireland'. Cooper, 34.
41. Cooper, 63.
42. Ibid., 65.
43. 8th Earl Granard. Correspondence. PRONI T.3765/K/12/2.
44. Cooper, 68.
45. Ibid.

CHAPTER 10: GALLIPOLI: THE LANDING AT HELLES (P.100-113)

1. Hans Kannengiesser. *The Campaign in Gallipoli*. London: Hutchinson, 185.
2. Rev. O. Creighton. *With the Twenty-Ninth Division in Gallipoli*. London: Longman Green, 46.
3. McCance, vol. 2, 47.

4. Ibid., 48.

5. Ibid., 49.

6. Col. H.C. Whylly. *Neil's Blue Caps: the 1st Royal Dublin Fusiliers.* 2 vols., Dublin: Maunsell 1925, vol. 2, 30.

7. Ibid., 30–1.

8. Creighton, 67.

9. Ibid.

10. H.W. Nevinson. *The Dardanelles Campaign.* London: Nesbit 1918, 98.

11. Ibid., 97.

12. C.V. Wedgwood. *The Last of the Radicals.* London: Jonathan Cape 1951, 106.

13. McCance, vol. 2, 51.

14. Winston S. Churchill. *The World Crisis.* 2 vols., London: Odhams, vol. 2, 762.

15. Capt. A.J. Trousdell, 1st Royal Irish Fusiliers. Diary, LC.

16. Creighton, 74.

17. Whylly, *Blue Caps*, vol. 2, 38.

18. Maj. O'Hara, quoted by Whylly, *Blue Caps*, vol. 2, 39.

19. McCance, vol. 2, 53.

20. Arthur Bryant. *The Years of Victory.* London: Collins, 437.

21. McCance, vol. 2, 53.

22. Sir F. Fox. *The Royal Inniskillings in the Great War.* London: Constable 1928, 183.

23. Whylly, *Blue Caps*, vol. 2, 41.

24. Ibid.

25. Arthur, vol. 3, 145.

26. Brig.-Gen. C.E. Aspinall-Oglander. *Military Operations: Gallipoli.* 2 vols., London: Heinemann 1932, vol. 2, 91.

27. Ibid.

28. Ibid.

29. Maj. C. Cripps, 9th Somerset Light Infantry. Memoirs, LC.

30. Ibid.

31. Ibid.

32. *Soldiers Died.*

33. Aspinall-Oglander, vol. 2, 93.

CHAPTER 11: GALLIPOLI: ANZAC, 6–12 AUGUST 1915 (P.114-124)

1. Alan Moorhead. *Gallipoli.* London: Hamish Hamilton 1956, 281.

2. Kannengiesser, 207.

3. Campbell.

4. Ibid.

5. Ibid.

6. Cooper, 77.

7. Godley, 11.

8. Campbell.

9. Ibid.

10. Ibid.

11. Ibid.

12. Ibid.

13. H.C. Armstrong. *Grey Wolf*. London: Penguin 1937, 68.

14. Cooper, 84.

15. Ibid., 85.

16. Ibid., 89.

17. Cooper, 61.

18. Godley, 188.

19. Cooper, 104.

20. Ibid., 106.

21. Jourdain, vol. 3, 116.

22. Ibid., 33.

23. Lt. Owen L.D. Gill, 11th Division Signal Company, RE. Letter, courtesy of Col. M.N. Gill, Irish army (retd.).

24. Pte R. Bradford, 6th Green Howards. Memoirs, LC.

25. Maj.-Gen. R.F.H. Nalder. *The Royal Corps of Signals: a History of its Antecedents and Development*. London: Royal Signals Institute 1956, 161.

Chapter 12: Gallipoli: 10th Division at Suvla, 1915 (p.125-140)

1. Cooper, 126.

2. Aspinall-Oglander, vol. 2, 256.

3. Ibid., 266.

4. Ibid., 274.

5 Cooper, 133.

6. Hanna, 58.

7. Capt. Edward King, 5th Royal Inniskilling Fusiliers. 'Haphazard' (privately printed), and Memoirs, LC.

8. Sir Ian Hamilton, *Gallipoli Diary*. 2 vols., London: Edward Arnold 1920, vol. 2, 332.

9. Aspinall-Oglander, vol. 2, 286.

10. Hanna, 82.

11. Aspinall-Oglander, vol. 2, 295. 'Water was very scarce: none who was there will ever forget the supply laid on by the destroyer *Grampus*.' Vershoyle.

12. Cooper, 150.

13. Hamilton, *Diary*, vol. 2, 333.

14. Aspinall-Oglander, vol. 2, 262–3; see also Cooper, 146, and Ian Hamilton's *Final Despatch*, London: Newnes 1916, 96.

15. Cooper, 137–8.

16. Ibid., 146.

17. Aspinall-Oglander, vol. 2, 272.

18. Cooper, 207.

19. Aspinall-Oglander, vol. 2, 262.

20. Ibid., 275.

21. Dart.
22. Cooper, 146.
23. Granard Papers.
24. Cooper, 155.
25. Nevison, 330.
26. Vershoyle.
27. Cooper, 168.
28. Michael Moynihan. *God On Our Side: the British Padre in the First World War.* London: Leo Cooper 1983, 97–8.
29. Ibid.
30. Cooper, 174.
31. Ibid., 176.
32. Granard Papers.
33. Kannengiesser, 224.
34. Ibid., 225.
35. Hamilton, *Diary*, vol. 2, 329.
36. Aspinall-Oglander, vol. 2, 323.
37. Churchill, vol. 2, 874.
38. Field-Marshal Liman von Sanders. *Five Years in Turkey.* US Naval Institute 1927, 67.
39. Maj.-Gen. Sir A. Lynden-Bell, MGGS MEF. Memoirs, LC.
40. Moorhead, 308.
41. Ibid.

CHAPTER 13: GALLIPOLI: THE LAST DAYS (P.141-152)

1. Cowland, 20; and Falls, *Irish Rifles*, 52.
2. Cooper, 185.
3. Aspinall-Oglander, vol. 2, 347–54.
4. King, 'Haphazard', 52.
5. Jourdain, vol. 3, 38
6. Cooper, 191.
7. Jourdain, vol. 3, 43
8. Cooper, 191.
9. Ibid.
10. Ibid.
11. Jourdain, vol. 3, 48.
12. Aspinall-Oglander, vol. 2, 355–60.
13. Jourdain, vol. 3, 68.
14. Ibid., 71.
15. Cooper, 197.
16. Jourdain, vol. 3, 62.
17. Ibid.
18. Hamilton, *Final Despatch*, 122. 'The bitter fighting on Hill 60, still regarded by the Australians and New Zealanders as perhaps their sternest test at Gallipoli.'

Aspinall-Oglander, vol. 2, 360–2.

19. Hamilton, *Diary*, vol. 2, 138–9.

20. Quoted by Jourdain, vol. 3, 50–1.

21. Cooper, 234.

22. Ibid., 237.

23. Aspinall-Oglander, vol. 2, 275.

24. von Sanders, 67.

25. Arthur, vol. 3, 168.

26. Thomas Pakenham, *The Boer War*, London: Weidenfeld and Nicolson 1979, 468-70.

27. Ibid.

28. Hamilton, vol. 2, 333. Unlike Hamilton, Mahon was 'the soul of frankness.' Capt. C. Falls. *Military Operations: Macedonia*. 2 vols., London: HMSO, vol. 1, 99.

29. Granard Papers.

30. Hamilton, *Diary*, vol. 2, 313. This is a contradiction. Following his visit to Suvla on 9 August 1915, Hamilton wrote: 'My talk with Mahon made me happier. Here at least was someone who had an idea of what he was doing.' At the same time Hamilton noted Mahon's anger and frustration. 'He besought me to get Hill and his battalions back to their own command.' *Diary*, vol. 2, 75.

31. Granard Papers.

32. Moorhead, 296.

33. Becke, part 3a, 11.

34. Granard Papers.

35. Ibid.

36. Ibid.

36. *Sprig of Shillelagh* [journal of the Royal Inniskilling Fusiliers], Oct. 1915.

CHAPTER 14: THE BATTLE OF LOOS, 25 SEPTEMBER–15 OCTOBER 1915 (P.153-160)

1. Whitton, vol. 2, 135.

2. Ibid.

3. Sir Archibald Wavell. *Allenby*. London: Harrap, 163, n. 1.

4. Jervis, 21.

5. Brig.-Gen. F.C. Crozier. *The Men I Killed*. London: Michael Joseph 1930, 214. 'Good old Plunkett' was twice recommended for the Victoria Cross, once as RSM of 2nd Royal Irish after Mons and Le Cateau, and again as a battalion commander for his defence of Bourlon Wood in 1917. Op. cit., 186–7.

6. Edmonds, 1915, vol. 3, 214.

7. Ibid.

8. Edmonds, 1918, vol. 5, 598.

9. Sir C.E. Callwell. *Experiences of a Dug-Out*. London: Constable 1920, 207.

10. Edmonds, 1915, vol. 5, 126 n. 2.

11. Kipling, vol. 2, 6.

12. Edmonds, 1915, vol. 5, 129.

13. Ibid., 114.

14. Ibid., 165.
15. Ibid., 188.
16. Ibid., 218.
17. Jervis, 23.
18. Edmonds, 1915, vol. 5, 219–20.
19. Ibid., 326–32.
20. C. Headlam. *History of the Guards Division in the Great War*. London: Murray 1924, 58–9.
21. *Officers Died; Soldiers Died*.
22. Edmonds, 1915, vol. 5, 373.
23. Ibid.
24. Headlam, 90.
25. Whitton, vol. 2, 141.
26. Jourdain, vol. 1, 486–7.
27. Lucy, 345.
28. Kipling, vol. 2, 233.

CHAPTER 15: SALONIKA, OCTOBER–NOVEMBER 1915 (P.161-170)

1. Field-Marshal Sir William Robertson. *Soldiers and Statesmen, 1914–1918*. London: Cassell 1926, vol. 2, 93, 99, 101–2.
2. Falls, *Macedonia*, vol. 1, 44.
3. Ibid., 45.
4. Ibid. , 50.
5. Ibid.
6. Jourdain, vol. 3, 88.
7. Vershoyle.
8. Sir Thomas Harley. Papers, LC.
9. Falls, *Macedonia*, vol. 1, 54.
10. Nalder, 168.
11. Falls, *Macedonia*, vol. 1, 57.
12. Lt. R.C.McB. Broun, 6th Royal Dublin Fusiliers. Correspondence, LC.
13. Nalder, 168.
14. Jourdain, vol. 3, 94–5.
15. Ibid.
16. Lynden-Bell.
17. Falls, *Macedonia*, vol. 1, 102.
18. Lynden-Bell.

CHAPTER 16: SERBIA, 15 NOVEMBER–8 DECEMBER 1915 (P.171-180)

1. Jourdain, vol. 3, 104, 129.
2. Falls, *Macedonia*, vol. 1, 65.
3. Sir W.D. Macpherson. *History of the Great War: Medical Services*. 4 vols., London: HMSO 1923, vol. 2, *Hygiene of the War*, 486–7.
4. Vershoyle.
5. Broun.

6. Ibid.

7. McCance, vol. 2, 194.

8. Broun.

9. Falls, *Macedonia*, vol. 1, 66.

10. Ibid., 71.

11. Ibid., 65.

12. Ibid., 57, n. 1.

13. Ibid., 64.

14. Jourdain, vol. 3, 111.

15. Falls, *Macedonia*, vol. 1, 67.

16. Jourdain, vol. 3, 120.

17. Falls, *Macedonia*, vol. 1, 67.

18. Broun.

19. 'The men, being thoroughly uncomfortable, were riotously happy.' Whitton, vol. 2, 207.

20. Jourdain, vol. 3, 120.

21. Ibid., 119.

22. Ibid., 120.

23. McCance, vol. 2, 195.

24. Ibid.

25. Jourdain, vol. 3, 121.

26. Vershoyle.

27. Falls, *Macedonia*, vol. 1, 72.

28. Ibid.

CHAPTER 17: THE RETREAT TO SALONIKA, 10–18 DECEMBER 1915 (P.181-187)

1. Falls, *Macedonia*, vol. 1, 73.

2. Jourdain, vol. 3, 133–4.

3. Falls, *Macedonia*, vol. 1, 79.

4. Ibid., 76.

5. Ibid.

6. Ibid., 77–8.

7. Ibid., 81.

8. Trimble, 24.

9. Jourdain, vol. 3, 134.

10. Ibid., 135.

11. Falls, *Macedonia*, vol. 1, 82, quoting Lt.-Col. M. Lon, *Bulgaria en la Guerra Europea, 1915–18*.

12. Casualty figures are computed from Falls, *Macedonia*, vol. 1, 82, and *Soldiers Died*, parts 23, 32, 41, 67–9, and 71–3.

13. Falls, *Macedonia*, vol. 1, 115.

CHAPTER 18: RAISING AND TRAINING 16TH DIVISION (P.188-202)

1. Becke, part 3a, 68.

2. Geoghegan, vol. 2, 111.

3. Ibid.

4. *Soldiers Died*.

5. Geoghegan, vol. 2, 111–2.

6. Maj. W.H.K. Redmond. *Trench Pictures from France*. London: Melrose 1917, introduction, 20.

7. *Soldiers Died*.

8. Whitton, vol. 2, 99.

9. Ibid., 196.

10. Falls, *Irish Rifles*, 11.

11. Sir Francis Vane, *Agin the Governments*. London: Samson Low and Marston, 249.

12. Ibid., 254.

13. Prof. T.M. Kettle. *The Ways of War*. London: Constable 1917, 72.

14. Walker, 3.

15. Ibid.

16. Ibid., 4

17. De Montmorency, 247.

18. Lt. P. Heptenstall, RE, 16th Divisional Engineers. Memoirs, LC.

19. Ibid.

20. Ibid.

21. Ibid.

22. Ibid.

23. Walker, 3–4.

24. Ibid., 5.

25. Ibid., 4, 25.

26. Sir B.G. Seton and John Grant. *The Pipes of War*. New York: EP Publishing 1975, 194.

27. Walker, 10.

28. Geoghegan, vol. 2, 111–2.

29. Ibid., vol. 2, 112.

30. Lucy, 353–4. One battalion commander later wrote from France: 'The officers' messes of the Division, though they include many diamonds in the rough, are pleasant places to live in—full of good will and good cheer.' Feilding, 128.

31. Headlam, 40.

32. Gwynn, 397–8.

33. Ibid, 400-4.

34. Walker, 9.

35. Geoghegan, vol. 2, 112.

36. FM Viscount Slim. *Defeat Into Victory*. London: Cassell 1959, 3.

37. Gwynn, 397.

38. Walker, 16.

39. Ibid., 14–15.

40. Ibid.

41. Kenneth Rose. *King George V*. London: Weidenfeld and Nicolson, 181–2. About the King's injuries, FM Haig unfeelingly entered in his diary: 'Few bruises can have had so much attention.' Op. cit.

42. Arthur, vol. 3, 297–9.

43. Falls, *Irish Rifles*, 20.

44. Fr Joseph Wrafter SJ, chaplain, 6th Royal Irish Regiment. Correspondence, JAD.

45. Maj. Sir John Hall, 8th Royal Munster Fusiliers. Correspondence, LC.

46. Walker, 16.

47. Ibid.

48. Ibid., 25.

CHAPTER 19: THE LOOS SALIENT (P.203-215)

1. Brig. W S. Hickie: conversations with author.

2. Ibid.

3. Pakenham, 475–6.

4. Lt.-Col. R. Feilding. *War Letters to a Wife*. London: Medici Society 1929, 136.

5. Edmonds, 1916, vol. 1, 260.

6. Robert Blake. *The Private Papers of Douglas Haig*. London: Eyre and Spottiswoode 1953, 145.

7. Ibid.

8. Hall, J.

9. Sir H. de la P. Gough. *The Fifth Army*. London: Hodder and Stoughton 1931, 130.

10. Walker, 29.

11. Ibid.

12. McCance, vol. 2, 197.

13. Jourdain, vol. 3, 206.

14. Ibid., 209.

15. Geoghegan, vol. 2, 113.

16. Edmonds, 1915, vol. 3, 5.

17. Macpherson, *Medical Services: Diseases of the War*, vol. 2, 341.

18. Alfred O'Rahilly. *Father William Doyle SJ*. London: Longman Green 1939, 408.

19. Ibid., 409.

20. Jourdain, vol. 3, 211.

21. Hall, J.

22. Edmonds, 1916, vol. 1, 195 n. 1, 196 n. 2.

23. Hall, J.

24. Pte. D. Moore, 2nd Royal Inniskilling Fusiliers. *Sprig of Shillelagh*, spring 1915.

25. Edmonds, 1916, vol. 1, 196–7. 'Though the PH helmets gave good protection it was evident there were serious limitations to the protection afforded.' Macpherson, *Medical Services: Diseases of the War*, vol. 2, 341.

26. McCance, vol. 2, 197.

27. Ibid.

28. Ibid., 198.

29. Lucy, 252.

30. McCance, vol. 2, 133.

31 Whitton, vol. 2, 303.

32. Jourdain, vol. 3, 218.

33. Thomas H. Sheridan. 'Memories of the 6th Battalion,' *The Ranger* [journal of the Connaught Rangers], no. 75, Jul. 1967.

34. *Soldiers Died*.

35. O'Rahilly, photograph, opposite 408.

CHAPTER 20: RAISING AND TRAINING 36TH DIVISION, SEPTEMBER 1914–MAY 1915 (P.216-223)

1. Becke, part 3b, 67.

2. Crozier, *Brass Hat*, 18–19.

3. Falls, *36th Div.*, 8.

4. Becke, part 3b, 67.

5. Falls, *36th Div.*, 1–2.

6. Ibid., 3.

7. Ibid., 4.

8. Crozier, *Brass Hat*, 20.

9. Falls, *36th Div.*, 6.

10. Ibid., 16.

11. Crozier, *Brass Hat*, 28–9. About the same time in Finner Camp, Co. Donegal, 'the great storm in Autumn (1914) levelled all the tents and soaked all the occupants to the skin. There was much profane grousing.' Lt.-Col. F.S.N. McRory, 'Story of the 10th Royal Inniskilling Fusiliers', PRO WO 95/2491.

12. *Soldiers Died*, parts 23, 32, 67, 68, 69, 71, 72, 73.

13. Falls, *36th Div.*, 15.

14. Ibid., 12.

15. Crozier, *Brass Hat*, 30–3.

16. Falls, 12.

17. Ibid., 5.

18. Ibid., 14.

19. Ibid., 18.

20. *Irish Times*, 9 May 1915.

21. Becke, part 3b, 63.

22. Falls, *36th Div.*, 17.

23. Ibid., 19.

24. Becke, part 3b, 63.

25. Falls, *36th Div.*, 30–1.

26. Ibid., 21.

27. Ibid., 23.

28. Ibid., 24.

29. Ibid., 25.
30. Ibid.
31. Ibid.
32. Sgt.-Maj. Samuel McKeever, 12th Royal Irish Rifles. Memoirs, LC.

CHAPTER 21: THE SOMME: THIEPVAL (P.224-236)
1. Edmonds, 1916, vol. 1, 31–2.
2. *Statistics*, 490.
3. Falls, *36th Div.*, 21.
4. Edmonds, 1916, vol. 3, 288.
5. 9th Royal Inniskilling Fusiliers. ABR.
6. Quoted by Falls, *36th Div.*, 52.
7. Lt.-Col. Stewart Blacker, 9th Royal Irish Fusiliers. Letter to Col. Fitzgerald, Commanding Officer, the Depot, Royal Irish Fusiliers, 1916.
8. Cunliffe, 307.
9. McKeever.
10. Ibid.
11. Ibid.
12. *Soldiers Died*.
13. Edmonds, 1916, vol. 1, 406.
14. Blacker.
15. Fox, 69.
16. Rfn. James McRoberts, 14th Royal Irish Rifles. Memoirs, LC.
17. 9th RInnF. ABR.
18. Crozier, *Men I Killed*, 83.
19. 9th RInnF. ABR.
20. Crozier, *Brass Hat*, 97–8.
21. Fox, 69.
22. Ibid.
23. 9th RInnF. ABR.
24. 36th Div. OO. PRO WO 95/2491.
25. 9th RInnF. ABR.
26. Edmonds, 1916, vol. 1, 289, 490–3.
27. McRoberts.
28. Falls, *36th Div.*, 56.
29. 11th RInnF. ABR.
30. Ibid.
31. Falls, *36th Div.*, 58.
32. Ibid., 58.
33. Ibid., 59.
34. Ibid., 59.
35. *Officers Died* and *Soldiers Died*.
36. Falls, *36th Div.*, 63.
37. Edmonds, 1916, vol. 1, 408.

38. Falls, *36th Div.*, 52.

39. Crozier, *Brass Hat*, 97–8.

40. Blacker.

CHAPTER 22: THE SOMME: GUILLEMONT, 2–4 SEPTEMBER 1916 (P.237-245)

1. Walker, 65.

2. Ibid., 64.

3. John Brophy and Eric Partridge. *The Long, Long Trail*. London: André Deutsch 1965, 61.

4. Whitton, vol. 2, 308.

5. Capt. Wilfred Miles. *Military Operations: France and Belgium, 1916*, vol. 2, 245, n. 2.

6. Ernst Jünger. *Storm of Steel*. London: Chatto and Windus 1928, 99.

7. Maj. J.V. Holland, 7th Leinster Regiment. Recorded interview, LC.

8. Whitton, vol. 2, 309–10.

9. Holland.

10. Ibid.

11. Jourdain, vol. 3, 221.

12. Ibid., 222.

13. William Grattan. *Adventures of the Connaught Rangers*. London: Henry Colburn 1847, vol. 2, 59.

14. When a Ranger doing field punishment heard that Hughes was recommended for the VC he was quite indignant. Claiming to have been with Hughes throughout the action, he demanded similar recognition. 'Life is notoriously unjust... for want of corroboration the other man's only record for posterity is the award of F. P. No. 1.' Col. S. Jourdain, 'A subaltern's war', *The Ranger*, no. 74, Jul. 1966.

15. Seton and Grant, 193.

16. Jourdain, vol. 3, 222.

17. Miles, 1916, vol. 2, 256.

18. McCance, vol. 2, 202.

19. Jourdain, vol. 3, 222.

20. Miles, 1916, vol. 2, 257, n. 4.

21. Whitton, vol. 2, 310.

22. Ibid., 311.

23. Miles, 1916, vol. 2, 257.

24. Whitton, vol. 2, 313.

25. Jourdain, vol. 3, 222.

26. Miles, 1916, vol. 2, 258.

27. Walker, 27.

28. Miles, 1916, vol. 2, 259.

29. Walker, 65–6.

CHAPTER 23: THE SOMME: GINCHY, 5–10 SEPTEMBER 1916 (P.246-256)

1. Miles, 1916, vol. 2, 260.

2. Falls, *Irish Rifles*, 73.
3. Walker, 67.
4. Ibid., 69.
5. Ibid., 124.
6. Miles, 1916, vol. 2, 274.
7. Maj.-Gen. Sir N. Holmes, 2nd Royal Irish Regt, DAAG, HQ 16th Division, LC.
8. Col. S. Jourdain, 6th Connaught Rangers: conversations with author.
9. Capt. C.A. Brett. 'Snowball', 'The Hundred Days', *The Ranger*, no. 76, Jul. 1968.
10. Feilding, *War Letters*, 113.
11. S. Jourdain.
12. Falls, *Irish Rifles*, 73.
13. Ibid.
14. McCance, vol. 2, 66.
15. Miles, 1916, vol. 2, 274.
16. Ibid., 273.
17. Feilding, 115–6.
18. Ibid., 122.
19. Falls, *Irish Rifles*, 74.
20. Whitton, vol. 2, 318.
21. Rfn. M. Kane, 7th Royal Irish Rifles. Recorded interview, LC.
22. Kipling, vol. 2, 101–5.
23. John Buchan. *Nelson's History of the Great War*. 24 vols., London: Nelson 1915–19, vol. 16, 101.
24. *Soldiers Died*. Wellington cried when told of the number of casualties at the storming of Badajoz in the Peninsular War—3,500, of whom 760 were dead. (*Napier*, vol. 3, 122.) Clearly, First World War generals were made of sterner stuff. However, unlike Wellington, Gens. Hickie and Nugent justly praised their men. 'The spirit, courage and determination by all ranks was beyond praise.' 16th Div. ABR, PRO WO 95/1955. 'Nothing finer was done in the war than the attack of the Ulster Division on the 1st July.' 36th Div. order of the day. PRO WO 95/2201.
25. Edmonds, 1916, vol. 1, 483.
26. Godley, 215.
27. Kettle, 18–19.
28. Ibid.
29. Witherow.
3o. McRoberts.

CHAPTER 24: MACEDONIA, 1916–17 (P.257-268)
1. Jourdain, vol. 3, 143.
2. Sgt. H. Downs, 5th CR. Memoirs, LC; and Whitton, vol. 2, 285.
3. Jourdain, vol. 3, 142.
4. Whitton, vol. 2, 323–5.
5. C.T. Atkinson. *The Royal Hampshire Regiment*. Winchester: Regimental Headquarters 1952, 150.

6. Campbell.

7. Whitton, vol. 2, 287.

8. Campbell.

9. Rev. R. Skilbeck-Smith [captain, Indian army, retired]. *A Subaltern in Macedonia and Palestine.* London: Mitre Press 1930, 58.

10. Atkinson, 150.

11. Falls, *Macedonia*, vol. 1, 173.

12. Ibid. See also Macpherson, *Medical Services: General*, vol. 3, 103–4.

13. Macpherson, *Medical Services: General*, vol. 3, 108–9. Maj. T.J. Mitchell. *History of the Great War: Medical Services, Casualties and Medical Statistics.* London: HMSO, 194, 216.

14. Campbell.

15. Ibid.

16. Col. T.T. McCartney-Filgate, Royal Inniskilling Fusiliers. Recorded interview, LC.

17. Falls, *Macedonia*, vol. 1, 173.

18. Ibid., 175.

19. Ibid., 180.

20. Ibid.

21. Campbell.

22. Ibid.

23. McCartney-Filgate.

24. Geoghegan, vol. 2, 89.

25. Whitton, vol. 2, 212.

26. Falls, *Macedonia*, vol. 1, 183. Whitton, vol. 2, 212, says it was 32 miles, 'without a man falling out.' A mile here or there, it was superb marching considering the heat of the Struma valley during the month of June.

27. Skilbeck-Smith, 67.

28. McCartney-Filgate.

29. Macpherson, *Medical Services: General*, vol. 2, 108–9.

30. Falls, *Macedonia*, vol. 1, 184.

31. Skilbeck-Smith, 73.

32. Whitton, vol. 2, 215.

33. Skilbeck-Smith, 55–8.

34. Ibid.

35. Whitton, vol. 2, 400.

36. The 40–10s, nickname of the Leinsters; see chap. 1, n. 15.

37. Vershoyle.

38. McCartney-Filgate.

39. Ibid.

40. Ibid.

41. Ibid.

42. Cowland, 30.

CHAPTER 25: MESSINES, 1917 (P.269-281)

1 Walker, 82.

2. Hickie.

3. Walker, 82.

4. McRoberts.

5. Hickie.

6. Walker, 91.

7. Ibid., 96.

8. Col. E.A.P. Hobday, 16th Divisional Artillery. Papers, LC.

9. Ibid.

10. 16 Div Artillery ABR. Hobday.

11. Ibid.

12. Ibid.

13. Ibid.

14. 16 Div. OO. Hobday.

15. Ibid.

16. Falls, *36th Div.*

17. 16 Div. OO. Hobday.

18. Whitton, vol. 2, 410.

19. Ibid., 417.

20. Geoghegan, vol. 2, 116.

21. Whitton, vol. 2, 418.

22. Ibid.

23. McCance, vol. 2, 70.

24. Jourdain, vol. 3, 243.

25. Brig.-Gen. G.E. Pereira, 47 Brigade ABR. Hobday Papers, LC.

26. McCance, vol. 2, 71.

27. 7th/8th RIF. WD.

28. Ibid.

29. Ibid.

30. Ibid. and *Soldiers Died.*

31. 7th/8th RIF. WD.

32. 16 Div. Artillery ABR. Hobday.

33. Feilding, 191.

34. *Soldiers Died.*

35. Redmond, 30–1.

36. Feilding, 219.

37. Ibid.

38. Falls, *36th Div.*, 86.

39. Withrow.

40. Ibid.

41. Ibid.

42. Falls, *36th Div.*, 93.

CHAPTER 26: THIRD YPRES: 16TH DIVISION (P.282-291)
1. O'Rahilly, 510.
2. Ibid.
3. Ibid.
4. Thomas B. Sheridan. 'Memories of the 6th Battalion', *The Ranger*, no. 75, Jul. 1967.
5. Falls, *36th Div.*, 122.
6. Edmonds, 1917, vol. 2, 385.
7. Gough, 201–2.
8. 7th/8th RIF. WD.
9. Sheridan.
10. 7th/8th RIF. WD.
11. O'Rahilly, 529.
12. Ibid., 532.
13. Jourdain, vol. 3, 248.
14. Edmonds, 1917, vol. 2, 188.
15. Ibid.
16. Blake, 250.
17. Holmes.
18. Edmonds, 1917, vol. 2, 189.
19. Ibid., 190.
20. Farndale, 204.
21. Ibid.
22. Ibid.
23. Edmonds, 1917, vol. 2, 195.
24. Ibid.
25. Falls, *Irish Rifles*, 109.
26. Ibid.
27. Geoghegan, vol. 2, 52.
28. Edmonds, 1917, vol. 2, 197.
29. Falls, *Irish Rifles*, 109.
30. Ibid.
31. Edmonds, 1917, vol. 2, 196 n. 2.
32. Jourdain, vol. 3, 250.
33. *Glasgow Evening News*, 1 Sep. 1917, quoted by Moynihan.

CHAPTER 27: THIRD YPRES: 36TH DIVISION (P.292-301)
1. Withrow.
2. 11th RInnF. ABR.
3. Falls, *36th Div.*, 117.
4. Ibid., 116.
5. Ibid., 118.
6. Ibid., 118.
7. Ibid., 118.

8. *Soldiers Died* and Edmonds, 1917, vol. 2, 197–8, n. 1.

9. Falls, *36th Div.*, 117.

10. Maj.-Gen. Sir Oliver Nugent, GOC 36th (Ulster) Division. Correspondence, PRONI D3835/E/2/502. In addition to honesty, Gen. Nugent's pen and voice were known for their sharpness, subtlety and wit. Crozier, *Men I Killed*, 67.

11. Sir Philip Gibbs. *The Realities of War*. London: Heinemann 388–9. 'But possibly the holding of these trenches for the days preceding the actual advance had proved the greatest strain the Derrymen yet endured.' McRory, PRO WO 95/2491.

12. Holmes.

13. Ibid.

14. Blake, 272.

15. Ibid.

16. Edmonds, 1917, vol. 2, 385.

17. Gen. Sir Anthony Farrar-Hockley. *Goughie*. London: Hart-Davis MacGibbon 1973, 106.

18. Capt. Stair Gillon. *The Story of the 29th Division*. London: Nelson, 136. The songs were more probably 'nationalist' ones.

19. Ibid.

20. Edmonds, 1917, vol. 2, 358–9.

21. McCance, vol. 2, 146.

22. Ibid.

23. Ibid., 147.

24. Jervis, 41.

25. Whitton, vol. 2, 373–4.

CHAPTER 28: THE BATTLE OF CAMBRAI (P.302-317)

1. Whitton, vol. 2, 434.

2. Hall. J.

3. Feilding, 228.

4. Ibid.

5. 7th/8th RIF. WD.

6. Feilding, 232.

7. Ibid.

8. Whitton, vol. 2, 435–6.

9. Ibid., 436.

10. Hall, J.

11. McWeeney.

12. Hall, J.

13. Quoted by Feilding, 240–1.

14. Falls, *36th Div.*, 134.

15. Capt. R.S. Trousdell, 1st Royal Irish Fusiliers. Memoirs, LC.

16. An illustration of this is his praise of the Inniskilling brigade at Thiepval: 'Everything solid and thorough.' Falls, 52.

17. Falls, *36th Div.*, 164.
18. Nugent. PRONI D3835/E/2/545.
19. Kipling, vol. 2, 248–9.
20. Capt. Wilfred Miles. *Military Operations: France and Belgium, 1917*, vol. 3, *The Battle of Cambrai*, London: HMSO, 358–9.
21. Fox, 113.
22. Maj. Sir Hugh Stewart, Bt, 1st Royal Inniskilling Fusiliers. Memoirs, LC. Commenting on Irish soldiers, a commanding officer of Connaught Rangers wrote, 'They are, I should imagine, difficult to drive, but easy to lead' (Feilding, 121). Sherwood-Kelly was a driver.
23. Kipling, vol. 1, 251.
24. Ibid.
25. 1st Irish Guards. WD, quoted by Kipling, vol. 1, 255.
26. Ibid.
27. *Soldiers Died*, part 5, and Kipling, vol. 1, 257.
28. Falls, *36th Div.*, 173–4.
29. Ibid., 177.
30. Miles, *Cambrai*, 382.

CHAPTER 29: PALESTINE: THIRD BATTLE OF GAZA (P.318-327)

1. Wavell, *Allenby*, 188.
2. SSgt. A.L.G. Whyte, RAMC. LC.
3. Whitton, vol. 2, 325.
4. Ibid., 326.
5. Col. A.P. Wavell. *The Palestine Campaigns*. London: Constable 1938, 112.
6. Wavell, *Allenby*, 203.
7. Skilbeck-Smith, 124.
8. Whitton, vol. 2, 326.
9. Ibid.
10. Pte. James Kelly, 6th Leinster Regiment: conversations with author.
11. Whitton, vol. 2, 326.
12. Wavell, *Allenby*, 200.
13. FM Sir Philip Chetwode, Bt, XX Corps OO. Chetwode papers, LC.
14. Skilbeck-Smith, 128.
15. Chetwode.
16. Skilbeck-Smith, 134.
17. Wavell, *Allenby*, 216.
18. Geoghegan, vol. 2, 108.
19. Whitton, vol. 2, 330.
20. Capt. E. Faithfull, 1st Royal Irish Regiment. Correspondence, LC.
21. Capt. R. M. Preston. *The Desert Mounted Corps*. London: Constable 1921, 43.
22. Capt. C. Falls. *Military Operations: Palestine, 1917–18*. 2 parts, London: HMSO 1930, part 1, 109, n. 2.
23. Whitton, vol. 2, 331. 'So long as he comes out of it alive, his agonies and

contortions dodging death are fair game.' Kipling, vol. 2, 52.
24. Whitton, vol. 2, 331.
25. Whitton, vol. 2, 332.
26. Chetwode.

CHAPTER 30: THE CAPTURE AND DEFENCE OF JERUSALEM (P.328-337)
1. Whitton, vol. 2, 334.
2. Faithfull.
3. Skilbeck-Smith, 156.
4. Whitton, vol. 2, 339–40.
5. Geoghegan, vol. 2, 95.
6. Falls, *Palestine,* part 1, 286.
7. Skilbeck-Smith, 161.
8. Ibid., 183.
9. Geoghegan, vol. 2, 109.
10. Ibid., 95.
11. Ibid.
12. Falls, part 1, 318.
13. Faithfull.
14. Geoghegan, vol. 2, 97.
15. Faithfull.
16. Ibid.
17. *Soldiers Died.*
18. Jourdain, vol. 3, 178.
19. Military maps of Palestine, 1918.
20. Wavell, *Allenby,* 198.
21. Whitton, vol. 2, 481.

CHAPTER 31: THE FIFTH ARMY, MARCH 1918 (P.338-344)
1. Edmonds, 1918, vol. 1, 87.
2. Gough, 257.
3. Burrows, 177.
4. Gough, 241.
5. Ibid.
6. Macpherson, *Medical Services: General History,* vol. 3, 212–3. Macpherson commented that in siting some of its CCSs so far forward, Fifth Army Medical Services appeared to be preparing for an advance, not a withdrawal. Op. cit.
7. Ibid. No. 5 and 55 Casualty Clearing Stations, responsible for VII and XIX Corps battle casualties, were hastily evacuated from Tincourt on the morning of 21 March during the German bombardment. Op. cit.
8. Gough, 229.
9. Ibid., 232.
10. Ibid., 232–3.
11. Ibid., 253.

12. Ibid., 252.
13. Ibid.
14. Priestly, 259.
15. Gough, 263.
16. Ibid., 266.
17. Edmonds, 1918, vol. 1, 195.
18. Gough, 271.

CHAPTER 32: THE MARCH OFFENSIVE: 36TH DIVISION, ST QUENTIN, 12 JANUARY–22 MARCH 1918 (P.345-353)
1. Falls, *36th Div.*, 183.
2. Becke, part 3b, 65, n. 42 to 46.
3. Falls, *36th Div.*, 185.
4. Witherow.
5. Ibid.
6. Fr Henry Gill SJ, chaplain, 2nd Royal Irish Rifles. Correspondence. JAD.
7. Martin Middlebrook. *The Kaiser's Battle*. London: Book Club Associates, 327.
8. Nugent. PRONI D/3835/E/2/545.
9. Witherow.
10. Falls, *36th Div.*, 196.
11. Ibid., 196.
12. Ibid., 197.
13. Ibid., 197.
14. McKeever. The war diary of 12th Rifles gives the battalion losses on 21 March as twenty-two officers and 566 other ranks 'missing'. PRO WO 95/2506.
15. Falls, *36th Div.*, 198.
16. Edmonds, 1918, vol. 1, 186.
17. Citation, quoted by Falls, *36th Div.*, 316.
18. Edmonds, 1918, vol. 1, 211–2.
19. Falls, *36th Div.*, 203.
20. Nugent. PRONI D3835/E/2/602.
21. Rfn. Albert Wilson, 9th Royal Irish Rifles. Memoirs, LC.
22. *DNB*.
23. Edmonds, 1918, vol. 1, 276.
24. Ibid.
25. Ibid., 277.

CHAPTER 33: THE MARCH OFFENSIVE: 16TH DIVISION (P.354-363)
1. Maj. W.S. Mason, 16th Machine-Gun Battalion. Letter, courtesy of Martin Middlebrook.
2. Ibid.
3. Ibid.
4. Ibid.
5. Edmonds, 1918, vol. 1, 180.

6. Ibid.

7. Geoghegan, vol. 2, 119.

8. Edmonds, 1918, vol. 1, 180.

9. Geoghegan, vol. 2, 120.

10. Ibid., 121.

11. Ibid.

12. Ibid.

13. Ibid.

14. 2nd R. Irish ABR. Quoted by Geoghegan, vol. 2, 122.

15. *Soldiers Died*, part 23.

16. 7th/8th RInnF. WD. Maj-Gen. F.W. Ramsay, who commanded 48 Brigade during the battle, when presenting colours to 7th/8th Inniskillings after the war told them, 'And as we heard afterwards from prisoners, your men in strong-points were still holding out next day at mid-day.' Walker, 124.

17. *Soldiers Died*, part 32.

18. Maj. J.P.B. Condon, MOD, Stanmore.

19. Gough, 268.

20. Priestly, 263.

21. Whylly, *Crown and Company*, vol. 2, 101.

22. Ibid.

23. Ibid., 102.

24. Ibid.

25. *Soldiers Died*, part 73.

26. Whylly, *The Blue Caps*, vol. 2, 103.

27. Gough, 268.

28. W.S. Swallow. *The Fifth Army in March 1918*. London: Bodley Head 1923, 207–8.

29. McCance, vol. 2, 150.

30. Ibid., 151.

31. Ibid.

32. Ibid.

33. *Soldiers Died*, part 72.

34. Liddell Hart, 524.

35. Edmonds, 1918, vol. 1, 192 n. 2.

36. Ibid., 194.

CHAPTER 34: THE GERMAN OFFENSIVE, MARCH 1918 (P.364-371)

1. Jourdain, vol. 3, 266.

2. Capt. Desmond McWeeney. 'Fifteen days of the March Retreat', *The Ranger*, no. 76, 1968. 'Neither Leveson-Gower, the brigade commander, nor his B.M. appeared to have any accurate information… nevertheless the counter attack was mounted and the Battalion destroyed to no purpose.' Op. cit. GHQ instructions of 9 Feb. 1918 ordered that 'the battle was not to be fought out on the front then held by throwing in reinforcements or making counter-attacks to regain lost ground… It may well be desirable to fall back to the rearward defences of

Péronne... and preparing for counter-attack.' Edmonds, 1918, vol. 1, 98.

3. Feilding, 264.

4. Ibid., 266.

5. Lt. H. Eric F. Hall. 'The German officer wore gloves', *The Ranger*, no. 76, Jul. 1968.

6. Harrison, 221.

7. *Soldiers Died.*

8. Feilding, 267.

9. Edmonds, 1918, vol. 1, 125.

10. Maj. H. Kenyon Daniel. Letter published in preface to *The 5th Army in March 1918*, 1923, xxxiii–xxxvi, by W.S. Sparrow. Maj. Daniel was refuting allegations in Sparrow's book concerning 16th Division.

11. Ibid.

12. Ibid.

13. Ibid.

14. Ibid.

15. Farndale, 264.

16. Ibid.

17. Ibid.

18. S. Jourdain.

19. Edmonds, 1918, vol. 1, 258.

20. Atkinson, 321.

21. Jourdain, vol. 3, 268.

22. Edmonds, 1918, vol. 1, 291–2.

23. Ibid.

24. Jourdain, vol. 3, 268.

25. Edmonds, 1918, vol. 1, 293.

26. Capt. R.T. Roussel. ABR published as 'The last stand', *The Ranger*, no. 76, Jul. 1968.

27. Atkinson, 321.

28. Edmonds, 1918, vol. 1, 125.

29. *Officers Died* and *Soldiers Died.*

30 Edmonds, 1918, vol. 1, 125.

CHAPTER 35: THE GREAT RETREAT: 36TH DIVISION, 23–30 MARCH 1918 (P.372-377)

1. Falls, *36th Div.*, 211.

2. Edmonds, 1918, vol. 1, 343.

3. Falls, *36th Div.*, 212.

4. Ibid., 216.

5. Witherow.

6. Ibid.

7. Ibid.

8. Burrowes, 112.

9. Falls, *36th Div.*, 221.

10. Edmonds, 1918, vol. 2, 94 ('reduced to considerably less than half its infantry strength'). Op. cit., 18.

11. Witherow.

12. Edmonds, 1918, vol. 1, 462–3.

13. Burrowes, 112–3.

14. Ibid., 113.

15. Ibid.

16. Ibid.

17. Falls, *36th Div.*, 225.

18. Ibid.

19. Ibid.

20. Nugent. PRONI D3835/E/2/602.

CHAPTER 36: THE GREAT RETREAT: 16TH DIVISION, 23 MARCH–5 APRIL 1918 (P.378-390)

1. Edmonds, 1918, vol. 1, 353.

2. Ibid.

3. Feilding, 268.

4. Edmonds, 1918, vol. 1, 359.

5. Macpherson, *Medical Services: General*, vol. 3, 216–7.

6. McWeeney.

7. Jourdain, vol. 3, 270. The Lucknow CCS was at Péronne la Chapellette. It was equipped for 600 patients, to serve Indian troops in the locality. With the evacuation of 5 and 55 CCS from Tincourt, the Indian CCS was inundated with wounded. Many could not be evacuated, because of a lack of transport. The CO left just before the arrival of the Germans. On reporting to the DMS he was placed under arrest for deserting his wounded but was later released. Macpherson, *Medical Services: General*, vol. 3, 216–7.

8. Feilding, 273.

9. Macpherson, *Medical Services: General*, vol. 3, 216–21. Because of the precipitate withdrawal of its CCS, divisional advance dressing stations had a long distance to cover evacuating their wounded. They succeeded only with the help of Ford motor ambulances. Op. cit.

10. McWeeney.

11. Ibid.

12. Edmonds, 1918, vol. 1, 359.

13. Ibid.

14. Ibid., 473.

15. Ibid., 463.

16. Ibid., 467.

17. Ibid., 505.

18. Ibid., 505–6.

19. Ibid., 507.

20. Edmonds, 1918, vol. 2, 19. 'The retirement of the right of Third Army from Bray had provided them [the Germans] with a priceless opportunity. To this retirement the difficulties which encompassed the Fifth Army on 27th March may with justice be attributed.' Op. cit., 22. The formation directly affected by this retirement was of course 16th Division.

21. Quoted by Whitton, vol. 2, 456.

22. Ibid., 455–6.

23. Edmonds, 1918, vol. 2, 47.

24. McCance, vol. 2, 82.

25. Edmonds, 1918, vol. 2, 23 n. 2.

26. Ibid., 25.

27. Ibid., 24.

28. Whylly, *Crown and Company*, 106.

29. Jervis, 46.

30. Ibid., and *London Gazette*, 30 Jan. 1921.

31. Whylly, *Crown and Company*, vol. 2, 107.

32. Jervis, 48.

33. Edmonds, 1918, vol. 2, 24.

34. Ibid., 51.

35. Ibid.

36. Ibid., 2.

37. Farndale, 277.

38. Edmonds, 1918, vol. 2, 95.

39. Blake, 296.

40. Edmonds, 1918, vol. 2, 458.

41. Ibid., 491.

42. Ibid., 119.

43. Nugent Papers, PRONI D 3835/E/2/608.

44. Edmonds, 1918, vol. 2, 458.

CHAPTER 37: BACKS TO THE WALL, 9–29 APRIL 1918 (P.391-399)

1. John Terrain. *Douglas Haig: the Educated Soldier*. London: Hutchinson 1963, 432–3. 'Drafted in his own hand with only three corrections.'

2. *Officers Died* and *Soldiers Died*.

3. Falls, *36th Div.*, 233.

4. Edmonds, 1918, vol. 2, 272.

5. Falls, *36th Div.*, 239.

6. McWeeney.

7. Edmonds, 1918, vol. 5, 179.

8. David Lloyd George. *Memoirs*. 2 vols., London: Odhams, vol. 1, 942.

9. Churchill, vol. 2, 1320.

10. Edmonds, 1918, vol. 3, 13–14.

11. Geoghegan, vol. 2, 62.
12. Edmonds, 1918, vol. 3, 405.
13. Whylly, *Neil's Blue Caps*, vol. 2, 115.
14. Ibid., 121.

CHAPTER 38: VICTORY IN PALESTINE, SEPTEMBER–OCTOBER 1918 (P.400-410)
1. Jourdain, vol. 1, 508.
2. Ibid.
3. Wavell, *Allenby*, 263–4.
4. Whitton, vol. 2, 489.
5. Ibid., and Falls, *Palestine*, part 2, 427–8.
6. Wavell, *Allenby*, 269.
7. Jourdain, vol. 1, 560.
8. Ibid.
9. Chetwode.
10. Falls, *Palestine*, part 2, 492.
11. Ibid.
12. Whitton, vol. 2, 490.
13. Geoghegan, vol. 2, 99.
14. Whitton, vol. 2, 491.
15. Chetwode.
16. Whitton, vol. 2, 493.
17. Falls, *Palestine*, part 2, 498.
18. Ibid., 499.
19. Ibid., 496–7.
20 Geoghegan, vol. 2, 100.
21. Whitton, vol. 2, 495.
22. Falls, *Palestine*, part 2, 502. Almost exactly three months from Henry Wilson's memorandum recommending a consolidation on the existing line in Palestine, Allenby's victory despatch was written. 'My Lord, I have the honour to forward a Dispatch describing the operations which, commencing on 19th September, resulted in the destruction of the enemy's army, the liberation of Palestine and Syria, the occupation of Damascus and Allepo.' *Buchan*, vol. 23, 281.
23. Whitton, vol. 2, 494.
24. Geoghegan, vol. 2, 100.
25. Becke, part 3a, 18.
26. Maj.-Gen. J.F.C. Fuller (edited by John Terrain). *Decisive Battles of the Western World*. London: Granada, 353.

CHAPTER 39: THE LAST PHASE, SEPTEMBER–NOVEMBER 1918 (P.411-426)
1. Whylly, *Neil's Blue Caps*, vol. 2, 119–20
2. Hitchcock, 286.

3. Ibid., 287.
4. Lt. Cuthbert FitzHerbert, Grenadier Guards. Diary, LC.
5. John Ewing. *History of the 9th (Scottish) Division.* London: John Murray, 371.
6. Falls, *36th Div.,* 271.
7. Edmonds, 1918, vol. 5, 149.
8. Ibid., 166.
9. Sir A.A. Montgomery. *The Story of the Fourth Army.* London: Hodder and Stoughton, 183.
10. Edmonds, 1918, vol. 5, 162.
11. Ibid., 173.
12. Jervis, 51–2.
13. Edmonds, 1918, vol. 5, 178.
14. Geoghegan, vol. 2, 69.
15. Edmonds, 1918, vol. 5, 194.
16. Ibid.
17. Ibid.
18. Ibid., 195.
19. Jourdain, vol. 3, 190.
20. Bishop Harman Shanley. 'A memory of Serain', *The Ranger,* no. 76, Jul. 1968. Lt. H.J. Shanley had joined 5th C. R. in Salonika on 15 Oct. 1915.
21. Skilbeck-Smith, 21.
22. Jervis, 54.
23. Edmonds, 1918, vol. 5, 195.
24. Capt. C.A. Brett. 'The hundred days: Serain and Le Cateau', *The Ranger,* no. 76, Jul. 1968.
25. Montgomery, 201–2.
26. Ibid.
27. Edmonds, 1918, vol. 5, 309.
28. Ibid., 310.
29. Montgomery, 219–25.
30. Edmonds, 1918, vol. 5, 314.
31. Jourdain, vol. 3., 193.
32. Edmonds, 1918, vol. 5, 314.
33. Jervis, 56–7.
34. Ibid., 56.
35. Fus. G.T. Nevill, 6th Royal Dublin Fusiliers. Memoirs, LC.
36. Montgomery, 228.
37. Edmonds, 1918, vol. 5, 273.
38. Ibid., 42.
39. Ewing, 372.
40. Falls, *36th Div.,* 292.
41. Edmonds, 1918, vol. 5, 472.
42. Jervis, 61.
43. Ibid., 62.
44. Whylly, *Crown and Company,* vol. 2, 121.

45. Ibid., 123.
46. Jourdain, vol. 3, 202.
47. Geoghegan, vol. 2, 70.
48. Edmonds, 1918, vol. 5, 542.
49. Hitchcock, 312.
50. Edmonds, 1918, vol. 5, 541.
51. George R. Preedy. *Child of Chequer'd Fortune*. London: Herbert Jenkins, 227.

EPILOGUE (P.427-428)
1. Kipling, vol. 1, 341.
2. Hitchcock, 323.
3. Ibid., 327.
4. Kipling, vol. 1, 341.
5. Hickie.
6. 'The Irish National War Memorial: Its Meaning and Purpose', courtesy of Capt. H.C. Heather.
7. Fr S. Farragher CSSp. 'Rockmen and the Rising', *Blackrock College Annual*, 1966. The article asserts that most 'Rockmen' supported John Redmond's constitutional nationalism.
8. Fr Thomas Rock.

Select Bibliography

PUBLISHED SOURCES

Armstrong, H. C. *Grey Wolf*. London: Penguin 1937.

Army List, 1915, 1916, 1917, 1918.

Arthur, Sir George. *Life of Lord Kitchener*. London: Macmillan 1920.

Aspinall-Oglander, Brig.-Gen. C. E. *Military Operations: Gallipoli*. 2 vols., London: Heinemann 1932.

Atkinson. C.T. *The Hampshire Regiment*. Winchester: Regimental Headquarters 1952.

Bean, C.E.W. (selected and annotated by Kevin Fewster). *Gallipoli Correspondent: the Frontline Diary of C. E. W. Bean*. Sydney: Allen and Unwin 1983.

Becke, A.F. *The Order of Battle of Divisions*. London: HMSO.

Binyon, L.M. *For Dauntless France*. London: Hodder and Stoughton 1918.

Blake, Robert. *The Private Papers of Douglas Haig*. London: Eyre and Spottiswoode 1953.

Braddon, Russel. *The Siege*. London: Jonathan Cape 1969.

Bredin, Brig. A.E.C. *History of the Irish Soldier*. Belfast: Century Books 1987.

Brett, Capt. C.A. [6th Connaught Rangers]. 'The hundred days: Serain and Le Cateau', *Connaught Rangers Journal*, no. 76, Jul. 1968.

Brophy, John, and Partridge, Eric. *The Long, Long Trail*. London: André Deutsch 1965.

Buchan, John. *Nelson's History of the Great War*. 24 vols., London: Nelson 1915–19.

Burgoyne, Gerald Achilles. *The Burgoyne Diaries*. London: Harmsworth.

Burrowes, Brig.-Gen. A.R. *The 1st Bn the Faugh-A-Ballaghs in the Great War*. Aldershot: Gale and Polden.

Callwell, Maj.-Gen. Sir C.E. *Experiences of a Dug-Out*. London: Constable 1920.

Callwell, Maj.-Gen. Sir C.E. *Life and Diary of Field-Marshal Sir Henry Wilson*. London: Cassell 1927.

Capper, Maj.-Gen. Sir J. *Foreword to Stand-To: a Diary of the Trenches* (Hitchcock).

Cassar, George H. *Kitchener: Architect of Victory*. London: William Kimber 1977.

Churchill, Winston S. *The World Crisis*. London: Odhams.

Cooper, Maj. B. *The Tenth Irish Division in Gallipoli*. London: Herbert Jenkins 1918.

Cowland, W. S. *10th and 12 Battalions the Hampshire Regiment*. Winchester: Warren 1930.

Crighton. Rev. O. *With the Twenty-Ninth Division in Gallipoli*. London: Longman Green.

Crozier, Brig.-Gen. F.P. *A Brass Hat in No Man's Land*. London: Jonathan Cape 1930.

—*The Men I Killed*. London: Michael Joseph 1930.

Cunliffe, M. *The Royal Irish Fusiliers, 1793–1950*. Oxford: Oxford University Press 1971.

de Montmorency, H. *Sword and Stirrup*. London: Bell and Sons 1936.

Dictionary of National Biography.

Edmonds, Brig.-Gen. Sir James. *Military Operations: France and Belgium, 1914–18*. 16 vols., London: HMSO.

Ewing, John. *History of the 9th (Scottish) Division*. London: John Murray 1921.

Falls, Capt. C. *The History of the 36th Ulster Division.* Belfast: M'Caw, Stevenson and Orr 1922.

Falls, Capt. C. *Military Operations: Macedonia.* 2 vols., London: HMSO 1930.

Falls, C. *The History of the Royal Irish Rifles.* Aldershot: Gale and Polden 1925.

Falls, Capt. C. *Military Operations: Palastine, 1917-1918.* 2 vols., London: HMSO 1930.

Falls, Cyril. *Armageddon.* London: Weidenfeld and Nicolson 1964.

Farndale, Gen. Sir Martin. *The Royal Artillery, 1914–18.* Royal Artillery Institute 1986.

Farragher, Fr. S. 'Rockmen and the Rising', *Blackrock College Annual,* 1966.

Farrar-Hockley, Gen. Sir Anthony. *Goughie.* London: Hart-Davis 1975.

Feilding, Lt.-Col. R. *War Letters to a Wife.* London: Medici Society 1929.

Fox, Sir F. *The Royal Inniskilling Fusiliers in the Great War.* London: Constable 1928.

Fraser, Sir David. *Alanbrooke.* London: Collins.

Fuller, Maj.-Gen. J.F.C. (edited by John Terrain). *Decisive Battles of the Western World.* London: Granada.

Geoghegan, Brig.-Gen. S. *Campaigns and History of the Royal Irish Regiment.* 2 vols., Edinburgh: Blackwood 1927.

Gibbs, Philip. *The Realities of War.* London: William Heinemann.

Gillon. Capt. Stair. *The Story of the 29th Division.* London: Nelson.

Gleason, A.H. *Inside the British Isles.* New York: Century 1917.

Godley, Gen. Sir A. *The Life of an Irish Soldier.* London: John Murray 1939.

Gough, Sir H. de la P. *The Fifth Army.* London: Hodder and Stoughton 1931.

Gwynn, D. *The Life of John Redmond.* London: Harrap 1932.

Hall, H. Eric. F. 'The German officer wore gloves', *The Ranger,* no. 76, Jul. 1968.

Hamilton, Sir Ian. *Despatches from the Dardanelles.* London: George Newnes 1917.

Hamilton, Sir Ian. *Gallipoli Diary.* London: Edward Arnold 1920.

Hanna, H. *The Pals at Suvla: D Company, the 7th Royal Dublin Fusiliers.* Dublin: Ponsonby 1916.

Harris, Maj. H.E.D. *The Irish Regiments in the First World War.* Dublin: Mercier Press 1968.

Harrison, Maj. M.C.C., and Cartwright, Capt. H. A. *Within Four Walls.* London: Penguin 1940.

Headlam, C. *History of the Guards Division in the Great War.* London: Murray 1924.

Hitchcock, Capt. F.C. *Stand-To: a Diary of the Trenches.* London: Hurst and Blackett 1937.

Hyde, H. Montgomery. *Carson.* London: Constable 1987.

Ireland's War Memorial Record (the King's Copy at the British Library).

Jervis, Lt.-Col. H.S. *The 2nd Munsters in France.* Aldershot: Gale and Polden 1922.

Jourdain, Lt.-Col. H.F.N. Record of the 5th (S) Bn the Connaught Rangers. Oxford: Oxford University Press 1916.

Jourdain, Lt.-Col. H.F.N. *History of the Connaught Rangers.* 3 vols., Whitehall: Royal United Service Institution 1925–28.

Jourdain, Col. S. 'A subaltern's war', *The Ranger,* no. 74, Jul. 1966.

Jünger, Ernst. *Storm of Steel.* London: Chatto and Windus 1928.

Juvenis. *Suvla and After.* London: Hodder and Stoughton 1916.

Kannengiesser, Hans. *The Campaign in Gallipoli.* London: Hutchinson.

Kenyon Daniel, Maj. H. Letter published in introduction to the third impression of *The Fifth Army in the March Retreat* by W. S. Sparrow.

Kerr, S.P. *What The Irish Regiments Have Done.* London: Unwin 1916.

Kettle, Prof. T.M. *The Ways of War.* London: Constable 1917.

Kipling, Rudyard. The Irish Guard in the Great War. Macmillan, London 1923.

Kirschener, Prof. Dr. M. [senior surgeon of the reserve, 3rd Bavarian Army Corps]. *'Remarks on the action of the regular infantry bullet and of the dumdum bullet on the human body'* [translated from Münchener Medizinische Wochenschrift, 29 Dec. 1914], RAMC Journal, 1915.

Liddell Hart, B.H. *History of the First World War.* London: Book Club Associates.

Lloyd George, David. *The Memoirs of David Lloyd George.* London: Odhams.

London Gazette (various editions).

McCance, Capt. S. *The History of the Royal Munster Fusiliers.* 2 vols., Aldershot: Gale and Polden 1927.

Macdonagh, M. *The Irish at the Front.* London: Hodder and Stoughton 1916.

Macpherson, Sir W.D. *History of the Great War: Medical Services.* London: HMSO.

McWeeney, Desmond. 'Fifteen days of the March retreat', *The Ranger,* no. 76, Jul. 1968.

Masefield, John. *Gallipoli.* London: Heinemann 1926.

Merewether, J.W.B. *The Indian Corps in France.* London: Murray 1918.

Middlebrook, Martin. *The Kaiser's Battle.* London: Book Club Associates.

Miles, Capt. Wilfred. *Military Operations: France and Belgium, 1916,* vol. 2. London: HMSO.

Miles, Capt. Wilfred. *Military Operations: France and Belgium, 1917,* vol. 3: *The Battle of Cambrai.* London: HMSO.

Mitchell, Brian R. *European Historical Statistics, 1980.* London: Macmillan.

Mitchell, Maj. T.J. *History of the Great War: Medical Services, Casualties and Medical Statistics.* London: HMSO.

Montgomery, Sir A.A. *The Story of the Fourth Army.* London: Hodder and Stoughton 1920.

Moore, Pte. D. Letter in *Sprig of Shillelagh,* Jun. 1915.

Moorhead, Alan. *Gallipoli.* London: Hamish Hamilton 1956.

Moynihan, Michael. *God on our Side: the British Padre in the First World War.* London: Leo Cooper 1983.

Nalder, Maj.-Gen. R.F.H. *The Royal Corps of Signals: a History of its Antecedents and Development.* London: Royal Signals Institute 1956.

Napier, Sir William. *History of the War in the Peninsula and the South of France, 1807–1814.* London: Frederick Warne.

National University of Ireland. *War List: Roll of Honour.* Dublin: NUI.

Nevinson, H.W. *The Dardanelles Campaign.* London: Nesbit 1918.

O'Rahilly, Alfred. *Father William Doyle SJ.* London: Longman Green 1939.

Pakenham, Thomas. *The Boer War.* London: Weidenfeld and Nicolson 1979.

Parker, Capt. Robert. *Memoirs of the Most Remarkable Transactions.* London 1741.

Peal, Fr. Frederick, SJ. *War Jottings.* Calcutta: Catholic Orphan Press 1916.

Preedy, George R. *Child of Chequer'd Fortune.* London: Herbert Jenkins 1939.

Preston, Col. R.M. *The Desert Mounted Corps.* London: Constable 1921.

Price, G. Ward. *The Story of the Salonika Army.* London: Hodder and Stoughton 1918.

Priestly, Maj. R.E. *The Signal Service in the European War.* Chatham: Institute of Royal Engineers and the Signals Association 1980.

The Ranger [journal of the Connaught Rangers].

Redmond, Maj. W.H.K. Trench Pictures from France. London: Melrose 1917.

Rickard, Mrs. L. *Story of the Munsters at Etreux, Festubert, Rue de Bois and Hulloch.* London: Hodder and Stoughton 1918.

Robertson, Field-Marshal Sir William. *Soldiers and Statesmen, 1914–1918.* London: Cassell 1926.

Rose, Kenneth. *King George V.* London: Weidenfeld and Nicolson.

Rousell. Capt. R.T. 'The last stand', *The Ranger,* no. 76, Jul. 1968.

Seligman, V. J. *The Salonika Side-Show*. London: Allen and Unwin 1919.
Seton, Sir B.G., and Grant, John. *The Pipes of War*. New York: EP Publishing 1975.
Shanley, Bishop Harman. 'A memory of Serain', *The Ranger*, no. 76, Jul. 1968.
Sheridan, Thomas B. 'Memories of the 6th Battalion', *The Ranger*, no. 75, Jul. 1967.
Simkins, Peter. *Kitchener's Armies: the Raising of the New Armies, 1914–1916*. Manchester: Manchester University Press 1988.
Skilbeck-Smith, Rev. R. *A Subaltern in Macedonia and Palestine*. London: Mitre Press 1930.
Slim, Field-Marshal Viscount. *Defeat Into Victory*. London: Cassell 1959.
Sparrow, W.S. *The Fifth Army in the March Retreat*.
Sprig of Shillelagh [journal of the Royal Inniskilling Fusiliers].
Strawson, John. *Gentlemen in Khaki*. London: Secker and Warburg.
Terrain, John. *Haig: the Educated Soldier*. London: Hutchinson 1963.
The 6th Bn the Royal Inniskilling Fusiliers in the Great War. Enniskillen: Trimble Press.
Thompson, Col. H.N. 'An account of my capture and experiences In Germany', *RAMC Journal*, 1915.
Trinity College, Dublin. *War List*. Dublin: TCD 1922.
Vane, Sir Francis, Bt. *Agin The Governments*. London: Samson Low and Marston.
Walker, Maj. G.A.C. *The Book of the 7th Royal Inniskilling Fusiliers*. Dublin: Brindley 1920.
Wavell, Col. A.P. *The Palestine Campaigns*. London: Constable 1938.
Wavell, Sir A.P. *Allenby*. London: Harrap 1940.
War Office. *Officers Died in the Great War*. London: HMSO 1922.
War Office. *Soldiers Died in the Great War* (various parts). London: HMSO 1922.
War Office. *Statistics of the Military Effort of the British Empire During the Great War*. London: HMSO 1922.
Wedgwood, C.V. *The Last of the Radicals*. London: Jonathan Cape.
Whitton, Lt.-Col. F.E. *The History of the Prince of Wales's Leinster Regiment*. 2 vols., Aldershot: Gale and Polden 1926.
Willcocks, Sir J. *With the Indians in France*. London: Constable 1920.
Williams, Capt. B.W. *Raising and Training the New Armies*. London: Constable 1918.
Wilson, Sir Henry (edited by Keith Jeffrey). *The Military Correspondence, 1918–1922*. London: Bodley Head (for the Army Records Society) 1985.
Wylly, Col. H.C. *Crown and Company [2nd Bn, Royal Dublin Fusiliers]*. 2 vols., Aldershot: Gale and Polden
Wylly, Col H.C. *Neil's Blue Caps [1st Bn, Royal Dublin Fusiliers]*. 2 vols., Dublin: Maunsell 1925.

UNPUBLISHED SOURCES
After-battle reports of the formations and units as stated at reference.
Blacker, Lt.-Col. Stewart, 9th Royal Irish Fusiliers. Letter to Col Fitzgerald. Courtesy of the Royal Irish Fusilier Museum, Armagh.
Bland, Lt. J.G., 2nd Royal Irish Rifles. LC.
Bradford, R., 6th Green Howards. LC.
Brierly, Capt. L.B., RE, staff captain, HQ 49 Brigade. LC
Broun, 2/Lt. R.C. McB., 6th Royal Dublin Fusiliers. LC.
Campbell, Capt. D., 6th Royal Irish Rifles. LC.
Cardin-Roe, Brig. W., Royal Irish Fusiliers. LC.
Catholic Chaplains in the Great War. RAChD Depot, Bagshot. Courtesy Monsignor Joseph Mallon, RAChD.

Chetwode, Field-Marshal Sir Philip. LC.

Ching, Pte. F.H., 10th Divisional Column, ASC. LC.

Cripps, Maj. G. 2/Lt. 9th SLI attached 1st Royal Dublin Fusiliers. LC.

Dart, Sgt. J.C., 10th Divisional Signal Company, RE. LC.

de Courcy Ireland, Lt.-Col. Gerald, 9th KRRC. LC.

Downs, Sgt Harry, 6th Connaught Rangers. LC.

Edwards, Patrick F., Custom House, Dublin, 1921: conversation with author.

Faithfull, Capt E., 1st Royal Irish Regiment. LC.

FitzHerbert, 2/Lt. Cuthbert, Grenadier Guards. LC.

Gill, Fr. Henry, SJ, chaplain, 2nd Royal Irish Rifles. JAD.

Gill, Lt. Owen, 11 Division Signal Company, Suvla. Courtesy of Col M. N. Gill.

Gleeson, Fr. Francis, chaplain, 2nd Royal Munster Fusiliers. Maher Papers, ADA.

Granard, Col. 8th Earl, CO 5th Royal Irish Regiment. Correspondence. PRONI.

Hall, Maj. Sir J.H., 8th Royal Munster Fusiliers, Brigade Major, HQ 47 Brigade. LC.

Harley, Sir Thomas. Correspondence. LC.

Heptenstall, Lt. P., 16th Divisional Engineers. RE. LC.

Hobday, Col. E.A.P., CO 16th Division DAC, RA. LC.

Holland, Maj. J.V. 7th Leinster Regiment. LC.

Holmes, Maj.-Gen. Sir N., Royal Irish Regt, DAAG, HQ 16th Division. LC.

Jourdain, Col. Seymour, lieutenant, 6th Connaught Rangers and HQ 16th Division: conversation with author.

Kane, Rfn. M., 7th Royal Irish Rifles. LC.

Kelly, Pte. James, 6th Leinster Regiment: conversation with author.

King, Capt. Edward, 5th Royal Inniskilling Fusiliers. LC and 'Haphazard'.

Lynden-Bell, Maj.-Gen. Sir A., Major-General, General Staff, HQ NEF. LC.

Mason, Maj. W.S., 16th Machine-Gun Battalion. Courtesy of Mr Martin Middlebrook.

McCartney-Filgate, Col. T.T., lieutenant, 6th Royal Inniskilling Fusiliers. LC.

McKeever, CSM Samuel, 12th Royal Irish Rifles. LC.

McRoberts, Rfn. James, 14th Royal Irish Rifles. LC.

MacRory, Lt.-Col. F.S.N. History of the 10th Royal Inniskilling Fusiliers: a Contribution to the History of the 36th (Ulster) Division. PRO. WO 95/2491.

Muirhead, Brig. Sir John, UPM.

Nevill, Fus. G.H., 7th Royal Dublin Fusiliers. LC.

Nugent, Maj.-Gen. Sir Oliver, GOC 36th (Ulster) Division. Correspondence, PRONI. Queen's University, Belfast. Roll of Honour, 1914–17.

Stewart, Maj. Sir Hugh, Bt, 1st Royal Inniskilling Fusiliers. LC.

Stonham, Col. H.F., East Surrey Regiment. LC.

Trousdell, Capt. A.J., 1st Royal Irish Fusiliers. LC.

Vershoyle, Maj. Terence, 6th Royal Inniskilling Fusiliers. LC.

West, Air-Commodore F., captain, Royal Munster Fusiliers and Royal Flying Corps. LC.

Wilson, Rfn. Albert, 9th Royal Irish Rifles. LC.

Withrow, Rev. T.H., lieutenant, 8th and 2nd Royal Irish Rifles. LC.

Wrafter, Fr. Joseph, SJ, chaplain, 6th Royal Irish Regiment and 7th Leinsters Regiment. JAD.

Wythe, SSgt A.L.G. RAMC. LC.

Index